Peregrine Books

D. H. Lawrence

# A SELECTION FROM PHOENIX

David Herbert Lawrence was born at Eastwood, Notts,
in 1885, the fourth child of a miner. At thirteen he won a
scholarship to Nottingham High School, which he left
for a job with a firm of surgical goods manufacturers at
a wage of thirteen shillings a week. He soon abandoned
this to become a teacher at Eastwood.

While attending Nottingham University for his teacher's
certificate he began his first novel, *The White Peacock*,
which was published by Heinemann in 1911. From that
time onwards, with the exception of a short period as a
schoolmaster in Croydon, he lived entirely by his writing.
For two years he travelled in Germany and Italy, and,
returning to England, was married in July 1914 to Frieda
von Richthofen. In 1919 the Lawrences left England and
travelled, first in Europe and then in Australia and
America.

They settled for a while in New Mexico, but came back
finally to Europe in 1929. In that year Lawrence became
seriously ill, and he died of tuberculosis on 2 March 1930.

D. H. Lawrence

# A SELECTION
# FROM PHOENIX
Edited by A. A. M. Inglis

Penguin Books

Penguin Books Ltd, Harmondsworth,
Middlesex, England
Penguin Books Australia Ltd, Ringwood,
Victoria, Australia

*Phoenix* first published by
William Heinemann Ltd 1936
*Phoenix II* first published by
William Heinemann Ltd 1968
This selection first published in
Peregrine Books 1971
*Phoenix II* copyright © the Estate of
Frieda Lawrence Ravagli, 1968

Made and printed in Great Britain by
Hazell Watson & Viney Ltd, Aylesbury, Bucks
Set in Linotype Times

# Contents

## 4. Censorship

## 5. Men and Women

## 6. Consciousness, Being, Selfhood

## 7. Myths

# A Note on this Selection

In *Phoenix: The posthumous papers of D. H. Lawrence* (1936) E. D. McDonald brought together most of the essays, reviews, introductions, sketches and articles that had lain unpublished or uncollected since Lawrence's death. In *Phoenix II* (1968) Warren Roberts and Harry T. Moore offered a supplementary gathering of fugitive and unpublished stories and essays and reprinted two groups of essays once collected by Lawrence – *Reflections on the Death of a Porcupine* (1925) and the lively journalism of *Assorted Articles* (1930). The present selection makes available in cheap format rather more than a third of the contents (apart from the fiction) of *Phoenix* and *Phoenix II*.

The quality of Lawrence's criticism of life and literature and the range of manner, matter and scale among items in such a miscellany have combined to make choice difficult. The four longest essays alone would have occupied two thirds of this volume had they all been included. 'Education of the People' did not easily furnish excerpts, and because of its length it could not be included entire; but the Magnus Introduction is here in full, with most of the 'Study of Thomas Hardy' and a representative section of 'The Crown'. (Except those two essays, and one other, everything in the selection is printed in full.) For the rest, the selection emphasizes Lawrence's writings on fiction and on modern civilization, somewhat at the expense of his nature and travel writings (many of which are already in print in cheap editions), of his criticism of American literature (because there, *Studies in Classic American Literature* is clearly the book to start with) and of his reviewing which, though penetrating, exemplary and never dull, was by its nature comparatively ephemeral and tangential.

## A Note on this Selection

'Mercury' and 'Flowery Tuscany' and the introductions to Verga's *Mastro-don Gesualdo* and to *The Paintings of D. H. Lawrence* would command a place here if they did not already appear in the *Selected Essays* (Penguin) edited by the late Richard Aldington, which this selection is not intended to supersede. 'Nottingham and the Mining Countryside', 'New Mexico', 'Nobody Loves Me', 'Reflections on the Death of a Porcupine', the essays on Galsworthy and on Democracy, and four shorter articles have forced their way into this volume although they also appear in *Selected Essays*.

The arrangement of the volume is fairly loose and arbitrary – necessarily so, with an author who explores the relation between Law and Love by comparing Rembrandt and Michelangelo and who proceeds quite naturally to embody the whole discussion in an essay on Hardy. The Index will be more useful than the Contents to a reader seeking to turn up some particular passage, or to find Lawrence's remarks on some specific topic. Arrangement by main subject-matter still seemed more promising and useful than any discernible alternative. Within the sections of the book, essays have been arranged to form readable sequences with their neighbours – an unemphatic indication of some of Lawrence's recurring concerns, not a covert imposition of linear intellectual development on the man who wrote 'There is a curious spiral rhythm, and the mind approaches again and again the point of concern, repeats itself, goes back, destroys the time-sequence entirely ...'

To each essay is prefixed a brief note of date of composition (when this differs materially from date of publication), date of first publication in a periodical, and date of first publication as or in a volume. There are no other notes, but probably I should point out that no known poem by Swift corresponds to the account Lawrence gives on pages 304 and 332, and that the quoted line appears (once in each) in two poems which satirize taboo and idealization.

A. A. H. INGLIS

# 1. Personal

# Autobiographical Sketch

*Sunday Dispatch*, 17 February 1929; *Assorted Articles*, 1930

They ask me: 'Did you find it very hard to get on and to become a success?' And I have to admit that if I can be said to have got on, and if I can be called a success, then I *did not* find it hard.

I never starved in a garret, nor waited in anguish for the post to bring me an answer from editor or publisher, nor did I struggle in sweat and blood to bring forth mighty works, nor did I ever wake up and find myself famous.

I was a poor boy. I *ought* to have wrestled in the fell clutch of circumstance, and undergone the bludgeonings of chance before I became a writer with a very modest income and a very questionable reputation. But I didn't. It all happened by itself and without any groans from me.

It seems a pity. Because I was undoubtedly a poor boy of the working classes, with no apparent future in front of me. But after all, what am I now?

I was born among the working classes and brought up among them. My father was a collier, and only a collier, nothing praiseworthy about him. He wasn't even respectable, in so far as he got drunk rather frequently, never went near a chapel, and was usually rather rude to his little immediate bosses at the pit.

He practically never had a good stall all the time he was a

butty, because he was always saying tiresome and foolish things about the men just above him in control at the mine. He offended them all, almost on purpose, so how could he expect them to favour him? Yet he grumbled when they didn't.

My mother was, I suppose, superior. She came from town, and belonged really to the lower bourgeoisie. She spoke King's English, without an accent, and never in her life could even imitate a sentence of the dialect which my father spoke, and which we children spoke out of doors.

She wrote a fine Italian hand, and a clever and amusing letter when she felt like it. And as she grew older she read novels again, and got terribly impatient with *Diana of the Crossways* and terribly thrilled by *East Lynne*.

But she was a working man's wife, and nothing else, in her shabby little black bonnet and her shrewd, clear, 'different' face. And she was very much respected, just as my father was not respected. Her nature was quick and sensitive, and perhaps really superior. But she was down, right down in the working class, among the mass of poorer colliers' wives.

I was a delicate pale brat with a snuffy nose, whom most people treated quite gently as just an ordinary delicate little lad. When I was twelve I got a county council scholarship, twelve pounds a year, and went to Nottingham High School.

After leaving school I was a clerk for three months, then had a very serious pneumonia illness, in my seventeenth year, that damaged my health for life.

A year later I became a school-teacher, and after three years' savage teaching of collier lads I went to take the 'normal' course in Nottingham University.

As I was glad to leave school, I was glad to leave college. It had meant mere disillusion, instead of the living contact of men. From college I went down to Croydon, near London, to teach in a new elementary school at a hundred pounds a year.

It was while I was at Croydon, when I was twenty-three, that the girl who had been the chief friend of my youth, and who was herself a school-teacher in a mining village at home, copied out some of my poems, and without telling me, sent them to the *Eng-*

*lish Review*, which had just had a glorious re-birth under Ford Madox Hueffer.

Hueffer was most kind. He printed the poems, and asked me to come and see him. The girl had launched me, so easily, on my literary career, like a princess cutting a thread, launching a ship.

I had been tussling away for four years, getting out *The White Peacock* in inchoate bits, from the underground of my consciousness. I must have written most of it five or six times, but only in intervals, never as a task or a divine labour, or in the groans of parturition.

I would dash at it, do a bit, show it to the girl; she always admired it; then realize afterwards it wasn't what I wanted, and have another dash. But at Croydon I had worked at it fairly steadily, in the evenings after school.

Anyhow, it was done, after four or five years' spasmodic effort. Hueffer asked at once to see the manuscript. He read it immediately, with the greatest cheery sort of kindness and bluff. And in his queer voice, when we were in an omnibus in London, he shouted in my ear: 'It's got every fault that the English novel can have.'

Just then the English novel was supposed to have so many faults, in comparison with the French, that it was hardly allowed to exist at all. 'But', shouted Hueffer in the 'bus, 'you've got GENIUS.'

This made me want to laugh, it sounded so comical. In the early days they were always telling me I had got genius, as if to console me for not having their own incomparable advantages.

But Hueffer didn't mean that. I always thought he had a bit of genius himself. Anyhow, he sent the MS. of *The White Peacock* to William Heinemann, who accepted it at once, and made me alter only four little lines whose omission would now make anybody smile. I was to have £50 when the book was published.

Meanwhile Hueffer printed more poems and some stories of mine in the *English Review*, and people read them and told me so, to my embarrassment and anger. I hated being an author, in people's eyes. Especially as I was a teacher.

When I was twenty-five my mother died, and two months later

*The White Peacock* was published, but it meant nothing to me. I went on teaching for another year, and then again a bad pneumonia illness intervened. When I got better I did not go back to school. I lived henceforward on my scanty literary earnings.

It is seventeen years since I gave up teaching and started to live an independent life of the pen. I have never starved, and never even felt poor, though my income for the first ten years was no better, and often worse, than it would have been if I had remained an elementary school-teacher.

But when one has been born poor a very little money can be enough. Now my father would think I am rich, if nobody else does. And my mother would think I have risen in the world, even if I don't think so.

But something is wrong, either with me or with the world, or with both of us. I have gone far and met people, of all sorts and all conditions, and many whom I have genuinely liked and esteemed.

People, *personally*, have nearly always been friendly. Of critics we will not speak, they are different fauna from people. And I have *wanted* to feel truly friendly with some, at least, of my fellow-men.

Yet I have never quite succeeded. Whether I get on *in* the world is a question; but I certainly don't get on very well *with* the world. And whether I am a worldly success or not I really don't know. But I feel, somehow, not much of a human success.

By which I mean that I don't feel there is any very cordial or fundamental contact between me and society, or me and other people. There is a breach. And my contact is with something that is non-human, non-vocal.

I used to think it had something to do with the oldness and the worn-outness of Europe. Having tried other places, I know that is not so. Europe is, perhaps, the least worn-out of the continents, because it is the most lived in. A place that is lived in lives.

It is since coming back from America that I ask myself seriously: Why is there so little contact between myself and the people whom I know? Why has the contact no vital meaning?

And if I write the question down, and try to write the answer down, it is because I feel it is a question that troubles many men.

The answer, as far as I can see, has something to do with class. Class makes a gulf, across which all the best human flow is lost. It is not exactly the triumph of the middle classes that has made the deadness, but the triumph of the middle-class *thing*.

As a man from the working class, I feel that the middle class cut off some of my vital vibration when I am with them. I admit them charming and educated and good people often enough. *But they just stop some part of me from working.* Some part has to be left out.

Then why don't I live with my working people? Because their vibration is limited in another direction. They are narrow, but still fairly deep and passionate, whereas the middle class is broad and shallow and passionless. Quite passionless. At the best they substitute affection, which is the great middle-class positive emotion.

But the working class is narrow in outlook, in prejudice, and narrow in intelligence. This again makes a prison. One can belong absolutely to no class.

Yet I find, here in Italy, for example, that I live in a certain silent contact with the peasants who work the land of this villa. I am not intimate with them, hardly speak to them save to say good day. And they are not working for me; I am not their *padrone*.

Yet it is they, really, who form my *ambiente*, and it is from them that the human flow comes to me. I don't want to live with them in their cottages; that would be a sort of prison. But I want them to be there, about the place, their lives going on along with mine, and in relation to mine. I don't idealize them. Enough of that folly! It is worse than setting school-children to express themselves in self-conscious twaddle. I don't expect them to make any millennium here on earth, neither now nor in the future. But I want to live near them, because their life still flows.

And now I know, more or less, why I cannot follow in the foot-steps even of Barrie or of Wells, who both came from the common people also and are both such a success. Now I know why I cannot rise in the world and become even a little popular and rich.

17

*Personal*

I cannot make the transfer from my own class into the middle class. I cannot, not for anything in the world, forfeit my passional consciousness and my old blood-affinity with my fellow-men and the animals and the land, for that other thin, spurious mental conceit which is all that is left of the mental consciousness once it has made itself exclusive.

# Hymns in a Man's Life

*Evening News*, 13 October 1928; *Assorted Articles*, 1930

Nothing is more difficult than to determine what a child takes in, and does not take in, of its environment and its teaching. This fact is brought home to me by the hymns which I learned as a child, and never forgot. They mean to me almost more than the finest poetry, and they have for me a more permanent value, somehow or other.

It is almost shameful to confess that the poems which have meant most to me, like Wordsworth's 'Ode to Immortality' and Keats's Odes, and pieces of *Macbeth* or *As You Like It* or *Midsummer Night's Dream*, and Goethe's lyrics, such as 'Über allen Gipfeln ist Ruh', and Verlaine's 'Ayant poussé la porte qui chancelle' – all these lovely poems which after all give the ultimate shape to one's life; all these lovely poems woven deep into a man's consciousness, are still not woven so deep in me as the rather banal Nonconformist hymns that penetrated through and through my childhood.

> Each gentle dove
> And sighing bough
> That makes the eve
> So fair to me
> Has something far
> Diviner now

> To draw me back
> To Galilee.
> O Galilee, sweet Galilee
> Where Jesus loved so much to be,
> O Galilee, sweet Galilee,
> Come sing thy songs again to me!

To me the word Galilee has a wonderful sound. The Lake of Galilee! I don't want to know where it is. I never want to go to Palestine. Galilee is one of those lovely, glamorous worlds, not places, that exist in the golden haze of a child's half-formed imagination. And in my man's imagination it is just the same. It has been left untouched. With regard to the hymns which had such a profound influence on my childish consciousness, there has been no crystallizing out, no dwindling into actuality, no hardening into the commonplace. They are the same to my man's experience as they were to me nearly forty years ago.

The moon, perhaps, has shrunken a little. One has been forced to learn about orbits, eclipses, relative distances, dead worlds, craters of the moon, and so on. The crescent at evening still startles the soul with its delicate flashing. But the mind works automatically and says: 'Ah, she is in her first quarter. She is all there, in spite of the fact that we see only this slim blade. The earth's shadow is over her.' And, willy-nilly, the intrusion of the mental processes dims the brilliance, the magic of the first apperception.

It is the same with all things. The sheer delight of a child's apperception is based on *wonder*; and deny it as we may, knowledge and wonder counteract one another. So that as knowledge increases wonder decreases. We say again: Familiarity breeds contempt. So that as we grow older, and become more familiar with phenomena, we become more contemptuous of them. But that is only partly true. It has taken some races of men thousands of years to become contemptuous of the moon, and to the Hindu the cow is still wondrous. It is not familiarity that breeds contempt: it is the assumption of knowledge. Anybody who looks at the moon and says, 'I know all about that poor orb,' is, of course, bored by the moon.

Now the great and fatal fruit of our civilization, which is a civilization based on knowledge, and hostile to experience, is boredom. All our wonderful education and learning is producing a grand sum-total of boredom. Modern people are inwardly thoroughly bored. Do as they may, they are bored.

They are bored because they experience nothing. And they experience nothing because the wonder has gone out of them. And when the wonder has gone out of a man he is dead. He is henceforth only an insect.

When all comes to all, the most precious element in life is wonder. Love is a great emotion, and power is power. But both love and power are based on wonder. Love without wonder is a sensational affair, and power without wonder is mere force and compulsion. The one universal element in consciousness which is fundamental to life is the element of wonder. You cannot help feeling it in a bean as it starts to grow and pulls itself out of its jacket. You cannot help feeling it in the glisten of the nucleus of the amoeba. You recognize it, willy-nilly, in an ant busily tugging at a straw; in a rook, as it walks the frosty grass.

They all have their own obstinate will. But also they all live with a sense of wonder. Plant consciousness, insect consciousness, fish consciousness, all are related by one permanent element, which we may call the religious element inherent in all life, even in a flea: the sense of wonder. That is our sixth sense. And it is the *natural* religious sense.

Somebody says that mystery is nothing, because mystery is something you don't know, and what you don't know is nothing to you. But there is more than one way of knowing.

Even the real scientist works in the sense of wonder. The pity is, when he comes out of his laboratory he puts aside his wonder along with his apparatus, and tries to make it all perfectly didactic. Science in its true condition of wonder is as religious as any religion. But didactic science is as dead and boring as dogmatic religion. Both are wonderless and productive of boredom, endless boredom.

Now we come back to the hymns. They live and glisten in the depths of the man's consciousness in undimmed wonder, because they have not been subjected to any criticism or analysis. By the time I was sixteen I had criticized and got over the Christian dogma.

It was quite easy for me; my immediate forebears had already done it for me. Salvation, heaven, Virgin birth, miracles, even the Christian dogmas of right and wrong – one soon got them adjusted. I never could really worry about them. Heaven is one of the instinctive dreams. Right and wrong is something you can't dogmatize about; it's not so easy. As for my soul, I simply don't and never did understand how I could 'save' it. One can save one's pennies. But how can one save one's soul? One can only *live* one's soul. The business is to live, really alive. And this needs wonder.

So that the miracle of the loaves and fishes is just as good to me now as when I was a child. I don't care whether it is historically a fact or not. What does it matter? It is part of the genuine wonder. The same with all the religious teaching I had as a child, *apart* from the didacticism and sentimentalism. I am eternally grateful for the wonder with which it filled my childhood.

> Sun of my soul, thou Saviour dear,
> It is not night if Thou be near –

That was the last hymn at the board-school. It did not mean to me any Christian dogma or any salvation. Just the words, 'Sun of my soul, thou Saviour dear', penetrated me with wonder and the mystery of twilight. At another time the last hymn was:

> Fair waved the golden corn
> In Canaan's pleasant land –

And again I loved 'Canaan's pleasant land'. The wonder of 'Canaan', which could never be localized.

I think it was good to be brought up a Protestant: and among Protestants, a Nonconformist, and among Nonconformists, a Congregationalist. Which sounds pharisaic. But I should have missed bitterly a direct knowledge of the Bible, and a direct relation to Galilee and Canaan, Moab and Kedron, those places that never existed on earth. And in the Church of England one would hardly have escaped those snobbish hierarchies of class, which spoil so much for a child. And the Primitive Methodists, when I was a boy, were always having 'revivals' and being 'saved', and I always had a horror of being saved.

So, altogether, I am grateful to my 'Congregational' upbringing. The Congregationalists are the oldest Nonconformists, descendants of the Oliver Cromwell Independents. They still had the Puritan tradition of no ritual. But they avoided the personal emotionalism which one found among the Methodists when I was a boy.

I liked our chapel, which was tall and full of light, and yet still; and colour-washed pale green and blue, with a bit of lotus pattern. And over the organ-loft, 'O worship the Lord in the beauty of holiness', in big letters.

That was a favourite hymn, too:

> O worship the Lord, in the beauty of holiness,
>  Bow down before him, his glory proclaim;
> With gold of obedience and incense of lowliness
>  Kneel and adore him, the Lord is his name.

I don't know what the 'beauty of holiness' is exactly. It easily becomes cant, or nonsense. But if you don't think about it – and why should you? – it has a magic. The same with the whole verse. It is rather bad, really, 'gold of obedience' and 'incense of lowliness'. But in me, to the music, it still produces a sense of splendour.

I am always glad we had the Bristol hymn-book, not Moody and Sankey. And I am glad our Scotch minister on the whole avoided sentimental messes such as 'Lead, Kindly Light', or even 'Abide with Me'. He had a healthy preference for healthy hymns.

> At even, ere the sun was set,
>  The sick, O Lord, around Thee lay.
> Oh, in what divers pains they met!
>  Oh, in what joy they went away!

And often we had 'Fight the good fight with all thy might'.
In Sunday School I am eternally grateful to old Mr Reming-

ton, with his round white beard and his ferocity. He made us sing! And he loved the martial hymns:

> Sound the battle-cry,
> See, the foe is nigh.
> Raise the standard high
> For the Lord.

The ghastly sentimentalism that came like a leprosy over religion had not yet got hold of our colliery village. I remember when I was in Class II in the Sunday School, when I was about seven, a woman teacher trying to harrow us about the Crucifixion. And she kept saying: 'And aren't you sorry for Jesus? Aren't you sorry?' And most of the children wept. I believe I shed a crocodile tear or two, but very vivid is my memory of saying to myself: 'I don't *really* care a bit.' And I could never go back on it. I never *cared* about the Crucifixion, one way or another. Yet the *wonder* of it penetrated very deep in me.

Thirty-six years ago men, even Sunday School teachers, still believed in the fight for life and the fun of it. 'Hold the fort, for I am coming.' It was far, far from any militarism or gun-fighting. But it was the battle-cry of a stout soul, and a fine thing too.

> Stand up, stand up for Jesus,
> Ye soldiers of the Lord.

Here is the clue to the ordinary Englishman – in the Nonconformist hymns.

# Introduction to *A Bibliography*
*of D. H. Lawrence* by Edward D. McDonald

Written 1924, published 1925

There doesn't seem much excuse for me, sitting under a little cedar tree at the foot of the Rockies, looking at the pale desert disappearing westward, with hummocks of shadow rising in the stillness of incipient autumn, this morning, the near pine trees perfectly still, the sunflowers and the purple Michaelmas daisies moving for the first time, this morning, in an invisible breath of breeze, to be writing an introduction to a bibliography.

Books to me are incorporate things, voices in the air, that do not disturb the haze of autumn, and visions that don't blot the sunflowers. What do I care for first or last editions? I have never read one of my own published works. To me, no book has a date, no book has a binding.

What do I care if 'e' is somewhere upside down, or 'g' comes from the wrong fount? I really don't.

And when I force myself to remember, what pleasure is there in that? The very first copy of *The White Peacock* that was ever sent out, I put into my mother's hands when she was dying. She looked at the outside, and then at the title-page, and then at me, with darkening eyes. And though she loved me so much, I think she doubted whether it could be much of a book, since no one more important than I had written it. Somewhere, in the helpless privacies of her being, she had wistful respect for me. But for me

25

in the face of the world, not much. This David would never get a stone across at Goliath. And why try? Let Goliath alone! Anyway, she was beyond reading my first immortal work. It was put aside, and I never wanted to see it again. She never saw it again.

After the funeral, my father struggled through half a page, and it might as well have been Hottentot.

'And what dun they gi'e thee for that, lad?'

'Fifty pounds, father.'

'Fifty pounds!' He was dumbfounded, and looked at me with shrewd eyes, as if I were a swindler. 'Fifty pounds! An' tha's niver done a day's hard work in thy life.'

I think to this day, he looks upon me as a sort of cleverish swindler, who gets money for nothing: a sort of Ernest Hooley. And my sister says, to my utter amazement: 'You always were lucky!'

Somehow, it is the actual corpus and substance, the actual paper and rag volume of any of my works, that calls up these personal feelings and memories. It is the miserable tome itself which somehow delivers me to the vulgar mercies of the world. The voice inside is mine for ever. But the beastly marketable chunk of published volume is a bone which every dog presumes to pick with me.

William Heinemann published *The White Peacock*. I saw him once; and then I realized what an immense favour he was doing me. As a matter of fact, he treated me quite well.

I remember at the last minute, when the book was all printed and ready to bind: some even bound: they sent me in great haste a certain page with a marked paragraph. Would I remove this paragraph, as it might be considered 'objectionable', and substitute an exactly identical number of obviously harmless words. Hastily I did so. And later, I noticed that the two pages, on one of which was the altered paragraph, were rather loose, not properly bound into the book. Only my mother's copy had the paragraph unchanged.

I have wondered often if Heinemann's just altered the 'objectionable' bit in the first little batch of books they sent out, then left the others as first printed. Or whether they changed all but the one copy they sent me ahead.

It was my first experience of the objectionable. Later, William Heinemann said he thought *Sons and Lovers* one of the dirtiest books he had ever read. He refused to publish it. I should not have thought the deceased gentleman's reading had been so circumspectly narrow.

I forget the first appearance of *The Trespasser* and *Sons and Lovers*. I always hide the fact of publication from myself as far as possible. One writes, even at this moment, to some mysterious presence in the air. If that presence were not there, and one thought of even a single solitary actual reader, the paper would remain for ever white.

But I always remember how, in a cottage by the sea, in Italy, I re-wrote almost entirely that play, *The Widowing of Mrs Holroyd*, right on the proofs which Mitchell Kennerley had sent me. And he nobly forbore with me.

But then he gave me a nasty slap. He published *Sons and Lovers* in America, and one day, joyful, arrived a cheque for twenty pounds. Twenty pounds in those days was a little fortune: and as it was a windfall, it was handed over to Madame; the first pin-money she had seen. Alas and alack, there was an alteration in the date of the cheque, and the bank would not cash it. It was returned to Mitchell Kennerley, but that was the end of it. He never made good, and never to this day made any further payment for *Sons and Lovers*. Till this year of grace 1924, America has had that, my most popular book, for nothing – as far as I am concerned.

Then came the first edition of *The Rainbow*. I'm afraid I set my rainbow in the sky too soon, before, instead of after, the deluge. Methuen published that book, and he almost wept before the magistrate, when he was summoned for bringing out a piece of indecent literature. He said he did not know the dirty thing he had been handling, he had not read the work, his reader had misadvised him – and *Peccavi! Peccavi!* wept the now be-knighted gentleman. Then around me arose such a fussy sort of interest, as when a really scandalous bit of scandal is being whispered about one. In print my fellow-authors kept scrupulously silent, lest a bit of the tar might stick to them. Later Arnold Bennett and May Sinclair raised a kindly protest. But John Galsworthy told me, very calmly and *ex cathedra*, he thought the book a failure as a work of art. They think as they please. But why not wait till I ask them, before they deliver an opinion to me? Especially as impromptu opinions by elderly authors are apt to damage him who gives as much as him who takes.

There is no more indecency or impropriety in *The Rainbow* than there is in this autumn morning – I, who say so, ought to know. And when I open my mouth, let no dog bark.

So much for the first edition of *The Rainbow*. The only copy of any of my books I ever keep is my copy of Methuen's *Rainbow*. Because the American editions have all been mutilated. And this is almost my favourite among my novels: this, and *Women in Love*. And I should really be best pleased if it were never reprinted at all, and only those blue, condemned volumes remained extant.

Since *The Rainbow*, one submits to the process of publication as to a necessary evil: as souls are said to submit to the necessary evil of being born into the flesh. The wind bloweth where it listeth. And one must submit to the processes of one's day. Personally, I have no belief in the vast public. I believe that only the winnowed few can care. But publishers, like thistle, must set innumerable seeds on the wind, knowing most will miscarry.

To the vast public, the autumn morning is only a sort of stage background against which they can display their own mechanical importance. But to some men still the trees stand up and look around at the daylight, having woven the two ends of darkness together into visible being and presence. And soon, they will let go the two ends of darkness again, and disappear. A flower laughs once, and having had his laugh, chuckles off into seed, and is gone. Whence? Whither? Who knows, who cares? That little laugh of achieved being is all.

So it is with books. To every man who struggles with his own soul in mystery, a book that is a book flowers once, and seeds, and is gone. First editions or forty-first are only the husks of it.

Yet if it amuses a man to save the husks of the flower that opened once for the first time, one can understand that too. It is like the costumes that men and women used to wear, in their youth, years ago, and which now stand up rather faded in museums. With a jolt they reassemble for us the day-to-day actuality of the bygone people, and we see the trophies once more of man's eternal fight with inertia.

# Introduction to *Memoirs of the Foreign Legion* by Maurice Magnus*

Written 1922, published 1924.

On a dark, wet, wintry evening in November 1919, I arrived in Florence, having just got back to Italy for the first time since 1914. My wife was in Germany, gone to see her mother, also for the first time since that fatal year 1914. We were poor; who was going to bother to publish me and to pay for my writings, in 1918 and 1919? I landed in Italy with nine pounds in my pocket and about twelve pounds lying in the bank in London. Nothing more. My wife, I hoped, would arrive in Florence with two or three pounds remaining. We should have to go very softly, if we were to house ourselves in Italy for the winter. But after the desperate weariness of the war, one could not bother.

So I had written to N— D— to get me a cheap room somewhere in Florence, and to leave a note at Cook's. I deposited my bit of luggage at the station, and walked to Cook's in the Via Tornabuoni. Florence was strange to me: seemed grim and dark and rather awful on the cold November evening. There was a note from D—, who has never left me in the lurch. I went down the Lung 'Arno to the address he gave.

I had just passed the end of the Ponte Vecchio, and was watch-

---

*For further information see Lawrence's Letter to the *New Statesman* dated 20 February 1926, reprinted in D. H. Lawrence's *Selected Essays*, Penguin Books.

ing the first lights of evening and the last light of day on the swollen river as I walked, when I heard D—'s voice:

'Isn't that Lawrence? Why of course it is, of course it is, beard and all! Well, how are you, eh? You got my note? Well now, my dear boy, you just go on to the Cavelotti – straight ahead, straight ahead – you've got the number. There's a room for you there. We shall be there in half an hour. Oh, let me introduce you to M—.'

I had unconsciously seen the two men approaching, D— tall and portly, the other man rather short and strutting. They were both buttoned up in their overcoats, and both had rather curly little hats. But D— was decidedly shabby and a gentleman, with his wicked red face and tufted eyebrows. The other man was almost smart, all in grey, and he looked at first sight like an actor-manager, common. There was a touch of down-on-his-luck about him too. He looked at me, buttoned up in my old thick overcoat, and with my beard bushy and raggy because of my horror of entering a strange barber's shop, and he greeted me in a rather fastidious voice, and a little patronizingly. I forgot to say I was carrying a small hand-bag. But I realized at once that I ought, in this little grey-sparrow man's eyes – he stuck his front out tubbily, like a bird, and his legs seemed to perch behind him, as a bird's do – I ought to be in a cab. But I wasn't. He eyed me in that shrewd and rather impertinent way of the world of actor-managers: cosmopolitan, knocking shabbily round the world.

He looked a man of about forty, spruce and youngish in his deportment, very pink-faced, and very clean, very natty, very alert, like a sparrow painted to resemble a tom-tit. He was just the kind of man I had never met: little smart man of the shabby world, very much on the spot, don't you know.

'How much does it cost?' I asked D—, meaning the room.

'Oh, my dear fellow, a trifle. Ten francs a day. Third rate, tenth rate, but not bad at the price. Pension terms of course – everything included – except wine. '

'Oh no, not at all bad for the money,' said M—. 'Well now, shall we be moving? You want the post office, D—?' His voice was precise and a little mincing, and it had an odd high squeak.

'I do,' said D—.

'Well then come down here –' M— turned to a dark little alley.

'Not at all,' said D—. 'We turn down by the bridge.'

'This is quicker,' said M—. He had a twang rather than an accent in his speech – not definitely American.

He knew all the short cuts of Florence. Afterwards I found that he knew all the short cuts in all the big towns of Europe.

I went on to the Cavelotti and waited in an awful plush and gilt drawing-room, and was given at last a cup of weird muddy brown slush called tea, and a bit of weird brown mush called jam on some bits of bread. Then I was taken to my room. It was far off, on the third floor of the big, ancient, deserted Florentine house. There I had a big and lonely, stone-comfortless room looking on to the river. Fortunately it was not very cold inside, and I didn't care. The adventure of being back in Florence again after the years of war made one indifferent.

After an hour or so someone tapped. It was D— coming in with his grandiose air – now a bit shabby, but still very courtly.

'Why here you are – miles and miles from human habitation! I *told* her to put you on the second floor, where we are. What does she mean by it? Ring that bell. Ring it.'

'No,' said I, 'I'm all right here.'

'What!' cried D—. 'In this Spitzbergen! Where's that bell?'

'Don't ring it,' said I, who have a horror of chambermaids and explanations.

'Not ring it! Well you're a man, you are! Come on then. Come on down to my room. Come on. Have you had some tea – filthy muck they call tea here? I never drink it.'

I went down to D—'s room on the lower floor. It was a littered mass of books and typewriter and papers: D— was just finishing his novel. M— was resting on the bed, in his shirt sleeves: a tubby, fresh-faced little man in a suit of grey, faced cloth bound at the edges with grey silk braid. He had light blue eyes, tired underneath, and crisp, curly, dark brown hair just grey at the temples. But everything was neat and even finicking about his person.

'Sit down! Sit down!' said D—, wheeling up a chair. 'Have a whisky?'

'Whisky!' said I.

'Twenty-four francs a bottle – and a find at that,' moaned D—. I must tell that the exchange was then about forty-five lire to the pound.

'Oh N—,' said M—, 'I didn't tell you. I was offered a bottle of 1913 Black and White for twenty-eight lire.'

'Did you buy it?'

'No. It's your turn to buy a bottle.'

'Twenty-eight francs – my dear fellow!' said D—, cocking up his eyebrows. 'I shall have to starve myself to do it.'

'Oh no you won't, you'll eat here just the same,' said M—.

'Yes, and I'm starved to death. Starved to death by the muck – the absolute muck they call food here. I can't face twenty-eight francs, my dear chap – can't be done, on my honour.'

'Well look here, N—. We'll both buy a bottle. And you can get the one at twenty-two, and I'll buy the one at twenty-eight.'

So it always was, M— indulged D—, and spoilt him in every way. And of course D— wasn't grateful. *Au contraire!* And M—'s pale blue smallish round eyes, in his cockatoo-pink face, would harden to indignation occasionally.

The room was dreadful. D— never opened the windows: didn't believe in opening windows. He believed that a certain amount of nitrogen – I should say a great amount – is beneficial. The queer smell of a bedroom which is slept in, worked in, lived in, smoked in, and in which men drink their whiskies, was something new to me. But I didn't care. One had got away from the war.

We drank our whiskies before dinner. M— was rather yellow under the eyes, and irritable; even his pink fattish face went yellowish.

'Look here,' said D—. 'Didn't you say there was a turkey for dinner? What? Have you been to the kitchen to see what they're doing to it?'

'Yes,' said M— testily. 'I forced them to prepare it to roast.'

'With chestnuts – stuffed with chestnuts?' said D—.

'They *said* so,' said M—.

'Oh, but go down and see that they're doing it. Yes, you've got to keep your eye on them, got to. The most awful howlers if you don't. You go now and see what they're up to.' D— used his most irresistible grand manner.

'It's too late,' persisted M—, testy.

'It's *never* too late. You just run down and absolutely prevent them from boiling that bird in the old soup-water,' said D—. 'If you need force, fetch me.'

M— went. He was a great epicure, and knew how things should be cooked. But of course his irruptions into the kitchen roused considerable resentment, and he was getting quaky. However, he went. He came back to say the turkey was being roasted, but without chestnuts.

'What did I tell you! What did I tell you!' cried D—. 'They are absolute—! If you don't hold them by the neck while they peel the chestnuts, they'll stuff the bird with old boots, to save themselves trouble. Of course you should have gone down sooner, M—.'

Dinner was always late, so the whisky was usually two whiskies. Then we went down, and were merry in spite of all things. That is, D— always grumbled about the food. There was one unfortunate youth who was boots and porter and waiter and all. He brought the big dish to D—, and D— always poked and pushed among the portions, and grumbled frantically, sotto voce, in Italian to the youth Beppo, getting into a nervous frenzy. Then M— called the waiter to himself, picked the nicest bits off the dish and gave them to D—, then helped himself.

The food was not good, but with D— it was an obsession. With the waiter he was terrible – 'Cos' e? Zuppa? Grazie. No niente per me. *No – No!* Quest' acqua sporca non bevo io. I don't drink this dirty water. What – What's that in it – a piece of dish clout? Oh holy Dio, I can't eat another thing this evening –'

And he yelled for more bread – bread being war rations and very limited in supply – so M— in nervous distress gave him his piece, and D— threw the crumb part on the floor, anywhere, and called for another litre. We always drank heavy dark red wine at three francs a litre. D— drank two thirds, M— drank least. He loved his liquors, and did not care for wine. We were noisy and unabashed at table. The old Danish ladies at the other end of the room, and the rather impecunious young Duca and family not far off were not supposed to understand English. The Italians rather liked the noise, and the young signorina with the high-up yellow hair eyed us with profound interest. On we sailed, gay and noisy, D— telling witty anecdotes and grumbling wildly and only half whimsically about the food. We sat on till most people had finished – then went up to more whisky – one more perhaps – in M—'s room.

When I came down in the morning I was called into M—'s room. He was like a little pontiff in a blue kimono-shaped dressing-gown with a broad border of reddish purple: the blue was a soft mid-blue, the material a dull silk. So he minced about, in demi-toilette. His room was very clean and neat, and slightly perfumed with essences. On his dressing-table stood many cut glass bottles and silver-topped bottles with essences and pomades and powders, and heaven knows what. A very elegant little prayer book lay by his bed – and a life of St Benedict. For M— was a Roman Catholic convert. All he had was expensive and finicking: thick leather silver-studded suit-cases standing near the wall, trouser-stretcher all nice, hair-brushes and clothes-brush with old ivory backs. I wondered over him and his niceties and little pomposities. He was a new bird to me.

For he wasn't at all just the common person he looked. He was queer and sensitive as a woman with D—, and patient and fastidious. And yet he *was* common, his very accent was common, and D— despised him.

And M— rather despised me because I did not spend money. I paid for a third of the wine we drank at dinner, and bought the third bottle of whisky we had during M—'s stay. After all, he only stayed three days. But I would not spend for myself. I had no money to spend, since I knew I must live and my wife must live.

'Oh,' said M—. 'Why, that's the very time to spend money, when you've got none. If you've got none, why try to save it? That's been my philosophy all my life; when you've got no money, you may just as well spend it. If you've got a good deal, that's the time to look after it.' Then he laughed his queer little laugh, rather squeaky. These were his exact words.

'Precisely,' said D—. 'Spend when you've nothing to spend, my boy. Spend *hard* then.'

'No,' said I. 'If I can help it, I will never let myself be penniless while I live. I mistrust the world too much.'

'But if you're going to live in fear of the world,' said M—, 'what's the good of living at all? Might as well die.'

I think I give his words almost verbatim. He had a certain impatience of me and of my presence. Yet we had some jolly times – mostly in one or other of their bedrooms, drinking a whisky and talking. We drank a bottle a day – I had very little, preferring the wine at lunch and dinner, which seemed delicious after the war famine. D— would bring up the remains of the second litre in the evening, to go on with before the coffee came.

I arrived in Florence on the Wednesday or Thursday evening; I think Thursday. M— was due to leave for Rome on the Saturday. I asked D— who M— was. 'Oh, you never know what he's at. He was manager for Isadora Duncan for a long time – knows all the capitals of Europe: St Petersburg, Moscow, Tiflis, Constantinople, Berlin, Paris – knows them as you and I know Florence. He's been mostly in that line – theatrical. Then a journalist. He edited the *Roman Review* till the war killed it. Oh, a many-sided sort of fellow.'

'But how do you know him?' said I.

'I met him in Capri years and years ago – oh, sixteen years ago – and clean forgot all about him till somebody came to me one day in Rome and said: You're N— D—. *I* didn't know who he was. But he'd never forgotten me. Seems to be smitten by me, somehow or other. All the better for me, ha-ha! – if he *likes* to run round for me. My dear fellow, I wouldn't prevent him, if it amuses him. Not for worlds.'

And that was how it was. M— ran D—'s errands, forced the other man to go to the tailor, to the dentist, and was almost a guardian angel to him.

'Look here!' cried D—. '*I can't* go to that damned tailor. Let the thing wait, I can't go.'

'Oh yes. Now look here N—, if you don't get it done now while I'm here you'll never get it done. I made the appointment for three o'clock –'

'To hell with you! Details! Details! I can't stand it, I tell you.'

D— chafed and kicked, but went.

'A little fussy fellow,' he said. 'Oh yes, fussing about like a woman. Fussy, you know, fussy. I *can't stand* these fussy –' And D— went off into improprieties.

Well, M— ran round and arranged D—'s affairs and settled his little bills, and was so benevolent, and so impatient and nettled at the ungrateful way in which the benevolence was accepted. And D— despised him all the time as a little busybody and an inferior. And I there between them just wondered. It seemed to me M— would get very irritable and nervous at midday and before dinner, yellow round the eyes and played out. He wanted his whisky. He was tired after running round on a thousand errands and quests which I never understood. He always took his morning coffee at dawn, and was out to early Mass and pushing his affairs before eight o'clock in the morning. But what his affairs were I still do not know. Mass is all I am certain of.

However, it was his birthday on the Sunday, and D— would not let him go. He had once said he would give a dinner for his birthday, and this he was not allowed to forget. It seemed to me M— rather wanted to get out of it. But D— was determined to have that dinner.

'You aren't going before you've given us that hare, don't you imagine it, my boy. I've got the smell of that hare in my imagination, and I've damned well got to set my teeth in it. Don't you imagine you're going without having produced that hare.'

So poor M—, rather a victim, had to consent. We discussed what we should eat. It was decided the hare should have truffles, and a dish of champignons, and cauliflower, and zabaioni – and I forget what else. It was to be on Saturday evening. And M— would leave on Sunday for Rome.

Early on the Saturday morning he went out, with the first daylight, to the old market, to get the hare and the mushrooms. He went himself because he was a connoisseur.

*Personal*

On the Saturday afternoon D— took me wandering round to buy a birthday present.

'I shall have to buy him something – have to – have to –' he said fretfully. He only wanted to spend about five francs. We trailed over the Ponte Vecchio, looking at the jewellers' booths there. It was before the foreigners had come back, and things were still rather dusty and almost at pre-war prices. But we could see nothing for five francs except the little saint-medals. D— wanted to buy one of those. It seemed to me infra dig. So at last coming down to the Mercato Nuovo we saw little bowls of Volterra marble, a natural amber colour, for four francs.

'Look, buy one of those,' I said to D—, 'and he can put his pins or studs or any trifle in, as he needs.'

So we went in and bought one of the little bowls of Volterra marble.

M— seemed so touched and pleased with the gift.

'Thank you a thousand times, N—,' he said. 'That's charming! That's exactly what I want.'

The dinner was quite a success, and, poorly fed as we were at the pension, we stuffed ourselves tight on the mushrooms and the hare and the zabaioni, and drank ourselves tight with the good red wine which swung in its straw flask in the silver swing on the table. A flask has two and a quarter litres. We were four persons, and we drank almost two flasks. D— made the waiter measure the remaining half-litre and take it off the bill. But good, good food, and cost about twelve francs a head the whole dinner.

Well, next day was nothing but bags and suit-cases in M—'s room, and the misery of departure with luggage. He went on the midnight train to Rome: first-class.

'I always travel first-class,' he said, 'and I always shall, while I can buy the ticket. Why should I go second? It's beastly enough to travel at all.'

'My dear fellow, I came up third the last time I came from Rome,' said D—. 'Oh, not bad, not bad. Damned fatiguing journey anyhow.'

So the little outsider was gone, and I was rather glad. I don't think he liked me. Yet one day he said to me at table:

'How lovely your hair is – such a lovely colour! What do you dye it with?'

I laughed, thinking he was laughing too. But no, he meant it.

'It's got no particular colour at all,' I said, 'so I couldn't dye it that!'

'It's a lovely colour,' he said. And I think he didn't believe me, that I didn't dye it. It puzzled me, and it puzzles me still.

But he was gone. D— moved into M—'s room, and asked me to come down to the room he himself was vacating. But I preferred to stay upstairs.

M— was a fervent Catholic, taking the religion, alas, rather unctuously. He had entered the Church only a few years before. But he had a bishop for a god-father, and seemed to be very intimate with the upper clergy. He was very pleased and proud because he was a constant guest at the famous old monastery south of Rome. He talked of becoming a monk; a monk in that aristocratic and well-bred order. But he had not even begun his theological studies: or any studies of any sort. And D— said he only chose the Benedictines because they lived better than any of the others.

But I had said to M— that when my wife came and we moved south, I would like to visit the monastery some time, if I might. 'Certainly,' he said. 'Come when I am there. I shall be there in about a month's time. Do come! Do be sure and come. It's a wonderful place – oh, wonderful. It will make a great impression on you. Do come. Do come. And I will tell Don Bernardo, who is my *greatest* friend, and who is guest-master, about you. So that if you wish to go when I am not there, write to Don Bernardo. But do come when I am there.'

My wife and I were due to go into the mountains south of Rome, and stay there some months. Then I was to visit the big, noble monastery that stands on a bluff hill like a fortress crowning a great precipice, above the little town and the plain between the mountains. But it was so icy cold and snowy among the mountains, it was unbearable. We fled south again, to Naples, and to Capri. Passing, I saw the monastery crouching there above, world-famous, but it was impossible to call then.

I wrote and told M— of my move. In Capri I had an answer from him. It had a wistful tone – and I don't know what made me think that he was in trouble, in monetary difficulty. But I felt it acutely – a kind of appeal. Yet he said nothing direct. And he wrote from an expensive hotel in Anzio, on the sea near Rome.

At the moment I had just received twenty pounds unexpected and joyful from America – a gift too. I hesitated for some time, because I felt unsure. Yet the curious appeal came out of the letter, though nothing was said. And I felt also I owed M— that dinner, and I didn't want to owe him anything, since he despised me a little for being careful. So partly out of revenge, perhaps, and partly because I felt the strange wistfulness of him appealing to me, I sent him five pounds, saying perhaps I was mistaken in imagining him very hard up, but if so, he wasn't to be offended.

It is strange to me even now, how I knew he was appealing to me. Because it was all as vague as I say. Yet I felt it so strongly. He replied: 'Your cheque has saved my life. Since I last saw you I have fallen down an abyss. But I will tell you when I see you. I shall be at the monastery in three days. Do come – and come alone.' I have forgotten to say that he was a rabid woman-hater.

This was just after Christmas. I thought his 'saved my life' and 'fallen down an abyss' was just the American touch of 'very, very —'. I wondered what on earth the abyss could be, and I decided it must be that he had lost his money or his hopes. It seemed to me that some of his old buoyant assurance came out again in this letter. But he was now very friendly, urging me to come to the monastery, and treating me with a curious little tenderness and protectiveness. He had a queer delicacy of his own, varying with a bounce and a commonness. He was a common little bounder. And then he had this curious delicacy and tenderness and wistfulness.

I put off going north. I had another letter urging me – and it seemed to me that, rather assuredly, he was expecting more money. Rather cockily, as if he had a right to it. And that made me not want to give him any. Besides, as my wife said, what right had I to give away the little money we had, and we there stranded in the south of Italy with no resources if once we were spent up.

And I have always been determined *never* to come to my last shilling – if I have to reduce my spending almost to nothingness. I have always been determined to keep a few pounds between me and the world.

I did not send any money. But I wanted to go to the monastery, so wrote and said I would come for two days. I always remember getting up in the black dark of the January morning, and making a little coffee on the spirit-lamp, and watching the clock, the big-faced, blue old clock on the campanile in the piazza in Capri, to see I wasn't late. The electric light in the piazza lit up the face of the campanile. And we were then a stone's throw away, high in the Palazzo Ferraro, opposite the bubbly roof of the little duomo. Strange dark winter morning, with the open sea beyond the roofs, seen through the side window, and the thin line of the lights of Naples twinkling far, far off.

At ten minutes to six I went down the smelly dark stone stairs of the old palazzo, out into the street. A few people were already hastening up the street to the terrace that looks over the sea to the bay of Naples. It was dark and cold. We slid down in the funicular to the shore, then in little boats were rowed out over the dark sea to the steamer that lay there showing her lights and hooting.

It was three long hours across the sea to Naples, with dawn coming slowly in the east, beyond Ischia, and flushing into lovely colour as our steamer pottered along the peninsula, calling at Massa and Sorrento and Piano. I always loved hanging over the side and watching the people come out in boats from the little places of the shore, that rose steep and beautiful. I love the movement of these watery Neapolitan people, and the naïve trustful way they clamber in and out the boats, and their softness, and their dark eyes. But when the steamer leaves the peninsula and begins to make away round Vesuvius to Naples, one is already tired, and cold, cold, cold in the wind that comes piercing from the snowcrests away there along Italy. Cold, and reduced to a kind of stony apathy by the time we come to the mole in Naples, at ten o'clock – or twenty past ten.

We were rather late, and I missed the train. I had to wait till two o'clock. And Naples is a hopeless town to spend three hours in. However, time passes. I remember I was calculating in my mind whether they had given me the right change at the ticket-window. They hadn't – and I hadn't counted in time. Thinking of this, I got in the Rome train. I had been there ten minutes when I heard a trumpet blow.

'Is this the Rome train?' I asked my fellow-traveller.

'Si.'

'The express?'

'No, it is the slow train.'

'It leaves?'

'At ten past two.'

I almost jumped through the window. I flew down the platform. 'The diretto! ' I cried to a porter.

'Parte! Eccolo là!' he said, pointing to a big train moving inevitably away.

I flew with wild feet across the various railway lines and seized the end of the train as it travelled. I had caught it. Perhaps if I had missed it fate would have been different. So I sat still for about three hours. Then I had arrived.

There is a long drive up the hill from the station to the monastery. The driver talked to me. It was evident he bore the monks no good will.

'Formerly,' he said, 'if you went up to the monastery you got a glass of wine and a plate of macaroni. But now they kick you out of the door.'

'Do they?' I said. 'It is hard to believe.'

'They kick you out of the gate,' he vociferated.

We twisted up and up the wild hillside, past the old castle of the town, past the last villa, between trees and rocks. We saw no one. The whole hill belongs to the monastery. At last at twilight we turned the corner of the oak wood and saw the monastery like a huge square fortress-palace of the sixteenth century crowning the near distance. Yes, and there was M— just stepping through the huge old gateway and hastening down the slope to where the carriage must stop. He was bare-headed, and walking with his perky, busy little stride, seemed very much at home in the place. He looked up to me with a tender, intimate look as I got down from the carriage. Then he took my hand.

'So *very* glad to see you,' he said. 'I'm so *pleased* you've come.'

And he looked into my eyes with that wistful, watchful tenderness rather like a woman who isn't quite sure of her lover. He had a certain charm in his manner; and an odd pompous touch with it at this moment, welcoming his guest at the gate of the vast monastery which reared above us from its buttresses in the rock, was rather becoming. His face was still pink, his eyes pale blue and sharp, but he looked greyer at the temples.

'Give me your bag,' he said. 'Yes do – and come along. Don Bernardo is just at Evensong, but he'll be here in a little while. Well now, tell me all the news.'

'Wait,' I said. 'Lend me five francs to finish paying the driver – he has no change.'

'Certainly, certainly,' he said, giving the five francs.

I had no news – so asked him his.

'Oh, I have none either,' he said. 'Very short of money, that of course is *no* news.' And he laughed his little laugh. 'I'm so glad to be here,' he continued. 'The peace, and the rhythm of the life is so *beautiful*! I'm sure you'll love it.'

We went up the slope under the big, tunnel-like entrance and were in the grassy courtyard, with the arched walk on the far sides, and one or two trees. It was like a grassy cloister, but still busy. Black monks were standing chatting, an old peasant was just driving two sheep from the cloister grass, and an old monk was darting into the little post-office which one recognized by the shield with the national arms over the doorway. From under the far arches came an old peasant carrying a two-handed saw.

And there was Don Bernardo, a tall monk in a black, well-shaped gown, young, good-looking, gentle, hastening forward with a quick smile. He was about my age, and his manner seemed fresh and subdued, as if he were still a student. One felt one was at college with one's college mates.

We went up the narrow stair and into the long, old, naked white corridor, high and arched. Don Bernardo had got the key of my room: two keys, one for the dark antechamber, one for the bedroom. A charming and elegant bedroom, with an engraving of English landscape, and outside the net curtain a balcony looking down on the garden, a narrow strip beneath the walls, and beyond, the clustered buildings of the farm, and the oak woods and arable fields of the hill summit: and beyond again, the gulf where the world's valley was, and all the mountains that stand in Italy on the plains as if God had just put them down ready made. The sun had already sunk, the snow on the mountains was full of a rosy glow, the valleys were full of shadow. One heard, far below, the trains shunting, the world clinking in the cold air.

'Isn't it wonderful! Ah, the most wonderful place on earth!' said M—. 'What now could you wish better than to end your days here? The peace, the beauty, the eternity of it.' He paused and sighed. Then he put his hand on Don Bernardo's arm and smiled at him with that odd, rather wistful smirking tenderness that made him such a quaint creature in my eyes.

'But I'm going to enter the order. You're going to let me be a monk and be one of you, aren't you, Don Bernardo?'

'We will see,' smiled Don Bernardo. 'When you have begun your studies.'

'It will take me two years,' said M—. 'I shall have to go to the college in Rome. When I have got the money for the fees –' He talked away, like a boy planning a new rôle.

'But I'm sure Lawrence would like to drink a cup of tea,' said Don Bernardo. He spoke English as if it were his native language. 'Shall I tell them to make it in the kitchen, or shall we go to your room?'

'Oh, we'll go to my room. How thoughtless of me! Do forgive me, won't you?' said M—, laying his hand gently on my arm. 'I'm so awfully sorry, you know. But we get so excited and enchanted when we talk of the monastery. But come along, come along, it will be ready in a moment on the spirit-lamp.'

We went down to the end of the high, white, naked corridor. M— had a quite sumptuous room, with a curtained bed in one part, and under the window his writing-desk with papers and photographs, and nearby a sofa and an easy table, making a little sitting-room, while the bed and toilet things, pomades and bottles were all in the distance, in the shadow. Night was fallen. From the window one saw the world far below, like a pool the flat plain, a deep pool of darkness with little twinkling lights, and rows and bunches of light that were the railway station.

I drank my tea, M— drank a little liqueur, Don Bernardo in his black winter robe sat and talked with us. At least he did very little talking. But he listened and smiled and put in a word or two as we talked, seated round the table on which stood the green-shaded electric lamp.

The monastery was cold as the tomb. Couched there on the top of its hill, it is not much below the winter snow-line. Now by the end of January all the summer heat is soaked out of the vast, ponderous stone walls, and they become masses of coldness cloaking around. There is no heating apparatus whatsoever – none. Save the fire in the kitchen, for cooking, nothing. Dead, silent, stone cold everywhere.

At seven we went down to dinner. Capri in the daytime was hot, so I had brought only a thin old dust-coat. M— therefore made me wear a big coat of his own, a coat made of thick, smooth black cloth, and lined with black sealskin, and having a collar of silky black sealskin. I can still remember the feel of the silky fur. It was queer to have him helping me solicitously into this coat, and buttoning it at the throat for me.

'Yes, it's a beautiful coat. Of course!' he said. 'I hope you find it warm.'

'Wonderful,' said I. 'I feel as warm as a millionaire.'

'I'm so glad you do,' he laughed.

'You don't mind my wearing your grand coat?' I said.

'Of course not! Of course not! It's a pleasure to me if it will keep you warm. We don't want to die of cold in the monastery, do we? That's one of the mortifications we will do our best to avoid. What? Don't you think? Yes, I think this coldness is going almost too far. I had that coat made in New York fifteen years ago. Of course in Italy –' he said It'ly – 'I've never worn it, so it is as good as new. And it's a beautiful coat, fur and cloth of the very best. *And* the tailor.' He laughed a little, self-approving laugh. He liked to give the impression that he dealt with the *best* shops,

45

don't you know, and stayed in the *best* hotels, etc. I grinned inside the coat, detesting best hotels, best shops, and best overcoats. So off we went, he in his grey overcoat and I in my sealskin millionaire monster, down the dim corridor to the guests' refectory. It was a bare room with a long white table. M— and I sat at the near end. Further down was another man, perhaps the father of one of the boy students. There is a college attached to the monastery.

We sat in the icy room, muffled up in our overcoats. A lay-brother with a bulging forehead and queer, fixed eyes waited on us. He might easily have come from an old Italian picture. One of the adoring peasants. The food was abundant – but alas, it had got cold in the long cold transit from the kitchen. And it was roughly cooked, even if it was quite wholesome. Poor M— did not eat much, but nervously nibbled his bread. I could tell the meals were a trial to him. He could not bear the cold food in that icy, empty refectory. And his phthisickiness offended the lay-brothers. I could see that his little pomposities and his 'superior' behaviour and his long stay made them have that old monastic grudge against him, silent but very obstinate and effectual – the same now as six hundred years ago. We had a decanter of good red wine – but he did not care for much wine. He was glad to be peeling the cold orange which was dessert.

After dinner he took me down to see the church, creeping like two thieves down the dimness of the great, prison-cold white corridors, on the cold flag floors. Stone cold: the monks must have invented the term. These monks were at Compline. So we went by our two secret little selves into the tall dense nearly-darkness of the church. M—, knowing his way about here as in the cities, led me, poor wondering worldling, by the arm through the gulfs of the tomb-like place. He found the electric light switches inside the church, and stealthily made me a light as we went. We looked at the lily marble of the great floor, at the pillars, at the Benvenuto Cellini casket, at the really lovely pillars and slabs of different coloured marbles, all coloured marbles, yellow and grey and rose and green and lily white, veined and mottled and splashed: lovely, lovely stones – And Benvenuto

46

had used pieces of lapis lazuli, blue as cornflowers. Yes, yes, all very rich and wonderful.

We tiptoed about the dark church stealthily, from altar to altar, and M— whispered ecstasies in my ear. Each time we passed before an altar, whether the high altar or the side chapels, he did a wonderful reverence, which he must have practised for hours, bowing waxily down and sinking till his one knee touched the pavement, then rising like a flower that rises and unfolds again, till he had skipped to my side and was playing cicerone once more. Always in his grey overcoat, and in whispers: me in the big black overcoat, millionairish. So we crept into the chancel and examined all the queer fat babies of the choir stalls, carved in wood and rolling on their little backs between monk's place and monk's place – queer things for the chanting monks to have between them, these shiny, polished, dark brown fat babies, all different, and all jolly and lusty. We looked at everything in the church – and then at everything in the ancient room at the side where surplices hang and monks can wash their hands.

Then we went down to the crypt, where the modern mosaics glow in wonderful colours, and sometimes in fascinating little fantastic trees and birds. But it was rather like a scene in the theatre, with M— for the wizard and myself a sort of Parsifal in the New York coat. He switched on the lights, the gold mosaic of the vaulting glittered and bowed, the blue mosaic glowed out, the holy of holies gleamed theatrically, the stiff mosaic figures posed around us. To tell the truth I was glad to get back to the normal human room and sit on a sofa huddled in my overcoat, and look at photographs which M— showed me: photographs of everywhere in Europe. Then he showed me a wonderful photograph of a picture of a lovely lady – asked me what I thought of it, and seemed to expect me to be struck to bits by the beauty. His almost sanctimonious expectation made me tell the truth, that I thought it just a bit cheap, trivial. And then he said, dramatic:

'That's my mother.'

It looked so unlike anybody's mother, much less M—'s, that I was startled. I realized that she was his great stunt, and that I had put my foot in it. So I just held my tongue. Then I said, for I felt he was going to be silent forever:

'There are so few portraits, unless by the really great artists, that aren't a bit cheap. She must have been a beautiful woman.'

'Yes, she *was*,' he said curtly. And we dropped the subject.

He locked all his drawers *very* carefully, and kept the keys on a chain. He seemed to give the impression that he had a great many secrets, perhaps dangerous ones, locked up in the drawers of his writing-table there. And I always wonder what the secrets can be, that are able to be kept so tight under lock and key.

Don Bernardo tapped and entered. We all sat round and sipped a funny liqueur which I didn't like. M— lamented that the bottle was finished. I asked him to order another and let me pay for it. So he said he would tell the postman to bring it up next day from the town. Don Bernardo sipped his tiny glass with the rest of us, and he told me, briefly, his story – and we talked politics till nearly midnight. Then I came out of the black overcoat and we went to bed.

In the morning a fat, smiling, nice old lay-brother brought me my water. It was a sunny day. I looked down on the farm cluster and the brown fields and the sere oak woods of the hill-crown, and the rocks and bushes savagely bordering it round. Beyond, the mountains with their snow were blue-glistery with sunshine, and seemed quite near, but across a sort of gulf. All was still and sunny. And the poignant grip of the past, the grandiose, violent past of the Middle Ages, when blood was strong and unquenched and life was flamboyant with splendours and horrible miseries, took hold of me till I could hardly bear it. It was really agony to me to be in the monastery and to see the old farm and the bullocks slowly working in the fields below, and the black pigs rooting among weeds, and to see a monk sitting on a parapet in the sun, and an old, old man in skin sandals and white bunched, swathed legs come driving an ass slowly to the monastery gate, slowly, with all that lingering nonchalance and wildness of the Middle Ages, and yet to know that I was myself, child of the present. It was so strange from M—'s window to look down on the plain and see the white road going straight past a mountain that stood like a loaf of sugar, the river meandering in loops, and the railway with glistening lines making a long black swoop across the flat and into the hills. To see trains come steaming, with white smoke flying. To see the station like a little harbour where trucks like shipping stood anchored in rows in the black bay of railway. To see trains stop in the station and tiny people swarming like flies! To see all this from the monastery, where the Middle Ages live on in a sort of agony, like Tithonus, and cannot die, this was almost a violation to my soul, made almost a wound.

Immediately after coffee we went down to Mass. It was celebrated in a small crypt chapel underground, because that was warmer. The twenty or so monks sat in their stalls, one monk officiating at the altar. It was quiet and simple, the monks sang sweetly and well, there was no organ. It seemed soon to pass by. M— and I sat near the door. He was very devoted and scrupulous in his going up and down. I was an outsider. But it was pleasant – not too sacred. One felt the monks were very human in their likes and their jealousies. It was rather like a group of dons in the dons' room at Cambridge, a cluster of professors in any college. But during Mass they, of course, just sang their responses. Only I could tell some watched the officiating monk rather with ridicule – he was one of the ultra-punctilious sort, just like a don. And some boomed their responses with a grain of defiance against some brother monk who had earned dislike. It was human, and more like a university than anything. We went to Mass every morning, but I did not go to Evensong.

After Mass M— took me round and showed me everything of the vast monastery. We went into the Bramante Courtyard, all stone, with its great well in the centre, and the colonnades of arches going round, full of sunshine, gay and Renaissance, a little bit ornate but still so jolly and gay, sunny pale stone waiting for the lively people, with the great flight of pale steps sweeping up to the doors of the church, waiting for gentlemen in scarlet trunk-hose, slender red legs, and ladies in brocade gowns, and page-boys with fluffed, golden hair. Splendid, sunny, gay Bramante Courtyard of lively stone. But empty. Empty of life. The gay red-legged gentry dead forever. And when pilgrimages do come and throng in, it is horrible artisan excursions from the great town, and the sordidness of industrialism.

We climbed the little watchtower that is now an observatory, and saw the vague and unshaven Don Giovanni among all his dust and instruments. M— was very familiar and friendly, chattering in his quaint Italian, which was more wrong than any Italian I have ever heard spoken; very familiar and friendly, and a tiny bit deferential to the monks, and yet, and yet – rather patronizing. His little pomposity and patronizing tone coloured even his deferential yearning to be admitted to the monastery. The monks were rather brief with him. They no doubt have their likes and dislikes greatly intensified by the monastic life.

We stood on the summit of the tower and looked at the world below: the town, the castle, the white roads coming straight as judgement out of the mountains north, from Rome, and piercing into the mountains south, towards Naples, traversing the flat, flat plain. Roads, railway, river, streams, a world in accurate and lively detail, with mountains sticking up abruptly and rockily, as the old painters painted it. I think there is no way of painting Italian landscape except that way – that started with Lorenzetti and ended with the sixteenth century.

We looked at the ancient cell away under the monastery, where all the sanctity started. We looked at the big library that belongs to the State, and at the smaller library that belongs still to the abbot. I was tired, cold, and sick among the books and illuminations. I could not bear it any more. I felt I must be outside, in the sun, and see the world below, and the way out.

That evening I said to M—:

'And what was the abyss, then?'

'Oh well, you know,' he said, 'it was a cheque which I made out at Anzio. There should have been money to meet it, in my bank in New York. But it appears the money had never been paid in by the people that owed it me. So there was I in a very nasty hole, an unmet cheque, and no money at all in Italy. I really had to escape here. It is an *absolute* secret that I am here, and it must be, till I can get this business settled. Of course I've written to

*Introduction to* Memoirs of the Foreign Legion

America about it. But as you see, I'm in a very nasty hole. That five francs I gave you for the driver was the last penny I had in the world: absolutely the last penny. I haven't even anything to buy a cigarette or a stamp.' And he laughed chirpily, as if it were a joke. But he didn't really think it a joke. Nor was it a joke.

I had come with only two hundred lire in my pocket, as I was waiting to change some money at the bank. Of this two hundred I had one hundred left or one hundred and twenty-five. I should need a hundred to get home. I could only give M— the twenty-five, for the bottle of drink. He was rather crestfallen. But I didn't want to give him money this time: because he expected it.

However, we talked about his plans: how he was to earn something. He told me what he had written. And I cast over in my mind where he might get something published in London, wrote a couple of letters on his account, told him where I thought he had best send his material. There wasn't a great deal of hope, for his smaller journalistic articles seemed to me very self-conscious and poor. He had one about the monastery, which I thought he might sell because of the photographs.

That evening he first showed me the Legion manuscript. He had got it rather raggedly typed out. He had a typewriter, but felt he ought to have somebody to do his typing for him, as he hated it and did it unwillingly. That evening and when I went to bed and when I woke in the morning I read this manuscript. It did not seem very good – vague and diffuse where it shouldn't have been – lacking in sharp detail and definite event. And yet there was something in it that made me want it done properly. So we talked about it, and discussed it carefully, and he unwillingly promised to tackle it again. He was curious, always talking about his work, even always working, but never *properly* doing anything.

We walked out in the afternoon through the woods and across the rocky bit of moorland which covers most of the hill-top. We were going to the ruined convent which lies on the other brow of the monastery hill, abandoned and sad among the rocks and heath and thorny bushes. It was sunny and warm. A barefoot little boy was tending a cow and three goats and a pony, a barefoot little girl had five geese in charge. We came to the convent and looked in. The further part of the courtyard was still entire, the place was a sort of farm, two rooms occupied by a peasant-farmer. We climbed about the ruins. Some creature was crying – crying, crying, crying with a strange, inhuman persistence, leaving off and crying again. We listened and listened – the sharp, poignant crying. Almost it might have been a sharp-voiced baby. We scrambled about, looking. And at last outside a little cave-like place found a blind black puppy crawling miserably on the floor, unable to walk, and crying incessantly. We put it back in the little cave-like shed, and went away. The place was deserted save for the crying puppy.

On the road outside however was a man, a peasant, just drawing up to the arched convent gateway with an ass under a load of brushwood. He was thin and black and dirty. He took off his hat, and we told him of the puppy. He said the bitch-mother had gone off with his son with the sheep. Yes, she had been gone all day. Yes, she would be back at sunset. No, the puppy had not drunk all day. Yes, the little beast cried, but the mother would come back to him.

They were the old-world peasants still about the monastery, with the hard, small bony heads and deep-lined faces and utterly blank minds, crying their speech as crows cry, and living their lives as lizards among the rocks, blindly going on with the little job in hand, the present moment, cut off from all past and future, and having no idea and no sustained emotion, only that eternal will-to-live which makes a tortoise wake up once more in spring, and makes a grasshopper whistle on in the moonlight nights even of November. Only these peasants don't whistle much. The whistlers go to America. It is the hard, static, unhoping souls that persist in the old life. And still they stand back, as one passes them in the corridors of the great monastery, they press themselves back against the whitewashed walls of the still place, and drop their heads, as if some mystery were passing by, some God-mystery, the higher beings, which they must not look closely upon. So also this old peasant – he was not old, but deep-lined like a gnarled bough. He stood with his hat down in his hands as we spoke to him and answered the short, hard, insentient answers, as a tree might speak.

'The monks keep their peasants humble,' I said to M—.

'Of course!' he said. 'Don't you think they are quite right? Don't you think they should be humble?' And he bridled like a little turkey-cock on his hind legs.

'Well,' I said, 'if there's any occasion for humility, I do.'

'Don't you think there is occasion?' he cried. 'If there's one thing worse than another, it's this *equality* that has come into the world. Do you believe in it yourself?'

'No,' I said. 'I don't believe in equality. But the problem is, wherein does superiority lie.'

'Oh,' chirped M— complacently. 'It lies in many things. It lies in birth and in upbringing and so on, but it is chiefly in *mind*. Don't you think? Of course I don't mean that the physical qualities aren't *charming*. They are, and nobody appreciates them more than I do. Some of the peasants are *beautiful* creatures, perfectly beautiful. But that passes. And the mind endures.'

I did not answer. M— was not a man one talked far with. But I thought to myself, I *could* not accept M—'s superiority to the peasant. If I had really to live always under the same roof with either one of them, I would have chosen the peasant. If I had had to choose, I would have chosen the peasant. Not because the peasant was wonderful and stored with mystic qualities. No, I don't give much for the wonderful mystic qualities in peasants. Money is their mystery of mysteries, absolutely. No, if I chose the peasant it would be for what he *lacked* rather than for what he had. He lacked that complacent mentality that M— was so proud of, he lacked all the trivial trash of glib talk and more glib thought, all the conceit of our shallow consciousness. For his mindlessness I would have chosen the peasant: and for his strong blood-presence. M— wearied me with his facility and his readiness to rush into speech, and for the exhaustive nature of his presence. As if he had no strong blood in him to sustain him, only this modern parasitic lymph which cries for sympathy all the time.

'Don't you think yourself that you are superior to that peasant?' he asked me, rather ironically. He half expected me to say no.

'Yes, I do,' I replied. 'But I think most middle-class, most so-called educated people are inferior to the peasant. I do that.'

'Of course,' said M— readily. 'In their *hypocrisy*—' He was great against hypocrisy – especially the English sort.

'And if I think myself superior to the peasant, it is only that I feel myself like the growing tip, or one of the growing tips of the tree, and him like a piece of the hard, fixed tissue of the branch or trunk. We're part of the same tree: and it's the same sap,' said I.

'Why, exactly! Exactly!' cried M—. 'Of course! The Church would teach the same doctrine. We are all one in Christ – but between our souls and our duties there are great differences.'

It is terrible to be agreed with, especially by a man like M—. All that one says, and means, turns to nothing.

'Yes,' I persisted. 'But it seems to me the so-called culture, education, the so-called leaders and leading-classes today, are only parasites – like a great flourishing bush of parasitic consciousness flourishing on top of the tree of life, and sapping it. The consciousness of today doesn't rise from the roots. It is just parasitic in the veins of life. And the middle and upper classes are just parasitic upon the body of life which still remains in the lower classes.'

'What!' said M— acidly. 'Do you believe in the democratic lower classes?'

'Not a bit,' said I.

'I should think not, indeed!' he cried complacently.

'No, I don't believe the lower classes can ever make life whole again, till they *do* become humble, like the old peasants, and yield themselves to real leaders. But not to great negators like Lloyd George or Lenin or Briand.'

'Of course! of course!' he cried. 'What you need is the Church in power again. The Church has a place for everybody.'

'You don't think the Church belongs to the past?' I asked.

'Indeed I don't, or I shouldn't be here. No,' he said sententiously, 'the Church is eternal. It puts people in their proper place. It puts women down into *their* proper place, which is the first thing to be done –'

He had a great dislike of women, and was very acid about them.

Not because of their sins, but because of their virtues: their economies, their philanthropies, their spiritualities. Oh, how he loathed women. He had been married, but the marriage had not been a success. He smarted still. Perhaps his wife had despised him, and he had not *quite* been able to defeat her contempt.

So, he loathed women, and wished for a world of men. 'They talk about love between men and women,' he said. 'Why it's all a *fraud*. The woman is just taking all and giving nothing, and feeling sanctified about it. All she tries to do is to thwart a man in whatever he is doing. No, I have found my life in my *friendships*. Physical relationships are very attractive, of course, and one tries to keep them as decent and all that as one can. But one knows they will pass and be finished. But one's *mental* friendships last for ever.'

'With me, on the contrary,' said I. 'If there is no profound blood-sympathy, I know the mental friendship is trash. If there is real, deep blood response, I will stick to that if I have to betray all the mental sympathies I ever made, or all the lasting spiritual loves I ever felt.'

He looked at me, and his face seemed to fall. Round the eyes he was yellow and tired and nervous. He watched me for some time.

'Oh!' he said, in a queer tone, rather cold. 'Well, my experience has been the opposite.'

We were silent for some time.

'And you,' I said, 'even if you do manage to do all your studies and enter the monastery, do you think you will be satisfied?'

'If I can be so fortunate, I do really,' he said. 'Do you doubt it?'

'Yes,' I said. 'Your nature is worldly, more worldly than mine. Yet I should die if I had to stay up here.'

'Why?' he asked, curiously.

'Oh, I don't know. The past, the past. The beautiful, the wonderful past, it seems to prey on my heart, I can't bear it.'

He watched me closely.

'Really!' he said stoutly. 'Do you feel like that? But don't you think it is a far preferable life up here than down there? Don't you think the past is far preferable to the future, with all this *socialismo* and these *communisti* and so on?'

*Personal*

We were seated, in the sunny afternoon, on the wild hill-top high above the world. Across the stretch of pale, dry, standing thistles that peopled the waste ground, and beyond the rocks was the ruined convent. Rocks rose behind us, the summit. Away on the left were the woods which hid us from the great monastery. This was the mountain top, the last foothold of the old world. Below we could see the plain, the straight white road, straight as a thought, and the more flexible black railway with the railway station. There swarmed the *ferrovieri* like ants. There was democracy, industrialism, socialism, the red flag of the communists and the red, white and green tricolor of the fascisti. That was another world. And how bitter, how barren a world! Barren like the black cinder-track of the railway, with its two steel lines.

And here above, sitting with the little stretch of pale, dry thistles around us, our back to a warm rock, we were in the Middle Ages. Both worlds were agony to me. But here, on the mountain top was worst: the past, the poignancy of the not-quite-dead past.

'I think one's got to go through with the life down there – get somewhere beyond it. One can't go back,' I said to him.

'But do you call the monastery going back?' he said. 'I don't. The peace, the eternity, the concern with things that matter. I consider it the happiest fate that could happen to me. Of course it means putting physical things aside. But when you've done that – why, it seems to me perfect.'

'No,' I said. 'You're too worldly.'

'But the monastery is worldly too. We're not Trappists. Why the monastery is one of the centres of the world – one of the most active centres.'

'Maybe. But that impersonal activity, with the blood suppressed and going sour – no, it's too late. It is too abstract – political maybe –'

'I'm sorry you think so,' he said, rising. 'I don't.'

'Well,' I said. 'You'll never be a monk here, M——. You see if you are.'

'You don't think I shall?' he replied, turning to me. And there was a catch of relief in his voice. Really, the monastic state must have been like going to prison for him.

'You haven't a vocation,' I said.

'I may not *seem* to have, but I hope I actually have.'

'You haven't.'

'Of course, if you're so sure,' he laughed, putting his hand on my arm.

He seemed to understand so much, round about the questions that trouble one deepest. But the quick of the question he never felt. He had no real middle, no real centre bit to him. Yet, round and round about all the questions, he was so intelligent and sensitive.

We went slowly back. The peaks of those Italian mountains in the sunset, the extinguishing twinkle of the plain away below, as the sun declined and grew yellow; the intensely powerful medieval spirit lingering on this wild hill summit, all the wonder of the medieval past; and then the huge mossy stones in the wintry wood, that was once a sacred grove; the ancient path through the wood, that led from temple to temple on the hill summit, before Christ was born; and then the great Cyclopean wall one passes at the bend of the road, built even before the pagan temples; all this overcame me so powerfully this afternoon, that I was almost speechless. That hill-top must have been one of man's intense sacred places for three thousand years. And men die generation after generation, races die, but the new cult finds root in the old sacred place, and the quick spot of earth dies very slowly. Yet at last it too dies. But this quick spot is still not quite dead. The great monastery couchant there, half empty, but also not quite dead. And M— and I walking across as the sun set yellow and the cold of the snow came into the air, back home to the monastery! And I feeling as if my heart had once more broken: I don't know why. And he feeling his fear of life, that haunted him, and his fear of his own self and its consequences, that never left him for long. And he seemed to walk close to me, very close. And we had neither of us anything more to say.

Don Bernardo was looking for us as we came up under the archway, he hatless in the cold evening, his black dress swinging voluminous. There were letters for M—. There was a small cheque for him from America – about fifty dollars – from some

newspaper in the Middle West that had printed one of his articles.
He had to talk with Don Bernardo about this.

I decided to go back the next day. I could not stay any longer.
M— was very disappointed, and begged me to remain. 'I thought
you would stay a week at least,' he said. 'Do stay over Sunday.
Oh do!' But I couldn't, I didn't want to. I could see that his days
were a torture to him – the long, cold days in that vast quiet
building, with the strange and exhausting silence in the air, and the
sense of the past preying on one, and the sense of the silent, suppressed scheming struggle of life going on still in the sacred place.

It was a cloudy morning. In the green courtyard the big Don
Anselmo had just caught the little Don Lorenzo round the waist
and was swinging him over a bush, like lads before school. The
Prior was just hurrying somewhere, following his long fine nose.
He bade me good-bye; pleasant, warm, jolly, with a touch of
wistfulness in his deafness. I parted with real regret from Don
Bernardo.

M— was coming with me down the hill – not down the carriage
road, but down the wide old paved path that swoops so wonderfully from the top of the hill to the bottom. It feels thousands of
years old. M— was quiet and friendly. We met Don Vincenzo, he
who has the care of the land and crops, coming slowly, slowly uphill in his black cassock, treading slowly with his great thick
boots. He was reading a little book. He saluted us as we passed.
Lower down a strapping girl was watching three merino sheep
among the bushes. One sheep came on its exquisite slender legs
to smell of me, with that insatiable curiosity of a pecora. Her
nose was silken and elegant as she reached it to sniff at me, and
the yearning, wondering, inquisitive look in her eyes, made me
realize that the Lamb of God must have been such a sheep as this.

M— was miserable at my going. Not so much at my going, as
at being left alone up there. We came to the foot of the hill, on to
the town highroad. So we went into a little cave of a wine-kitchen
to drink a glass of wine. M— chatted a little with the young
woman. He chatted with everybody. She eyed us closely – and
asked if we were from the monastery. We said we were. She
seemed to have a little lurking antagonism round her nose, at the

mention of the monastery. M— paid for the wine – a franc. So we went out on the highroad, to part.

'Look,' I said. 'I can only give you twenty lire, because I shall need the rest for the journey –'

But he wouldn't take them. He looked at me wistfully. Then I went on down to the station, he turned away uphill. It was market in the town, and there were clusters of bullocks, and women cooking a little meal at a brazier under the trees, and goods spread out on the floor to sell, and sacks of beans and corn standing open, clustered round the trunks of the mulberry trees, and wagons with their shafts on the ground. The old peasants in their brown homespun frieze and skin sandals were watching for the world. And there again was the Middle Ages.

It began to rain, however. Suddenly it began to pour with rain, and my coat was wet through, and my trouser-legs. The train from Rome was late – I hoped not very late, or I should miss the boat. She came at last: and was full. I had to stand in the corridor. Then the man came to say dinner was served, so I luckily got a place and had my meal too. Sitting there in the dining-car, among the fat Neapolitans eating their macaroni, with the big glass windows steamed opaque and the rain beating outside, I let myself be carried away, away from the monastery, away from M—, away from everything.

At Naples there was a bit of sunshine again, and I had time to go on foot to the Immacolatella, where the little steamer lay. There on the steamer I sat in a bit of sunshine, and felt that again the world had come to an end for me, and again my heart was broken. The steamer seemed to be making its way away from the old world, that had come to another end in me.

It was after this I decided to go to Sicily. In February, only a few days after my return from the monastery, I was on the steamer for Palermo, and at dawn looking out on the wonderful coast of Sicily. Sicily, tall, forever rising up to her gem-like summits, all golden in dawn, and always glamorous, always hovering as if inaccessible, and yet so near, so distinct. Sicily unknown to me, and amethystine-glamorous in the Mediterranean dawn: like the dawn of our day, the wonder-morning of our epoch.

I had various letters from M—. He had told me to go to Girgenti. But I arrived in Girgenti when there was a strike of sulphur-miners, and they threw stones. So I did not want to live in Girgenti. M— hated Taormina – he had been everywhere, tried everywhere, and was not, I found, in any good odour in most places. He wrote however saying he hoped I would like it. And later he sent the Legion manuscript. I thought it was good, and told him so. It was offered to publishers in London, but rejected.

In early April I went with my wife to Syracuse for a few days: lovely, lovely days, with the purple anemones blowing in the Sicilian fields, and Adonis-blood red on the little ledges, and the corn rising strong and green in the magical, malarial places, and Etna flowing now to the northward, still with her crown of snow. The lovely, lovely journey from Catania to Syracuse, in spring, winding round the blueness of that sea, where the tall pink asphodel was dying, and the yellow asphodel like a lily showing her silk. Lovely, lovely Sicily, the dawn-place, Europe's dawn, with Odysseus pushing his ship out of the shadows into the blue. Whatever had died for me, Sicily had then not died: dawn-lovely Sicily, and the Ionian sea.

We came back, and the world was lovely: our own house above the almond trees, and the sea in the cove below. Calabria glimmering like a changing opal away to the left, across the blue, bright straits and all the great blueness of the lovely dawn-sea in front, where the sun rose with a splendour like trumpets every morning, and me rejoicing like a madness in this dawn, day-dawn, life-dawn, the dawn which is Greece, which is me.

Well, into this lyricism suddenly crept the serpent. It was a lovely morning, still early. I heard a noise on the stairs from the lower terrace, and went to look. M— on the stairs, looking up at me with a frightened face.

'Why!' I said. 'Is it you?'

'Yes,' he replied. 'A terrible thing has happened.'

He waited on the stairs, and I went down. Rather unwillingly, because I detest terrible things, and the people to whom they happen. So we leaned on the creeper-covered rail of the terrace, under festoons of creamy bignonia flowers, and looked at the pale blue, ethereal sea.

'When did you get back?' said he.

'Last evening.'

'Oh! I came before. The contadini said they thought you would come yesterday evening. I've been here several days.'

'Where are you staying?'

'At the San Domenico.'

The San Domenico being then the most expensive hotel here, I thought he must have money. But I knew he wanted something of me.

'And are you staying some time?'

He paused a moment, and looked round cautiously.

'Is your wife there?' he asked, sotto voce.

'Yes, she's upstairs.'

'Is there anyone who can hear?'

'No – only old Grazia down below, and she can't understand anyhow.'

'Well,' he said, stammering. 'Let me tell you what's happened. I had to escape from the monastery. Don Bernardo had a telephone message from the town below, that the carabinieri were looking for an Americano – my name – Of course you can guess how I felt, up there! Awful! Well –! I had to fly at a moment's notice. I just put two shirts in a handbag and went. I slipped down a path – or rather, it isn't a path – down the back of the hill. Ten minutes after Don Bernardo had the message I was running down the hill.'

'But what did they want you for?' I asked dismayed.

'Well,' he faltered. 'I told you about the cheque at Anzio, didn't I? Well it seems the hotel people applied to the police. Anyhow,' he added hastily, 'I couldn't let myself be arrested up there, could I? So awful for the monastery!'

'Did they know then that you were in trouble?' I asked.

'Don Bernardo knew I had no money,' he said. 'Of course he had to know. Yes – he knew I was in *difficulty*. But, of course, he didn't know – well – *everything*.' He laughed a little, comical laugh over the *everything*, as if he was just a little bit naughtily proud of it: most ruefully also.

'No,' he continued, 'that's what I'm most afraid of – that they'll find out everything at the monastery. Of course it's *dreadful* – the Americano, been staying there for months, and everything so nice and – well you know how they are, they imagine every American is a millionaire, if not a multi-millionaire. And suddenly to be wanted by the police! Of course it's *dreadful*! Anything rather than a scandal at the monastery – anything. Oh, how awful it was! I can tell you, in that quarter of an hour, I sweated blood. Don Bernardo lent me two hundred lire of the monastery money – which he'd no business to do. And I escaped down the back of the hill, I walked to the next station up the line, and took the next train – the slow train – a few stations up towards Rome. And there I changed and caught the diretto for Sicily. I came straight to you – Of course I was in *agony*: imagine it! I spent most of the time as far as Naples in the lavatory.' He laughed his little jerky laugh.

'What class did you travel?'

'Second. All through the night. I arrived more dead than alive, not having had a meal for two days – only some sandwich stuff I bought on the platform.'

'When did you come then?'

'I arrived on Saturday evening. I came out here on Sunday morning, and they told me you were away. Of course, imagine what it's like! I'm in torture every minute, in torture, of course. Why just imagine!' And he laughed his little laugh.

'But how much money have you got?'

'Oh – I've just got twenty-five francs and five soldi.' He laughed as if it was rather a naughty joke.

'But,' I said, 'if you've got no money, why do you go to the San Domenico? How much do you pay there?'

'Fifty lire a day. Of course it's *ruinous* –'

'But at the Bristol you only pay twenty-five – and at Fichera's only twenty.'

'Yes, I know you do,' he said. 'But I stayed at the Bristol once, and I loathed the place. Such an offensive manager. And I couldn't touch the food at Fichera's.'

'But who's going to pay for the San Domenico, then?' I asked.

'Well, I thought,' he said, 'you know all those manuscripts of mine? Well, you think they're some good, don't you? Well, I thought if I made them over to you, and you did what you could with them and just kept me going till I can get a new start – or till I can get away –'

I looked across the sea: the lovely morning-blue sea towards Greece.

'Where do you want to get away to?' I said.

'To Egypt. I know a man in Alexandria who owns newspapers there. I'm sure if I could get over there he'd give me an editorship or something. And of course money will come. I've written to —, who was my *greatest* friend, in London. He will send me something –'

'And what else do you expect?'

'Oh, my article on the monastery was accepted by *Land and Water* – thanks to you and your kindness, of course. I thought if I might stay very quietly with you, for a time, and write some things I'm wanting to do, and collect a little money – and then get away to Egypt –'

He looked up into my face, as if he were trying all he could on me. First thing I knew was that I could not have him in the house with me: and even if I could have done it, my wife never could.

'You've got a lovely place here, perfectly beautiful,' he said. 'Of course, if it had to be Taormina, you've chosen far the best place here. I like this side so much better than the Etna side. Etna always there and people raving about it gets on my nerves. And a *charming* house, *charming*.'

He looked round the loggia and along the other terrace.

'Is it all yours?' he said.

'We don't use the ground floor. Come in here.'

So we went into the salotta.

'Oh, what a beautiful room,' he cried. 'But perfectly palatial. Charming! Charming! *Much* the nicest house in Taormina.'

'No,' I said, 'as a house it isn't very grand, though I like it for myself. It's just what I want. And I love the situation. But I'll go and tell my wife you are here.'

'Will you?' he said, bridling nervously. 'Of course I've never met your wife.' And he laughed the nervous, naughty, jokey little laugh.

I left him, and ran upstairs to the kitchen. There was my wife, with wide eyes. She had been listening to catch the conversation. But M—'s voice was too hushed.

'M—!' said I softly. 'The carabinieri wanted to arrest him at the monastery, so he has escaped here, and wants me to be responsible for him.'

'Arrest him what for?'

'Debts, I suppose. Will you come down and speak to him?'

M— of course was very charming with my wife. He kissed her hand humbly, in the correct German fashion, and spoke with an air of reverence that infallibly gets a woman.

'Such a beautiful place you have here,' he said, glancing through the open doors of the room, at the sea beyond. 'So clever of you to find it.'

'Lawrence found it,' said she. 'Well, and you are in all kinds of difficulty!'

'Yes, isn't it terrible!' he said, laughing as if it were a joke – rather a wry joke. 'I felt dreadful at the monastery. So dreadful for them, if there was any sort of scandal. And after I'd been so well received there – and so much the Signor Americano – Dreadful, don't you think?' He laughed again, like a naughty boy.

We had an engagement to lunch that morning. My wife was dressed, so I went to get ready. Then we told M— we must go out, and he accompanied us to the village. I gave him just the hundred francs I had in my pocket, and he said could he come and see me that evening? I asked him to come next morning.

'You're so awfully kind,' he said, simpering a little.

But by this time I wasn't feeling kind.

'He's quite nice,' said my wife. 'But he's rather an impossible little person. And you'll see, he'll be a nuisance. Whatever do you pick up such dreadful people for?'

'Nay,' I said. 'You can't accuse me of picking up dreadful people. He's the first. And even he isn't dreadful.'

The next morning came a letter from Don Bernardo addressed to me, but only enclosing a letter to M—. So he was using my address. At ten o'clock he punctually appeared: slipping in as if to avoid notice. My wife would not see him, so I took him out on the terrace again.

'Isn't it beautiful here!' he said. 'Oh, so beautiful! If only I had peace of mind. Of course I sweat blood every time anybody comes through the door. You are splendidly private out here.'

'Yes,' I said. 'But M—, there isn't a room for you in the house. There isn't a spare room anyway. You'd better think of getting something cheaper in the village.'

'But what can I get?' he snapped.

That rather took my breath away. Myself, I had never been near the San Domenico hotel. I knew I simply could not afford it.

'What made you go to the San Domenico in the first place?' I said. 'The most expensive hotel in the place!'

'Oh, I'd stayed there for two months, and they knew me, and I knew they'd ask no questions. I knew they wouldn't ask for a deposit or anything.'

'But nobody dreams of asking for a deposit,' I said.

'Anyhow I shan't take my meals there. I shall just take coffee in the morning. I've had to eat there so far, because I was starved to death, and had no money to go out. But I had two meals in that little restaurant yesterday; disgusting food.'

'And how much did that cost?'

'Oh fourteen francs and fifteen francs, with a quarter of wine – and such a poor meal!'

Now I was annoyed, knowing that I myself should have bought bread and cheese for one franc, and eaten it in my room. But also I realized that the modern creed says, if you sponge, sponge thoroughly: and also that every man has a 'right to live', and that if he can manage to live well, no matter at whose expense, all credit to him. This is the kind of talk one accepts in one's slipshod moments; now it was actually tried on me, I didn't like it at all.

'But who's going to pay your bill at the San Domenico?' I said.

'I thought you'd advance me the money on those manuscripts.'

'It's no good talking about the money on the manuscripts,' I said. 'I should have to give it to you. And as a matter of fact, I've got just sixty pounds in the bank in England, and about fifteen hundred lire here. My wife and I have got to live on that. We don't spend as much in a week as you spend in three days at the San Domenico. It's no good your thinking I can advance money on the manuscripts. I can't. If I was rich, I'd give you money. But I've got no money, and never have had any. Have you nobody you can go to?'

'I'm waiting to hear from ——. When I go back into the village, I'll telegraph to him,' replied M—, a little crestfallen. 'Of course I'm in torture night and day, or I wouldn't appeal to you like this. I know it's unpleasant for you –' and he put his hand on my arm and looked up beseechingly. 'But what am I to do?'

'You must get out of the San Domenico,' I said. 'That's the first thing.'

'Yes,' he said, a little piqued now. 'I know it is. I'm going to ask Pancrazio Melenga to let me have a room in his house. He knows me quite well – he's an awfully nice fellow. He'll do *anything* for me – *anything*. I was just going there yesterday afternoon when you were coming from Timeo. He was out, so I left word with his wife, who is a charming little person. If he has a room to spare, I know he will let me have it. And he's a *splendid* cook – splendid. By far the nicest food in Taormina.'

'Well,' I said. 'If you settle with Melenga, I will pay your bill at the San Domenico, but I can't do any more. I simply can't.'

'But what am I to *do*?' he snapped.

'I don't know,' I said. 'You must think.'

'I came here,' he said, 'thinking you would help me. What am I to do, if you won't? I shouldn't have come to Taormina at all, save for you. Don't be unkind to me – don't speak so coldly to me –' He put his hand on my arm, and looked up at me with tears swimming in his eyes. Then he turned aside his face, overcome with tears. I looked away at the Ionian sea, feeling my blood turn to ice and the sea go black. I loathe scenes such as this.

'Did you telegraph to —?' I said.

'Yes. I have no answer yet. I hope you don't mind – I gave your address for a reply.'

'Oh,' I said. 'There's a letter for you from Don Bernardo.'

He went pale. I was angry at his having used my address in this manner.

'Nothing further has happened at the monastery,' he said. 'They rang up from the Questura, from the police station, and Don Bernardo answered that the Americano had left for Rome. Of course I did take the train for Rome. And Don Bernardo wanted me to go to Rome. He advised me to do so. I didn't tell him I was here till I had got here. He thought I should have had more resources in Rome, and of course I should. I should certainly have gone there, if it hadn't been for *you here –*'

Well, I was getting tired and angry. I would not give him any more money at the moment. I promised, if he would leave the hotel I would pay his bill, but he must leave it at once. He went off to settle with Melenga. He asked again if he could come in the afternoon: I said I was going out.

He came nevertheless while I was out. This time my wife found him on the stairs. She was for hating him, of course. So she stood immovable on the top stair, and he stood two stairs lower, and he kissed her hand in utter humility. And he pleaded with her, and as he looked up to her on the stairs the tears ran down his face and he trembled with distress. And her spine crept up and down with distaste and discomfort. But he broke into a few phrases of touching German, and I know he broke down her reserve and she promised him all he wanted. This part she would never confess, though. Only she was shivering with revulsion and excitement and even a sense of power, when I came home.

That was why M— appeared more impertinent than ever, next morning. He had arranged to go to Melenga's house the following day, and to pay ten francs a day for his room, his meals extra. So that was something. He made a long tale about not eating any of his meals in the hotel now, but pretending he was invited out, and eating in the little restaurants where the food was so bad. And he had now only fifteen lire left in his pocket. But I was cold, and wouldn't give him any more. I said I would give him money next day, for his bill.

He had now another request, and a new tone.

'Won't you do *one more* thing for me?' he said. 'Oh do! Do do this one thing for me. I want you to go to the monastery and bring away my important papers and some clothes and my important trinkets. I have made a list of the things here – and where you'll find them in my writing-table and in the chest of drawers. I don't think you'll have any trouble. Don Bernardo has the keys. He will open everything for you. And I beg you, *in the name of God*, don't let anybody else see the things. Not even Don Bernardo. Don't, whatever you do, let him see the papers and manuscripts you are bringing. If he sees them, there's an end to me at the monastery. I can *never* go back there. I am ruined in their eyes for ever. As it is – although Don Bernardo is the best person in the world and my dearest friend, still – you know what people are – especially monks. A little curious, don't you know, a little inquisitive. Well, let us hope for the best as far as that goes. But you will do this for me, won't you? I shall be so eternally grateful.'

Now a journey to the monastery meant a terrible twenty hours in the train each way – all that awful journey through Calabria to Naples and northwards. It meant mixing myself up in this man's affairs. It meant appearing as his accomplice at the monastery. It meant travelling with all his 'compromising' papers and his valuables. And all this time, I never knew what mischiefs he had really been up to, and I didn't trust him, not for one single second. He would tell me nothing save that Anzio hotel cheque. I knew that wasn't all, by any means. So I mistrusted him. And with a feeling of utter mistrust goes a feeling of contempt and dislike – And finally, it would have cost me at least ten pounds sterling, which I simply did not want to spend in waste.

'I don't want to do that,' I said.

'Why not?' he asked, sharp, looking green. He had planned it all out.

'No, I don't want to.'

'Oh, but I *can't* remain here as I am. I've got no *clothes* – I've got nothing to *wear*. I *must* have my things from the monastery. What can I do? What can I do? I came to you, if it hadn't been for you I should have gone to Rome. I came to you – Oh yes, you *will* go. You *will* go, won't you? You *will* go to the monastery for my things?' And again he put his hand on my arm, and the tears began to fall from his upturned eyes. I turned my head aside. Never had the Ionian sea looked so sickening to me.

'I don't *want* to,' said I.

'But you *will*! You will! You *will* go to the monastery for me, won't you? Everything else is no good if you won't. I've nothing to wear. I haven't got my manuscripts to work on, I can't do the things I am doing. Here I live in a sweat of anxiety. I try to work, and I can't settle. I can't do anything. It's dreadful. I shan't have a minute's peace till I have got those things from the monastery, till I know they can't get at my private papers. You will do this for me! You will, won't you? Please do! Oh please do!' And again tears.

And I with my bowels full of bitterness, loathing the thought of that journey there and back, on such an errand. Yet not quite sure that I ought to refuse. And he pleaded and struggled, and tried to bully me with tears and entreaty and reproach, to do his will. And I couldn't quite refuse. But neither could I agree.

At last I said:

'I don't want to go, and I tell you. I won't promise to go. And I won't say that I will not go. I won't say until tomorrow. Tomorrow I will tell you. Don't come to the house. I will be in the Corso at ten o'clock.'

'I didn't doubt for a minute you would do this for me,' he said. 'Otherwise I should never have come to Taormina.' As if he had done me an honour in coming to Taormina; and as if I had betrayed *him*.

'Well,' I said. 'If you make these messes you'll have to get out of them yourself. I don't know why you are *in* such a mess.'

'Any man may make a mistake,' he said sharply, as if correcting me.

'Yes, a *mistake*!' said I. 'If it's a question of a mistake.'

So once more he went, humbly, beseechingly, and yet, one could not help but feel, with all that terrible insolence of the humble. It is the humble, the wistful, the would-be-loving souls today who bully us with their charity-demanding insolence. They just make up their minds, these needful sympathetic souls, that one is there to do their will. Very good.

I decided in the day I would *not* go. Without reasoning it out, I knew I *really* didn't want to go. I plainly didn't want it. So I wouldn't go.

The morning came again hot and lovely. I set off to the village. But there was M— watching for me on the path beyond the valley. He came forward and took my hand warmly, clingingly. I turned back, to remain in the country. We talked for a minute of his leaving the hotel – he was going that afternoon, he had asked for his bill. But he was waiting for the other answer.

'And I have decided,' I said, 'I won't go to the monastery.'

'You won't.' He looked at me. I saw how yellow he was round the eyes, and yellow under his reddish skin.

'No,' I said.

And it was final. He knew it. We went some way in silence. I turned in at the garden gate. It was a lovely, lovely morning of hot sun. Butterflies were flapping over the rosemary hedges and over a few little red poppies, the young vines smelt sweet in flower, very sweet, the corn was tall and green, and there were still some wild, rose-red gladiolus flowers among the watery green of the wheat. M— had accepted my refusal. I expected him to be angry. But no, he seemed quieter, wistfuller, and he seemed almost to love me for having refused him. I stood at a bend in the path. The sea was heavenly blue, rising up beyond the vines and olive leaves, lustrous pale lacquer blue as only the Ionian sea can be. Away at the brook below the women were washing, and one could hear the chock-chock-chock of linen beaten against the stones. I felt M— then an intolerable weight and like a clot of dirt over everything.

'May I come in?' he said to me.

'No,' I said. 'Don't come to the house. My wife doesn't want it.'

Even that he accepted without any offence, and seemed only to like me better for it. That was a puzzle to me. I told him I would leave a letter and a cheque for him at the bank in the Corso that afternoon.

I did so, writing a cheque for a few pounds, enough to cover his bill and leave a hundred lire or so over, and a letter to say I could *not* do any more, and I didn't want to see him any more.

So, there was an end of it for a moment. Yet I felt him looming in the village, waiting. I had rashly said I would go to tea with him to the villa of one of the Englishmen resident here, whose acquaintance I had not made. Alas, M— kept me to the promise. As I came home he appealed to me again. He was rather insolent. What good to him, he said, were the few pounds I had given him? He had got a hundred and fifty lire left. What good was that? I realized it really was not a solution, and said nothing. Then he spoke of his plans for getting to Egypt. The fare, he had found out, was thirty-five pounds. And where were thirty-five pounds coming from? Not from me.

I spent a week avoiding him, wondering what on earth the poor devil was doing, and yet *determined* he should not be a parasite on me. If I could have given him fifty pounds and sent him to Egypt to be a parasite on somebody else, I would have done so. Which is what we call charity. However, I couldn't.

My wife chafed, crying: 'What have you done! We shall have him on our hands all our life. We can't let him starve. It is degrading, degrading, to have him hanging on to us.'

'Yes,' I said. 'He must starve or work or something. I am not God who is responsible for him.'

M— was determined not to lose his status as a gentleman. In a way I sympathized with him. He would never be out at elbows. That is your modern rogue. He will not degenerate outwardly. Certain standards of a gentleman he *would* keep up: he would be well-dressed, he would be lavish with borrowed money, he would be as far as possible honourable in his small transactions of daily life. Well, very good. I sympathized with him to a certain degree. If he could find his own way out, well and good. Myself, I was not his way out.

Ten days passed. It was hot and I was going about the terrace in pyjamas and a big old straw hat, when suddenly, a Sicilian, handsome, in the prime of life, and in his best black suit, smiling at me and taking off his hat!

71

And could he speak to me. I threw away my straw hat, and we went into the salotta. He handed me a note.

'Il Signor M— mi ha dato questa lettera per Lei!' he began, and I knew what was coming. Melenga had been a waiter in good hotels, had saved money, built himself a fine house which he let to foreigners. He was a pleasant fellow, and at his best now, because he was in a rage. I must repeat M—'s letter from memory – 'Dear Lawrence, would you do me another kindness. *Land and Water* sent a cheque for seven guineas for the article on the monastery, and Don Bernardo forwarded this, to me under Melenga's name. But unfortunately he made a mistake, and put Orazio instead of Pancrazio, so the post office would not deliver the letter, and have returned it to the monastery. This morning Melenga insulted me, and I cannot stay in his house another minute. Will you be so kind as to advance me these seven guineas, and I shall leave Taormina at once, for Malta.'

I asked Melenga what had happened, and read him the letter. He was handsome in his rage, lifting his brows and suddenly smiling:

'Ma senta, Signore! Signor M— has been in my house for ten days, and lived well, and eaten well, and drunk well, and I have not seen a single penny of his money. I go out in the morning and buy all the things, all he wants, and my wife cooks it, and he is very pleased, very pleased, has never eaten such good food in his life, and everything is splendid, splendid. And he never pays a penny. Not a penny. Says he is waiting for money from England, from America, from India. But the money never comes. And I am a poor man, Signore, I have a wife and child to keep. I have already spent three hundred lire for this Signor M—, and I never see a penny of it back. And he says the money is coming, it is coming – But when? He never says he has got no money. He says he is expecting. Tomorrow – always tomorrow. It will come tonight, it will come tomorrow. This makes me in a rage. Till at last this morning I said to him I would bring nothing in, and he shouldn't have not so much as a drop of coffee in my house until he paid for it. It displeases me, Signore, to say such a thing. I have known Signor M— for many years, and he has always had money, and always been pleasant, molto bravo, and also generous with his money. Si, lo so! And my wife, poverina, she cries and says if the man has no money he must eat. But he doesn't say he has no money. He says always it is coming, it is coming, today, to-morrow, today, tomorrow. E non viene mai niente. And this enrages me, Signore. So I said that to him this morning. And he said he wouldn't stay in my house, and that I had insulted him, and he sends me this letter to you, Signore, and says you will send him the money. Ecco come!'

Between his rage he smiled at me. One thing however I could see: he was not going to lose his money, M— or no M—.

'Is it true that a letter came which the post would not deliver?' I asked him.

'Si signore, e vero. It came yesterday, addressed to me. And why, signore, why do his letters come addressed in my name? Why? Unless he has done something –?'

He looked at me inquiringly. I felt already mixed up in shady affairs.

'Yes,' I said, 'there is something. But I don't know exactly what. I don't ask, because I don't want to know in these affairs. It is better not to know.'

'Gia! Gia! Molto meglio, signore. There will be something. There will be something happened that he had to escape from that monastery. And it will be some affair of the police.'

'Yes, I think so,' said I. 'Money and the police. Probably debts. I don't ask. He is only an acquaintance of mine, not a friend.'

'Sure it will be an affair of the police,' he said with a grimace. 'If not, why does he use my name! Why don't his letters come in his own name? Do you believe, signore, that he has any money? Do you think this money will come?'

'I'm sure he's *got* no money,' I said. 'Whether anybody will send him any I don't know.'

The man watched me attentively.

'He's got nothing?' he said.

'No. At the present he's got nothing.'

Then Pancrazio exploded on the sofa.

'Allora! Well then! Well then, why does he come to my house, why does he come and take a room in my house, and ask me to buy food, good food as for a gentleman who can pay, and a flask of wine, and everything, if he has no money? If he has no money, why does he come to Taormina? It is many years that he has been in Italy – ten years, fifteen years. And he has no money. Where has he had his money from before? Where?'

'From his writing, I suppose.'

'Well then why doesn't he get money for his writing now? He writes. He writes, he works, he says it is for the big newspapers.'

'It is difficult to sell things.'

'Heh! then why doesn't he live on what he made before? He hasn't a soldo. He hasn't a penny – But how! How did he pay his bill at the San Domenico?'

'I had to lend him the money for that. He really hadn't a penny.'

'You! You! Well then, he has been in Italy all these years. How is it he has nobody that he can ask for a hundred lire or two? Why does he come to you? Why? Why has he nobody in Rome, in Florence, anywhere?'

'I wonder that myself.'

'Siccuro! He's been all these years here. And why doesn't he speak proper Italian? After all these years, and speaks all upside-down, it isn't Italian, an ugly confusion. Why? Why? He passes for a signore, for a man of education. And he comes to take the bread out of my mouth. And I have a wife and child, I am a poor man, I have nothing to eat myself if everying goes to a mezzo-signore like him. Nothing! He owes me now three hundred lire. But he will not leave my house, he will not leave Taormina till he has paid. I will go to the Prefettura, I will go to the Questura, to the police. I will not be swindled by such a mezzo-signore. What does he want to do? If he has no money, what does he want to do?'

'To go to Egypt where he says he can earn some,' I replied briefly. But I was feeling bitter in the mouth. When the man called M— a mezzo-signore, a half-gentleman, it was so true. And at the same time it was so cruel, and so rude. And Melenga – there I sat in my pyjamas and sandals – probably he would be calling me also a mezzo-signore, or a quarto-signore even. He was a

Sicilian who feels he is being done out of his money – and that is saying everything.

'To Egypt! And who will pay for him to go? Who will give him money? But he must pay me first. He must pay me first.'

'He says,' I said, 'that in the letter which went back to the monastery there was a cheque for seven pounds – some six hundred lire – and he asks me to send him this money, and when the letter is returned again I shall have the cheque that is in it.'

Melenga watched me.

'Six hundred lire –' he said.

'Yes.'

'Oh well then. If he pays me, he can stay –' he said; he almost added: 'till the six hundred is finished.' But he left it unspoken.

'But am I going to send the money? Am I sure that what he says is true?'

'I think it is true. I think it is true,' said he. 'The letter *did* come.'

I thought for a while.

'First,' I said, 'I will write and ask him if it is quite true, and to give me a guarantee.'

'Very well,' said Melenga.

I wrote to M—, saying that if he could assure me that what he said about the seven guineas was quite correct, and if he would give me a note to the editor of *Land and Water*, saying that the cheque was to be paid to me, I would send the seven guineas.

Melenga was back in another half hour. He brought a note which began:

'Dear Lawrence, I seem to be living in an atmosphere of suspicion. First Melenga this morning, and now you –' Those are the exact opening words. He went on to say that of course his word was true, and he enclosed a note to the editor, saying the seven guineas were to be transferred to me. He asked me please to send the money, as he could not stay another night at Melenga's house, but would leave for Catania, where, by the sale of some trinkets, he hoped to make some money and to see once more about a passage to Egypt. He had been to Catania once already – travelling *third class*! – but had failed to find any cargo boat that would take him to Alexandria. He would get away now to

Malta. His things were being sent down to Syracuse from the monastery.

I wrote and said I hoped he would get safely away, and enclosed the cheque.

'This will be for six hundred lire,' said Melenga.

'Yes,' said I.

'Eh, va bene! If he pays the three hundred lire, he can stop in my house for thirty lire a day.'

'He says he won't sleep in your house again.'

'Ma! Let us see. If he likes to stay. He has always been a bravo signore. I have always liked him quite well. If he wishes to stay and pay me thirty lire a day –'

The man smiled at me rather greenly.

'I'm afraid he is offended,' said I.

'Eh, va bene! Ma senta, Signore. When he was here before – you know I have this house of mine to let. And you know the English signorina goes away in the summer. Oh, very well. Says M—, he writes for a newspaper, he owns a newspaper, I don't know what, in Rome. He will put in an advertisement advertising my villa. And so I shall get somebody to take it. Very well. And he put in the advertisement. He sent me the paper and I saw it there. But no one came to take my villa. Va bene! But after a year, in the January, that is, came a bill for me for twenty-two lire to pay for it. Yes, I had to pay the twenty-two lire, for nothing – for the advertisement which Signore M— put in the paper.'

'Bah!' said I.

He shook hands with me and left. The next day he came after me in the street and said that M— had departed the previous evening for Catania. As a matter of fact the post brought me a note of thanks from Catania. M— was never indecent, and one could never dismiss him just as a scoundrel. He was not. He was one of these modern parasites who must assume their right to live and live well, leaving the payment to anybody who can, will, or must pay. The end is inevitably swindling.

There came also a letter from Rome, addressed to me. I opened it unthinking. It was for M—, from an Italian lawyer, stating that inquiry had been made about the writ against M—, and that it

76

Introduction *to* Memoirs of the Foreign Legion

was for *qualche affaro di truffa*, some affair of swindling: that
the lawyer had seen this, that and the other person, but nothing
could be done. He regretted, etc., etc. I forwarded this letter to
M— at Syracuse, and hoped to God it was ended. Ah, I breathed
free now he had gone.

But no. A friend who was with us dearly wanted to go to Malta.
It is only about eighteen hours' journey from Taormina – easier
than going to Naples. So our friend invited us to take the trip with
her, as her guests. This was rather jolly. I calculated that M—, who
had been gone a week or so, would easily have got to Malta. I
had had a friendly letter from him from Syracuse, thanking me
for the one I had forwarded, and enclosing an I.O.U. for the
various sums of money he had had.

So, on a hot, hot Thursday, we were sitting in the train again
running south, the four and a half hours' journey to Syracuse.
And M— dwindled now into the past. If we should see him! But
no, it was impossible. After all the wretchedness of that affair
we were in holiday spirits.

The train ran into Syracuse station. We sat on, to go the few
yards further into the port. A tout climbed on the foot-board:
were we going to Malta? Well, we couldn't. There was a strike of
the steamers, we couldn't go. When would the steamer go? Who
knows? Perhaps tomorrow.

We got down crestfallen. What should we do? There stood the
express train about to start off back northwards. We could be
home again that evening. But no, it would be too much of a
fiasco. We let the train go, and trailed off into the town, to the
Grand Hotel, which is an old Italian place just opposite the port.
It is rather a dreary hotel – and many bloodstains of squashed
mosquitoes on the bedroom walls. Ah, vile mosquitoes!

However, nothing to be done. Syracuse port is fascinating too,
a tiny port with the little Sicilian ships having the slanting eyes
painted on the prow, to see the way, and a coal boat from Cardiff,
and one American and two Scandinavian steamers – no more.
But there were two torpedo boats in the harbour, and it was like
a festa, a strange, lousy festa.

Beautiful the round harbour where the Athenian ships came.

77

And wonderful, beyond, the long sinuous sky-line of the long flat-topped table-land hills which run along the southern coast, so different from the peaky, pointed, bunched effect of many-tipped Sicily in the north. The sun went down behind that lovely, sinuous sky-line, the harbour water was gold and red, the people promenaded in thick streams under the pomegranate trees and hibiscus trees. Arabs in white burnouses and fat Turks in red and black alpaca long coats strolled also – waiting for the steamer.

Next day it was very hot. We went to the consul and the steamer agency. There was real hope that the brute of a steamer might actually sail that night. So we stayed on, and wandered round the town on the island, the old solid town, and sat in the church looking at the grand Greek columns embedded there in the walls.

When I came in to lunch the porter said there was a letter for me. Impossible! said I. But he brought me a note. Yes. M—! He was staying at the other hotel along the front. 'Dear Lawrence, I saw you this morning, all three of you walking down the Via Nazionale, but you would not look at me. I have got my visés and everything ready. The strike of the steamboats has delayed me here. I am sweating blood. I have a last request to make of you. Can you let me have ninety lire, to make up what I need for my hotel bill? If I cannot have this I am lost. I hoped to find you at the hotel but the porter said you were out. I am at the Casa Politi, passing every half hour in agony. If you can be so kind as to stretch your generosity to this last loan, of course I shall be eternally grateful. I can pay you back once I get to Malta –'

Well, here was a blow! The worst was that he thought I had cut him – a thing I wouldn't have done. So after luncheon behold me going through the terrific sun of that harbour front of Syracuse, an enormous and powerful sun, to the Casa Politi. The porter recognized me and looked inquiringly. M— was out, and I said I would call again at four o'clock.

It happened we were in the town eating ices at four, so I didn't get to his hotel till half past. He was out – gone to look for me. So I left a note saying I had not seen him in the Via Nazionale,

that I had called twice, and that I should be in the Grand Hotel
in the evening.

When we came in at seven, M— in the hall, sitting, the picture
of misery and endurance. He took my hand in both his, and
bowed to the women, who nodded and went upstairs. He and I
went and sat in the empty lounge. Then he told me the trials he
had had – how his luggage had come, and the station had charged
him eighteen lire a day for deposit – how he had had to wait on
at the hotel because of the ship – how he had tried to sell his trinkets, and had today parted with his opal sleevelinks – so that now
he only wanted seventy, not ninety lire. I gave him a hundred note,
and he looked into my eyes, his own eyes swimming with tears,
and he said he was sweating blood.

Well, the steamer went that night. She was due to leave at ten.
We went on board after dinner. We were going second class.
And so, for once, was M—. It was only an eight hours' crossing,
yet, in spite of all the blood he had sweated, he would not go third
class. In a way I admired him for sticking to his principles. I
should have gone third myself, out of shame of spending somebody else's money. He would not give way to such weakness. He
knew that as far as the world goes, you're a first-class gentleman
if you have a first-class ticket; if you have a third, no gentleman
at all. It behoved him to be a gentleman. I understood his point,
but the women were indignant. And I was just rather tired of him
and his gentlemanliness.

It amused me very much to lean on the rail of the upper deck
and watch the people coming on board – first going into the little
customs house with their baggage, then scuffling up the gangway
on board. The tall Arabs in their ghostly white woollen robes
came carrying their sacks: they were going on to Tripoli. The fat
Turk in his fez and long black alpaca coat with white drawers
underneath came beaming up to the second class. There was a
great row in the customs house: and then, simply running like a
beetle with rage, there came on board a little Maltese or Greek
fellow, followed by a tall lantern-jawed fellow: both seedy-
looking scoundrels suckled in scoundrelism. They raved and
nearly threw their arms away into the sea, talking wildly in some

weird language with the fat Turk, who listened solemnly, away
below on the deck. Then they rushed to somebody else. Of course,
we were dying with curiosity. Thank heaven I heard men talking
in Italian. It appears the two seedy fellows were trying to smuggle
silver coin in small sacks and rolls out of the country. They were
detected. But they declared they had a right to take it away, as it
was foreign specie, English florins and half-crowns, and South
American dollars and Spanish money. The customs-officers however detained the lot. The little enraged beetle of a fellow ran
back and forth from the ship to the customs, from the customs to
the ship, afraid to go without his money, afraid the ship would
go without him.

At five minutes to ten, there came M—: very smart in his little
grey overcoat and grey curly hat, walking very smart and erect
and genteel, and followed by a porter with a barrow of luggage.
They went into the customs, M— in his grey suède gloves passing
rapidly and smartly in, like the grandest gentleman on earth, and
with his grey suède hands throwing open his luggage for inspec-
tion. From on board we could see the interior of the little customs
shed.

Yes, he was through. Brisk, smart, superb, like the grandest
little gentleman on earth, strutting because he was late, he crossed
the bit of flagged pavement and came up the gangway, haughty
as you can wish. The carabinieri were lounging by the foot of the
gangway, fooling with one another. The little gentleman passed
them with his nose in the air, came quickly on board, followed
by his porter, and in a moment disappeared. After about five
minutes the porter reappeared – a red-haired fellow, I knew him
– he even saluted me from below, the brute. But M— lay in
hiding.

I trembled for him at every unusual stir. There on the quay
stood the English consul with his bull-dog, and various elegant
young officers with yellow on their uniforms, talking to elegant
young Italian ladies in black hats with stiff ospreys and bunchy
furs, and gangs of porters and hotel people and onlookers. Then
came a tramp-tramp-tramp of a squad of soldiers in red fezzes
and baggy grey trousers. Instead of coming on board they

camped on the quay. I wondered if all these had come for poor M—. But apparently not.

So the time passed, till nearly midnight, when one of the elegant young lieutenants began to call the names of the soldiers: and the soldiers answered: and one after another filed on board with their kit. So, they were on board, on their way to Africa.

Now somebody called out – and the visitors began to leave the boat. Barefooted sailors and a boy ran to raise the gangway. The last visitor or official with a bunch of papers stepped off the gangway. People on shore began to wave handkerchiefs. The red-fezzed soldiers leaned like so many flower-pots over the lower rail. There was a calling of farewells. The ship was fading into the harbour, the people on shore seemed smaller, under the lamp, in the deep night – without one's knowing why.

So, we passed out of the harbour, passed the glittering lights of Ortygia, past the two lighthouses, into the open Mediterranean. The noise of a ship in the open sea! It was a still night, with stars, only a bit chill. And the ship churned through the water.

Suddenly, like a *revenant*, appeared M— near us, leaning on the rail and looking back at the lights of Syracuse sinking already forlorn and little on the low darkness. I went to him.

'Well,' he said, with his little smirk of a laugh. 'Good-bye Italy!'

'Not a sad farewell either,' said I.

'No, my word, not this time,' he said. 'But what an awful long time we were starting! A brutta mezz'ora for me, indeed. Oh, my word, I begin to breathe free for the first time since I left the monastery! How awful it's been! But of course, in Malta, I shall be all right. Don Bernardo has written to his friends there. They'll have everything ready for me that I want, and I can pay you back the money you so kindly lent me.'

We talked for some time, leaning on the inner rail of the upper deck.

'Oh,' he said, 'there's Commander So-and-so, of the British fleet. He's stationed in Malta. I made his acquaintance in the hotel. I hope we're going to be great friends in Malta. I hope I shall have an opportunity to introduce you to him. Well, I

81

suppose you will want to be joining your ladies. So long, then. Oh, for tomorrow morning! I never longed so hard to be in the British Empire –' He laughed, and strutted away.

In a few minutes we three, leaning on the rail of the second-class upper deck, saw our little friend large as life on the first-class deck, smoking a cigar and chatting in an absolutely first-class-ticket manner with the above mentioned Commander. He pointed us out to the Commander, and we felt the first-class passengers were looking across at us second-class passengers with pleasant interest. The women went behind a canvas heap to laugh, I hid my face under my hat-brim to grin and watch. Larger than any first-class ticketer leaned our little friend on the first-class rail, and whiffed at his cigar. So *dégagé* and so genteel he could be. Only I noticed he wilted a little when the officers of the ship came near.

He was still on the first-class deck when we went down to sleep. In the morning I came up soon after dawn. It was a lovely summer Mediterranean morning, with the sun rising up in a gorgeous golden rage, and the sea so blue, so fairy blue, as the Mediterranean is in summer. We were approaching quite near to a rocky, pale yellow island with some vineyards, rising magical out of the swift blue sea into the morning radiance. The rocks were almost as pale as butter, the islands were like golden shadows loitering in the midst of the Mediterranean, lonely among all the blue.

M— came up to my side.

'Isn't it lovely! Isn't it beautiful!' he said. 'I love approaching these islands in the early morning.' He had almost recovered his assurance, and the slight pomposity and patronizing tone I had first known in him. 'In two hours I shall be free! Imagine it! Oh what a beautiful feeling!' I looked at him in the morning light. His face was a good deal broken by his last month's experience, older looking, and dragged. Now that the excitement was nearing its end, the tiredness began to tell on him. He was yellowish round the eyes, and the whites of his round, rather impudent blue eyes were discoloured.

Malta was drawing near. We saw the white fringe of the sea upon the yellow rocks, and a white road looping on the yellow rocky hillside. I thought of St Paul, who must have been blown this way, must have struck the island from this side. Then we saw the heaped glitter of the square facets of houses, Valletta, splendid above the Mediterranean, and a tangle of shipping and Dreadnoughts and watch-towers in the beautiful, locked-in harbour.

We had to go down to have passports examined. The officials sat in the long saloon. It was a horrible squash and squeeze of the first- and second-class passengers. M— was a little ahead of me. I saw the American eagle on his passport. Yes, he passed all right. Once more he was free. As he passed away he turned and gave a condescending affable nod to me and to the Commander, who was just behind me.

The ship was lying in Valletta harbour. I saw M—, quite superb and brisk now, ordering a porter with his luggage into a boat. The great rocks rose above us, yellow and carved, cut straight by man. On top were all the houses. We got at last into a boat and were rowed ashore. Strange to be on British soil and to hear English. We got a carriage and drove up the steep highroad through the cutting in the rock, up to the town. There, in the big square we had coffee, sitting out of doors. A military band went by playing splendidly in the bright, hot morning. The Maltese lounged about, and watched. Splendid the band, and the soldiers! One felt the splendour of the British Empire, let the world say what it likes. But alas, as one stayed on even in Malta, one felt the old lion had gone foolish and amiable. Foolish and amiable, with the weak amiability of old age.

We stayed in the Great Britain Hotel. Of course one could not be in Valletta for twenty-four hours without meeting M—. There he was, in the Strada Reale, strutting in a smart white duck suit, with a white piqué cravat. But alas, he had no white shoes: they had got lost or stolen. He had to wear black boots with his summer finery.

He was staying in an hotel a little further down our street, and he begged me to call and see him, he begged me to come to lunch. I promised and went. We went into his bedroom, and he rang for more sodas.

'How wonderful it is to be here!' he said brightly. 'Don't you like it immensely? And oh, how wonderful to have a whisky and soda! Well now, say when.'

He finished one bottle of Black and White, and opened another. The waiter, a good-looking Maltese fellow, appeared with two syphons. M— was very much the signore with him, and at the same time very familiar: as I should imagine a rich Roman of the merchant class might have been with a pet slave. We had quite a nice lunch, and whisky and soda and a bottle of French wine. And M— was the charming and attentive host.

After lunch we talked again of manuscripts and publishers and how he might make money. I wrote one or two letters for him. He was anxious to get something under way. And yet the trouble of these arrangements was almost too much for his nerves. His face looked broken and old, but not like an old man, like an old boy, and he was really very irritable.

For my own part I was soon tired of Malta, and would gladly have left after three days. But there was the strike of steamers still, we had to wait on. M— professed to be enjoying himself hugely, making excursions every day, to St Paul's Bay and to the other islands. He had also made various friends or acquaintances. Particularly two young men, Maltese, who were friends of Don Bernardo. He introduced me to these two young men: one Gabriel Mazzaiba and the other Salonia. They had small businesses down on the wharf. Salonia asked M— to go for a drive in a motor-car round the island, and M— pressed me to go too. Which I did. And swiftly, on a Saturday afternoon, we dodged about in the car upon that dreadful island, first to some fearful and stony bay, arid, treeless, desert, a bit of stony desert by the sea, with unhappy villas and a sordid, scrap-iron front: then away inland up long and dusty roads, across a bone-dry, bone-bare, hideous landscape. True, there was ripening corn, but this was all of a colour with the dust-yellow, bone-bare island. Malta is all a pale, softish, yellowish rock, just like bathbrick: this goes into fathomless dust. And the island is stark as a corpse, no trees, no bushes even: a fearful landscape, cultivated, and weary with ages of weariness, and old weary houses here and there.

We went to the old capital in the centre of the island, and this is interesting. The town stands on a bluff of hill in the middle of the dreariness, looking at Valletta in the distance, and the sea. The houses are all pale yellow, and tall, and silent, as if forsaken. There is a cathedral, too, and a fortress outlook over the sun-blazed, sun-dried, disheartening island. Then we dashed off to another village and climbed a church-dome that rises like a tall blister on the plain, with houses round and corn beyond and dust that has no glamour, stale, weary, like bone-dust, and thorn hedges sometimes, and some tin-like prickly pears. In the dusk we came round by St Paul's Bay, back to Valletta.

The young men were very pleasant, very patriotic for Malta, very Catholic. We talked politics and a thousand things. M— was gently patronizing, and seemed, no doubt, to the two Maltese a very elegant and travelled and wonderful gentleman. They, who had never seen even a wood, thought how wonderful a forest must be, and M— talked to them of Russia and of Germany.

But I was glad to leave that bone-dry, hideous island. M— begged me to stay longer: but not for worlds! He was establishing himself securely: was learning the Maltese language, and cultivating a thorough acquaintance with the island. And he was going to establish himself. Mazzaiba was exceedingly kind to him, helping him in every way. In Rabato, the suburb of the old town – a quiet, forlorn little yellow street – he found a tiny house of two rooms and a tiny garden. This would cost five pounds a year. Mazzaiba lent the furniture – and when I left, M— was busily skipping back and forth from Rabato to Valletta, arranging his little home, and very pleased with it. He was also being very Maltese, and rather anti-British, as is essential, apparently, when one is not a Britisher and finds oneself in any part of the British Empire. M— was very much the American gentleman.

Well, I was thankful to be home again and to know that he was safely shut up in that beastly island. He wrote me letters, saying how he loved it all, how he would go down to the sea – five or six miles' walk – at dawn, and stay there all day, studying Maltese and writing for the newspapers. The life was fascinating, the summer was blisteringly hot, and the Maltese were *most* attractive, especially when they knew you were not British. Such good-looking fellows, too, and do anything you want. Wouldn't I come and spend a month? – I did not answer – felt I had had enough. Came a postcard from M—: 'I haven't had a letter from you, nor any news at all. I am afraid you are ill, and feel so anxious. Do write –' But no, I didn't want to write.

During August and September and half October we were away in the north. I forgot my little friend: hoped he was gone out of my life. But I had that fatal sinking feeling that he *hadn't* really gone out of it yet.

In the beginning of November a little letter from Don Bernardo – did I know that M— had committed suicide in Malta? Following that, a scrubby Maltese newspaper, posted by Salonia, with a marked notice: 'The suicide of an American gentleman at Rabato. Yesterday the American M— M—, a well-built man in the prime of life, was found dead in his bed in his house at Rabato. By the bedside was a bottle containing poison. The deceased had evidently taken his life by swallowing prussic acid. Mr M— had been staying for some months on the island, studying the language and the conditions with a view to writing a book. It is understood that financial difficulties were the cause of this lamentable event.'

Then Mazzaiba wrote asking me what I knew of M—, and saying the latter had borrowed money which he, Mazzaiba, would like to recover. I replied at once, and then received the following letter from Salonia. 'Valletta, 20 November, 1920. My dear Mr Lawrence, some time back I mailed you our *Daily Malta Chronicle* which gave an account of the death of M—. I hope you have received same. As the statements therein given were very vague and not quite correct, please accept the latter part of this letter as a more correct version.

'The day before yesterday Mazzaiba received your letter which he gave me to read. As you may suppose we were very much astonished by its general purport. Mazzaiba will be writing to you in a few days, in the meantime I volunteered to give you the details you asked for.

'Mazzaiba and I have done all in our power to render M—'s

stay here as easy and pleasant as possible from the time we first met him in your company at the Great Britain Hotel. [This is not correct. They were already quite friendly with M— before that motor-drive, when I saw these two Maltese for the first time.] He lived in an embarrassed mood since then, and though we helped him as best we could both morally and financially he never confided to us his troubles. To this very day we cannot but look on his coming here and his stay amongst us, to say the least of the way he left us, as a huge farce wrapped up in mystery, a painful experience unsolicited by either of us and a cause of grief unrequited except by our own personal sense of duty towards a stranger.

'Mazzaiba out of mere respect did not tell me of his commitments towards M— until about a month ago, and this he did in a most confidential and private manner merely to put me on my guard, thinking, and rightly, too, that M— would be falling on me next time for funds; Mazzaiba having already given him about £55 and would not possibly commit himself any further. Of course, we found him all along a perfect gentleman. Naturally, he hated the very idea that we or anybody else in Malta should look upon him in any other light. He never asked directly, though Mazzaiba (later myself) was always quick enough to interpret rightly what he meant and obliged him forthwith.

'At this stage, to save the situation, he made up a scheme that the three of us should exploit the commercial possibilities in Morocco. It very nearly materialized, everything was ready, I was to go with him to Morocco, Mazzaiba was to take charge of affairs here and to dispose of transactions we initiated there. Fortunately, for lack of the necessary funds the idea had to be dropped, and there it ended, thank God, after a great deal of trouble I had in trying to set it well on foot.

'Last July, the Police, according to our law, advised him that he was either to find a surety or to deposit a sum of money with them as otherwise at the expiration of his three months' stay he would be compelled to leave the place. Money he had none, so he asked Mazzaiba to stand as surety. Mazzaiba could not as he was already guarantor for his alien cousins who were here at the time.

Mazzaiba (not M—) asked me and I complied, thinking that the responsibility was just moral and only exacted as a matter of form.

'When, as stated before, Mazzaiba told me that M— owed him £55 and that he owed his grocer and others at Notabile (the old town, of which Rabato is the suburb) over £10, I thought I might as well look up my guarantee and see if I was directly responsible for any debts he incurred here. The words of his declaration which I endorsed stated that "I hereby solemnly promise that I will not be a burden to the inhabitants of these islands, etc.", and deeming that unpaid debts to be more or less a burden, I decided to withdraw my guarantee, which I did on the 23rd ult. The reason I gave to the police was that he was outliving his income and that I did not intend to shoulder any financial responsibility in the matter. On the same day I wrote to him up at Notabile saying that for family reasons I was compelled to withdraw his surety. He took my letter in the sense implied and no way offended at my procedure.

'M—, in his resourceful way, knowing that he would with great difficulty find another guarantor, wrote at once to the police saying that he understood from Mr Salonia that he (S) had withdrawn his guarantee, but as he (M) would be leaving the island in about three weeks' time (still intending to exploit Morocco) he begged the Commissioner to allow him this period of grace, without demanding a new surety. In fact he asked me to find him a cheap passage to Gib. in an ingoing tramp steamer. The police did not reply to his letter at all, no doubt they had everything ready and well thought out. He was alarmed in not receiving an acknowledgement, and, knowing full well what he imminently expected at the hands of the Italian police, he decided to prepare for the last act of his drama.

'We had not seen him for three or four days when he came to Mazzaiba's office on Wednesday, 3rd inst., in the forenoon. He stayed there for some time talking on general subjects and looking somewhat more excited than usual. He went up to town alone at noon as Mazzaiba went to Singlea. I was not with them in the morning, but in the afternoon about 4.30, whilst I was talking to

Mazzaiba in his office, M— again came in looking very excited, and, being closing time, we went up, the three of us, to town, and there left him in the company of a friend.

'On Thursday morning, 4th inst., at about 10 a.m., two detectives in plain clothes met him in a street at Notabile. One of them quite casually went up to him and said very civilly that the inspector of police wished to see him *re* a guarantee or something, and that he was to go with him to the police station. This was an excuse as the detective had about him a warrant for his arrest for frauding an hotel in Rome, and that he was to be extradited at the request of the authorities in Italy. M— replied that as he was in his sandals he would dress up and go with them immediately, and, accompanying him to his house at No. 1 Strada S. Pietro, they allowed him to enter. He locked the door behind him, leaving them outside.

'A few minutes later he opened his bedroom window and dropped a letter addressed to Don Bernardo which he asked a boy in the street to post for him, and immediately closed the window again. One of the detectives picked up the letter and we do not know to this day if same was posted at all. Some time elapsed and he did not come out. The detectives were by this time very uneasy and as another police official came up they decided to burst open the door. As the door did not give way they got a ladder and climbed over the roof, and there they found M— in his bedroom dying from poisoning, outstretched on his bed and a glass of water close by. A priest was immediately called in who had just time to administer Extreme Unction before he died at 11.45 a.m.

'At 8.0 a.m. the next day his body was admitted for examination at the Floriana Civil Hospital and death was certified to be from poisoning with hydrocyanic acid. His age was given as 44, being buried on his birthday (7th Novr), with R. Catholic Rites at the expense of *His Friends in Malta.*

'Addenda: Contents of Don Bernardo's letter: –

' "I leave it to you and to Gabriel Mazzaiba to arrange my affairs. I cannot live any longer. Pray for me."

'Document found on his writing-table:

' "In case of my unexpected death inform American consul.

' "I want to be buried first class, my wife will pay.

' "My little personal belongings to be delivered to my wife. (Address.)

' "My best friend here, Gabriel Mazzaiba, inform him. (Address.)

' "My literary executor N— D—. (Address.)

' "All manuscripts and books for N— D—. I leave my literary property to N— D— to whom half of the results are to accrue. The other half my debts are to be paid with:

' "Furniture, etc., belong to Coleiro, Floriana.

' "Silver spoons, etc., belong to Gabriel Mazzaiba. (Address.)"

'The American Consul is in charge of all his personal belongings. I am sure he will be pleased to give you any further details you may require. By the way, his wife refused to pay his burial expenses, but five of his friends in Malta undertook to give him a decent funeral. His mourners were: The consul, the vice-consul, Mr A., an American citizen, Gabriel Mazzaiba and myself.

'Please convey to Mrs Lawrence an expression of our sincere esteem and high regard and you will kindly accept equally our warmest respects, whilst soliciting any information you would care to pass on to us regarding the late M—. Believe me, My dear Mr Lawrence, etc.'

[Mrs M— refunded the burial expenses through the American consul about two months after her husband's death.]

When I had read this letter the world seemed to stand still for me. I knew that in my own soul I had said, 'Yes, he must die if he cannot find his own way.' But for all that, now I *realized* what it must have meant to be the hunted, desperate man: everything seemed to stand still. I could, by giving half my money, have saved his life. I had chosen not to save his life.

Now, after a year has gone by, I keep to my choice. I still would not save his life. I respect him for dying when he was cornered. And for this reason I feel still connected with him: still have this to discharge, to get his book published, and to give him his place, to present him just as he was as far as I knew him myself.

The worst thing I have against him, is that he abused the confidence, the kindness, and the generosity of unsuspecting people like Mazzaiba. He did not *want* to, perhaps. But he did it. And he leaves Mazzaiba swindled, distressed, confused, and feeling sold in the best part of himself. What next? What is one to feel towards one's strangers, after having known M—? It is this Judas treachery to *ask* for sympathy and for generosity, to take it when given – and then : 'Sorry, but anybody may make a mistake!' It is this betraying with a kiss which makes me still say: 'He should have died sooner.' No, I would not help to keep him alive, not if I had to choose again. I would let him go over into death. He shall and should die, and so should all his sort: and so they will. There are so many kiss-giving Judases. He was not a criminal: he was obviously well intentioned: but a Judas every time, selling the good feeling he had tried to arouse, and had aroused, for any handful of silver he could get. A little loving vampire!

Yesterday arrived the manuscript of the Legion, from Malta. It is exactly two years since I read it first in the monastery. Then I was moved and rather horrified. Now I am chiefly amused; because in my mind's eye is the figure of M— in the red trousers and the blue coat with lappets turned up, swinging like a little indignant pigeon across the drill yards and into the canteen of Bel-Abbès. He *is* so indignant, so righteously and morally indignant, and so funny. All the horrors of the actuality fade before the indignation, his little, tuppenny indignation.

Oh, M— is a prime hypocrite. *How* loudly he rails against the *Boches*! *How* great his enthusiasm for the pure, the spiritual Allied cause. Just so long as he is in Africa, and it suits his purpose! His scorn for the German tendencies of the German legionaries: even Count de R. secretly leans towards Germany. 'Blood is thicker than water,' says our hero glibly. Some blood, thank God. Apparently not his own. For according to all showing he was, by blood, pure German: father and mother: even Hohenzollern blood ! ! ! Pure German! Even his speech, his *mother-tongue*, was German and not English! And then the little mongrel! – !

But perhaps something happens to blood when once it has been taken to America.

And then, once he is in Valbonne, lo, a change! Where now is sacred France and the holy Allied Cause! Where is our hero's fervour? It is *worse than* Bel-Abbès! Yes, indeed, far less human, more hideously cold. One is driven by very rage to wonder if he was really a spy, a German spy whom Germany cast off because he was no good.

The little *gentleman*! God damn his white-blooded gentility. The legionaries must have been gentlemen, that they didn't kick him every day to the lavatory and back.

'You are a journalist?' said the Colonel.

'No, a *littérateur*,' said M— perkily.

'That is something more?' said the Colonel.

Oh, I would have given a lot to have seen it and heard it. The *littérateur*! Well, I hope this book will establish his fame as such. I hope the editor, if it gets one, won't alter any more of the marvellously staggering sentences and the joyful French mistakes. The *littérateur*! – the impossible little pigeon!

But the Bel-Abbès part is alive and interesting. It should be read only by those who have the stomach. Ugly, foul – alas, it is no uglier and no fouler than the reality. M— himself was near enough to being a scoundrel, thief, forger, etc., etc. – what lovely strings of names he hurls at them! – to be able to appreciate his company. He himself was such a liar, that he was not taken in. But his conceit as a gentleman *keeping up appearances* gave him a real standpoint from which to see the rest. The book is in its way a real creation. But I would hate it to be published and taken at its face value, with M— as a spiritual dove among vultures of lust. Let us first put a pinch of salt on the tail of this dove. What he did in this way of vice, even in Bel-Abbès, I never chose to ask him.

Yes, yes, he sings another note when he is planted right among the sacred Allies, with never a German near. Then the gorgeousness goes out of his indignation. He takes it off with the red trousers. Now he is just a sordid little figure in filthy corduroys. There is no vice to purple his indignation, the little holy liar. There is only sordidness and automatic, passionless, colourless awful mud. When all is said and done, mud, cold, hideous, foul, engulfing mud, up to the waist, this is the final symbol of the Great War. Hear some of the horrified young soldiers. They dare hardly speak of it yet.

The Valbonne part is worse, really, than the Bel-Abbès part. Passionless, barren, utterly, coldly foul and hopeless. The ghastly emptiness, and the slow mud-vortex, the brink of it.

Well, now M— has gone himself. Yes, and he would be gone in the common mud and dust himself, if it were not that the blood still beats warm and hurt and kind in some few hearts. M— 'hinted' at Mazzaiba for money, in Malta, and Mazzaiba gave it to him, thinking him a man in distress. He thought him a gentleman, and lovable, and in trouble! And Mazzaiba – it isn't his real name, but there he is, real enough – still has this feeling of grief for M—. So much so that now he has had the remains taken from the public grave in Malta, and buried in his own, the Mazzaiba grave, so that they shall not be lost. For my part, I would have said that the sooner they mingled with the universal dust, the better. But one is glad to see a little genuine kindness and gentleness, even if it is wasted on the bones of that selfish little scamp of a M—. He despised his 'physical friendships – though he didn't forgo them. So why should anyone rescue his physique from the public grave?

But there you are – there was his power: to arouse affection and a certain tenderness in the hearts of others, for himself. And on this he traded. One sees the trick working all the way through the Legion book. God knows how much warm kindness, generosity, was showered on him during the course of his forty-odd years. And selfish little scamp, he took it as a greedy boy takes cakes off a dish, quickly, to make the most of his opportunity while it lasted. And the cake once eaten: *buona sera!* He patted his own little paunch and felt virtuous. Merely physical feeling, you see! He had a way of saying 'physical' – a sort of American way, as if it were spelt 'fisacal' – that made me want to kick him.

Not that he was mean, while he was about it. No, he would give very freely: even a little ostentatiously, always feeling that he was being a *liberal gentleman*. Ach, the liberality and the gentility he prided himself on! *Ecco!* And he gave a large tip, with a

93

little winsome smile. But in his heart of hearts it was always himself he was thinking of, while he did it. Playing his role of the gentleman who was awfully *nice* to everybody : so long as they were nice to him, or so long as it served his advantage. Just private charity!

Well, poor devil, he is dead: which is all the better. He had his points, the courage of his own terrors, quick-wittedness, sensitiveness to certain things in his surroundings. I prefer him, scamp as he is, to the ordinary respectable person. He ran his risks: he *had* to be running risks with the police, apparently. And he poisoned himself rather than fall into their clutches. I like him for that. And I like him for the sharp and quick way he made use of every one of his opportunities to get out of that beastly army. There I admire him: a courageous isolated little devil, facing his risks, and like a good rat, *determined* not to be trapped. I won't forgive him for trading on the generosity of others, and so dropping poison into the heart of all warm-blooded faith. But I am glad after all that Mazzaiba has rescued his bones from the public grave. I wouldn't have done it myself, because I don't forgive him his 'fisacal' impudence and parasitism. But I am glad Mazzaiba has done it. And, for my part, I will put his Legion book before the world if I can. Let him have his place in the world's consciousness.

Let him have his place, let his word be heard. He went through vile experiences: he looked them in the face, braved them through, and kept his manhood in spite of them. For manhood is a strange quality, to be found in human rats as well as in hot-blooded men. M— carried the human consciousness through circumstances which would have been too much for me. I would have died rather than be so humiliated, I could never have borne it. Other men, I know, went through worse things in the war. But then, horrors, like pain, are their own anaesthetic. Men lose their normal consciousness, and go through in a sort of delirium. The bit of Stendhal which Dos Passos quotes in front of *Three Soldiers* is frighteningly true. There are certain things which are *so* bitter, *so* horrible, that the contemporaries just cannot know them, cannot contemplate them. So it is with a great deal of the late war. It was so foul, and humanity in Europe fell suddenly into such ignominy and inhuman ghastliness, that we shall *never* fully realize what it was. We just cannot bear it. We haven't the soul-strength to contemplate it.

And yet, humanity can only finally conquer by realizing. It is human destiny, since Man fell into consciousness and self-consciousness, that we can only go forward step by step through realization, full, bitter, conscious realization. This is true of all the great terrors and agonies and anguishes of life: sex, and war, and even crime. When Flaubert in his story – it is so long since I read it – makes his saint have to kiss the leper, and naked clasp the leprous awful body against his own, that is what we must at last do. It is the great command *Know Thyself*. We've got to *know* what sex is, let the sentimentalists wiggle as they like. We've got to know the greatest and most shattering human passions, let the puritans squeal as they like for screens. And we've got to know humanity's criminal tendency, look straight at humanity's great deeds of crime against the soul. We have to fold this horrible leper against our naked warmth: because life and the throbbing blood and the believing soul are greater even than leprosy. Knowledge, true knowledge is like vaccination. It prevents the continuing of ghastly moral disease.

And so it is with the war. Humanity in Europe fell horribly into a hatred of the living soul, in the war. There is no gainsaying it. We all fell. Let us not try to wriggle out of it. We fell into hideous depravity of hating the human soul; a purulent small-pox of the spirit we had. It was shameful, shameful, shameful, in every country and in all of us. Some tried to resist, and some didn't. But we were all drowned in shame. A purulent small-pox of the vicious spirit, vicious against the deep soul that pulses in the blood.

We haven't got over it. The small-pox sores are running yet in the spirit of mankind. And we have got to take this putrid spirit to our bosom. There's nothing else for it. Take the foul rotten spirit of mankind, full of the running sores of the war, to our bosom, and cleanse it there. Cleanse it not with blind love: ah no, that won't help. But with bitter and wincing realization. We have to take the disease into our consciousness and let it go through our soul, like some virus. We have got to realize. And then we can surpass.

M— went where I could never go. He carried the human consciousness unbroken through circumstances I could not have borne. It is not heroism to rush on death. It is cowardice to accept a martyrdom today. That is the feeling one has at the end of Dos Passos' book. To let oneself be absolutely trapped? Never! I prefer M—. He drew himself out of the thing he loathed, despised, and feared. He fought it, for his own spirit and liberty. He fought it open-eyed. He went through. They were more publicly heroic, they won war medals. But the lonely terrified courage of the isolated spirit which grits its teeth and stares the horrors in the face and *will* not succumb to them, but fights its way through them, *knowing* that it must surpass them: this is the rarest courage. And this courage M— had: and the man in the Dos Passos book didn't *quite* have it. And so, though M— poisoned himself, and I would not wish him *not* to have poisoned himself: though as far as warm life goes, I don't forgive him; yet, as far as the eternal and unconquerable spirit of man goes, I am with him through eternity. I am grateful to him, he beat out for me boundaries of human experience which I could not have beaten out for myself. The *human* traitor he was. But he was not traitor to the spirit. In the great spirit of human consciousness he was a hero, little, quaking and heroic: a strange, quaking little star.

Even the dead ask only for *justice*: not for praise or exoneration. Who dares humiliate the dead with excuses for their living? I hope I may do M— justice; and I hope his restless spirit may be appeased. I do not try to forgive. The living blood knows no forgiving. Only the overweening spirit takes on itself to dole out forgiveness. But Justice is a sacred human right. The overweening spirit pretends to perch above justice. But I am a man, not a spirit, and men with blood that throbs and throbs and throbs can only live at length by being just, can only die in peace if they have justice. Forgiveness gives the whimpering dead no rest. Only deep, true justice.

There is M—'s manuscript then, like a map of the lower places of mankind's activities. There is the war: foul, foul, unutterably foul. As foul as M— says. Let us make up our minds about it.

It is the only help: to realize, *fully*, and then make up our minds. The war was *foul*. As long as I am a man, I say it and assert it, and further I say, as long as I am a man such a war shall never occur again. It shall not, and it shall not. All modern militarism is foul. It shall go. A man I am, and above machines, and it shall go, forever, because I have found it vile, vile, too vile ever to experience again. Cannons shall go. Never again shall trenches be dug. They *shall* not, for I am a man, and such things are within the power of man, to break and make. I have said it, and as long as blood beats in my veins, I mean it. Blood beats in the veins of many men who mean it as well as I.

Man perhaps *must* fight. Mars, the great god of war, will be a god forever. Very well. Then if fight you must, fight you shall, and without engines, without machines. Fight if you like, as the Roman fought, with swords and spears, or like the Red Indian, with bows and arrows and knives and war paint. But never again shall you fight with the foul, base, fearful, monstrous machines of war which man invented for the last war. You shall not. The diabolic mechanisms are man's, and I am a man. Therefore they are mine. And I smash them into oblivion. With every means in my power, *except* the means of these machines, I smash them into oblivion. I am at war! I, a man, am at war! – with these foul machines and contrivances that men have conjured up. Men have conjured them up. I, a man, will conjure them down again. Won't I? – but I will! I am not one man, I am many, I am most.

So much for the war! So much for M—'s manuscript. Let it be read. It is not this that will do harm, but sloppy sentiment and cant. Take the bitterness and cleanse the blood.

Now would you believe it, that little scamp M— spent over a hundred pounds of borrowed money during his four months in Malta, when his expenses, he boasted to me, need not have been more than a pound a week, once he got into the little house in Notabile. That is, he spent at least seventy pounds too much. Heaven knows what he did with it, apart from 'guzzling'. And this hundred pounds must be paid back in Malta. Which it never will be, unless this manuscript pays it back. Pay the gentleman's last debts, if no others.

He had to be a gentleman. I didn't realize till after his death. I never suspected him of royal blood. But there you are, you never know where it will crop out. He was the grandson of an emperor. His mother was the illegitimate daughter of the German Kaiser: D— says, of the old Kaiser Wilhelm I, Don Bernardo says, of Kaiser Frederick Wilhelm, father of the present ex-Kaiser. She was born in Berlin on the 31 October 1845: and her portrait, by Paul, now hangs in a gallery in Rome. Apparently there had been some injustice against her in Berlin – for she seems once to have been in the highest society there, and to have attended at court. Perhaps she was discreetly banished by Wilhelm II, hence M—'s hatred of that monarch. She lies buried in the Protestant Cemetery in Rome, where she died in 1912, with the words *Filia Regis* on her tomb. M— adored her, and she him. Part of his failings one can *certainly* ascribe to the fact that he was an only son, an adored son, in whose veins the mother imagined only royal blood. And she must have thought him so beautiful, poor thing! Ah well, they are both dead. Let us be just and wish them Lethe.

M— himself was born in New York, 7 November 1876; so at least it says on his passport. He entered the Catholic Church in England in 1902. His father was a Mr L— M—, married to the mother in 1867.

So poor M— had Hohenzollern blood in his veins: close kin to the ex-Kaiser William. Well, that itself excuses him a great deal: because of the cruel illusion of importance *manqué*, which it must have given him. He never breathed a word of this to me. Yet apparently it is accepted at the monastery, the great monastery which knows most European secrets of any political significance. And for myself, I believe it is true. And if he was a scamp and a treacherous little devil, he had also qualities of nerve and breeding undeniable. He faced his way through that Legion experience: royal nerves dragging themselves through the sewers, without giving way. But alas, for royal blood! Like most other blood, it has gradually gone white, during our spiritual era. Bunches of nerves! And whitish, slightly acid blood. And no bowels of deep compassion and kindliness. Only charity – a little more than kin, and less than kind.

*Also – M—! Ich grüsse dich, in der Ewigkeit. Aber hier, im Herzblut, hast du Gift und Leid nachgelassen* – to use your own romantic language.

# 2. Peoples and Places

# Nottingham and the Mining Countryside

Written 1929, published in *New Adelphi*, June–August
1930; *Phoenix*, 1936

I was born nearly forty-four years ago, in Eastwood, a mining
village of some three thousand souls, about eight miles from Nottingham, and one mile from the small stream, the Erewash, which
divides Nottinghamshire from Derbyshire. It is hilly country,
looking west to Crich and towards Matlock, sixteen miles away,
and east and north-east towards Mansfield and the Sherwood
Forest district. To me it seemed, and still seems, an extremely
beautiful countryside, just between the red sandstone and the oak-
trees of Nottingham, and the cold limestone, the ash-trees, the
stone fences of Derbyshire. To me, as a child and a young man, it
was still the old England of the forest and agricultural past; there
were no motor-cars, the mines were, in a sense, an accident in the
landscape, and Robin Hood and his merry men were not very far
away.

The string of coal-mines of B. W. & Co. had been opened some
sixty years before I was born, and Eastwood had come into being
as a consequence. It must have been a tiny village at the beginning
of the nineteenth century, a small place of cottages and fragmentary rows of little four-roomed miners' dwellings, the homes of
the old colliers of the eighteenth century, who worked in the bits
of mines, foot-rill mines with an opening in the hillside into which
the miners walked, or windlass mines, where the men were wound

up one at a time, in a bucket, by a donkey. The windlass mines were still working when my father was a boy – and the shafts of some were still there, when I was a boy.

But somewhere about 1820 the company must have sunk the first big shaft – not very deep – and installed the first machinery of the real industrial colliery. Then came my grandfather, a young man trained to be a tailor, drifting from the south of England, and got the job of company tailor for the Brinsley mine. In those days the company supplied the men with the thick flannel vests, or singlets, and the moleskin trousers lined at the top with flannel, in which the colliers worked. I remember the great rolls of coarse flannel and pit-cloth which stood in the corner of my grandfather's shop when I was a small boy, and the big, strange old sewing-machine, like nothing else on earth, which sewed the massive pit-trousers. But when I was only a child the company discontinued supplying the men with pit-clothes.

My grandfather settled in an old cottage down in a quarry-bed, by the brook at Old Brinsley, near the pit. A mile away, up at Eastwood, the company built the first miners' dwellings – it must be nearly a hundred years ago. Now Eastwood occupies a lovely position on a hilltop, with the steep slope towards Derbyshire and the long slope towards Nottingham. They put up a new church, which stands fine and commanding, even if it has no real form, looking across the awful Erewash Valley at the church of Heanor, similarly commanding, away on a hill beyond. What opportunities, what opportunities! These mining villages *might* have been like the lovely hill-towns of Italy, shapely and fascinating. And what happened?

Most of the little rows of dwellings of the old-style miners were pulled down, and dull little shops began to rise along the Nottingham Road, while on the down-slope of the north side the company erected what is still known as the New Buildings, or the Square. These New Buildings consist of two great hollow squares of dwellings planked down on the rough slope of the hill, little four-room houses with the 'front' looking outward into the grim, blank street, and the 'back', with a tiny square brick yard, a low wall, and a w.c. and ash-pit, looking into the desert of the square, hard, uneven, jolting black earth tilting rather steeply down, with these little back yards all round, and openings at the corners. The squares were quite big, and absolutely desert, save for the posts for clothes lines, and people passing, children playing on the hard earth. And they were shut in like a barracks enclosure, very strange.

Even fifty years ago the squares were unpopular. It was 'common' to live in the Square. It was a little less common to live in the Breach, which consisted of six blocks of rather more pretentious dwellings erected by the company in the valley below, two rows of three blocks, with an alley between. And it was most 'common', most degraded of all, to live in Dakins Row, two rows of the old dwellings, very old, black, four-roomed little places, that stood on the hill again, not far from the Square.

So the place started. Down the steep street between the squares, Scargill Street, the Wesleyans' chapel was put up, and I was born in the little corner shop just above. Across the other side of the Square the miners themselves built the big, barn-like Primitive Methodist chapel. Along the hill-top ran the Nottingham Road, with its scrappy, ugly mid-Victorian shops. The little market-place, with a superb outlook, ended the village on the Derbyshire side, and was just left bare, with the Sun Inn on one side, the chemist across, with the gilt pestle-and-mortar, and a shop at the other corner, the corner of Alfreton Road and Nottingham Road.

In this queer jumble of the old England and the new, I came into consciousness. As I remember, little local speculators already began to straggle dwellings in rows, always in rows, across the fields: nasty red-brick, flat-faced dwellings with dark slate roofs. The bay-window period only began when I was a child. But most of the country was untouched.

There must be three or four hundred company houses in the squares and the streets that surround the squares, like a great barracks wall. There must be sixty or eighty company houses in the Breach. The old Dakins Row will have thirty to forty little holes. Then counting the old cottages and rows left with their old gardens down the lanes and along the twitchells, and even in the midst of Nottingham Road itself, there were houses enough for the population, there was no need for much building. And not much building went on when I was small.

We lived in the Breach, in a corner house. A field-path came down under a great hawthorn hedge. On the other side was the brook, with the old sheep-bridge going over into the meadows. The hawthorn hedge by the brook had grown tall as tall trees, and we used to bathe from there in the dipping-hole, where the sheep were dipped, just near the fall from the old mill-dam, where the water rushed. The mill only ceased grinding the local corn when I was a child. And my father, who always worked in Brinsley pit, and who always got up at five o'clock, if not at four, would set off in the dawn across the fields at Coney Grey, and hunt for mushrooms in the long grass, or perhaps pick up a skulking rabbit, which he would bring home at evening inside the lining of his pit-coat.

So that the life was a curious cross between industrialism and the old agricultural England of Shakespeare and Milton and Fielding and George Eliot. The dialect was broad Derbyshire, and always 'thee' and 'thou'. The people lived almost entirely by instinct, men of my father's age could not really read. And the pit did not mechanize men. On the contrary. Under the butty system, the miners worked underground as a sort of intimate community, they knew each other practically naked, and with curious close intimacy, and the darkness and the underground remoteness of the pit 'stall', and the continual presence of danger, made the physical, instinctive, and intuitional contact between men very highly developed, a contact almost as close as touch, very real and very powerful. This physical awareness and intimate *togetherness* was at its strongest down pit. When the men came up into the light, they blinked. They had, in a measure, to change their flow. Nevertheless, they brought with them above ground the curious dark intimacy of the mine, the naked sort of contact, and if I think of my childhood, it is always as if there was a lustrous sort of inner darkness, like the gloss of coal, in which we moved and had our real being. My father loved the pit. He was hurt badly, more than once, but he would never stay away. He loved the contact, the intimacy, as men in the war loved the intense male comradeship of the dark days. They did not know what they had lost till they lost it. And I think it is the same with the young colliers of today.

Now the colliers had also an instinct of beauty. The colliers' wives had not. The colliers were deeply alive, instinctively. But they had no daytime ambition, and no daytime intellect. They avoided, really, the rational aspect of life. They preferred to take life instinctively and intuitively. They didn't even care very profoundly about wages. It was the women, naturally, who nagged on this score. There was a big discrepancy, when I was a boy, between the collier who saw, at the best, only a brief few hours of daylight – often no daylight at all during the winter weeks – and the collier's wife, who had all the day to herself when the man was down pit.

The great fallacy is, to pity the man. He didn't dream of pitying himself, till agitators and sentimentalists taught him to. He was happy: or more than happy, he was fulfilled. Or he was fulfilled on the receptive side, not on the expressive. The collier went to the pub and drank in order to continue his intimacy with his mates. They talked endlessly, but it was rather of wonders and marvels, even in politics, than of facts. It was hard facts, in the shape of wife, money, and nagging home necessities, which they fled away from, out of the house to the pub, and out of the house to the pit.

The collier fled out of the house as soon as he could, away from the nagging materialism of the woman. With the women it was always: This is broken, now you've got to mend it! or else: We want this, that and the other, and where is the money coming from? The collier didn't know and didn't care very deeply – his life was otherwise. So he escaped. He roved the countryside with his dog, prowling for a rabbit, for nests, for mushrooms, anything. He loved the countryside, just the indiscriminating feel of it. Or he loved just to sit on his heels and watch – anything or nothing. He was not intellectually interested. Life for him did not consist in facts, but in a flow. Very often, he loved his garden. And very often he had a genuine love of the beauty of flowers. I have known it often and often, in colliers.

Now the love of flowers is a very misleading thing. Most women love flowers as possessions, and as trimmings. They can't look at a flower, and wonder a moment, and pass on. If they see a flower that arrests their attention, they must at once pick it, pluck it. Possession! A possession! Something added on to *me*! And most of the so-called love of flowers today is merely this reaching out of possession and egoism: something I've *got*: something that embellishes *me*. Yet I've seen many a collier stand in his back garden looking down at a flower with that odd, remote sort of contemplation which shows a *real* awareness of the presence of beauty. It would not even be admiration, or joy, or delight, or any of those things which so often have a root in the possessive instinct. It would be a sort of contemplation: which shows the incipient artist.

The real tragedy of England, as I see it, is the tragedy of ugliness. The country is so lovely: the man-made England is so vile. I know that the ordinary collier, when I was a boy, had a peculiar sense of beauty, coming from his intuitive and instinctive consciousness, which was awakened down pit. And the fact that he met with just cold ugliness and raw materialism when he came up into daylight, and particularly when he came to the Square or the Breach, and to his own table, killed something in him, and in a sense spoiled him as a man. The woman almost invariably nagged about material things. She was taught to do it; she was encouraged to do it. It was a mother's business to see that her sons 'got on', and it was the man's business to provide the money. In my father's generation, with the old wild England behind them, and the lack of education, the man was not beaten down. But in my generation, the boys I went to school with, colliers now, have all been beaten down, what with the din-din-dinning of Board Schools, books, cinemas, clergymen, the whole national and human consciousness hammering on the fact of material prosperity above all things.

The men are beaten down, there is prosperity for a time, in their defeat – and then disaster looms ahead. The root of all disaster is disheartenment. And the men are disheartened. The men of England, the colliers in particular, are disheartened. They have been betrayed and beaten.

Now though perhaps nobody knew it, it was ugliness which

really betrayed the spirit of man, in the nineteenth century. The great crime which the moneyed classes and promoters of industry committed in the palmy Victorian days was the condemning of the workers to ugliness, ugliness, ugliness: meanness and formless and ugly surroundings, ugly ideals, ugly religion, ugly hope, ugly love, ugly clothes, ugly furniture, ugly houses, ugly relationship between workers and employers. The human soul needs actual beauty even more than bread. The middle classes jeer at the colliers for buying pianos – but what is the piano, often as not, but a blind reaching out for beauty. To the woman it is a possession and a piece of furniture and something to feel superior about. But see the elderly colliers trying to learn to play, see them listening with queer alert faces to their daughter's execution of 'The Maiden's Prayer', and you will see a blind, unsatisfied craving for beauty. It is far more deep in the men than the women. The women want show. The men want beauty, and still want it.

If the company, instead of building those sordid and hideous Squares, then, when they had that lovely site to play with, there on the hill top: if they had put a tall column in the middle of the small market-place, and run three parts of a circle of arcade round the pleasant space, where people could stroll or sit, and with handsome houses behind! If they had made big, substantial houses, in apartments of five or six rooms, and with handsome entrances. If above all, they had encouraged song and dancing – for the miners still sang and danced – and provided handsome space for these. If only they had encouraged some form of beauty in dress, some form of beauty in interior life – furniture, decoration. If they had given prizes for the handsomest chair or table, the loveliest scarf, the most charming room that the men or women could make! If only they had done this, there would never have been an industrial problem. The industrial problem arises from the base forcing of all human energy into a competition of mere acquisition.

You may say the working man would not have accepted such a form of life: the Englishman's home is his castle, etc., etc. – 'my own little home'. But if you can hear every word the next-door people say, there's not much castle. And if you can see everybody in the square if they go to the w.c.! And if your one desire is to get out of your 'castle' and your 'own little home'! – well, there's not much to be said for it. Anyhow, it's only the woman who idolizes 'her own little home' – and it's always the woman at her worst, her most greedy, most possessive, most mean. There's nothing to be said for the 'little home' any more: a great scrabble of ugly pettiness over the face of the land.

As a matter of fact, till 1800 the English people were strictly a rural people – very rural. England has had towns for centuries, but they have never been real towns, only clusters of village streets. Never the real *urbs*. The English character has failed to develop the real *urban* side of a man, the civic side. Siena is a bit of a place, but it is a real city, with citizens intimately connected with the city. Nottingham is a vast place sprawling towards a million, and it is nothing more than an amorphous agglomeration. There *is* no Nottingham, in the sense that there is Siena. The Englishman is stupidly undeveloped, as a citizen. And it is partly due to his 'little home' stunt, and partly to his acceptance of hopeless paltriness in his surrounding. The new cities of America are much more genuine cities, in the Roman sense, than is London or Manchester. Even Edinburgh used to be more of a true city than any town England ever produced.

That silly little individualism of 'the Englishman's home is his castle' and 'my own little home' is out of date. It would work almost up to 1800, when every Englishman was still a villager, and a cottager. But the industrial system has brought a great change. The Englishman still likes to think of himself as a 'cottager' – 'my home, my garden'. But it is puerile. Even the farm-labourer today is psychologically a town-bird. The English are town-birds through and through, today, as the inevitable result of their complete industrialization. Yet they don't know how to build a city, how to think of one, or how to live in one. They are all suburban, pseudo-cottagy, and not one of them knows how to be truly urban – the citizen as the Romans were citizens – or the Athenians – or even the Parisians, till the war came.

And this is because we have frustrated that instinct of community which would make us unite in pride and dignity in the

110

bigger gesture of the citizen, not the cottager. The great city means beauty, dignity, and a certain splendour. This is the side of the Englishman that has been thwarted and shockingly betrayed. England is a mean and petty scrabble of paltry dwellings called 'homes'. I believe in their heart of hearts all Englishmen loathe their little homes – but not the women. What we want is a bigger gesture, a greater scope, a certain splendour, a certain grandeur, and beauty, big beauty. The American does far better than we, in this.

And the promoter of industry, a hundred years ago, dared to perpetrate the ugliness of my native village. And still more monstrous, promoters of industry today are scrabbling over the face of England with miles and square miles of red-brick 'homes', like horrible scabs. And the men inside these little red rat-traps get more and more helpless, being more and more humiliated, more and more dissatisfied, like trapped rats. Only the meaner sort of women go on loving the little home which is no more than a rat-trap to her man.

Do away with it all, then. At no matter what cost, start in to alter it. Never mind about wages and industrial squabbling. Turn the attention elsewhere. Pull down my native village to the last brick. Plan a nucleus. Fix the focus. Make a handsome gesture of radiation from the focus. And then put up big buildings, handsome, that sweep to a civic centre. And furnish them with beauty. And make an absolute clean start. Do it place by place. Make a new England. Away with little homes! Away with scrabbling pettiness and paltriness. Look at the contours of the land, and build up from these, with a sufficient nobility. The English may be mentally or spiritually developed. But as citizens of splendid cities they are more ignominious than rabbits. And they nag, nag, nag all the time about politics and wages and all that, like mean narrow housewives.

# Paris Letter

Written 1924, published in *Laughing Horse*,
April 1926; *Phoenix*, 1936

I promised to write a letter to you from Paris. Probably I should have forgotten, but I saw a little picture – or sculpture – in the Tuileries, of Hercules slaying the Centaur, and that reminded me. I had so much rather the Centaur had slain Hercules, and men had never developed souls. Seems to me they're the greatest ailment humanity ever had. However, they've got it.

Paris is still monumental and handsome. Along the river where its splendours are, there's no denying its man-made beauty. The poor, pale little Seine runs rapidly north to the sea, the sky is pale, pale jade overhead, greenish and Parisian, the trees of black wire stand in rows,and flourish their black wire brushes against a low sky of jade-pale cobwebs, and the huge dark-grey palaces rear up their masses of stone and slope off towards the sky still with a massive, satisfying suggestion of pyramids. There is something noble and man-made about it all.

My wife says she wishes that grandeur still squared its shoulders on the earth. She wishes she could sit sumptuously in the river windows of the Tuileries, and see a royal spouse – who wouldn't be me – cross the bridge at the head of a tossing, silk and silver cavalcade. She wishes she had a bevy of ladies-in-waiting around her, as a peacock has its tail, as she crossed the weary expanses of pavement in the Champs Elysées.

Well, she can have it. At least, she can't. The world has lost its faculty for splendour, and Paris is like an old, weary peacock that sports a bunch of dirty twigs at its rump, where it used to have a tail. Democracy has collapsed into more and more democracy, and men, particularly Frenchmen, have collapsed into little, rather insignificant, rather wistful, rather nice and helplessly common-place little fellows who rouse one's mother-instinct and make one feel they should be tucked away in bed and left to sleep, like Rip Van Winkle, till the rest of the storms rolled by.

It's a queer thing to sit in the Tuileries on a Sunday afternoon and watch the crowd drag through the galleries. Instead of a gay and wicked court, the weary, weary crowd, that looks as if it had nothing at heart to keep it going. As if the human creature had been dwindling and dwindling through the processes of demo-cracy, amid the ponderous ridicule of the aristocratic setting, till soon he will dwindle right away.

Oh, those galleries. Oh, those pictures and those statues of nude, nude women: nude, nude, insistently and hopelessly nude. At last the eyes fall in absolute weariness, the moment they catch sight of a bit of pink-and-white painting, or a pair of white marble *fesses*. It becomes an inquisition: like being forced to go on eating pink marzipan icing. And yet there is a fat and very undistinguished bourgeois with a little beard and a fat and hopelessly petit-bourgeoise wife and awful little girl, standing in front of a huge heap of twisting marble, while he, with a goose-grease unctuous simper, strokes the marble hip of the huge marble female, and points out its niceness *to his wife*. She is not in the least jealous. She knows, no doubt, that her own hip and the marble hip are the only ones he will stroke without paying prices, one of which, and the last he could pay, would be the price of spunk.

It seems to me the French are just worn out. And not nearly so much with the late great war as with the pink nudities of women. The men are just worn out, making offerings on the shrine of Aphrodite in elastic garters. And the women are worn out, keep-ing the men up to it. The rest is all nervous exasperation.

And the table. One shouldn't forget that other, four-legged mis-tress of man, more unwitherable than Cleopatra. The table.

The good kindly tables of Paris, with Coquilles Saint Martin, and escargots and oysters and châteaubriants and the good red wine. If they can afford it, the men sit and eat themselves pink. And no wonder. But the Aphrodite in a hard black hat opposite, when she has eaten herself also pink, is going to insist on further delights, to which somebody has got to play up. Weariness isn't the word for it.

May the Lord deliver us from our own enjoyments, we gasp at last. And he won't. We actually have to deliver ourselves.

One goes out again from the restaurant comfortably fed and soothed with a food and drink, to find the pale-jade sky of Paris crumbling in a wet dust of rain; motor-cars skidding till they turn clean around, and are facing south when they were going north: a boy on a bicycle coming smack, and picking himself up with his bicycle pump between his legs: and the men still fishing, as if it were a Sisyphus penalty, with long sticks fishing for invisible fishes in the Seine: and the huge buildings of the Louvre and the Tuileries standing ponderously, with their Parisian suggestion of pyramids.

And no, in the old style of grandeur I never want to be grand. That sort of regality, that builds itself up in piles of stone and masonry, and prides itself on living inside the monstrous heaps, once they're built, is not for me. My wife asks why she can't live in the Petit Palais, while she's in Paris. Well, even if she might, she'd live alone.

I don't believe any more in democracy. But I can't believe in the old sort of aristocracy, either, nor can I wish it back, splendid as it was. What I believe in is the old Homeric aristocracy, when the grandeur was inside the man, and he lived in a simple wooden house. Then, the men that were grand inside themselves, like Ulysses, were the chieftains and the aristocrats by instinct and by choice. At least we'll hope so. And the Red Indians only knew the aristocrat by instinct. The leader was leader in his own being, not because he was somebody's son or had so much money.

It's got to be so again. They say it won't work. I say, why not? If men could once recognize the natural aristocrat when they set eyes on him, they can still. They can still choose him if they would.

But this business of dynasties is weariness. House of Valois, House of Tudor! Who would want to be a House, or a bit of a House! Let a man be a man, and damn the House business. I'm absolutely a democrat as far as that goes.

But that men are all brothers and all equal is a greater lie than the other. Some men are always aristocrats. But it doesn't go by birth. A always contains B, but B is not contained in C.

Democracy, however, says that there is no such thing as an aristocrat. All men have two legs and one nose, *ergo*, they are all alike. Nosily and leggily, maybe. But otherwise, very different.

Democracy says that B is not contained in C, and neither is it contained in A. B, that is, the aristocrat, does not exist.

Now this is palpably a greater lie than the old dynastic life. Aristocracy truly does not go by birth. But it still goes. And the tradition of aristocracy will help it a lot.

The aristocrats tried to fortify themselves inside these palaces and these splendours. Regal Paris built up the external evidences of her regality. But the two-limbed man inside these vast shells died, poor worm, of over-encumbrance.

The natural aristocrat has got to fortify himself inside his own will, according to his own strength. The moment he builds himself external evidences, like palaces, he builds himself in, and commits his own doom. The moment he depends on his jewels, he has lost his virtue.

It always seems to me that the next civilization won't want to raise these ponderous, massive, deadly buildings that refuse to crumble away with their epoch and weigh men helplessly down. Neither palaces nor cathedrals nor any other hugenesses. Material simplicity is after all the highest sign of civilization. Here in Paris one knows it finally. The ponderous and depressing museum that is regal Paris. And living humanity like poor worms struggling inside the shell of history, all of them inside the museum. The dead life and the living life, all one museum.

Monuments, museums, permanencies, and ponderosities are all anathema. But brave men are for ever born, and nothing else is worth having.

# A Letter from Germany

Written 1924, published in the *New Statesman and Nation*, 13 October 1934; *Phoenix*, 1936

We are going back to Paris tomorrow, so this is the last moment to write a letter from Germany. Only from the fringe of Germany, too.

It is a miserable journey from Paris to Nancy, through that Marne country, where the country still seems to have had the soul blasted out of it, though the dreary fields are ploughed and level, and the pale wire trees stand up. But it is all void and null. And in the villages, the smashed houses in the street rows, like rotten teeth between good teeth.

You come to Strasbourg, and the people still talk Alsatian German, as ever, in spite of French shop-signs. The place feels dead. And full of cotton goods, white goods, from Mülhausen, from the factories that once were German. Such cheap white cotton goods, in a glut.

The cathedral front rearing up high and flat and fanciful, a sort of darkness in the dark, with round rose windows and long, long prisons of stone. Queer, that men should have ever wanted to put stone upon fanciful stone to such a height, without having it fall down. The Gothic! I was always glad when my card-castle fell. But these Goths and Alemans seemed to have a craze for peaky heights.

The Rhine is still the Rhine, the great divider. You feel it as you cross. The flat, frozen, watery places. Then the cold and curving river. Then the other side, seeming so cold, so empty, so frozen, so forsaken. The train stands and steams fiercely. Then it draws through the flat Rhine plain, past frozen pools of flood-water, and frozen fields, in the emptiness of this bit of occupied territory.

Immediately you are over the Rhine, the spirit of place has changed. There is no more attempt at the bluff of geniality. The marshy places are frozen. The fields are vacant. There seems nobody in the world.

It is as if the life had retreated eastwards. As if the Germanic life were slowly ebbing away from contact with western Europe, ebbing to the deserts of the east. And there stand the heavy, ponderous, round hills of the Black Forest, black with an inky blackness of Germanic trees, and patched with a whiteness of snow. They are like a series of huge, involved black mounds, obstructing the vision eastwards. You look at them from the Rhine plain, and know that you stand on an actual border, up against something.

The moment you are in Germany, you know. It feels empty, and, somehow, menacing. So must the Roman soldiers have watched those black, massive round hills: with a certain fear, and with the knowledge that they were at their own limit. A fear of the invisible natives. A fear of the invisible life lurking among the woods. A fear of their own opposite.

So it is with the French: this almost mystic fear. But one should not insult even one's fears.

Germany, this bit of Germany, is very different from what it was two-and-a-half years ago, when I was here. Then it was still open to Europe. Then it still looked to western Europe for a reunion, for a sort of reconciliation. Now that is over. The inevitable, mysterious barrier has fallen again, and the great leaning of the Germanic spirit is once more eastwards, towards Russia, towards Tartary. The strange vortex of Tartary has become the positive centre again, the positivity of western Europe is broken. The positivity of our civilization has broken. The influences that come, come invisibly out of Tartary. So that all Germany reads *Beasts, Men and Gods* with a kind of fascination. Returning

117

again to the fascination of the destructive East, that produced Attila.

So it is at night. Baden-Baden is a little quiet place, all its guests gone. No more Turgenevs or Dostoyevskys or Grand Dukes or King Edwards coming to drink the waters. All the outward effect. of a world-famous watering-place. But empty now, a mere Black Forest village with the wagon-loads of timber going through, to the French.

The Rentenmark, the new gold mark of Germany, is abominably dear. Prices are high in England, but English money buys less in Baden than it buys in London, by a long chalk. And there is no work – consequently no money. Nobody buys anything, except absolute necessities. The shop-keepers are in despair. And there is less and less work.

Everybody gives up the telephone – can't afford it. The tramcars don't run, except about three times a day to the station. Up to the Annaberg, the suburb, the lines are rusty, no trams ever go. The people can't afford the ten pfennigs for the fare. Ten pfennigs is an important sum now: one penny. It is really a hundred milliards of marks.

Money becomes insane, and people with it.

At night the place is almost dark, economizing light. Economy, economy, economy – that too becomes an insanity. Luckily the government keeps bread fairly cheap.

But at night you feel strange things stirring in the darkness, strange feelings stirring out of this still-unconquered Black Forest. You stiffen your backbone and you listen to the night. There is a sense of danger. It is not the people. They don't seem dangerous. Out of the very air comes a sense of danger, a queer, *bristling* feeling of uncanny danger.

Something has happened. Something has happened which has not yet eventuated. The old spell of the old world has broken, and the old, bristling, savage spirit has set in. The war did not break the old peace-and-production hope of the world, though it gave it a severe wrench. Yet the old peace-and-production hope still governs, at least the consciousness. Even in Germany it has not quite gone.

But it feels as if, virtually, it were gone. The last two years have done it. The hope in peace-and-production is broken. The old flow, the old adherence is ruptured. And a still older flow has set in. Back, back to the savage polarity of Tartary, and away from the polarity of civilized Christian Europe. This, it seems to me, has already happened. And it is a happening of far more profound import than any actual *event*. It is the father of the next phase of events.

And the feeling never relaxes. As you travel up the Rhine valley, still the same latent sense of danger, of silence, of suspension. Not that the people are actually planning or plotting or preparing. I don't believe it for a minute. But something has happened to the human soul, beyond all help. The human soul recoiling now from unison, and making itself strong elsewhere. The ancient spirit of pre-historic Germany coming back, at the end of history.

The same in Heidelberg. Heidelberg full, full, full of people. Students the same, youths with rucksacks the same, boys and maidens in gangs come down from the hills. The same, and not the same. These queer gangs of *Young Socialists*, youths and girls, with their non-materialistic professions, their half-mystic assertions, they strike one as strange. Something primitive, like loose, roving gangs of broken, scattered tribes, so they affect one. And the swarms of people somehow produce an impression of silence, of secrecy, of stealth. It is as if everything and everybody recoiled away from the old unison, as barbarians lurking in a wood recoil out of sight. The old habits remain. But the bulk of the people have no money. And the whole stream of feeling is reversed.

So you stand in the woods above the town and see the Neckar flowing green and swift and slippery out of the gulf of Germany, to the Rhine. And the sun sets slow and scarlet into the haze of the Rhine valley. And the old, pinkish stone of the ruined castle across looks sultry, the marshalry is in shadow below, the peaked roofs of old, tight Heidelberg compressed in its river gateway glimmer and glimmer out. There is a blue haze.

And it all looks as if the years were wheeling swiftly backwards, no more onwards. Like a spring that is broken, and whirls

119

swiftly back, so time seems to be whirling with mysterious swiftness to a sort of death. Whirling to the ghost of the old Middle Ages of Germany, then to the Roman days, then to the days of the silent forest and the dangerous, lurking barbarians.

Something about the Germanic races is unalterable. White-skinned, elemental, and dangerous. Our civilization has come from the fusion of the dark-eyes with the blue. The meeting and mixing and mingling of the two races has been the joy of our ages. And the Celt has been there, alien, but necessary as some chemical reagent to the fusion. So the civilization of Europe rose up. So these cathedrals and these thoughts.

But now the Celt is the disintegrating agent. And the Latin and southern races are falling out of association with the northern races, the northern Germanic impulse is recoiling towards Tartary, the destructive vortex of Tartary.

It is a fate; nobody now can alter it. It is a fate. The very blood changes. Within the last three years, the very constituency of the blood has changed, in European veins. But particularly in Germanic veins.

At the same time, we have brought it about ourselves – by a Ruhr occupation, by an English nullity, and by a German false will. We have done it ourselves. But apparently it was not to be helped.

*Quos vult perdere Deus, dementat prius.*

# Au Revoir, U.S.A.

*Laughing Horse*, December 1923; *Phoenix*, 1936

> Say au revoir
> But not good-bye
> This parting brings
> A bitter sigh ...

It really does, when you find yourself in an unkempt Pullman trailing through endless deserts, south of El Paso, fed on doubtful scraps at enormous charge and at the will of a rather shoddy smallpox-marked Mexican Pullman-boy who knows there's been a revolution and that his end is up. Then you remember the neat and nice nigger who looked after you as far as El Paso, before you crossed the Rio Grande into desert and chaos, and you sigh, if you have time before a curse chokes you.

Yet, U.S.A., you do put a strain on the nerves. Mexico puts a strain on the temper. Choose which you prefer. Mine's the latter. I'd rather be in a temper than be pulled taut. Which is what the U.S.A. did to me. Tight as a fiddle string, tense over the bridge of the solar plexus. Anyhow the solar plexus goes a bit loose and has a bit of play down here.

I still don't know why the U.S.A. pulls one so tight and makes one feel like a chicken that is being drawn. The people on the whole are quite as amenable as people anywhere else. They don't pick your pocket, or even your personality. They're not unfriendly. It's not the people. Something in the air tightens one's nerves like fiddle strings, screws them up, squeak-squeak! ... till one's nerves will give out nothing but a shrill fine shriek of overwroughtness. Why, in the name of heaven? Nobody knows. It's just the spirit of the place.

You cross the Rio Grande and change from tension into exasperation. You feel like hitting the impudent Pullman waiter with a beer-bottle. In the U.S.A. you don't even think of such a thing.

Of course, one might get used to a state of tension. And then one would pine for the United States. Meanwhile one merely snarls back at the dragons of San Juan Teotihuacan.

It's a queer continent – as much as I've seen of it. It's a fanged continent. It's got a rattlesnake coiled in its heart, has this democracy of the New World. It's a dangerous animal, once it lifts its head again. Meanwhile, the dove still nests in the coils of the rattlesnake, the stone coiled rattlesnake of Aztec eternity. The dove lays her eggs on his flat head.

The old people had a marvellous feeling for snakes and fangs, down here in Mexico. And after all, Mexico is only the sort of solar plexus of North America. The great paleface overlay hasn't gone into the soil half an inch. The Spanish churches and palaces stagger, the most rickety things imaginable, always just on the point of falling down. And the peon still grins his Indian grin behind the Cross. And there's quite a lively light in his eyes, much more so than in the eyes of the northern Indian. He knows his gods.

These old civilizations down here, they never got any higher than Quetzalcoatl. And he's just a sort of feathered snake. Who needed the smoke of a little heart's-blood now and then, even he.

'Only the ugly is aesthetic now,' said the young Mexican artist. Personally, he seems as gentle and self-effacing as the nicest of lambs. Yet his caricatures are hideous, hideous without mirth or whimsicality. Blood-hideous. Grim, earnest hideousness.

Like the Aztec things, the Aztec carvings. They all twist and bite. That's all they do. Twist and writhe and bite, or crouch in lumps. And coiled rattlesnakes, many, like dark heaps of excrement. And out at San Juan Teotihuacan where are the great pyramids of a vanished, pre-Aztec people, as we are told – and the so-called Temple of Quetzalcoatl – there, behold you, huge gnashing heads jut out jagged from the wall-face of the low pyramid, and a huge snake stretches along the base, and one grasps at a carved fish, that swims in old stone and for once seems harmless. Actually a harmless fish!

But look out! The great stone heads snarl at you from the wall, trying to bite you: and one great dark, green blob of an obsidian eye, you never saw anything so blindly malevolent: and then white fangs. Great white fangs, smooth today, the white fangs, with tiny cracks in them. Enamelled. These bygone pyramid-building Americans, who were a dead-and-gone mystery even to the Aztecs, when the Spaniards arrived, they applied their highest art to the enamelling of the great fangs of these venomous stone heads, and there is the enamel today, white and smooth. You can stroke the great fang with your finger and see. And the blob of an obsidian eye looks down at you.

It's a queer continent. The anthropologists may make what prettiness they like out of myths. But come here, and you'll see that the gods bit. There is none of the phallic preoccupation of the old Mediterranean. Here they hadn't got even as far as hot-blooded sex. Fangs, and cold serpent folds, and bird-snakes with fierce cold blood and claws.

I admit that I feel bewildered. There is always something a bit amiably comic about Chinese dragons and contortions. There's nothing amiably comic in these ancient monsters. They're dead in earnest about biting and writhing, snake-blooded birds.

And the Spanish white superimposition, with rococo church-towers among pepper-trees and column cactuses, seems so rickety and temporary, the pyramids seem so indigenous, rising like hills out of the earth itself. The one goes down with a clatter, the other remains.

And this is what seems to me the difference between Mexico and the United States. And this is why, it seems to me, Mexico exasperates, whereas the U.S.A. puts an unbearable tension on one. Because here in Mexico the fangs are still obvious. Everybody knows the gods are going to bite within the next five minutes. While in the United States, the gods have had their teeth pulled, and their claws cut, and their tails docked, till they seem real mild lambs. Yet all the time, inside, it's the same old dragon's blood. The same old American dragon's blood.

And that discrepancy of course is a strain on the human psyche.

# New Mexico

Written 1928, published in *Survey Graphic*,
1 May 1931; *Phoenix*, 1936

Superficially, the world has become small and known. Poor little globe of earth, the tourists trot round you as easily as they trot round the Bois or round Central Park. There is no mystery left, we've been there, we've seen it, we know all about it. We've done the globe, and the globe is done.

This is quite true, superficially. On the superficies, horizontally, we've been everywhere and done everything, we know all about it. Yet the more we know, superficially, the less we penetrate, vertically. It's all very well skimming across the surface of the ocean, and saying you know all about the sea. There still remain the terrifying under-deeps, of which we have utterly no experience.

The same is true of land travel. We skim along, we get there, we see it all, we've done it all. And as a rule, we never once go through the curious film which railroads, ships, motor-cars, and hotels stretch over the surface of the whole earth. Peking is just the same as New York, with a few different things to look at; rather more Chinese about, etc. Poor creatures that we are, we crave for experience, yet we are like flies that crawl on the pure and transparent mucous-paper in which the world like a bon-bon is wrapped so carefully that we can never get at it, though we see it there all the time as we move about it, apparently in contact, yet actually as far removed as if it were the moon.

As a matter of fact, our great-grandfathers, who never went anywhere, in actuality had more experience of the world than we have, who have seen everything. When they listened to a lecture with lantern-slides, they really held their breath before the unknown, as they sat in the village school-room. We, bowling along in a rickshaw in Ceylon, say to ourselves: 'It's very much what you'd expect.' We really know it all.

We are mistaken. The know-it-all state of mind is just the result of being outside the mucous-paper wrapping of civilization. Underneath is everything we don't know and are afraid of knowing.

I realized this with shattering force when I went to New Mexico.

New Mexico, one of the United States, part of the U.S.A. New Mexico, the picturesque reservation and playground of the eastern states, very romantic, old Spanish, Red Indian, desert mesas, pueblos, cowboys, penitentes, all that film-stuff. Very nice, the great South-West, put on a sombrero and knot a red kerchief round your neck, to go out in the great free spaces!

That is New Mexico wrapped in the absolutely hygienic and shiny mucous-paper of our trite civilization. That is the New Mexico known to most of the Americans who know it at all. But break through the shiny sterilized wrapping, and actually *touch* the country, and you will never be the same again.

I think New Mexico was the greatest experience from the outside world that I have ever had. It certainly changed me for ever. Curious as it may sound, it was New Mexico that liberated me from the present era of civilization, the great era of material and mechanical development. Months spent in holy Kandy, in Ceylon, the holy of holies of southern Buddhism, had not touched the great psyche of materialism and idealism which dominated me. And years, even in the exquisite beauty of Sicily, right among the old Greek paganism that still lives there, had not shattered the essential Christianity on which my character was established. Australia was a sort of dream or trance, like being under a spell, the self remaining unchanged, so long as the trance did not last too long. Tahiti, in a mere glimpse, repelled me: and so did California, after a stay of a few weeks. There seemed a strange brut-

126

ality in the spirit of the western coast, and I felt: O, let me get away!

But the moment I saw the brilliant, proud morning shine high up over the deserts of Santa Fé, something stood still in my soul, and I started to attend. There was a certain magnificence in the high-up day, a certain eagle-like royalty, so different from the equally pure, equally pristine and lovely morning of Australia, which is so soft, so utterly pure in its softness, and betrayed by green parrot flying. But in the lovely morning of Australia one went into a dream. In the magnificent fierce morning of New Mexico one sprang awake, a new part of the soul woke up suddenly, and the old world gave way to a new.

There are all kinds of beauty in the world, thank God, though ugliness is homogeneous. How lovely is Sicily, with Calabria across the sea like an opal, and Etna with her snow in a world above and beyond! How lovely is Tuscany, with little red tulips wild among the corn: or bluebells at dusk in England, or mimosa in clouds of pure yellow among the grey-green dun foliage of Australia, under a soft, blue, unbreathed sky! But for a *greatness* of beauty I have never experienced anything like New Mexico. All those mornings when I went with a hoe along the ditch to the Cañon, at the ranch, and stood, in the fierce, proud silence of the Rockies, on their foothills, to look far over the desert to the blue mountains away in Arizona, blue as chalcedony, with the sagebrush desert sweeping grey-blue in between, dotted with tiny cube-crystals of houses, the vast amphitheatre of lofty, indomitable desert, sweeping round to the ponderous Sangre de Cristo mountains on the east, and coming up flush at the pine-dotted foot-hills of the Rockies! What splendour! Only the tawny eagle could really sail out into the splendour of it all. Leo Stein once wrote to me: It is the most aesthetically-satisfying landscape I know. To me it was much more than that. It had a splendid silent terror, and a vast far-and-wide magnificence which made it way beyond mere aesthetic appreciation. Never is the light more pure and overweening than there, arching with a royalty almost cruel over the hollow, uptilted world. For it is curious that the land which has produced modern political democracy at its highest pitch

127

should give one the greatest sense of overweening, terrible proudness and mercilessness: but so beautiful, God! so beautiful! Those that have spent morning after morning alone there pitched among the pines above the great proud world of desert will know, almost unbearably, how beautiful it is, how clear and unquestioned is the might of the day. Just day itself is tremendous there. It is so easy to understand that the Aztecs gave hearts of men to the sun. For the sun is not merely hot or scorching, not at all. It is of a brilliant and unchallengeable purity and haughty serenity which would make one sacrifice the heart to it. Ah, yes, in New Mexico the heart is sacrificed to the sun and the human being is left stark, heartless, but undauntingly religious.

And that was the second revelation out there. I had looked over all the world for something that would strike *me* as religious. The simple piety of some English people, the semi-pagan mystery of some Catholics in southern Italy, the intensity of some Bavarian peasants, the semi-ecstasy of Buddhists or Brahmins : all this had seemed religious all right, as far as the parties concerned were involved, but it didn't involve me. I looked on at their religiousness from the outside. For it is still harder to feel religion at will than to love at will.

I had seen what I felt was a hint of wild religion in the so-called devil dances of a group of naked villagers from the far-remote jungle in Ceylon, dancing at midnight under the torches, glittering wet with sweat on their dark bodies as if they had been gilded, at the celebration of the Pera-hera, in Kandy, given to the Prince of Wales. And the utter dark absorption of these naked men, as they danced with their knees wide apart, suddenly affected me with a *sense* of religion, I *felt* religion for a moment. For religion is an experience, an uncontrollable sensual experience, even more so than love: I use sensual to mean an experience deep down in the senses, inexplicable and inscrutable.

But this experience was fleeting, gone in the curious turmoil of the Pera-hera, and I had no permanent feeling of religion till I came to New Mexico and penetrated into the old human race experience there. It is curious that it should be in America, of all places, that a European should really experience religion, after

touching the old Mediterranean and the East. It is curious that
one should get a sense of living religion from the Red Indians,
having failed to get it from Hindus or Sicilian Catholics or Cin-
galese.

Let me make a reservation. I don't stand up to praise the Red
Indian as he reveals himself in contact with white civilization.
From that angle, I am forced to admit he *may* be thoroughly
objectionable. Even my small experience knows it. But also I
know he *may* be thoroughly nice, even in his dealings with
white men. It's a question of individuals, a good deal, on both
sides.

But in this article, I don't want to deal with the everyday or
superficial aspect of New Mexico, outside the mucous-paper
wrapping, I *want* to go beneath the surface. But therefore the
American Indian in his behaviour as an American citizen doesn't
really concern me. What concerns me is what he is – or what he
seems to me to be, in his ancient, ancient race-self and religious-
self.

For the Red Indian seems to me much older than Greeks, or
Hindus or any Europeans or even Egyptians. The Red Indian,
as a civilized and truly religious man, civilized beyond taboo and
totem, as he is in the south, is religious in perhaps the oldest sense,
and deepest, of the word. That is to say, he is a remnant of the
most deeply religious race still living. So it seems to me.

But again let me protect myself. The Indian who sells you bas-
kets on Albuquerque station or who slinks around Taos plaza
may be an utter waster and an indescribably low dog. Personally
he may be even less religious than a New York sneak-thief. He
may have broken with his tribe, or his tribe itself may have collapsed finally from its old religious integrity, and ceased, really, to
exist. Then he is only fit for rapid absorption into white civilization, which must make the best of him.

But while a tribe retains its religion and keeps up its religious
practices, and while any member of the tribe shares in those practices, then there is a tribal integrity and a living tradition going
back far beyond the birth of Christ, beyond the pyramids, beyond Moses. A vast old religion which once swayed the earth

lingers in unbroken practice there in New Mexico, older, perhaps, than anything in the world save Australian aboriginal taboo and totem, and that is not yet religion.

You can feel it, the atmosphere of it, around the pueblos. Not, of course, when the place is crowded with sight-seers and motor-cars. But go to Taos pueblo on some brilliant snowy morning and see the white figure on the roof: or come riding through at dusk on some windy evening, when the black skirts of the silent women blow around the white wide boots, and you will feel the old, old root of human consciousness still reaching down to depths we know nothing of: and of which, only too often, we are jealous. It seems it will not be long before the pueblos are uprooted.

But never shall I forget watching the dancers, the men with the fox-skin swaying down from their buttocks, file out at San Geronimo, and the women with seed rattles following. The long, streaming, glistening black hair of the men. Even in ancient Crete long hair was sacred in a man, as it is still in the Indians. Never shall I forget the utter absorption of the dance, so quiet, so steadily, timelessly rhythmic, and silent, with the ceaseless down-tread, always to the earth's centre, the very reverse of the upflow of Dionysiac or Christian ecstasy. Never shall I forget the deep singing of the men at the drum, swelling and sinking, the deepest sound I have heard in all my life, deeper than thunder, deeper than the sound of the Pacific Ocean, deeper than the roar of a deep waterfall: the wonderful deep sound of men calling to the unspeakable depths.

Never shall I forget coming into the little pueblo of San Filipi one sunny morning in spring, unexpectedly, when bloom was on the trees in the perfect little pueblo more old, more utterly peaceful and idyllic than anything in Theocritus, and seeing a little casual dance. Not impressive as a spectacle, only, to me, profoundly moving because of the truly terrifying religious absorption of it.

Never shall I forget the Christmas dances at Taos, twilight, snow, the darkness coming over the great wintry mountains and the lonely pueblo, then suddenly, again, like dark calling to dark, the deep Indian cluster-singing around the drum, wild and awful, suddenly rousing on the last dusk as the procession starts. And then the bonfires leaping suddenly in pure spurts of high flame, columns of sudden flame forming an alley for the procession.

Never shall I forget the khiva of birch-trees, away in the Apaché country, in Arizona this time, the tepees and flickering fires, the neighing of horses unseen under the huge dark night, and the Apachés all abroad, in their silent moccasined feet: and in the khiva, beyond a little fire, the old man reciting, reciting in the unknown Apaché speech, in the strange wild Indian voice that re-echoes away back to before the Flood, reciting apparently the traditions and legends of the tribe, going on and on, while the young men, the *braves* of today, wandered in, listened, and wandered away again, overcome with the power and majesty of that utterly old tribal voice, yet uneasy with their half-adherence to the modern civilization, the two things in contact. And one of these *braves* shoved his face under my hat, in the night, and stared with his glittering eyes close to mine. He'd have killed me then and there, had he dared. He didn't dare: and I knew it: and he knew it.

Never shall I forget the Indian races, when the young men, even the boys, run naked, smeared with white earth and stuck with bits of eagle fluff for the swiftness of the heavens, and the old men brush them with eagle feathers, to give them power. And they run in the strange hurling fashion of the primitive world, hurled forward, not making speed deliberately. And the race is not for victory. It is not a contest. There is no competition. It is a great cumulative effort. The tribe this day is adding up its male energy and exerting it to the utmost – for what? To get power, to get strength: to come, by sheer cumulative, hurling effort of the bodies of men, into contact with the great cosmic source of vitality which gives strength, power, energy to the men who can grasp it, energy for the zeal of attainment.

It was a vast old religion, greater than anything we know: more starkly and nakedly religious. There is no God, no conception of a god. All is god. But it is not the pantheism we are accustomed to, which expresses itself as 'God is everywhere, God is in everything.' In the oldest religion, everything was alive, not supernaturally but naturally alive. There were only deeper and deeper streams of life, vibrations of life more and more vast. So rocks were alive, but a mountain had a deeper, vaster life than a rock, and it was much harder for a man to bring his spirit, or his energy, into contact with the life of the mountain, and so draw strength from the mountain, as from a great standing well of life, than it was to come into contact with the rock. And he had to put forth a great religious effort. For the whole life-effort of man was to get his life into direct contact with the elemental life of the cosmos, mountain-life, cloud-life, thunder-life, air-life, earth-life, sun-life. To come into immediate *felt* contact, and so derive energy, power, and a dark sort of joy. This effort into sheer naked contact, *without an intermediary or mediator*, is the root meaning of religion, and at the sacred races the runners hurled themselves in a terrible cumulative effort, through the air, to come at last into naked contact with the very life of the air, which is the life of the clouds, and so of the rain.

It was a vast and pure religion, without idols or images, even mental ones. It is the oldest religion, a cosmic religion the same for all peoples, not broken up into specific gods or saviours or systems. It is the religion which precedes the god-concept, and is therefore greater and deeper than any god-religion.

And it lingers still, for a little while, in New Mexico: but long enough to have been a revelation to me. And the Indian, however objectionable he may be on occasion, has still some of the strange beauty and pathos of the religion that brought him forth and is now shedding him away into oblivion. When Trinidad, the Indian boy, and I planted corn at the ranch, my soul paused to see his brown hands softly moving the earth over the maize in pure ritual. He was back in his old religious self, and the ages stood still. Ten minutes later he was making a fool of himself with the horses. Horses were never part of the Indian's religious life, never would be. He hasn't a tithe of the feeling for them that he has for a bear, for example. So horses don't like Indians.

But there it is: the newest democracy ousting the oldest religion! And once the oldest religion is ousted, one feels the democracy and all its paraphernalia will collapse, and the oldest religion, which comes down to us from man's pre-war days, will start again. The sky-scraper will scatter on the winds like thistle-down, and the genuine America, the America of New Mexico, will start on its course again. This is an interregnum.

# Europe Versus America

*Laughing Horse,* April 1926; *Phoenix,* 1936

A young American said to me : 'I am not very keen on Europe, but should like to see it, and have done with it.' He is an ass. How can one 'see' Europe and have done with it? One might as well say: I want to see the moon next week and have done with it. If one doesn't want to see the moon, he doesn't look. And if he doesn't want to see Europe, he doesn't look either. But neither of 'em will go away because he's not looking.

There's no 'having done with it'. Europe is here, and will be here, long after he has added a bit of dust to America. To me, I simply don't see the point of that American trick of saying one is 'through with a thing', when the thing is a good deal better than oneself.

I can hear that young man saying: 'Oh, I'm through with the moon, she's played out. She's a dead old planet anyhow, and was never more than a side issue.' So was Eve only a side issue. But when a man is through with her, he's through with most of his life.

It's the same with Europe. One may be sick of certain aspects of European civilization. But they're in ourselves, rather than in Europe. As a matter of fact, coming back to Europe, I realize how much more *tense* the European civilization is, in the Americans, than in the Europeans. The Europeans still have a vague idea that the universe is greater than they are, and isn't going to change

134

very radically, not for all the telling of all men put together. But the Americans are tense, somewhere inside themselves, as if they felt that once they slackened, the world would really collapse. It wouldn't. If the American tension snapped tomorrow, only that bit of the world which is tense and American would come to an end. Nothing more.

How could I say: I am through with America? America is a great continent; it won't suddenly cease to be. Some part of me will always be conscious of America. But probably some part greater still in me will always be conscious of Europe, since I am a European.

As for Europe's being old, I find it much younger than America. Even these countries of the Mediterranean, which have known quite a bit of history, seem to me much, much younger even than Taos, not to mention Long Island, or Coney Island.

In the people here there is still, at the bottom, the old, young insouciance. It isn't that the young *don't care*: it is merely that, at the bottom of them there *isn't* care. Instead there is a sort of bubbling-in of life. It isn't till we grow old that we grip the very sources of our life with care, and strangle them.

And that seems to me the rough distinction between an American and a European. They are both of the same civilization, and all that. But the American grips himself, at the very sources of his consciousness, in a grip of care: and then, to so much of the rest of life, is indifferent. Whereas, the European hasn't got so much care in him, so he cares much more for life and living.

That phrase again of wanting to see Europe and have done with it shows that strangle-hold so many Americans have got on themselves. Why don't they say: I'd like to see Europe, and then, if it means something to me, good! and if it doesn't mean much to me, so much the worse for both of us. *Vogue la galère!*

I've been a fool myself, saying: Europe is finished for me. It wasn't Europe at all, it was myself, keeping a strangle-hold on myself. And that strangle-hold I carried over to America; as many a man – and woman, worse still – has done before me.

Now, back in Europe, I feel a real relief. The past is too big, and too intimate, for one generation of men to get a strangle-hold on it. Europe is squeezing the life out of herself, with her mental education and fixed ideas. But she hasn't got her hands round her own throat not half so far as America has hers; here the grip is already falling slack; and if the system collapses, it'll only be another system collapsed, of which there have been plenty. But in America, where men grip themselves so much more intensely and suicidally – the women worse – the system has its hold on the very sources of consciousness, so God knows what would happen, if the system broke.

No, it's a relief to be by the Mediterranean, and gradually let the tight coils inside oneself come slack. There is much more life in a deep insouciance, which really is the clue to faith, than in this frenzied, keyed-up care, which is characteristic of our civilization, but which is at its worst, or at least its intensest, in America.

# On Coming Home

Written 1923, published in *Phoenix II*, 1968

> Breathes there a man with soul so dead
> Who never to himself hath said
> This is my own, my native land –

With a vengeance!

It is four years since I saw, under a little winter snow, the death-grey coast of Kent go out. After four years, down, down on the horizon, with the last sunset still in the west, right down under the eyelid of the shut cold sky, the faintest spark, like a message. It is the Land's End light. And I, who am a bit short-sighted, saw it almost first. One sees by divination. The infinitesimal sparking of the Land's End light, so absolutely remote, as one approaches from over the sea, from the Gulf of Mexico, after sunset.

I won't pretend my heart was dead. It exploded again in my chest. 'This is my own, my native land!' My God, what lies behind that spark of light!

One goes out on deck again, two hours later, to find a vast light towering out of the dark, as if someone were swinging an immense white beam of communication in the black boughs of the tree of night. And the ship creeps invisible under the pure white branches of the light of men, down on the little lustre of the sea. We are entering Plymouth Sound.

'Breathes there a man with soul so dead –?'

There are the small lights on the soft blackness that must be land. Far off, ahead, a tiny row of lights that must be the Hoe. And the ship slowly pulses forward, at half speed, venturing in.

England! So still! So remote-seeming! Across what mysterious belt of isolation does England lie! 'It doesn't seem like a big civilized country,' says the Cuban behind me. 'It seems as if there were no people in it.'

'Yes!' cries the German woman. 'So still! So still! As if one could never come to it.'

And that is how it seems, as you slowly steam up the Sound in the night, and watch the little lights that must be land, on the unspeaking darkness. The darkness doesn't speak, as the darkness of the coast of America, or of Spain for example, speaks in the night when you are passing.

Slowly the ship lapses to silence in mid-water. A tender lit up with red and white and yellow lights – the German woman calls it the Christmas-tree boat – hovers round the stern and comes up on the leeward side. It looks curiously empty, in spite of its lights. And with strange quick quietness, the English sailors make fast. Queer to hear English voices below on the tender, so curiously quiet and withheld, against the noise of Spanish and German we are used to on board.

It is the same with English voices of sailors making fast the ropes, as with the sight of land. They do not stir the darkness. They do not come through. Quickly, quietly, the ladder is put up. Quickly, quietly, the police and passport people come on board. All is strangely still, and the ship, which at tea-time was still lively with mixed nationalities, seems deserted. England is on board – everything has fallen silent.

Quietly, quickly, softly, everything is done, and we are landed. There is a strange absence of something, an absentness is felt in everything and in everybody. I think, in the ordinary come-and-go of life, only the Englishman is really civilized. So, the soft, quiet, vague landing, the vague looking at the luggage, the vague finding oneself in the hotel in Plymouth. Everything soft, vague, with the quiet of accomplished civilization. Accomplished, that

138

is, in these matters of landing from a ship and finding oneself in an hotel.

And it is the first night ashore, in the curious stillness. I cannot say wherein lies the almost deathly sense of stillness one gets, returning to England from the west. Landing in San Francisco gave me the feeling of intolerable crackling noise. But London gives me a dead muffled sense of stillness, as if nothing had any resonance. Everything muffled, or muted, and no sharp contact, no sharp reaction anywhere. As if all the traffic went on deep sand, heavily, straining the heart, and hushed.

I must confess, this curious mutedness of my native land frightens me more than the noise of New York or of Mexico City. Since the sparking of the Land's End light, and the great strong beaming of the lighthouse overhead, tall overhead like a great tree, at the entrance to the Sound, I have not had one single sharp impression in England. Everything seems sand-bagged, like when a ship hangs bags of sand over her side to deaden the bump with the wharf. So it is here. Every impact, every contact is sand-bagged, deadened. Everything that everybody says is modified beforehand, to prevent any kind of bump. Everything that everybody feels is keyed down, and muted, so as not to impinge on anybody else's feelings.

And this, in the end, becomes a madness. One sits in the breakfast car in the train, coming to London. There is a strange tension. What is the curious unease that holds the car spell-bound? In America the Pullmans, being much heavier, don't shake like our cars. And there seems more room, inside and out, morally and physically. It is possible the American manners are not so good, though I doubt if I agree, even there. The silent bad manners of the Englishman when he happens to decide that he is not among his own 'sort', take a lot of beating. But of course, he never says or does anything, so he is perfectly safe and proper in his circumstance.

But there one sits in a breakfast car on the Great Western. The train shakes terribly. The waiters are quick and soft and attentive, but the food isn't very good, and one feels as if one were some sort of ghost being waited on by men who have long ago gone to sleep, and are serving one in their sleep. The place feels tight: one would like to smash something. Outside, a tight little landscape goes by, just unbelievable, with sunshine like thin water, a horizon half a mile away, and everything crowded forward into one's face till one gasps for space and breath, and tries to jerk one's head back, as one does when someone pushes his face right under one's hat-brim. Too horribly close!

Inside, we eat kippers and bacon. The place is full. The other people, mostly men, all keep themselves modified and muted, as if they didn't want their aura to stray beyond the four legs of their chair. Inside this charmed circle of their self-constraint they seem to sit and smile with pleasant English faces. And, of course, they are all trying to be a bit 'grander' than they really are: to give the impression that they have more servants in the kitchen than they really have, and so on. That is part of the English naïveté! If they have two servants, they want to give the impression of four: not less than four.

Essentially, however, and apart from being 'grand', each one of them sits complacent inside a crystal bubble, smiling and eating and sprinkling sugar on porridge, and then half-furtively glancing through the transparency of their bubble, to see if there is anything outside. They will never allow anything outside: except, of course, other bubbles of varying 'grandness'.

In the small things of life, the Englishman is the only perfectly civilized being. But God save me from such civilization. God in heaven deliver me. The trick lies in tensely withholding oneself, tensely withholding one's aura, till it forms a perfect and transparent little globe around one. At the centre of this little globe sits the Englishman, his own little god unto himself, terribly complacent, and at the same time, terribly self-deprecating. He seems to say: My dear man, I know I am no more than what I am. I wouldn't trespass on what you are, not for worlds. Oh, not for worlds! Because when all's said and done, what you are means nothing to me. I am god inside my own crystal world, the strictly limited domain of myself, which after all no one can deny is my own. I am only god within the bubble of my own self-contained being, dear sir; but there, god I am, so how could I pos-

140

sibly desire to trespass? I only urge that all other people shall be as self-contained and as little inclined to trespass. And they may be gods inside their own bubbles if they like.

Hence the feeling of intolerable shut-in-edness. One enters from the open sea, to the Channel: first box. Into Plymouth Sound: second box. Into the customs place: third box. Into the hotel: fourth. Into the dining car of the train: fifth. And so on and so on, like those Chinese boxes that fit one inside the other, and at the very middle is a tiny porcelain figure half an inch long. That is how one feels. Like a tiny porcelain figure shut in inside box after box of repeated and intensified shut-in-edness. It is enough to send one mad.

That is coming home, home to one's fellow countrymen! In one sense – the small ways of life – they are the nicest and most civilized people in the world. But there they are: each one of them a perfect little accomplished figure, enclosed first and foremost within the box, or bubble, of his own self-contained ego, and afterwards in all the other boxes he has made for himself, for his own safety.

At the centre of himself he is complacent, and even 'superior'. It strikes one very hard, coming home, that every Englishman sits there feeling subtly 'superior'. He wouldn't impose anything on anybody, dear me no. That is part of his own superiority. He is too superior to make any imposition of himself in any way. But like a pleased image, there he sits at the centre of his own bubble, and feels superior. Superior to what? Oh, nothing in particular, don't you know. Just superior. And well – if you press him – superior to everything. Just damn superior to everything. There inside the bubble of his own self-constraint, his own illusion, the strange germ of his unnatural conceit.

> This is my own, my native land.

He seems to have accomplished the trick of being at his ease, the gentleman in the breakfast car, sprinkling sugar on his porridge. He knows he has a pretty way of sprinkling sugar on porridge: he knows he can put the spoon back prettily into the sugar-bowl: he knows his voice is cultured and his smile charming, compared to the rest of the world. It is quite obvious he means no one ill. Surely it is obvious he would like to give every man the best that man could have. If it were his, to give, which it isn't. And finally he knows he is able to contain himself. He is an Englishman and he is himself, he is able to contain and to constrain himself, and to live within the unbroken bubble of his own self-constraint, without letting his aura stray and get at cross-purposes with other people's auras. The dear, dangerless patrician!

Yet something does stray out of him. Look into his nice, bright, apparently-smiling English eyes. They are not smiling. And look again at his nice fresh English face, that seems so pleased with life. It also is not smiling, any more than Mr Lloyd George is really smiling. The eyes are not really at ease, and the nice, fresh face is not at ease either. At the centre of the eyes, where the smile twinkles, there is fear. Even at the middle of this amiable and all-tolerant English complacency, there is fear. And the smile-wrinkles on the fresh, pleased face, they give odd quivers, and look like spite wrinkles. There strays out of him, in spite of all his self-constraining, the faint effluence of fear, and the sense of impotence, and a quiver of spite, of subdued malice. Underneath the soft civilizedness of him, fear, impotence, and malice.

> Whose heart within him ne'er hath burned
> As home his wandering steps he turned
> From travelling in a foreign land.

That's how one finds the Englishman at home. And then one understands the bitterness of Englishmen abroad in the world, especially Englishmen in responsible positions.

There is no denying this: that since the war, England's prestige has declined terribly, all over the world. Ah, says the Englishman, that's because America has the dollars. And there you hear the voice of England's own downfall.

England's prestige wasn't based on money. It was based on the imagination of men. England was supposed to be proud, and

at the same time, free. Proud in her freedom, and free, to a certain extent generous, truly generous, in her pride.

This was the England that led the world. Myself, I think this
was a true conception of England at her best. This was how the
other nations accepted her: at her best. And the individual
Englishman got his certain honour, in the world, on the strength
of it.

Now? Now he still receives the remnants of honour, but mock-
ingly, as poor Russian counts receive a little mocking distinction,
now that they have to sell newspapers. The real English pride
has gone, and 'superiority' takes its place: a really imbecile
superiority, which the world laughs at.

As far as the wide world is concerned, England is anything
but superior. She is just humiliated. From day to day she makes
a more humiliated spectacle of herself in the eyes of the world.
Weak, vacillating, without purpose or policy, without even the
last vestige of pride, she continues to apologize and deprecate on
the platform of the world.

And of course individual Englishmen abroad feel it. You
rarely meet an Englishman far from home, but he is burning with
impatience, disgust, and even contempt, of home. Home seems a
shoddy place. And when you get here, it's even shoddier than it
seems from afar.

If, abroad, you meet an Englishman in office, he is speechless,
almost cynical with rage. 'What can I do!' he says. 'What can I
do, against the orders from home. I get orders that I must give no
loop-hole for offence against America. All I have to do is
to guard against giving offence, above all to America. I must be
on my knees all the time, in front of America, begging her not to
take offence, when she hasn't the faintest intention even of taking
offence.'

This is from a man who has lived out in the world, and who
knows that the moment you go down on your knees to a man, he
spits on you: and quite right too. Men have no business on their
knees.

'I have an Englishman wants to go into the United States:
Washington has given him a visa, and said: Yes, you can enter

whenever you like. Comes a cable from London: Prevent this man from crossing into the United States, Washington might not like it. What can one do?'

The same story everywhere. A man is building a railway with nigger labour. Some insolent Jamaica nigger – British subject, larger than life – brings a charge against his boss. Solemn trial by the British, influence from the government, the Englishman is reprimanded, and the nigger smiles and spits in his face.

Long live the bottom dog! May he devour us all.

Same story from India, from Egypt, from China. At home, a lot of queer, insane, half-female-seeming men, not quite men at all, and certainly not women! The women would be far braver. Then abroad, a few Englishmen still struggling.

England seems to me the one really soft spot, the rotten spot in the empire. If ever men had to think in world terms, they have to think in world terms today. And here you get an island no bigger than a back garden, chock-full of people who never realize there is anything outside their back garden, pretending to direct the destinies of the world. It is pathetic and ridiculous. And the 'superiority' is bathetic to lunacy.

These poor 'superior' gentry, all that is left to them is to blame the Americans. It amazes me, the rancour with which English people speak of Americans. Just because the republican eagle of the west doesn't choose to be a pelican for other people's convenience. Why should it?

After all, rancour is a bad sign in a superior person. It is a sign of impotence. The superior Englishman feels impotent against the American dollar, so he is wildly rancorous, in private, when America can't hear him.

Now I am an Englishman. And I know, that if my countrymen still have a soul to sell, they'll sell it for American dollars, and drive a hard bargain.

Which is what I call being truly superior to the dollar.

This is my own, my native land.

It was such a brave country, for so many years: the old brave, reckless, manly England. Even a man with dyed whiskers, like

144

Palmerston. Too brave and reckless to be treacherous. My England.

Look at us now. Not a man left inside all the millions of pairs of trousers. Not a man left. A host of would-be-amiable cowards shut up each in his own bubble of conceit, and the whole lot within box after box of safeguards.

One could shout with laughter at the figures inside these endless safety boxes. Except that one is still English, and therefore flabbergasted. My own, my native land just leaves me flabbergasted.

# Return to Bestwood

Written 1926, published in *Phoenix II*, 1968

I came home to the Midlands for a few days, at the end of September. Not that there is any home, for my parents are dead. But there are my sisters, and the district one calls home; that mining district between Nottingham and Derby.

It always depresses me to come to my native district. Now I am turned forty, and have been more or less a wanderer for nearly twenty years, I feel more alien, perhaps, in my home place than anywhere else in the world. I can feel at ease in Canal Street, New Orleans, or in the Avenue Madero, in Mexico City, or in George Street, Sydney, in Trincomallee Street, Kandy, or in Rome or Paris or Munich or even London. But in Nottingham Road, Bestwood, I feel at once a devouring nostalgia and an infinite repulsion. Partly I want to get back to the place as it was when I was a boy, and I waited so long to be served in the Co-op. I remember our Co-op number, 1553A.L., better than the date of my birth – and when I came out hugging a string net of groceries. There was a little hedge across the road from the Co-op then, and I used to pick the green buds which we called bread-and-cheese. And there were no houses in Gabes Lane. And at the corner of Queen Street, Butcher Bob was huge and fat and taciturn.

Butcher Bob is long dead, and the place is all built up. I am never quite sure where I am, in Nottingham Rd. Walker Street is not very much changed though because the ash tree was cut down when I was sixteen, when I was ill. The houses are still only on one side the street, the fields on the other. And still one looks across at the amphitheatre of hills which I still find beautiful, though there are new patches of reddish houses and a darkening of smoke. Crich is still on the sky line to the west, and the woods of Annesley to the north, and Coney Grey Farm still lies in front. And there is still a certain glamour about the country-side. Curiously enough, the more motor-cars and tram-cars and omnibuses there are rampaging down the roads, the more the country retreats into its own isolation, and becomes more mysteriously inaccessible.

When I was a boy, the whole population lived very much more *with* the country. Now, they rush and tear along the roads, and have joyrides and outings, but they never seem to touch the reality of the country-side. There are many more people, for one thing: and all these new contrivances, for another.

The country seems, somehow, fogged over with people, and yet not really touched. It seems to lie back, away, unreached and asleep. The roads are hard and metalled and worn with ever-lasting rush. The very field-paths seem wider and more trodden and squalid. Wherever you go, there is the sordid sense of humanity.

And yet the fields and the woods in between the roads and paths sleep as in a heavy, weary dream, disconnected from the modern world.

This visit, this September, depresses me peculiarly. The weather is soft and mild, mildly sunny in that hazed, dazed, un-canny sunless sunniness which makes the Midlands peculiarly fearsome to me. I cannot, cannot accept as sunshine this thin luminous vaporousness which passes as a fine day in the place of my birth. Oh Phoebus Apollo! Surely you have turned your face aside!

But the special depression this time is the great coal strike, still going on. In house after house, the families are now living on bread and margarine and potatoes. The colliers get up before

147

dawn, and are away into the last recesses of the country-side, scouring the country for blackberries, as if there were a famine. But they will sell the blackberries at fourpence a pound, and so they'll be fourpence in pocket.

But when I was a boy, it was utterly *infra dig.* for a miner to be picking blackberries. He would never have demeaned himself to such an unmanly occupation. And as to walking home with a little basket – he would almost rather have committed murder. The children might do it, or the women, or even the half grown youths. But a married, manly collier!

But nowadays, their pride is in their pocket, and the pocket has a hole in it.

It is another world. There are policemen everywhere, great big strange policemen with faces like a leg of mutton. Where they come from, heaven only knows: Ireland or Scotland, presumably, for they are no Englishmen. And they exist, along the country-side, in thousands. The people call them 'blue-bottles', and 'meat-flies'. And you can hear a woman call across the street to another: 'Seen any blow-flies about?' – Then they turn to look at the alien policemen, and laugh shrilly.

And this in my native place! Truly, one no longer knows the palm of his own hand. When I was a boy, we had our own police sergeant, and two young constables. And the women would as leave have thought of calling Sergeant Mellor a 'blue-bottle' as calling Queen Victoria one. The Sergeant was a quiet, patient man, who spent his life trying to keep people out of trouble. He was another sort of shepherd, and the miners and their children were a flock to him. The women had the utmost respect for him.

But the women seem to have changed most in this, that they have no respect for anything. There was a scene in the market-place yesterday, a Mrs Hufton and a Mrs Rowley being taken off to court to be tried for insulting and obstructing the police. The police had been escorting the black-legs from the mines, after a so-called day's work, and the women had made the usual row. They were two women from decent homes. In the past they would have died of shame, at having to go to court. But now, not at all.

They had a little gang of women with them in the market-place, waving red flags and laughing loudly and using occasional bad language. There was one, the decent wife of the postman. I had known her and played with her as a girl. But she was waving her red flag, and cheering as the motor-bus rolled up.

The two culprits got up, hilariously, into the bus.

'Good luck, old girl! Let 'em have it! Give it the blue-bottles in the neck! Tell 'em what for! Three cheers for Bestwood! Strike while the iron's hot, girls!'

'So long! So long, girls! See you soon! Merry home coming, what, eh?'

'Have a good time, now! Have a good time! Stick a pin in their fat backsides, if you can't move 'em any other road. We s'll be thinking of you!'

'So long! So long! See you soon! Who says Walker!'

'E-eh! E-eh!'

The bus rolled heavily off, with the shouting women, amid the strange hoarse cheering of the women in the little market-place. The draughty little market-place where my mother shopped on Friday evenings, in her rusty little black bonnet, and where now a group of decent women waved little red flags and hoarsely cheered two women going to court!

O mamma mia! – as the Italians say. My dear mother, your little black bonnet would fly off your head in horrified astonishment, if you saw it now. You were so keen on progress: a decent working man, and a good wage! You paid my father's union pay for him, for so many years! You believed so firmly in the Co-op! You were at your Women's Guild when they brought you word your father, the old tyrannus, was dead! At the same time, you believed so absolutely in the ultimate benevolence of all the masters, of all the upper classes. One had to be grateful to them, after all!

Grateful! You can have your cake and eat it, while the cake lasts. When the cake comes to an end, you can hand on your indigestion. Oh my dear and virtuous mother, who believed in a Utopia of goodness, so that your own people were never quite good enough for you – not even the spoiled delicate boy, myself!

149

– oh my dear and virtuous mother, behold the indigestion we have inherited, from the cake of perfect goodness you baked too often! Nothing was good enough! We must all rise into the upper classes! Upper! Upper! Upper!

Till at last the boots are all uppers, the sole is worn out, and we yell as we walk on stones.

My dear, dear mother, you were so tragic, because you had nothing to be tragic about! We, on the other side, having a moral and social indigestion that would raise the wind for a thousand explosive tragedies, let off a mild crepitus ventris and shout: Have a good time, old girl! Enjoy yourself, old lass!

Nevertheless, we have all of us 'got on'. The reward of goodness, in my mother's far-off days, less than twenty years ago, was that you should 'get on'. *Be good, and you'll get on in life.*

Myself, a snotty-nosed little collier's lad, I call myself at home when I sit in a heavy old Cinque-cento Italian villa, of which I rent only half, even then – surely I can be considered to have 'got-on'. When I wrote my first book, and it was going to be published – sixteen years ago – and my mother was dying, a fairly well-known editor wrote to my mother and said, of me: 'By the time he is forty, he will be riding in his carriage.'

To which my mother is supposed to have said, sighing, 'Ay, if he lives to be forty!'

Well, I am forty-one, so there's one in the eye for that sighing remark. I was always weak in health, but my life was strong. Why had they all made up their minds that I was to die? Perhaps they thought I was too good to live. Well, in that case they were had!

And when I was forty, I was not even in my own motor-car. But I did drive my own two horses in a light buggy (my own) on a little ranch (also my own, or my wife's, through me) away on the western slope of the Rocky Mountains. And sitting in my corduroy trousers and blue shirt, calling: 'Get up Aaron! *Ambrose!*' then I thought of Justin Harrison's prophecy. Oh Oracle of Delphos! Oracle of Dodona! 'Get up, Ambrose!' Bump! went the buggy over a rock, and the pine-needles slashed my face! See him driving in his carriage, at forty! – driving it pretty badly too! Put the brake on!

So I suppose I've got on, snotty-nosed little collier's lad, of whom most of the women said: 'He's a *nice* little lad!' They don't say it now: if ever they say anything, which is doubtful. They've forgotten me entirely.

But my sister's 'getting on' is much more concrete than mine. She is almost on the spot. Within six miles of that end dwelling in The Breach, which is the house I first remember – an end house of hideous rows of miners' dwellings, though I loved it, too – stands my sister's new house, 'a lovely house!' – and her garden: 'I wish mother could see my garden in June!'

And if my mother did see it, what then? It is wonderful the flowers that bloom in these Midlands, in June. A northern Persephone seems to steal out from the Plutonic, coal-mining depths and give a real hoot of blossoms. But if my mother *did* return from the dead, and see that garden in full bloom, and the glass doors open from the hall of the new house, what then? Would she then say: It is reached! Consummatum est!

When Jesus gave up the ghost, he cried: It is finished. Consummatum est! But was it? And if so, what? What was it that was consummate?

Likewise, before the war, in Germany I used to see advertised in the newspapers a moustache-lifter, which you tied on at night and it would make your moustache stay turned up, like the immortal moustache of Kaiser Wilhelm II, whose moustache alone is immortal. This moustache-lifter was called: Es ist erreicht! In other words: It is reached! Consummatum est!

Was it? Was it reached? With the moustache-lifter?

So the ghost of my mother, in my sister's garden. I see it each time I am there, bending over the violas, or looking up at the almond tree. Actually an almond tree! And I always ask, of the grey-haired, good little ghost: 'Well what of it, my dear? What is the verdict?'

But she never answers, though I press her:

'Do look at the house, my dear! Do look at the tiled hall, and the rug from Mexico, and the brass from Venice, seen through the open doors, beyond the lilies and the carnations of the lawn beds! Do look! And do look at me, and see if I'm not a gentleman! Do say that I'm almost upper class!'

But the dear little ghost says never a word.

'Do say we've got on! Do say, we've arrived. Do say, it is reached, es ist erreicht, consummatum est!'

But the little ghost turns aside, she knows I am teasing her. She gives me one look, which is a look I know, and which says: 'I shan't tell you, so you can't laugh at me. You must find out for yourself.' And she steals away, to her place, wherever it may be. – 'In my father's house are many mansions. If it were not so, I would have told you.'

The black-slate roofs beyond the wind-worn young trees at the end of the garden are the same thick layers of black roofs of blackened brick houses, as ever. There is the same smell of sulphur from the burning pit bank. Smuts fly on the white violas. There is a harsh sound of machinery. Persephone couldn't quite get out of hell, so she let Spring fall from her lap along the upper workings.

But no! There are no smuts, there is even no smell of the burning pit bank. They cut the bank, and the pits are not working. The strike has been going on for months. It is September, but there are lots of roses on the lawn beds.

'Where shall we go this afternoon? Shall we go to Hardwick?'

Let us go to Hardwick. I have not been for twenty years. Let us go to Hardwick:

> Hardwick Hall
> More window than wall.

Built in the days of good Queen Bess, by that other Bess, termagant and tartar, Countess of Shrewsbury.

Butterley, Alfreton, Tibshelf – what was once the Hardwick district is now the Notts-Derby coal area. The country is the same, but scarred and splashed all over with mines and mining settlements. Great houses loom from hill-brows, old villages are smothered in rows of miners' dwellings, Bolsover Castle rises from the mass of the colliery village of Bolsover. – Böwser, we called it, when I was a boy.

Hardwick is shut. On the gates, near the old inn, where the atmosphere of the old world lingers perfect, is a notice: 'This park is closed to the public and to all traffic until further notice. No admittance.'

Of course! The strike! They are afraid of vandalism.

Where shall we go? Back into Derbyshire, or to Sherwood Forest.

Turn the car. We'll go on through Chesterfield. If I can't ride in my own carriage, I can still ride in my sister's motor-car.

It is a still September afternoon. By the ponds in the old park, we see colliers slowly loafing, fishing, poaching in spite of all notices.

And at every lane end there is a bunch of three or four policemen, 'blue-bottles', big, big-faced, stranger policemen. Every field path, every stile seems to be guarded. There are great pits, coal mines, in the fields. And at the end of the paths coming out of the field from the colliery, along the high-road, the colliers are squatted on their heels, on the wayside grass, silent and watchful. Their faces are clean, white, and all the months of the strike have given them no colour and no tan. They are pit-bleached. They squat in silent remoteness, as if in the upper galleries of hell. And the policemen, alien, stand in a group near the stile. Each lot pretends not to be aware of the others.

It is past three. Down the path from the pit come straggling what my little nephew calls 'the dirty ones'. They are the men who have broken strike, and gone back to work. They are not many: their faces are black, they are in their pit-dirt. They linger till they have collected, a group of a dozen or so 'dirty ones', near the stile, then they trail off down the road, the policemen, the alien 'blue-bottles', escorting them. And the 'clean ones', the colliers still on strike, squat by the wayside and watch without looking. They say nothing. They neither laugh nor stare. But here they are, a picket, and with their bleached faces they see without looking, and they register with the silence of doom, squatted down in rows by the road-side.

The 'dirty ones' straggle off in the lurching, almost slinking walk of colliers, swinging their heavy feet and going as if the mine-roof were still over their heads. The big blue policemen follow at a little distance. No voice is raised : nobody seems aware of anybody else. But there is the silent, hellish registering in the consciousness of all three groups, clean ones, dirty ones and bluebottles.

So it is now all the way into Chesterfield, whose crooked spire lies below. The men who have gone back to work – they seem few, indeed – are lurching and slinking in quiet groups, home down the high-road, the police at their heels. And the pickets, with bleached faces, squat and lean and stand, in silent groups, with a certain fatality, like Hell, upon them.

And I, who remember the homeward-trooping of the colliers when I was a boy, the ringing of the feet, the red mouths and the quick whites of the eyes, the swinging pit bottles, and the strange voices of men from the underworld calling back and forth, strong and, it seemed to me, gay with the queer, absolved gaiety of miners – I shiver, and feel I turn into a ghost myself. The colliers were noisy, lively, with strong underworld voices such as I have never heard in any other men, when I was a boy. And after all, it is not so long ago. I am only forty-one.

But after the war, the colliers went silent: after 1920. Till 1920 there was a strange power of life in them, something wild and urgent, that one could hear in their voices. They were always excited, in the afternoon, to come up above-ground: and excited, in the morning, at going down. And they called in the darkness with strong, strangely evocative voices. And at the little local foot-ball matches, on the damp, dusky Saturday afternoons of winter, great, full-throated cries came howling from the foot-ball field, in the zest and the wildness of life.

But now, the miners go by to the foot-ball match in silence like ghosts, and from the field comes a poor, ragged shouting. These are the men of my own generation, who went to the board school with me. And they are almost voiceless. They go to the welfare clubs, and drink with a sort of hopelessness.

I feel I hardly know any more the people I come from, the colliers of the Erewash Valley district. They are changed, and I suppose I am changed. I find it so much easier to live in Italy. And they have got a new kind of shallow consciousness, all newspaper and cinema, which I am not in touch with. At the same time, they have, I think, an underneath ache and heaviness very much like my own. It must be so, because when I see them, I feel it so strongly.

They are the only people who move me strongly, and with whom I feel myself connected in deeper destiny. It is they who are, in some peculiar way, 'home' to me. I shrink away from them, and I have an acute nostalgia for them.

And now, this last time, I feel a doom over the country, and a shadow of despair over the hearts of the men, which leaves me no rest. Because the same doom is over me, wherever I go, and the same despair touches my heart.

Yet it is madness to despair, while we still have the course of destiny open to us.

One is driven back to search one's own soul, for a way out into a new destiny.

A few things I know, with inner knowledge.

I know that what I am struggling for is life, more life ahead, for myself and the men who will come after me: struggling against fixations and corruptions.

I know that the miners at home are men very much like me, and I am very much like them: ultimately, we want the same thing. I know they are, in the life sense of the word, good.

I know that there is ahead the mortal struggle for property.

I know that the ownership of property has become, now, a problem, a religious problem. But it is one we can solve.

I know I want to own a few things: my personal things. But I also know I want to own no more than those. I don't want to own a house, nor land, nor a motor-car, nor shares in anything. I don't want a fortune – not even an assured income.

At the same time, I don't want poverty and hardship. I know I need enough money to leave me free in my movements, and I want to be able to earn that money without humiliation.

I know that most decent people feel very much the same in this respect: and the indecent people must, in their indecency, be subordinated to the decent.

I know that we could, if we would, establish little by little a true democracy in England: we could nationalize the land and industries and means of transport, and make the whole thing work infinitely better than at present, *if we would*. It all depends on the spirit in which the thing is done.

I know we are on the brink of a class war.

I know we had all better hang ourselves at once, than enter on a struggle which shall be a fight for the ownership or non-ownership of property, pure and simple, and nothing beyond.

I know the ownership of property is a problem that may have to be fought out. But beyond the fight must lie a new hope, a new beginning.

I know our vision of life is all wrong. We must be prepared to have a new conception of what it means, *to live*. And everybody should try to help to build up this new conception, and everybody should be prepared to destroy, bit by bit, our old conception.

I know that man cannot live by his own will alone. With his soul, he must search for the sources of the power of life. It is life we want.

I know that where there is life, there is essential beauty. Genuine beauty, which fills the soul, is an indication of life, and genuine ugliness, which blasts the soul, is an indication of morbidity. – But prettiness is opposed to beauty.

I know that, first and foremost, we must be sensitive to life and to its movements. If there is power, it must be sensitive power.

I know that we must look after the quality of life, not the quantity. Hopeless life should be put to sleep, the idiots and the hopeless sick and the true criminal. And the birth-rate should be controlled.

I know we must take up the responsibility for the future, now. A great change is coming, and must come. What we need is some glimmer of a vision of a world that shall be, beyond the change. Otherwise we shall be in for a great débâcle.

What is alive, and open, and active, is good. All that makes for inertia, lifelessness, dreariness, is bad. This is the essence of morality.

What we should live for is life and the beauty of aliveness, imagination, awareness, and contact. To be perfectly alive is to be immortal.

I know these things, along with other things. And it is nothing very new to know these things. The only new thing would be to act on them.

And what is the good of saying these things, to men whose whole education consists in the fact that twice two are four? – which, being interpreted, means that twice tuppence is fourpence. All our education, the whole of it, is formed upon this little speck of dust.

# 3. The Novel and Novelists

# The Novel

*Reflections on the Death of a Porcupine*, 1925

Somebody says the novel is doomed. Somebody else says it is the green bay tree getting nearer. Everybody says something, so why shouldn't I!

Mr Santayana sees the modern novel expiring because it is getting so thin; which means, Mr Santayana is bored.

I am rather bored myself. It becomes harder and harder to read the *whole* of any modern novel. One reads a bit, and knows the rest; or else one doesn't want to know any more.

This is sad. But again, I don't think it's the novel's fault. Rather the novelists'.

You can put anything you like in a novel. So why do people *always* go on putting the same thing? Why is the *vol au vent* always chicken! Chicken *vol au vents* may be the rage. But who sickens first shouts first for something else.

The novel is a great discovery: far greater than Galileo's telescope or somebody else's wireless. The novel is the highest form of human expression so far attained. Why? Because it is so incapable of the absolute.

In a novel, everything is relative to everything else, if that novel is art at all. There may be didactic bits, but they aren't the novel. And the author may have didactic 'purpose' up his sleeve. Indeed most great novelists have, as Tolstoy had his Christian-socialism,

*The Novel and Novelists*

and Hardy his pessimism, and Flaubert his intellectual desperation. But even a didactic purpose so wicked as Tolstoy's or Flaubert's cannot put to death the novel.

You can tell me, Flaubert had a 'philosophy', not 'purpose'.
But what is a novelist's philosophy but a purpose on a rather
higher level? And since every novelist who amounts to anything
has a philosophy – even Balzac – any novel of importance has a
purpose. If only the 'purpose' be large enough, and not at outs
with the passional inspiration.

Vronsky sinned, did he? But also the sinning was a consummation devoutly to be wished. The novel makes that obvious: in
spite of old Leo Tolstoy. And the would-be-pious Prince in
*Resurrection* is a muff, with his piety that nobody wants or believes in.

There you have the greatness of the novel itself. It won't *let*
you tell didactic lies, and put them over. Nobody in the world is
anything but delighted when Vronsky gets Anna Karenina. Then
what about the sin? – Why, when you look at it, all the tragedy
comes from Vronsky's and Anna's fear of *society*. The monster
was social, not phallic at all. They couldn't live in the pride of
their sincere passion, and spit in Mother Grundy's eye. And that,
that cowardice, was the real 'sin'. The novel makes it obvious,
and knocks all old Leo's teeth out. 'As an officer I am still useful.
But as a man, I am a ruin,' says Vronsky – or words to that effect.
Well what a skunk, collapsing as a man and a male, and remaining merely as a social instrument; an 'officer', God love us! –
merely because people at the opera turn backs on him! As if
people's backs weren't preferable to their faces, anyhow!

And old Leo tries to make out it was all because of the phallic
sin. Old liar! Because where would any of Leo's books be, without the phallic splendour? And then to blame the column of
blood, which really gave him all his life riches! The Judas!
Cringe to a mangy, bloodless Society, and try to dress up that
dirty old Mother Grundy in a new bonnet and face-powder of
Christian-socialism. Brothers indeed! Sons of a castrated
Father!

162

The novel itself gives Vronsky a kick in the behind, and knocks old Leo's teeth out, and leaves us to learn.

It is such a bore that nearly all great novelists have a didactic purpose, otherwise a philosophy, directly opposite to their passional inspiration. In their passional inspiration, they are all phallic worshippers. From Balzac to Hardy, it is so. Nay, from Apuleius to E. M. Forster. Yet all of them, when it comes to their philosophy, or what they think-they-are, they are all crucified Jesuses. What a bore! And what a burden for the novel to carry!

But the novel has carried it. Several thousands of thousands of lamentable crucifixions of self-heroes and self-heroines. Even the silly duplicity of *Resurrection*, and the wickeder duplicity of Salammbô, with that flayed phallic Matho, tortured upon the Cross of a gilt Princess.

You can't fool the novel. Even with man crucified upon a woman: his 'dear cross'. The novel will show you how dear she was: dear at any price. And it will leave you with a bad taste of disgust against these heroes who *turn* their women into a 'dear cross', and *ask* for their own crucifixion.

You can fool pretty nearly every other medium. You can make a poem pietistic, and still it will be a poem. You can write *Hamlet* in drama: if you wrote him in a novel, he'd be half comic, or a trifle suspicious: a suspicious character, like Dostoyevsky's Idiot. Somehow, you sweep the ground a bit too clear in the poem or the drama, and you let the human Word fly a bit too freely. Now in a novel there's always a tom-cat, a black tom-cat that pounces on the white dove of the Word, if the dove doesn't watch it; and there is a banana-skin to trip on; and you know there is a water-closet on the premises. All these things help to keep the balance.

If, in Plato's *Dialogues*, somebody had suddenly stood on his head and given smooth Plato a kick in the wind, and set the whole school in an uproar, then Plato would have been put into a much truer relation to the universe. Or if, in the midst of the *Timaeus*, Plato had only paused to say: 'And now, my dear Cleon – (or whoever it was) – I have a bellyache, and must retreat to the privy: this too is part of the Eternal Idea of man', then we never need have fallen so low as Freud.

And if, when Jesus told the rich man to take all he had and give it to the poor, the rich man had replied: '*All right, old sport! You are poor, aren't you? Come on, I'll give you a fortune. Come on!*' Then a great deal of snivelling and mistakenness would have been spared us all, and we might never have produced a Marx and a Lenin. If only Jesus had *accepted* the fortune!

Yes, it's a pity of pities that Matthew, Mark, Luke, and John didn't write straight novels. They did write novels; but a bit crooked. The *Evangels* are wonderful novels, by authors 'with a purpose'. Pity there's so much Sermon-on-the-Mounting.

> Matthew, Mark, Luke and John
> Went to bed with their breeches on! –

as every child knows. Ah, if only they'd taken them off!

Greater novels, to my mind, are the books of the Old Testament, Genesis, Exodus, Samuel, Kings, by authors whose purpose was so big, it didn't quarrel with their passionate inspiration. The purpose and the inspiration were almost one. Why, in the name of everything bad, the two ever should have got separated, is a mystery! But in the modern novel they are hopelessly divorced. When there *is* any inspiration there, to be divorced from.

This, then, is what is the matter with the modern novel. The modern novelist is possessed, hag-ridden, by such a stale old 'purpose', or idea-of-himself, that his inspiration succumbs. Of course he denies having any didactic purpose at all: because a purpose is supposed to be like catarrh, something to be ashamed of. But he's got it. They've all got it: the same snivelling purpose.

They're all little Jesuses in their own eyes, and their 'purpose' is to prove it. Oh Lord! – *Lord Jim*! *Sylvestre Bonnard*! *If Winter Comes*! *Main Street*! *Ulysses*! *Pan*! They are all pathetic or sympathetic or antipathetic little Jesuses *accomplis* or *manqués*. And there is a heroine who is always 'pure', usually, nowadays, on the muck-heap! Like the Green Hatted Woman. She is all the time at the feet of Jesus, though her behaviour there may be misleading. Heaven knows what the Saviour really makes of it: whether she's a Green Hat or a Constant Nymph (eighteen months of constancy, and her heart failed), or any of the rest of 'em. They are all, heroes and heroines, novelists and she-novelists, little Jesuses or Jesusesses. They may be wallowing in the mire: but then didn't Jesus harrow Hell! *A la bonne heure!*

Oh, they are all novelists with an idea of themselves! Which is a 'purpose', with a vengeance! For what a weary, false, sickening idea it is nowadays! The novel gives them away. They can't fool the novel.

Now really, it's time we left *off* insulting the novel any further. If your purpose is to prove your own Jesus qualifications, and the thin stream of your inspiration is 'sin', then dry up, for the interest is dead. *Life as it is!* What's the good of pretending that the lives of a set of tuppenny Green Hats and Constant Nymphs is Life-as-it-is, when the novel itself proves that all it amounts to a life as it is isn't life, but a sort of everlasting and intricate and boring habit: of Jesus peccant and *Jesusa peccante.*

These wearisome sickening little personal novels! After all, they aren't novels at all. In every great novel, who is the hero all the time? Not any of the characters, but some unnamed and nameless flame behind them all. Just as God is the pivotal interest in the books of the Old Testament. But just a trifle too intimate, too *frère et cochon*, there. In the great novel, the felt but unknown flame stands behind all the characters, and in their words and gestures there is a flicker of the presence. If you are *too personal, too human*, the flicker fades out, leaving you with something awfully lifelike, and as lifeless as most people are.

We have to choose between the quick and the dead. The quick is God-flame, in everything. And the dead is dead. In this room where I write, there is a little table that is dead: it doesn't even weakly exist. And there is a ridiculous little iron stove, which for some unknown reason is quick. And there is an iron wardrobe trunk, which for some still more mysterious reason is quick. And there are several books, whose mere corpus is dead, utterly dead and non-existent. And there is a sleeping cat, very quick. And a glass lamp, alas, is dead.

What makes the difference? *Quién sabe!* But difference there is. And I *know* it.

And the sum and source of all quickness, we will call God. And the sum and total of all deadness we may call human.

And if one tries to find out wherein the quickness of the quick lies, it is in a certain weird relationship between that which is quick and – I don't know; perhaps all the rest of the things. It seems to consist in an odd sort of fluid, changing, grotesque or beautiful relatedness. That silly iron stove somehow *belongs*. Whereas this thin-shanked table doesn't belong. It is a mere disconnected lump, like a cut-off finger.

And now we see the great, great merits of the novel. It can't exist without being 'quick'. The ordinary unquick novel, even if it be a best seller, disappears into absolute nothingness, the dead burying their dead with surprising speed. For even the dead like to be tickled. But the next minute, they've forgotten both the tickling and the tickler.

Secondly, the novel contains no didactic absolute. All that is quick, and all that is said and done by the quick, is in some way godly. So that Vronsky's taking Anna Karenina we must count godly, since it is quick. And that Prince in *Resurrection*, following the convict girl, we must count dead. The convict train is quick and alive. But that would-be-expiatory Prince is as dead as lumber.

The novel itself lays down these laws for us, and we spend our time evading them. The man in the novel must be 'quick'. And this means one thing, among a host of unknown meaning: it means he must have a quick relatedness to all the other things in the novel: snow, bed-bugs, sunshine, the phallus, trains, silk-hats, cats, sorrow, people, food, diphtheria, fuchsias, stars, ideas, God, tooth-paste, lightning, and toilet-paper. He must be in quick relation to all these things. What he says and does must be relative to them all.

And this is why Pierre, for example, in *War and Peace*, is more dull and less quick than Prince André. Pierre is quite nicely related to ideas, tooth-paste, God, people, foods, trains, silk-hats, sorrow, diphtheria, stars. But his relation to snow and sunshine, cats, lightning and the phallus, fuchsias and toilet-paper, is sluggish and mussy. He's not quick enough.

The really quick, Tolstoy loved to kill them off or muss them over. Like a true Bolshevist. One can't help feeling Natasha is rather mussy and unfresh, married to that Pierre.

Pierre was what we call 'so human'. Which means 'so limited'. Men clotting together into social masses in order to limit their individual liabilities: this is humanity. And this is Pierre. And this is Tolstoy, the philosopher with a very nauseating Christian-brotherhood idea of himself. Why limit man to a Christian-brotherhood? I myself, I could belong to the sweetest Christian-brotherhood one day, and ride after Attila with a raw beefsteak for my saddle-cloth, to see the red cock crow in flame over all Christendom, next day.

And that is man! That, really, was Tolstoy. That, even, was Lenin, God in the machine of Christian-brotherhood, that hashes men up into social sausage-meat.

Damn all absolutes. Oh damn, damn, damn all absolutes! I tell you, no absolute is going to make the lion lie down with the lamb: unless, like the limerick, the lamb is inside.

> They returned from the ride
> With lamb Leo inside
> And a smile on the face of the tiger!
> Sing fol-di-lol-lol!
> Fol-di-lol-lol!
> Fol-di-lol-ol-di-lol-olly!

For man, there is neither absolute nor absolution. Such things should be left to monsters like the right-angled triangle, which does only exist in the ideal consciousness. A man can't have a square on his hypotenuse, let him try as he may.

Ay! Ay! Ay! – Man handing out absolutes to man, as if we were all books of geometry with axioms, postulates and definitions in front. God with a pair of compasses! Moses with a set square! Man a geometric bifurcation, not even a radish!

Holy Moses!

'Honour thy father and thy mother!' That's awfully cute! But supposing they are not honourable? How then, Moses?

Voice of thunder from Sinai: *'Pretend to honour them!'*

'Love thy neighbour as thyself.'

Alas, my neighbour happens to be mean and detestable.

Voice of the lambent Dove, cooing: *'Put it over him, that you love him.'*

Talk about the cunning of serpents! I never saw even a serpent kissing his instinctive enemy.

Pfui! I wouldn't blacken my mouth, kissing my neighbour, who, I repeat, to me is mean and detestable.

Dove, go home!

The Goat and Compasses, indeed!

Everything is relative. Every Commandment that ever issued out of the mouth of God or man is strictly relative: adhering to the particular time, place and circumstance.

And this is the beauty of the novel; everything is true in its own relationship, and no further.

For the relatedness and interrelatedness of all things flows and changes and trembles like a stream, and like a fish in the stream the characters in the novel swim and drift and float and turn belly-up when they're dead.

So, if a character in a novel wants two wives – or three – or thirty: well, that is true of that man, at that time, in that circumstance. It may be true of other men, elsewhere and elsewhen. But to infer that all men at all times want two, three, or thirty wives; or that the novelist himself is advocating furious polygamy; is just imbecility.

It has been just as imbecile to infer that, because Dante worshipped a remote Beatrice, every man, all men, should go worshipping remote Beatrices.

And that wouldn't have been so bad, if Dante had put the thing in its true light. Why do we slur over the actual fact that Dante had a cosy bifurcated wife in his bed, and a family of lusty little Dantinos? Petrarch, with his Laura in the distance, had *twelve* little legitimate Petrarchs of his own, between his knees. Yet all we hear is *Laura! Laura! Beatrice! Beatrice! Distance! Distance!*

What bunk! Why didn't Dante and Petrarch chant in chorus:

> Oh be my spiritual concubine
>   Beatrice! ⎱
>   Laura!   ⎰
> My old girl's got several babies that are mine,
> But *thou* be my spiritual concubine,
>   Beatrice! ⎱
>   Laura!   ⎰

Then there would have been an honest relation between all the bunch. Nobody grudges the gents their spiritual concubines. But keeping a wife and family – twelve children – up one's sleeve, has always been recognized as a dirty trick.

Which reveals how *immoral* the absolute is! Invariably keeping some vital fact dark! Dishonourable!

Here we come upon the third essential quality of the novel. Unlike the essay, the poem, the drama, the book of philosophy, or the scientific treatise: all of which may beg the question, when they don't downright filch it; the novel inherently is and must be:

1. Quick.

2. Interrelated in all its parts, vitally, organically.

3. Honourable.

I call Dante's *Commedia* slightly dishonourable, with never a mention of the cosy bifurcated wife, and the kids. And *War and Peace* I call downright dishonourable, with that fat, diluted Pierre for a hero, stuck up as preferable and desirable, when everybody knows that he *wasn't* attractive, even to Tolstoy.

Of course Tolstoy, being a great creative artist, was true to his characters. But being a man with a philosophy, he wasn't true to his *own character*.

Character is a curious thing. It is the flame of a man, which burns brighter or dimmer, bluer or yellower or redder, rising or sinking or flaring according to the draughts of circumstance and the changing air of life, changing itself continually, yea remaining

169

one single, separate flame, flickering in a strange world: unless it be blown out at last by too much adversity.

If Tolstoy had looked into the flame of his own belly, he would have seen that he didn't really like the fat, fuzzy Pierre, who was a poor tool, after all. But Tolstoy was a personality even more than a character. And a personality is a self-conscious *I am*: being all that is left in us of a once-almighty Personal God. So being a personality and almighty *I am*, Leo proceeded deliberately to lionize that Pierre, who was a domestic sort of house-dog.

Doesn't anybody call that dishonourable on Leo's part? He might just as well have been true to *himself*! But no! His self-conscious personality was superior to his own belly and knees, so he thought he'd improve on himself, by creeping inside the skin of a lamb; the doddering old lion that he was! Leo! Léon!

Secretly, Leo worshipped the human male, man as a column of rapacious and living blood. He could hardly meet three lusty, roisterous young guardsmen in the street, without crying with envy: and ten minutes later, fulminating on them black oblivion and annihilation, utmost moral thunder-bolts.

How boring, in a great man! And how boring, in a great nation like Russia, to let its old-Adam manhood be so improved upon by these reformers, who all feel themselves short of something, and therefore live by spite, that at last there's nothing left but a lot of shells of men, improving themselves steadily emptier and emptier, till they rattle with words and formulae, as if they'd swallowed the whole encyclopedia of socalism.

But wait! There is life in the Russians. Something new and strange will emerge out of their weird transmogrification into Bolshevists.

When the lion swallows the lamb, fluff and all, he usually gets a pain, and there's a rumpus. But when the lion tries to force himself down the throat of the huge and popular lamb – a nasty old sheep, really – then it's a phenomenon. Old Leo did it: wedged himself bit by bit down the throat of woolly Russia. And now out of the mouth of the Bolshevist lambkin still waves an angry, mistaken, tufted leonine tail, like an agitated exclamation mark.

Meanwhile it's a deadlock.

But what a dishonourable thing for that claw-biting little Leo to do! And in his novels you see him at it. So that the papery lips of *Resurrection* whisper: '*Alas! I would have been a novel. But Leo spoiled me.*'

Count Tolstoy had that last weakness of a great man: he wanted the absolute: the absolute of love, if you like to call it that. Talk about the 'last infirmity of noble minds'! It's a perfect epidemic of senility. He wanted to *be* absolute: a universal brother. Leo was too tight for Tolstoy. He wanted to puff, and puff, and puff, till he became Universal Brotherhood itself, the great gooseberry of our globe.

Then pop went Leo! And from the bits sprang up Bolshevists.

It's all bunk. No man can be absolute. No man can be absolutely good or absolutely right, nor absolutely lovable, nor absolutely beloved, nor absolutely loving. Even Jesus, the paragon, was only relatively good and relatively right. Judas could take him by the nose.

No god, that men can conceive of, could possibly be absolute or absolutely right. All the gods that men ever discovered are still God: and they contradict one another and fly down one another's throats, marvellously. Yet they are *all* God: the incalculable Pan.

It is rather nice, to know what a lot of gods there are, and have been, and will be, and that they are all of them God all the while. Each of them utters an absolute: which, in the ears of all the rest of them, falls flat. This makes even eternity lively.

But man, poor man, bobbing like a cork in the stream of time, must hitch himself to some absolute star of righteousness overhead. So he throws out his line, and hooks on. Only to find, after a while, that his star is slowly falling: till it drops into the stream of time with a fizzle, and there's *another* absolute star gone out.

Then we scan the heavens afresh.

As for the babe of love, we're simply tired of changing its napkins. Put the brat down, and let it learn to run about, and manage its own little breeches.

But it's nice to think that all the gods are God all the while.

And if a god only genuinely feels to you like God, then it *is* God. But if it doesn't feel quite, quite altogether like God to you, then wait awhile, and you'll hear him fizzle.

The novel knows all this, irrevocably. 'My dear,' it kindly says, 'one God is relative to another god, until he gets into a machine; and then it's a case for the traffic cop!'

'But what am I to do!' cries the despairing novelist. 'From Amon and Ra to Mrs Eddy, from Ashtaroth and Jupiter to Annie Besant, I don't know where I am.'

'Oh yes you do, my dear!' replies the novel. 'You are where you are, so you needn't hitch yourself on to the skirts either of Ashtaroth or Eddy. If you meet them, say *how-do-you-do!* to them quite courteously. But don't hook on, or I shall turn you down.'

'Refrain from hooking on!' says the novel.

'But be honourable among the host!' he adds.

Honour! Why, the gods are like the rainbow, all colours and shades. Since light itself is invisible, a manifestation has got to be pink or black or blue or white or yellow or vermilion, or 'tinted'.

You may be a theosophist, and then you will cry: *Avaunt! Thou dark-red aura! Away!!! – Oh come! Thou pale-blue or thou primrose aura, come!*

This you may cry if you are a theosophist. And if you put a theosophist in a novel, he or she may cry *avaunt!* to the heart's content.

But a theosophist cannot be a novelist, as a trumpet cannot be a regimental band. A theosophist, or a Christian, or a Holy Roller, may be *contained* in a novelist. But a novelist may not put up a fence. The wind bloweth where it listeth, and auras will be red when they want to.

As a matter of fact, only the Holy Ghost knows truly what righteousness is. And heaven only knows what the Holy Ghost is! But it sounds all right. So the Holy Ghost hovers among the flames, from the red to the blue and the black to the yellow, putting brand to brand and flame to flame, as the wind changes, and life travels in flame from the unseen to the unseen, men will never know how or why. Only travel it must, and not die down in nasty fumes.

And the honour, which the novel demands of you, is only that you shall be true to the flame that leaps in you. When that Prince in *Resurrection* so cruelly betrayed and abandoned the girl, at the beginning of her life, he betrayed and wetted on the flame of his own manhood. When, later, he bullied her with his repentant benevolence, he again betrayed and slobbered upon the flame of his waning manhood, till in the end his manhood is extinct, and he's just a lump of half-alive elderly meat.

It's the oldest Pan-mystery. God is the flame-life in all the universe; multifarious, multifarious flames, all colours and beauties and pains and sombrenesses. Whichever flame flames in your manhood, that is you, for the time being. It is your manhood, don't make water on it, says the novel. A man's manhood is to honour the flames in him, and to know that none of them is absolute: even a flame is only relative.

But see old Leo Tolstoy wetting on the flame. As if even his wet were absolute!

Sex is flame, too, the novel announces. Flame burning against every absolute, even against the phallic. For sex is so much more than phallic, and so much deeper than functional desire. The flame of sex singes your absolute, and cruelly scorches your ego. What, will you assert your ego in the universe? Wait till the flames of sex leap at you like striped tigers.

> They returned from the ride
> With the lady inside,
> And a smile on the face of the tiger.

You will play with sex, will you! You will tickle yourself with sex as with an ice-cold drink from a soda-fountain! You will pet your best girl, will you, and spoon with her, and titillate yourself and her, and do as you like with your sex?

Wait! Only wait till the flame you have dribbled on flies back at you; later! Only wait!

Sex is a life-flame, a dark one, reserved and mostly invisible. It is a deep reserve in a man, one of the core-flames of his manhood.

What, would you play with it? Would you make it cheap and nasty!

Buy a king-cobra, and try playing with that.

Sex is even a majestic reserve in the sun.

Oh, give me the novel! Let me hear what the novel says.

As for the novelist, he is usually a dribbling liar.

# Morality and the Novel

*Calendar of Modern Letters*, December 1925;
*Phoenix*, 1936

The business of art is to reveal the relation between man and his circumambient universe, at the living moment. As mankind is always struggling in the toils of old relationships, art is always ahead of the 'times', which themselves are always far in the rear of the living moment.

When van Gogh paints sunflowers, he reveals, or achieves, the vivid relation between himself, as man, and the sunflower, as sunflower, at that quick moment of time. His painting does not represent the sunflower itself. We shall never know what the sunflower itself is. And the camera will *visualize* the sunflower far more perfectly than van Gogh can.

The vision on the canvas is a third thing, utterly intangible and inexplicable, the offspring of the sunflower itself and van Gogh himself. The vision on the canvas is for ever incommensurable with the canvas, or the paint, or van Gogh as a human organism, or the sunflower as a botanical organism. You cannot weigh nor measure nor even describe the vision on the canvas. It exists, to tell the truth, only in the much-debated fourth dimension. In dimensional space it has no existence.

It is a revelation of the perfected relation, at a certain moment, between a man and a sunflower. It is neither man-in-the-mirror nor flower-in-the-mirror, neither is it above nor below nor across

175

anything. It is in between everything, in the fourth dimension.

And this perfected relation between man and his circumambient universe is life itself, for mankind. It has the fourth-dimensional quality of eternity and perfection. Yet it is momentaneous.

Man and the sunflower both pass away from the moment, in the process of forming a new relationship. The relation between all things changes from day to day, in a subtle stealth of change. Hence art, which reveals or attains to another perfect relationship, will be for ever new.

At the same time, that which exists in the non-dimensional space of pure relationship is deathless, lifeless, and eternal. That is, it gives us the *feeling* of being beyond life or death. We say an Assyrian lion or an Egyptian hawk's head 'lives'. What we really mean is that it is beyond life, and therefore beyond death. It gives us that feeling. And there is something inside us which must also be beyond life and beyond death, since that 'feeling' which we get from an Assyrian lion or an Egyptian hawk's head is so infinitely precious to us. As the evening star, that spark of pure relation between night and day, has been precious to man since time began.

If we think about it, we find that our life *consists in* this achieving of a pure relationship between ourselves and the living universe about us. This is how I 'save my soul' by accomplishing a pure relationship between me and another person, me and other people, me and a nation, me and a race of men, me and the animals, me and the trees or flowers, me and the earth, me and the skies and sun and stars, me and the moon: an infinity of pure relations, big and little, like the stars of the sky: that makes our eternity, for each one of us, me and the timber I am sawing, the lines of force I follow; me and the dough I knead for bread, me and the very motion with which I write, me and the bit of gold I have got. This, if we knew it, is our life and our eternity: the subtle, perfected relation between me and my whole circumambient universe.

And morality is that delicate, for ever trembling and changing *balance* between me and my circumambient universe, which precedes and accompanies a true relatedness.

Now here we see the beauty and the great value of the novel. Philosophy, religion, science, they are all of them busy nailing things down, to get a stable equilibrium. Religion, with its nailed-down One God, who says *Thou shalt, Thou shan't*, and hammers home every time; philosophy, with its fixed ideas; science with its 'laws': they, all of them, all the time, want to nail us on to some tree or other.

But the novel, no. The novel is the highest example of subtle inter-relatedness that man has discovered. Everything is true in its own time, place, circumstance, and untrue outside of its own place, time, circumstance. If you try to nail anything down, in the novel, either it kills the novel, or the novel gets up and walks away with the nail.

Morality in the novel is the trembling instability of the balance. When the novelist puts his thumb in the scale, to pull down the balance to his own predilection, that is immorality.

The modern novel tends to become more and more immoral, as the novelist tends to press his thumb heavier and heavier in the pan; either on the side of love, pure love: or on the side of licentious 'freedom'.

The novel is not, as a rule, immoral because the novelist has any dominant *idea*, or *purpose*. The immorality lies in the novelist's helpless, unconscious predilection. Love is a great emotion. But if you set out to write a novel, and you yourself are in the throes of the great predilection for love, love as the supreme, the only emotion worth living for, then you will write an immoral novel.

Because *no* emotion is supreme, or exclusively worth living for. *All* emotions go to the achieving of a living relationship between a human being and the other human being or creature or thing he becomes purely related to. All emotions, including love and hate, and rage and tenderness, go to the adjusting of the oscillating, unestablished balance between two people who amount to anything. If the novelist puts his thumb in the pan, for love, tenderness, sweetness, peace, then he commits an immoral act: he *prevents* the possibility of a pure relationship, a pure relatedness, the only thing that matters: and he makes inevitable the horrible

177

reaction, when he lets his thumb go, towards hate and brutality, cruelty and destruction.

Life is so made that opposites sway about a trembling centre of balance. The sins of the fathers are visited on the children. If the fathers drag down the balance on the side of love, peace, and production, then in the third or fourth generation the balance will swing back violently to hate, rage, and destruction. We must balance as we go.

And of all the art forms, the novel most of all demands the trembling and oscillating of the balance. The 'sweet' novel is more falsified, and therefore more immoral, than the blood-and-thunder novel.

The same with the smart and smudgily cynical novel, which says it doesn't matter what you do, because one thing is as good as another, anyhow, and prostitution is just as much 'life' as anything else.

This misses the point entirely. A thing isn't life just because somebody does it. This the artist ought to know perfectly well. The ordinary bank clerk buying himself a new straw hat isn't 'life' at all: it is just existence, quite all right, like everyday dinners: but not 'life'.

By life, we mean something that gleams, that has the fourth-dimensional quality. If the bank clerk feels really piquant about his hat, if he establishes a lively relation with it, and goes out of the shop with the new straw on his head, a changed man, be-aureoled, then that is life.

The same with the prostitute. If a man establishes a living relation to her, if only for one moment, then it is life. But if he *doesn't*: if it is just money and function, then it is not life, but sordidness, and a betrayal of living.

If a novel reveals true and vivid relationships, it is a moral work, no matter what the relationships may consist in. If the novelist *honours* the relationship in itself, it will be a great novel.

But there are so many relationships which are not real. When the man in *Crime and Punishment* murders the old woman for sixpence, although it is *actual* enough, it is never quite real. The

balance between the murderer and the old woman is gone entirely; it is only a mess. It is actuality, but it is not 'life', in the living
sense.

The popular novel, on the other hand, dishes up a réchauffé
of old relationships: *If Winter Comes*. And old relationships
dished up are likewise immoral. Even a magnificent painter like
Raphael does nothing more than dress up in gorgeous new
dresses relationships which have already been experienced. And
this gives a gluttonous kind of pleasure to the mass: a voluptuousness, a wallowing. For centuries, men say of their volup-
tuously ideal woman: 'She is a Raphael Madonna.' And women
are only just learning to take it as an insult.

A new relation, a new relatedness hurts somewhat in the attaining; and will always hurt. So life will always hurt. Because real
voluptuousness lies in re-acting old relationships, and at the
best, getting an alcoholic sort of pleasure out of it, slightly de-
praving.

Each time we strive to a new relation, with anyone or anything,
it is bound to hurt somewhat. Because it means the struggle with
and the displacing of old connexions, and this is never pleasant.
And moreover, between living things at least, an adjustment
means also a fight, for each party, inevitably, must 'seek its own'
in the other, and be denied. When, in the two parties, each of
them seeks his own, her own, absolutely, then it is a fight to the
death. And this is true of the thing called 'passion'. On the other
hand, when, of the two parties, one yields utterly to the other,
this is called sacrifice, and it also means death. So the Constant
Nymph died of her eighteen months of constancy.

It isn't the nature of nymphs to be constant. She should have
been constant in her nymph-hood. And it is unmanly to accept
sacrifices. He should have abided by his own manhood.

There is, however, the third thing, which is neither sacrifice nor
fight to the death: when each seeks only the true relatedness to
the other. Each must be true to himself, herself, his own manhood, her own womanhood, and let the relationship work out of
itself. This means courage above all things: and then discipline.
Courage to accept the life-thrust from within oneself, and from

179

the other person. Discipline, not to exceed oneself any more than one can help. Courage, when one has exceeded oneself, to accept the fact and not whine about it.

Obviously, to read a really new novel will *always* hurt, to some extent. There will always be resistance. The same with new pictures, new music. You may judge of their reality by the fact that they do arouse a certain resistance, and compel, at length, a certain acquiescence.

The great relationship, for humanity, will always be the relation between man and woman. The relation between man and man, woman and woman, parent and child, will always be subsidiary.

And the relation between man and woman will change for ever, and will for ever be the new central clue to human life. It is the *relation itself* which is the quick and the central clue to life, not the man, nor the woman, nor the children that result from the relationship, as a contingency.

It is no use thinking you can put a stamp on the relation between man and woman, to keep it in the *status quo*. You can't. You might as well try to put a stamp on the rainbow or the rain.

As for the bond of love, better put it off when it galls. It is an absurdity, to say that men and women *must love*. Men and women will be for ever subtly and changingly related to one another; no need to yoke them with any 'bond' at all. The only morality is to have man true to his manhood, woman to her womanhood, and let the relationship form of itself, in all honour. For it is, to each, *life itself*.

If we are going to be moral, let us refrain from driving pegs through anything, either through each other or through the third thing, the relationship, which is for ever the ghost of both of us. Every sacrificial crucifixion needs five pegs, four short ones and a long one, each one an abomination. But when you try to nail down the relationship itself, and write over it *Love* instead of *This is the King of the Jews*, then you can go on putting in nails for ever. Even Jesus called it the Holy Ghost, to show you that you can't lay salt on its tail.

The novel is a perfect medium for revealing to us the changing rainbow of our living relationships. The novel can help us to live, as nothing else can: no didactic Scripture, anyhow. If the novelist keeps his thumb out of the pan.

But when the novelist *has* his thumb in the pan, the novel becomes an unparalleled perverter of men and women. To be compared only, perhaps, to that great mischief of sentimental hymns, like 'Lead, Kindly Light', which have helped to rot the marrow in the bones of the present generation.

# Why the Novel Matters

Written in the middle 1920s, published in *Phoenix*, 1936

We have curious ideas of ourselves. We think of ourselves as a body with a spirit in it, or a body with a soul in it, or a body with a mind in it. *Mens sana in corpore sano.* The years drink up the wine, and at last throw the bottle away, the body, of course, being the bottle.

It is a funny sort of superstition. Why should I look at my hand, as it so cleverly writes these words, and decide that it is a mere nothing compared to the mind that directs it? Is there really any huge difference between my hand and my brain? Or my mind? My hand is alive, it flickers with a life of its own. It meets all the strange universe in touch, and learns a vast number of things, and knows a vast number of things. My hand, as it writes these words, slips gaily along, jumps like a grasshopper to dot an *i*, feels the table rather cold, gets a little bored if I write too long, has its own rudiments of thought, and is just as much *me* as is my brain, my mind, or my soul. Why should I imagine that there is a *me* which is more *me* than my hand is? Since my hand is absolutely alive, me alive.

Whereas, of course, as far as I am concerned, my pen isn't alive at all. My pen *isn't me* alive. Me alive ends at my finger-tips.

Whatever is me alive is me. Every tiny bit of my hands is alive, every little freckle and hair and fold of skin. And whatever is me alive is me. Only my finger-nails, those ten little weapons between me and an inanimate universe, they cross the mysterious Rubicon between me alive and things like my pen, which are not alive, in my own sense.

So, seeing my hand is all alive, and me alive, wherein is it just a bottle, or a jug, or a tin can, or a vessel of clay, or any of the rest of that nonsense? True, if I cut it it will bleed, like a can of cherries. But then the skin that is cut, and the veins that bleed, and the bones that should never be seen, they are all just as alive as the blood that flows. So the tin can business, or vessel of clay, is just bunk.

And that's what you learn, when you're a novelist. And that's what you are very liable *not* to know, if you're a parson, or a philosopher, or a scientist, or a stupid person. If you're a parson, you talk about souls in heaven. If you're a novelist, you know that paradise is in the palm of your hand, and on the end of your nose, because both are alive; and alive, and man alive, which is more than you can say, for certain, of paradise. Paradise is after life, and I for one am not keen on anything that is *after* life. If you are a philosopher, you talk about infinity, and the pure spirit which knows all things. But if you pick up a novel, you realize immediately that infinity is just a handle to this self-same jug of a body of mine; while as for knowing, if I find my finger in the fire, I know that fire burns, with a knowledge so emphatic and vital, it leaves Nirvana merely a conjecture. Oh, yes, my body, me alive, *knows*, and knows intensely. And as for the sum of all knowledge, it can't be anything more than an accumulation of all the things I know in the body, and you, dear reader, know in the body.

These damned philosophers, they talk as if they suddenly went off in steam, and were then much more important than they are when they're in their shirts. It is nonsense. Every man, philosopher included, ends in his own finger-tips. That's the end of his man alive. As for the words and thoughts and sighs and aspirations that fly from him, they are so many tremulations in the ether, and not alive at all. But if the tremulations reach another man alive, he may receive them into his life, and his life may

183

take on a new colour, like a chameleon creeping from a brown rock on to a green leaf. All very well and good. It still doesn't alter the fact that the so-called spirit, the message or teaching of the philosopher or the saint, isn't alive at all, but just a tremulation upon the ether, like a radio message. All this spirit stuff is just tremulations upon the ether. If you, as man alive, quiver from the tremulation of the ether into new life, that is because you are man alive, and you take sustenance and stimulation into your alive man in a myriad ways. But to say that the message, or the spirit which is communicated to you, is more important than your living body, is nonsense. You might as well say that the potato at dinner was more important.

Nothing is important but life. And for myself, I can absolutely see life nowhere but in the living. Life with a capital L is only man alive. Even a cabbage in the rain is cabbage alive. All things that are alive are amazing. And all things that are dead are subsidiary to the living. Better a live dog than a dead lion. But better a live lion than a live dog. *C'est la vie!*

It seems impossible to get a saint, or a philosopher, or a scientist, to stick to this simple truth. They are all, in a sense, renegades. The saint wishes to offer himself up as spiritual food for the multitude. Even Francis of Assisi turns himself into a sort of angel-cake, of which anyone may take a slice. But an angel-cake is rather less than man alive. And poor St Francis might well apologize to his body, when he is dying: 'Oh, pardon me, my body, the wrong I did you through the years!' It was no wafer, for others to eat.

The philosopher, on the other hand, because he can think, decides that nothing but thoughts matter. It is as if a rabbit, because he can make little pills, should decide that nothing but little pills matter. As for the scientist, he has absolutely no use for me so long as I am man alive. To the scientist, I am dead. He puts under the microscope a bit of dead me, and calls it me. He takes me to pieces, and says first one piece, and then another piece, is me. My heart, my liver, my stomach have all been scientifically me, according to the scientist; and nowadays I am either a brain, or nerves, or glands, or something more up-to-date in the tissue line.

184

Now I absolutely flatly deny that I am a soul, or a body, or a mind, or an intelligence, or a brain, or a nervous system, or a bunch of glands, or any of the rest of these bits of me. The whole is greater than the part. And therefore, I, who am man alive, am greater than my soul, or spirit, or body, or mind, or consciousness, or anything else that is merely a part of me. I am a man, and alive. I am man alive, and as long as I can, I intend to go on being man alive.

For this reason I am a novelist. And being a novelist, I consider myself superior to the saint, the scientist, the philosopher, and the poet, who are all great masters of different bits of man alive, but never get the whole hog.

The novel is the one bright book of life. Books are not life. They are only tremulations on the ether. But the novel as a tremulation can make the whole man alive tremble. Which is more than poetry, philosophy, science, or any other book-tremulation can do.

The novel is the book of life. In this sense, the Bible is a great confused novel. You may say, it is about God. But it is really about man alive. Adam, Eve, Sarai, Abraham, Isaac, Jacob, Samuel, David, Bath-Sheba, Ruth, Esther, Solomon, Job, Isaiah, Jesus, Mark, Judas, Paul, Peter: what is it but man alive, from start to finish? Man alive, not mere bits. Even the Lord is another man alive, in a burning bush, throwing the tablets of stone at Moses's head.

I do hope you begin to get my idea, why the novel is supremely important, as a tremulation on the ether. Plato makes the perfect ideal being tremble in me. But that's only a bit of me. Perfection is only a bit, in the strange make-up of man alive. The Sermon on the Mount makes the selfless spirit of me quiver. But that, too, is only a bit of me. The Ten Commandments set the old Adam shivering in me, warning me that I am a thief and a murderer, unless I watch it. But even the old Adam is only a bit of me.

I very much like all these bits of me to be set trembling with life and the wisdom of life. But I do ask that the whole of me shall tremble in its wholeness, some time or other.

And this, of course, must happen in me, living.

But as far as it can happen from a communication, it can only happen when a whole novel communicates itself to me. The Bible – but *all* the Bible – and Homer, and Shakespeare: these are the supreme old novels. These are all things to all men. Which means that in their wholeness they affect the whole man alive, which is the man himself, beyond any part of him. They set the whole tree trembling with a new access of life, they do not just stimulate growth in one direction.

I don't want to grow in any one direction any more. And, if I can help it, I don't want to stimulate anybody else into some particular direction. A particular direction ends in a *cul-de-sac*. We're in a *cul-de-sac* at present.

I don't believe in any dazzling revelation, or in any supreme Word. 'The grass withereth, the flower fadeth, but the Word of the Lord shall stand for ever.' That's the kind of stuff we've drugged ourselves with. As a matter of fact, the grass withereth, but comes up all the greener for that reason, after the rains. The flower fadeth, and therefore the bud opens. But the Word of the Lord, being man-uttered and a mere vibration on the ether, becomes staler and staler, more and more boring, till at last we turn a deaf ear and it ceases to exist, far more finally than any withered grass. It is grass that renews its youth like the eagle, not any Word.

We should ask for no absolutes, or absolute. Once and for all and for ever, let us have done with the ugly imperialism of any absolute. There is no absolute good, there is nothing absolutely right. All things flow and change, and even change is not absolute. The whole is a strange assembly of apparently incongruous parts, slipping past one another.

Me, man alive, I am a very curious assembly of incongruous parts. My yea! of today is oddly different from my yea! of yesterday. My tears of tomorrow will have nothing to do with my tears of a year ago. If the one I love remains unchanged and unchanging, I shall cease to love her. It is only because she changes and startles me into change and defies my inertia, and is herself staggered in her inertia by my changing, that I can continue to love her. If she stayed put, I might as well love the pepper-pot.

In all this change, I maintain a certain integrity. But woe betide me if I try to put my finger on it. If I say of myself, I am this, I am that! – then, if I stick to it, I turn into a stupid fixed thing like a lamp-post. I shall never know wherein lies my integrity, my individuality, my me. I *can* never know it. It is useless to talk about my ego. That only means that I have made up an *idea* of myself, and that I am trying to cut myself out to pattern. Which is no good. You can cut your cloth to fit your coat, but you can't clip bits off your living body, to trim it down to your idea. True, you can put yourself into ideal corsets. But even in ideal corsets, fashions change.

Let us learn from the novel. In the novel, the characters can do nothing but *live*. If they keep on being good, according to pattern, or bad, according to pattern, or even volatile, according to pattern, they cease to live, and the novel falls dead. A character in a novel has got to live, or it is nothing.

We, likewise, in life have got to live, or we are nothing.

What we mean by living is, of course, just as indescribable as what we mean by *being*. Men get ideas into their heads, of what they mean by Life, and they proceed to cut life out to pattern. Sometimes they go into the desert to seek God, sometimes they go into the desert to seek cash, sometimes it is wine, woman, and song, and again it is water, political reform, and votes. You never know what it will be next: from killing your neighbour with hideous bombs and gas that tears the lungs, to supporting a Foundlings Home and preaching infinite Love, and being co-respondent in a divorce.

In all this wild welter, we need some sort of guide. It's no good inventing Thou Shalt Nots!

What then? Turn truly, honourably to the novel, and see wherein you are man alive, and wherein you are dead man in life. You may love a woman as man alive, and you may be making love to a woman as sheer dead man in life. You may eat your dinner as man alive, or as a mere masticating corpse. As man alive you may have a shot at your enemy. But as a ghastly simulacrum of life you may be firing bombs into men who are neither your enemies nor your friends, but just things you are

187

dead to. Which is criminal, when the things happen to be alive.

To be alive, to be man alive, to be whole man alive: that is the point. And at its best, the novel, and the novel supremely, can help you. It can help you not to be dead man in life. So much of a man walks about dead and a carcass in the street and house, to-day: so much of women is merely dead. Like a pianoforte with half the notes mute.

But in the novel you can see, plainly, when the man goes dead, the woman goes inert. You can develop an instinct for life, if you will, instead of a theory of right and wrong, good and bad.

In life, there is right and wrong, good and bad, all the time. But what is right in one case is wrong in another. And in the novel you see one man becoming a corpse, because of his so-called goodness, another going dead because of his so-called wickedness. Right and wrong is an instinct: but an instinct of the whole consciousness in a man, bodily, mental, spiritual at once. And only in the novel are *all* things given full play, or at least, they may be given full play, when we realize that life itself, and not inert safety, is the reason for living. For out of the full play of all things emerges the only thing that is anything, the wholeness of a man, the wholeness of a woman, man alive, and live woman.

# Surgery for the Novel – or a Bomb

*Literary Digest International Book Review*, April 1923; *Phoenix*, 1936

You talk about the future of the baby, little cherub, when he's in the cradle cooing; and it's a romantic, glamorous subject. You also talk, with the parson, about the future of the wicked old grandfather who is at last lying on his death-bed. And there again you have a subject for much vague emotion, chiefly of fear this time.

How do we feel about the novel? Do we bounce with joy thinking of the wonderful novelistic days ahead? Or do we grimly shake our heads and hope the wicked creature will be spared a little longer? Is the novel on his death-bed, old sinner? Or is he just toddling round his cradle, sweet little thing? Let us have another look at him before we decide this rather serious case.

There he is, the monster with many faces, many branches to him, like a tree: the modern novel. And he is almost dual, like Siamese twins. On the one hand, the pale-faced, high-browed, earnest novel, which you have to take seriously; on the other, that smirking, rather plausible hussy, the popular novel.

Let us just for the moment feel the pulses of *Ulysses* and of Miss Dorothy Richardson and M. Marcel Proust, on the earnest side of Briareus; on the other, the throb of *The Sheik* and Mr Zane Grey, and, if you will, Mr Robert Chambers and the rest. Is *Ulysses* in his cradle? Oh, dear! What a grey face! And *Pointed*

*Roofs*, are they a gay little toy for nice little girls? And M. Proust? Alas! You can hear the death-rattle in their throats. They can hear it themselves. They are listening to it with acute interest, trying to discover whether the intervals are minor thirds or major fourths. Which is rather infantile, really.

So there you have the 'serious' novel, dying in a very long-drawn-out fourteen-volume death-agony, and absorbedly, childishly interested in the phenomenon. 'Did I feel a twinge in my little toe, or didn't I?' asks every character of Mr Joyce or of Miss Richardson or M. Proust. Is my aura a blend of frankincense and orange pekoe and boot-blacking, or is it myrrh and bacon-fat and Shetland tweed? The audience round the death-bed gapes for the answer. And when, in a sepulchral tone, the answer comes at length, after hundreds of pages: 'It is none of these, it is abysmal chloro-coryambasis,' the audience quivers all over, and murmurs: 'That's just how I feel myself.'

Which is the dismal, long-drawn-out comedy of the death-bed of the serious novel. It is self-consciousness picked into such fine bits that the bits are most of them invisible, and you have to go by smell. Through thousands and thousands of pages Mr Joyce and Miss Richardson tear themselves to pieces, strip their smallest emotions to the finest threads, till you feel you are sewed inside a wool mattress that is being slowly shaken up, and you are turning to wool along with the rest of the woolliness.

It's awful. And it's childish. It really is childish, after a certain age, to be absorbedly self-conscious. One has to be self-conscious at seventeen: still a little self-conscious at twenty-seven; but if we are going it strong at thirty-seven, then it is a sign of arrested development, nothing else. And if it is still continuing at forty-seven, it is obvious senile precocity.

And there's the serious novel: senile-precocious. Absorbedly, childishly concerned with *what I am*. 'I am this, I am that, I am the other. My reactions are such, and such, and such. And, oh, Lord, if I liked to watch myself closely enough, if I liked to analyse my feelings minutely, as I unbutton my gloves, instead of saying crudely I unbuttoned them, then I could go on to a million pages instead of a thousand. In fact, the more I come to think of it, it is gross, it is uncivilized bluntly to say: I unbuttoned my gloves. After all, the absorbing adventure of it! Which button did I begin with?' etc.

The people in the serious novels are so absorbedly concerned with themselves and what they feel and don't feel, and how they react to every mortal button; and their audience as frenziedly absorbed in the application of the author's discoveries to their own reactions: 'That's me! That's exactly it! I'm just finding myself in this book!' Why, this is more than death-bed, it is almost post-mortem behaviour.

Some convulsion or cataclysm will have to get this serious novel out of its self-consciousness. The last great war made it worse. What's to be done? Because, poor thing, it's really young yet. The novel has never become fully adult. It has never quite grown to years of discretion. It has always youthfully hoped for the best, and felt rather sorry for itself on the last page. Which is just childish. The childishness has become very long-drawn-out. So very many adolescents who drag their adolescence on into their forties and their fifties and their sixties! There needs some sort of surgical operation, somewhere.

Then the popular novels – the *Sheiks* and *Babbitts* and Zane Grey novels. They are just as self-conscious, only they do have more illusions about themselves. The heroines do think they are lovelier, and more fascinating, and purer. The heroes do see themselves more heroic, braver, more chivalrous, more fetching. The mass of the populace 'find themselves' in the popular novels. But nowadays it's a funny sort of self they find. A Sheik with a whip up his sleeve, and a heroine with weals on her back, but adored in the end, adored, the whip out of sight, but the weals still faintly visible.

It's a funny sort of self they discover in the popular novels. And the essential moral of *If Winter Comes*, for example, is so shaky. 'The gooder you are, the worse it is for you, poor you, oh, poor you. Don't you be so blimey good, it's not good enough.' Or *Babbitt*: 'Go on, you make your pile, and then pretend you're too good for it. Put it over the rest of the grabbers that way.

191

They're only pleased with themselves when they've made their pile. You go one better.'

Always the same sort of baking-powder gas to make you rise: the soda counteracting the cream of tartar, and the tartar counteracted by the soda. Sheik heroines, duly whipped, wildly adored. Babbitts with solid fortunes, weeping from self-pity. Winter-Comes heroes as good as pie, hauled off to jail. *Moral*: Don't be too good, because you'll go to jail for it. *Moral*: Don't feel sorry for yourself till you've made your pile and don't need to feel sorry for yourself. *Moral*: Don't let him adore you till he's whipped you into it. Then you'll be partners in mild crime as well as in holy matrimony.

Which again is childish. Adolescence which *can't* grow up. Got into the self-conscious rut and going crazy, quite crazy in it. Carrying on their adolescence into middle age and old age, like the looney Cleopatra in *Dombey and Son*, murmuring 'Rose-coloured curtains' with her dying breath.

The future of the novel? Poor old novel, it's in a rather dirty, messy tight corner. And it's either got to get over the wall or knock a hole through it. In other words, it's got to grow up. Put away childish things like: 'Do I love the girl, or don't I?' – 'Am I pure and sweet, or am I not?' – 'Do I unbutton my right glove first, or my left?' – 'Did my mother ruin my life by refusing to drink the cocoa which my bride had boiled for her?' These questions and their answers don't really interest me any more, though the world still goes sawing them over. I simply don't care for any of these things now, though I used to. The purely emotional and self-analytical stunts are played out in me. I'm finished. I'm deaf to the whole band. But I'm neither *blasé* nor cynical, for all that. I'm just interested in something else.

Supposing a bomb were put under the whole scheme of things, what would we be after? What feelings do we want to carry through into the next epoch? What feelings will carry us through? What is the underlying impulse in us that will provide the motive power for a new state of things, when this democratic-industrial-lovey-dovey-darling-take-me-to-mamma state of things is bust?

*What next?* That's what interests me. 'What now?' is no fun any more.

If you wish to look into the past for what-next books, you can go back to the Greek philosophers. Plato's Dialogues are queer little novels. It seems to me it was the greatest pity in the world, when philosophy and fiction got split. They used to be one, right from the days of myth. Then they went and parted, like a nagging married couple, with Aristotle and Thomas Aquinas and that beastly Kant. So the novel went sloppy, and philosophy went abstract-dry. The two should come together again – in the novel.

You've got to find a new impulse for new things in mankind, and it's really fatal to find it through abstraction. No, no; philosophy and religion, they've both gone too far on the algebraical tack: Let X stand for sheep and Y for goats: then X minus Y equals Heaven, and X plus Y equals Earth, and Y minus X equals Hell. Thank you! But what coloured shirt does X have on?

The novel has a future. It's got to have the courage to tackle new propositions without using abstractions; it's got to present us with new, really new feelings, a whole line of new emotion, which will get us out of the emotional rut. Instead of snivelling about what is and has been, or inventing new sensations in the old line, it's got to break a way through, like a hole in the wall. And the public will scream and say it is sacrilege: because, of course, when you've been jammed for a long time in a tight corner, and you get really used to its stuffiness and its tightness, till you find it suffocatingly cosy; then, of course, you're horrified when you see a new glaring hole in what was your cosy wall. You're horrified. You back away from the cold stream of fresh air as if it were killing you. But gradually, first one and then another of the sheep filters through the gap, and finds a new world outside.

# *From* Study of Thomas Hardy

Written 1914, published in *Phoenix*, 1936

CHAPTER III

*Containing Six Novels and the Real Tragedy*

This is supposed to be a book about the people in Thomas Hardy's novels. But if one wrote everything they give rise to, it would fill the Judgement Book.

One thing about them is that none of the heroes and heroines care very much for money, or immediate self-preservation, and all of them are struggling hard to come into being. What exactly the struggle into being consists in, is the question. But most obviously, from the Wessex novels, the first and chiefest factor is the struggle into love and the struggle with love: by love, meaning the love of a man for a woman and a woman for a man. The *via media* to being, for man or woman, is love, and love alone. Having achieved and accomplished love, then the man passes into the unknown. He has become himself, his tale is told. Of anything that is complete there is no more tale to tell. The tale is about becoming complete, or about the failure to become complete.

It is urged against Thomas Hardy's characters that they do unreasonable things – quite, quite unreasonable things. They are always going off unexpectedly and doing something that nobody would do. That is quite true, and the charge is amusing. These people of Wessex are always bursting suddenly out of bud and taking a wild flight into flower, always shooting suddenly out of a tight convention, a tight, hide-bound cabbage state into some-

194

thing quite madly personal. It would be amusing to count the number of special marriage licences taken out in Hardy's books. Nowhere, except perhaps in Jude, is there the slightest development of personal action in the characters: it is all explosive. Jude, however, does see more or less what he is doing, and acts from choice. He is more consecutive. The rest explode out of the convention. They are people each with a real, vital, potential self, even the apparently wishy-washy heroines of the earlier books, and this self suddenly bursts the shell of manner and convention and commonplace opinion, and acts independently, absurdly, without mental knowledge or acquiescence.

And from such an outburst the tragedy usually develops. For there does exist, after all, the great self-preservation scheme, and in it we must all live. Now to live in it after bursting out of it was the problem these Wessex people found themselves faced with. And they never solved the problem, none of them except the comically, insufficiently treated Ethelberta.

This because they must subscribe to the system in themselves. From the more immediate claims of self-preservation they could free themselves: from money, from ambition for social success. None of the heroes or heroines of Hardy cared much for these things. But there is the greater idea of self-preservation, which is formulated in the State, in the whole modelling of the community. And from this idea, the heroes and heroines of Wessex. like the heroes and heroines of almost anywhere else, could not free themselves. In the long run, the State, the Community, the established form of life remained, remained intact and impregnable, the individual, trying to break forth from it, died of fear, of exhaustion, or of exposure to attacks from all sides, like men who have left the walled city to live outside in the precarious open.

This is the tragedy of Hardy, always the same: the tragedy of those who, more or less pioneers, have died in the wilderness, whither they had escaped for free action, after having left the walled security, and the comparative imprisonment, of the established convention. This is the theme of novel after novel: remain quite within the convention, and you are good, safe, and happy in the long run, though you never have the vivid pang of sympathy on your side: or, on the other hand, be passionate, individual, wilful, you will find the security of the convention a walled prison, you will escape, and you will die, either of your own lack of strength to bear the isolation and the exposure, or by direct revenge from the community, or from both. This is the tragedy, and only this: it is nothing more metaphysical than the division of a man against himself in such a way: first, that he is a member of the community, and must, upon his honour, in no way move to disintegrate the community, either in its moral or its practical form; second, that the convention of the community is a prison to his natural, individual desire, a desire that compels him, whether he feel justified or not to break the bounds of the community, lands him outside the pale, there to stand alone, and say: 'I was right, my desire was real and inevitable; if I was to be myself I must fulfil it, convention or no convention,' or else, there to stand alone, doubting, and saying: 'Was I right, was I wrong? If I was wrong, oh, let me die!' – in which case he courts death.

The growth and the development of this tragedy, the deeper and deeper realization of this division and this problem, the coming towards some conclusion, is the one theme of the Wessex novels.

And therefore the books must be taken chronologically, to reveal the development and to advance towards the conclusion.

1. *Desperate Remedies.*

Springrove, the dull hero, fast within convention, dare not tell Cytherea that he is already engaged, and thus prepares the complication. Manston, represented as fleshily passionate, breaks the convention and commits murder, which is very extreme, under compulsion of his desire for Cytherea. He is aided by the darkly passionate, lawless Miss Aldclyffe. He and Miss Aldclyffe meet death, and Springrove and Cytherea are united to happiness and success.

2. *Under the Greenwood Tree.*

After a brief excursion from the beaten track in the pursuit of social ambition and satisfaction of the imagination, figured by the Clergyman, Fancy, the little school-mistress, returns to Dick, renounces imagination, and settles down to steady, solid, physically satisfactory married life, and all is as it should be. But Fancy will carry in her heart all her life many unopened buds that will die unflowered; and Dick will probably have a bad time of it.

3. *A Pair of Blue Eyes.*

Elfride breaks down in her attempt to jump the first little hedge of convention, when she comes back after running away with Stephen. She cannot stand even a little alone. Knight, his conventional ideas backed up by selfish instinct, cannot endure Elfride when he thinks she is not virgin, though now she loves him beyond bounds. She submits to him, and owns the conventional idea entirely right, even whilst she is innocent. An aristocrat walks off with her whilst the two men hesitate, and she, poor innocent victim of passion not vital enough to overthrow the most banal conventional ideas, lies in a bright coffin, while the three confirmed lovers mourn, and say how great the tragedy is.

4. *Far from the Madding Crowd.*

The unruly Bathsheba, though almost pledged to Farmer Boldwood, a ravingly passionate, middle-aged bachelor pretendant, who has suddenly started in mad pursuit of some unreal conception of woman, personified in Bathsheba, lightly runs off and marries Sergeant Troy, an illegitimate aristocrat, unscrupulous and yet sensitive in taking his pleasures. She loves Troy, he does not love her. All the time she is loved faithfully and persistently by the good Gabriel, who is like a dog that watches the bone and bides the time. Sergeant Troy treats Bathsheba badly, never loves her, though he is the only man in the book who knows anything about her. Her pride helps her to recover. Troy is killed by Boldwood; exit the unscrupulous, but discriminative, almost cynical young soldier and the mad, middle-aged pursuer of the Fata Morgana; enter the good, steady Gabriel, who marries Bathsheba because he will make her a good husband, and the flower of imaginative first love is dead for her with Troy's scorn of her.

5. *The Hand of Ethelberta.*

Ethelberta, a woman of character and of brilliant parts, sets out in pursuit of social success, finds that Julius, the only man she is inclined to love, is too small for her, hands him over to the good little Picotee, and she herself, sacrificing almost cynically what is called her heart, marries the old scoundrelly Lord Mountclerc, runs him and his estates and governs well, a sound, strong pillar of established society, now she has nipped off the bud of her heart. Moral: it is easier for the butler's daughter to marry a lord than to find a husband with her love, if she be an exceptional woman.

*The Hand of Ethelberta* is the one almost cynical comedy. It marks the zenith of a certain feeling in the Wessex novels, the zenith of the feeling that the best thing to do is to kick out the craving for 'Love' and substitute commonsense, leaving sentiment to the minor characters.

This novel is a shrug of the shoulders, and a last taunt to hope, it is the end of the happy endings, except where sanity and a little cynicism again appear in *The Trumpet Major*, to bless where they despise. It is the hard, resistant, ironical announcement of personal failure, resistant and half-grinning. It gives way to violent, angry passions and real tragedy, real killing of beloved people, self-killing. Till now, only Elfride among the beloved, has been killed; the good men have always come out on top.

6. *The Return of the Native*.

This is the first tragic and important novel. Eustacia, dark, wild, passionate, quite conscious of her desires and inheriting no tradition which would make her ashamed of them, since she is of a novelistic Italian birth, loves, first, the unstable Wildeve, who does not satisfy her, then casts him aside for the newly returned Clym, whom she marries. What does she want? She does not know, but it is evidently some form of self-realization: she wants to be herself, to attain herself. But she does not know how, by what means, so romantic imagination says, Paris and the *beau monde*. As if that would have stayed her unsatisfaction.

Clym has found out the vanity of Paris and the *beau monde*. What, then, does he want? He does not know; his imagination tells him he wants to serve the moral system of the community, since the material system is despicable. He wants to teach little Egdon boys in school. There is as much vanity in this, easily, as in Eustacia's Paris. For what is the moral system but the ratified form of the material system? What is Clym's altruism but a deep, very subtle cowardice, that makes him shirk his own being whilst apparently acting nobly; which makes him choose to improve mankind rather than to struggle at the quick of himself into being. He is not able to undertake his own soul, so he will take a commission for society to enlighten the souls of others. It is a subtle equivocation. Thus both Eustacia and he sidetrack from themselves, and each leaves the other unconvinced, unsatisfied, unrealized. Eustacia, because she moves outside the convention, must die; Clym, because he identified himself with the community, is transferred from Paris to preaching. He had never become an integral man, because when faced with the demand to produce himself, he remained under cover of the community and excused by his altruism.

His remorse over his mother is adulterated with sentiment; it is exaggerated by the push of tradition behind it. Even in this he does not ring true. He is always according to pattern, producing his feelings more or less on demand, according to the accepted standard. Practically never is he able to act or even feel in his original self: he is always according to the convention. His punishment is his final loss of all his original self: he is left preaching, out of sheer emptiness.

Thomasin and Venn have nothing in them turbulent enough to push them to the bounds of the convention. There is always room for them inside. They are genuine people, and they get the prize within the walls.

Wildeve, shifty and unhappy, attracted always from outside and never driven from within, can neither stand with nor without the established system. He cares nothing for it, because he is unstable, has no positive being. He is an eternal assumption.

The other victim, Clym's mother, is the crashing-down of one of the old, rigid pillars of the system. The pressure on her is too great. She is weakened from the inside also, for her nature is non-conventional; it cannot own the bounds.

So, in this book, all the exceptional people, those with strong feelings and unusual characters, are reduced; only those remain who are steady and genuine, if commonplace. Let a man will for himself, and he is destroyed. He must will according to the established system.

The real sense of tragedy is got from the setting. What is the great, tragic power in the book? It is Egdon Heath. And who are the real spirits of the Heath? First, Eustacia, then Clym's mother, then Wildeve. The natives have little or nothing in common with the place.

What is the real stuff of tragedy in the book? It is the Heath. It is the primitive, primal earth, where the instinctive life heaves up. There, in the deep, rude stirring of the instincts, there was the reality that worked the tragedy. Close to the body of things, there can be heard the stir that makes us and destroys us. The heath heaved with raw instinct. Egdon, whose dark soil was strong and crude and organic as the body of a beast. Out of the body of this crude earth are born Eustacia, Wildeve, Mistress Yeobright, Clym, and all the others. They are one year's accidental crop. What matters if some are drowned or dead, and others preaching or married: what matter, any more than the withering heath, the reddening berries, the seedy furze, and the dead fern of one autumn of Egdon? The Heath persists. Its body is strong and fecund, it will bear many more crops beside this. Here is the sombre, latent power that will go on producing, no matter what happens to the product. Here is the deep, black source from whence all these little contents of lives are drawn. And the contents of the small lives are spilled and wasted. There is savage satisfaction in it: for so much more remains to come, such a black, powerful fecundity is working there that what does it matter?

Three people die and are taken back into the Heath; they mingle their strong earth again with its powerful soil, having been broken off at their stem. It is very good. Not Egdon is futile, sending forth life on the powerful heave of passion. It cannot be futile, for it is eternal. What is futile is the purpose of man.

Man has a purpose which he has divorced from the passionate purpose that issued him out of the earth into being. The Heath threw forth its shaggy heather and furze and fern, clean into being. It threw forth Eustacia and Wildeve and Mistress Yeobright

From Study of Thomas Hardy

and Clym, but to what purpose? Eustacia thought she wanted the hats and bonnets of Paris. Perhaps she was right. The heavy, strong soil of Egdon, breeding original native beings, is under Paris as well as under Wessex, and Eustacia sought herself in the gay city. She thought life there, in Paris, would be tropical, and all her energy and passion out of Egdon would there come into handsome flower. And if Paris real had been Paris as she imagined it, no doubt she was right, and her instinct was soundly expressed. But Paris real was not Eustacia's imagined Paris. Where was her imagined Paris, the place where her powerful nature could come to blossom? Beside some strong-passioned, unconfined man, her mate.

Which mate Clym might have been. He was born out of passionate Egdon to live as a passionate being whose strong feelings moved him ever further into being. But quite early his life became narrowed down to a small purpose: he must of necessity go into business, and submit his whole being, body and soul as well as mind, to the business and to the greater system it represented. His feelings, that should have produced the man, were suppressed and contained, he worked according to a system imposed from without. The dark struggle of Egdon, a struggle into being as the furze struggles into flower, went on in him, but could not burst the enclosure of the idea, the system which contained him. Impotent to *be*, he must transform himself, and live in an abstraction, in a generalization, he must identify himself with the system. He must live as Man or Humanity, or as the Community, or as Society, or as Civilization.

An inner strenuousness was preying on his outer symmetry, and they rated his look as singular. . . . His countenance was overlaid with legible meanings. Without being thought-worn, he yet had certain marks derived from a perception of his surroundings, such as are not infrequently found on man at the end of the four or five years of endeavour which follow the close of placid pupilage. He already showed that thought is a disease of the flesh, and indirectly bore evidence that ideal physical beauty is incompatible with emotional development and a full recognition of the coil of things. Mental luminousness must be fed with the oil of life, even if there is already a physical seed for it; and the pitiful sight of two demands on one supply was just showing itself here.

But did the face of Clym show that thought is a disease of flesh, or merely that in his case a dis-ease, an un-ease, of flesh produced thought? One does not catch thought like a fever: one produces it. If it be in any way a disease of flesh, it is rather the rash that indicates the disease than the disease itself. The 'inner strenuousness' of Clym's nature was not fighting against his physical symmetry, but against the limits imposed on his physical movement. By nature, as a passionate, violent product of Egdon, he should have loved and suffered in flesh and in soul from love, long before this age. He should have lived and moved and had his being, whereas he had only his business, and afterwards his inactivity. His years of pupilage were past, 'he was one of whom something original was expected', yet he continued in pupilage. For he produced nothing original in being or in act, and certainly no original thought. None of his ideas were original. Even he himself was not original. He was over-taught, had become an echo. His life had been arrested, and his activity turned into repetition. Far from being emotionally developed, he was emotionally undeveloped, almost entirely. Only his mental faculties were developed. And, hid, his emotions were obliged to work according to the label he put upon them: a ready-made label.

Yet he remained for all that an original, the force of life was in him, however much he frustrated and suppressed its natural movement. 'As is usual with bright natures, the deity that lies ignominiously chained within an ephemeral human carcass shone out of him like a ray.' But was the deity chained within his ephemeral human carcass, or within his limited human consciousness? Was it his blood, which rose dark and potent out of Egdon, which hampered and confined the deity, or was it his mind, that house built of extraneous knowledge and guarded by his will, which formed the prison?

He came back to Egdon – what for? To re-unite himself with the strong, free flow of life that rose out of Egdon as from a source? No – 'to preach to the Egdon eremites that they might rise to a serene comprehensiveness without going through the process of enriching themselves'. As if the Egdon eremites had not already far more serene comprehensiveness than ever he had himself, rooted as they were in the soil of all things, and living from the root! What did it matter how they enriched themselves, so long as they kept this strong, deep root in the primal soil, so long as their instincts moved out to action and to expression? The system was big enough for them, and had no power over their instincts. They should have taught him rather than he them.

And Egdon made him marry Eustacia. Here was action and life, here was a move into being on his part. But as soon as he got her, she became an idea to him, she had to fit in his system of ideas. According to his way of living, he knew her already, she was labelled and classed and fixed down. He had got into this way of living, and he could not get out of it. He had identified himself with the system, and he could not extricate himself. He did not know that Eustacia had her being beyond his. He did not know that she existed untouched by his system and his mind, where no system had sway and where no consciousness had risen to the surface. He did not know that she was Egdon, the powerful, eternal origin seething with production. He thought he knew. Egdon to him was the tract of common land, producing familiar rough herbage, and having some few unenlightened inhabitants. So he skated over heaven and hell, and having made a map of the surface, thought he knew all. But underneath and among his mapped world, the eternal powerful fecundity worked on heedless of him and his arrogance. His preaching, his superficiality made no difference. What did it matter if he had calculated a moral chart from the surface of life? Could that affect life, any more than a chart of the heavens affects the stars, affects the whole stellar universe which exists beyond our knowledge? Could the sound of his words affect the working of the body of Egdon, where in the unfathomable womb was begot and conceived all that would ever come forth? Did not his own heart beat far removed and immune from his thinking and talking? Had he been able to put even his own heart's mysterious resonance upon his map, from which he charted the course of lives in his moral system? And how much more completely, then, had he left out, in utter ignorance, the dark, powerful source whence all things rise into being, whence they will always continue to rise, to struggle forward to further being? A little of the static surface he could see, and map out. Then he thought his map was the thing itself. How blind he was, how utterly blind to the tremendous movement carrying and producing the surface. He did not know that the greater part of every life is underground, like roots in the dark in contact with the beyond. He preached, thinking lives could be moved like hen-houses from here to there. His blindness indeed brought on the calamity. But what matter if Eustacia or Wildeve or Mrs Yeobright died: what matter if he himself became a mere rattle of repetitive words – what did it matter? It was regrettable; no more. Egdon, the primal impulsive body, would go on producing all that was to be produced, eternally, though the will of man should destroy the blossom yet in bud, over and over again. At last he must learn what it is to be at one, in his mind and will, with the primal impulses that rise in him. Till then, let him perish or preach. The great reality on which the little tragedies enact themselves cannot be detracted from. The will and words which militate against it are the only vanity.

This is a constant revelation in Hardy's novels: that there exists a great background, vital and vivid, which matters more than the people who move upon it. Against the background of dark, passionate Egdon, of the leafy, sappy passion and sentiment of the woodlands, of the unfathomed stars, is drawn the lesser scheme of lives: *The Return of the Native, The Woodlanders,* or *Two on a Tower.* Upon the vast, incomprehensible pattern of some primal morality greater than ever the human mind can grasp, is drawn the little, pathetic pattern of man's moral life and struggle, pathetic, almost ridiculous. The little fold of law and order, the little walled city within which man has to defend himself from the waste enormity of nature, becomes always too small, and the pioneers venturing out with the code of the walled city upon them, die in the bonds of that code, free and yet unfree, preaching the walled city and looking to the waste.

This is the wonder of Hardy's novels, and gives them their

beauty. The vast, unexplored morality of life itself, what we call the immorality of nature, surrounds us in its eternal incomprehensibility, and in its midst goes on the little human morality play, with its queer frame of morality and its mechanized movement; seriously, portentously, till some one of the protagonists chances to look out of the charmed circle, weary of the stage, to look into the wilderness raging round. Then he is lost, his little drama falls to pieces, or becomes mere repetition, but the stupendous theatre outside goes on enacting its own incomprehensible drama, untouched. There is this quality in almost all Hardy's work, and this is the magnificent irony it all contains, the challenge, the contempt. Not the deliberate ironies, little tales of widows or widowers, contain the irony of human life as we live it in our self-aggrandized gravity, but the big novels, *The Return of the Native*, and the others.

And this is the quality Hardy shares with the great writers, Shakespeare or Sophocles or Tolstoy, this setting behind the small action of his protagonists the terrific action of unfathomed nature; setting a smaller system of morality, the one grasped and formulated by the human consciousness within the vast, uncomprehended and incomprehensible morality of nature or of life itself, surpassing human consciousness. The difference is, that whereas in Shakespeare or Sophocles the greater, uncomprehended morality, or fate, is actively transgressed and gives active punishment, in Hardy and Tolstoy the lesser, human morality, the mechanical system is actively transgressed, and holds, and punishes the protagonist, whilst the greater morality is only passively, negatively transgressed, it is represented merely as being present in background, in scenery, not taking any active part, having no direct connexion with the protagonist. Oedipus, Hamlet, Macbeth set themselves up against, or find themselves set up against, the unfathomed moral forces of nature, and out of this unfathomed force comes their death. Whereas Anna Karenina, Eustacia, Tess, Sue, and Jude find themselves up against the established system of human government and morality, they cannot detach themselves, and are brought down. Their real tragedy is that they are unfaithful to the greater unwritten morality, which would have bidden Anna Karenina be patient and wait until she, by virtue of greater right, could take what she needed from society; would have bidden Vronsky detach himself from the system, become an individual, creating a new colony of morality with Anna; would have bidden Eustacia fight Clym for his own soul, and Tess take and claim her Angel, since she had the greater light; would have bidden Jude and Sue endure for very honour's sake, since one must bide by the best that one has known, and not succumb to the lesser good.

Had Oedipus, Hamlet, Macbeth been weaker, less full of real, potent life, they would have made no tragedy; they would have comprehended and contrived some arrangement of their affairs, sheltering in the human morality from the great stress and attack of the unknown morality. But being, as they are, men to the fullest capacity, when they find themselves, daggers drawn, with the very forces of life itself, they can only fight till they themselves are killed, since the morality of life, the greater morality, is eternally unalterable and invincible. It can be dodged for some time, but not opposed. On the other hand, Anna, Eustacia, Tess or Sue – what was there in their position that was necessarily tragic? Necessarily painful it was, but they were not at war with God, only with Society. Yet they were all cowed by the mere judgement of man upon them, and all the while by their own souls they were right. And the judgement of men killed them, not the judgement of their own souls or the judgement of Eternal God.

Which is the weakness of modern tragedy, where transgression against the social code is made to bring destruction, as though the social code worked our irrevocable fate. Like Clym, the map appears to us more real than the land. Shortsighted almost to blindness, we pore over the chart, map out journeys, and confirm them: and we cannot see life itself giving us the lie the whole time.

*From* CHAPTER V

*Work and the Angel and the Unbegotten Hero*

We start the wrong way round: thinking, by learning what we are not, to know what we as individuals are: whereas the whole of the human consciousness contains, as we know, not a tithe of what *is*, and therefore it is hopeless to proceed by a method of elimination; and thinking, by discovering the motion life has made, to be able therefrom to produce the motion it will make: whereas we know that, in life, the new motion is not the resultant of the old, but something quite new, quite other, according to our perception.

So we struggle mechanically, unformed, unbegotten, unborn, repeating some old process of life, unable to become ourselves, unable to produce anything new.

Looking over the Hardy novels, it is interesting to see which of the heroes one would call a distinct individuality, more or less achieved, which an unaccomplished potential individuality, and which an impure, unindividualized life embedded in the matrix, either achieving its own lower degree of distinction, or not achieving it.

In *Desperate Remedies* there are scarcely any people at all, particularly when the plot is working. The tiresome part about Hardy is that, so often, he will neither write a morality play nor a novel. The people of the first book, as far as the plot is concerned, are not people: they are the heroine, faultless and white; the hero, with a small spot on his whiteness; the villainess, red and black, but more red than black; the villain, black and red; the Murderer, aided by the Adulteress, obtains power over the Virgin, who, rescued at the last moment by the Virgin Knight, evades the evil clutch. Then the Murderer, overtaken by vengeance, is put to death, whilst Divine Justice descends upon the Adulteress. Then the Virgin unites with the Virgin Knight, and receives Divine Blessing.

That is a morality play, and if the morality were vigorous and original, all well and good. But, between-whiles, we see that the Virgin is being played by a nice, rather ordinary girl.

In *The Laodicean*, there is all the way through a *prédilection d'artiste* for the aristrocrat, and all the way through a moral condemnation of him, a substituting the middle or lower-class personage with bourgeois virtues into his place. This was the root of Hardy's pessimism. Not until he comes to Tess and Jude does he ever sympathize with the aristocrat – unless it be in *The Mayor of Casterbridge*, and then he sympathizes only to slay. He always, always represents them the same, as having some vital weakness, some radical ineffectuality. From first to last it is the same.

Miss Aldclyffe and Manston, Elfride and the sickly lord she married, Troy and Farmer Boldwood, Eustacia Vye and Wildeve, de Stancy in *The Laodicean*, Lady Constantine in *Two on a Tower*, the Mayor of Casterbridge and Lucetta, Mrs Charmond and Dr Fitzpiers in *The Woodlanders*, Tess and Alec d'Urberville, and, though different, Jude. There is also the blond, passionate, yielding man: Sergeant Troy, Wildeve, and, in spirit, Jude.

These are all, in their way, the aristocrat-characters of Hardy. They must every one die, every single one.

Why has Hardy this *prédilection d'artiste* for the aristocrat, and why, at the same time, this moral antagonism to him?

It is fairly obvious in *The Laodicean*, a book where, the spirit being small, the complaint is narrow. The heroine, the daughter of a famous railway engineer, lives in the castle of the old de Stancys. She sighs, wishing she were of the de Stancy line: the tombs and portraits have a spell over her. 'But,' says the hero to her, 'have you forgotten your father's line of ancestry: Archimedes, Newcomen, Watt, Tylford, Stephenson?' – 'But I have a *prédilection d'artiste* for ancestors of the other sort,' sighs Paula. And the hero despairs of impressing her with the list of his architect ancestors: Phidias, Ictinus and Callicrates, Chersiphron, Vitruvius, Wilars of Cambray, William of Wykeham. He deplores her marked preference for an 'animal pedigree'.

But what is this 'animal pedigree'? If a family pedigree of her ancestors, working-men and burghers, had been kept, Paula would not have gloried in it, animal though it were. Hers was a *prédilection d'artiste*.

And this because the aristocrat alone has occupied a position where he could afford to *be*, to be himself, to create himself, to live as himself. That is his eternal fascination. This is why the preference for him is a *prédilection d'artiste*. The preference for the architect line would be a *prédilection de savant*, the preference for the engineer pedigree would be a *prédilection d'economiste.*

The *prédilection d'artiste* – Hardy has it strongly, and it is rooted deeply in every imaginative human being. The glory of mankind has been to produce lives, to produce vivid, independent, individual men, not buildings or engineering works or even art, not even the public good. The glory of mankind is not in a host of secure, comfortable, law-abiding citizens, but in the few more fine, clear lives, beings, individuals, distinct, detached, single as may be from the public.

And these the artist of all time has chosen. Why, then, must the aristocrat always be condemned to death, in Hardy? Has the community come to consciousness in him, as in the French Revolutionaries, determined to destroy all that is not the average? Certainly in the Wessex novels, all but the average people die. But why? Is there the germ of death in these more single, distinguished people, or has the artist himself a bourgeois taint, a jealous vindictiveness that will now take revenge, now that the community, the average, has gained power over the aristocrat, the exception?

It is evident that both is true. Starting with the bourgeois morality, Hardy makes every exceptional person a villain, all exceptional or strong individual traits he holds up as weaknesses or wicked faults. So in *Desperate Remedies, Under the Greenwood Tree, Far from the Madding Crowd, The Hand of Ethelberta, The Return of the Native* (but in *The Trumpet-Major* there is an ironical dig in the ribs to this civic communial morality), *The Laodicean, Two on a Tower, The Mayor of Casterbridge,* and *Tess,* in steadily weakening degree. The blackest villain is Manston, the next, perhaps, Troy, the next Eustacia, and Wildeve, always becoming less villainous and more human. The first show of real sympathy, nearly conquering the bourgeois or commune morality, is for Eustacia, whilst the dark villain is becoming merely a weak, pitiable person in Dr Fitzpiers. In *The Mayor of Casterbridge* the dark villain is already almost the hero. There is a lapse in the maudlin, weak but not wicked Dr Fitzpiers, duly condemned. Alec d'Urberville is not unlikable, and Jude is a complete tragic hero, at once the old Virgin Knight and Dark Villain.

The condemnation gradually shifts over from the dark villain to the blond bourgeois virgin hero, from Alec d'Urberville to Angel Clare, till in Jude they are united and loved, though the preponderance is of a dark villain, now dark, beloved, passionate hero. The condemnation shifts over at last from the dark villain to the white virgin, the bourgeois in soul: from Arabella to Sue. Infinitely more subtle and sad is the condemnation at the end, but there it is: the virgin knight is hated with intensity, yet still loved; the white virgin, the beloved, is the arch-sinner against life at last, and the last note of hatred is against her.

It is a complete and devastating shift-over, it is a complete *volte-face* of moralities. Black does not become white, but it takes white's place as good; white remains white, but it is found bad. The old, communal morality is like a leprosy, a white sickness: the old, anti-social, individualist morality is alone on the side of life and health.

But yet, the aristocrat must die, all the way through: even Jude. Was the germ of death in him at the start? Or was he merely at outs with his times, the times of the Average in triumph? Would Manston, Troy, Farmer Boldwood, Eustacia, de Stancy, Henchard, Alec d'Urberville, Jude have been real heroes in heroic times, without tragedy? It seems as if Manston, Boldwood, Eustacia, Henchard, Alec d'Urberville, and almost Jude, might have been. In an heroic age they might have lived and more or less triumphed. But Troy, Wildeve, de Stancy, Fitzpiers, and Jude have something fatal in them. There is a rottenness at the core of them. The failure, the misfortune, or the tragedy, whichever it may be, was inherent in them: as it was in Elfride, Lady Constantine, Marty South in *The Woodlanders*, and Tess. They have all passionate natures, and in them all failure is inherent.

So that we have, of men, the noble Lord in *A Pair of Blue Eyes*, Sergeant Troy, Wildeve, de Stancy, Fitzpiers, and Jude, all passionate, aristocratic males, doomed by their very being, to tragedy, or to misfortune in the end.

Of the same class among women are Elfride, Lady Constantine, Marty South, and Tess, all aristocratic, passionate, yet necessarily unfortunate females.

We have also, of men, Manston, Farmer Boldwood, Henchard, Alec d'Urberville, and perhaps Jude, all passionate, aristocratic males, who fell before the weight of the average, the lawful crowd, but who, in more primitive times, would have formed romantic rather than tragic figures.

Of women in the same class are Miss Aldclyffe, Eustacia, Lucetta, Mrs Charmond.

The third class, of bourgeois or average hero, whose purpose is to live and have his being in the community, contains the successful hero of *Desperate Remedies*, the unsuccessful but not very much injured two heroes of *A Pair of Blue Eyes*, the successful Gabriel Oak, the unsuccessful, left-preaching Clym, the unsuccessful but not very much injured astronomer of *Two on a Tower*, the successful Scotchman of Casterbridge, the unsuccessful and expired Giles Winterborne of *The Woodlanders*, the arch-type, Angel Clare, and perhaps a little of Jude.

The companion women to these men are: the heroine of *Desperate Remedies*, Bathsheba, Thomasin, Paula, Henchard's daughter, Grace in *The Woodlanders*, and Sue.

This, then, is the moral conclusion drawn from the novels:

1. The physical individual is in the end an inferior thing which must fall before the community: Manston, Henchard, etc.

2. The physical and spiritual individualist is a fine thing which must fall because of its own isolation, because it is a sport, not in the true line of life: Jude, Tess, Lady Constantine.

3. The physical individualist and spiritual bourgeois or communist is a thing, finally, of ugly, undeveloped, non-distinguished or perverted physical instinct, and must fall physically. Sue, Angel Clare, Clym, Knight. It remains, however, fitted into the community.

4. The undistinguished, bourgeois or average being with average or civic virtues usually succeeds in the end. If he fails, he is left practically uninjured. If he expire during probation, he has flowers on his grave.

By individualist is meant, not a selfish or greedy person, anxious to satisfy appetites, but a man of distinct being, who must act in his own particular way to fulfil his own individual nature. He is a man who, being beyond the average, chooses to rule his own life to his own completion, and as such is an aristocrat.

The artist always has a predilection for him. But Hardy, like Tolstoy, is forced in the issue always to stand with the community in condemnation of the aristocrat. He cannot help himself, but must stand with the average against the exception, he must, in his ultimate judgement, represent the interests of humanity, or the community as a whole, and rule out the individual interest.

To do this, however, he must go against himself. His private sympathy is always with the individual against the community: as is the case with the artist. Therefore he will create a more or less blameless individual and, making him seek his own fulfilment, his highest aim, will show him destroyed by the community, or by that in himself which represents the community, or by some close embodiment of the civic idea. Hence the pessimism. To do this, however, he must select his individual with a definite weakness, a certain coldness of temper, inelastic, a certain inevitable and inconquerable adhesion to the community.

This is obvious in Troy, Clym, Tess, and Jude. They have naturally distinct individuality but, as it were, a weak life-flow, so that they cannot break away from the old adhesion, they cannot separate themselves from the mass which bore them, they cannot detach themselves from the common. Therefore they are pathetic rather than tragic figures. They have not the necessary strength: the question of their unfortunate end is begged in the beginning.

Whereas Oedipus or Agamemnon or Clytemnestra or Orestes, or Macbeth or Hamlet or Lear, these are destroyed by their own conflicting passions. Out of greed for adventure, a desire to be off, Agamemnon sacrifices Iphigenia: moreover he has his love-affairs outside Troy: and this brings on him death from the mother of his daughter, and from his pledged wife. Which is the working of the natural law. Hamlet, a later Orestes, is commanded by the Erinyes of his father to kill his mother and his uncle: but his maternal filial feeling tears him. It is almost the same tragedy as Orestes, without any goddess or god to grant peace.

In these plays, conventional morality is transcended. The action is between the great, single, individual forces in the nature of Man, not between the dictates of the community and the original passion. The Commandment says: 'Thou shalt not kill.' But doubtless Macbeth had killed many a man who was in his way. Certainly Hamlet suffered no qualms about killing the old man behind the curtain. Why should he? But when Macbeth killed Duncan, he divided himself in twain, into two hostile parts. It was all in his own soul and blood: it was nothing outside himself: as it was, really, with Clym, Troy, Tess, Jude. Troy would probably have been faithful to his little unfortunate person, had she been a lady, and had he not felt himself cut off from society in his very being, whilst all the time he cleaved to it. Tess allowed herself to be condemned, and asked for punishment from Angel Clare. Why? She had done nothing particularly, or at least irrevocably, unnatural, were her life young and strong. But she sided with the community's condemnation of her. And almost the bitterest, most pathetic, deepest part of Jude's misfortune was his failure to obtain admission to Oxford, his failure to gain his place and standing in the world's knowledge, in the world's work.

There is a lack of sternness, there is a hesitating betwixt life and public opinion, which diminishes the Wessex novels from the rank of pure tragedy. It is not so much the eternal, immutable laws of being which are transgressed, it is not that vital life-forces are set in conflict with each other, bringing almost inevitable tragedy – yet not necessarily death, as we see in the most splendid Aeschylus. It is, in Wessex, that the individual succumbs to what is in its shallowest, public opinion, in its deepest, the human compact by which we live together, to form a community.

CHAPTER IX

*A Nos Moutons*

Most fascinating in all artists is this antinomy between Law and Love, between the Flesh and the Spirit, between the Father and the Son.

For the moralist it is easy. He can insist on that aspect of the Law or Love which is in the immediate line of development for his age, and he can sternly and severely exclude or suppress all the rest.

So that all morality is of temporary value, useful to its times. But Art must give a deeper satisfaction. It must give fair play all round.

Yet every work of art adheres to some system of morality. But if it be really a work of art, it must contain the essential criticism on the morality to which it adheres. And hence the antinomy, hence the conflict necessary to every tragic conception.

The degree to which the system of morality, or the metaphysic, of any work of art is submitted to criticism within the work of art makes the lasting value and satisfaction of that work. Aeschylus, having caught the oriental idea of Love, correcting the tremendous Greek conception of the Law with this new idea, produces the intoxicating satisfaction of the Orestean trilogy. The Law, and Love, they are here the Two-in-One in all their magnificence. But Euripides, with his aspiration towards Love, Love the supreme, and his almost hatred of the Law, Law the Triumphant but Base Closer of Doom, is less satisfactory, because of the very fact that he holds Love always Supreme, and yet must endure the chagrin of seeing Love perpetually transgressed and overthrown. So he makes his tragedy: the higher thing eternally pulled down by the lower. And this unfairness in the use of terms, higher and lower, but above all, the unfairness of showing Love always violated and suffering, never supreme and triumphant, makes us disbelieve Euripides in the end. For we have to bring in pity, we must admit that Love is at a fundamental disadvantage before the Law, and cannot therefore ever hold its own. Which is weak philosophy.

If Aeschylus had a metaphysic to his art, this metaphysic is that Love and Law are Two, eternally in conflict, and eternally being reconciled. This is the tragic significance of Aeschylus.

But the metaphysic of Euripides is that the Law and Love are two eternally in conflict, and unequally matched, so that Love must always be borne down. In Love a man shall only suffer. There is also a Reconciliation, otherwise Euripides were not so great. But there is always the unfair matching, this disposition insisted on, which at last leaves one cold and unbelieving.

The moments of pure satisfaction come in the choruses, in the pure lyrics, when Love is put into true relations with the Law, apart from knowledge, transcending knowledge, transcending the metaphysic, where the aspiration to Love meets the acknowledgement of the Law in a consummate marriage, for the moment.

Where Euripides adheres to his metaphysic, he is unsatisfactory. Where he transcends his metaphysic, he gives that supreme equilibrium wherein we know satisfaction.

The adherence to a metaphysic does not necessarily give artistic form. Indeed the over-strong adherence to a metaphysic usually destroys any possibility of artistic form. Artistic form is a revelation of the two principles of Love and the Law in a state of conflict and yet reconciled: pure motion struggling against and yet reconciled with the Spirit: active force meeting and overcoming and yet not overcoming inertia. It is the conjunction of the two which makes form. And since the two must always meet under fresh conditions, form must always be different. Each work of art has its own form, which has no relation to any other form. When a young painter studies an old master, he studies, not the form, that is an abstraction which does not exist: he studies maybe the method of the old great artist: but he studies chiefly to understand how the old great artist suffered in himself the conflict of Love and Law, and brought them to a reconciliation. Apart from artistic method, it is not Art that the young man is studying, but the State of Soul of the great old artist, so that he, the young artist, may understand his own soul and gain a reconciliation between the aspiration and the resistant.

It is most wonderful in poetry, this sense of conflict contained within a reconciliation:

> Hail to thee, blithe Spirit!
>     Bird thou never wert,
> That from Heaven, or near it,
>     Pourest thy full heart
> In profuse strains of unpremeditated art.

215

Shelley wishes to say, the skylark is a pure, untrammelled spirit, a pure motion. But the very 'Bird thou never wert' admits that the skylark *is* in very fact a bird, a concrete, momentary thing. If the line ran, 'Bird though never art', that would spoil it all. Shelley wishes to say, the song is poured out of heaven: but 'or near it', he admits. There is the perfect relation between heaven and earth. And the last line is the tumbling sound of a lark's singing, the real Two-in-One.

The very adherence to rhyme and regular rhythm is a concession to the Law, a concession to the body, to the being and requirements of the body. They are an admission of the living, positive inertia which is the other half of life, other than the pure will to motion. In this consummation, they are the resistance and response of the Bride in the arms of the Bridegroom. And according as the Bride and Bridegroom come closer together, so is the response and resistance more fine, indistinguishable, so much the more, in this act of consummation, is the movement that of Two-in-One, indistinguishable each from the other, and not the movement of two brought together clumsily.

So that in Swinburne, where almost all is concession to the body, so that the poetry becomes almost a sensation and not an experience or a consummation, justifying Spinoza's 'Amor est titillatio, concomitante idea causae externae', we find continual adherence to the body, to the Rose, to the Flesh, the physical in everything, in the sea, in the marshes; there is an overbalance in the favour of Supreme Law; Love is not Love, but passion, part of the Law; there is no Love, there is only Supreme Law. And the poet sings the Supreme Law to gain rebalance in himself, for he hovers always on the edge of death, of Not-Being, he is always out of reach of the Law, bodiless, in the faintness of Love that has triumphed and denied the Law, in the dread of an over-developed, over-sensitive soul which exists always on the point of dissolution from the body.

But he is not divided against himself. It is the novelists and dramatists who have the hardest task in reconciling their metaphysic, their theory of being and knowing, with their living sense of being. Because a novel is a microcosm, and because man in

viewing the universe must view it in the light of a theory, therefore every novel must have the background or the structural
skeleton of some theory of being, some metaphysic. But the
metaphysic must always subserve the artistic purpose beyond the
artist's conscious aim. Otherwise the novel becomes a treatise.

And the danger is, that a man shall make himself a metaphysic
to excuse or cover his own faults or failure. Indeed, a sense of
fault or failure is the usual cause of a man's making himself a
metaphysic, to justify himself.

Then, having made himself a metaphysic of self-justification,
or a metaphysic of self-denial, the novelist proceeds to apply the
world to this, instead of applying this to the world.

Tolstoy is a flagrant example of this. Probably because of
profligacy in his youth, because he had disgusted himself in his
own flesh, by excess or by prostitution, therefore Tolstoy, in his
metaphysic, renounced the flesh altogether, later on, when he had
tried and had failed to achieve complete marriage in the flesh.
But above all things, Tolstoy was a child of the Law, he belonged
to the Father. He had a marvellous sensuous understanding, and
very little clarity of mind.

So that, in his metaphysic, he had to deny himself, his own
being, in order to escape his own disgust of what he had done to
himself, and to escape admission of his own failure.

Which made all the later part of his life a crying falsity and
shame. Reading the reminiscences of Tolstoy, one can only feel
shame at the way Tolstoy denied all that was great in him, with
vehement cowardice. He degraded himself infinitely, he perjured
himself far more than did Peter when he denied Christ. Peter re-
pented. But Tolstoy denied the Father, and propagated a great
system of his recusancy, elaborating his own weakness, blaspheming his own strength. 'What difficulty is there in writing about
how an officer fell in love with a married woman?' he used to say
of his *Anna Karenina*; 'there's no difficulty in it, and, above all,
no good in it.'

Because he was mouthpiece to the Father in uttering the law of
passion, he said there was no difficulty in it, because it came
naturally to him. Christ might just as easily have said, there was

no difficulty in the Parable of the Sower, and no good in it, either, because it flowed out of him without effort.

And Thomas Hardy's metaphysic is something like Tolstoy's. 'There is no reconciliation between Love and the Law,' says Hardy. 'The spirit of Love must always succumb before the blind, stupid, but overwhelming power of the Law.'

Already as early as *The Return of the Native* he has come to this theory, in order to explain his own sense of failure. But before that time, from the very start, he has had an overweening theoretic antagonism to the Law. 'That which is physical, of the body, is weak, despicable, bad,' he said at the very start. He represented his fleshy heroes as villains, but very weak and maundering villains. At its worst, the Law is a weak, craven sensuality: at its best, it is a passive inertia. It is the gap in the armour, it is the hole in the foundation.

Such a metaphysic is almost silly. If it were not that man is much stronger in feeling than in thought, the Wessex novels would be sheer rubbish, as they are already in parts. *The Well-Beloved* is sheer rubbish, fatuity, as is a good deal of *The Dynasts* conception.

But it is not as a metaphysician that one must consider Hardy. He makes a poor show there. For nothing in his work is so pitiable as his clumsy efforts to push events into line with his theory of being, and to make calamity fall on those who represent the principle of Love. He does it exceedingly badly, and owing to this effort his form is execrable in the extreme.

His feeling, his instinct, his sensuous understanding is, however, apart from his metaphysic, very great and deep, deeper than that, perhaps, of any other English novelist. Putting aside his metaphysic, which must always obtrude when he thinks of people, and turning to the earth, to landscape, then he is true to himself.

Always he must start from the earth, from the great source of the Law, and his people move in his landscape almost insignificantly, somewhat like tame animals wandering in the wild. The earth is the manifestation of the Father, of the Creator, Who made us in the Law. God still speaks aloud in His Works, as to Job, so to Hardy, surpassing human conception and the human law. 'Dost thou know the balancings of the clouds, the wondrous works of him which is perfect in knowledge? How thy garments are warm, when he quieteth the earth by the south wind? Hast thou with him spread out the sky, which is strong?'

This is the true attitude of Hardy – 'With God is terrible majesty.' The theory of knowledge, the metaphysic of the man, is much smaller than the man himself. So with Tolstoy.

Knowest thou the time when the wild goats of the rock bring forth? Or canst thou mark when the hinds do calve? Canst thou number the months that they fulfil? Or knowest thou the time when they bring forth? They bow themselves, they bring forth their young ones, they cast out their sorrows. Their young ones are good in liking, they grow up with corn; they go forth, and return not unto them.

There is a good deal of this in Hardy. But in Hardy there is more than the concept of Job, protesting his integrity. Job says in the end:

Therefore have I uttered that I understood not; things too wonderful for me, which I knew not.

I have heard of thee by hearing of the ear; but now mine eye seeth thee.

Wherefore I abhor myself, and repent in dust and ashes.

But Jude ends where Job began, cursing the day and the services of his birth, and in so much cursing the act of the Lord, 'Who made him in the womb.'

It is the same cry all through Hardy, this curse upon the birth in the flesh, and this unconscious adherence to the flesh. The instincts, the bodily passions are strong and sudden in all Hardy's men. They are too strong and sudden. They fling Jude into the arms of Arabella, years after he has known Sue, and against his own will.

For every man comprises male and female in his being, the male always struggling for predominance. A woman likewise consists in male and female, with female predominant.

And a man who is strongly male tends to deny, to refute the female in him. A real 'man' takes no heed for his body, which is

219

the more female part of him. He considers himself only as an instrument, to be used in the service of some idea.

The true female, on the other hand, will eternally hold herself superior to any idea, will hold full life in the body to be the real happiness. The male exists in doing, the female in being. The male lives in the satisfaction of some purpose achieved, the female in the satisfaction of some purpose contained.

In Aeschylus, in the *Eumenides*, there is Apollo, Loxias, the Sun God, the prophet, the male: there are the Erinyes, daughters of primeval Mother Night, representing here the female risen in retribution for some crime against the flesh; and there is Pallas, unbegotten daughter of Zeus, who is as the Holy Spirit in the Christian religion, the spirit of wisdom.

Orestes is bidden by the male god, Apollo, to avenge the murder of his father, Agamemnon, by his mother: that is, the male, murdered by the female, must be avenged by the male. But Orestes is child of his mother. He is in himself female. So that in himself the conscience, the madness, the violated part of his own self, his own body, drives him to the Furies. On the male side, he is right; on the female, wrong. But peace is given at last by Pallas, the Arbitrator, the spirit of wisdom.

And although Aeschylus in his consciousness makes the Furies hideous, and Apollo supreme, yet, in his own self and in very fact, he makes the Furies wonderful and noble, with their tremendous hymns, and makes Apollo a trivial, sixth-form braggart and ranter. Clytemnestra also, wherever she appears, is wonderful and noble. Her sin is the sin of pride : she was the first to be injured. Agamemnon is a feeble thing beside her.

So Aeschylus adheres still to the Law, to Right, to the Creator who created man in His Own Image, and in His Law. What he has learned of Love, he does not yet quite believe.

Hardy has the same belief in the Law, but in conceit of his own understanding, which cannot understand the Law, he says that the Law is nothing, a blind confusion.

And in conceit of understanding, he deprecates and destroys both women and men who would represent the old primeval Law, the great Law of the Womb, the primeval Female principle.

220

The Female shall not exist. Where it appears, it is a criminal tendency, to be stamped out.

This in Manston, Troy, Boldwood, Eustacia, Wildeve, Henchard, Tess, Jude, everybody. The women approved of are not Female in any real sense. They are passive subjects to the male, the re-echo from the male. As in the Christian religion, the Virgin worship is no real Female worship, but worship of the Female as she is passive and subjected to the male. Hence the sadness of Botticelli's Virgins.

Thus Tess sets out, not as any positive thing, containing all purpose, but as the acquiescent complement to the male. The female in her has become inert. Then Alec d'Urberville comes along, and possesses her. From the man who takes her Tess expects her own consummation, the singling out of herself, the addition of the male complement. She is of an old line, and has the aristocratic quality of respect for the other being. She does not see the other person as an extension of herself, existing in a universe of which she is the centre and pivot. She knows that other people are outside her. Therein she is an aristocrat. And out of this attitude to the other person came her passivity. It is not the same as the passive quality in the other little heroines, such as the girl in *The Woodlanders*, who is passive because she is small.

Tess is passive out of self-acceptance, a true aristocratic quality, amounting almost to self-indifference. She knows she is herself incontrovertibly, and she knows that other people are not herself. This is a very rare quality, even in a woman. And in a civilization so unequal, it is almost a weakness.

Tess never tries to alter or to change anybody, neither to alter nor to change nor to divert. What another person decides, that is his decision. She respects utterly the other's right to be. She is herself always.

But the others do not respect her right to be. Alec d'Urberville sees her as the embodied fulfilment of his own desire: something, that is, belonging to him. She cannot, in his conception, exist apart from him nor have any being apart from his being. For she is the embodiment of his desire.

This is very natural and common in men, this attitude to the world. But in Alec d'Urberville it applies only to the woman of his desire. He cares only for her. Such a man adheres to the female like a parasite.

It is a male quality to resolve a purpose to its fulfilment. It is the male quality, to seek the motive power in the female, and to convey this to a fulfilment; to receive some impulse into his senses, and to transmit it into expression.

Alec d'Urberville does not do this. He is male enough, in his way; but only physically male. He is constitutionally an enemy of the principle of self-subordination, which principle is inherent in every man. It is this principle which makes a man, a true male, see his job through, at no matter what cost. A man is strictly only himself when he is fulfilling some purpose he has conceived: so that the principle is not of self-subordination, but of continuity, of development. Only when insisted on, as in Christianity, does it become self-sacrifice. And this resistance to self-sacrifice on Alec d'Urberville's part does not make him an individualist, an egoist, but rather a non-individual, an incomplete, almost a fragmentary thing.

There seems to be in d'Urberville an inherent antagonism to any progression in himself. Yet he seeks with all his power for the source of stimulus in woman. He takes the deep impulse from the female. In this he is exceptional. No ordinary man could really have betrayed Tess. Even if she had had an illegitimate child to another man, to Angel Clare, for example, it would not have shattered her as did her connexion with Alec d'Urberville. For Alec d'Urberville could reach some of the real sources of the female in a woman, and draw from them. Troy could also do this. And, as a woman instinctively knows, such men are rare. Therefore they have a power over a woman. They draw from the depth of her being.

And what they draw, they betray. With a natural male, what he draws from the source of the female, the impulse he receives from the source he transmits through his own being into utterance, motion, action, expression. But Troy and Alec d'Urberville, what they received they knew only as gratification in the senses;

some perverse will prevented them from submitting to it, from becoming instrumental to it.

Which was why Tess was shattered by Alec d'Urberville, and why she murdered him in the end. The murder is badly done, altogether the book is botched, owing to the way of thinking in the author, owing to the weak yet obstinate theory of being. Nevertheless, the murder is true, the whole book is true, in its conception.

Angel Clare has the very opposite qualities to those of Alec d'Urberville. To the latter, the female in himself is the only part of himself he will acknowledge: the body, the senses, that which he shares with the female, which the female shares with him. To Angel Clare, the female in himself is detestable, the body, the senses, that which he will share with a woman, is held degraded. What he wants really is to receive the female impulse other than through the body. But his thinking has made him criticize Christianity, his deeper instinct has forbidden him to deny his body any further, a deadlock in his own being, which denies him any purpose, so that he must take to hand, labour out of sheer impotence to resolve himself, drives him unwillingly to woman. But he must see her only as the Female Principle, he cannot bear to see her as the Woman in the Body. Her he thinks degraded. To marry her, to have physical marriage with her, he must overcome all his ascetic revulsion, he must, in his own mind, put off his own divinity, his pure maleness, his singleness, his pure completeness, and descend to the heated welter of the flesh. It is objectionable to him. Yet his body, his life, is too strong for him.

Who is he, that he shall be pure male, and deny the existence of the female? This is the question the Creator asks of him. Is then the male the exclusive whole of life? – is he even the higher or supreme part of life? Angel Clare thinks so: as Christ thought.

Yet it is not so, as even Angel Clare must find out. Life, that is Two-in-One, Male and Female. Nor is either part greater than the other.

It is not Angel Clare's fault that he cannot come to Tess when he finds that she has, in his words, been defiled. It is the result of generations of ultra-Christian training, which had left in him an inherent aversion to the female, and to all in himself which pertained to the female. What he, in his Christian sense, conceived of as Woman, was only the servant and attendant and administering spirit to the male. He had no idea that there was such a thing as positive Woman, as the Female, another great living Principle counterbalancing his own male principle. He conceived of the world as consisting of the One, the Male Principle.

Which conception was already gendered in Botticelli, whence the melancholy of the Virgin. Which conception reached its fullest in Turner's pictures, which were utterly bodiless; and also in the great scientists or thinkers of the last generation, even Darwin and Spencer and Huxley. For these last conceived of evolution, of one spirit or principle starting at the far end of time, and lonelily traversing Time. But there is not one principle, there are two, travelling always to meet, each step of each one lessening the distance between the two of them. And Space, which so frightened Herbert Spencer, is as a Bride to us. And the cry of Man does not ring out into the Void. It rings out to Woman, whom we know not.

This Tess knew, unconsciously. An aristocrat she was, developed through generations to the belief in her own self-establishment. She could help, but she could not be helped. She could give, but she could not receive. She could attend to the wants of the other person, but no other person, save another aristocrat – and there is scarcely such a thing as another aristocrat – could attend to her wants, her deepest wants.

So it is the aristocrat alone who has any real and vital sense of 'the neighbour', of the other person; who has the habit of submerging himself, putting himself entirely away before the other person: because he expects to receive nothing from the other person. So that now he has lost much of his initiative force, and exists almost isolated, detached, and without the surging ego of the ordinary man, because he has controlled his nature according to the other man, to exclude him.

And Tess, despising herself in the flesh, despising the deep Female she was, because Alec d'Urberville had betrayed her very source loved Angel Clare, who also despised and hated the flesh.
224

She did not hate d'Urberville. What a man did, he did, and if he did it to her, it was her look-out. She did not conceive of him as having any human duty towards her.

The same with Angel Clare as with Alec d'Urberville. She was very grateful to him for saving her from her despair of contamination, and from her bewildered isolation. But when he accused her, she could not plead or answer. For she had no right to his goodness. She stood alone.

The female was strong in her. She was herself. But she was out of place, utterly out of her element and her times. Hence her utter bewilderment. This is the reason why she was so overcome. She was outwearied from the start, in her spirit. For it is only by receiving from all our fellows that we are kept fresh and vital. Tess was herself, female, intrinsically a woman.

The female in her was indomitable, unchangeable, she was utterly constant to herself. But she was, by long breeding, intact from mankind. Though Alec d'Urberville was of no kin to her, yet, in the book, he has always a quality of kinship. It was as if only a kinsman, an aristocrat, could approach her. And this to her undoing. Angel Clare would never have reached her. She would have abandoned herself to him, but he would never have reached her. It needed a physical aristocrat. She would have lived with her husband, Clare, in a state of abandon to him, like a coma. Alec d'Urberville forced her to realize him, and to realize herself. He came close to her, as Clare could never have done. So she murdered him. For she was herself.

And just as the aristocratic principle had isolated Tess, it had isolated Alec d'Urberville. For though Hardy consciously made the young betrayer a plebeian and an impostor, unconsciously, with the supreme justice of the artist, he made him the same as de Stancy, a true aristocrat, or as Fitzpiers, or Troy. He did not give him the tiredness, the touch of exhaustion necessary, in Hardy's mind, to an aristocrat. But he gave him the intrinsic qualities.

With the men as with the women of old descent: they have nothing to do with mankind in general, they are exceedingly personal. For many generations they have been accustomed to regard their own desires as their own supreme laws. They have not been bound by the conventional morality: this they have transcended, being a code unto themselves. The other person has been always present to their imagination, in the spectacular sense. He has always existed to them. But he has always existed as something other than themselves.

Hence the inevitable isolation, detachment of the aristocrat. His one aim, during centuries, has been to keep himself detached. At last he finds himself, by his very nature, cut off.

Then either he must go his own way, or he must struggle towards reunion with the mass of mankind. Either he must be an incomplete individualist, like de Stancy, or like the famous Russian nobles, he must become a wild humanitarian and reformer.

For as all the governing power has gradually been taken from the nobleman, and as, by tradition, by inherent inclination, he does not occupy himself with profession other than government, how shall he use that power which is in him and which comes into him?

He is, by virtue of breed and long training, a perfect instrument. He knows, as every pure-bred thing knows, that his root and source is in his female. He seeks the motive power in the woman. And, having taken it, has nothing to do with it, can find, in this democratic, plebeian age, no means by which to transfer it into action, expression, utterance. So there is a continual gnawing of unsatisfaction, a constant seeking of another woman, still another woman. For each time the impulse comes fresh, everything seems all right.

It may be, also, that in the aristocrat a certain weariness makes him purposeless, vicious, like a form of death. But that is not necessary. One feels that in Manston, and Troy, and Fitzpiers, and Alec d'Urberville, there is good stuff gone wrong. Just as in Angel Clare, there is good stuff gone wrong in the other direction.

There can never be one extreme of wrong, without the other extreme. If there had never been the extravagant Puritan idea, that the Female Principle was to be denied, cast out by man from his soul, that only the Male Principle, of Abstraction, of Good, of

Public Good, of the Community, embodied in 'Thou shalt love
thy neighbour as thyself', really existed, there would never have
been produced the extreme Cavalier type, which says that only
the Female Principle endures in man, that all the Abstraction,
the Good, the Public Elevation, the Community, was a grovelling cowardice, and that man lived by enjoyment, through his
senses, enjoyment which ended in his senses. Or perhaps better,
if the extreme Cavalier type had never been produced, we should
not have had the Puritan, the extreme correction.

The one extreme produces the other. It is inevitable for Angel
Clare and for Alex d'Urberville mutually to destroy the woman
they both loved. Each does her the extreme of wrong, so she is
destroyed.

The book is handled with very uncertain skill, botched and
bungled. But it contains the elements of the greatest tragedy:
Alec d'Urberville, who has killed the male in himself, as Clytemnestra symbolically for Orestes killed Agamemnon; Angel
Clare, who has killed the female in himself, as Orestes killed Clytemnestra: and Tess, the Woman, the Life, destroyed by a mechanical fate, in the communal law.

There is no reconciliation. Tess, Angel Clare, Alec d'Urberville, they are all as good as dead. For Angel Clare, though still
apparently alive, is in reality no more than a mouth, a piece of
paper, like Clym left preaching.

There is no reconciliation, only death. And so Hardy really
states his case, which is not his consciously stated metaphysic,
by any means, but a statement how man has gone wrong and
brought death on himself: how man has violated the Law, how
he has supererogated himself, gone so far in his male conceit as
to supersede the Creator, and win death as a reward. Indeed, the
works of supererogation of our male assiduity help us to a better
salvation.

Jude is only Tess turned round about. Instead of the heroine
containing the two principles, male and female, at strife within
her one being, it is Jude who contains them both, whilst the two
women with him take the place of the two men to Tess. Arabella

is Alec d'Urberville, Sue is Angel Clare. These represent the same pair of principles.

But, first, let it be said again that Hardy is a bad artist. Because he must condemn Alec d'Urberville, according to his own personal creed, therefore he shows him a vulgar intriguer of coarse lasses, and a ridiculous convert to evangelism. But Alec d'Urberville, by the artist's account, is neither of these. It is, in actual life, a rare man who seeks and seeks among women for one of such character and intrinsic female being as Tess. The ordinary sensualist avoids such characters. They implicate him too deeply. An ordinary sensualist would have been much too common, much too afraid, to turn to Tess. In a way, d'Urberville was her mate. And his subsequent passion for her is in its way noble enough. But whatever his passion, as a male, he must be a betrayer, even if he had been the most faithful husband on earth. He betrayed the female in a woman, by taking her, and by responding with no male impulse from himself. He roused her, but never satisfied her. He could never satisfy her. It was like a soul-disease in him: he was, in the strict though not the technical sense, impotent. But he must have wanted, later on, not to be so. But he could not help himself. He was spiritually impotent in love.

Arabella was the same. She, like d'Urberville, was converted by an evangelical preacher. It is significant in both of them. They were not just shallow, as Hardy would have made them out.

He is, however, more contemptuous in his personal attitude to the woman than to the man. He insists that she is a pig-killer's daughter; he insists that she drag Jude into pig-killing; he lays stress on her false tail of hair. That is not the point at all. This is only Hardy's bad art. He himself, as an artist, manages in the whole picture of Arabella almost to make insignificant in her these pig-sticking, false-hair crudities. But he must have his personal revenge on her for her coarseness, which offends him, because he is something of an Angel Clare.

The pig-sticking and so forth are not so important in the real picture. As for the false tail of hair, few women dared have been so open and natural about it. Few women, indeed, dared have made Jude marry them. It may have been a case with Arabella of 'fools rush in'. But she was not such a fool. And her motives are explained in the book. Life is not, in the actual, such a simple affair of getting a fellow and getting married. It is, even for Arabella, an affair on which she places her all. No barmaid marries anybody, the first man she can lay hands on. She cannot. It must be a personal thing to her. And no ordinary woman would want Jude. Moreover, no ordinary woman could have laid her hands on Jude.

It is an absurd fallacy this, that a small man wants a woman bigger and finer than he is himself. A man is as big as his real desires. Let a man, seeing with his eyes a woman of force and being, want her for his own, then that man is intrinsically an equal of that woman. And the same with a woman.

A coarse, shallow woman does not want to marry a sensitive, deep-feeling man. She feels no desire for him, she is not drawn to him, but repelled, knowing he will contemn her. She wants a man to correspond to herself: that is, if she is a young woman looking for a mate, as Arabella was.

What an old, jaded, yet still unsatisfied woman or man wants is another matter. Yet not even one of these will take a young creature of real character, superior in force. Instinct and fear prevent it.

Arabella was, under all her disguise of pig-fat and false hair, and vulgar speech, in character somewhat an aristocrat. She was, like Eustacia, amazingly lawless, even splendidly so. She believed in herself and she was not altered by any outside opinion of herself. Her fault was pride. She thought herself the centre of life, that all which existed belonged to her in so far as she wanted it.

In this she was something like Job. His attitude was 'I am strong and rich, and, also, I am a good man.' He gave out of his own sense of bounty, and felt no indebtedness. Arabella was almost the same. She felt also strong and abundant, arrogant in her hold on life. She needed a complement; and the nearest thing to her satisfaction was Jude. For as she, intrinsically, was a strong female, by far overpowering her Annies and her friends, so was he a strong male.

The difference between them was not so much a difference of quality, or degree, as a difference of form. Jude, like Tess, wanted full consummation. Arabella, like Alec d'Urberville, had that in her which resisted full consummation, wanted only to enjoy herself in contact with the male. She would have no transmission.

There are two attitudes to love. A man in love with a woman says either: 'I, the man, the male, am the supreme, I am the one, and the woman is administered unto me, and this is her highest function, to be administered unto me.' This was the conscious attitude of the Greeks. But their unconscious attitude was the reverse: they were in truth afraid of the female principle, their vaunt was empty, they went in deep, inner dread of her. So did the Jews, so do the Italians. But after the Renaissance, there was a change. Then began conscious Woman-reverence, and a lack of instinctive reverence, rather only an instinctive pity. It is according to the balance between the Male and Female principles.

The other attitude of a man in love, besides this of 'she is administered unto my maleness', is, 'She is the unknown, the undiscovered, into which I plunge to discovery, losing myself.'

And what we call real love has always this latter attitude.

The first attitude, which belongs to passion, makes a man feel proud, splendid. It is a powerful stimulant to him, the female administered to him. He feels full of blood, he walks the earth like a Lord. And it is to this state Nietzsche aspires in his *Wille zur Macht*. It is this the passionate nations crave.

And under all this there is, naturally, the sense of fear, transition, and the sadness of mortality. For, the female being herself an independent force, may she not withdraw, and leave a man empty, like ash, as one sees a Jew or an Italian so often?

This first attitude, too, of male pride receiving the female administration may, and often does, contain the corresponding intense fear and reverence of the female, as of the unknown. So that, starting from the male assertion, there came in the old days the full consummation; as often there comes the full consummation now.

But not always. The man may retain all the while the sense of himself, the primary male, receiving gratification. This constant
230

reaction upon himself at length dulls his senses and his sensibility, and makes him mechanical, automatic. He grows gradually incapable of receiving any gratification from the female, and becomes a *roué*, only automatically alive, and frantic with the knowledge thereof.

It is the tendency of the Parisian – or has been – to take this attitude to love, and to intercourse. The woman knows herself all the while as the primary female receiving administration of the male. So she becomes hard and external, and inwardly jaded, tired out. It is the tendency of English women to take this attitude also. And it is this attitude of love, more than anything else, which devitalizes a race, and makes it barren.

It is an attitude natural enough to start with. Every young man must think that it is the highest honour he can do to a woman, to receive from her her female administration to his male being, whilst he meanwhile gives her the gratification of himself. But intimacy usually corrects this, love, or use, or marriage: a married man ceases to think of himself as the primary male: hence often his dullness. Unfortunately, he also fails in many cases to realize the gladness of a man in contact with the unknown in the female, which gives him a sense of richness and oneness with all life, as if, by being part of life, he were infinitely rich. Which is different from the sense of power, of dominating life. The *Wille zur Macht* is a spurious feeling.

For a man who dares to look upon, and to venture within the unknown of the female, losing himself, like a man who gives himself to the sea, or a man who enters a primeval, virgin forest, feels, when he returns, the utmost gladness of singing. This is certainly the gladness of a male bird in his singing, the amazing joy of return from the adventure into the unknown, rich with addition to his soul, rich with the knowledge of the utterly illimitable depth and breadth of the unknown; the every-yielding extent of the unacquired, the unattained; the inexhaustible riches lain under unknown skies over unknown seas, all the magnificence that *is*, and yet which is unknown to any of us. And the knowledge of the reality which it awaits me, the male, the knowledge of the calling and struggling of all the unknown, illimitable Female towards me, unembraced as yet, towards those men who will endlessly follow me, who will endlessly struggle after me, beyond me, further into this calling, unrealized vastness, nearer to the outstretched, eager, advancing unknown in the woman.

It is for this sense of All the magnificence that is unknown to me, of All that which stretches forth arms and breast to the Inexhaustible Embrace of all the ages, towards me, whose arms are outstretched, for this moment's embrace which gives me the inkling of the Inexhaustible Embrace that every man must and does yearn. And whether he be a *roué*, and vicious, or young and virgin, this is the bottom of every man's desire, for the embrace, for the advancing into the unknown, for the landing on the shore of the undiscovered half of the world, where the wealth of the female lies before us.

What is true of men is so of women. If we turn our faces west, towards nightfall and the unknown within the dark embrace of a wife, they turn their faces east, towards the sunrise and the brilliant, bewildering, active embrace of a husband. And as we are dazed with the unknown in her, so is she dazed with the unknown in us. It is so. And we throw up our joy to heaven like towers and spires and fountains and leaping flowers, so glad we are.

But always, we are divided within ourselves. Is it not that I am wonderful? Is it not a gratification for me when a stranger shall land on my shores and enjoy what he finds there? Shall I not also enjoy it? Shall I not enjoy the strange motion of the stranger, like a pleasant sensation of silk and warmth against me, stirring unknown fibres? Shall I not take this enjoyment without venturing out in dangerous waters, losing myself, perhaps destroying myself seeking the unknown? Shall I not stay at home, and by feeling the swift, soft airs blow out of the unknown upon my body, shall I not have rich pleasure of myself?

And, because they were afraid of the unknown, and because they wanted to retain the full-veined gratification of self-pleasure, men have kept their women tightly in bondage. But when the men were no longer afraid of the unknown, when they deemed it exhausted, they said, 'There are no women; there are only daughters of men' – as we say now, as the Greeks tried to say. Hence the 'Virgin' conception of woman, the passionless, passive conception, progressing from Fielding's Amelia to Dickens' Agnes, and on to Hardy's Sue.

Whereas Arabella in *Jude the Obscure* has what one might call the selfish instinct for love, Jude himself has the other, the unselfish. She sees in him a male who can gratify her. She takes him, and is gratified by him. Which makes a man of him. He becomes a grown, independent man in the arms of Arabella, conscious of having met, and satisfied, the female demand in him. This makes a man of any youth. He is proven unto himself as a male being, initiated into the freedom of life.

But Arabella refused his purpose. She refused to combine with him in one purpose. Just like Alec d'Urberville, she had from the outset an antagonism to the submission to any change in herself, to any development. She had the will to remain where she was, static, and to receive and exhaust all impulse she received from the male, in her senses. Whereas in a normal woman, impulse received from the male drives her on to a sense of joy and wonder and glad freedom in touch with the unknown of which she is made aware, so that she exists on the edge of the unknown half in rapture. Which is the state the writers wish to portray in 'Amelia' and 'Agnes', but particularly in the former; which Reynolds wishes to portray in his pictures of women.

To all this Arabella was antagonistic. It seems like a perversion in her, as if she played havoc with the stuff she was made of, as Alec d'Urberville did. Nevertheless she remained always unswervable female, she never truckled to the male idea, but was self-responsible, without fear. It is easier to imagine such a woman, out of one's desires, than to find her in real life. For, where a half-criminal type, a reckless, dare-devil type resembling her, may be found on the outskirts of society, yet these are not Arabella. Which criminal type, or reckless, low woman, would want to marry Jude? Arabella wanted Jude. And it is evident she was not too coarse for him, since she made no show of refinement from the first. The female in her, reckless and unconstrained, was strong enough to draw him after her, as her male, right to the end. Which other woman could have done this? At least let acknowledgement be made to her great female force of character. Her coarseness seems to me exaggerated to make the moralist's case good against her.

Jude could never hate her. She did a great deal for the true making of him, for making him a grown man. She gave him to himself.

And there was danger at the outset that he should never become a man, but that he should remain incorporeal, smothered out under his idea of learning. He was somewhat in Angel Clare's position. Not that generations of particular training had made him almost rigid and paralysed to the female: but that his whole passion was concentrated away from woman to reinforce in him the male impulse towards extending the consciousness. His family was a difficult family to marry. And this because, whilst the men were physically vital, with a passion towards the female from which no moral training had restrained them, like a plant tied to a stick and diverted, they had at the same time an inherent complete contempt of the female, valuing only that which was male. So that they were strongly divided against themselves, with no external hold, such as a moral system, to grip to.

It would have been possible for Jude, monkish, passionate, medieval, belonging to woman yet striving away from her, refusing to know her, to have gone on denying one side of his nature, adhering to his idea of learning, till he had stultified the physical impulse of his being and perverted it entirely. Arabella brought him to himself, gave him himself, made him free, sound as a physical male.

That she would not, or could not, combine her life with him for the fulfilment of a purpose was their misfortune. But at any rate, his purpose of becoming an Oxford don was a cut-and-dried purpose which had no connexion with his living body, and for which probably no woman could have united with him.

No doubt Arabella hated his books, and hated his whole attitude to study. What had he, a passionate, emotional nature, to do with learning for learning's sake, with mere academics? Any woman must know it was ridiculous. But he persisted with the tenacity of all perverseness. And she, in this something of an aristocrat, like Tess, feeling that she had no right to him, no right to receive anything from him, except his sex, in which she felt she gave and did not receive, for she conceived of herself as the primary female, as that which, in taking the male, conferred on him his greatest boon, she left him alone. Her attitude was, that he would find all he desired in coming to her. She was occupied with herself. It was not that she wanted *him*. She wanted to have the sensation of herself in contact with him. His being she refused. She allowed only her own being.

Therefore she scarcely troubled him, when he earned little money and took no notice of her. He did not refuse to take notice of her because he hated her, or was deceived by her, or disappointed in her. He was not. He refused to consider her seriously because he adhered with all his pertinacity to the idea of study, from which he excluded her.

Which she saw and knew, and allowed. She would not force him to notice her, or to consider her seriously. She would compel him to nothing. She had had a certain satisfaction of him, which would be no more if she stayed for ever. For she was non-developing. When she knew him in her senses she knew the end of him, as far as she was concerned. That was all.

So she just went her way. He did not blame her. He scarcely missed her. He returned to his books.

Really, he had lost nothing by his marriage with Arabella: neither innocence nor belief nor hope. He had indeed gained his manhood. She left him the stronger and completer.

And now he would concentrate all on his male idea, of arresting himself, of becoming himself a non-developing quality, an academic mechanism. That was his obsession. That was his craving: to have nothing to do with his own life. This was the same as Tess when she turned to Angel Clare. She wanted life merely in the secondary, outside form, in the consciousness.

It was another form of the disease, or decay of old family, which possessed Alec d'Urberville; a different form, but closely related. D'Urberville wanted to arrest all his activity in his senses. Jude Fawley wanted to arrest all his activity in his mind. Each of them wanted to become an impersonal force working automatically. Each of them wanted to deny, or escape the responsibility and trouble of living as a complete person, a full individual.

And neither was able to bring it off. Jude's real desire was, not to live in the body. He wanted to exist only in his mentality. He was as if bored, or *blasé*, in the body, just like Tess. This seems to be the result of coming of an old family, that had been long conscious, long self-conscious, specialized, separate, exhausted.

This drove him to Sue. She was his kinswoman, as d'Urberville was kinsman to Tess. She was like himself in her being and her desire. Like Jude, she wanted to live partially, in the consciousness, in the mind only. She wanted no experience in the senses, she wished only to know.

She belonged, with Tess, to the old woman-type of witch or prophetess, which adhered to the male principle, and destroyed the female. But in the true prophetess, in Cassandra, for example, the denial of the female cost a strong and almost maddening effect. But in Sue it was done before she was born.

She was born with the vital female atrophied in her: she was almost male. Her *will* was male. It was wrong for Jude to take her physically, it was a violation of her. She was not the virgin type, but the witch type, which has no sex. Why should she be forced into intercourse that was not natural to her?

It was not natural for her to have children. It is inevitable that her children die. It is not natural for Tess nor for Angel Clare to have children, nor for Arabella nor for Alec d'Urberville. Because none of these wished to give of themselves to the lover, none of them wished to mate: they only wanted their own experience. For Jude alone it was natural to have children, and this in spite of himself.

Sue wished to identify herself utterly with the male principle. That which was female in her she wanted to consume within the male force, to consume it in the fire of understanding, of giving utterance. Whereas an ordinary woman knows that she *contains* all understanding, that she is the unutterable which man must for ever continue to try to utter, Sue felt that all must be uttered, must be given to the male, that, in truth, only Male existed, that everything was the Word, and the Word was everything.

Sue is the production of the long selection by man of the woman in whom the female is subordinated to the male principle. A long line of Amelias and Agneses, those women who submitted to the man-idea, flattered the man, and bored him, the Gretchens and the Turgenev heroines, those who have betrayed the female and who therefore only seem to exist to be betrayed by their men, these have produced at length a Sue, the pure thing. And as soon as she is produced she is execrated.

What Cassandra and Aspasia became to the Greeks, Sue has become to the northern civilization. But the Greeks never pitied Woman. They did not show her that highest impertinence – not even Euripides.

But Sue is scarcely a woman at all, though she is feminine enough. Cassandra submitted to Apollo, and gave him the Word of affiance, brought forth prophecy to him, not children. She received the embrace of the spirit, He breathed His Grace upon her: and she conceived and brought forth a prophecy. It was still a marriage. Not the marriage of the Virgin with the Spirit, but the marriage of the female spirit with the male spirit, bodiless.

With Sue, however, the marriage was no marriage, but a submission, a service, a slavery. Her female spirit did not wed with the male spirit: she could not prophesy. Her spirit submitted to the male spirit, owned the priority of the male spirit, wished to become the male spirit. That which was female in her, resistant, gave her only her critical faculty. When she sought out the physical quality in the Greeks, that was her effort to make even the unknowable physique a part of knowledge, to contain the body within the mind.

One of the supremest products of our civilization is Sue, and a product that well frightens us. It is quite natural that, with all her mental alertness, she married Phillotson without ever considering the physical quality of marriage. Deep instinct made her avoid the consideration. And the duality of her nature made her

237

extremely liable to self-destruction. The suppressed, atrophied female in her, like a potent fury, was always there, suggesting to her to make the fatal mistake. She contained always the rarest, most deadly anarchy in her own being.

It needed that she should have some place in society where the clarity of her mental being, which was in itself a form of death, could shine out without attracting any desire for her body. She needed a refinement on Angel Clare. For she herself was a more specialized, more highly civilized product on the female side, than Angel Clare on the male. Yet the atrophied female in her would still want the bodily male.

She attracted to herself Jude. His experience with Arabella had for the time being diverted his attention altogether from the female. His attitude was that of service to the pure male spirit. But the physical male in him, that which knew and belonged to the female, was potent, and roused the female in Sue as much as she wanted it roused, so much that it was a stimulant to her, making her mind the brighter.

It was a cruelly difficult position. She must, by the constitution of her nature, remain quite physically intact, for the female was atrophied in her, to the enlargement of the male activity. Yet she wanted some quickening for this atrophied female. She wanted even kisses. That the new rousing might give her a sense of life. But she could only *live* in the mind.

Then, where could she find a man who would be able to feed her with his male vitality, through kisses, proximity, without demanding the female return? For she was such that she could only receive quickening from a strong male, for she was herself no small thing. Could she then find a man, a strong, passionate male, who would devote himself entirely to the production of the mind in her, to the production of male activity, or of female activity critical to the male?

She could only receive the highest stimulus, which she must inevitably seek, from a man who put her in constant jeopardy. Her essentiality rested upon her remaining intact. Any suggestion of the physical was utter confusion to her. Her principle was the ultra-Christian principle – of living entirely according to the

Spirit, to the One, male spirit, which knows, and utters, and shines, but exists beyond feeling, beyond joy or sorrow, or pain, exists only in Knowing. In tune with this, she was herself. Let her, however, be turned under the influence of the other dark, silent, strong principle, of the female, and she would break like a fine instrument under discord.

Yet, to live at all in tune with the male spirit, she must receive the male stimulus from a man. Otherwise she was as an instrument without a player. She must feel the hands of a man upon her, she must be infused with his male vitality, or she was not alive.

Here then was her difficulty: to find a man whose vitality could infuse her and make her live, and who would not, at the same time, demand of her a return, the return of the female impulse into him. What man could receive this drainage, receiving nothing back again? He must either die, or revolt.

One man had died. She knew it well enough. She knew her own fatality. She knew she drained the vital, male stimulus out of a man, producing in him only knowledge of the mind, only mental clarity: which man must always strive to attain, but which is not life in him, rather the product of life.

Just as Alec d'Urberville, on the other hand, drained the female vitality out of a woman, and gave her only sensation, only experience in the senses, a sense of herself, nothing to the soul or spirit, thereby exhausting her.

Now Jude, after Arabella, and following his own *idée fixe*, haunted this mental clarity, this knowing, above all. What he contained in himself, of male and female impulse, he wanted to bring forth, to draw into his mind, to resolve into understanding, as a plant resolves that which it contains into flower.

This Sue could do for him. By creating a vacuum, she could cause the vivid flow which clarified him. By rousing him, by drawing from him his turgid vitality, made thick and heavy and physical with Arabella, she could bring into consciousness that which he contained. For he was heavy and full of unrealized life, clogged with untransmuted knowledge, with accretion of his senses. His whole life had been till now an indrawing, ingestion.

Arabella had been a vital experience for him, received into his blood. And how was he to bring out all this fulness into knowledge or utterance? For all the time he was being roused to new physical desire, new life-experience, new sense-enrichening, and he could not perform his male function of transmitting this into expression, or action. The particular form his flowering should take, he could not find. So he hunted and studied, to find the call, the appeal which should call out of him that which was in him.

And great was his transport when the appeal came from Sue. She wanted, at first, only his words. That of him which could come to her through speech, through his consciousness, her mind, like a bottomless gulf, cried out for. She wanted satisfaction through the mind, and cried out for him to satisfy her through the mind.

Great, then, was his joy at giving himself out to her. He gave, for it was more blessed to give than to receive. He gave, and she received some satisfaction. But where she was not satisfied, there he must try still to satisfy her. He struggled to bring it all forth. She was, as himself, asking himself what he was. And he strove to answer, in a transport.

And he answered in a great measure. He singled himself out from the old matrix of the accepted idea, he produced an individual flower of his own.

It was for this he loved Sue. She did for him quickly what he would have done for himself slowly, through study. By patient, diligent study, he would have used up the surplus of that turgid energy in him, and would, by long contact with old truth, have arrived at the form of truth which was in him. What he indeed wanted to get from study was, not a store of learning, nor the vanity of education, a sort of superiority of educational wealth, though this also gave him pleasure. He wanted, through familiarity with the true thinkers and poets, particularly with the classic and theological thinkers, because of their comparative sensuousness, to find conscious expression for that which he held in his blood. And to do this, it was necessary for him to resolve and to reduce his blood, to overcome the female sensuousness in himself, to transmute his sensuous being into another state, a

From *Study of Thomas Hardy*

state of clarity, of consciousness. Slowly, laboriously, struggling with the Greek and the Latin, he would have burned down his thick blood as fuel, and have come to the true light of himself.

This Sue did for him. In marriage, each party fulfils a dual function with regard to the other: exhaustive and enrichening. The female at the same time exhausts and invigorates the male, the male at the same time exhausts and invigorates the female. The exhaustion and invigoration are both temporary and relative. The male, making the effort to penetrate into the female, exhausts himself and invigorates her. But that which, at the end, he discovers and carries off from her, some seed of being, enrichens him and exhausts her. Arabella, in taking Jude, accepted very little from him. She absorbed very little of his strength and vitality into herself. For she only wanted to be aware of herself in contact with him, she did not want him to penetrate into her very being, till he moved her to her very depths, till she loosened to him some of her very self for his enrichening. She was intrinsically impotent, as was Alec d'Urberville.

So that in her Jude went very little further in Knowledge, or in Self-Knowledge. He took only the first steps: of knowing himself sexually, as a sexual male. That is only the first, the first necessary, but rudimentary, step.

When he came to Sue, he found her physically impotent, but spiritually potent. That was what he wanted. Of Knowledge in the blood he had a rich enough store: more than he knew what to do with. He wished for the further step, of reduction, of essentializing into Knowledge. Which Sue gave to him.

So that his experience with Arabella, plus his first experience of trembling intimacy and incandescent realization with Sue made one complete marriage: that is, the two women added together made One Bride.

When Jude had exhausted his surplus self, in spiritual intimacy with Sue, when he had gained through her all the wonderful understanding she could evoke in him, when he was clarified to himself, then his marriage with Sue was over. Jude's marriage with Sue was over before he knew her physically. She had, physically, nothing to give him.

Which, in her deepest instinct, she knew. She made no mistake in marrying Phillotson. She acted according to the pure logic of her nature. Phillotson was a man who wanted no marriage whatsoever with the female. Sexually, he wanted her as an instrument through which he obtained relief, and some gratification: but, really, relief. Spiritually, he wanted her as a thing to be wondered over and delighted in, but quite separately from himself. He knew quite well he could never marry her. He was a human being as near to mechanical function as a human being can be. The whole process of digestion, masticating, swallowing, digesting, excretion, is a sort of super-mechanical process. And Phillotson was like this. He was an organ, a function-fulfilling organ, he had no separate existence. He could not create a single new movement or thought or expression. Everything he did was a repetition of what had been. All his study was a study of what had been. It was a mechanical, functional process. He was a true, if small, form of the *Savant*. He could understand only the functional laws of living, but these he understood honestly. He was true to himself, he was not overcome by any cant or sentimentalizing. So that in this he was splendid. But it is a cruel thing for a complete, or a spiritual, individuality to be submitted to a functional organism.

The Widow Edlin said that there are some men no woman of any feeling could touch, and Phillotson was one of them. If the Widow knew this, why was Sue's instinct so short?

But Mrs Edlin was a full human being, creating life in a new form through her personality. She must have known Sue's deficiency. It was natural for Sue to read and to turn again to:

> Thou hast conquered, O pale Galilean!
> The world has grown grey from Thy breath.

In her the pale Galilean had indeed triumphed. Her body was as insentient as hoar-frost. She knew well enough that she was not alive in the ordinary human sense. She did not, like an ordinary woman, receive all she knew through her senses, her instincts, but through her consciousness. The pale Galilean had a pure disciple in her: in her He was fulfilled. For the senses, the body, did not exist in her; she existed as a consciousness. And this is so much so, that she was almost an Apostate. She turned to look at Venus and Apollo. As if she could know either Venus or Apollo, save as ideas. Nor Venus nor Aphrodite had anything to do with her, but only Pallas and Christ.

She was unhappy every moment of her life, poor Sue, with the knowledge of her own non-existence within life. She felt all the time the ghastly sickness of dissolution upon her, she was as a void unto herself.

So she married Phillotson, the only man she could, in reality, marry. To him she could be a wife: she could give him the sexual relief he wanted of her, and supply him with the transcendence which was a pleasure to him; it was hers to seal him with the seal which made an honourable human being of him. For he felt, deep within himself, something a reptile feels. And she was his guarantee, his crown.

Why does a snake horrify us, or even a newt? Why was Phillotson like a newt? What is it, in our life or in our feeling, to which a newt corresponds? Is it that life has the two sides, of growth and of decay, symbolized most acutely in our bodies by the semen and the excreta? Is it that the newt, the reptile, belong to the putrescent activity of life; the bird, the fish to the growth activity? Is it that the newt and the reptile are suggested to us through those sensations connected with excretion? And was Phillotson more or less connected with the decay activity of life? Was it his function to reorganize the life-excreta of the ages? At any rate, one can honour him, for he was true to himself.

Sue married Phillotson according to her true instinct. But being almost pure Christian, in the sense of having no physical life, she had turned to the Greeks, and with her mind was an Aphrodite-worshipper. In craving for the highest form of that which she lacked, she worshipped Aphrodite. There are two sets of Aphrodite-worshippers: daughters of Aphrodite and the almost neutral daughters of Mary of Bethany. Sue was, oh, cruelly far from being a daughter of Aphrodite. She was the furthest alien from Aphrodite. She might excuse herself through her Venus Urania – but it was hopeless.

Therefore, when she left Phillotson, in whose marriage she consummated her own crucifixion, to go to Jude, she was deserting the God of her being for the God of her hopeless want. How much could she become a living, physical woman? But she would get away from Phillotson.

She went to Jude to continue the spiritual marriage, bodiless. That was all very well, if he had been satisfied. If he had been satisfied, they might have lived in this spiritual intimacy, without physical contact, for the rest of their lives, so strong was her true instinct for herself.

He, however, was not satisfied. He reached the point where he was clarified, where he had reduced from his blood into his consciousness all that was uncompounded before. He had become himself as far as he could, he had fulfilled himself. All that he had gathered in his youth, all that he had gathered from Arabella, was assimilated now, fused and transformed into one clear Jude.

Now he wants that which is necessary for him if he is to go on. He wants, at its lowest, the physical, sexual relief. For continually baulked sexual desire, or necessity, makes a man unable to live freely, scotches him, stultifies him. And where a man is roused to the fullest pitch, as Jude was roused by Sue, then the principal connexion becomes a necessity, if only for relief. Anything else is a violation.

Sue ran away to escape physical connexion with Phillotson, only to find herself in the arms of Jude. But Jude wanted of her more than Phillotson wanted. This was what terrified her to the bottom of her nature. Whereas Phillotson always only wanted sexual relief of her, Jude wanted the consummation of marriage. He wanted that deepest experience, that penetrating far into the unknown and undiscovered which lies in the body and blood of man and woman, during life. He wanted to receive from her the quickening, the primitive seed and impulse which should start him to a new birth. And for this he must go back deep into the primal, unshown, unknown life of the blood, the thick source-stream of life in her.

And she was terrified lest he should find her out, that it was wanting in her. This was her deepest dread, to see him inevitably disappointed in her. She could not bear to be put into the balance, wherein she knew she would be found wanting.

For she knew in herself that she was cut off from the source and origin of life. For her, the way back was lost irrevocably. And when Jude came to her, wanting to retrace with her the course right back to the springs and the welling-out, she was more afraid than of death. For she could not. She was like a flower broken off from the tree, that lives a while in water, and even puts forth. So Sue lived sustained and nourished by the rarefied life of books and art, and by the inflow from the man. But, owing to centuries and centuries of weaning away from the body of life, centuries of insisting upon the supremacy and bodilessness of Love, centuries of striving to escape the conditions of being and of striving to attain the condition of Knowledge, centuries of pure Christianity, she had gone too far. She had climbed and climbed to be near the stars. And now, at last, on the topmost pinnacle, exposed to all the horrors and the magnificence of space, she could not go back. Her strength had fallen from her. Up at that great height, with scarcely any foothold, but only space, space all round her, rising up to her from beneath, she was like a thing suspended, supported almost at the point of extinction by the density of the medium. Her body was lost to her, fallen away, gone. She existed there as a point of consciousness, no more, like one swooned at a great height, held up at the tip of a fine pinnacle that drove upwards into nothingness.

Jude rose to that height with her. But he did not die as she died. Beneath him the foothold was more, he did not swoon. There came a time when he wanted to go back, down to earth. But she was fastened like Andromeda.

Perhaps, if Jude had not known Arabella, Sue might have persuaded him that he too was bodiless, only a point of consciousness. But she was too late; another had been before her and given her the lie.

Arabella was never so jealous of Sue as Sue of Arabella. How shall the saint that tips the pinnacle, Saint Simon Stylites thrust on the highest needle that pricks the heavens, be envied by the man who walks the horizontal earth? But Sue was cruelly anguished with jealousy of Arabella. It was only this, this knowledge that Jude wanted Arabella, which made Sue give him access to her own body.

When she did that, she died. The Sue that had been till then, the glimmering, pale, star-like Sue, died and was revoked on the night when Arabella called at their house at Aldbrickham, and Jude went out in his slippers to look for her, and did not find her, but came back to Sue, who in her anguish gave him then the access to her body. Till that day, Sue had been, in her will and in her very self, true to one motion, to Love, to Knowledge, to the Light, to the upward motion. Phillotson had not altered this. When she had suffered him, she had said: 'He does not touch me; I am beyond him.'

But now she must give her body to Jude. At that moment her light began to go out, all she had lived for and by began to turn into a falseness, Sue began to nullify herself.

She could never become physical. She could never return down to earth. But there, lying bound at the pinnacle-tip, she had to pretend she was lying on the horizontal earth, prostrate with a man.

It was a profanation and a pollution, worse than the pollution of Cassandra or of the Vestals. Sue had her own form: to break this form was to destroy her. Her destruction began only when she said to Jude, 'I give in.'

As for Jude, he dragged his body after his consciousness. His instinct could never have made him actually desire physical connexion with Sue. He was roused by an appeal made through his consciousness. This appeal automatically roused his senses. His consciousness desired Sue. So his senses were forced to follow his consciousness.

But he must have felt, in knowing her, the *frisson* of sacrilege, something like the Frenchman who lay with a corpse. Her body, the body of a Vestal, was swooned into that state of bloodless ecstasy wherein it was dead to the senses. Or it was the body of an insane woman, whose senses are directed from the disordered mind, whose mind is not subjected to the senses.

From *Study of Thomas Hardy*

But Jude was physically undeveloped. Altogether he was medieval. His senses were vigorous but not delicate. He never realized what it meant to *him*, his taking Sue. He thought he was satisfied.

But if it was death to her, or profanation, or pollution, or breaking, it was unnatural to him, blasphemy. How could he, a living, loving man, warm and productive, take with his body the moonlit cold body of a woman who did not live to him, and did not want him? It was monstrous, and it sent him mad.

She knew it was wrong, she knew it should never be. But what else could she do? Jude loved her now with his will. To have left him to Arabella would have been to destroy him. To have shared him with Arabella would have been possible to Sue, but impossible to him, for he had the strong, purist idea that a man's body should follow and be subordinate to his spirit, his senses should be subordinate to and subsequent to his mind. Which idea is utterly false.

So Jude and Sue are damned, partly by their very being, but chiefly by their incapacity to accept the conditions of their own and each other's being. If Jude could have known that he did not want Sue physically, and then have made his choice, they might not have wasted their lives. But he could not know.

If he could have known, after a while, after he had taken her many times, that it was wrong, still they might have made a life. He must have known that, after taking Sue, he was depressed as she was depressed. He must have known worse than that. He must have felt the devastating sense of the unlivingness of life, things must have ceased to exist for him, when he rose from taking Sue, and he must have felt that he walked in a ghastly blank, confronted just by space, void.

But he would acknowledge nothing of what he felt. He must feel according to his idea and his will. Nevertheless, they were too truthful ever to marry. A man as real and personal as Jude cannot, from his deeper religious sense, marry a woman unless indeed he can marry her, unless with her he can find or approach the real consummation of marriage. And Sue and Jude could not lie to themselves, in their last and deepest feelings. They knew it was no marriage; they knew it was wrong, all along; they knew they were sinning against life, in forcing a physical marriage between themselves.

How many people, man and woman, live together, in England, and have children, and are never, never asked whether they have been through the marriage ceremony together? Why then should Jude and Sue have been brought to task? Only because of their own uneasy sense of wrong, of sin, which they communicated to other people. And this wrong or sin was not against the community, but against their own being, against life. Which is why they were, the pair of them, instinctively disliked.

They never knew happiness, actual, sure-footed happiness, not for a moment. That was incompatible with Sue's nature. But what they knew was a very delightful but poignant and unhealthy condition of lightened consciousness. They reacted on each other to stimulate the consciousness. So that, when they went to the flower-show, her sense of the roses, and Jude's sense of the roses, would be most, most poignant. There is always this pathos, this poignancy, this trembling on the verge of pain and tears, in their happiness.

'Happy?' he murmured. She nodded.

The roses, how the roses glowed for them! The flowers had more being than either he or she. But as their ecstasy over things sank a little, they felt, the pair of them, as if they themselves were wanting in real body, as if they were too unsubstantial, too thin and evanescent in substance, as if the other solid people might jostle right through them, two wandering shades as they were.

This they felt themselves. Hence their uncertainty in contact with other people, hence their abnormal sensitiveness. But they had their own form of happiness, nevertheless, this trembling on the verge of ecstasy, when, the senses strongly roused to the service of the consciousness, the things they contemplated took flaming being, became flaming symbols of their own emotions to them.

So that the real marriage of Jude and Sue was in the roses. Then, in the third state, in the spirit, these two beings met upon the roses and in the roses were symbolized in consummation.

The rose is the symbol of marriage-consummation in its beauty. To them it is more than a symbol, it is a fact, a flaming experience.

They went home tremblingly glad. And then the horror when, because of Jude's unsatisfaction, he must take Sue sexually. The flaming experience became a falsity, or an *ignis fatuus* leading them on.

They exhausted their lives, he in the consciousness, she in the body. She was glad to have children, to prove she was a woman. But in her it was a perversity to wish to prove she was a woman. She was no woman. And her children, the proof thereof, vanished like hoar-frost from her.

It was not the stone-masonry that exhausted him and weakened him and made him ill. It was this continuous feeding of his consciousness from his senses, this continuous state of incandescence of the consciousness, when his body, his vital tissues, the very protoplasm in him, was being slowly consumed away. For he had no life in the body. Every time he went to Sue, physically, his inner experience must have been a shock back from life and from the form of outgoing, like that of a man who lies with a corpse. He had no life in the senses: he had no inflow from the source to make up for the enormous wastage. So he gradually became exhausted, burned more and more away, till he was frail as an ember.

And she, her body also suffered. But it was in the mind that she had had her being, and it was in the mind she paid her price. She tried and tried to receive and to satisfy Jude physically. She bore him children, she gave herself to the life of the body.

But as she was formed she was formed, and there was no altering it. She needed all the life that belonged to her, and more, for the supplying of her mind, since such a mind as hers is found only, healthily, in a person of powerful vitality. For the mind, in a common person, is created out of the surplus vitality, or out of the remainder after all the sensuous life has been fulfilled.

She needed all the life that belonged to her, for her mind. It was her form. To disturb that arrangement was to make her into somebody else, not herself. Therefore, when she became a physical wife and a mother, she forswore her own being. She abjured her own mind, she denied it, took her faith, her belief, her very living away from it.

It is most probable she lived chiefly in her children. They were her guarantee as a physical woman, the being to which she now laid claim. She had forsaken the ideal of an independent mind.

She would love her children with anguish, afraid always for their safety, never certain of their stable existence, never assured of their real reality. When they were out of her sight, she would be uneasy, uneasy almost as if they did not exist. There would be a gnawing at her till they came back. She would not be satisfied till she had them crushed on her breast. And even then, she would not be sure, she would not be sure. She could not be sure, in life, of anything. She could only be sure, in the old days, of what she saw with her mind. Of that she was absolutely sure.

Meanwhile Jude became exhausted in vitality, bewildered, aimless, lost, pathetically nonproductive.

Again one can see what instinct, what feeling it was which made Arabella's boy bring about the death of the children and of himself. He, sensitive, so bodiless, so selfless as to be a sort of automaton, is very badly suggested, exaggerated, but one can see what is meant. And he feels, as any child will feel, as many children feel today, that they are really anachronisms, accidents, fatal accidents, unreal, false notes in their mothers' lives, that, according to her, they have no being: that, if they have being, then she has not. So he takes away all the children.

And then Sue ceases to be: she strikes the line through her own existence, cancels herself. There exists no more Sue Fawley. She cancels herself. She wishes to cease to exist, as a person, she wishes to be absorbed away, so that she is no longer self-responsible.

For she denied and forsook and broke her own real form, her own independent, cool-lighted mind-life. And now her children are not only dead, but self-slain, those pledges of the physical life for which she abandoned the other.

She has a passion to expiate, to expiate, to expiate. Her children should never have been born: her instinct always knew this.

Now their dead bodies drive her mad with a sense of blasphemy. And she blasphemed the Holy Spirit, which told her she is guilty of their birth and their death, of the horrible nothing which they are. She is even guilty of their little, palpitating sufferings and joys of mortal life, now made nothing. She cannot bear it – who could? And she wants to expiate, doubly expiate. Her mind, which she set up in her conceit, and then forswore, she must stamp it out of existence, as one stamps out fire. She would never again think or decide for herself. The world, the past, should have written every decision for her. The last act of her intellect was the utter renunciation of her mind and the embracing of utter orthodoxy, where every belief, every thought, every decision was made ready for her, so that she did not exist self-responsible. And then her loathed body, which had committed the crime of bearing dead children, which had come to life only to spread nihilism like a pestilence, that too should be scourged out of existence. She chose the bitterest penalty in going back to Phillotson.

There was no more Sue. Body, soul, and spirit, she annihilated herself. All that remained of her was the will by which she annihilated herself. That remained fixed, a locked centre of self-hatred, life-hatred so utter that it had no hope of death. It knew that life is life, and there is no death for life.

Jude was too exhausted himself to save her. He says of her she was not worth a man's love. But that was not the point. It was not a question of her worth. It was a question of her being. If he had said she was not capable of receiving a man's love as he wished to bestow it, he might have spoken nearer the truth. But she practically told him this. She made it plain to him what she wanted, what she could take. But he overrode her. She tried hard to abide by her own form. But he forced her. He had no case against her, unless she made the great appeal for him, that he should flow to her, whilst at the same time she could not take him completely, body and spirit both.

She asked for what he could not give – what perhaps no man can give: passionate love without physical desire. She had no blame for him: she had no love for him. Self-love triumphed in

251

her when she first knew him. She almost deliberately asked for more, far more, than she intended to give. Self-hatred triumphed in the end. So it had to be.

As for Jude, he had been dying slowly, but much quicker than she, since the first night she took him. It was best to get it done quickly in the end.

And this tragedy is the result of over-development of one principle of human life at the expense of the other; an over-balancing; a laying of all the stress on the Male, the Love, the Spirit, the Mind, the Consciousness; a denying, a blaspheming against the Female, the Law, the Soul, the Senses, the Feelings. But she is developed to the very extreme, she scarcely lives in the body at all. Being of the feminine gender, she is yet no woman at all, nor male; she is almost neuter. He is nearer the balance, nearer the centre, nearer the wholeness. But the whole human effort, towards pure life in the spirit, towards becoming pure Sue, drags him along; he identifies himself with this effort, destroys himself and her in his adherence to this identification.

But why, in casting off one or another form of religion, has man ceased to be religious altogether? Why will he not recognize Sue and Jude, as Cassandra was recognized long ago, and Achilles, and the Vestals, and the nuns, and the monks? Why must being be denied altogether?

Sue had a being, special and beautiful. Why must not Jude recognize it in all its speciality? Why must man be so utterly irreverent, that he approaches each being as if it were no-being? Why must it be assumed that Sue is an 'ordinary' woman – as if such a thing existed? Why must she feel ashamed if she is specialized? And why must Jude, owing to the conception he is brought up in, force her to act as if she were his 'ordinary' abstraction, a woman?

She was not a woman. She was Sue Bridehead, something very particular. Why was there no place for her? Cassandra had the Temple of Apollo. Why are we so foul that we have no reverence for that which we are and for that which is amongst us? If we had reverence for our life, our life would take at once religious form. But as it is, in our filthy irreverence, it remains a disgusting slough, where each one of us goes so thoroughly disguised in dirt that we are all alike and indistinguishable.

If we had reverence for what we are, our life would take real form, and Sue would have a place, as Cassandra had a place; she would have a place which does not yet exist, because we are all so vulgar, we have nothing.

# Translator's Preface to *Cavalleria Rusticana* by Giovanni Verga

Written 1927, published 1928

*Cavalleria Rusticana* is in many ways the most interesting of the Verga books. The volume of short stories under this title appeared in 1880, when the author was forty years old, and when he had just 'retired' from the world.

The Verga family owned land around Vizzini, a biggish village in southern Sicily; and here, in and around Vizzini, the tragedies of Turiddu and La Lupa and Jeli take place. But it was only in middle life that the drama of peasant passion really made an impression on Giovanni Verga. His earlier imagination, naturally, went out into the great world.

The family of the future author lived chiefly at Catania, the seaport of east Sicily, under Etna. And Catania was really Verga's home town, just as Vizzini was his home village.

But as a young man of twenty he already wanted to depart into the bigger world of 'the Continent', as the Sicilians called the mainland of Italy. It was the Italy of 1860, the Italy of Garibaldi, and the new era. Verga seems to have taken little interest in politics. He had no doubt the southern idea of himself as a gentleman and an aristocrat, beyond politics. And he had the ancient southern thirst for show, for lustre, for glory, a desire to figure grandly among the first society of the world. His nature was proud and unmixable. At the same time, he had the southern passionate yearning for tenderness and generosity. And so he ventured into the world, without much money; and, in true southern fashion, he was dazzled. To the end of his days he was dazzled by elegant ladies in elegant equipages: one sees it, amusingly, in all his books.

He was a handsome man, by instinct haughty and reserved: because, partly, he was passionate and emotional, and did not choose to give himself away. A true provincial, he had to try to enter the *beau monde*. He lived by journalism, more or less: certainly the Vizzini lands would not keep him in affluence. But still, in his comparative poverty, he must enter the *beau monde*.

He did so: and apparently with a certain success. And for nearly twenty years he lived in Milan, in Florence, in Naples, writing, and imagining he was fulfilling his thirst for glory by having love-affairs with elegant ladies: most elegant ladies, as he assures us.

To this period belong the curiously unequal novels of the city world: *Eva, Tigre Reale, Eros*. They are interesting, alive, bitter, somewhat unhealthy, smelling of the seventies and of the Paris of the Goncourts, and, in some curious way, abortive. The man had not found himself. He was in his wrong element, fooling himself and being fooled by show, in a true Italian fashion.

Then, towards the age of forty, came the recoil, and the *Cavalleria Rusticana* volume is the first book of the recoil. It was a recoil away from the *beau monde* and the 'Continent', back to Sicily, to Catania, to the peasants. Verga never married: but he was deeply attached to his own family. He lived in Catania, with his sister. His brother, or brother-in-law, who had looked after the Vizzini property, was ill. So for the first time in his life Giovanni Verga had to undertake the responsibility for the family estate and fortune. He had to go to Vizzini and more or less manage the farm work – at least keep an eye on it. He said he hated the job, that he had no capacity for business, and so on. But we may be sure he managed very well. And certainly from this experience he gained his real fortune, his genuine sympathy with peasant life, instead of his spurious sympathy with elegant ladies. His great books all followed *Cavalleria Rusticana*: and

255

*Mastro-don Gesualdo* and the *Novelle Rusticane* ('Little Novels of Sicily') and most of the sketches have their scenes laid in or around Vizzini.

So that *Cavalleria Rusticana* marks a turning-point in the man's life. Verga still looks back to the city elegance, and makes such a sour face over it, it is really funny. The sketch he calls 'Fantasticheria' ('Caprice') and the last story in the book, 'Il Come, il Quando, e il Perché' ('The How, When, and Where-fore') both deal with the elegant little lady herself. The sketch 'Caprice' we may take as autobiographical – the story not entirely so. But we have enough data to go on.

The elegant little lady is the same, pretty, spoilt, impulsive, emotional, but without passion. The lover, Polidori, is only half-sketched. But evidently he is a passionate man who *thinks* he can play at love and then is mortified to his very soul because he finds it is only a game. The tone of mortification is amusingly evident both in the sketch and in the story. Verga is profoundly and everlastingly offended with the little lady, with all little ladies, for not taking him absolutely seriously as an amorous male, when all the time he doesn't quite take himself seriously, and doesn't take the little lady seriously at all.

Nevertheless, the moment of sheer roused passion is serious in the man: and apparently not so in the woman. Each time the moment comes, it involves the whole nature of the man and does not involve the whole nature of the woman: she still clings to her social safeguards. It is the difference between a passionate nature and an emotional nature. But then the man goes out deliberately to make love to the emotional elegant woman who is truly social and not passionate. So he has only himself to blame if his passionate nose is out of joint.

It is most obviously out of joint. His little picture of the elegant little lady jingling her scent-bottle and gazing in nervous anxiety for the train from Catania which will carry her away from Aci-Trezza and her too-intense lover, back to her light, gay, secure world on the mainland is one of the most amusingly biting things in the literature of love. How glad she must have been to get away from him! And how bored she must have been by his preaching the virtues of the humble poor, holding them up before her to make her feel small. We may be sure she doesn't feel small, only nervous and irritable. For apparently she had no deep warmth or generosity of nature.

So Verga recoiled to the humble poor, as we see in his 'Caprice' sketch. Like a southerner, what he did he did wholesale. Floods of savage and tragic pity he poured upon the humble fisher-folk of Aci-Trezza, whether they asked for it or not – partly to spite the elegant little lady. And this particular flood spreads over the whole of his long novel concerning the fisher-folk of Aci-Trezza: *I Malavoglia.* It is a great novel, in spite of the pity: but always in spite of it.

In *Cavalleria Rusticana,* however, Verga had not yet come to the point of letting loose his pity. He is still too much and too profoundly offended, as a passionate male. He recoils savagely away from the sophistications of the city life of elegant little ladies, to the peasants in their most crude and simple, almost brute-like aspect.

When one reads, one after the other, the stories of Turiddu, La Lupa, Jeli, Brothpot, Rosso Malpelo, one after the other, stories of crude killing, it seems almost too much, too crude, too violent, too much a question of mere brutes.

As a matter of fact, the judgement is unjust. Turiddu is not a brute: neither is Alfio. Both are men of sensitive and even honourable nature. Turiddu knows he is wrong, and would even let himself be killed, he says, but for the thought of his old mother. The elegant Maria and her Erminia are never so sensitive and direct in expressing themselves; not so frankly warm-hearted.

As for Jeli, who could call him a brute? or Nanni? or Brothpot? They are perhaps not brutal enough. They are too gentle and forbearing, too delicately naïve. And so grosser natures trespass on them unpardonably; and the revenge flashes out.

His contemporaries abused Verga for being a realist of the Zola school. The charge is unjust. The base of the charge against Zola is that he made his people too often merely physical-functional arrangements, physically and materially functioning without any 'higher' nature. The charge against Zola is often justifiable. It is completely justifiable against the earlier d'Annunzio. In fact, the Italian tends on the one hand to be this creature of physical-functional activity and nothing else, spasmodically sensual and materialist; hence the violent Italian outcry against the portrayal of such creatures, and d'Annunzio's speedy transition to neurotic Virgins of the Rocks and ultra-refinements.

But Verga's people are always people in the purest sense of the word. They are not intellectual, but then neither was Hector nor Ulysses intellectual. Verga, in his recoil, mistrusted everything that smelled of sophistication. He had a passion for the most naïve, the most unsophisticated manifestation of human nature. He was not seeking the brute, the animal man, the so-called cave-man. Far from it. He knew already too well that the brute and the cave-man lie quite near under the skin of the ordinary successful man of the world. There you have the predatory cave-man of vulgar imagination, thinly hidden under expensive cloth.

What Verga's soul yearned for was the purely naïve human being, in contrast to the sophisticated. It seems as if Sicily, in some way, under all her amazing forms of sophistication and corruption, still preserves some flower of pure human candour: the same thing that fascinated Theocritus. Theocritus was an Alexandrine courtier, singing from all his 'musk and insolence' of the pure idyllic Sicilian shepherds. Verga is the Theocritus of the nineteenth century, born among the Sicilian shepherds, and speaking of them in prose more sadly than Theocritus, yet with some of the same eternal Sicilian dawn-freshness in his vision. It is almost bitter to think that Rosso Malpelo must often have looked along the coast and seen the rocks that the Cyclops flung at Ulysses; and that Jeli must some time or other have looked to the yellow temple-ruins of Girgenti.

Verga was fascinated, after his mortification in the *beau monde*, by pure naïveté and by the spontaneous passion of life, that spurts beyond all convention or even law. Yet as we read, one after the other, of these betrayed husbands killing the co-respondents, it seems a little mechanical. Alfio, Jeli, Brothpot,

Gramigna ending their life in prison: it seems a bit futile and hopeless, mechanical again.

The fault is partly Verga's own, the fault of his own obsession. He felt himself in some way deeply mortified, insulted in his ultimate sexual or male self, and he enacted over and over again the drama of revenge. We think to ourselves, ah, how stupid of Alfio, of Jeli, of Brothpot, to have to go killing a man and getting themselves shut up in prison for life, merely because the man had committed adultery with their wives. Was it worth it? Was the wife worth one year of prison, to a man, let alone a lifetime?

We ask the question with our reason, and with our reason we answer No! Not for a moment was any of these women worth it. Nowadays we have learnt more sense, and we let her go her way. So the stories are too old-fashioned.

And again, it was not for love of their wives that Jeli and Alfio and Brothpot killed the other man. It was because people talked. It was because of the fiction of 'honour'. We have got beyond all that.

We are so much more reasonable. All our life is so much more reasoned and reasonable. *Nous avons changé tout cela.*

And yet, as the years go by, one wonders if mankind is so radically changed. One wonders whether reason, sweet reason, has really changed us, or merely delayed or diverted our reactions. Are Alfio and Jeli and Gramigna utterly out of date, a thing superseded for ever? Or are they eternal?

Is man a sweet and reasonable creature? Or is he, basically, a passional phenomenon? Is man a phenomenon on the face of the earth, or a rational consciousness? Is human behaviour to be reasonable, throughout the future, reasoned and rational? – or will it always display itself in strange and violent phenomena?

Judging from all experience, past and present, one can only decide that human behaviour is ultimately one of the natural phenomena, beyond all reason. Part of the phenomenon, for the time being, is human reason, the control of reason, and the power of the Word. But the Word and the reason are themselves only part of the coruscating phenomenon of human existence; they are, so to speak, one rosy shower from the rocket, which gives

259

way almost instantly to the red shower of ruin or the green shower of despair.

Man is a phenomenon on the face of the earth. But the phenomena have their laws. One of the laws of the phenomenon called a human being is that, hurt this being mortally at its sexual root, and it will recoil ultimately into some form of killing. The recoil may be prompt, or delay by years or even by generations. But it will come. We may take it as a law.

We may take it as another law that the very deepest quick of a man's nature is his own pride and self-respect. The human being, weird phenomenon, may be patient for years and years under insult, insult to his very quick, his pride in his own natural being. But at last, O phenomenon, killing will come of it. All bloody revolutions are the result of the long, slow, accumulated insult to the quick of pride in the mass of men.

A third law is that the naïve or innocent core in a man is always his vital core, and infinitely more important than his intellect or his reason. It is only from his core of unconscious naïveté that the human being is ultimately a responsible and dependable being. Break this human core of naïveté – and the evil of the world all the time tries to break it, in Jeli, in Rosso Malpelo, in Brothpot, in all these Verga characters – and you get either a violent reaction, or, as is usual nowadays, a merely rational creature whose core of spontaneous life is dead. Now the rational creature, who is merely rational, by some cruel trick of fate remains rational only for one or two generations at best. Then he is quite mad. It is one of the terrible qualities of the reason that it has no life of its own, and unless continually kept nourished or modified by the naïve life in man and woman, it becomes a purely parasitic and destructive thing. Make any human being a really rational being, and you have made him a parasitic and destructive force. Make any people mainly rational in their life, and their inner activity will be the activity of destruction. The more the populations of the world become only rational in their consciousness, the swifter they bring about their destruction pure and simple.

Verga, like every great artist, had sensed this. What he bewails really, as the tragedy of tragedies, in this book, is the ugly trespass of the sophisticated greedy ones upon the naïve life of the true human being: the death of the naïve, pure being – or his lifelong imprisonment – and the triumph or the killing of the sophisticated greedy ones.

This is the tragedy of tragedies in all time, but particularly in our epoch: the killing off of the naïve innocent life in all of us, by which alone we can continue to live, and the ugly triumph of the sophisticated greedy.

It may be urged that Verga commits the Tolstoyan fallacy, of repudiating the educated world and exalting the peasant. But this is not the case. Verga is very much the gentleman, exclusively so, to the end of his days. He did not dream of putting on a peasant's smock, or following the plough. What Tolstoy somewhat perversely worshipped in the peasants was poverty itself, and humility, and what Tolstoy perversely hated was instinctive pride or spontaneous passion. Tolstoy has a perverse pleasure in making the later Vronsky abject and pitiable: because Tolstoy so meanly envied the healthy passionate male in the young Vronsky. Tolstoy cut off his own nose to spite his face. He envied the reckless passionate male with a carking envy, because he must have felt himself in some way wanting in comparison. So he exalts the peasant: not because the peasant may be a more natural and spontaneous creature than the city man or the guardsman, but just because the peasant is poverty-stricken and humble. This is malice, the envy of weakness and deformity.

We know now that the peasant is no better than anybody else; no better than a prince or a selfish young army officer or a governor or a merchant. In fact, in the mass, the peasant is worse than any of these. The peasant mass is the ugliest of all human masses, most greedily selfish and brutal of all. Which Tolstoy, leaning down from the gold bar of heaven, will have had opportunity to observe. If we have to trust to a *mass*, then better trust the upper or middle-class mass, all masses being odious.

But Verga by no means exalts the peasants as a class: nor does he believe in their poverty and humility. Verga's peasants are certainly not Christ-like, whatever else they are. They are most normally ugly and low, the bulk of them. And individuals are sensitive and simple.

Verga turns to the peasants only to seek for a certain something which, as a healthy artist, he worshipped. Even Tolstoy, as a healthy artist, worshipped it the same. It was only as a moralist and a personal being that Tolstoy was perverse. As a true artist, he worshipped, as Verga did, every manifestation of pure, spontaneous, passionate life, life kindled to vividness. As a perverse moralist with a sense of some subtle deficiency in himself, Tolstoy tries to insult and to damp out the vividness of life. Imagine any great artist making the vulgar social condemnation of Anna and Vronsky figure as divine punishment! Where now is the society that turned its back on Vronsky and Anna? Where is it? And what is its condemnation worth, today?

Verga turned to the peasants to find, *in individuals*, the vivid spontaneity of sensitive, passionate life, non-moral and non-didactic. He found it always *defeated*. He found the vulgar and the greedy always destroying the sensitive and the passionate. The vulgar and the greedy are themselves usually peasants: Verga was far too sane to put an aureole round the whole class. Still more are the women greedy and egoistic. But even so, Turiddu and Jeli and Rosso Malpelo and Nanni and Gramigna and Brothpot are not humble. They have no saint-like, self-sacrificial qualities. They are only naïve, passionate, and natural. They are 'defeated' not because there is any glory or sanctification in defeat; there is no martyrdom about it. They are defeated because they are too unsuspicious, not sufficiently armed and ready to do battle with the greedy and the sophisticated. When they do strike, they destroy themselves too. So the real tragedy is that they are not sufficiently conscious and developed to defend their own naïve sensitiveness against the inroads of the greedy and the vulgar. The greedy and the vulgar win all the time: which, alas, is only too true, in Sicily as everywhere else. But Giovanni Verga certainly doesn't help them, by preaching humility. He does show them the knife of revenge at their throat.

And these stories, instead of being out of date, just because the manners depicted are more or less obsolete, even in Sicily, which is a good deal Americanized and 'cleaned up', as the reformers would say; instead of being out of date, they are dynamically perhaps the most up to date of stories. The Chekhovian after-influenza effect of inertia and will-lessness is wearing off, all over Europe. We realize we've had about enough of being null. And if Chekhov represents the human being driven into an extremity of self-consciousness and faintly-wriggling inertia, Verga represents him as waking suddenly from inaction into the stroke of revenge. We shall see which of the two visions is more deeply true to life.

'Cavalleria Rusticana' and 'La Lupa' have always been hailed as masterpieces of brevity and gems of literary form. Master-pieces they are, but one is now a little sceptical of their form. After the enormous diffusiveness of Victor Hugo, it was perhaps necessary to make the artist more self-critical and self-effacing. But any wholesale creed in art is dangerous. Hugo's romanti-cism, which consisted in letting himself go, in an orgy of effusive self-conceit, was not much worse than the next creed the French invented for the artist, of self-effacement. Self-effacement is quite as self-conscious, and perhaps even more conceited than letting oneself go. Maupassant's self-effacement becomes more blatant than Hugo's self-effusion. As for the perfection of form achieved – Mérimée achieved the highest, in his dull stories like 'Mateo Falcone' and 'L'Enlèvement de la Redoute'. But they are hope-lessly literary, fabricated. So is most of Maupassant. And if *Madame Bovary* has form, it is a pretty flat form.

But Verga was caught up by the grand idea of self-effacement in art. Anything more confused, more silly, really, than the pages prefacing the excellent story 'Gramigna's Lover' would be hard to find, from the pen of a great writer. The moment Verga starts talking theories, our interest wilts immediately. The theories were none of his own: just borrowed from the literary smarties of Paris. And poor Verga looks a sad sight in Paris ready-mades. And when he starts putting his theories into practice, and effac-ing himself, one is far more aware of his interference than when he just goes ahead. Naturally! Because self-effacement is, of course, self-conscious, and any form of emotional self-consciousness hinders a first-rate artist: though it may help the second-rate.

Therefore in 'Cavalleria Rusticana' and in 'La Lupa' we are just a bit too much aware of the author and his scissors. He has clipped too many away. The transitions are too abrupt. All is over in a gasp: whereas a story like 'La Lupa' covers at least several years of time.

As a matter of fact, we need more looseness. We need an apparent formlessness, definite form is mechanical. We need more easy transition from mood to mood and from deed to deed. A great deal of the meaning of life and of art lies in the apparently dull spaces, the pauses, the unimportant passages. They are truly passages, the places of passing over.

So that Verga's deliberate missing-out of transition passages is, it seems to me, often a defect. And for this reason a story like 'La Lupa' loses a great deal of its life. It may be a masterpiece of concision, but it is hardly a masterpiece of narration. It is so short, our acquaintance with Nanni and Maricchia is so fleeting, we forget them almost at once. 'Jeli' makes a far more profound impression, so does 'Rosso Malpelo'. These seem to me the finest stories in the book, and among the finest stories ever written. Rosso Malpelo is an extreme of the human consciousness, subtle and appalling as anything done by the Russians, and at the same time substantial, not introspective vapours. You will never forget him.

And it needed a deeper genius to write 'Rosso Malpelo' than to write 'Cavalleria Rusticana' or 'La Lupa'. But the literary smarties, being so smart, have always praised the latter two above the others.

This business of missing out transition passages is quite deliberate on Verga's part. It is perhaps most evident in this volume, because it is here that Verga practises it for the first time. It was a new dodge, and he handled it badly. The sliding-over of the change from Jeli's boyhood to his young manhood is surely too deliberately confusing!

But Verga had a double motive. First was the Frenchy idea of self-effacement, which, however, didn't go very deep, as Verga was too much of a true southerner to know quite what it meant. But the second motive was more dynamic. It was connected with Verga's whole recoil from the sophisticated world, and it effected a revolution in his style. Instinctively he had come to hate the tyranny of a persistently logical sequence, or even a persistently chronological sequence. Time and the syllogism both seemed to represent the sophisticated falsehood and a sort of bullying, to him.

He tells us himself how he came across his new style:

I had published several of my first novels. They went well: I was preparing others. One day, I don't know how, there came into my hands a sort of broadside, a halfpenny sheet, sufficiently ungrammatical and disconnected, in which a sea-captain succinctly relates all the vicissitudes through which his sailing-ship has passed. Seaman's language, short, without an unnecessary phrase. It struck me, and I read it again; it was what I was looking for, without definitely knowing it. Sometimes, you know, just a sign, an indication is enough. It is a revelation...

This passage explains all we need to know about Verga's style, which is perhaps at its most extreme in this volume. He was trying to follow the workings of the unsophisticated mind, and trying to reproduce the pattern.

Now the emotional mind, if we may be allowed to say so, is not logical. It is a psychological fact, that when we are thinking emotionally or passionately, thinking and feeling at the same time, we do not think rationally: and therefore, and therefore, and therefore. Instead, the mind makes curious swoops and circles. It touches the point of pain or interest, then sweeps away again in a cycle, coils round and approaches again the point of pain or interest. There is a curious spiral rhythm, and the mind approaches again and again the point of concern, repeats itself, goes back, destroys the time-sequence entirely, so that time ceases to exist, as the mind stoops to the quarry, then leaves it without striking, soars, hovers, turns, swoops, stoops again, still does not strike, yet is nearer, nearer, reels away again, wheels off into the air, even forgets, quite forgets, yet again turns, bends, circles

265

slowly, swoops and stoops again, until at last there is the closing-in, and the clutch of a decision or a resolve.

This activity of the mind is strictly timeless, and illogical. Afterwards you can deduce the logical sequence and the time sequence, as historians do from the past. But in the happening, the logical and the time sequence do not exist.

Verga tried to convey this in his style. It gives at first the sense of jumble and incoherence. The beginning of the story 'Brothpot' is a good example of this breathless muddle of the peasant mind. When one is used to it, it is amusing, and a new movement in deliberate consciousness: though the humorists have used the form before. But at first it may be annoying. Once he starts definitely narrating, however, Verga drops the 'muddled' method, and seeks only to be concise, often too concise, too abrupt in the transition. And in the matter of punctuation he is, perhaps, deliberately, a puzzle, aiming at the same muddled swift effect of the emotional mind in its movements. He is doing, as a great artist, what men like James Joyce do only out of contrariness and desire for a sensation. The emotional mind, however apparently muddled, has its own rhythm, its own commas and colons and full-stops. They are not always as we should expect them, but they are there, indicating that other rhythm.

Everybody knows, of course, that Verga made a dramatized version of 'Cavalleria Rusticana', and that this dramatized version is the libretto of the ever-popular little opera of the same name. So that Mascagni's rather feeble music has gone to immortalize a man like Verga, whose only *popular* claim to fame is that he wrote the aforesaid libretto. But that is fame's fault, not Verga's.

# Preface to *The Grand Inquisitor* by F. M. Dostoyevsky

Written and published 1930

It is a strange experience, to examine one's reaction to a book over a period of years. I remember when I first read *The Brothers Karamazov*, in 1913, how fascinated yet unconvinced it left me. And I remember Middleton Murry saying to me: 'Of course the whole clue to Dostoyevsky is in that Grand Inquisitor story.' And I remember saying: 'Why? It seems to me just rubbish.'

And it was true. The story seemed to me just a piece of showing off: a display of cynical-satanical pose which was simply irritating. The cynical-satanical pose always irritated me, and I could see nothing else in that black-a-vised Grand Inquisitor talking at Jesus at such length. I just felt it was all pose; he didn't really mean what he said; he was just showing off in blasphemy.

Since then I have read *The Brothers Karamazov* twice, and each time found it more depressing because, alas, more drearily true to life. At first it had been lurid romance. Now I read *The Grand Inquisitor* once more, and my heart sinks right through my shoes. I still see a trifle of cynical-satanical showing-off. But under that I hear the final and unanswerable criticism of Christ. And it is a deadly, devastating summing-up, unanswerable because borne out by the long experience of humanity. It is reality versus illusion, and the illusion was Jesus's, while time itself retorts with the reality.

If there is any question: Who is the Grand Inquisitor? – then surely we must say it is Ivan himself. And Ivan is the thinking mind of the human being in rebellion, thinking the whole thing out to the bitter end. As such he is, of course, identical with the Russian revolutionary of the thinking type. He is also, of course, Dostoyevsky himself, in his thoughtful, as apart from his passional and inspirational self. Dostoyevsky half hated Ivan. Yet, after all, Ivan is the greatest of the three brothers, pivotal. The passionate Dmitri and the inspired Alyosha are, at last, only offsets to Ivan.

And we cannot doubt that the Inquisitor speaks Dostoyevsky's own final opinion about Jesus. The opinion is, baldly, this: Jesus, you are inadequate. Men must correct you. And Jesus in the end gives the kiss of acquiescence to the Inquisitor, as Alyosha does to Ivan. The two inspired ones recognize the inadequacy of their inspiration: the thoughtful one has to accept the responsibility of a complete adjustment.

We may agree with Dostoyevsky or not, but we have to admit that his criticism of Jesus is the final criticism, based on the experience of two thousand years (he says fifteen hundred) and on a profound insight into the nature of mankind. Man can but be true to his own nature. No inspiration whatsoever will ever get him permanently beyond his limits.

And what are the limits? It is Dostoyevsky's first profound question. What are the limits to the nature, not of Man in the abstract, but of men, mere men, everyday men?

The limits are, says the Grand Inquisitor, three. Mankind in the bulk can never be 'free', because man on the whole makes three grand demands on life, and cannot endure unless these demands are satisfied.

1. He demands bread, and not merely as foodstuff, but as a miracle, given from the hand of God.

2. He demands mystery, the sense of the miraculous in life.

3. He demands somebody to bow down to, and somebody before whom all men shall bow down.

These three demands, for miracle, mystery and authority, prevent men from being 'free'. They are man's 'weakness'. Only a few men, the elect, are capable of abstaining from the absolute demand for bread, for miracle, mystery, and authority. These are the strong, and they must be as gods, to be able to be Christians fulfilling all the Christ-demand. The rest, the millions and millions of men throughout time, they are as babes or children or geese, they are too weak, 'impotent, vicious, worthless and rebellious' even to be able to share out the earthly bread, if it is left to them.

This, then, is the Grand Inquisitor's summing-up of the nature of mankind. The inadequacy of Jesus lies in the fact that Christianity is too difficult for men, the vast mass of men. It could only be realized by the few 'saints' or heroes. For the rest, man is like a horse harnessed to a load he cannot possibly pull. 'Hadst Thou respected him less, Thou wouldst have demanded less of him, and that would be nearer to love, for his burden would be lighter.'

Christianity, then, is the ideal, but is it impossible. It is impossible because it makes demands greater than the nature of man can bear. And therefore, to get a livable, working scheme, some of the elect, such as the Grand Inquisitor himself, have turned round to 'him', that other great Spirit, Satan, and have established Church and State on 'him'. For the Grand Inquisitor finds that to be able to live at all, mankind must be loved more tolerantly and more contemptuously than Jesus loved it, loved, for all that, more truly, since it is loved for itself, for what it is, and not for what it ought to be. Jesus loved mankind for what it ought to be, free and limitless. The Grand Inquisitor loves it for what it is, with all its limitations. And he contends his is the kinder love. And yet he says it is Satan. And Satan, he says at the beginning, means annihilation, and not-being.

As always in Dostoyevsky, the amazing perspicacity is mixed with ugly perversity. Nothing is pure. His wild love for Jesus is mixed with perverse and poisonous hate of Jesus: his moral hostility to the devil is mixed with secret worship of the devil. Dostoyevsky is always perverse, always impure, always an evil thinker and a marvellous seer.

Is it true that mankind demands, and will always demand, miracle, mystery, and authority? Surely it is true. Today, man gets his sense of the miraculous from science and machinery, radio, aeroplane, vast ships, zeppelins, poison gas, artificial silk: these things nourish man's sense of the miraculous as magic did in the past. But now, man is master of the mystery, there are no occult powers. The same with mystery: medicine, biological experiment, strange feats of the psychic people, spiritualists, Christian scientists – it is all mystery. And as for authority, Russia destroyed the Tsar to have Lenin and the present mechanical despotism, Italy has the rationalized despotism of Mussolini, and England is longing for a despot.

Dostoyevsky's diagnosis of human nature is simple and unanswerable. We have to submit, and agree that men are like that. Even over the question of sharing the bread, we have to agree that man is too weak, or vicious, or something, to be able to do it. He has to hand the common bread over to some absolute authority, Tsar or Lenin, to be shared out. And yet the mass of men are *incapable* of looking on bread as a mere means of sustenance, by which man sustains himself for the purpose of true living, true life being the 'heavenly bread'. It seeems a strange thing that men, the mass of men, cannot understand that *life* is the great reality, that true living fills us with vivid life, 'the heavenly bread', and earthly bread merely supports this. No, men cannot understand, never have understood that simple fact. They cannot see the distinction between bread, or property, money, and vivid life. They think that property and money are the same thing as vivid life. Only the few, the potential heroes or the 'elect', can see the simple distinction. The mass *cannot* see it, and will never see it.

Dostoyevsky was perhaps the first to realize this devastating truth, which Christ had not seen. A truth it is, none the less, and once recognized it will change the course of history. All that remains is for the elect to take charge of the bread – the property, the money – and then give it back to the masses as if it were really the gift of life. In this way, mankind might live happily, as the Inquisitor suggests. Otherwise, with the masses making the terrible mad mistake that money is life, and that therefore no one shall control the money, men shall be 'free' to get what they can, we are brought to a condition of competitive insanity and ultimate suicide.

So far, well and good, Dostoyevsky's diagnosis stands. But is it then to betray Christ and turn over to Satan if the elect should at last realize that instead of refusing Satan's three offers, the heroic Christian must now accept them. Jesus refused the three offers out of pride and fear: he wanted to be greater than these, and 'above' them. But we now realize, no man, not even Jesus, is really 'above' miracle, mystery, and authority. The one thing that Jesus is truly above, is the confusion between money and life. Money is not life, says Jesus, therefore you can ignore it and leave it to the devil.

Money is not life, it is true. But ignoring money and leaving it to the devil means handing over the great mass of men to the devil, for the mass of men *cannot* distinguish between money and life. It is hard to believe: certainly Jesus didn't believe it: and yet, as Dostoyevsky and the Inquisitor point out, it is so.

Well, and what then? Must we therefore go over to the devil? After all, the whole of Christianity is not contained in the rejection of the three temptations. The essence of Christianity is a love of mankind. If a love of mankind entails accepting the bitter limitation of the mass of men, their inability to distinguish between money and life, then accept the limitation, and have done with it. Then take over from the devil the money (or bread), the miracle, and the sword of Caesar, and, for the love of mankind, give back to men the bread, with its wonder, and give them the miracle, the marvellous, and give them, in a hierarchy, someone, some men, in higher and higher degrees, to bow down to. Let them bow down, let them bow down *en masse*, for the mass, who do not understand the difference between money and life, should always bow down to the elect, who do.

And is that serving the devil? It is certainly not serving the spirit of annihilation and not-being. It is serving the great wholeness of mankind, and in that respect, it is Christianity. Anyhow, it is the service of Almighty God, who made men what they are, limited and unlimited.

Where Dostoyevsky is perverse is in his making the old, old, wise governor of men a Grand Inquisitor. The recognition of the weakness of man has been a common trait in all great, wise rulers of people, from the Pharaohs and Darius through the great patient Popes of the early Church right down to the present day. They have known the weakness of men, and felt a certain tenderness. This is the spirit of all great government. But it was not the spirit of the Spanish Inquisition. The Spanish Inquisition in 1500 was a new-fangled thing, peculiar to Spain, with her curious death-lust and her bullying, and, strictly, a Spanish-political instrument, not Catholic at all, but rabidly national. The Spanish Inquisition actually was diabolic. It could not have produced a Grand Inquisitor who put Dostoyevsky's sad questions to Jesus. And the man who put those sad questions to Jesus could not possibly have been a Spanish Inquisitor. He could not possibly have burnt a hundred people in an *auto-da-fé*. He would have been too wise and far-seeing.

So that, in this respect, Dostoyevsky showed his epileptic and slightly criminal perversity. The man who feels a certain tenderness for mankind in its weakness or limitation is not therefore diabolic. The man who realizes that Jesus asked too much of the mass of men, in asking them to choose between earthly and heavenly bread, and to judge between good and evil, is not therefore satanic. Think how difficult it is to know the difference between good and evil! Why, sometimes it is evil to be good. And how is the ordinary man to understand that? He can't. The extraordinary men have to understand it for him. And is that going over to the devil? Or think of the difficulty in choosing between the earthly and heavenly bread. Lenin, surely a pure soul, rose to great power simply to give men – what? The earthly bread. And what was the result? Not only did they lose the heavenly bread, but even the earthly bread disappeared out of wheat-producing Russia. It is most strange. And all the socialists and the generous thinkers of today, what are they striving for? The same: to share out more evenly the earthly bread. Even *they*, who are practising Christianity *par excellence*, cannot properly choose between the heavenly and earthly bread. For the poor, they choose the earthly bread, and once more the heavenly bread is lost: and once more, as soon as it is really chosen, the earthly bread begins to

272

disappear. It is a great mystery. But today, the most passionate believers in Christ believe that all you have to do is to struggle to give earthly bread (good houses, good sanitation, etc.) to the poor, and that is in itself the heavenly bread. But it isn't. Especially for the poor, it isn't. It is for them the loss of heavenly bread. And the poor are the vast majority. Poor things, how everybody hates them today! For benevolence is a form of hate.

What then is the heavenly bread? Every generation must answer for itself. But the heavenly bread is life, is living. Whatever makes life vivid and delightful is the heavenly bread. And the earthly bread must come as a by-product of the heavenly bread. The vast mass will never understand this. Yet it is the essential truth of Christianity, and of life itself. The few will understand. Let them take the responsibility.

Again, the Inquisitor says that it is a weakness in men, that they must have miracle, mystery and authority. But is it? Are they not bound up in our emotions, always and for ever, these three demands of miracle, mystery, and authority? If Jesus cast aside miracle in the Temptation, still there is miracle again in the Gospels. And if Jesus refused the earthly bread, still he said: 'In my Father's house are many mansions.' And for authority: 'Why call ye me Lord, Lord, and do not the things which I say?'

The thing Jesus was trying to do was to supplant physical emotion by moral emotion. So that earthly bread becomes, in a sense, immoral, as it is to many refined people today. The Inquisitor sees that this is the mistake. The earthly bread must in itself be the miracle, and be bound up with the miracle.

And here, surely, he is right. Since man began to think and to feel vividly, seed-time and harvest have been the two great sacred periods of miracle, rebirth, and rejoicing. Easter and harvest-home are festivals of the earthly bread, and they are festivals which go to the roots of the soul. For it is the earthly bread as a miracle, a yearly miracle. All the old religions saw it: the Catholic still sees it, by the Mediterranean. And this is not weakness. This is *truth*. The rapture of the Easter kiss, in old Russia, is intimately bound up with the springing of the seed and the first footstep of the new earthly bread. It is the rapture of the Easter kiss which

273

makes the bread worth eating. It is the absence of the Easter kiss which makes the Bolshevist bread barren, dead. They eat dead bread, now.

The earthly bread is leavened with the heavenly bread. The heavenly bread is life, is contact, and is consciousness. In sowing the seed man has his contact with earth, with sun and rain: and he *must not* break the contact. In the awareness of the springing of the corn he has his ever-renewed consciousness of miracle, wonder, and mystery: the wonder of creation, procreation, and re-creation, following the mystery of death and the cold grave. It is the grief of Holy Week and the delight of Easter Sunday. And man must not, must not lose this supreme state of consciousness out of himself, or he has lost the best part of him. Again, the reaping and the harvest are another contact, with earth and sun, a rich touch of the cosmos, a living stream of activity, and then the contact with harvesters, and the joy of harvest-home. All this is life, life, it is the heavenly bread which we eat in the course of getting the earthly bread. Work is, or should be, our heavenly bread of activity, contact and consciousness. All work that is not this, is anathema. True, the work is hard; there is the sweat of the brow. But what of it? In decent proportion, this is life. The sweat of the brow is the heavenly butter.

I think the older Egyptians understood this, in the course of their long and marvellous history. I think that probably, for thousands of years, the masses of the Egyptians were happy, in the hierarchy of the State.

Miracle and mystery run together, they merge. Then there is the third thing, authority. The word is bad: a policeman has authority, and no one bows down to him. The Inquisitor means: 'that which men bow down to'. Well, they bowed down to Caesar, and they bowed down to Jesus. They will bow down, first, as the Inquisitor saw, to the one who has the power to control the bread.

The bread, the earthly bread, while it is being reaped and grown, it is life. But once it is harvested and stored, it becomes a commodity, it becomes riches. And then it becomes a danger. For men think, if they only possessed the hoard, they need not work;

274

which means, really, they need not live. And that is the real blasphemy. For while we live we must live, we must not wither or rot inert.

So that ultimately men bow down to the man, or group of men, who can and dare take over the hoard, the store of bread, the riches, to distribute it among the people again. The lords, the givers of bread. How profound Dostoyevsky is when he says that the people will forget that it is their own bread which is being given back to them. While they keep their own bread, it is not much better than stone to them – inert possessions. But given back to them from the great Giver, it is divine once more, it has the quality of miracle to make it taste well in the mouth and in the belly.

Men bow down to the lord of bread, first and foremost. For, by knowing the difference between earthly and heavenly bread, he is able calmly to distribute the earthly bread, and to give it, for the commonalty, the heavenly taste which they can never give it. That is why, in a democracy, the earthly bread loses its taste, the salt loses its savour, and there is no one to bow down to.

It is not man's weakness that he needs someone to bow down to. It is his nature, and his strength, for it puts him into touch with far, far greater life than if he stood alone. All life bows to the sun. But the sun is very far away to the common man. It needs someone to bring it to him. It needs a lord: what the Christians call one of the elect, to bring the sun to the common man, and put the sun in his heart. The sight of a true lord, a noble, a nature-hero puts the sun into the heart of the ordinary man, who is no hero, and therefore cannot know the sun direct.

This is one of the real mysteries. As the Inquisitor says, the mystery of the elect is one of the inexplicable mysteries of Christianity, just as the lord, the natural lord among men, is one of the inexplicable mysteries of humanity throughout time. We must accept the mystery, that's all.

But to do so is not diabolic.

And Ivan need not have been so tragic and satanic. He had made a discovery about men, which was due to be made. It was the rediscovery of a fact which was known universally almost till the end of the eighteenth century, when the illusion of the perfectibility of men, of all men, took hold of the imagination of the civilized nations. It was an illusion. And Ivan has to make a restatement of the old truth, that most men *cannot* choose between good and evil, because it is so extremely difficult to know which is which, especially in crucial cases: and that most men *cannot* see the difference between life-values and money-values: they can only see money-values; even nice simple people who *live* by the life-values, kind and natural, yet can only estimate value in terms of money. So let the specially gifted few make the decision between good and evil, and establish the life-values against the money-values. And let the many accept the decision, with gratitude, and bow down to the few, in the hierarchy. What is there diabolical or satanic in that? Jesus kisses the Inquisitor: Thank you, you are right, wise old man! Alyosha kisses Ivan: Thank you, brother, you are right, you take a burden off me! So why should Dostoyevsky drag in Inquisitors and *autos-da-fé*, and Ivan wind up so morbidly suicidal? Let them be glad they've found the truth again.

# German Books: Thomas Mann

*Blue Review*, July 1913; *Phoenix*, 1936

Thomas Mann is perhaps the most famous of German novelists now writing. He, and his elder brother, Heinrich Mann, with Jakob Wassermann, are acclaimed the three artists in fiction of present-day Germany.

But Germany is now undergoing that craving for form in fiction, that passionate desire for the mastery of the medium of narrative, that will of the writer to be greater than and undisputed lord over the stuff he writes, which is figured to the world in Gustave Flaubert.

Thomas Mann is over middle age, and has written three or four books. *Buddenbrooks*, a novel of the patrician life of Lübeck; *Tristan*, a collection of six *Novellen*; *Königliche Hoheit*, an unreal Court romance; various stories, and lastly, *Der Tod in Venedig*. The author himself is the son of a Lübeck *Patrizier*.

It is as an artist rather than as a story-teller that Germany worships Thomas Mann. And yet it seems to me, this craving for form is the outcome, not of artistic conscience, but of a certain attitude to life. For form is not a personal thing like style. It is impersonal like logic. And just as the school of Alexander Pope was logical in its expressions, so it seems the school of Flaubert is, as it were, logical in its aesthetic form. 'Nothing outside the definite line of the book', is a maxim. But can the human mind fix

277

absolutely the definite line of a book, any more than it can fix absolutely any definite line of action for a living being?

Thomas Mann, however, is personal, almost painfully so, in his subject-matter. In 'Tonio Kröger', the long *Novelle* at the end of the *Tristan* volume, he paints a detailed portrait of himself as a youth and younger man, a careful analysis. And he expresses at some length the misery of being an artist. 'Literature is not a calling, it is a curse.' Then he says to the Russian painter girl: 'There is no artist anywhere but longs again, my love, for the common life.' But any young artist might say that. It is because the stress of life in a young man, but particularly in an artist, is very strong, and has as yet found no outlet, so that it rages inside him in *Sturm und Drang*. But the condition is the same, only more tragic, in the Thomas Mann of fifty-three. He has never found any outlet for himself, save his art. He has never given himself to anything but his art. This is all well and good, if his art absorbs and satisfies him, as it has done some great men, like Corot. But then there are the other artists, the more human, like Shakespeare and Goethe, who must give themselves to life as well as to art. And if these were afraid, or despised life, then with their surplus they would ferment and become rotten. Which is what ails Thomas Mann. He is physically ailing, no doubt. But his complaint is deeper: it is of the soul.

And out of this soul-ailment, this unbelief, he makes his particular art, which he describes, in 'Tonio Kröger', as *'wählerisch, erlesen, kostbar, fein, reizbar gegen das Banale, und aufs höchste empfindlich in Fragen des Taktes und Geschmacks'*. He is a disciple, in method, of the Flaubert who wrote: 'I worked sixteen hours yesterday, today the whole day, and have at last finished one page.' In writing of the *Leitmotiv* and its influence, he says:

Now this method alone is sufficient to explain my slowness. It is the result neither of anxiety nor indigence, but of an overpowering sense of responsibility for the choice of every word, the coining of every phrase ... a responsibility that longs for perfect freshness, and which, after two hours' work, prefers not to undertake an important sentence. For which sentence is important, and which not? Can one know before hand whether a sentence, or part of a sentence may not be called upon to appear again as *Motiv*, peg, symbol, citation or connexion? And a sentence which must be heard twice must be fashioned accordingly. It must – I do not speak of beauty – possess a certain high level, and symbolic suggestion, which will make it worthy to sound again in any epic future. So every point becomes a standing ground, every adjective a decision, and it is clear that such work is not to be produced off-hand.

This, then, is the method. The man himself was always delicate in constitution. 'The doctors said he was too weak to go to school, and must work at home.' I quote from Aschenbach, in *Der Tod in Venedig*. 'When he fell, at the age of fifty-three, one of his closest observers said of him: "Aschenbach has always lived like this" – and he gripped his fist hard clenched; "never like this" – and he let his open hand lie easily on the arm of the chair.'

He forced himself to write, and kept himself to the work. Speaking of one of his works, he says:

It was pardonable, yea, it showed plainly the victory of his morality, that the uninitiated reader supposed the book to have come of a solid strength and one long breath; whereas it was the result of small daily efforts and hundreds of single inspirations.

And he gives the sum of his experience in the belief: *'dass beinahe alles Grosse, was dastehe, als ein Trotzdem dastehe, trotz Kummer und Qual, Armut, Verlassenheit, Körperschwäche, Laster, Leidenschaft und tausend hemmnischen Zuständen gekommen sei.'* And then comes the final revelation, difficult to translate. He is speaking of life as it is written into his books:

For endurance of one's fate, grace in suffering, does not only mean passivity, but is an active work, a positive triumph, and the Sebastian figure is the most beautiful symbol, if not of all art, yet of the art in question. If one looked into this portrayed world and saw the elegant self-control that hides from the eyes of the world to the last moment the inner undermining, the biological decay; saw the yellow ugliness which, sensuously at a disadvantage, could blow its choking heat of desire to a pure flame, and even rise to sovereignty in the kingdom of beauty; saw the pale impotence which draws out of the glowing depths of its intellect sufficient strength to subdue a whole vigorous people,

279

bring them to the foot of the Cross, to the feet of impotence; saw the amiable bearing in the empty and severe service of Form; saw the quickly enervating longing and art of the born swindler: if one saw such a fate as this, and all the rest it implied, then one would be forced to doubt whether there were in reality any other heroism than that of weakness. Which heroism, in any case, is more of our time than this?

Perhaps it is better to give the story of *Der Tod in Venedig*, from which the above is taken, and to whose hero it applies.

Gustav von Aschenbach, a fine, famous author, over fifty years of age, coming to the end of a long walk one afternoon, sees as he is approaching a burying place, near Munich, a man standing between the chimeric figures of the gateway. This man in the gate of the cemetery is almost the *Motiv* of the story. By him, Aschenbach is infected with a desire to travel. He examines himself minutely, in a way almost painful in its frankness, and one sees the whole soul of this author of fifty-three. And it seems, the artist has absorbed the man, and yet the man is there, like an exhausted organism on which a parasite has fed itself strong. Then begins a kind of Holbein *Totentanz*. The story is quite natural in appearance, and yet there is the gruesome sense of symbolism throughout. The man near the burying ground has suggested travel – but whither? Aschenbach sets off to a watering place on the Austrian coast of the Adriatic, seeking some adventure, some passionate adventure, to which his sick soul and unhealthy body have been kindled. But finding himself on the Adriatic, he knows it is not thither that his desire draws him, and he takes ship for Venice. It is all real, and yet with a curious sinister unreality, like decay, the 'biological decay'. On board there is a man who reminds one of the man in the gateway, though there is no connexion. And then, among a crowd of young Poles who are crossing, is a ghastly fellow, whom Aschenbach sees is an old man dressed up as young, who capers unsuspected among the youths, drinks hilariously with them, and falls hideously drunk at last on the deck, reaching to the author, and slobbering about '*dem allerliebsten, dem schönsten Liebchen*'. Suddenly the upper plate of his false teeth falls on his underlip.

Aschenbach takes a gondola to the Lido, and again the gondolier reminds one of the man in the cemetery gateway. He is, moreover, one who will make no concession, and, in spite of Aschenbach's demand to be taken back to St Mark's, rows him in his black craft to the Lido, talking to himself softly all the while. Then he goes without payment.

The author stays in a fashionable hotel on the Lido. The adventure is coming, there by the pallid sea. As Aschenbach comes down into the hall of the hotel, he sees a beautiful Polish boy of about fourteen, with honey-coloured curls clustering round his pale face, standing with his sisters and their governess.

Aschenbach loves the boy – but almost as a symbol. In him he loves life and youth and beauty, as Hyacinth in the Greek myth. This, I suppose, is blowing the choking heat to pure flame, and raising it to the kingdom of beauty. He follows the boy, watches him all day long on the beach, fascinated by beauty concrete before him. It is still the *Künstler* and his abstraction: but there is also the 'yellow ugliness, sensually at a disadvantage', of the elderly man below it all. But the picture of the writer watching the folk on the beach gleams and lives with a curious, gold-phosphorescent light, touched with the brightness of Greek myth, and yet a modern seashore with folks on the sands, and a half-threatening, diseased sky.

Aschenbach, watching the boy in the hotel lift, finds him delicate, almost ill, and the thought that he may not live long fills the elderly writer with a sense of peace. It eases him to think the boy should die.

Then the writer suffers from the effect of the *sirocco*, and intends to depart immediately from Venice. But at the station he finds with joy that his luggage has gone wrong, and he goes straight back to the hotel. There, when he sees Tadzin again, he knows why he could not leave Venice.

There is a month of hot weather, when Aschenbach follows Tadzin about, and begins to receive a look, loving, from over the lad's shoulder. It is wonderful, the heat, the unwholesomeness, the passion in Venice. One evening comes a street singer, smelling of carbolic acid, and sings beneath the veranda of the hotel. And this

281

time, in gruesome symbolism, it is the man from the burying ground distinctly.

The rumour is, that the black cholera is in Venice. An atmosphere of secret plague hangs over the city of canals and palaces. Aschenbach verifies the report at the English bureau, but cannot bring himself to go away from Tadzin, nor yet to warn the Polish family. The secretly pest-smitten days go by. Aschenbach follows the boy through the stinking streets of the town and loses him. And on the day of the departure of the Polish family, the famous author dies of the plague.

It is absolutely, almost intentionally, unwholesome. The man is sick, body and soul. He portrays himself as he is, with wonderful skill and art, portrays his sickness. And since any genuine portrait is valuable, this book has its place. It portrays one man, one atmosphere, one sick vision. It claims to do no more. And we have to allow it. But we know it is unwholesome – it does not strike me as being morbid for all that, it is too well done – and we give it its place as such.

Thomas Mann seems to me the last sick sufferer from the complaint of Flaubert. The latter stood away from life as from a leprosy. And Thomas Mann, like Flaubert, feels vaguely that he has in him something finer than ever physical life revealed. Physical life is a disordered corruption, against which he can fight with only one weapon, his fine aesthetic sense, his feeling for beauty, for perfection, for a certain fitness which soothes him, and gives him an inner pleasure, however corrupt the stuff of life may be. There he is, after all these years, full of disgusts and loathing of himself as Flaubert was, and Germany is being voiced, or partly so, by him. And so, with real suicidal intention, like Flaubert's, he sits, a last too-sick disciple, reducing himself grain by grain to the statement of his own disgust, patiently, self-destructively, so that his statement at least may be perfect in a world of corruption. But he is so late.

Already I find Thomas Mann, who, as he says, fights so hard against the banal in his work, somewhat banal. His expression may be very fine. But by now what he expresses is stale. I think we have learned our lesson, to be sufficiently aware of the fulsomeness of life. And even while he has a rhythm in style, yet his work has none of the rhythm of a living thing, the rise of a poppy, then the after uplift of the bud, the shedding of the calyx and the spreading wide of the petals, the falling of the flower and the pride of the seed-head. There is an unexpectedness in this such as does not come from their carefully plotted and arranged developments. Even *Madame Bovary* seems to me dead in respect to the living rhythm of the whole work. While it is there in *Macbeth* like life itself.

But Thomas Mann is old – and we are young. Germany does not feel very young to me.

# John Galsworthy

Written 1927, published in *Scrutinies*, 1928

Literary criticism can be no more than a reasoned account of the feeling produced upon the critic by the book he is criticizing. Criticism can never be a science: it is, in the first place, much too personal, and in the second, it is concerned with values that science ignores. The touchstone is emotion, not reason. We judge a work of art by its effect on our sincere and vital emotion, and nothing else. All the critical twiddle-twaddle about style and form, all this pseudo-scientific classifying and analysing of books in an imitation-botanical fashion, is mere impertinence and mostly dull jargon.

A critic must be able to *feel* the impact of a work of art in all its complexity and its force. To do so, he must be a man of force and complexity himself, which few critics are. A man with a paltry, impudent nature will never write anything but paltry, impudent criticism. And a man who is *emotionally* educated is rare as a phoenix. The more scholastically educated a man is generally, the more he is an emotional boor.

More than this, even an artistically and emotionally educated man must be a man of good faith. He must have the courage to admit what he feels, as well as the flexibility to *know* what he feels. So Sainte-Beuve remains, to me, a great critic. And a man like Macaulay, brilliant as he is, is unsatisfactory, because he is not honest. He is emotionally very alive, but he juggles his feelings. He prefers a fine effect to the sincere statement of the aesthetic and emotional reaction. He is quite intellectually capable of giving us a true account of what he feels. But not morally. A critic must be emotionally alive in every fibre, intellectually capable and skilful in essential logic, and then morally very honest.

Then it seems to me a good critic should give his reader a few standards to go by. He can change the standards for every new critical attempt, so long as he keeps good faith. But it is just as well to say : This and this is the standard we judge by.

Sainte-Beuve, on the whole, set up the standard of the 'good man'. He sincerely believed that the great man was essentially the good man in the widest range of human sympathy. This remained his universal standard. Pater's standard was the lonely philosopher of pure thought and pure aesthetic truth. Macaulay's standard was tainted by a political or democratic bias, he must be on the side of the weak. Gibbon tried a purely moral standard, individual morality.

Reading Galsworthy again – or most of him, for all is too much – one feels oneself in need of a standard, some conception of a real man and a real woman, by which to judge all these Forsytes and their contemporaries. One cannot judge them by the standard of the good man, nor of the man of pure thought, nor of the treasured humble nor the moral individual. One would like to judge them by the standard of the human being, but what, after all, is that? This is the trouble with the Forsytes. They are human enough, since anything in humanity is human, just as anything in nature is natural. Yet not one of them seems to be a really vivid human being. They are social beings. And what do we mean by that?

It remains to define, just for the purpose of this criticism, what we mean by a social being as distinct from a human being. The necessity arises from the sense of dissatisfaction which these Forsytes give us. Why can't we admit them as human beings? Why can't we have them in the same category as Sairey Gamp for example, who is satirically conceived, or of Jane Austen's people, who are social enough? We can accept Mrs Gamp or Jane Austen's characters or even George Meredith's Egoist as human beings in the same category as ourselves. Whence arises this repulsion from the Forsytes, this refusal, this emotional refusal, to have them identified with our common humanity? Why do we feel so instinctively that they are inferiors?

It is because they seem to us to have lost caste as human beings, and to have sunk to the level of the social being, that peculiar creature that takes the place in our civilization of the slave in the old civilizations. The human individual is a queer animal, always changing. But the fatal change today is the collapse from the psychology of the free human individual into the psychology of the social being, just as the fatal change in the past was a collapse from the freeman's psyche to the psyche of the slave. The free moral and the slave moral, the human moral and the social moral: these are the abiding antitheses.

While a man remains a man, a true human individual, there is at the core of him a certain innocence or naïveté which defies all analysis, and which you cannot bargain with, you can only deal with it in good faith from your own corresponding innocence or naïveté. This does not mean that the human being is nothing but naïve or innocent. He is Mr Worldly Wiseman also to his own degree. But in his essential core he is naïve, and money does not touch him. Money, of course, with every man living goes a long way. With the alive human being it may go as far as his penultimate feeling. But in the last naked him it does not enter.

With the social being it goes right through the centre and is the controlling principle no matter how much he may pretend, nor how much bluff he may put up. He may give away all he has to the poor and still reveal himself as a social being swayed finally and helplessly by the money-sway, and by the social moral, which is inhuman.

It seems to me that when the human being becomes too much divided between his subjective and objective consciousness, at last something splits in him and he becomes a social being. When he becomes too much aware of objective reality, and of his own isolation in the face of a universe of objective reality, the core of his identity splits, his nucleus collapses, his innocence or his naïveté perishes, and he becomes only a subjective-objective reality, a divided thing hinged together but not strictly individual.

While a man remains a man, before he falls and becomes a social individual, he innocently feels himself altogether within the great continuum of the universe. He is not divided nor cut off. Men may be against him, the tide of affairs may be rising to sweep him away. But he is one with the living continuum of the universe. From this he cannot be swept away. Hamlet and Lear feel it, as does Oedipus or Phaedra. It is the last and deepest feeling that is in a man while he remains a man. It is there the same in a deist like Voltaire or a scientist like Darwin: it is there, imperishable, in every great man: in Napoleon the same, till material things piled too much on him and he lost it and was doomed. It is the essentiál innocence and naïveté of the human being, the sense of being at one with the great universe-continuum of space-time-life, which is vivid in a great man, and a pure nuclear spark in every man who is still free.

But if a man loses his mysterious naïve assurance, which is his innocence; if he gives *too* much importance to the external objective reality and so collapses in his natural innocent pride, then he becomes obsessed with the idea of objectives or material assurance; he wants to *insure* himself, and perhaps everybody else: universal insurance. The impulse rests on fear. Once the individual loses his naïve at-oneness with the living universe he falls into a state of fear and tries to insure himself with wealth. If he is an altruist he wants to insure everybody, and feels it is the tragedy of tragedies if this can't be done. But the whole necessity for thus materially insuring oneself with wealth, money, arises from the state of fear into which a man falls who has lost his at-oneness with the living universe, lost his peculiar nuclear innocence and fallen into fragmentariness. Money, material salvation is the only salvation. What is salvation is God. Hence money is God. The social being may rebel even against this god, as do many of Galsworthy's characters. But that does not give them back their innocence. They are only anti-materialists instead of positive materialists. And the anti-materialist is a social being just the same as the materialist, neither more nor less. He is castrated just the same, made a neuter by having lost his innocence, the bright little individual spark of his at-oneness.

When one reads Mr Galsworthy's books it seems as if there were not on earth one single human individual. They are all these social beings, positive and negative. There is not a free soul among them, not even Pendyce, or June Forsyte. If money does not actively determine their being, it does negatively. Money, or property, which is the same thing. Mrs Pendyce, lovable as she is, is utterly circumscribed by property. Ultimately, she is not lovable at all, she is part of the fraud, she is prostituted to property. And there is nobody else. Old Jolyon is merely a sentimental materialist. Only for one moment do we see a man, and that is the road-sweeper in *Fraternity* after he comes out of prison and covers his face. But even *his* manhood has to be explained away by a wound in the head: an abnormality.

Now it looks as if Mr Galsworthy set out to make that very point: to show that the Forsytes were not full human individuals, but social beings fallen to a lower level of life. They have lost that bit of free manhood and free womanhood which makes men and women. *The Man of Property* has the elements of a very great novel, a very great satire. It sets out to reveal the social being in all his strength and inferiority. But the author has not the courage to carry it through. The greatness of the book rests in its new and sincere and amazingly profound satire. It is the ultimate satire on modern humanity, and done from the inside, with really consummate skill and sincere creative passion, something quite new. It seems to be a real effort to show up the social being in all his weirdness. And then it fizzles out.

Then, in the love affair of Irene and Bosinney, and in the sentimentalizing of old Jolyon Forsyte, the thing is fatally blemished. Galsworthy had not quite enough of the superb courage of his satire. He faltered, and gave in to the Forsytes. It is a thousand pities. He might have been the surgeon the modern soul needs so badly, to cut away the proud flesh of our Forsytes from the living body of men who are fully alive. Instead, he put down the knife and laid on a soft, sentimental poultice, and helped to make the corruption worse.

Satire exists for the very purpose of killing the social being, showing him what an inferior he is and, with all his parade of social honesty, how subtly and corruptly debased. Dishonest to life, dishonest to the living universe on which he is parasitic as a louse. By ridiculing the social being, the satirist helps the true individual, the real human being, to rise to his feet again and go on with the battle. For it is always a battle, and always will be.

Not that the majority are necessarily social beings. But the majority is only *conscious* socially: humanly, mankind is helpless and unconscious, unaware even of the thing most precious to any human being, that core of manhood or womanhood, naïve, innocent at-oneness with the living universe-continuum, which alone makes a man individual and, as an individual, *essentially* happy, even if he be driven mad like Lear. Lear was essentially happy, even in his greatest misery. A happiness from which Goneril and Regan were excluded as lice and bugs are excluded from happiness, being social beings, and, as such, parasites, fallen from true freedom and independence.

But the tragedy today is that men are only materially and socially conscious. They are unconscious of their own manhood, and so they let it be destroyed. Out of free men we produce social beings by the thousand every week.

The Forsytes are all parasites, and Mr Galsworthy set out, in a really magnificent attempt, to let us see it. They are parasites upon the thought, the feelings, the whole body of life of really living individuals who have gone before them and who exist alongside with them. All they can do, having no individual life of their own, is out of fear to rake together property, and to feed upon the life that has been given by living men to mankind. They have no life, and so they live for ever, in perpetual fear of death, accumulating property to ward off death. They can keep up convention, but they cannot carry on a tradition. There is a tremendous difference between the two things. To carry on a tradition you must add something to the tradition. But to keep up a convention needs only the monotonous persistency of a parasite, the endless endurance of the craven, those who fear life because they are not alive, and who cannot die because they cannot live – the social beings.

As far as I can see, there is nothing but Forsyte in Galsworthy's books: Forsyte positive or Forsyte negative, Forsyte successful or Forsyte *manqué*. That is, every single character is determined by money: either the getting it, or the having it, or the wanting it, or the utter lacking it. Getting it are the Forsytes as such; having it are the Pendyces and patricians and Hilarys and Biancas and all that lot; wanting it are the Irenes and Bosinneys and young Jolyons; and utterly lacking it are all the charwomen and squalid poor who form the background – the shadows of the 'having' ones, as old Mr Stone says. This is the whole Galsworthy gamut, all absolutely determined by money, and not an individual soul among them. They are all fallen, all social beings, a castrated lot.

Perhaps the overwhelming numerousness of the Forsytes frightened Mr Galsworthy from utterly damning them. Or perhaps it was something else, something more serious in him. Perhaps it was his utter failure to see what you were when you *weren't* a Forsyte. What was there *besides* Forsytes in all the wide human world? Mr Galsworthy looked, and found nothing. Strictly and truly, after his frightened search, he had found nothing. But he came back with Irene and Bosinney, and offered us that. Here! he seems to say. Here is the anti-Forsyte! Here! Here you have it! Love! Pa-assion! P A S S I O N.

We look at this love, this P A S S I O N, and we see nothing but a doggish amorousness and a sort of anti-Forsytism. They are the *anti* half of the show. Runaway dogs of these Forsytes, running in the back garden and furtively and ignominiously copulating – this is the effect, on me, of Mr Galsworthy's grand love affairs, Dark Flowers or Bosinneys, or Apple Trees or George Pendyce – whatever they be. About every one of them something ignominious and doggish, like dogs copulating in the street, and looking round to see if the Forsytes are watching.

Alas! this is the Forsyte trying to be freely sensual. He can't do it; he's lost it. He can only be doggishly messy. Bosinney is not only a Forsyte, but an anti-Forsyte, with a vast grudge against property. And the thing a man has a vast grudge against is the man's determinant. Bosinney is a property hound, but he has run away from the kennels, or been born outside the kennels, so he is a rebel. So he goes sniffing round the property bitches, to get even with the successful property hounds that way. One cannot help preferring Soames Forsyte, in a choice of evils.

Just as one prefers June or any of the old aunts to Irene. Irene seems to me a sneaking, creeping, spiteful sort of bitch, an anti-Forsyte, absolutely living off the Forsytes – yes, to the very end; absolutely living off their money and trying to do them dirt. She is like Bosinney, a property mongrel doing dirt in the property kennels. But she is a real property prostitute, like the little model in *Fraternity*. Only she is *anti*! It is a type recurring again and again in Galsworthy: the parasite upon the parasites, 'Big fleas have little fleas, etc.' And Bosinney and Irene, as well as the vagabond in *The Island Pharisees*, are among the little fleas. And as a tramp loves his own vermin, so the Forsytes and the Hilarys love these, their own particular body parasites, their *antis*.

It is when he comes to sex that Mr Galsworthy collapses finally. He becomes nastily sentimental. He wants to make sex important, and he only makes it repulsive. Sentimentalism is the working off on yourself of feelings you haven't really got. We all *want* to have certain feelings : feelings of love, of passionate sex, of kindliness, and so forth. Very few people really feel love, or sex passion, or kindliness, or anything else that goes at all deep. So the mass just fake these feelings inside themselves. Faked feelings! The world is all gummy with them. They are better than real feelings, because you can spit them out when you brush your teeth; and then tomorrow you can fake them afresh.

Shelton, in *The Island Pharisees*, is the first of Mr Galsworthy's lovers, and he might as well be the last. He is almost comical. All we know of his passion for Antonia is that he feels at the beginning a 'hunger' for her, as if she were a beefsteak. And towards the end he once kisses her, and expects her, no doubt, to fall instantly at his feet overwhelmed. He never for a second feels a moment of gentle sympathy with her. She is class-bound, but she doesn't seem to have been inhuman. The inhuman one was the lover. He can gloat over her in the distance, as if she were a dish of pig's trotters, *pieds truffés*: she can be an angelic *vision* to him a little way off, but when the poor thing has to be just a rather ordinary middle-class girl to him, quite near, he hates her with a comical, rancorous hate. It is most queer. He is helplessly *anti*. He hates her for even existing as a woman of her own class, for even having her own existence. Apparently she should just be a floating female sex-organ, hovering round to satisfy his little 'hungers', and then *basta*. Anything of the real meaning of sex, which involves the whole of a human being, never occurs to him. It is a function, and the female is a sort of sexual appliance, no more.

And so we have it again and again, in this low and bastard level, all the human correspondence lacking. The sexual level is extraordinarily low, like dogs. The Galsworthy heroes are all weirdly in love with themselves, when we know them better, afflicted with chronic narcissism. They know just three types of women: the Pendyce mother, prostitute to property; the Irene, the essential *anti* prostitute, the floating, flaunting female organ; and the social woman, the mere lady. All three are loved and hated in turn by the recurrent heroes. But it is all on the debased level of property, positive or *anti*. It is all a doggy form of prostitution. Be quick and have done.

One of the funniest stories is *The Apple Tree*. The young man finds, at a lonely Devon farm, a little Welsh farm-girl who, being a Celt and not a Saxon, at once falls for the Galsworthian hero. This young gentleman, in the throes of narcissistic love for his marvellous self, falls for the maid because she has fallen so utterly and abjectly for him. She doesn't call him 'My King', not being Wellsian; she only says: 'I can't live away from you. Do what you like with me. Only let me come with you!' The proper prostitutional announcement!

For this, of course, a narcissistic young gentleman just down from Oxford falls at once. Ensues a grand pa-assion. He goes to buy her a proper frock to be carried away in, meets a college friend with a young lady sister, has jam for tea and stays the night, and the grand pa-assion has died a natural death by the time he spreads the marmalade on his bread. He has returned to his own class, and nothing else exists. He marries the young lady, true to his class. But to fill the cup of his vanity, the maid drowns herself. It is funny that maids only seem to do it for these narcissistic young gentlemen who, looking in the pool for their own image, desire the added satisfaction of seeing the face of drowned Ophelia there as well; saving them the necessity of taking the narcissus plunge in person. We have gone one better than the myth. Narcissus, in Mr Galsworthy, doesn't drown himself. He asks Ophelia, or Megan, kindly to drown herself instead. And in this fiction she actually does. And he feels so *wonderful* about it!

Mr Galsworthy's treatment of passion is really rather shameful. The whole thing is doggy to a degree. The man has a temporary 'hunger'; he is 'on the heat' as they say of dogs. The heat passes. It's done. Trot away, if you're not tangled. Trot off, looking shamefacedly over your shoulder. People have been watching! Damn them! But never mind, it'll blow over. Thank God, the bitch is trotting in the other direction. She'll soon have another trail of dogs after her. That'll wipe out my traces. Good for that! Next time I'll get properly married and do my doggishness in my own house.

With the fall of the individual, sex falls into a dog's heat. Oh, if only Mr Galsworthy had had the strength to satirize this too, instead of pouring a sauce of sentimental savouriness over it. Of course, if he had done so he would never have been a popular writer, but he would have been a great one.

However, he chose to sentimentalize and glorify the most doggy sort of sex. Setting out to satirize the Forsytes, he glorifies the *anti*, who is one worse. While the individual remains real and unfallen, sex remains a vital and supremely important thing. But once you have the fall into social beings, sex becomes disgusting, like dogs on the heat. Dogs are social beings, with no true canine individuality. Wolves and foxes don't copulate on the pavement. Their sex is wild and in act utterly private. Howls you may hear, but you will never see anything. But the dog is tame – and he makes excrement and he copulates on the pavement, as if to spite you. He is the Forsyte *anti*.

The same with human beings. Once they become tame they become, in a measure, exhibitionists, as if to spite everything. They have no real feelings of their own. Unless somebody 'catches them at it' they don't really feel they've felt anything at all. And this is how the mob is today. It is Forsyte *anti*. It is the social being spiting society.

Oh, if only Mr Galsworthy had satirized *this* side of Forsytism, the anti-Forsyte posturing of the 'rebel', the narcissus and the exhibitionist, the dogs copulating on the pavement! Instead of that, he glorified it, to the eternal shame of English literature.

The satire, which in *The Man of Property* really had a certain noble touch, soon fizzles out, and we get that series of Galsworthian 'rebels' who are, like all the rest of the modern middle-class rebels, not in rebellion at all. They are merely social beings behaving in an anti-social manner. They worship their own class, but they pretend to go one better and sneer at it. They are Forsyte *antis*, feeling snobbish about snobbery. Nevertheless, they want to attract attention and make money. That's why they are *anti*. It is the vicious circle of Forsytism. Money means more to them than it does to a Soames Forsyte, so they pretend to go one better, and despise it, but they will do anything to have it – things which Soames Forsyte would not have done.

If there is one thing more repulsive than the social being positive, it is the social being negative, the mere *anti*. In the great débâcle of decency this gentleman is the most indecent. In a subtle way Bosinney and Irene are more dishonest and more indecent than Soames and Winifred, but they are *anti*, so they are glorified. It is pretty sickening.

The introduction to *The Island Pharisees* explains the whole show:

Each man born into the world is born to go a journey, and for the most part he is born on the high road. ... As soon as he can toddle, he moves, by the queer instinct we call the love of life, along this road: ... his fathers went this way before him, they made this road for him to tread, and, when they bred him, passed into his fibre the love of doing things as they themselves had done them. So he walks on and on. ... Suddenly, one day, without intending to, he notices a path or opening in the hedge, leading to right or left, and he stands looking at the undiscovered. After that he stops at all the openings in the hedge; one day, with a beating heart, he tries one. And this is where the fun begins.

Nine out of ten get back to the broad road again, and sidetrack no more. They snuggle down comfortably in the next inn, and think where they might have been. 'But the poor silly tenth is faring on. Nine times out of ten he goes down in a bog; the undiscovered has engulfed him.' But the tenth time he gets across, and a new road is opened to mankind.

It is a class-bound consciousness, or at least a hopeless social consciousness which sees life as a high road between two hedges. And the only way out is gaps in the hedge and excursions into naughtiness! These little *anti* excursions, from which the wayfarer slinks back to solid comfort nine times out of ten; an odd one goes down in a bog; and a very rare one finds a way across and opens out a new road.

In Mr Galsworthy's novels we see the nine, the ninety-nine, the nine hundred and ninety-nine slinking back to solid comfort; we see an odd Bosinney go under a bus, because he hadn't guts enough to do something else, the poor *anti*! but that rare figure sidetracking into the unknown we do *not* see. Because, as a matter of fact, the whole figure is faulty at that point. If life is a great highway, then it must forge on ahead into the unknown. Sidetracking gets nowhere. That is mere *anti*. The tip of the road is always unfinished, in the wilderness. If it comes to a precipice and a cañon – well, then, there is need for some exploring. But we see Mr Galsworthy, after *The Country House*, very safe on the old highway, very secure in comfort, wealth, and renown. He at least has gone down in no bog, nor lost himself striking new paths. The hedges nowadays are ragged with gaps, anybody who likes strays out on the little trips of 'unconventions'. But the Forsyte road has not moved on at all. It has only become dishevelled and sordid with excursionists doing the *anti* tricks and being 'unconventional', and leaving tin cans behind.

In the three early novels, *The Island Pharisees, The Man of Property, Fraternity*, it looked as if Mr Galsworthy might break through the blind end of the highway with the dynamite of satire, and help us out on to a new lap. But the sex ingredient of his dynamite was damp and muzzy, the explosion gradually fizzled off in sentimentality, and we are left in a worse state than before.

The later novels are purely commercial, and, if it had not been for the early novels, of no importance. They are popular, they sell well, and there's the end of them. They contain the explosive powder of the first books in minute quantities, fizzling as silly squibs. When you arrive at *To Let*, and the end, at least the *promised* end, of the Forsytes, what have you? Just money! Money, money, money and a certain snobbish silliness, and many more *anti* tricks and poses. Nothing else. The story is feeble, the characters have no blood and bones, the emotions are faked, faked, faked. It is one great fake. Not necessarily of Mr Galsworthy. The characters fake their own emotions. But that doesn't help us. And if you look closely at the characters, the meanness and low-level vulgarity are very distasteful. You have all the Forsyte meanness, with none of the energy. Jolyon and Irene are meaner and more treacherous to their son than the older Forsytes were to theirs. The young ones are of a limited, mechanical, vulgar egoism far surpassing that of Swithin or James, their ancestors. There is in it all a vulgar sense of being rich, and therefore we do as we like: an utter incapacity for anything like *true* feeling, especially in the women. Fleur, Irene, Annette, June: a glib crassness, a youthful spontaneity which is just impertinence and lack of feeling; and all the time, a creeping, 'having' sort of vulgarity of money and self-will, money and self-will, so that we wonder sometimes if Mr Galsworthy is not treating his public in real bad faith, and being cynical and rancorous under his rainbow sentimentalism.

Fleur he destroys in one word: she is 'having'. It is perfectly true. We don't blame the young Jon for clearing out. Irene he destroys in a phrase out of Fleur's mouth to June: 'Didn't she spoil your life too?' – and it is precisely what she did. Sneaking and mean, Irene prevented June from getting her lover. Sneaking and mean, she prevents Fleur. She is the bitch in the manger. She is the sneaking *anti*. Irene, the most beautiful woman on earth! And Mr Galsworthy, with the cynicism of a successful old sentimentalist, turns it off by making June say: 'Nobody can spoil a life, my dear. That's nonsense. Things happen, but we bob up.'

This is the final philosophy of it all. 'Things happen, but we bob up.' Very well, then, write the book in that key, the keynote of a frank old cynic. There's no point in sentimentalizing it and being a sneaking old cynic. Why pour out masses of feelings that pretend to be genuine and then turn it all off with: 'Things happen, but we bob up'?

It is quite true, things happen, and we bob up. If we are vulgar sentimentalists, we bob up just the same, so nothing has happened and nothing can happen. All is vulgarity. But it pays. There is money in it.

Vulgarity pays, and cheap cynicism smothered in sentimentalism pays better than anything else. Because nothing *can* happen to the degraded social being. So let's pretend it does, and then bob up!

It is time somebody began to spit out the jam of sentimentalism, at least, which smothers the 'bobbing-up' philosophy. It is time we turned a straight light on this horde of rats, these younger Forsyte sentimentalists whose name is legion. It is sentimentalism which is stifling us. Let the social beings keep on bobbing up while ever they can. But it is time an effort was made to turn a hosepipe on the sentimentalism they ooze over everything. The world is one sticky mess, in which the little Forsytes indeed may keep on bobbing still, but in which an honest feeling can't breathe.

But if the sticky mess gets much deeper, even the little Forsytes won't be able to bob up any more. They'll be smothered in their own slime along with everything else. Which is a comfort.

# 4. Censorship

# Introduction to the Privately Printed Edition of *Pansies* by D. H. Lawrence

Written and published 1929

This little bunch of fragments is offered as a bunch of *pensées*, *anglicé* pansies; a handful of thoughts. Or, if you will have the other derivation of pansy, from *panser*, to dress or soothe a wound, these are my tender administrations to the mental and emotional wounds we suffer from. Or you can have heartsease if you like, since the modern heart could certainly do with it.

Each little piece is a thought; not a bare idea or an opinion or a didactic statement, but a true thought, which comes as much from the heart and the genitals as from the head. A thought, with its own blood of emotion and instinct running in it like the fire in a fire-opal, if I may be so bold. Perhaps if you hold up my pansies properly to the light, they may show a running vein of fire. At least, they do not pretend to be half-baked lyrics or melodies in American measure. They are thoughts which run through the modern mind and body, each having its own separate existence, yet each of them combining with all the others to make up a complete state of mind.

It suits the modern temper better to have its state of mind made up of apparently irrelevant thoughts that scurry in different directions, yet belong to the same nest: each thought trotting down the page like an independent creature, each with its own small head and tail, trotting its own little way, then curling up to sleep. We prefer it, at least the young seem to prefer it to those solid blocks of mental pabulum packed like bales in the pages of a proper heavy book. Even we prefer it to those slightly didactic opinions and slices of wisdom which are laid horizontally across the pages of Pascal's *Pensées* or La Bruyère's *Caractères*, separated only by *pattes de mouches*, like faint sprigs of parsley. Let every *pensée* trot on its own little paws, not be laid like a cutlet trimmed with a *patte de mouche*.

Live and let live, and each pansy will tip you its separate wink. The fairest thing in nature, a flower, still has its roots in earth and manure; and in the perfume there hovers still the faint strange scent of earth, the under-earth in all its heavy humidity and darkness. Certainly it is so in pansy-scent, and in violet-scent; mingled with the blue of the morning the black of the corrosive humus. Else the scent would be just sickly sweet.

So it is: we all have our roots in earth. And it is our roots that now need a little attention, need the hard soil eased away from them, and softened so that a little fresh air can come to them, and they can breathe. For by pretending to have no roots, we have trodden the earth so hard over them that they are starving and stifling below the soil. We have roots, and our roots are in the sensual, instinctive and intuitive body, and it is here we need fresh air of open consciousness.

I am abused most of all for using the so-called 'obscene' words. Nobody quite knows what the word 'obscene' itself means, or what it is intended to mean: but gradually all the *old* words that belong to the body below the navel, have come to be judged obscene. Obscene means today that the policeman thinks he has a right to arrest you, nothing else.

Myself, I am mystified at this horror over a mere word, a plain simple word that stands for a plain simple thing. 'In the beginning was the Word, and the Word was God and the Word was with God.' If that is true, then we are very far from the beginning. When did the Word 'fall'? When did the Word become unclean 'below the navel'? Because today, if you suggest that the word arse was in the beginning and was God and was with God, you will just be put in prison at once. Though a doctor might say the same word *ischial tuberosity,* and all the old ladies would piously murmur 'Quite!' Now that sort of thing is idiotic and humiliating. Whoever the God was that made us, He made us complete. He didn't stop at the navel and leave the rest to the devil. It is too childish. And the same with the Word which is God. If the Word is God – which in the sense of the human it is – then you can't suddenly say that all the words which belong below the navel are obscene. The word arse is as much god as the word face. It must be so, otherwise you cut off your god at the waist.

What is obvious is that the words in these cases have been dirtied by the mind, by unclean mental associations. The words themselves are clean, so are the things to which they apply. But the mind drags in a filthy association, calls up some repulsive emotion. Well then, cleanse the mind, that is the real job. It is the mind which is the Augean stables, not language. The word arse is clean enough. Even the part of the body it refers to is just as much me as my hand and my brain are me. It is not for *me* to quarrel with my own natural make-up. If I am, I am all that I am. But the impudent and dirty mind won't have it. It hates certain parts of the body, and makes the words representing these parts scapegoats. It pelts them out of the consciousness with filth, and there they hover, never dying, never dead, slipping into the consciousness again unawares, and pelted out again with filth, haunting the margins of the consciousness like jackals or hyenas. And they refer to parts of our own living bodies, and to our most essential acts. So that man has turned himself into a thing of shame and horror. And his consciousness shudders with horrors that he has made for himself.

That sort of thing has got to stop. We can't have the consciousness haunted any longer by repulsive spectres which are no more than poor simple scapegoat words representing parts of man himself; words that the cowardly and unclean mind has driven out into the limbo of the unconscious, whence they return upon us looming and magnified out of all proportion, frightening us beyond all reasons. We must put an end to that. It is the self divided against itself most dangerously. The simple and natural 'obscene' words must be cleaned up of all their depraved fear-associations, and readmitted into the consciousness to take their natural place. Now they are magnified out of all proportion, so is the mental fear they represent. We must accept the word arse as we accept the word face, since arses we have and always shall have. We can't start cutting off the buttocks of unfortunate mankind, like the ladies in the Voltaire story, just to fit the mental expulsion of the word.

This scapegoat business does the mind itself so much damage. There is a poem of Swift's which should make us pause. It is written to Celia, his Celia – and every verse ends with the mad, maddened refrain: 'But – Celia, Celia, Celia shits!' Now that, stated blandly, is so ridiculous it is almost funny. But when one remembers the gnashing insanity to which the great mind of Swift was reduced by that and similar thoughts, the joke dies away. Such thoughts poisoned him, like some terrible constipation. They poisoned his mind. And why, in heaven's name? The *fact* cannot have troubled him, since it applied to himself and to all of us. It was not the fact that Celia shits which so deranged him, it was the *thought*. His mind couldn't bear the thought. Great wit as he was, he could not see how ridiculous his revulsions were. His arrogant mind overbore him. He couldn't even see how much worse it would be if Celia didn't shit. His physical sympathies were too weak, his guts were too cold to sympathize with poor Celia in her natural functions. His insolent and sickly squeamish mind just turned her into a thing of horror, because she was merely natural and went to the w.c. It is monstrous! One feels like going back across all the years to poor Celia, to say to her: It's all right, don't take any notice of that mental lunatic.

And Swift's form of madness is very common today. Men with cold guts and over-squeamish minds are always thinking those things and squirming. Wretched man is the victim of his own little revulsions, which he magnifies into great horrors and terrifying taboos. We are all savages, we all have taboos. The Australian black may have the kangaroo for his taboo. And then he will probably die of shock and terror if a kangaroo happens to touch him. Which is what I would call a purely unnecessary death. But

304

modern men have even more dangerous taboos. To us, certain words, certain ideas are taboos, and if they come upon us and we don't drive them away, we die or go mad with a degraded sort of terror. Which is what happened to Swift. He was such a great wit. And the modern mind altogether is falling into this form of degraded taboo-insanity. I call it a waste of sane human consciousness. But it is very dangerous, dangerous to the individual and utterly dangerous to society as a whole. Nothing is so fearful in a mass-civilization like ours as a mass-insanity.

The remedy is, of course, the same in both cases: lift off the taboo. The kangaroo is a harmless animal, the word shit is a harmless word. Make either into a taboo, and it becomes more dangerous. The result of taboo is insanity. And insanity, especially mob-insanity, mass-insanity, is the fearful danger that threatens our civilization. There are certain persons with a sort of rabies, who live only to infect the mass. If the young do not watch out, they will find themselves, before so very many years are past, engulfed in a howling manifestation of mob-insanity, truly terrifying to think of. It will be better to be dead than to live to see it. Sanity, wholeness, is everything. In the name of piety and purity, what a mass of disgusting insanity is spoken and written. We shall have to fight the mob, in order to keep sane, and to keep society sane.

# Pornography and Obscenity

*This Quarter*, July–September 1929; *Pornography and Obscenity*, 1929

What they are depends, as usual, entirely on the individual. What is pornography to one man is the laughter of genius to another.

The word itself, we are told, means 'pertaining to harlots' – the graph of the harlot. But nowadays, what is a harlot? If she was a woman who took money from a man in return for going to bed with him – really, most wives sold themselves, in the past, and plenty of harlots gave themselves, when they felt like it, for nothing. If a woman hasn't got a tiny streak of a harlot in her, she's a dry stick as a rule. And probably most harlots had somewhere a streak of womanly generosity. Why be so cut and dried? The law is a dreary thing, and its judgements have nothing to do with life.

The same with the word *obscene*: nobody knows what it means. Suppose it were derived from *obscena*: that which might not be represented on the stage; how much further are you? None! What is obscene to Tom is not obscene to Lucy or Joe, and really, the meaning of a word has to wait for majorities to decide it. If a play shocks ten people in an audience, and doesn't shock the remaining five hundred, then it is obscene to ten and innocuous to five hundred; hence, the play is not obscene, by majority. But *Hamlet* shocked all the Cromwellian Puritans, and shocks nobody today, and some of Aristophanes shocks everybody today, and didn't galvanize the later Greeks at all, apparently. Man is a changeable beast, and words change their meanings with him, and things are not what they seemed, and what's what becomes what isn't, and if we think we know where we are it's only because we are so rapidly being translated to somewhere else. We have to leave everything to the majority, everything to the majority, everything to the mob, the mob, the mob. They know what is obscene and what isn't, they do. If the lower ten million doesn't know better than the upper ten men, then there's something wrong with mathematics. Take a vote on it! Show hands, and prove it by count! *Vox populi, vox Dei. Odi profanum vulgum! Profanum vulgum.*

So it comes down to this: if you are talking to the mob, the meaning of your words is the mob-meaning, decided by majority. As somebody wrote to me: the American law on obscenity is very plain, and America is going to enforce the law. Quite, my dear, quite, quite, quite! The mob knows all about obscenity. Mild little words that rhyme with spit or farce are the height of obscenity. Supposing a printer put 'h' in the place of 'p', by mistake, in that mere word spit? Then the great American public knows that this man has committed an obscenity, an indecency, that his act was lewd, and as a compositor he was pornographical. You can't tamper with the great public, British or American. *Vox populi, vox Dei*, don't you know. If you don't we'll let you know it. At the same time, this *vox Dei* shouts with praise over moving-pictures and books and newspaper accounts that seem, to a sinful nature like mine, completely disgusting and obscene. Like a real prude and Puritan, I have to look the other way. When obscenity becomes mawkish, which is its palatable form for the public, and when the *Vox populi, vox Dei* is hoarse with sentimental indecency, then I have to steer away, like a Pharisee, afraid of being contaminated. There is a certain kind of sticky universal pitch that I refuse to touch.

So again, it comes down to this: you accept the majority, the mob, and its decisions, or you don't. You bow down before the *Vox populi, vox Dei*, or you plug your ears not to hear its obscene howl. You perform your antics to please the vast public,

## Censorship

*Deus ex machina*, or you refuse to perform for the public at all, unless now and then to pull its elephantine and ignominious leg.

When it comes to the meaning of anything, even the simplest word, then you must pause. Because there are two great categories of meaning, for ever separate. There is mob-meaning, and there is individual meaning. Take even the word *bread*. The mob-meaning is merely: stuff made with white flour into loaves that you eat. But take the individual meaning of the word bread: the white, the brown, the corn-pone, the home-made, the small of bread just out of the oven, the crust, the crumb, the unleavened bread, the shewbread, the staff of life, sour-dough bread, cottage loaves, French bread, Viennese bread, black bread, a yesterday's loaf, rye, graham, barley, rolls, *Bretzeln*, *Kringeln*, scones, damper, matsen – there is no end to it all, and the word bread will take you to the ends of time and space, and far-off down avenues of memory. But this is individual. The word bread will take the individual off on his own journey, and its meaning will be his own meaning, based on his own genuine imagination reactions. And when a word comes to us in its individual character, and starts in us the individual responses, it is great pleasure to us. The American advertisers have discovered this, and some of the cunningest American literature is to be found in advertisements of soap-suds, for example. These advertisements are *almost* prose-poems. They give the word soap-suds a bubbly, shiny individual meaning, which is very skilfully poetic, would, perhaps, be quite poetic to the mind which could forget that the poetry was bait on a hook.

Business is discovering the individual, dynamic meaning of words, and poetry is losing it. Poetry more and more tends to far-fetch its word-meanings, and this results once again in mob-meanings, which arouse only a mob-reaction in the individual. For every man has a mob-self and an individual self, in varying proportions. Some men are almost all mob-self, incapable of imaginative individual responses. The worst specimens of mob-self are usually to be found in the professions, lawyers, professors, clergymen and so on. The business man, much maligned, has a tough outside mob-self, and a scared, floundering yet still alive individual self. The public, which is feeble-minded like an idiot, will never be able to preserve its individual reactions from the tricks of the exploiter. The public is always exploited and always will be exploited. The methods of exploitation merely vary. Today the public is tickled into laying the golden egg. With imaginative words and individual meanings it is tricked into giving the great goose-cackle of mob-acquiescence. *Vox populi, vox Dei*. It has always been so, and will always be so. Why? Because the public has not enough wit to distinguish between mob-meanings and individual meanings. The mass is for ever vulgar, because it can't distinguish between its own original feelings and feelings which are diddled into existence by the exploiter. The public is always profane, because it is controlled from the outside, by the trickster, and never from the inside, by its own sincerity. The mob is always obscene, because it is always second-hand.

Which brings us back to our subject of pornography and obscenity. The reaction to any word may be, in any individual, either a mob-reaction or an individual reaction. It is up to the individual to ask himself: Is my reaction individual, or am I merely reacting from my mob-self?

When it comes to the so-called obscene words, I should say that hardly one person in a million escapes mob-reaction. The first reaction is almost sure to be mob-reaction, mob-indignation, mob-condemnation. And the mob gets no further. But the real individual has second thoughts and says: Am I really shocked? Do I *really* feel outraged and indignant? And the answer of any individual is bound to be: No, I am not shocked, not outraged, nor indignant. I know the word, and take it for what it is, and I am not going to be jockeyed into making a mountain out of a mole-hill, not for all the law in the world.

Now if the use of a few so-called obscene words will startle man or woman out of a mob-habit into an individual state, well and good. And word prudery is so universal a mob-habit that it is time we were startled out of it.

But still we have only tackled obscenity, and the problem of pornography goes even deeper. When a man is startled into his

309

individual self, he still may not be able to know, inside himself, whether Rabelais is or is not pornographic: and over Aretino or even Boccaccio he may perhaps puzzle in vain, torn between different emotions.

One essay on pornography, I remember, comes to the conclusion that pornography in art is that which is calculated to arouse sexual desire, or sexual excitement. And stress is laid on the fact, whether the author or artist *intended* to arouse sexual feelings. It is the old vexed question of intention, become so dull today, when we know how strong and influential our unconscious intentions are. And why a man should be held guilty of his conscious intentions, and innocent of his unconscious intentions, I don't know, since every man is more made up of unconscious intentions than of conscious ones. I am what I am, not merely what I think I am.

However! We take it, I assume, that *pornography* is something base, something unpleasant. In short, we don't like it. And why don't we like it? Because it arouses sexual feelings?

I think not. No matter how hard we may pretend otherwise, most of us rather like a moderate rousing of our sex. It warms us, stimulates us like sunshine on a grey day. After a century or two of Puritanism, this is still true of most people. Only the mob-habit of condemning any form of sex is too strong to let us admit it naturally. And there are, of course, many people who are genuinely repelled by the simplest and most natural stirrings of sexual feeling. But these people are perverts who have fallen into hatred of their fellow men: thwarted, disappointed, unfulfilled people, of whom, alas, our civilization contains so many. And they nearly always enjoy some unsimple and unnatural form of sex excitement, secretly.

Even quite advanced art critics would try to make us believe that any picture or book which had 'sex appeal' was *ipso facto* a bad book or picture. This is just canting hypocrisy. Half the great poems, pictures, music, stories of the whole world are great by virtue of the beauty of their sex appeal. Titian or Renoir, the Song of Solomon or *Jane Eyre*, Mozart or 'Annie Laurie', the loveliness is all interwoven with sex appeal, sex stimulus, call it what you will. Even Michelangelo, who rather hated sex, can't help filling the Cornucopia with phallic acorns. Sex is a very powerful, beneficial and necessary stimulus in human life, and we are all grateful when we feel its warm, natural flow through us, like a form of sunshine.

So we can dismiss the idea that sex appeal in art is pornography. It may be so to the grey Puritan, but the grey Puritan is a sick man, soul and body sick, so why should we bother about his hallucinations? Sex appeal, of course, varies enormously. There are endless different kinds, and endless degrees of each kind. Perhaps it may be argued that a mild degree of sex appeal is not pornographical, whereas a high degree is. But this is a fallacy. Boccaccio at his hottest seems to me less pornographical than *Pamela* or *Clarissa Harlowe* or even *Jane Eyre*, or a host of modern books or films which pass uncensored. At the same time Wagner's *Tristan and Isolde* seems to me very near to pornography, and so, even, do some quite popular Christian hymns.

What is it, then? It isn't a question of sex appeal, merely: nor even a question of deliberate intention on the part of the author or artist to arouse sexual excitement. Rabelais sometimes had a deliberate intention, so in a different way, did Boccaccio. And I'm sure poor Charlotte Brontë, or the authoress of *The Sheik*, did not have any deliberate intention to stimulate sex feelings in the reader. Yet I find *Jane Eyre* verging towards pornography and Boccaccio seems to me always fresh and wholesome.

The late British Home Secretary, who prides himself on being a very sincere Puritan, grey, grey in every fibre, said with indignant sorrow in one of his outbursts on improper books: '– and these two young people, who had been perfectly pure up till that time, after reading this book went and had sexual intercourse together ! ! !' *One up to them!* is all we can answer. But the grey Guardian of British Morals seemed to think that if they had murdered one another, or worn each other to rags of nervous prostration, it would have been much better. The grey disease!

Then what is pornography, after all this? It isn't sex appeal or sex stimulus in art. It isn't even a deliberate intention on the part of the artist to arouse or excite sexual feelings. There's noth-

311

ing wrong with sexual feelings in themselves, so long as they are straightforward and not sneaking or sly. The right sort of sex stimulus is invaluable to human daily life. Without it the world grows grey. I would give everybody the gay Renaissance stories to read, they would help to shake off a lot of grey self-importance, which is our modern civilized disease.

But even I would censor genuine pornography, rigorously. It would not be very difficult. In the first place, genuine pornography is almost always underworld, it doesn't come into the open. In the second, you can recognize it by the insult it offers, invariably, to sex, and to the human spirit.

Pornography is the attempt to insult sex, to do dirt on it. This is unpardonable. Take the very lowest instance, the picture postcard sold under hand, by the underworld, in most cities. What I have seen of them have been of an ugliness to make you cry. The insult to the human body, the insult to a vital human relationship! Ugly and cheap they make the human nudity, ugly and degraded they make the sexual act, trivial and cheap and nasty.

It is the same with the books they sell in the underworld. They are either so ugly they make you ill, or so fatuous you can't imagine anybody but a cretin or a moron reading them, or writing them.

It is the same with the dirty limericks that people tell after dinner, or the dirty stories one hears commercial travellers telling each other in a smoke-room. Occasionally there is a really funny one, that redeems a great deal. But usually they are just ugly and repellent, and the so-called 'humour' is just a trick of doing dirt on sex.

Now the human nudity of a great many modern people is just ugly and degraded, and the sexual act between modern people is just the same, merely ugly and degrading. But this is nothing to be proud of. It is the catastrophe of our civilization. I am sure no other civilization, not even the Roman, has showed such a vast proportion of ignominious and degraded nudity, and ugly, squalid dirty sex. Because no other civilization has driven sex into the underworld, and nudity to the w.c.

The intelligent young, thank heaven, seem determined to alter in these two respects. They are rescuing their young nudity from the stuffy, pornographical hole-and-corner underworld of their elders, and they refuse to sneak about the sexual relation. This is a change the elderly grey ones of course deplore, but it is in fact a very great change for the better, and a real revolution.

But it is amazing how strong is the will in ordinary, vulgar people, to do dirt on sex. It was one of my fond illusions, when I was young, that the ordinary healthy-seeming sort of men, in railway carriages, or the smoke-room of an hotel or a pullman, were healthy in their feelings and had a wholesome rough devil-may-care attitude towards sex. All wrong! All wrong! Experience teaches that common individuals of this sort have a disgusting attitude towards sex, a disgusting contempt of it, a disgusting desire to insult it. If such fellows have intercourse with a woman, they triumphantly feel that they have done her dirt, and now she is lower, cheaper, more contemptible than she was before.

It is individuals of this sort that tell dirty stories, carry indecent picture post-cards, and know the indecent books. This is the great pornographical class – the really common men-in-the-street and women-in-the-street. They have as great a hate and contempt of sex as the greyest Puritan, and when an appeal is made to them, they are always on the side of the angels. They insist that a film-heroine shall be a neuter, a sexless thing of washed-out purity. They insist that real sex-feeling shall only be shown by the villain or villainess, low lust. They find a Titian or a Renoir really indecent, and they don't want their wives and daughters to see it.

Why? Because they have the grey disease of sex-hatred, coupled with the yellow disease of dirt-lust. The sex functions and the excrementory functions in the human body work so close together, yet they are, so to speak, utterly different in direction. Sex is a creative flow, the excrementory flow is towards dissolution, de-creation, if we may use such a word. In the really healthy human being the distinction between the two is instant, our profoundest instincts are perhaps our instincts of opposition between the two flows.

But in the degraded human being the deep instincts have gone dead, and then the two flows become identical. *This* is the secret of really vulgar and of pornographical people: the sex flow and the excrement flow is the same to them. It happens when the psyche deteriorates, and the profound controlling instincts collapse. Then sex is dirt and dirt is sex, and sexual excitement becomes a playing with dirt, and any sign of sex in a woman becomes a show of her dirt. This is the condition of the common, vulgar human being whose name is legion, and who lifts his voice and it is the *Vox populi, vox Dei.* And this is the source of all pornography .

And for this reason we must admit that *Jane Eyre* or Wagner's *Tristan* are much nearer to pornography than is Boccaccio. Wagner and Charlotte Brontë were both in the state where the strongest instincts have collapsed, and sex has become something slightly obscene, to be wallowed in, but despised. Mr Rochester's sex passion is not 'respectable' till Mr Rochester is burned, blinded, disfigured, and reduced to helpless dependence. Then, thoroughly humbled and humiliated, it may be merely admitted. All the previous titillations are slightly indecent, as in *Pamela* or *The Mill on the Floss* or *Anna Karenina.* As soon as there is sex excitement with a desire to spite the sexual feeling, to humiliate it and degrade it, the element of pornography enters.

For this reason, there is an element of pornography in nearly all nineteenth-century literature and very many so-called pure people have a nasty pornographical side to them, and never was the pornographical appetite stronger than it is today. It is a sign of a diseased condition of the body politic. But the way to treat the disease is to come out into the open with sex and sex stimulus. The real pornographer truly dislikes Boccaccio, because the fresh healthy naturalness of the Italian story-teller makes the modern pornographical shrimp feel the dirty worm he is. Today Boccaccio should be given to everybody young or old, to read if they like. Only a natural fresh openness about sex will do any good, now we are being swamped by secret or semi-secret pornography. And perhaps the Renaissance story-tellers, Boccaccio, Lasca, and the rest, are the best antidote we can find now, just as more plasters of Puritanism are the most harmful remedy we can resort to.

The whole question of pornography seems to me a question of secrecy. Without secrecy there would be no pornography. But secrecy and modesty are two utterly different things. Secrecy has always an element of fear in it, amounting very often to hate. Modesty is gentle and reserved. Today, modesty is thrown to the winds, even in the presence of the grey guardians. But secrecy is hugged, being a vice in itself. And the attitude of the grey ones is: Dear young ladies, you may abandon all modesty, so long as you hug your dirty little secret.

This 'dirty little secret' has become infinitely precious to the mob of people today. It is a kind of hidden sore or inflammation which, when rubbed or scratched, gives off sharp thrills that seem delicious. So the dirty little secret is rubbed and scratched more and more, till it becomes more and more secretly inflamed, and the nervous and psychic health of the individual is more and more impaired. One might easily say that half the love novels and half the love films today depend entirely for their success on the secret rubbing of the dirty little secret. You can call this sex excitement if you like, but it is sex excitement of a secretive, furtive sort, quite special. The plain and simple excitement, quite open and wholesome, which you find in some Boccaccio stories is not for a minute to be confused with the furtive excitement aroused by rubbing the dirty little secret in all secrecy in modern best-sellers. This furtive, sneaking, cunning rubbing of an inflamed spot in the imagination is the very quick of modern pornography, and it is a beastly and very dangerous thing. You can't so easily expose it, because of its very furtiveness and its sneaking cunning. So the cheap and popular modern love novel and love film flourishes and is even praised by moral guardians, because you get the sneaking thrill fumbling under all the purity of dainty underclothes, without one single gross word to let you know what is happening.

Without secrecy there would be no pornography. But if pornography is the result of sneaking secrecy, what is the result of pornography? What is the effect on the individual?

The effect on the individual is manifold, and always pernicious. But one effect is perhaps inevitable. The pornography of today, whether it be the pornography of the rubber-goods shop or the pornography of the popular novel, film, and play, is an invariable stimulant to the vice of self-abuse, onanism, masturbation, call it what you will. In young or old, man or woman, boy or girl, modern pornography is a direct provocative of masturbation. It cannot be otherwise. When the grey ones wail that the young man and the young woman went and had sexual intercourse, they are bewailing the fact that the young man and the young woman didn't go separately and masturbate. Sex must go somewhere, especially in young people. So, in our glorious civilization, it goes in masturbation. And the mass of our popular literature, the bulk of our popular amusements just exists to provoke masturbation. Masturbation is the one thoroughly secret act of the human being, more secret even than excrementation. It is the one functional result of sex-secrecy, and it is stimulated and provoked by our glorious popular literature of pretty pornography, which rubs on the dirty secret without letting you know what is happening.

Now I have heard men, teachers and clergymen, commend masturbation as the solution of an otherwise insoluble sex problem. This at least is honest. The sex problem is there, and you can't just will it away. There it is, and under the ban of secrecy and taboo in mother and father, teacher, friend, and foe, it has found its own solution, the solution of masturbation.

But what about the solution? Do we accept it? Do all the grey ones of this world accept it? If so, they must now accept it openly. We can none of us pretend any longer to be blind to the fact of masturbation, in young and old, man and woman. The moral guardians who are prepared to censor all open and plain portrayal of sex must now be made to give their only justification: We prefer that the people shall masturbate. If this preference is open and declared, then the existing forms of censorship are justified. If the moral guardians prefer that the people shall masturbate, then their present behaviour is correct, and popular amusements are as they should be. If sexual intercourse is deadly sin, and masturbation is comparatively pure and harmless, then all is well. Let things continue as they now are.

Is masturbation so harmless, though? Is it even comparatively pure and harmless? Not to my thinking. In the young, a certain amount of masturbation is inevitable, but not therefore natural. I think, there is no boy or girl who masturbates without feeling a sense of shame, anger, and futility. Following the excitement comes the shame, anger, humiliation, and the sense of futility. This sense of futility and humiliation deepens as the years go on, into a suppressed rage, because of the impossibility of escape. The one thing that it seems impossible to escape from, once the habit is formed, is masturbation. It goes on and on, on into old age, in spite of marriage or love affairs or anything else. And it always carries this secret feeling of futility and humiliation, futility and humiliation. And this is, perhaps, the deepest and most dangerous cancer of our civilization. Instead of being a comparatively pure and harmless vice, masturbation is certainly the most dangerous sexual vice that a society can be afflicted with, in the long run. Comparatively pure it may be – purity being what it is. But harmless! ! !

The great danger of masturbation lies in its merely exhaustive nature. In sexual intercourse, there is a give and take. A new stimulus enters as the native stimulus departs. Something quite new is added as the old surcharge is removed. And this is so in all sexual intercourse where two creatures are concerned, even in the homosexual intercourse. But in masturbation there is nothing but loss. There is no reciprocity. There is merely the spending away of a certain force, and no return. The body remains. in a sense, a corpse, after the act of self-abuse. There is no change, only deadening. There is what we call dead loss. And this is not the case in any act of sexual intercourse between two people. Two people may destroy one another in sex. But they cannot just produce the null effect of masturbation.

The only positive effect of masturbation is that it seems to release a certain mental energy, in some people. But it is mental energy which manifests itself always in the same way, in a vicious circle of analysis and impotent criticism, or else a vicious circle of false and easy sympathy, sentimentalities. The sentimentalism and the niggling analysis, often self-analysis, of most of our modern literature, is a sign of self-abuse. It is the manifestation of masturbation, the sort of conscious activity stimulated by masturbation, whether male or female. The outstanding feature of such consciousness is that there is no real object, there is only subject. This is just the same whether it be a novel or a work of science. The author never escapes from himself, he pads along within the vicious circle of himself. There is hardly a writer living who gets out of the vicious circle of himself – or a painter either. Hence the lack of creation, and the stupendous amount of production. It is a masturbation result, within the vicious circle of the self. It is self-absorption made public.

And of course the process is exhaustive. The real masturbation of Englishmen began only in the nineteenth century. It has continued with an increasing emptying of the real vitality and the real *being* of men, till now people are little more than shells of people. Most of the responses are dead, most of the awareness is dead, nearly all the constructive activity is dead, and all that remains is a sort of shell, a half-empty creature fatally self-preoccupied and incapable of either giving or taking. Incapable either of giving or taking, in the vital self. And this is masturbation result. Enclosed within the vicious circle of the self, with no vital contacts outside, the self becomes emptier and emptier, till it is almost a nullus, a nothingness.

But null or nothing as it may be, it still hangs on to the dirty little secret, which it must still secretly rub and inflame. For ever the vicious circle. And it has a weird, blind will of its own.

One of my most sympathetic critics wrote: 'If Mr Lawrence's attitude to sex were adopted, then two things would disappear, the love lyric and the smoking-room story.' And this, I think, is true. But it depends on which love lyric he means. If it is the: *Who is Sylvia, what is she?* – then it may just as well disappear. All that pure and noble and heaven-blessed stuff is only the counterpart to the smoking-room story. *Du bist wie eine Blume!* Jawohl! One can see the elderly gentleman laying his hands on

the head of the pure maiden and praying God to keep her for ever
so pure, so clean and beautiful. Very nice for him! Just pornography! Tickling the dirty little secret and rolling his eyes to
heaven! He knows perfectly well that if God keeps the maiden
so clean and pure and beautiful – in his vulgar sense of clean and
pure – for a few more years, then she'll be an unhappy old maid,
and not pure nor beautiful at all, only stale and pathetic. Sentimentality is a sure sign of pornography. Why should 'sadness
strike through the heart' of the old gentleman, because the maid
was pure and beautiful? Anybody but a masturbator would have
been glad and would have thought: What a lovely bride for some
lucky man! – But no, not the self-enclosed, pornographic masturbator. Sadness has to strike into his beastly heart! – Away
with such love lyrics, we've had too much of their pornographic
poison, tickling the dirty little secret and rolling the eyes to
heaven.

But if it is a question of the sound love lyric, *My love is like a
red, red rose –!* then we are on other ground. My love is like a
red, red rose only when she's *not* like a pure, pure lily. And
nowadays the pure, pure lilies are mostly festering, anyhow.
Away with them and their lyrics. Away with the pure, pure lily
lyric, along with the smoking-room story. They are counter-
parts, and the one is as pornographic as the other. *Du bist wie
eine Blume* is really as pornographic as a dirty story: tickling the
dirty little secret and rolling the eyes to heaven. But oh, if only
Robert Burns had been accepted for what he is, then love might
still have been like a red, red rose.

The vicious circle, the vicious circle! The vicious circle of masturbation! The vicious circle of self-consciousness that is never
*fully* self-conscious, never fully and openly conscious, but always
harping on the dirty little secret. The vicious circle of secrecy, in
parents, teachers, friends – everybody. The specially vicious
circle of family. The vast conspiracy of secrecy in the press, and
at the same time, the endless tickling of the dirty little secret. The
needless masturbation! and the endless purity! The vicious
circle!

How to get out of it? There is only one way: Away with the

secret! No more secrecy! The only way to stop the terrible mental itch about sex is to come out quite simply and naturally into the open with it. It is terribly difficult, for the secret is cunning as a crab. Yet the thing to do is to make a beginning. The man who said to his exasperating daughter: 'My child, the only pleasure I ever had out of you was the pleasure I had in begetting you' has already done a great deal to release both himself and her from the dirty little secret.

How to get out of the dirty little secret! It is, as a matter of fact, extremely difficult for us secretive moderns. You can't do it by being wise and scientific about it, like Dr Marie Stopes: though to be wise and scientific like Dr Marie Stopes is better than to be utterly hypocritical, like the grey ones. But by being wise and scientific in the serious and earnest manner you only tend to disinfect the dirty little secret, and either kill sex altogether with too much seriousness and intellect, or else leave it a miserable disinfected secret. The unhappy 'free and pure' love of so many people who have taken out the dirty little secret and thoroughly disinfected it with scientific words is apt to be more pathetic even than the common run of dirty-little-secret love. The danger is, that in killing the dirty little secret, you kill dynamic sex altogether, and leave only the scientific and deliberate mechanism.

This is what happens to many of those who become seriously 'free' in their sex, free and pure. They have mentalized sex till it is nothing at all, nothing at all but a mental quality. And the final result is disaster, every time.

The same is true, in an even greater proportion, of the emancipated bohemians: and very many of the young are bohemian today, whether they ever set foot in Bohemia or not. But the bohemian is 'sex free'. The dirty little secret is no secret either to him or her. It is, indeed, a most blatantly open question. There is nothing they don't say: everything that can be revealed is revealed. And they do as they wish.

And then what? They have apparently killed the dirty little secret, but somehow, they have killed everything else too. Some of the dirt still sticks, perhaps; sex remains still dirty. But the

320

thrill of secrecy is gone. Hence the terrible dreariness and depression of modern Bohemia, and the inward dreariness and emptiness of so many young people of today. They have killed, they imagine, the dirty little secret. The thrill of secrecy is gone. Some of the dirt remains. And for the rest, depression, inertia, lack of life. For sex is the fountain-head of our energetic life, and now the fountain ceases to flow.

Why? For two reasons. The idealists along the Marie Stopes line, and the young bohemians of today have killed the dirty little secret as far as their personal self goes. But they are still under its dominion socially. In the social world, in the press, in literature, film, theatre, wireless, everywhere purity and the dirty little secret reign supreme. At home, at the dinner table, it is just the same. It is the same wherever you go. The young girl, and the young woman is by tacit assumption pure, virgin, sexless. *Du bist wie eine Blume.* She, poor thing, knows quite well that flowers, even lilies, have tippling yellow antlers and a sticky stigma, sex, rolling sex. But to the popular mind flowers are sexless things, and when a girl is told she is like a flower, it means she is sexless and ought to be sexless. She herself knows quite well she isn't sexless and she isn't merely like a flower. But how bear up against the great social life forced on her? She can't! She succumbs, and the dirty little secret triumphs. She loses her interest in sex, as far as men are concerned, but the vicious circle of masturbation and self-consciousness encloses her even still faster.

This is one of the disasters of young life today. Personally, and among themselves, a great many, perhaps a majority of the young people of today have come out into the open with sex and laid salt on the tail of the dirty little secret. And this is a very good thing. But in public, in the social world, the young are still entirely under the shadow of the grey elderly ones. The grey elderly ones belong to the last century, the eunuch century, the century of the mealy-mouthed lie, the century that has tried to destroy humanity, the nineteenth century. All our grey ones are left over from this century. And they rule us. They rule us with the grey, mealy-mouthed, canting lie of that great century of lies which, thank God, we are drifting away from. But they rule us

321

still with the lie, for the lie, in the name of the lie. And they are too heavy and too numerous, the grey ones. It doesn't matter what government it is. They are all grey ones, left over from the last century, the century of mealy-mouthed liars, the century of purity and the dirty little secret.

So there is one cause for the depression of the young: the public reign of the mealy-mouthed lie, purity and the dirty little secret, which they themselves have privately overthrown. Having killed a good deal of the lie in their own private lives, the young are still enclosed and imprisoned within the great public lie of the grey ones. Hence the excess, the extravagance, the hysteria, and then the weakness, the feebleness, the pathetic silliness of the modern youth. They are all in a sort of prison, the prison of a great lie and a society of elderly liars. And this is one of the reasons, perhaps the main reason why the sex-flow is dying out of the young, the real energy is dying away. They are enclosed within a lie, and the sex won't flow. For the length of a complete lie is never more than three generations, and the young are the fourth generation of the nineteenth-century lie.

The second reason why the sex-flow is dying is of course, that the young, in spite of their emancipation, are still enclosed within the vicious circle of self-conscious masturbation. They are thrown back into it, when they try to escape, by the enclosure of the vast public lie of purity and the dirty little secret. The most emancipated bohemians, who swank most about sex, are still utterly self-conscious and enclosed within the narcissus-masturbation circle. They have perhaps less sex even than the grey ones. The whole thing has been driven up into their heads. There isn't even the lurking hole of a dirty little secret. Their sex is more mental than their arithmetic; and as vital physical creatures they are more non-existent than ghosts. The modern bohemian is indeed a kind of ghost, not even narcissus, only the image of narcissus reflected on the face of the audience. The dirty little secret is most difficult to kill. You may put it to death publicly a thousand times, and still it reappears, like a crab, stealthily from under the submerged rocks of the personality. The French, who are supposed to be so open about sex, will perhaps be the last to kill the dirty little secret. Perhaps they don't want to. Anyhow, mere publicity won't do it.

You may parade sex abroad, but you will not kill the dirty little secret. You may read all the novels of Marcel Proust, with everything there in all detail. Yet you will not kill the dirty little secret. You will perhaps only make it more cunning. You may even bring about a state of utter indifference and sex-inertia, still without killing the dirty little secret. Or you may be the most wispy and enamoured little Don Juan of modern days, and still the core of your spirit merely be the dirty little secret. That is to say, you will still be in the narcissus-masturbation circle, the vicious circle of self-enclosure. For whenever the dirty little secret exists, it exists as the centre of the vicious circle of masturbation self-enclosure. And whenever you have the vicious circle of masturbation self-enclosure, you have at the core the dirty little secret. And the most high-flown sex-emancipated young people today are perhaps the most fatally and nervously enclosed within the masturbation self-enclosure. Nor do they want to get out of it, for there would be nothing left to come out.

But some people surely do want to come out of the awful self-enclosure. Today, practically everybody is self-conscious and imprisoned in self-consciousness. It is the joyful result of the dirty little secret. Vast numbers of people don't want to come out of the prison of their self-consciousness: they have so little left to come out with. But some people, surely, want to escape this doom of self-enclosure which is the doom of our civilization. There is surely a proud minority that wants once and for all to be free of the dirty little secret.

And the way to do it is, first, to fight the sentimental lie of purity and the dirty little secret wherever you meet it, inside yourself or in the world outside. Fight the great lie of the nineteenth century, which has soaked through our sex and our bones. It means fighting with almost every breath, for the lie is ubiquitous.

Then secondly, in his adventure of self-consciousness a man must come to the limits of himself and become aware of something beyond him. A man must be self-conscious enough to know his own limits, and to be aware of that which surpasses him.

## Censorship

What surpasses me is the very urge of life that is within me, and this life urges me to forget myself and to yield to the stirring half-born impulse to smash up the vast lie of the world, and make a new world. If my life is merely to go on in a vicious circle of self-enclosure, masturbating self-consciousness, it is worth nothing to me. If my individual life is to be enclosed within the huge corrupt lie of society today, purity and the dirty little secret, then it is worth not much to me. Freedom is a very great reality. But it means, above all things, freedom from lies. It is first, freedom from myself, from the lie of myself, from the lie of my all-importance, even to myself; it is freedom from the self-conscious masturbating thing I am, self-enclosed. And second, freedom from the vast lie of the social world, the lie of purity and the dirty little secret. All the other monstrous lies lurk under the cloak of this one primary lie. The monstrous lie of money lurks under the cloak of purity. Kill the purity-lie, and the money-lie will be defenceless.

We have to be sufficiently conscious, and self-conscious, to know our own limits and to be aware of the greater urge within us and beyond us. Then we cease to be primarily interested in ourselves. Then we learn to leave ourselves alone, in all the affective centres: not to force our feelings in any way, and never to force our sex. Then we make the great onslaught on to the outside lie, the inside lie being settled. And that is freedom and the fight for freedom.

The greatest of all lies in the modern world is the lie of purity and the dirty little secret. The grey ones left over from the nineteenth century are the embodiment of this lie. They dominate in society, in the press, in literature, everywhere. And, naturally, they lead the vast mob of the general public along with them.

Which means, of course, perpetual censorship of anything that would militate against the lie of purity and the dirty little secret, and perpetual encouragement of what may be called permissible pornography, pure, but tickling the dirty little secret under the delicate underclothing. The grey ones will pass and will commend floods of evasive pornography, and will suppress every outspoken word.

324

The law is a mere figment. In his article on the 'Censorship of Books', in the *Nineteenth Century*, Viscount Brentford, the late Home Secretary, says:

Let it be remembered that the publishing of an obscene book, the issue of an obscene post-card or pornographic photograph – are all offences against the law of the land, and the Secretary of State who is the general authority for the maintenance of law and order most clearly and definitely cannot discriminate between one offence and another in discharge of his duty.

So he winds up, *ex cathedra* and infallible. But only ten lines above he has written:

I agree, that if the law were pushed to its logical conclusion, the printing and publication of such books as *The Decameron*, Benvenuto Cellini's *Life*, and Burton's *Arabian Nights* might form the subject of proceedings. But the ultimate sanction of all law is public opinion, and I do not believe for one moment that prosecution in respect of books that have been in circulation for many centuries would command public support.

Ooray then for public opinion! It only needs that a few more years shall roll. But now we see that the Secretary of State most clearly and definitely *does* discriminate between one offence and another in discharge of his duty. Simple and admitted discrimination on his part! Yet what is this public opinion? Just more lies on the part of the grey ones. They would suppress Benvenuto tomorrow, if they dared. But they would make laughing-stocks of themselves, because *tradition* backs up Benvenuto. It isn't public opinion at all. It is the grey ones afraid of making still bigger fools of themselves. But the case is simple. If the grey ones are going to be backed by a general public, then every new book that would smash the mealy-mouthed lie of the nineteenth century will be suppressed as it appears. Yet let the grey ones beware. The general public is nowadays a very unstable affair, and no longer loves its grey ones so dearly, with their old lie. And there is another public, the small public of the minority, which hates the lie and the grey ones that perpetuate the lie, and which has its own dynamic ideas about pornography and obscenity. You can't fool all the people all the time, even with purity and a dirty little secret.

And this minority public knows well that the books of many contemporary writers, both big and lesser fry, are far more pornographical than the liveliest story in *The Decameron*: because they tickle the dirty little secret and excite to private masturbation, which the wholesome Boccaccio never does. And the minority public knows full well that the most obscene painting on a Greek vase – *Thou still unravished bride of quietness* – is not as pornographical as the close-up kisses on the film, which excite men and women to secret and separate masturbation.

And perhaps one day even the general public will desire to look the thing in the face, and see for itself the difference between the sneaking masturbation pornography of the press, the film, and present-day popular literature, and then the creative portrayals of the sexual impulse that we have in Boccaccio or the Greek vase-paintings or some Pompeian art, and which are necessary for the fulfilment of our consciousness.

As it is, the public mind is today bewildered on this point, bewildered almost to idiocy. When the police raided my picture show, they did not in the least know what to take. So they took every picture where the smallest bit of the sex organ of either man or woman showed. Quite regardless of subject or meaning or anything else: they would allow anything, these dainty policemen in a picture show, except the actual sight of a fragment of the human *pudenda*. This was the police test. The dabbing on of a postage stamp – especially a green one that could be called a leaf – would in most cases have been quite sufficient to satisfy this 'public opinion'.

It is, we can only repeat, a condition of idiocy. And if the purity-with-a-dirty-little-secret lie is kept up much longer, the mass of society will really be an idiot, and a dangerous idiot at that. For the public is made up of individuals. And each individual has sex, and is pivoted on sex. And if, with purity and dirty little secrets, you drive every individual into the masturbation self-enclosure, and keep him there, then you will produce a state of general idiocy. For the masturbation self-enclosure produces idiots. Perhaps if we are all idiots, we shan't know it. But God preserve us.

# A Propos of *Lady Chatterley's Lover*

Written 1929; this version published 1930

Owing to the existence of various pirated editions of *Lady Chatter-ley's Lover*, I brought out in 1929 a cheap popular edition, pro-duced in France and offered to the public at sixty francs, hoping at least to meet the European demand. The pirates, in the United States certainly, were prompt and busy. The first stolen edition was being sold in New York almost within a month of the arrival in America of the first genuine copies from Florence. It was a facsimile of the original, produced by the photographic method, and was sold, even by reliable booksellers, to the unsuspecting public as if it were the original first edition. The price was usually fifteen dollars, whereas the price of the original was ten dollars: and the purchaser was left in fond ignorance of the fraud.

This gallant attempt was followed by others. I am told there was still another facsimile edition produced in New York or Philadelphia: and I myself possess a filthy-looking book bound in a dull orange cloth, with green label, smearily produced by photography, and containing my signature forged by the little boy of the piratical family. It was when this edition appeared in Lon-don, from New York, towards the end of 1928, and was offered to the public at thirty shillings, that I put out from Florence my little second edition of two hundred copies, which I offered at a guinea. I had wanted to save it for a year or more, but had to launch it against the dirty orange pirate. But the number was too small. The orange pirate persisted.

Then I have had in my hand a very funereal volume, bound in black and elongated to look like a bible or long hymn-book, gloomy. This time the pirate was not only sober, but earnest. He has not one, but two title-pages, and on each is a vignette representing the American Eagle, with six stars round his head and lightning splashing from his paw, all surrounded by a laurel wreath in honour of his latest exploit in literary robbery. Altogether it is a sinister volume – like Captain Kidd with his face blackened, reading a sermon to those about to walk the plank. Why the pirate should have elongated the page, by adding a false page-heading, I don't know. The effect is peculiarly depressing, sinisterly high-brow. For of course this book also was produced by the photographic process. The signature anyhow is omitted. And I am told this lugubrious tome sells for ten, twenty, thirty, and fifty dollars, according to the whim of the bookseller and the gullibility of the purchaser.

That makes three pirated editions in the United States for certain. I have heard mentioned the report of a fourth, another facsimile of the original. But since I haven't seen it, I want not to believe in it.

There is, however, the European pirated edition of fifteen hundred, produced by a Paris firm of booksellers, and stamped *Imprimé en Allemagne*: Printed in Germany. Whether printed in Germany or not, it was certainly printed, not photographed, for some of the spelling errors of the original are corrected. And it is a very respectable volume, a very close replica of the original, but lacking the signature and it gives itself away also by the green-and-yellow silk edge of the back-binding. This edition is sold to the trade at one hundred francs, and offered to the public at three hundred, four hundred, five hundred francs. Very unscrupulous booksellers are said to have forged the signature and offered the book as the original signed edition. Let us hope it is not true. But it all sounds very black against the 'trade'. Still there is some relief. Certain booksellers will not handle the pirated edition at all. Both sentimental and business scruples prevent them. Others handle it, but not very warmly. And apparently they would all rather handle the authorized edition. So that sentiment does genuinely enter in, against the pirates, even if not strong enough to keep them out altogether.

None of these pirated editions has received any sort of authorization from me, and from none of them have I received a penny. A semi-repentant bookseller of New York did, however, send me some dollars which were, he said, my ten-per-cent royalty on all copies sold in his shop. 'I know', he wrote, 'it is but a drop in the bucket'. He meant of course, a drop out of the bucket. And since, for a drop, it was quite a nice little sum, what a beautiful bucketful there must have been for the pirates!

I received a belated offer from the European pirates, who found the booksellers stiff-necked, offering me a royalty on all copies sold in the past as well as the future, if I would authorize their edition. Well, I thought to myself, in a world of: Do him or you will be done by him, – why not? – When it came to the point, however, pride rebelled. It is understood that Judas is always ready with a kiss. But that I should have to kiss him back –!

So I managed to get published the little cheap French edition, photographed down from the original, and offered at sixty francs. English publishers urge me to make an expurgated edition, promising large returns, perhaps even a little bucket, one of those children's sea-side pails! – and insisting that I should show the public that here is a fine novel, apart from all 'purple' and all 'words'. So I begin to be tempted and start in to expurgate. But impossible! I might as well try to clip my own nose into shape with scissors. The book bleeds.

And in spite of all antagonism, I put forth this novel as an honest, healthy book, necessary for us today. The words that shock so much at first don't shock at all after a while. Is this because the mind is depraved by habit? Not a bit. It is that the words merely shocked the eye, they never shocked the mind at all. People without minds may go on being shocked, but they don't matter. People with minds realize that they aren't shocked, and never really were : and they experience a sense of relief.

And that is the whole point. We are today, as human beings, evolved and cultured far beyond the taboos which are inherent in our culture. This is a very important fact to realize. Probably, to the Crusaders, mere words were potent and evocative to a degree we can't realize. The evocative power of the so-called obscene words must have been very dangerous to the dim-minded, obscure, violent natures of the Middle Ages, and perhaps is still too strong for slow-minded, half-evoked lower natures today. But real culture makes us give to a word only those mental and imaginative reactions which belong to the mind, and saves us from violent and indiscriminate physical reactions which may wreck social decency. In the past, man was too weak-minded, or crude-minded, to contemplate his own physical body and physical functions, without getting all messed up with physical reactions that overpowered him. It is no longer so. Culture and civilization have taught us to separate the reactions. We now know the act does not necessarily follow on the thought. In fact, thought and action, word and deed, are two separate forms of consciousness, two separate lives which we lead. We need, very sincerely, to keep a connexion. But while we think, we do not act, and while we act we do not think. The great necessity is that we should act according to our thoughts, and think according to our acts. But while we are in thought we cannot really act, and while we are in action we cannot really think. The two conditions, of thought and action, are mutually exclusive. Yet they should be related in harmony.

And this is the real point of this book. I want men and women to be able to think sex, fully, completely, honestly and cleanly.

Even if we can't act sexually to our complete satisfaction, let us at least think sexually, complete and clear. All this talk of young girls and virginity, like a blank white sheet on which nothing is written, is pure nonsense. A young girl and a young boy is a tormented tangle, a seething confusion of sexual feelings and sexual thoughts which only the years will disentangle. Years of honest thoughts of sex, and years of struggling action in sex will bring us at last where we want to get, to our real and accomplished chastity, our completeness, when our sexual act and our

330

sexual thought are in harmony, and the one does not interfere with the other.

Far be it from me to suggest that all women should go running after gamekeepers for lovers. Far be it from me to suggest that they should be running after anybody. A great many men and women today are happiest when they abstain and stay sexually apart, quite clean: and at the same time, when they understand and realize sex more fully. Ours is the day of realization rather than action. There has been so much action in the past, especially sexual action, a wearying repetition over and over, without a corresponding thought, a corresponding realization. Now our business is to realize sex. Today the full conscious realization of sex is even more important than the act itself. After centuries of obfuscation, the mind demands to know and know fully. The body is a good deal in abeyance, really. When people act in sex, nowadays, they are half the time acting up. They do it because they think it is expected of them. Whereas as a matter of fact it is the mind which is interested, and the body has to be provoked. The reason being that our ancestors have so assiduously acted sex without ever thinking it or realizing it, that now the act tends to be mechanical, dull and disappointing, and only fresh mental realization will freshen up the experience.

The mind has to catch up, in sex: indeed, in all the physical acts. Mentally, we lag behind in our sexual thought, in a dimness, a lurking, grovelling fear which belongs to our raw, somewhat bestial ancestors. In this one respect, sexual and physical, we have left the mind unevolved. Now we have to catch up, and make a balance between the consciousness of the body's sensations and experiences, and these sensations and experiences themselves. Balance up the consciousness of the act, and the act itself. Get the two in harmony. It means having a proper reverence for sex, and a proper awe of the body's strange experience. It means being able to use the so-called obscene words, because these are the natural part of the mind's consciousness of the body. Obscenity only comes in when the mind despises and fears the body, and the body hates and resists the mind.

When we read of the case of Colonel Barker, we see what is the matter. Colonel Barker was a woman who masqueraded as a man. The 'Colonel' married a wife, and lived five years with her in 'conjugal happiness'. And the poor wife thought all the time she was married normally and happily to a real husband. The revelation at the end is beyond all thought cruel for the poor woman. The situation is monstrous. Yet there are thousands of women today who might be so deceived, and go on being deceived. Why? Because they know nothing, they can't think sexually at all; they are morons in this respect. It is better to give all girls this book, at the age of seventeen.

The same with the case of the venerable schoolmaster and clergyman, for years utterly 'holy and good': and at the age of sixty-five, tried in the police courts for assaulting little girls. This happens at the moment when the Home Secretary, himself growing elderly, is most loudly demanding and enforcing a mealy-mouthed silence about sexual matters. Doesn't the experience of that other elderly, most righteous and 'pure' gentleman, make him pause at all?

But so it is. The mind has an old grovelling fear of the body and the body's potencies. It is the mind we have to liberate, to civilize on these points. The mind's terror of the body has probably driven more men mad than ever could be counted. The insanity of a great mind like Swift's is at least partly traceable to this cause. In the poem to his mistress Celia, which has the maddened refrain 'But – Celia, Celia, Celia s***s', (the word rhymes with spits), we see what can happen to a great mind when it falls into panic. A great wit like Swift could not see how ridiculous he made himself. Of course Celia s***s! Who doesn't? And how much worse if she didn't. It is hopeless. And then think of poor Celia, made to feel iniquitous about her proper natural function, by her 'lover'. It is monstrous. And it comes from having taboo words, and from not keeping the mind sufficiently developed in physical and sexual consciousness.

In contrast to the puritan hush! hush!, which produces the sexual moron, we have the modern young jazzy and high-brow person who has gone one better, and won't be hushed in any respect, and just 'does as she likes'. From fearing the body, and denying its existence, the advanced young go to the other extreme and treat it as a sort of toy to be played with, a slightly nasty toy, but still you can get some fun out of it, before it lets you down. These young people scoff at the importance of sex, take it like a cocktail, and flout their elders with it. These young ones are advanced and superior. They despise a book like *Lady Chatterley's Lover*. It is much too simple and ordinary for them. The naughty words they care nothing about, and the attitude to love they find old-fashioned. Why make a fuss about it? Take it like a cocktail! The book, they say, shows the mentality of a boy of fourteen. But perhaps the mentality of a boy of fourteen, who still has a little natural awe and proper fear in fact of sex, is more wholesome than the mentality of the young cocktaily person who has no respect for anything and whose mind has nothing to do but play with the toys of life, sex being one of the chief toys, and who loses his mind in the process. Heliogabulus, indeed!

So, between the stale grey puritan who is likely to fall into sexual indecency in advanced age, and the smart jazzy person of the young world, who says: 'We can do anything. If we can think a thing we can do it', and then the low uncultured person with a dirty mind, who looks for dirt – this book has hardly a space to turn in. But to them all I say the same: Keep your perversions if you like them – your perversion of puritanism, your perversion of smart licentiousness, your perversion of a dirty mind. But I stick to my book and my position: Life is only bearable when the mind and body are in harmony, and there is a natural balance between them, and each has a natural respect for the other.

And it is obvious, there is no balance and no harmony now. The body is at the best the tool of the mind, at the worst, the toy. The business man keeps himself 'fit', that is, keeps his body in good working order, for the sake of his business, and the usual young person who spends much time on keeping fit does so as a rule out of self-conscious self-absorption, narcissism. The mind has a stereotyped set of ideas and 'feelings', and the body is made to act up, like a trained dog: to beg for sugar, whether it wants sugar or whether it doesn't, to shake hands when it would dearly like to snap the hand it has to shake. The body of men and women today is just a trained dog. And of no one is this more true than of the free and emancipated young. Above all, their bodies are the bodies of trained dogs. And because the dog is trained to do things the old-fashioned dog never did, they call themselves free, full of real life, the real thing.

But they know perfectly well it is false. Just as the business man knows, somewhere, that he's all wrong. Men and women aren't really dogs: they only look like it and behave like it. Somewhere inside there is a great chagrin and a gnawing discontent. The body is, in its spontaneous natural self, dead or paralysed. It has only the secondary life of a circus dog, acting up and showing off: and then collapsing.

What life could it have, of itself? The body's life is the life of sensations and emotions. The body feels real hunger, real thirst, real joy in the sun or the snow, real pleasure in the smell of roses or the look of a lilac bush; real anger, real sorrow, real love, real tenderness, real warmth, real passion, real hate, real grief. All the emotions belong to the body, and are only recognized by the mind. We may hear the most sorrowful piece of news, and only feel a mental excitement. Then, hours after, perhaps in sleep, the awareness may reach the bodily centres, and true grief wrings the heart.

How different they are, mental feelings and real feelings. Today, many people live and die without having had any real feelings – though they have had a 'rich emotional life' apparently, having showed strong mental feeling. But it is all counterfeit. In magic, one of the so-called 'occult' pictures represents a man standing, apparently, before a flat table mirror, which reflects him from the waist to the head, so that you have the man from head to waist, then his reflection downwards from waist to head again. And whatever it may mean in magic, it means what we are today, creatures whose active emotional self has no real existence, but is all reflected downwards from the mind. Our education from the start has *taught* us a certain range of emotions, what to feel and what not to feel, and how to feel the feelings we allow ourselves to feel. All the rest is just non-existent. The vulgar criticism of any new good book is: Of course nobody ever felt like that! – People allow themselves to feel a certain number of finished feelings. So it was in the last century. This feeling only what you allow yourselves to feel at last kills all capacity for feeling, and in the higher emotional range you feel nothing at all. This has come to pass in our present century. The higher emotions are strictly dead. They have to be faked.

And by higher emotions we mean love in all its manifestations, from genuine desire to tender love, love of our fellowmen, and love of God: we mean love, joy, delight, hope, true indignant anger, passionate sense of justice and injustice, truth and untruth, honour and dishonour, and real belief in *anything*: for belief is a profound emotion that has the mind's connivance. All these things, today, are more or less dead. We have in their place the loud and sentimental counterfeit of all such emotion.

Never was an age more sentimental, more devoid of real feeling, more exaggerated in false feeling, than our own. Sentimentality and counterfeit feeling have become a sort of game, everybody trying to outdo his neighbour. The radio and the film are mere counterfeit emotion all the time, the current press and literature the same. People wallow in emotion: counterfeit emotion. They lap it up: they live in it and on it. They ooze with it.

And at times, they seem to get on very well with it all. And then, more and more, they break down. They go to pieces. You can fool yourself for a long time about your own feelings. But not forever. The body itself hits back at you, and hits back remorselessly in the end.

As for other people – you can fool most people all the time, and all people most of the time, but not all people all the time, with false feelings. A young couple fall in counterfeit love, and fool themselves and each other completely. But, alas, counterfeit love is good cake but bad bread. It produces a fearful emotional indigestion. Then you get a modern marriage, and a still more modern separation.

The trouble with counterfeit emotion is that nobody is really happy, nobody is really contented, nobody has any peace. Everybody keeps on rushing to get away from the counterfeit emotion which is in themselves worst of all. They rush from the false

335

feelings of Peter to the false feelings of Adrian, from the counterfeit emotions of Margaret to those of Virginia, from film to radio, from Eastbourne to Brighton, and the more it changes the more it is the same thing.

Above all things love is a counterfeit feeling today. Here, above all things, the young will tell you, is the greatest swindle. That is, if you take it seriously. Love is all right if you take it lightly, as an amusement. But if you begin taking it seriously you are let down with a crash.

There are, the young women say, no *real* men to love. And there are, the young men say, no *real* girls to fall in love with. So they go on falling in love with unreal ones, on either side; which means, if you can't have real feelings, you've got to have counterfeit ones: since some feelings you've *got* to have: like falling in love. There are still some young people who would *like* to have real feelings, and they are bewildered to death to know why they can't. Especially in love.

But especially in love, only counterfeit emotions exist nowadays. We have all been taught to mistrust everybody emotionally, from parents downwards, or upwards. Don't trust *anybody* with your real emotions: if you've got any: that is the slogan of today. Trust them with your money, even, but *never* with your feelings. They are bound to trample on them.

I believe there has never been an age of greater mistrust between persons than ours today: under a superficial but quite genuine social trust. Very few of my friends would pick my pocket, or let me sit on a chair where I might hurt myself. But practically all my friends would turn my real emotions to ridicule. They can't help it; it's the spirit of the day. So there goes love, and there goes friendship: for each implies a fundamental emotional sympathy. And hence, counterfeit love, which there is no escaping.

And with counterfeit emotions there is no real sex at all. Sex is the one thing you cannot really swindle; and it is the centre of the worst swindling of all, emotional swindling. Once come down to sex, and the emotional swindle must collapse. But in all the approaches to sex, the emotional swindle intensifies more and more. Till you get there. Then collapse.

Sex lashes out against counterfeit emotion, and is ruthless, devastating against false love. The peculiar hatred of people who have not loved one another, but who have pretended to, even perhaps have imagined they really did love, is one of the phenomena of our time. The phenomenon, of course, belongs to all time. But today it is almost universal. People who thought they loved one another dearly, dearly, and went on for years, ideal: lo! suddenly the most profound and vivid hatred appears. If it doesn't come out fairly young, it saves itself till the happy couple are nearing fifty, the time of the great sexual change – and then – cataclysm!

Nothing is more startling. Nothing is more staggering, in our age, than the intensity of the hatred people, men and women, feel for one another when they have once 'loved' one another. It breaks out in the most extraordinary ways. And when you know people intimately, it is almost universal. It is the charwoman as much as the mistress, and the duchess as much as the policeman's wife.

And it would be too horrible, if one did not remember that in all of them, men and women alike, it is the organic reaction against counterfeit love. All love today is counterfeit. It is a stereotyped thing. All the young know just how they ought to feel and how they ought to behave, in love. And they feel and they behave like that. And it is counterfeit love. So that revenge will come back at them, tenfold. The sex, the very sexual organism in man and woman alike accumulates a deadly and desperate rage, after a certain amount of counterfeit love has been palmed off on it, even if itself has given nothing but counterfeit love. The element of counterfeit in love at last maddens, or else kills, sex, the deepest sex in the individual. But perhaps it would be safe to say that it *always* enrages the inner sex, even if at last it kills it. There is always the period of rage. And the strange thing is, the worst offenders in the counterfeit-love game fall into the greatest rage. Those whose love has been a bit sincere are always gentler, even though they have been most swindled.

Now the real tragedy is here: that we are none of us all of a piece, none of us *all* counterfeit, or *all* true love. And in many a marriage, in among the counterfeit there flickers a little flame of the true thing, on both sides. The tragedy is, that in an age peculiarly conscious of counterfeit, peculiarly suspicious of substitute and swindle in emotion, particularly sexual emotion, the rage and mistrust against the counterfeit element is likely to overwhelm and extinguish the small, true flame of real loving communion, which might have made two lives happy. Herein lies the danger of harping only on the counterfeit and the swindle of emotion, as most 'advanced' writers do. Though they do it, of course, to counterbalance the hugely greater swindle of the sentimental 'sweet' writers.

Perhaps I shall have given some notion of my feeling about sex, for which I have been so monotonously abused. When a 'serious' young man said to me the other day: 'I can't believe in the regeneration of England by sex, you know', I could only say, 'I'm sure you can't.' He had no sex anyhow: poor, self-conscious, uneasy, narcissus-monk as he was. And he didn't know what it meant, to have any. To him, people only had minds, or no minds, mostly no minds, so they were only there to be gibed at, and he wandered round ineffectively seeking for gibes or for truth, tight shut in inside his own ego.

Now when brilliant young people like this talk to me about sex: or scorn to: I say nothing. There is nothing to say. But I feel a terrible weariness. To them, sex means just plainly and simply, a lady's underclothing, and the fumbling therewith. They have read all the love literature, *Anna Karenina*, all the rest, and looked at statues and pictures of Aphrodite, all very laudable. Yet when it comes to actuality, to today, sex means to them meaningless young women and expensive underthings. Whether they are young men from Oxford, or working-men, it is the same. The story from the modish summer-resort, where city ladies take up with young mountaineer 'dancing partners' for a season – or less – is typical. It was end of September, the summer visitors had almost all gone. Young John, the young mountain farmer, had said good-bye to his 'lady' from the capital, and was lounging about alone. 'Ho, John! you'll be missing your lady!' 'Nay!' he said. 'Only she had such nice underclothes.'

That is all sex means to them: just the trimmings. The regeneration of England with that? Good God! Poor England, she will have to regenerate the sex in her young people, before they do any regenerating of her. It isn't England that needs regeneration, it is her young.

They accuse me of barbarism. I want to drag England down to the level of savages. But it is this crude stupidity, deadness, about sex which I find barbaric and savage. The man who finds a woman's underclothing the most exciting part about her is a savage. Savages are like that. We read of the woman-savage who wore three overcoats on top of one another to excite her man: and did it. That ghastly crudity of seeing in sex nothing but a functional act and a certain fumbling with clothes is, in my opinion, a low degree of barbarism, savagery. And as far as sex goes, our white civilization is crude, barbaric, and uglily savage: especially England and America.

Witness Bernard Shaw, one of the greatest exponents of our civilization. He says clothes arouse sex and lack of clothes tends to kill sex – speaking of muffled-up women or our present bare-armed and bare-legged sisters: and scoffs at the Pope for wanting to cover women up; saying that the last person in the world to know anything about sex is the Chief Priest of Europe: and that the one person to ask about it would be the chief Prostitute of Europe, if there were such a person.

Here we see the flippancy and vulgarity of our chief thinkers, at least. The half-naked women of today certainly do not rouse much sexual feeling in the muffled-up men of today – who don't rouse much sexual feeling in the women, either. – But why? Why does the bare woman of today rouse so much less sexual feeling than the muffled-up woman of Mr Shaw's muffled-up eighties? It would be silly to make it a question of mere muffling.

When a woman's sex is in itself dynamic and alive, then it is a power in itself, beyond her reason. And of itself it emits its peculiar spell, drawing men in the first delight of desire. And the woman has to protect herself, hide herself as much as possible. She veils herself in timidity and modesty, because her sex is a power in itself, exposing her to the desire of men. If a woman in

339

whom sex was alive and positive were to expose her naked flesh as women do today, then men could go mad for her. As David was mad for Bathsheba.

But when a woman's sex has lost its dynamic call, and is in a sense dead or static, then the woman *wants* to attract men, for the simple reason that she finds she no longer does attract them. So all the activity that used to be unconscious and delightful becomes conscious and repellent. The woman exposes her flesh more and more, and the more she exposes, the more men are sexually repelled by her. But let us not forget that the men are *socially* thrilled, while sexually repelled. The two things are opposites, today. Socially, men like the gesture of the half-naked woman, half-naked in the street. It is *chic*, it is a declaration of defiance and independence, it is modern, it is free, it is popular because it is strictly a-sexual, or anti-sexual. Neither men nor women *want* to feel real desire, today. They want the counterfeit, mental substitute.

But we are very mixed, all of us, and creatures of many diverse and often opposing desires. The very men who encourage women to be most daring and sexless complain most bitterly of the sexlessness of women. The same with women. The women who adore men so tremendously for their social smartness and sexlessness as males, hate them most bitterly for not being 'men'. In public, *en masse*, and socially, everybody today wants counterfeit sex. But at certain hours in their lives, all individuals hate counterfeit sex with deadly and maddened hate, and those who have dealt it out most perhaps have the wildest hate of it, in the other person – or persons.

The girls of today could muffle themselves up to the eyes, wear crinolines and chignons and all the rest, and though they would not, perhaps, have the peculiar hardening effect on the hearts of men that our half-naked women truly have, neither would they exert any more real sexual attraction. If there is no sex to muffle up, it's no good muffling. Or not much good. Man is often willing to be deceived – for a time – even by muffled-up nothingness.

The point is, when women are sexually alive and quivering and helplessly attractive, beyond their will, then they always
340

cover themselves, and drape themselves with clothes, gracefully. The extravagance of 1880 bustles and such things was only a forewarning of approaching sexlessness.

While sex is a power in itself, women try all kinds of fascinating disguise, and men flaunt. When the Pope insists that women shall cover their naked flesh in church, it is not sex he is opposing, but the sexless tricks of female immodesty. The Pope, and the priests, conclude that the flaunting of naked women's flesh in street and church produces a bad, 'unholy' state of mind both in men and women. And they are right. But not because the exposure arouses sexual desire: it doesn't, or very rarely: even Mr Shaw knows that. But when women's flesh arouses no sort of desire, something is specially wrong! Something is sadly wrong. For the naked arms of women today arouse a feeling of flippancy, cynicism and vulgarity which is indeed the very last feeling to go to church with, if you have any respect for the Church. The bare arms of women in an Italian church are really a mark of disrespect, given the tradition.

The Catholic Church, especially in the south, is neither antisexual, like the northern Churches, nor a-sexual, like Mr Shaw and such social thinkers. The Catholic Church recognizes sex, and makes of marriage a sacrament based on the sexual communion, for the purpose of procreation. But procreation in the south is not the bare and scientific fact, and act, that it is in the north. The act of procreation is still charged with all the sensual mystery and importance of the old past. The man is potential creator, and in this has his splendour. All of which has been stripped away by the northern Churches and the Shavian logical triviality.

But all this which has gone in the north, the Church has tried to keep in the south, knowing that it is of basic importance in life. The sense of being a potential creator and law-giver, as father and husband, is perhaps essential to the day-by-day life of a man, if he is to live full and satisfied. The sense of the eternality of marriage is perhaps necessary to the inward peace, both of men and women. Even if it carry a sense of doom, it is necessary. The Catholic Church does not spend its time reminding the people

341

that in heaven there is no marrying nor giving in marriage. It insists: if you marry, you marry for ever! And the people accept the decree, the doom and the dignity of it. To the priest, sex is the clue to marriage and marriage is the clue to the daily life of the people and the Church is the clue to the greater life.

So that sexual lure in itself is not deadly to the Church. Much more deadly is the anti-sexual defiance of bare arms and flippancy, 'freedom', cynicism, irreverence. Sex may be obscene in church, or blasphemous, but never cynical and atheist. Potentially, the bare arms of women today are cynical, atheist, in the dangerous, vulgar form of atheism. Naturally the Church is against it. The Chief Priest of Europe knows more about sex than Mr Shaw does, anyhow, because he knows more about the essential nature of the human being. Traditionally, he has a thousand years' experience. Mr Shaw jumped up in a day. And Mr Shaw, as a dramatist, has jumped up to play tricks with the counterfeit sex of the modern public. No doubt he can do it. So can the cheapest film. But it is equally obvious that he *cannot* touch the deeper sex of the real individual, whose existence he hardly seems to suspect.

And, as a parallel to himself, Mr Shaw suggests that the Chief Prostitute of Europe would be the one to consult about sex, not the Chief Priest. The parallel is just. The Chief Prostitute of Europe would know truly as much about sex as Mr Shaw himself does. Which is, not much. Just like Mr Shaw, the Chief Prostitute of Europe would know an immense amount about the counterfeit sex of men, the shoddy thing that is worked by tricks. And just like him, she would know nothing at all about the real sex in a man, that has the rhythm of the seasons and the years, the crisis of the winter solstice and the passion of Easter. This the Chief Prostitute would know nothing about, positively, because to be a prostitute she would have to have lost it. But even then, she would know more than Mr Shaw. She would know that the profound, rhythmic sex of a man's inward life *existed*. She would know, because time and again she would have been up against it. All the literature of the world shows the prostitute's ultimate impotence in sex, her inability to keep a man, her rage against the profound instinct of fidelity in a man, which is, as shown by world-history, just a little deeper and more powerful than his instinct of faithless sexual promiscuity. All the literature of the world shows how profound is the instinct of fidelity in both man and woman, how men and women both hanker restlessly after the satisfaction of this instinct, and fret at their own inability to find the real mode of fidelity. The instinct of fidelity is perhaps the deepest instinct in the great complex we call sex. Where there is real sex there is the underlying passion for fidelity. And the prostitute knows this, because she is up against it. She can only keep men who have no real sex, the counterfeits: and these she despises. The men with real sex leave her inevitably, as unable to satisfy their real desire.

The Chief Prostitute knows so much. So does the Pope, if he troubles to think of it, for it is all in the traditional consciousness of the Church. But the Chief Dramatist knows nothing of it. He has a curious blank in his make-up. To him, all sex in infidelity and only infidelity is sex. Marriage is sexless, null. Sex is only manifested in infidelity, and the queen of sex is the chief prostitute. If sex crops up in marriage, it is because one party falls in love with somebody else, and wants to be unfaithful. Infidelity is sex, and prostitutes know all about it. Wives know nothing and are nothing, in that respect.

This is the teaching of the Chief Dramatists and Chief Thinkers of our generation. And the vulgar public agrees with them entirely. Sex is a thing you don't have except to be naughty with. Apart from naughtiness, that is, apart from infidelity and fornication, sex doesn't exist. Our chief thinkers, ending in the flippantly cocksure Mr Shaw, have taught this trash so thoroughly, that it has almost become a fact. Sex is almost non-existent, apart from the counterfeit forms of prostitution and shallow fornication. And marriage is empty, hollow.

Now this question of sex and marriage is of paramount importance. Our social life is established on marriage, and marriage, the sociologists say, is established upon property. Marriage has been found the best method of conserving property and stimulating production. Which is all there is to it.

But is it? We are just in the throes of a great revolt against marriage, a passionate revolt against its ties and restrictions. In fact, at least three quarters of the unhappiness of modern life could be laid at the door of marriage. There are few married people today, and few unmarried, who have not felt an intense and vivid hatred against marriage itself, marriage as an institution and an imposition upon human life. Far greater than the revolt against governments is this revolt against marriage.

And everybody, pretty well, takes it for granted that as soon as we can find a possible way out of it, marriage will be abolished. The Soviet abolishes marriage: or did. If new 'modern' states spring up, they will almost certainly follow suit. They will try to find some social substitute for marriage, and abolish the hated yoke of conjugality. State support of motherhood, state support of children, and independence of women. It is on the programme of every great scheme of reform. And it means, of course, the abolition of marriage.

The only question to ask ourselves is, do we really want it? Do we want the absolute independence of women. State support of motherhood and of children, and consequent doing away with the necessity of marriage? Do we want it? Because all that matters is that men and women shall do what they *really* want to do. Though here, as everywhere, we must remember that man has a double set of desires, the shallow and the profound, the personal, superficial, temporary desires, and the inner, impersonal, great desires that are fulfilled in long periods of time. The desires of the moment are easy to recognize, but the others, the deeper ones, are difficult. It is the business of our Chief Thinkers to tell us of our deeper desires, not to keep shrilling our little desires in our ears.

Now the Church is established upon a recognition of some, at least, of the greatest and deepest desires in man, desires that take years, or a life-time, or even centuries to fulfil. And the Church, celibate as its priesthood may be, built as it may be upon the lonely rock of Peter, or of Paul, really rests upon the indissolubility of marriage. Make marriage in any serious degree unstable, dissoluble, destroy the permanency of marriage, and the Church falls. Witness the enormous decline of the Church of England.

The reason being that the Church is established upon the element of *union* in mankind. And the first element of union in the Christian world is the marriage-tie. The marriage-tie, the marriage bond, take it which way you like, is the fundamental connecting link in Christian society. Break it, and you will have to go back to the overwhelming dominance of the State, which existed before the Christian era. The Roman State was all-powerful, the Roman Fathers represented the State, the Roman family was the father's estate, held more or less in fee for the State itself. It was the same in Greece, with not so much feeling for the *permanence* of property, but rather a dazzling splash of the moment's possessions. The family was much more insecure in Greece than in Rome.

But, in either case, the family was the man, as representing the State. There are States where the family is the woman: or there have been. There are States where the family hardly exists, priest States where the priestly control is everything, even functioning as family control. Then there is the Soviet State, where again family is not supposed to exist, and the State controls every individual direct, mechanically, as the great religious States, such as early Egypt, may have controlled every individual direct, through priestly surveillance and ritual.

Now the question is, do we want to go back, or forward, to any of these forms of State control? Do we want to be like the Romans under the Empire, or even under the Republic? Do we want to be, as far as our family and our freedom is concerned, like the Greek citizens of a City State in Hellas? Do we want to imagine ourselves in the strange priest-controlled, ritual-fulfilled condition of the earlier Egyptians? Do we want to be bullied by a Soviet?

For my part, I have to say NO! every time. And having said it, we have to come back and consider the famous saying, that perhaps the greatest contribution to the social life of man made by Christianity is – marriage. Christianity brought marriage into the world: marriage as we know it. Christianity established the little autonomy of the family within the greater rule of the State. Christianity made marriage in some respects inviolate, not to be violated by the State. It is marriage, perhaps, which had given man the best of his freedom, given him his little kingdom of his own within the big kingdom of the State, given him his foothold of independence on which to stand and resist an unjust State. Man and wife, a king and queen with one or two subjects, and a few square yards of territory of their own: this, really, is marriage. It is a true freedom because it is a true fulfilment, for man, woman, and children.

Do we, then, want to break marriage? If we do break it, it means we all fall to a far greater extent under the direct sway of the State. Do we want to fall under the direct sway of the State, any State? For my part, I don't.

And the Church created marriage by making it a sacrament, a sacrament of man and woman united in the sex communion, and never to be separated, except by death. And even when separated by death, still not freed from the marriage. Marriage, as far as the individual went, eternal. Marriage, making one complete body out of two incomplete ones, and providing for the complex development of the man's soul and the woman's soul in unison, throughout a life-time. Marriage sacred and inviolable, the great way of earthly fulfilment for man and woman, in unison, under the spiritual rule of the Church.

This is Christianity's great contribution to the life of man, and it is only too easily overlooked. Is it, or is it not, a great step in the direction of life-fulfilment, for men and women? Is it, or is it not? Is marriage a great help to the fulfilment of man and woman, or is it a frustration? It is a very important question indeed, and every man and woman must answer it.

If we are to take the Nonconformist, protestant idea of ourselves: that we are all isolated individual souls, and our supreme business is to save our own souls; then marriage surely is a hindrance. If I am only out to save my own soul, I'd better leave marriage alone. As the monks and hermits knew. But also, if I am only out to save other people's souls, I had also best leave marriage alone, as the apostles knew, and the preaching saints.

But supposing I am neither bent on saving my own soul nor other people's souls? Supposing Salvation seems incomprehensible to me, as I confess it does. 'Being saved' seems to me just jargon, the jargon of self-conceit. Supposing, then, that I cannot

346

see this Saviour and Salvation stuff, supposing that I see the soul as something which must be developed and fulfilled throughout a life-time, sustained and nourished, developed and further fulfilled, to the very end; what then?

Then I realize that marriage, or something like it, is essential, and that the Old Church knew best the enduring needs of man, beyond the spasmodic needs of today and yesterday. The Church established marriage for life, for the fulfilment of the soul's living life, not postponing it till the after-death.

The old Church knew that life is here our portion, to be lived, to be lived in fulfilment. The stern rule of Benedict, the wild flights of Francis of Assisi, these were coruscations in the steady heaven of the Church. The rhythm of life itself was preserved by the Church hour by hour, day by day, season by season, year by year, epoch by epoch, down among the people, and the wild coruscations were accommodated to this permanent rhythm. We feel it, in the south, in the country, when we hear the jangle of the bells at dawn, at noon, at sunset, marking the hours with the sound of mass or prayers. It is the rhythm of the daily sun. We feel it in the festivals, the processions, Christmas, the Three Kings, Easter, Pentecost, St John's Day, All Saints, All Souls. This is the wheeling of the year, the movement of the sun through solstice and equinox, the coming of the seasons, the going of the seasons. And it is the inward rhythm of man and woman, too, the sadness of Lent, the delight of Easter, the wonder of Pentecost, the fires of St John, the candles on the graves of All Souls, the lit-up tree of Christmas, all representing kindled rhythmic emotions in the souls of men and women. And men experience the great rhythm of emotion man-wise, women experience it woman-wise, and in the unison of men and women it is complete.

Augustine said that God created the universe new every day: and to the living, emotional soul, this is true. Every dawn dawns upon an entirely new universe, every Easter lights up an entirely new glory of a new world opening in utterly new flower. And the soul of man and the soul of woman is new in the same way, with the infinite delight of life and the evernewness of life. So a man and a woman are new to one another throughout a life-time, in the rhythm of marriage that matches the rhythm of the year.

Sex is the balance of male and female in the universe, the attraction, the repulsion, the transit of neutrality, the new attraction, the new repulsion, always different, always new. The long neuter spell of Lent, when the blood is low, and the delight of the Easter kiss, the sexual revel of spring, the passion of midsummer, the slow recoil, revolt, and grief of autumn, greyness again, then the sharp stimulus of winter of the long nights. Sex goes through the rhythm of the year, in man and woman, ceaselessly changing: the rhythm of the sun in his relation to the earth. Oh, what a catastrophe for man when he cut himself off from the rhythm of the year, from his unison with the sun and the earth. Oh, what a catastrophe, what a maiming of love when it was made a personal, merely personal feeling, taken away from the rising and the setting of the sun, and cut off from the magic connexion of the solstice and the equinox! This is what is the matter with us. We are bleeding at the roots, because we are cut off from the earth and sun and stars, and love is a grinning mockery, because, poor blossom, we plucked it from its stem on the tree of Life, and expected it to keep on blooming in our civilized vase on the table.

Marriage is the clue to human life, but there is no marriage apart from the wheeling sun and the nodding earth, from the straying of the planets and the magnificence of the fixed stars. Is not a man different, utterly different, at dawn from what he is at sunset? and a woman too? And does not the changing harmony and discord of their variation make the secret music of life?

And is it not so throughout life? A man is different at thirty, at forty, at fifty, at sixty, at seventy: and the woman at his side is different. But is there not some strange conjunction in their differences? Is there not some peculiar harmony, through youth, the period of child-birth, the period of florescence and young children, the period of the woman's change of life, painful yet also a renewal, the period of waning passion but mellowing delight of affection, the dim, unequal period of the approach of death, when the man and woman look at one another with the dim apprehension of separation that is not really a separation: is there not, throughout it all, some unseen, unknown interplay of balance, harmony, completion, like some soundless symphony which moves with a rhythm from phase to phase, so different, so very different in the various movements, and yet one symphony, made out of the soundless singing of two strange and incompatible lives, a man's and a woman's?

This is marriage, the mystery of marriage, marriage which fulfils itself here, in this life. We may well believe that in heaven there is no marrying or giving in marriage. All this has to be fulfilled here, and if it is not fulfilled here, it will never be fulfilled. The great saints only live, even Jesus only lives to add a new fulfilment and a new beauty to the permanent sacrament of marriage.

But – and this *but* crashes through our heart like a bullet – marriage is no marriage that is not basically and permanently phallic, and that is not linked up with the sun and the earth, the moon and the fixed stars and the planets, in the rhythm of days, in the rhythm of months, in the rhythm of quarters, of years, of decades and of centuries. Marriage is no marriage that is not a correspondence of blood. For the blood is the substance of the soul, and of the deepest consciousness. It is by blood that we are: and it is by the heart and the liver that we live and move and have our being. In the blood, knowing and being, or feeling, are one and undivided: no serpent and no apple has caused a split. So that only when the conjunction is of the blood, is marriage truly marriage. The blood of man and the blood of woman are two eternally different streams, that can never be mingled. Even scientifically we know it. But therefore they are the two rivers that encircle the whole of life, and in marriage the circle is complete, and in sex the two rivers touch and renew one another, without ever commingling or confusing. We know it. The phallus is a column of blood that fills the valley of blood of a woman. The great river of male blood touches to its depths the great river of female blood – yet neither breaks its bounds. It is the deepest of all communions, as all the religions, in practice, know. And it is one of the greatest mysteries, in fact, the greatest, as almost every initiation shows, showing the supreme achievement of the mystic marriage.

And this is the meaning of the sexual act: this Communion, this touching on one another of the two rivers, Euphrates and Tigris – to use old jargon – and the enclosing of the land of Mesopotamia, where Paradise was, or the Park of Eden, where man had his beginning. This is marriage, this circuit of the two rivers, this communion of the two blood-streams, this, and nothing else: as all the religions know.

Two rivers of blood, are man and wife, two distinct eternal streams, that have the power of touching and communing and so renewing, making new one another, without any breaking of the subtle confines, any confusing or commingling. And the phallus is the connecting-link between the two rivers, that establishes the two streams in a oneness, and gives out of their duality a single circuit, forever. And this, this oneness gradually accomplished throughout a life-time in twoness, is the highest achievement of time or eternity. From it all things human spring, children and beauty and well-made things; all the true creations of humanity. And all we know of the will of God is that He wishes this, this oneness, to take place, fulfilled over a life-time, this oneness within the great dual blood-stream of humanity.

Man dies, and woman dies, and perhaps separate the souls go back to the Creator. Who knows? But we know that the oneness of the blood-stream of man and woman in marriage completes the universe, as far as humanity is concerned, completes the streaming of the sun and the flowing of the stars.

There is, of course, the counterpart to all this, the counterfeit. There is counterfeit marriage, like nearly all marriage today. Modern people are just personalities, and modern marriage takes place when two people are 'thrilled' by each other's personality: when they have the same tastes in furniture or books or sport or amusement, when they love 'talking' to one another, when they admire one another's 'minds'. Now this, this affinity of mind and personality is an excellent basis of friendship between the sexes, but a disastrous basis for marriage. Because marriage inevitably starts the sex-activity, and the sex-activity is, and always was and

350

will be, in some way hostile to the mental, *personal* relationship between man and woman. It is almost an axiom that the marriage of two *personalities* will end in a startling physical hatred. People who are personally devoted to one another at first end by hating one another with a hate which they cannot account for, which they try to hide, for it makes them ashamed, and which is none-theless only too painfully obvious, especially to one another. In people of strong individual feeling the irritation that accumulates in marriage increases only too often to a point of rage that is close akin to madness. And, apparently, all without reason.

But the real reason is, that the exclusive sympathy of nerves and mind and personal interest is, alas, hostile to blood-sympathy, in the sexes. The modern cult of personality is excellent for friend-ship between the sexes, and fatal for marriage. On the whole, it would be better if modern people didn't marry. They could re-main so much more true to what they are, to their own person-ality.

But marriage or no marriage, the fatal thing happens. If you have only known personal sympathy and personal love, then rage and hatred will sooner or later take possession of the soul, be-cause of the frustration and denial of blood-sympathy, blood-contact. In celibacy, the denial is withering and souring, but in marriage, the denial produces a sort of rage. And we can no more avoid this, nowadays, than we can avoid thunderstorms. It is part of the phenomenon of the psyche. The important point is that sex itself comes to subserve the personality and the personal 'love' entirely, without ever giving sexual satisfaction or fulfil-ment. In fact, there is probably far more sexual activity in a 'per-sonal' marriage than in a blood-marriage. Woman sighs for a perpetual lover: and in the personal marriage, relatively, she gets him. And how she comes to hate him, with his never-ending desire, which never gets anywhere or fulfils anything!

It is a mistake I have made, talking of sex I have always in-ferred that sex meant blood-sympathy and blood-contact. Tech-nically this is so. But as a matter of fact, nearly all modern sex is a pure matter of nerves, cold and bloodless. This is personal sex. And this white, cold, nervous, 'poetic' personal sex, which is prac-

351

tically all the sex that moderns know, has a very peculiar physiological effect, as well as psychological. The two blood-streams are brought into contact, in man and woman, just the same as in the urge of blood-passion and blood-desire. But whereas the contact in the urge of blood-desire is positive, making a newness in the blood, in the insistence of this nervous, personal desire the blood-contact becomes frictional and destructive, there is a resultant whitening and impoverishment of the blood. Personal or nervous or spiritual sex is destructive to the blood, has a katabolistic activity, whereas coition in warm blood-desire is an activity of metabolism. The katabolism of 'nervous' sex-activity may produce for a time a sort of ecstasy and a heightening of consciousness. But this, like the effect of alcohol or drugs, is the result of the decomposition of certain corpuscles in the blood, and is a process of impoverishment. This is one of the many reasons for the failure of energy in modern people; sexual activity, which ought to be refreshing and renewing, becomes exhaustive and debilitating. So that when the young man fails to believe in the regeneration of England by sex, I am constrained to agree with him. Since modern sex is practically all personal and nervous, and, in effect, exhaustive, disintegrative. The disintegrative effect of modern sex-activity is undeniable. It is only less fatal than the disintegrative effect of masturbation, which is more deadly still.

So that at last I begin to see the point of my critics' abuse of my exalting of sex. They only know one form of sex: in fact, to them there *is* only one form of sex: the nervous, personal, disintegrative sort, the 'white' sex. And this, of course, is something to be flowery and false about, but nothing to be very hopeful about. I quite agree. And I quite agree, we can have no hope of the regeneration of England from such sort of sex.

At the same time, I cannot see any hope of regeneration for a sexless England. An England that has lost its sex seems to me nothing to feel very hopeful about. And nobody feels very hopeful about it. Though I may have been a fool for insisting on sex where the current sort of sex is just what I *don't* mean and *don't* want, still I can't go back on it all and believe in the regeneration

352

of England by pure sexlessness. A sexless England! – it doesn't ring very hopeful, to me.

And the other, the warm blood-sex that establishes the living and revitalizing connexion between man and woman, how are we to get that back? I don't know. Yet get it back we must: or the younger ones must, or we are all lost. For the bridge to the future is the phallus, and there's the end of it. But not the poor, nervous counterfeit phallus of modern 'nervous' love. Not that.

For the new impulse to life will never come without blood-contact; the true, positive blood-contact, not the nervous negative reaction. And the essential blood-contact is between man and woman, always has been so, always will be. The contact of positive sex. The homosexual contacts are secondary, even if not merely substitutes of exasperated reaction from the utterly unsatisfactory nervous sex between men and women.

If England is to be regenerated – to use the phrase of the young man who seemed to think there was need of *regeneration* – the very word is his – then it will be by the arising of a new blood-contact, a new touch, and a new marriage. It will be a phallic rather than a sexual regeneration. For the phallus is only the great old symbol of godly vitality in a man, and of immediate contact.

It will also be a renewal of marriage: the true phallic marriage. And, still further, it will be marriage set again in relationship to the rhythmic cosmos. The rhythm of the cosmos is something we cannot get away from, without bitterly impoverishing our lives. The Early Christians tried to kill the old pagan rhythm of cosmic ritual, and to some extent succeeded. They killed the planets and the zodiac, perhaps because astrology had already become debased to fortune-telling. They wanted to kill the festivals of the year. But the Church, which knows that man doth not live by man alone, but by the sun and moon and earth in their revolutions, restored the sacred days and feasts almost as the pagans had them, and the Christian peasants went on very much as the pagan peasants had gone, with the sunrise pause for worship, and the sunset, and noon, the three great daily moments of the sun: then the new holy-day, one in the ancient seven-cycle: then Easter and the dying and rising of God, Pentecost, Midsummer Fire, the November dead and the spirits of the grave, then Christmas, then Three Kings. For centuries the mass of people lived in this rhythm, under the Church. And it is down in the mass that the roots of religion are eternal. When the mass of a people loses the religious rhythm, that people is dead, without hope. But Protestantism came and gave a great blow to the religious and ritualistic rhythm of the year, in human life. Nonconformity *almost* finished the deed. Now you have a poor, blind, disconnected people with nothing but politics and bank-holidays to satisfy the eternal human need of living in ritual adjustment to the cosmos in its revolutions, in eternal submission to the great laws. And marriage, being one of the greater necessities, has suffered the same from the loss of the sway of the greater laws, the cosmic rhythms which should sway life always, Mankind has got to get back to the rhythm of the cosmos, and the permanence of marriage.

All this is post-script, or afterthought, to my novel, *Lady Chatterley's Lover*. Man has little needs and deeper needs. We have fallen into the mistake of living from our little needs till we have almost lost our deeper needs in a sort of madness. There is a little morality, which concerns persons and the little needs of man: and this, alas, is the morality we live by. But there is a deeper morality, which concerns all womanhood, all manhood, and nations, and races, and classes of men. This greater morality affects the destiny of mankind over long stretches of time, applies to man's greater needs, and is often in conflict with the little morality of the little needs. The tragic consciousness has taught us, even, that one of the greater needs of man is a knowledge and experience of death; every man needs to know death in his own body. But the greater consciousness of the pre-tragic and post-tragic epochs teaches us – though we have not yet reached the post-tragic epoch – that the greatest need of man is the renewal forever of the complete rhythm of life and death, the rhythm of the sun's year, the body's year of a lifetime, and the greater year of the stars, the soul's year of immortality. This is our need, our imperative need. It is a need of the mind and soul, body, spirit and sex: all. It is no use asking for a Word to fulfil such a need.

No Word, no Logos, no Utterance will ever do it. The Word is uttered, most of it: we need only pay true attention. But who will call us to the Deed, the great Deed of the Seasons and the year, the Deed of the soul's cycle, the Deed of a woman's life at one with a man's, the little Deed of the moon's wandering, the bigger Deed of the sun's, and the biggest, of the great still stars? It is the *Deed* of life we have now to learn: we are supposed to have learnt the Word, but, alas, look at us. Word-perfect we may be, but Deed-demented. Let us prepare now for the death of our present 'little' life, and the re-emergence in a bigger life, in touch with the moving cosmos.

It is a question, practically, of relationship. We *must* get back into relation, vivid and nourishing relation to the cosmos and the universe. The way is through daily ritual, and the re-awakening. We *must* once more practise the ritual of dawn and noon and sunset, the ritual of the kindling fire and pouring water, the ritual of the first breath, and the last. This is an affair of the individual and the household, a ritual of day. The ritual of the moon in her phases, of the morning star and the evening star is for men and women separate. Then the ritual of the seasons, with the Drama and the Passion of the soul embodied in procession and dance, this is for the community, an act of men and women, a whole community, in togetherness. And the ritual of the great events in the year of stars is for nations and whole peoples. To these rituals we must return: or we must evolve them to suit our needs. For the truth is, we are perishing for lack of fulfilment of our greater needs, we are cut off from the great sources of our inward nourishment and renewal, sources which flow eternally in the universe. Vitally, the human race is dying. It is like a great up-rooted tree, with its roots in the air. We must plant ourselves again in the universe.

It means a return to ancient forms. But we shall have to create these forms again, and it is more difficult than the preaching of an evangel. The Gospel came to tell us we were all saved. We look at the world today and realize that humanity, alas, instead of being saved from sin, whatever that may be, is almost completely lost, lost to life, and near to nullity and extermination.

We have to go back, a long way, before the idealist conceptions began, before Plato, before the tragic idea of life arose, to get on to our feet again. For the gospel of salvation through the Ideals and escape from the body coincided with the tragic conception of human life. Salvation and tragedy are the same thing, and they are now both beside the point.

Back, before the idealist religions and philosophies arose and started man on the great excursion of tragedy. The last three thousand years of mankind have been an excursion into ideals, bodilessness, and tragedy and now the excursion is over. And it is like the end of a tragedy in the theatre. The stage is strewn with dead bodies, worse still, with meaningless bodies, and the curtain comes down.

But in life, the curtain never comes down on the scene. There the dead bodies lie, and the inert ones, and somebody has to clear them away, somebody has to carry on. It is the day after. Today is already the day after the end of the tragic and idealist epoch. Utmost inertia falls on the remaining protagonists. Yet we have to carry on.

Now we have to re-establish the great relationships which the grand idealists, with their underlying pessimism, their belief that life is nothing but futile conflict, to be avoided even unto death, destroyed for us. Buddha, Plato, Jesus, they were all three utter pessimists as regards life, teaching that the only happiness lay in abstracting oneself from life, the daily, yearly, seasonal life of birth and death and fruition, and in living in the 'immutable' or eternal spirit. But now, after almost three thousand years, now that we are almost abstracted entirely from the rhythmic life of the seasons, birth and death and fruition, now we realize that such abstraction is neither bliss nor liberation, but nullity. It brings null inertia. And the great saviours and teachers only cut us off from life. It was the tragic *excursus*.

The universe is dead for us, and how is it to come to life again? 'Knowledge' has killed the sun, making it a ball of gas, with spots; 'knowledge' has killed the moon, it is a dead little earth fretted with extinct craters as with smallpox; the machine has killed the earth for us, making it a surface, more or less bumpy, that you travel over. How, out of all this, are we to get back the grand orbs of the soul's heavens, that fill us with unspeakable joy? How are we to get back Apollo, and Attis, Demeter, Persephone, and the halls of Dis? How even see the star Hesperus, or Betelgeuse?

We've got to get them back, for they are the world our soul, our greater consciousness, lives in. The world of reason and science, the moon, a dead lump of earth, the sun, so much gas with spots: this is the dry and sterile little world the abstracted mind inhabits. The world of our little consciousness, which we know in our pettifogging *apartness*. This is how we know the world when we know it apart from ourselves, in the mean separateness of everything. When we know the world in togetherness with ourselves, we know the earth hyacinthine or Plutonic, we know the moon gives us our body as delight upon us, or steals it away, we know the purring of the great gold lion of the sun, who licks us like a lioness her cubs, making us bold, or else, like the red, angry lion, dashes at us with open claws. There are many ways of knowing, there are many sorts of knowledge. But the two ways of knowing, for man, are knowing in terms of apartness, which is mental, rational, scientific, and knowing in terms of togetherness, which is religious and poetic. The Christian religion lost, in Protestantism finally, the togetherness with the universe, the togetherness of the body, the sex, the emotions, the passions, with the earth and sun and stars.

But relationship is threefold. First, there is the relation to the living universe. Then comes the relation of man to woman. Then comes the relation of man to man. And each is a blood-relationship, not mere spirit or mind. We have abstracted the universe into Matter and Force, we have abstracted men and women into separate personalities – personalities being isolated units, incapable of togetherness – so that all three great relationships are bodiless, dead.

None, however, is quite so dead as the man-to-man relationship. I think, if we came to analyse to the last what men feel about one another today, we should find that every man feels every other man as a menace. It is a curious thing, but the more

357

mental and ideal men are, the more they seem to feel the bodily presence of any other man a menace, a menace, as it were, to their very being. Every man that comes near me threatens my very existence: nay, more, my very being.

This is the ugly fact which underlies our civilization. As the advertisement of one of the war novels said, it is an epic of 'friendship and hope, mud and blood', which means, of course, that the friendship and hope must end in mud and blood.

When the great crusade against sex and the body started in full blast with Plato, it was a crusade for 'ideals', and for this 'spiritual' knowledge in apartness. Sex is the great unifier. In its big, slower vibration it is the warmth of heart which makes people happy together, in togetherness. The idealist philosophies and religions set out deliberately to kill this. And they did it. Now they have done it. The last great ebullition of friendship and hope was squashed out in mud and blood. Now men are all separate little entities. While 'kindness' is the glib order of the day – everybody *must* be 'kind' – underneath this 'kindness' we find a coldness of heart, a lack of heart, a callousness, that is very dreary. Every man *is* a menace to every other man.

Men only know one another in menace. Individualism has triumphed. If I am a sheer individual, then every other being, every other man especially, is over against me as a menace to me. This is the peculiarity of our society today. We are all extremely sweet and 'nice' to one another, because we merely fear one another.

The sense of isolation, followed by the sense of menace and of fear, is bound to arise as the feeling of oneness and community with our fellow-men declines, and the feeling of individualism and personality, which is existence in isolation, increases. The so-called 'cultured' classes are the first to develop 'personality' and individualism, and the first to fall into this state of unconscious menace and fear. The working-classes retain the old blood-warmth of oneness and togetherness some decades longer. Then they lose it too. And then class-consciousness becomes rampant, and class-hate. Class-hate and class-consciousness are only a sign that the old togetherness, the old blood-warmth has collapsed, and every man is really aware of himself in apartness. Then we have these hostile groupings of men for the sake of opposition, strife. Civil strife becomes a necessary condition of self-assertion.

This, again, is the tragedy of social life today. In the old England, the curious blood-connexion held the classes together. The squires might be arrogant, violent, bullying and unjust, yet in some ways they were *at one* with the people, part of the same blood-stream. We feel it in Defoe or Fielding. And then, in the mean Jane Austen, it is gone. Already this old maid typifies 'personality' instead of character, the sharp knowing in apartness instead of knowing in togetherness, and she is, to my feeling, thoroughly unpleasant, English in the bad, mean, snobbish sense of the word, just as Fielding is English in the good, generous sense.

So, in *Lady Chatterley's Lover* we have a man, Sir Clifford, who is purely a personality, having lost entirely all connexion with his fellowmen and women, except those of usage. All warmth is gone entirely, the hearth is cold, the heart does not humanly exist. He is a pure product of our civilization, but he is the death of the great humanity of the world. He is kind by rule, but he does not know what warm sympathy means. He is what he is. And he loses the woman of his choice.

The other man still has the warmth of a man, but he is being hunted down, destroyed. Even it is a question if the woman who turns to him will really stand by him and his vital meaning.

I have been asked many times if I intentionally made Clifford paralysed, if it is symbolic. And literary friends say, it would have been better to have left him whole and potent, and to have made the woman leave him nevertheless.

As to whether the 'symbolism' is intentional – I don't know. Certainly not in the beginning, when Clifford was created. When I created Clifford and Connie, I had no idea what they were or why they were. They just came, pretty much as they are. But the novel was written, from start to finish, three times. And when I read the first version, I recognized that the lameness of Clifford was symbolic of the paralysis, the deeper emotional or passional paralysis, of most men of his sort and class today. I realized that it was perhaps taking an unfair advantage of Connie, to paralyse him technically. It made it so much more vulgar of her to leave him. Yet the story came as it did, by itself, so I left it alone. Whether we call it symbolism or not, it is, in the sense of its happening, inevitable.

And these notes, which I write now almost two years after the novel was finished, are not intended to explain or expound anything: only to give the emotional beliefs which perhaps are necessary as a background to the book. It is so obviously a book written in defiance of convention that perhaps some reason should be offered for the attitude of defiance: since the silly desire to *épater le bourgeois*, to bewilder the commonplace person, is not worth entertaining. If I use the taboo words, there is a reason. We shall never free the phallic reality from the 'uplift' taint till we give it its own phallic language, and use the obscene words. The greatest blasphemy of all against the phallic reality is this 'lifting it to a higher plane'. Likewise, if the lady marries the gamekeeper – she hasn't done it yet – it is not class-spite, but in spite of class.

Finally, there are the correspondents who complain that I describe the pirated editions – some of them – but not the original. The original first edition, issued in Florence, is bound in hard covers, dullish mulberry-red paper with my phoenix (symbol of immortality, the bird rising new from the nest of flames) printed in black on the cover, and a white paper label on the back. The paper is good, creamy hand-rolled Italian paper, but the print, though nice, is ordinary, and the binding is just the usual binding of a little Florentine shop. There is no expert bookmaking in it: yet it is a pleasant volume, much more so than many far 'superior' books.

And if there are many spelling errors – there are – it is because the book was set up in a little Italian printing shop, such a family affair, in which nobody knew one word of English. They none of them knew any English at all, so they were spared all blushes: and the proofs were terrible. The printer would do fairly well for a few pages, then he would go drunk, or something. And then the words danced weird and *macabre*, but not English. So that if still some of the hosts of errors exist, it is a mercy they are not more.

Then one paper wrote pitying the poor printer who was deceived into printing the book. Not deceived at all. A white-moustached little man who has just married a second wife, he was told: Now the book contains such-and-such words, in English, and it describes certain things. Don't you print it if you think it will get you into trouble! – 'What does it describe?' he asked. And when told, he said, with the short indifference of a Florentine: 'Oh! *ma*! but we do it every day!' – And it seemed, to him, to settle the matter entirely. Since it was nothing political or out of the way, there was nothing to think about. Everyday concerns, commonplace.

But it was a struggle, and the wonder is the book came out as well as it did. There was just enough type to set up a half of it: so the half was set up, the thousand copies were printed and, as a measure of caution, the two hundred on ordinary paper, the little second edition, as well: then the type was distributed, and the second half set up.

Then came the struggle of delivery. The book was stopped by the American customs almost at once. Fortunately in England there was a delay. So that practically the whole edition – at least eight hundred copies, surely – must have gone to England.

Then came the storms of vulgar vituperation. But they were inevitable. 'But we do it every day,' says a little Italian printer. 'Monstrous and horrible!' shrieks a section of the British press. 'Thank you for a really sexual book about sex, at last. I am so tired of a-sexual books,' says one of the most distinguished citizens of Florence to me – an Italian. 'I don't know – I don't know – if it's not a bit too strong,' says a timid Florentine critic – an Italian. 'Listen, Signor Lawrence, you find it really necessary to *say* it?' I told him I did, and he pondered. – 'Well, one of them was a brainy vamp, and the other was a sexual moron,' said an American woman, referring to the two men in the book – 'so I'm afraid Connie had a poor choice – *as usual*!'

# 5. Men and Women

# The State of Funk

Written 1928 or 1929, published in *Assorted Articles*, 1930

What is the matter with the English, that they are so scared of everything? They are in a state of blue funk, and they behave like a lot of mice when somebody stamps on the floor. They are terrified about money, finance, about ships, about war, about work, about Labour, about Bolshevism, and funniest of all, they are scared stiff of the printed word. Now this is a very strange and humiliating state of mind, in a people which has always been so dauntless. And, for the nation, it is a very dangerous state of mind. When a people falls into a state of funk, then God help it. Because mass funk leads some time or other to mass panic, and then – one can only repeat, God help us.

There is, of course, a certain excuse for fear. The time of change is upon us. The need for change has taken hold of us. We are changing, we have got to change, and we can no more help it than leaves can help going yellow and coming loose in autumn, or than bulbs can help shoving their little green spikes out of the ground, in spring. We are changing, we are in the throes of change, and the change will be a great one. Instinctively, we feel it. Intuitively, we know it. And we are frightened. Because change hurts. And also, in the periods of serious transition, everything is uncertain, and living things are most vulnerable.

But what of it? Granted all the pains and dangers and uncertainties, there is no excuse for falling into a state of funk. If we come to think of it, every child that is begotten and born is a seed of change, a danger to its mother, at childbirth a great pain, and after birth, a new responsibility, a new change. If we feel in a state of funk about it, we should cease having children altogether. *If* we fall into a state of funk, indeed, the best thing is to have no children. But why fall into a state of funk?

Why not look things in the face like men, and like women? A woman who is going to have a child says to herself: Yes, I feel uncomfortable, sometimes I feel wretched, and I have a time of pain and danger ahead of me. But I have a good chance of coming through all right, especially if I am intelligent, and I bring a new life into the world. Somewhere I feel hopeful, even happy. So I must take the sour with the sweet. There is no birth without birth-pangs.

It is the business of men, of course, to take the same attitude towards the birth of new conditions, new ideas, new emotions. And sorry to say, most modern men don't. They fall into a state of funk. We all of us know that ahead of us lies a great social change, a great social readjustment. A few men look it in the face and try to realize what will be best. We none of us *know* what will be best. There is no ready-made solution. Ready-made solutions are almost the greatest danger of all. A change is a slow flux, which must happen bit by bit. And it must *happen*. You can't drive it like a steam engine. But all the time you can be alert and intelligent about it, and watch for the next step, and watch for the direction of the main trend. Patience, alertness, intelligence, and a human goodwill and fearlessness, that is what you want in a time of change. Not funk.

Now England is on the brink of great changes, radical changes. Within the next fifty years the whole framework of our social life will be altered, will be greatly modified. The old world of our grandfathers is disappearing like thawing snow, and is as likely to cause a flood. What the world of our grandchildren will be, fifty years hence, we don't know. But in its social form it will be very different from our world of today. We've got to change. And in our power to change, in our capacity to make new intelligent adaptation to new conditions, in our readiness to admit and fulfil new needs, to give expression to new desires and new feelings, lies our hope and our health. Courage is the great word. Funk spells sheer disaster.

There is a great change coming, bound to come. The whole money arrangement will undergo a change: what, I don't know. The whole industrial system will undergo a change. Work will be different and pay will be different. The owning of property will be different. Class will be different, and human relations will be modified and perhaps simplified. If we are intelligent, alert and undaunted, then life will be much better, more generous, more spontaneous, more vital, less basely materialistic. If we fall into a state of funk, impotence and persecution, then things may be very much worse than they are now. It is up to us. It is up to men to be men. While men are courageous and willing to change, nothing terribly bad can happen. But once men fall into a state of funk, with the inevitable accompaniment of bullying and repression, then only bad things can happen. To be firm is one thing. But bullying is another. And bullying of any sort whatsoever can have nothing but disastrous results. And when the mass falls into a state of funk, and you have mass bullying, then catastrophe is near.

Change in the whole social system is inevitable not merely because conditions change – though partly for that reason – but because people themselves change. We change, you and I, we change and change vitally, as the years go on. New feelings arise in us, old values depreciate, new values arise. Things we thought we wanted most intensely we realize we don't care about. The things we built our lives on crumble and disappear, and the process is painful. But it is not tragic. A tadpole that has so gaily waved its tail in the water must feel very sick when the tail begins to drop off and little legs begin to sprout. The tail was its dearest, gayest, most active member, all its little life was in its tail. And now the tail must go. It seems rough on the tadpole; but the little green frog in the grass is a new gem, after all.

As a novelist, I feel it is the change inside the individual which is my real concern. The great social change interests me and troubles me, but it is not my field. I know a change is coming – and I know we must have a more generous, more human system based on the life values and not on the money values. That I know. But what steps to take I don't know. Other men know better.

My field is to know the feelings inside a man, and to make new feelings conscious. What really torments civilized people is that they are full of feelings they know nothing about; they can't realize them, they can't fulfil them, they can't *live* them. And so they are tortured. It is like having energy you can't use – it destroys you. And feelings are a form of vital energy.

I am convinced that the majority of people today have good, generous feelings which they can never know, never experience, because of some fear, some repression. I do not believe that people would be villains, thieves, murderers, and sexual criminals if they were freed from legal restraint. On the contrary, I think the vast majority would be much more generous, good-hearted and decent if they felt they dared be. I am convinced that people want to be more decent, more good-hearted than our social system of money and grab allows them to be. The awful fight for money, into which we are all forced, hurts our good nature more than we can bear. I am sure this is true of a vast number of people.

And the same is true of our sexual feelings; only worse. There, we start all wrong. Consciously, there is supposed to be no such thing as sex in the human being. As far as possible, we never speak of it, never mention it, never, if we can help it, even think of it. It is disturbing. It is – somehow – wrong.

The whole trouble with sex is that we daren't speak of it and think of it naturally. We are not secretly sexual villains. We are not secretly sexually depraved. We are just human beings with living sex. We are all right, if we had not this unaccountable and disastrous *fear* of sex. I know, when I was a lad of eighteen, I used to remember with shame and rage in the morning the sexual thoughts and desires I had had the night before. Shame, and rage, and terror lest anybody else should have to know. And I *hated* the self that I had been, the night before.

Most boys are like that, and it is, of course, utterly wrong. The boy that had excited sexual thoughts and feelings was the living, warm-hearted, passionate me. The boy that in the morning remembered these feelings with such fear, shame and rage was the social mental me: perhaps a little priggish, and certainly in a state of funk. But the two were divided against one another. A boy divided against himself; a girl divided against herself; a people divided against itself; it is a disastrous condition.

And it was a long time before I was able to say to myself: I am *not* going to be ashamed of my sexual thoughts and desires, they are me myself, they are part of my life. I am going to accept myself sexually as I accept myself mentally and spiritually, and know that I am one time one thing, one time another, but I am always myself. My sex is me as my mind is me, and nobody will make me feel shame about it.

It is long since I came to that decision. But I remember how much freer I felt, how much warmer and more sympathetic towards people. I had no longer anything to hide from them, no longer anything to be in a funk about, lest they should find it out. My sex was me, like my mind and my spirit. And the other man's sex was him, as his mind was him, and his spirit was him. And the woman's sex was her, as her mind and spirit were herself too. And once this quiet admission is made, it is wonderful how much deeper and more real the human sympathy flows. And it is wonderful how difficult the admission is to make, for man or woman: the tacit, natural admission, that allows the natural warm flow of the blood-sympathy, without repression and holding back.

I remember when I was a very young man I was enraged when with a woman, if I was reminded of her sexual actuality. I only wanted to be aware of her personality, her mind and spirit. The other had to be fiercely shut out. Some part of the natural sympathy for a woman had to be shut away, cut off. There was a mutilation in the relationship all the time.

Now, in spite of the hostility of society, I have learned a little better. Now I know that a woman is her sexual self too, and I can feel the normal sex sympathy with her. And this silent sympathy is utterly different from desire or anything rampant or lurid. If I can really sympathize with a woman in her sexual self, it is just a form of warm-heartedness and compassionateness, the most natural life-flow in the world. And it may be a woman of seventy-five, or a child of two, it is the same. But our civilization, with its horrible fear and funk and repression and bullying, has almost destroyed the natural flow of common sympathy between men and men, and men and women.

And it is this that I want to restore into life: just the natural warm flow of common sympathy between man and man, man and woman. Many people hate it, of course. Many men hate it that one should tacitly take them for sexual, physical men instead of mere social and mental personalities. Many women hate it the same. Some, the worst, are in a state of rabid funk. The papers call me 'lurid'; and a 'dirty-minded fellow'. One woman, evidently a woman of education and means, wrote to me out of the blue: 'You, who are a mixture of the missing-link and the chimpanzee, etc.' – and told me my name stank in men's nostrils: though, since she was Mrs Something or other, she might have said women's nostrils. – And these people think they are being perfectly well-bred and perfectly 'right'. They are safe inside the convention, which also agrees that we are sexless creatures and social beings merely, cold and bossy and assertive, cowards safe inside a convention.

Now I am one of the least lurid mortals, and I don't at all mind being likened to a chimpanzee. If there is one thing I don't like it is cheap and promiscuous sex. If there is one thing I insist on it is that sex is a delicate, vulnerable, vital thing that you mustn't fool with. If there is one thing I deplore it is heartless sex. Sex must be a real flow, a real flow of sympathy, generous and warm, and not a trick thing, or a moment's excitation, or a mere bit of bullying.

And if I write a book about the sex relations of a man and a woman, it is not because I want all men and women to begin having indiscriminate lovers and love affairs, off the reel. All this horrid scramble of love affairs and prostitution is only part of the funk, bravado and *doing it on purpose*. And bravado and *doing it on purpose* is just as unpleasant and hurtful as repression, just as much a sign of secret fear.

What you have to do is to get out of the state of funk, sex funk. And to do so, you've got to be perfectly decent, and you have to accept sex fully in the consciousness. Accept sex in the consciousness, and let the normal physical awareness come back, between you and other people. Be tacitly and simply aware of the sexual being in every man and woman, child and animal; and unless the man or woman is a bully, be sympathetically aware. It is the most important thing just now, this gentle physical awareness. It keeps us tender and alive at a moment when the great danger is to go brittle, hard, and in some way dead.

Accept the sexual, physical being of yourself, and of every other creature. Don't be afraid of it. Don't be afraid of the physical functions. Don't be afraid of the so-called obscene words. There is nothing wrong with the words. It is your fear that makes them bad, your needless fear. It is your fear which cuts you off physically even from your nearest and dearest. And when men and women are physically cut off, they become at last dangerous, bullying, cruel. Conquer the fear of sex, and restore the natural flow. Restore even the so-called obscene words, which are part of the natural flow. If you don't, if you don't put back a bit of the old warmth into life, there is savage disaster ahead.

# The Real Thing

Written after 1927, published in *Scribner's Magazine*,
June 1930; *Phoenix*, 1936

Most revolutions are explosions: and most explosions blow up a
great deal more than was intended. It is obvious, from later
history, that the French didn't really want to blow up the whole
monarchic and aristocratic system, in the 1790s. Yet they did it,
and try as they might, they could never really put anything
together again. The same with the Russians: they want to blow a
gateway in a wall, and they blow the whole house down.

All fights for freedom, that succeed, go too far, and become in
turn the infliction of a tyranny. Like Napoleon or a soviet. And
like the freedom of women. Perhaps the greatest revolution of
modern times is the emancipation of women; and perhaps the
deepest fight for two thousand years and more has been the fight
for woman's independence, or freedom, call it what you will.
The fight was deeply bitter, and, it seems to me, it is won. It is
even going beyond, and becoming a tyranny of woman, of the
individual woman in the house, and of the feminine ideas and
ideals in the world. Say what we will, the world is swayed by feminine emotion today, and the triumph of the productive and domestic activities of man over all his previous military or adventurous
or flaunting activities is a triumph of the woman in the home.

The male is subservient to the female need, and outwardly, man
is submissive to the demands of woman.

But inwardly, what has happened? It cannot be denied that there has been a fight. Woman has not won her freedom without fighting for it; and she still fights, fights hard, even when there is no longer any need. For man has fallen. It would be difficult to point to a man in the world today who is not subservient to the great woman-spirit that sways modern mankind. But still not peacefully. Still the sway of a struggle, the sway of conflict.

Woman in the mass has fought her fight politically. But woman the individual has fought her fight with individual man, with father, brother, and particularly with husband. All through the past, except for brief periods of revolt, woman has played a part of submission to man. Perhaps the inevitable nature of man and woman demands such submission. But it must be an instinctive, unconscious submission, made in unconscious faith. At certain periods this blind faith of woman in man seems to weaken, then break. It always happens at the end of some great phase, before another phase sets in. It always seems to start, in man, an overwhelming worship of woman, and a glorification of queens. It always seems to bring a brief spell of glory, and a long spell of misery after. Man yields in glorifying the woman, the glory dies, the fight goes on.

It is not necessarily a sex struggle. The sexes are not by nature pitted against one another in hostility. It only happens so, in certain periods: when man loses his unconscious faith in himself, and woman loses her faith in him, unconsciously and then consciously. It is not biological sex struggle. Not at all. Sex is the great uniter, the great unifier. Only in periods of the collapse of instinctive life-assurance in men does sex become a great weapon and divider.

Man loses his faith in himself, and woman begins to fight him. Cleopatra really fought Antony – that's why he killed himself. But he had first lost faith in himself, and leaned on love, which is a sure sign of weakness and failure. And when woman once begins to fight her man, she fights and fights, as if for freedom. But it is not even freedom she wants. Freedom is a man's word: its meaning, to a woman, is really rather trivial. She fights to escape from a man who doesn't really believe in himself; she fights and fights, and there is no freedom from the fight. Woman is truly less free today than ever she has been since time began, in the womanly sense of freedom. Which means, she has less peace, less of that lovely womanly peace that flows like a river, less of the lovely, flower-like repose of a happy woman, less of the nameless joy in life, purely unconscious, which is the very breath of a woman's being, than she has had since she and man first set eyes on one another.

Today, woman is always tense and strung-up, alert, and bare-armed, not for love but for battle. In her shred of a dress and her little helmet of a hat, her cropped hair and her stark bearing she is a sort of soldier, and look at her as one may, one can see nothing else. It is not her fault. It is her doom. It happens when man loses his primary faith in himself and in his very life.

Now through the ages thousands of ties have been formed between men and women. In the ages of discredit, these ties are felt as bonds, and must be fought loose. It is a great tearing and snapping of sympathies, and of unconscious sympathetic connexions. It is a great rupture of unconscious tenderness and unconscious flow of strength between man and woman. Man and woman are not two separate and complete entities. In spite of all protestation, we must continue to assert it. Man and woman are not even two separate persons: not even two separate consciousnesses, or minds. In spite of vehement cries to the contrary, it is so. Man is connected with woman for ever, in connexions visible and invisible, in a complicated life-flow that can never be analysed. It is not only man and wife: the woman facing me in the train, the girl I buy cigarettes from, all send forth to me a stream, a spray, a vapour of female life that enters my blood and my soul, and makes me me. And back again, I send the stream of male life which soothes and satisfies and builds up the woman. So it still is, very often, in public contacts. The more general stream of life-flow between men and women is not so much broken and reversed as the private flow. Hence we all tend more and more to live in public. In public men and women are still kind to another, very often.

But in private, the fight goes on. It had started in our great-grandmothers; it was going strong in our grandmothers; and in our mothers it was the dominant factor in life. The women *thought* it was a fight for righteousness. They *thought* they were fighting the man to make him 'better', and to make life 'better' for the children.

We know now this ethical excuse was only an excuse. We know now that our fathers were fought and beaten by our mothers, not because our mothers really knew what was 'better', but because our fathers had lost their instinctive hold on the life-flow and the life-reality, that therefore the female had to fight them at any cost, blind, and doomed. We saw it going on as tiny children, the battle. We believed the moral excuse. But we lived to be men, and to be fought in turn. And now we know there is no excuse, moral or immoral. It is just phenomenal. And our mothers, who asserted such a belief in 'goodness', were tired of that self-same goodness even before their death.

No, the fight was, and is, for itself, and it is pitiless – except in spasms and pauses. A woman does not fight a man for his love – though she may say so a thousand times over. She fights him because she knows, instinctively, he *cannot* love. He has lost his peculiar belief in himself, his instinctive faith in his own life-flow, and so he cannot love. He *cannot*. The more he protests, the more he asserts, the more he kneels, the more he worships, the less he loves. A woman who is worshipped, or even adored, knows perfectly well, in her instinctive depths, that she is not loved, that she is being swindled. She encourages the swindle, oh enormously, it flatters her vanity. But in the end comes Nemesis and the Furies, pursuing the unfortunate pair. Love between man and woman is neither worship nor adoration, but something much deeper, much less showy and gaudy, part of the very breath, and as ordinary, if we may say so, as breathing. Almost as necessary. In fact, love between man and woman is really just a kind of breathing.

No woman ever got a man's love by fighting for it: at least, by fighting *him*. No man ever loved a woman until she left off fighting him. And when will she leave off fighting him? When he has, apparently, submitted to her (for the submission is always, at least partly, false and a fraud)? No, then least of all. When a man has submitted to a woman, she usually fights him worse than ever, more ruthlessly. Why doesn't she leave him? Often she does. But what then? She merely takes up with another man in order to resume the fight. The need to fight with man is upon her, inexorable.

Why can't she live alone? She can't. Sometimes she can join with other women, and keep up the fight in a group. Sometimes she *must* live alone, for no man will come forward to fight with her. Yet, sooner or later, the need for contact with a man comes over a woman again. It is imperative. If she is rich, she hires a dancing partner, a gigolo, and humiliates him to the last dregs. The fight is not ended. When the great Hector is dead, it is not enough. He must be trailed naked and defiled; tied by the heels to the tail of a contemptuous chariot.

When is the fight over? Ah when! Modern life seems to give no answer. Perhaps when a man finds his strength and his rooted belief in himself again. Perhaps when the man has died, and been painfully born again with a different breath, a different courage, and a different kind of care, or carelessness. But most men can't and daren't die in their old, fearful selves. They cling to their women in desperation, and come to hate them with cold and merciless hate, the hate of a child that is persistently ill-treated. Then when the hate dies, the man escapes into the final state of egoism, when he has no true feelings any more, and cannot be made to suffer.

That is where the young are now. The fight is more or less fizzling out, because both parties have become hollow. There is a perfect cynicism. The young men know that most of the 'benevolence' and 'motherly love' of their adoring mothers was simply egoism again, and an extension of self, and a love of having absolute power over another creature. Oh, these women who secretly lust to have absolute power over their own children – for their own good! Do they think the children are deceived? Not for a moment! You can read in the eyes of the small modern child: 'My mother is trying to bully me with every breath she draws, but though I am only six, I can really resist her.' It is the fight, the fight. It has degenerated into the mere fight to impose the will over some other creature, mostly now, mother over her children. She fails again, abjectly. But she goes on.

For the great fight with the man has come almost to an end. Why? Is it because man has found a new strength, has died the death in his old body and been born with a new strength and a new sureness? Alas, apparently not so at all. Man has dodged, side-tracked. Tortured and cynical and unbelieving, he has let all his feelings go out of him, and remains a shell of a man, very nice, very pleasant, in fact the best of modern men. Because nothing really moves him except one thing, a threat against his own safety. He is terrified of not feeling 'safe'. So he keeps his woman there between him and the world of dangerous feelings and demands.

But he feels nothing. It is the great *counterfeit* liberation, this counterfeit of Nirvana and the peace that passeth all understanding. It is a sort of Nirvana, and a sort of peace: in sheer nullity. At first, the woman cannot realize it. She rages, she goes mad. Woman after woman you can see smashing herself against the figure of a man who has achieved the state of false peace, false strength, false power: the egoist. The egoist, he who has no more spontaneous feelings, and can be made to suffer humanly no more. He who derives all his life henceforth at second-hand, and is animated by self-will and some sort of secret ambition to *impose* himself, either on the world or another individual. See a man or a woman trying to impose herself, himself, and you have an egoist in natural action. But the true *pose* of the modern egoist is that of perfect suaveness and kindness and humility: oh, always delicately humble!

When a man achieves this triumph of egoism: and many men have achieved it today, practically all the successful ones, certainly all the charming ones, and all the 'artistic' ones: then the woman concerned is apt to go really a little mad. She gets no more responses. The fight has suddenly given out. She throws herself against a man, and he is not there, only the sort of glassy image of him receives her shocks and feels nothing. She becomes wild, outrageous. The explanation of the impossible behaviour of some women in their thirties lies here. Suddenly nothing comes back at them in the fight, and they go crazy, demented, as if they were on the brink of a fearful abyss. Which they are.

And then they either go to pieces, or else, with one of those sudden turns typical of women, they suddenly realize. And then, almost instantly, their whole behaviour changes. It is over. The fight is finished. The man has side-tracked. He becomes, in a sense, negligible, though the basic animosity is only rarefied, made more subtle. And so you have the smart young woman in her twenties. She no longer fights her man – or men. She leaves him to his devices, and as far as possible invents her own. She may have a child to bully. But as a rule she pushes the child away as far as she can. No, she is now quite alone. If the man has no real feelings, she has none either. No matter how she feels about her husband, unless she is in a state of nervous rage she calls him angel of light, and winged messenger, and loveliest man, and my beautiful pet boy. She flips it all over him, like eau de cologne. And he takes it quite for granted, and suggests the next amusement. And their life is 'one round of pleasure', to use the old banality: until the nerves collapse. Everything is counterfeit: counterfeit complexion, counterfeit jewels, counterfeit elegance, counterfeit charm, counterfeit endearment, counterfeit passion, counterfeit culture, counterfeit love of Blake, or of *The Bridge of San Luis Rey*, or Picasso, or the latest film-star. Counterfeit sorrows and counterfeit delights, counterfeit woes and moans, counterfeit ecstasies, and, under all, a hard, hard realization that we live by money, and money alone: and a terrible lurking fear of nervous collapse, collapse.

These are, of course, the extreme cases of the modern young. They are those who have got way beyond tragedy or real seriousness, that old-fashioned stuff. They are – they don't know where they are. And they don't care. But they are at the far end of the great fight between men and women.

Judging them as a result, the fight hardly seems to have been worth it. But we are looking on them still as fighters. Perhaps there is something else, positive, as a result.

In their own way, many of these young ones who have gone through everything and reached a stage of emptiness and disillusion unparalleled since the decadent Romans of Ravenna, in the fifth century, they are now, in very fear and forlornness, beginning to put out feelers towards some other way of trust. They begin to realize that if they are not careful, they will have missed life altogether. Missed the bus! They, the smart young who are so swift at hopping onto a thing, to have missed life itself, not to have hopped onto it! Missed the bus! to use London slang. Let the great chance slip by, while they were fooling round! The young are just beginning uneasily to realize that this may be the case. They are just beginning uneasily to realize that all that 'life' which they lead, rushing around and being so smart, perhaps isn't life after all, and they are missing the real thing.

What then? What *is* the real thing? Ah, there's the rub. There are millions of ways of living, and it's all life. But what is the real thing in life? What is it that makes you *feel* right, makes life really feel good?

It is the great question. And the answers are old answers. But every generation must frame the answer in its own way. What makes life good to me is the sense that, even if I am sick and ill, I am alive, alive to the depths of my soul, and in touch somewhere in touch with the vivid life of the cosmos. Somehow my life draws strength from the depths of the universe, from the depths among the stars, from the great 'world'. Out of the great world comes my strength and my reassurance. One could say 'God', but the word 'God' is somehow tainted. But there *is* a flame or a Life Everlasting wreathing through the cosmos for ever and giving us our renewal, once we can get in touch with it.

It is when men lose their contact with this eternal life-flame, and become merely personal, things in themselves, instead of things kindled in the flame, that the fight between man and woman begins. It cannot be avoided; any more than nightfall or rain. The more conventional and correct a woman may be, the more outwardly devastating she is. Once she feels the loss of the greater control and the greater sustenance, she becomes emotionally destructive, she can no more help it than she can help being a woman, when the great connexion is lost.

And then there is nothing for men to do but to turn back to

life itself. Turn back to the life that flows invisibly in the cosmos, and will flow for ever, sustaining and renewing all living things. It is not a question of sins or morality, of being good or being bad. It is a question of renewal, of being renewed, vivified, made new and vividly alive and aware, instead of being exhausted and stale, as men are today. How to be renewed, reborn, revivified? That is the question men must ask themselves, and women too.

And the answer will be difficult. Some trick with glands or secretions, or raw food, or drugs won't do it. Neither will some wonderful revelation or message. It is not a question of knowing something, but of doing something. It is a question of getting into contact again with the *living* centre of the cosmos. And how are we to do it?

# Nobody Loves Me

Written 1928, published in *Life and Letters*, July 1930;
*Phoenix*, 1936

Last year, we had a little house up in the Swiss mountains, for
the summer. A friend came to tea: a woman of fifty or so, with
her daughter: old friends. 'And how are you all?' I asked, as she
sat, flushed and rather exasperated at the climb up to the chalet
on a hot afternoon, wiping her face with a too-small handker-
chief. 'Well!' she replied, glancing almost viciously out of the
window at the immutable slopes and peaks opposite, 'I don't
know how *you* feel about it – but – these mountains! – well! –
I've lost *all* my *cosmic consciousness*, and *all* my *love for
humanity*.'

She is, of course, New England of the old school – and usually
transcendentalist calm. So that her exasperated frenzy of the moment – it was really a frenzy – coupled with the New England
language and slight accent, seemed to me really funny. I laughed
in her face, poor dear, and said: 'Never mind! Perhaps you can
do with a rest from your cosmic consciousness and your love of
humanity.'

I have often thought of it since: of what she really meant. And
every time, I have had a little pang, realizing that I was a bit spiteful to her. I admit, her New England transcendental habit of
loving the cosmos *en bloc* and humanity *en masse* did rather get
on my nerves, always. But then she had been brought up that

way. And the fact of loving the cosmos didn't prevent her from being fond of her own garden – though it did, a bit; and her love of humanity didn't prevent her from having a real affection for her friends, except that she felt that she *ought* to love them in a selfless and general way, which was rather annoying. Nevertheless, that, to me, rather silly language about cosmic consciousness and love of humanity did stand for something that was not merely cerebral. It stood, and I realized it afterwards, for her peace, her inward peace with the universe and with man. And this she could *not* do without. One may be at war with society, and still keep one's deep peace with mankind. It is not pleasant to be at war with society, but sometimes it is the only way of preserving one's peace of soul, which is peace with the living, struggling, *real* mankind. And this latter one cannot afford to lose. So I had no right to tell my friend she could do with a rest from her love of humanity. She couldn't, and none of us can : if we interpret *love of humanity* as that feeling of being at one with the struggling soul, or spirit, or whatever it is, of our fellow-men.

Now the wonder to me is that the young do seem to manage to get on without any 'cosmic consciousness' or 'love of humanity'. They have, on the whole, shed the cerebral husk of generalizations from their emotional state: the cosmic and humanity touch. But it seems to me they have also shed the flower that was inside the husk. Of course, you can hear a girl exclaim: '*Really*, you know, the colliers are darlings, and it's a shame the way they're treated.' She will even rush off and register a vote for her darlings. But she doesn't really care – and one can sympathize with her. This caring about the wrongs of unseen people has been rather overdone. Nevertheless, though the colliers or cotton-workers or whatever they be are a long way off and we can't do anything about it, still, away in some depth of us, we know that we are connected vitally, if remotely, with these colliers or cotton-workers, we dimly realize that mankind is one, almost one flesh. It is an abstraction, but it is also a physical fact. In some way or other, the cotton-workers of Carolina, or the rice growers of China, are connected with me and, to a faint yet real degree, part of me. The vibration of life which they give off reaches me, touches me, and affects me all unknown to me. For we are more or less connected, all more or less in touch: all humanity. That is, until we have killed the sensitive responses in ourselves, which happens today only too often.

Dimly, this is what my transcendentalist meant by her 'love of humanity', though she tended to kill the real thing by labelling it so philanthropically and bossily. Dimly, she meant her sense of participating in the life of all humanity, which is a sense we all have, delicately and deeply, when we are at peace in ourselves. But let us lose our inward peace, and at once we are likely to substitute for this delicate inward sense of participating in the life of all mankind another thing, a nasty pronounced benevolence, which wants to do good to all mankind, and is only a form of self-assertion and of bullying. From this sort of love of humanity, good Lord deliver us! and deliver poor humanity. My friend was a tiny bit tainted with this form of self-importance, as all transcendentalists were. So if the mountains, in their brutality, took away the tainted love, good for them. But my dear Ruth – I shall call her Ruth – had more than this. She had, woman of fifty as she was, an almost girlish naïve sense of living at peace, real peace, with her fellow-men. And this she could not afford to lose. And save for that taint of generalization and *will*, she would never have lost it, even for that half-hour in the Swiss mountains. But she meant the 'cosmos' and 'humanity' to fit her will and her feelings, and the mountains made her realize that the cosmos *wouldn't*. When you come up against the cosmos, your consciousness is likely to suffer a jolt. And humanity, when you come down to it, is likely to give your 'love' a nasty jar. But there you are.

When we come to the younger generation, however, we realize that 'cosmos consciousness' and 'love of humanity' have really been left out of their composition. They are like a lot of brightly coloured bits of glass, and they only feel just what they bump against, when they're shaken. They make an accidental pattern with other people, and for the rest they know nothing and care nothing.

So that cosmic consciousness and love of humanity, to use the absurd New England terms, are really dead. They were tainted.

Both the cosmos and humanity were too much manufactured in New England. They weren't the real thing. They were, very often, just noble phrases to cover up self-assertion, self-importance, and malevolent bullying. They were just activities of the ugly, self-willed ego, determined that humanity and the cosmos should exist as New England allowed them to exist, or not at all. They were tainted with bullying egoism, and the young, having fine noses for this sort of smell, would have none of them.

The way to kill any feeling is to insist on it, harp on it, exaggerate it. Insist on loving humanity, and sure as fate you'll come to hate everybody. Because, of course, if you insist on loving humanity, then you insist that it shall be lovable: which half the time it isn't. In the same way, insist on loving your husband, and you won't be able to help hating him secretly. Because of course nobody is *always* lovable. If you insist they shall be, this imposes a tyranny over them, and they become less lovable, and if you force yourself to love them – or pretend to – when they are not lovable, you falsify everything, and fall into hate. The result of forcing any feeling is the death of that feeling, and the substitution of some sort of opposite. Whitman insisted on sympathizing with everything and everybody: so much so, that he came to believe in death only, not just his own death, but the death of all people. In the same way the slogan 'Keep Smiling!' produces at last a sort of savage rage in the breast of smilers, and the famous 'cheery morning greeting' makes the gall accumulate in all the cheery ones.

It is no good. Every time you force your feelings, you damage yourself and produce the opposite effect to the one you want. Try to force yourself to love somebody, and you are bound to end by detesting that same somebody. The only thing to do is to have the feelings you've really got, and not make up any of them. And that is the only way to leave the other person free. If you feel like murdering your husband, then don't say, 'Oh, but I love him dearly. I'm devoted to him.' That is not only bullying yourself, but bullying him. He doesn't want to be *forced*, even by love. Just say to yourself: 'I could murder him, and that's a fact. But I suppose I'd better not.' And then your true feelings will get their own balance.

The same is true of love of humanity. The last generation, and the one before that *insisted* on loving humanity. They cared terribly for the poor suffering Irish and Armenians and Congo rubber Negroes and all that. And it was a great deal of it fake, self-conceit, self-importance. The bottom of it was the egoistic thought: 'I'm so good, I'm so superior, I'm so benevolent, I care intensely about the poor suffering Irish and the martyred Armenians and the oppressed Negroes, and I'm going to save them, even if I have to upset the English and the Turks and the Belgians severely.' This love of mankind was half self-importance and half a desire to interfere and put a spoke in other people's wheels. The younger generation, smelling the rat under the lamb's-wool of Christian Charity, said to themselves: No love of humanity for me!

They have, if the truth be told, a secret detestation for all oppressed or unhappy people who need 'relief'. They rather hate 'the poor colliers', 'the poor cotton-workers', 'the poor starving Russians', and all that. If there came another war, how they would loathe 'the stricken Belgians'! And so it is: the father eats the pear, and the son's teeth are set on edge.

Having overdone the sympathy touch, especially the love of humanity, we have now got the recoil away from sympathy. The young don't sympathize, and they don't want to. They are egoists, and frankly so. They say quite honestly: 'I don't give a hoot in hell for the poor oppressed this-that-and-the-other.' And who can blame them? Their loving forebears brought on the Great War. If love of humanity brought on the Great War, let us see what frank and honest egoism will do. Nothing so horrible, we can bet.

The trouble about frank and accepted egoism is its unpleasant effect on the egoist himself. Honesty is very good, and it is good to cast off all the spurious sympathies and false emotions of the pre-war world. But casting off spurious sympathy and false emotion need not entail the death of all sympathy and all deep emotion, as it seems to do in the young. The young quite deliberately *play* at sympathy and emotion. 'Darling child, how lovely you look tonight! I *adore* to look at you!' – and in the next breath,

385

a little arrow of spite. Or the young wife to her husband: 'My beautiful love, I feel so precious when you hold me like that, my perfect dear! But shake me a cocktail, angel, would you? I need a good kick – you *angel* of light!'

The young, at the moment, have a perfectly good time strumming on the keyboard of emotion and sympathy, tinkling away at all the exaggerated phrases of rapture and tenderness, adoration and delight, while they feel – nothing, except a certain amusement at the childish game. It is so *chic* and charming to use all the most precious phrases of love and endearment amusingly, just amusingly, like the tinkling in a music-box.

And they would be very indignant if told they had no love of humanity. The English ones profess the most amusing and histrionic love of England, for example. 'There is only one thing I care about, except my beloved Philip, and that is England, our precious England. Philip and I are both prepared to die for England, at any moment.' At the moment, England does not seem to be in any danger of asking them, so they are quite safe. And if you gently inquire: 'But what, in your imagination, is England?' they reply fervently: 'The great tradition of the English, the great idea of England' – which seems comfortably elastic and non-committal.

And they cry: 'I would give anything for the cause of freedom. Hope and I have wept tears, and saddened our precious marriage-bed, thinking of the trespass on English liberty. But we are calmer now, and determined to fight calmly to the utmost.' Which calm fight consists in taking another cocktail and sending out a wildly emotional letter to somebody perfectly irresponsible. Then all is over, and freedom is forgotten, and perhaps religion gets a turn, or a wild outburst over some phrase in the burial service.

This is the advanced young of today. I confess it is amusing, while the coruscation lasts. The trying part is when the fireworks have finished – and they don't last very long, even with cocktails – and the grey stretches intervene. For with the advanced young, there is no warm daytime and silent night. It is all fireworks of excitement and stretches of grey emptiness; then more fireworks. And, let the grisly truth be owned, it is rather exhausting.

386

Now in the grey intervals in the life of the modern young one fact emerges in all its dreariness, and makes itself plain to the young themselves, as well as the onlooker. The fact that they are empty: that they care about nothing and nobody: not even the Amusement they seek so strenuously. Of course this skeleton is not to be taken out of the cupboard. 'Darling angel man, don't start being a nasty white ant. Play the game, angel-face, play the game; don't start saying unpleasant things and rattling a lot of dead men's bones! Tell us something nice, something amusing. Or let's be *really* serious, you know, and talk about Bolshevism or *la haute finance*. Do be an angel of light, and cheer us up, you nicest precious pet!'

As a matter of fact, the young are becoming afraid of their own emptiness. It's awful fun throwing things out of the window. But when you've thrown everything out, and you've spent two or three days sitting on the bare floor, your bones begin to ache, and you begin to wish for some of the old furniture, even if it was the ugliest Victorian horsehair.

At least, that's how it seems to me the young women begin to feel. They are frightened at the emptiness of their house of life, now they've thrown everything out of the window. Their young Philips and Peters and so on don't seem to make the slightest move to put any new furniture in the house of the young generation. The only new piece they can introduce is a cocktail-shaker and perhaps a wireless set. For the rest, it can stay blank.

And the young women begin to feel a little uneasy. Women don't like to feel empty. A woman hates to feel that she believes in nothing and stands for nothing. Let her be the silliest woman on earth, she will take something seriously: her appearance, her clothes, her house, something. And let her be not so very silly, and she wants more than that. She wants to feel, instinctively, that she amounts to something and that her life stands for something. Women, who so often are angry with men because men cannot 'just live', but must always be wanting some purpose in life, are themselves, perhaps, the very root of the male necessity for a purpose in life. It seems to me that in a woman the need to feel that her life *means* something, stands for something, and amounts to something is much more imperative than in a man. The woman herself may deny it emphatically; because, of course, it is the man's business to supply her life with this 'purpose'. But a man can be a tramp, purposeless, and be happy. Not so a woman. It is a very, very rare woman who can be happy if she feels herself 'outside' the great purpose of life. Whereas, I verily believe, vast numbers of men would gladly drift away as wasters, if there were anywhere to drift to.

A woman cannot bear to feel empty and purposeless. But a man may take a real pleasure in that feeling. A man can take real pride and satisfaction in pure negation: 'I am quite empty of feeling, I don't care the slightest bit in the world for anybody or anything except myself. But I do care for myself, and I'm going to survive in spite of them all, and I'm going to have my own success without caring the least in the world how I get it. Because I'm cleverer than they are, I'm cunninger than they are, even if I'm weak. I must build myself proper protections, and entrench myself, and then I'm safe. I can sit inside my glass tower and feel nothing and be touched by nothing, and yet exert my power, my will, through the glass walls of my ego.'

That, roughly, is the condition of a man who accepts the condition of true egoism, and emptiness, in himself. He has a certain pride in the condition, since in pure emptiness of real feeling he can still carry out his ambition, his will to egoistic success.

Now I doubt if any woman can feel like this. The most egoistic woman is always in a tangle of hate, if not of love. But the true male egoist neither hates nor loves. He is quite empty, at the middle of him. Only on the surface he has feelings: and these he is always trying to get away from. Inwardly, he feels nothing. And when he feels nothing, he exults in his ego and knows he is safe. Safe, within his fortifications, inside his glass tower.

But I doubt if women can even understand this condition in a man. They mistake the emptiness for depth. They think the false calm of the egoist who really feels nothing, is strength. And they imagine that all the defences which the confirmed egoist throws up, the glass tower of imperviousness, are screens to a real man, a positive being. And they throw themselves madly on the defences, to tear them down and come at the real man, little knowing that there *is* no real man, the defences are only there to protect a hollow emptiness, an egoism, not a human man.

But the young are beginning to suspect. The young women are beginning to respect the defences, for they are more afraid of coming upon the ultimate nothingness of the egoist, than of leaving him undiscovered. Hollowness, nothingness – it frightens the woman. They cannot be *real* nihilists. But men can. Men can have a savage satisfaction in the annihilation of all feeling and all connexion, in a resultant state of sheer negative emptiness, when there is nothing left to throw out of the window, and the window is sealed.

Women wanted freedom. The result is a hollowness, an emptiness which frightens the stoutest heart. Women then turn to women for love. But that doesn't last. It can't. Whereas the emptiness persists and persists.

The love of humanity is gone, leaving a great gap. The cosmic consciousness has collapsed upon a great void. The egoist sits grinning furtively in the triumph of his own emptiness. And now what is woman going to do? Now that the house of life is empty, now that she's thrown all the emotional furnishing out of the window, and the house of life, which is her eternal home, is empty as a tomb, now what is dear forlorn woman going to do?

# Women Are So Cocksure

Written in the later 1920s, published in *Phoenix*, 1936

My destiny has been cast among cocksure women. Perhaps when man begins to doubt himself, woman, who should be nice and peacefully hen-sure, becomes instead insistently cocksure. She develops convictions, or she catches them. And then woe betide everybody.

I began with my mother. She was convinced about some things: one of them being that a man ought not to drink beer. This conviction developed from the fact, naturally, that my father drank beer. He sometimes drank too much. He sometimes boozed away the money necessary for the young family. Therefore the drinking of beer became to my mother the cardinal sin. No other sin was so red, so red-hot. She was like a bull before this red sin. When my father came in tipsy, she saw scarlet.

We dear children were trained never, *never* to fall into this sin. We were sent to the Band of Hope, and told harrowing stories of drunkenness; we wept bitterly over the heroic youth who had taken the pledge and sworn never never to touch nor to taste, and who clenched his teeth when his cruel comrades tried to force beer down his throat: but alas, he had lost one of his front teeth, and through this narrow gap beer trickled even down his gullet. So he died of a broken heart.

My mother, though a woman with a real sense of humour, kept

her face straight and stern while we recounted this fearsome episode. And we were rigidly sent to the Band of Hope.

Years passed. Children became young men. It was evident my mother's sons were not going to hell down the beer-mug: they didn't care enough about it. My mother relaxed. She would even watch with pleasure while I drank a glass of ale, the fearful enemy, at supper. There was no longer a serpent in the glass, dash it down, dash it down.

'But, mother, if you don't mind if I drink a little beer, why did you mind so much about my father?'

'You don't realize what I had to put up with.'

'Yes, I do. But you made it seem a sin, a horror. You terrified our lives with the bogy of strong drink. You were absolutely sure it was utter evil. Why isn't it utter evil any more?'

'You're different from your father –'

But she was just a little shame-faced. Life changes our feelings. We may get mellower, or we may get harder, as time goes on. But we change. What outrages our feelings in the twenties will probably not outrage them in the fifties, not at all. And the change is much more striking in women than in men. Particularly in those women who are the moral force in the household, as my mother was.

My mother spoilt her life with her moral frenzy against John Barleycorn. To be sure she had occasion to detest the alcoholic stuff. But why the moral frenzy? It made a tragedy out of what was only a nuisance. And at fifty, when the best part of life was gone, she realized it. And then what would she not have given to have her life again, her young children, her tipsy husband, and a proper natural insouciance, to get the best out of it all. When woman tries to be too much mistress of fate, particularly of other people's fates, what a tragedy!

As sure as a woman has the whip-hand over her destiny and the destinies of those near her, so sure will she make a mess of her own destiny, and a muddle of the others'. And just as inevitably as the age of fifty will come upon her, so inevitably will come the realization that she has got herself into a hole. *She ought not to have been so cocksure.*

391

Beware, oh modern women, the age of fifty. It is then that the play is over, the theatre shuts, and you are turned out into the night. If you have been making a grand show of your life, all off your own bat, and being grand mistress of your destiny, all triumphant, the clock of years tolls fifty, and the play is over. You've had your turn on the stage. Now you must go, out into the common night, where you may or may not have a true place of shelter.

It is dangerous for anybody to be cocksure. But it is peculiarly dangerous for a woman. Being basically a creature of emotion, she will direct all her emotion force full on to what seems to her the grand aim of existence. For twenty, thirty years she may rush ahead to the grand goal of existence. And then the age of fifty approaches – the speed slackens – the driving force begins to fail – the grand goal is not only no nearer, it is all too near. It is all round about. It is a waste of unspeakable dreariness.

There were three sisters. One started out to be learned and to give herself to social reform. She was absolutely cocksure about being able to bring the world nearer salvation. The second obstinately decided to live her own life and to be herself. 'The aim of my life is to be myself.' She was cocksure about what her self was and how to be it. The aim of the third was to gather roses, whilst she might. She had real good times with her lovers, with her dressmakers, with her husband and her children. All three had everything life could offer.

The age of fifty draws near. All three are in the state of vital bankruptcy of the modern woman of that age. The one is quite cynical about reform, the other begins to realize that the 'self' she was so cocksure about doesn't exist, and she wonders what does exist. To the third the world is a dangerous and dirty place, and she doesn't know where to put herself.

Of all things, the most fatal to a woman is to have an aim, and be cocksure about it.

# Give Her a Pattern

*Daily Express*, 19 June 1929; *Assorted Articles*, 1930

The real trouble about women is that they must always go on trying to adapt themselves to men's theories of women, as they always have done. When a woman is thoroughly herself, she is being what her type of man wants her to be. When a woman is hysterical it's because she doesn't quite know what to be, which pattern to follow, which man's picture of woman to live up to.

For, of course, just as there are many men in the world, there are many masculine theories of what women should be. But men run to type, and it is the type, not the individual, that produces the theory, or 'ideal' of woman. Those very grasping gentry, the Romans, produced a theory or ideal of the matron, which fitted in very nicely with the Roman property lust. 'Caesar's wife should be above suspicion.' – So Caesar's wife kindly proceeded to be above it, no matter how far below it the Caesar fell. Later gentlemen like Nero produced the 'fast' theory of woman, and later ladies were fast enough for everybody. Dante arrived with a chaste and untouched Beatrice, and chaste and untouched Beatrices began to march self-importantly through the centuries. The Renaissance disovered the learned woman, and learned women buzzed mildly into verse and prose. Dickens invented the child-wife, so child-wives have swarmed ever since. He also fished out his version of the chaste Beatrice, a chaste but marriageable

Agnes. George Eliot imitated this pattern, and it became confirmed. The noble woman, the pure spouse, the devoted mother took the field, and was simply worked to death. Our own poor mothers were this sort. So we younger men, having been a bit frightened of our noble mothers, tended to revert to the child-wife. We weren't very inventive. Only the child-wife must be a boyish little thing – that was the new touch we added. Because young men are definitely frightened of the real female. She's too risky a quantity. She is too untidy, like David's Dora. No, let her be a boyish little thing, it's safer. So a boyish little thing she is.

There are, of course, other types. Capable men produce the capable woman ideal. Doctors produce the capable nurse. Business men produce the capable secretary. And so you get all sorts. You can produce the masculine sense of honour (whatever that highly mysterious quantity may be) in women, if you want to.

There is, also, the eternal secret ideal of men – the prostitute. Lots of women live up to this idea: just because men want them to.

And so, poor woman, destiny makes away with her. It isn't that she hasn't got a mind – she has. She's got everything that man has. The only difference is that she asks for a pattern. Give me a pattern to follow! That will always be woman's cry. Unless of course she has already chosen her pattern quite young, then she will declare she is herself absolutely, and no man's idea of women has any influence over her.

Now the real tragedy is not that women ask and must ask for a pattern of womanhood. The tragedy is not, even, that men give them such abominable patterns, child-wives, little-boy-baby-face girls, perfect secretaries, noble spouses, self-sacrificing mothers, pure women who bring forth children in virgin coldness, prostitutes who just make themselves low, to please the men; all the atrocious patterns of womanhood that men have supplied to woman; patterns all perverted from any real natural fulness of a human being. Man is willing to accept woman as an equal, as a man in skirts, as an angel, a devil, a baby-face, a machine, an instrument, a bosom, a womb, a pair of legs, a servant, an encyclopaedia, an ideal or an obscenity; the one thing he won't accept her as is a human being, a real human being of the feminine sex.

And, of course, women love living up to strange patterns, weird patterns – the more uncanny the better. What could be more uncanny than the present pattern of the Eton-boy girl with flowerlike artificial complexion? It is just weird. And for its very weirdness women like living up to it. What can be more gruesome than the little-boy-baby-face pattern? Yet the girls take it on with avidity.

But even that isn't the real root of the tragedy. The absurdity, and often, as in the Dante-Beatrice business, the inhuman nastiness of the pattern – for Beatrice had to go on being chaste and untouched all her life, according to Dante's pattern, while Dante had a cosy wife and kids at home – even that isn't the worst of it. The worst of it is, as soon as a woman has really lived up to the man's pattern, the man dislikes her for it. There is intense secret dislike for the Eton-young-man girl, among the boys, now that she is actually produced. Of course, she's very nice to show in public, absolutely the thing. But the very young men who have brought about her production detest her in private and in their private hearts are appalled by her.

When it comes to marrying, the pattern goes all to pieces. The boy marries the Eton-boy girl, and instantly he hates the *type*. Instantly his mind begins to play hysterically with all the other types, noble Agneses, chaste Beatrices, clinging Doras and lurid *filles de joie*. He is in a wild welter of confusion. Whatever pattern the poor woman tries to live up to, he'll want another. And that's the condition of modern marriage.

Modern woman isn't really a fool. But modern man is. That seems to me the only plain way of putting it. The modern man is a fool, and the modern young man a prize fool. He makes a greater mess of his women than men have ever made. Because he absolutely doesn't know *what* he wants her to be. We shall see the changes in the woman-pattern follow one another fast and furious now, because the young men hysterically don't know what they want. Two years hence women may be in crinolines – there was a pattern for you! – or a bead flap, like naked Negresses in mid-Africa – or they may be wearing brass armour, or the uniform of the Horse Guards. They may be anything. Because the young men are off their heads, and don't know what they want.

The women aren't fools, but they *must* live up to some pattern or other. They *know* the men are fools. They don't really respect the pattern. Yet a pattern they must have, or they can't exist.

Women are not fools. They have their own logic, even if it's not the masculine sort. Women have the logic of emotion, men have the logic of reason. The two are complementary and mostly in opposition. But the woman's logic of emotion is no less real and inexorable than the man's logic of reason. It only works differently.

And the woman never really loses it. She may spend years living up to a masculine pattern. But in the end, the strange and terrible logic of emotion will work out the smashing of that pattern, if it has not been emotionally satisfactory. This is the partial explanation of the astonishing changes in women. For years they go on being chaste Beatrices or child-wives. Then on a sudden – bash! The chaste Beatrice becomes something quite different, the child-wife becomes a roaring lioness! The pattern didn't suffice, emotionally.

Whereas men are fools. They are based on a logic of reason, or are supposed to be. And then they go and behave, especially with regard to women, in a more-than-feminine unreasonableness. They spend years training up the little-boy-baby-face type, till they've got her perfect. Then the moment they marry her, they want something else. Oh, beware, young women, of the young men who adore you! The moment they've got you they'll want something utterly different. The moment they marry the little-boy-baby face, instantly they begin to pine for the noble Agnes, pure and majestic, or the infinite mother with deep bosom of consolation, or the perfect business woman, or the lurid prostitute on black silk sheets: or, most idiotic of all, a combination of all the lot of them at once. And that is the logic of reason! When it comes to women, modern men are idiots. They don't know what they want, and so they never want, permanently, what they get. They want a cream cake that is at the same time ham and eggs and at the same time porridge. They are fools. If only women weren't bound by fate to play up to them!

For the fact of life is that women *must* play up to man's pattern. And she only gives her best to a man when he gives her a satisfactory pattern to play up to. But today, with a stock of ready-made, worn-out idiotic patterns to live up to, what can women give to men but the trashy side of their emotions? What could a woman possibly give to a man who wanted her to be a boy-baby face? What could she possibly give him but the dribblings of an idiot? – And, because women aren't fools, and aren't fooled even for very long at a time, she gives him some nasty cruel digs with her claws, and makes him cry for mother dear! – abruptly changing his pattern.

Bah! men are fools. If they want anything from women, let them give women a decent, satisfying idea of womanhood – not these trick patterns of washed-out idiots.

# Making Love to Music

Written 1927, published in *Phoenix*, 1936

'To me, dancing,' said Romeo, 'is just making love to music.'

'That's why you never will dance with me, I suppose,' replied Juliet.

'Well, you know, you are a bit too much of an individual.'

It is a curious thing, but the ideas of one generation become the instincts of the next. We are all of us, largely, the embodied ideas of our grandmothers, and, without knowing it, we behave as such. It is odd that the grafting works so quickly, but it seems to. Let the ideas change rapidly, and there follows a correspondingly rapid change in humanity. We become what we think. Worse still, we have become what our grandmothers thought. And our children's children will become the lamentable things that we are thinking. Which is the psychological visiting of the sins of the fathers upon the children. For we do not become just the lofty or beautiful thoughts of our grandmothers. Alas no! We are the embodiment of the most potent ideas of our progenitors, and these ideas are mostly private ones, not to be admitted in public, but to be transmitted as instincts and as the dynamics of behaviour to the third and fourth generation. Alas for the thing that our grandmothers brooded over in secret, and willed in private. That thing are we.

What did they wish and will? One thing is certain: they wished
398

to be made love to, to music. They wished man were not a coarse creature, jumping to his goal, and finished. They wanted heavenly strains to resound, while he held their hand, and a new musical movement to burst forth, as he put his arm round their waist. With infinite variations the music was to soar on, from level to level of love-making, in a delicious dance, the two things inextricable, the two persons likewise.

To end, of course, before the so-called consummation of love-making, which, to our grandmothers in their dream, and therefore to us in actuality, is the grand anti-climax. Not a consummation, but a humiliating anti-climax.

This is the so-called act of love itself, the actual knuckle of the whole bone of contention: a humiliating anti-climax. The bone of contention, of course, is sex. Sex is very charming and very delightful, so long as you make love to music, and you tread the clouds with Shelley, in a two-step. But to come at last to the grotesque bathos of capitulation: no, sir! Nay-nay!

Even a man like Maupassant, an apparent devotee of sex, says the same thing: and Maupassant is grandfather, or great-grandfather, to very many of us. Surely, he says, the act of copulation is the Creator's cynical joke against us. To have created in us all these beautiful and noble sentiments of love, to set the nightingale and all the heavenly spheres singing, merely to throw us into this grotesque posture, to perform this humiliating act, is a piece of cynicism worthy, not of a benevolent Creator, but of a mocking demon.

Poor Maupassant, there is the clue to his own catastrophe! He wanted to make love to music. And he realized, with rage, that copulate to music you cannot. So he divided himself against himself, and damned his eyes in disgust, then copulated all the more.

We, however, his grandchildren, are shrewder. Man *must* make love to music and woman *must* be made love to, to a string and saxophone accompaniment. It is our inner necessity. Because our grandfathers, and especially our great-grandfathers, left the music most severely out of their copulations. So now we leave the copulation most severely out of our musical love-making. We *must* make love to music: it is our grandmothers' dream, become an inward necessity in us, an unconscious motive force. Copulate you cannot, to music. So cut out that part, and solve the problem.

The popular modern dances, far from being 'sexual', are distinctly anti-sexual. But there, again, we must make a distinction. We should say, the modern jazz and tango and Charleston, far from being an incitement to copulation, are in direct antagonism to copulation. Therefore it is all nonsense for the churches to raise their voices against dancing, against 'making love to music'. Because the Church, and society at large, has no particular antagonism to sex. It would be ridiculous, for sex is so large and all-embracing that the religious passion itself is largely sexual. But, as they say, 'sublimated'. This is the great recipe for sex: only sublimate it! Imagine the quicksilver heated and passing off in weird, slightly poisonous vapour, instead of heavily rolling together and fusing: and there you have the process: sublimation: making love to music! Morality has really no quarrel at all with 'sublimated' sex. Most 'nice' things are 'sublimated sex'. What morality hates, what the Church hates, what modern *mankind* hates – for what, after all, is 'morality' except the instinctive revulsion of the majority? – is just copulation. The modern youth especially just have an instinctive aversion from copulation. They love sex. But they inwardly loathe copulation, even when they play at it. As for playing at it, what else are they to do, given the toys? But they don't like it. They do it in a sort of self-spite. And they turn away, with disgust and relief, from this bed-ridden act, to make love once more to music.

And really, surely this is all to the good. If the young don't really *like* copulation, then they are safe. As for marriage, they will marry, according to their grandmothers' dream, for quite other reasons. Our grandfathers, or great-grandfathers, married crudely and unmusically, for copulation. That was the actuality. So the dream was all of music. The dream was the mating of two souls, to the faint chiming of the Seraphim. We, the third and fourth generation, we are the dream made flesh. They dreamed of a marriage with all things gross – meaning especially copulation – left out, and only the pure harmony of equality and intimate companionship remaining. And the young live out the dream.

400

They marry: they copulate in a perfunctory and half-disgusted fashion, merely to show they can do it. And so they have children. But the marriage is made to music, the gramophone and the wireless orchestrate each small domestic act, and keep up the jazzing jig of connubial felicity, a felicity of companionship, equality, forbearance, and mutual sharing of everything the married couple have in common. Marriage set to music! The worn-out old serpent in this musical Eden of domesticity is the last, feeble instinct for copulation, which drives the married couple to clash upon the boring organic differences in one another, and prevents them from being twin souls in almost identical bodies. But we are wise, and soon learn to leave the humiliating act out altogether. It is the only wisdom.

We are such stuff as our grandmothers' dreams were made on, and our little life is rounded by a band.

The thing you wonder, as you watch the modern dancers making love to music, in a dance-hall, is what kind of dances will our children's children dance? Our mothers' mothers danced quadrilles and sets of Lancers, and the waltz was almost an indecent thing to them. Our mothers' mothers' mothers danced minuets and Roger de Coverleys, and smart and bouncing country-dances which worked up the blood and danced a man nearer and nearer to copulation.

But lo! even while she was being whirled round in the dance, our great-grandmother was dreaming of soft and throbbing music, and the arms of 'one person', and the throbbing and sliding unison of this one more elevated person, who would never coarsely bounce her towards bed and copulation, but would slide on with her for ever, down the dim and sonorous vistas, making love without end to music without end, and leaving out entirely that disastrous, music-less full-stop of copulation, the end of ends.

So she dreamed, our great-grandmother, as she crossed hands and was flung around, and buffeted and busked towards bed, and the bouncing of the *bête à deux dos*. She dreamed of men that were only embodied souls, not tiresome and gross males, lords and masters. She dreamed of 'one person' who was all men in one, universal, and beyond narrow individualism.

401

So that now, the great-granddaughter is made love to by all men – to music – as if it were one man. To music, all men, as if it were one man, make love to her, and she sways in the arms, not of an individual, but of the modern species. It is wonderful. And the modern man makes love, to music, to all women, as if she were one woman. All woman, as if she were one woman! It is almost like Baudelaire making love to the vast thighs of Dame Nature herself, except that that dream of our great-grandfather is still too copulative, though all-embracing.

But what is the dream that is simmering at the bottom of the soul of the modern young woman as she slides to music across the floor, in the arms of the species, or as she waggles opposite the species, in the Charleston? If she is content, there is no dream. But woman is never content. If she were content, the Charleston and the Black Bottom would not oust the tango.

She is not content. She is even less content, in the morning after the night before, than was her great-grandmother, who had been bounced by copulatory attentions. She is even less content; therefore her dream, though not risen yet to consciousness, is even more devouring and more rapidly subversive.

What is her dream, this slender, tender lady just out of her teens, who is varying the two-step with the Black Bottom? What can her dream be? Because what her dream is, that her children, and my children, or children's children, will become. It is the very ovum of the future soul, as my dream is the sperm.

There is not much left for her to dream of, because whatever she wants she can have. All men, or no men, this man or that, she has the choice, for she has no lord and master. Sliding down the endless avenues of music, having an endless love endlessly made to her, she has this too. If she wants to be bounced into copulation, at a dead end, she can have that too: just to prove how monkeyish it is, and what a fumbling in the cul-de-sac.

Nothing is denied her, so there is nothing to want. And without desire, even dreams are lame. Lame dreams! Perhaps she has lame dreams, and wishes, last wish of all, she had no dreams at all.

But while life lasts, and is an affair of sleeping and waking, this is the one wish that will never be granted. From dreams no man escapeth, no woman either. Even the little blonde who is preferred by gentlemen has a dream somewhere, if she, and we, and he, did but know it. Even a dream beyond emeralds and dollars.

What is it? What is the lame and smothered dream of the lady? Whatever it is, she will never know: not till somebody has told it her, and then gradually, and after a great deal of spiteful repudiation. she will recognize it, and it will pass into her womb.

Myself, I do not know what the frail lady's dream may be. But depend upon one thing, it will be something very different from the present business. The dream and the business! – an eternal antipathy. So the dream, whatever it may be, will *not* be 'making love to music'. It will be something else.

Perhaps it will be the re-capturing of a dream that started in mankind, and never finished, was never fully unfolded. The thought occurred to me suddenly when I was looking at the remains of paintings on the walls of Etruscan tombs at Tarquinia. There the painted women dance, in their transparent linen with heavier, coloured borders, opposite the naked-limbed men, in a splendour and an abandon which is not at all abandoned. There is a great beauty in them, as of life which has not finished. The dance is Greek, if you like, but not finished off like the Greek dancing. The beauty is not so pure, if you will, as the Greek beauty; but also it is more ample, not so narrowed. And there is not the slight element of abstraction, of inhumanity, which underlies all Greek expression, the tragic will.

The Etruscans, at least before the Romans smashed them, do not seem to have been tangled up with tragedy, as the Greeks were from the first. There seems to have been a peculiar large carelessness about them, very human and non-moral. As far as one can judge, they never said: certain acts are immoral, just because we say so! They seem to have had a strong feeling for taking life sincerely as a pleasant thing. Even death was a gay and lively affair.

Moralists will say: Divine law wiped them out. The answer to that is, divine law wipes everything out in time, even itself. And if the smashing power of the all-trampling Roman is to be identified with divine law, then all I can do is to look up another divinity.

No, I do believe that the unborn dream at the bottom of the soul of the shingled, modern young lady is this Etruscan young woman of mine, dancing with such abandon opposite her naked-limbed, strongly dancing young man, to the sound of the double flute. They are wild with a dance that is heavy and light at the same time, and not a bit anti-copulative, yet not bouncingly copulative either.

That was another nice thing about the Etruscans: there was a phallic symbol everywhere, so everybody was used to it, and they no doubt all offered it small offerings, as the source of inspiration. Being part of the everyday life, there was no need to get it on the brain, as we tend to do.

And apparently the men, the men slaves at least, went gaily and jauntily round with no clothes on at all, and being therefore of a good brown colour, wore their skin for livery. And the Etruscan ladies thought nothing of it. Why should they? We think nothing of a naked cow, and we still refrain from putting our pet-dogs into pants or petticoats: marvellous to relate: but then, our ideal is Liberty, after all! So if the slave was stark-naked, who gaily piped to the lady as she danced, and if her partner was three-parts naked, and herself nothing but a transparency, well, nobody thought anything about it; there was nothing to shy off from, and all the fun was in the dance.

There it is, the delightful quality of the Etruscan dance. They are neither making love to music, to avoid copulation, nor are they bouncing towards copulation with a brass band accompaniment. They are just dancing a dance with the elixir of life. And if they have made a little offering to the stone phallus at the door, it is because when one is full of life one is full of possibilities, and the phallus gives life. And if they have made an offering also to the queer ark of the female symbol, at the door of a woman's tomb, it is because the womb too is the source of life, and a great fountain of dance-movements.

It is we who have narrowed the dance down to two move-ments: either bouncing towards copulation, or sliding and shaking and waggling, to elude it. Surely it is ridiculous to make love to music, and to music to be made love to! Surely the music is to dance to! And surely the modern young woman feels this, somewhere deep inside.

To the music one should dance, and dancing, dance. The Etruscan young woman is going gaily at it, after two thousand five hundred years. She is not making love to music, nor is the dark-limbed youth, her partner. She is just dancing her very soul into existence, having made an offering on one hand to the lively phallus of man, on the other hand, to the shut womb-symbol of woman, and put herself on real good terms with both of them. So she is quite serene, and dancing herself as a very fountain of motion and of life, the young man opposite her dancing himself the same, in contrast and balance, with just the double flute to whistle round their naked heels.

And I believe this is, or will be, the dream of our pathetic, music-shunned young girl of today, and the substance of her children's children, unto the third and fourth generation.

# The 'Jeune Fille' Wants to Know

*Evening News*, 8 May 1928; *Assorted Articles*, 1930

If you are a writer, nothing is more confusing than the difference between the things you have to say and the things you are allowed to print. Talking to an intelligent girl, the famous '*jeune fille*' who is the excuse for the great Hush! Hush! in print, you find, not that you have to winnow your words and leave out all the essentials, but that she, the innocent girl in question, is flinging all sorts of fierce questions at your head, in all sorts of shameless language, demanding all sorts of impossible answers. You think to yourself: 'My heaven, *this* is the innocent young thing on whose behalf books are suppressed!' And you wonder: 'How on earth am I to answer her?'

You decide the only way to answer her is straight-forward. She smells an evasion in an instant, and despises you for it. She is no fool, this innocent maiden. Far from it. And she loathes an evasion. Talking to her father in the sanctum of his study, you have to winnow your words and watch your step, the old boy is so nervous, so tremulous lest anything be said that should hurt his feelings. But once away in the drawing-room or the garden, the innocent maiden looks at you anxiously, and it is all you can do to prevent her saying crudely, 'Please don't be annoyed with daddy. You see, he *is* like that, and we have to put up with him' – or else from blurting out, 'Daddy's an old fool, but he *is* a dear, isn't he?'

It is a queer reversal of the Victorian order. Father winces and bridles and trembles in his study or his library, and the innocent maiden knocks you flat with her outspokenness in the conservatory. And you have to admit that she is the man of the two; of the three, maybe. Especially when she says, rather sternly, 'I hope you didn't let daddy see what you thought of him!' 'But what *do* I think of him?' I gasp. 'Oh, it's fairly obvious!' she replies coolly, and dismisses the point.

I admit the young are a little younger than I am; or a little older, which is it? I really haven't spent my years cultivating prunes and prisms, yet, confronted with a young thing of twenty-two, I often find myself with a prune-stone in my mouth, and I don't know what to do with it.

'Why *is* daddy like that?' she says, and there is genuine pain in the question. 'Like what?' you ask. 'Oh, you know what I mean! Like a baby ostrich with its head in the sand! It only makes his rear so much the more conspicuous. And it's a pity, because he's awfully intelligent in other ways.'

Now, what is man to answer? '*Why* are they like that?' she insists. 'Who?' say I. 'Men!' she says; 'men like daddy!' 'I suppose it's a sort of funk,' say I. '*Exactly!*' she pounces on me like a panther. 'But what is there to be in a funk about?'

I have to confess I don't know. 'Of course not!' she says. 'There's nothing at all to be in a funk about. So why can't we make him see it?'

When the younger generation, usually the feminine half of it in her early twenties, starts firing off Whys? at me, I give in. Anything crosses her in the least – and she takes aim at it with the deadly little pistol of her inquiring spirit, and says '*Why?*' She is a deadly shot: Billy the Kid is nothing to her; she hits the nail on the head every time. 'Now, why can't I talk like a sensible human being to daddy?' 'I suppose he thinks it is a little early for you to be quite so sensible,' say I mildly. 'Cheek! What *cheek* of him to think he can measure out the amount of sense I ought to have!' she cries. 'Why does he think it?'

Why indeed? But once you start whying, there's no end to it. A hundred years ago, a few reformers piped up timorously, 'Why is man so infinitely superior to woman?' And on the slow years came the whisper 'He isn't!' Then the poor padded young of those days roused up. 'Why are fathers *always* in the right?' And the end of the century confessed that they weren't. Since then, the innocent maiden has ceased to be anaemic; all maidens were more or less anaemic thirty years ago; and though she is no less innocent, but probably more so, than her stuffy grandmother or mother before her, there isn't a thing she hasn't shot her Why? at, or her Wherefore? – the innocent maiden of today. And digging implements are called by their bare, their barest names. 'Why should daddy put his foot down upon love? He's been a prize muff at it himself, judging from mother.'

It's terrible, if all the sanctifications have to sit there like celluloid Aunt Sallies, while the young take pot shots at them. A real straight Why? aimed by sweet-and-twenty goes clean through them. Nothing but celluloid! and looking so important! Really, *why* ... ?

The answer seems to be, bogey! The elderly today seem to be ridden by a bogey, they grovel before the fetish of human wickedness. Every young man is out to 'ruin' every young maiden. Bogey! The young maiden knows a thing or two about that. She's not quite the raw egg she's supposed to be, in the first place. And as for most young men, they're only too nice, and it would grieve them bitterly to 'ruin' any young maid, even if they knew exactly how to set about it. Of which the young maiden is perfectly aware, and 'Why can't daddy see it?' He can, really. But he is so wedded to his bogey, that once the young man's back is turned, the old boy can see in the young boy nothing but a danger, a danger to my daughter! Wickedness in other people is an *idée fixe* of the elderly. 'Ah, my boy, you will find that in life every man's hand is against you!' As a matter of fact, my boy finds nothing of the sort. Every man has to struggle for himself, true. But most people are willing to give a bit of help where they can. The world may really be a bogey. But that isn't because individuals are wicked villains. At least ninety-nine per cent of individuals in this country, and in any other country as far as we have ever seen, are perfectly decent people who have a certain amount of struggle to get along, but who don't want to do anybody any harm, if they can help it.

This seems to be the general experience of the young, and so they can't appreciate the bogey of human wickedness which seems to dominate the minds of the old, in their relation to the succeeding generation. The young ask 'What, exactly, is this bogey, this wickedness we are to be shielded from?' And the old only reply, 'Of course, there is no danger to *us*. But to you, who are young and inexperienced ...!'

And the young, naturally, see nothing but pure hypocrisy. They have no desire to be shielded. If the bogey exists, they would like to set eyes on him, to take the measure of this famous 'wickedness'. But since they never come across it, since they find meanness and emptiness the worst crimes, they decide that the bogey doesn't and never did exist, that he is an invention of the elderly spirit, the last stupid stick with which the old can beat the young and feel self-justified. 'Of course, it's perfectly hopeless with mother and daddy, one has to treat them like mental infants,' say the young. But the mother sententiously reiterates, 'I don't mind, as far as I am concerned. But I have to protect my children.'

Protect, that is, some artificial children that only exist in parental imagination, from a bogey that likewise has no existence outside that imagination, and thereby derive a great sense of parental authority, importance and justification.

The danger for the young is that they will question everything out of existence, so that nothing is left. But that is no reason to stop questioning. The old lies must be questioned out of existence, even at a certain loss of things worth having. When everything is questioned out of existence, then the real fun will begin putting the right things back. But nothing is any good till the old lies are got rid of.

# Men Must Work and Women As Well

*Star Review*, November 1929; *Assorted Articles*, 1930

Supposing that circumstances go on pretty much in the same way they're going on in now, then men and women will go on pretty much in the same way they are now going on in. There is always an element of change, we know. But change is of two sorts: the next step, or a jump in another direction. The next step is called progress. If our society continues its course of gay progress along the given lines, then men and women will do the same: always along the given lines.

So what is important in that case is not so much men and women, but the given lines. The railway train doesn't matter particularly in itself. What matters is where it is going to. If I want to go to Crewe, then a train to Bedford is supremely uninteresting to me, no matter how full it may be. It will only arouse a secondary and temporal interest if it happens to have an accident.

And there you are with men and women today. They are not particularly interesting, and they are not, in themselves, particularly important. All the thousands and millions of bowler hats and neat handbags that go bobbing to business every day may represent so many immortal souls, but somehow we feel that is not for us to say. The clergyman is paid to tickle our vanity in these matters. What all the bowler hats and neat handbags represent to you and me and to each other is business, my dear, and a job.

So that, granted the present stream of progress towards better business and better jobs continues, the point is, not to consider the men and women bobbing in the stream, any more than you consider the drops of water in the Thames – but where the stream is flowing. Where is the stream flowing, indeed, the stream of progress? Everybody hopes, of course, it is flowing towards bigger business and better jobs. And what does that mean, again, to the man under the bowler hat and the woman who clutches the satchel?

It means, of course, more money, more congenial labours, and fewer hours. It means freedom from all irksome tasks. It means, apart from the few necessary hours of highly paid and congenial labour, that men and women shall have nothing to do except enjoy themselves. No beastly housework for the women, no beastly homework for the men. Free! free to enjoy themselves. More films, more motor-cars, more dances, more golf, more tennis and more getting completely away from yourself. And the goal of life is enjoyment.

Now if men and women want these things with sufficient intensity, they may really get them, and go on getting them. While the game is worth the candle, men and women will go on playing the game. And it seems today as if the motor-car, the film, the radio and the jazz were worth the candle. This being so, progress will continue from business to bigger business, and from job to better job. This is, in very simple terms, the plan of the universe laid down by the great magnates of industry like Mr Ford. And they know what they are talking about.

But – and the 'but' is a very big one – it is not easy to turn business into bigger business, and it is sometimes *impossible* to turn uncongenial jobs into congenial ones. This is where science really leaves us in the lurch, and calculation collapses. Perhaps in Mr Ford's super-factory of motor-cars all jobs may be made abstract and congenial. But the woman whose cook falls foul of the kitchen range, heated with coal, every day, hates that coal range herself even more darkly than the cook hates it. Yet many

411

housewives can't afford electric cooking. And if everyone could, it still doesn't make housework entirely congenial. All the inventions of modern science fail to make housework anything but uncongenial to the modern woman, be she mistress or servant-maid. Now the only decent way to get something done is to get it done by somebody who quite likes doing it. In the past, cooks really enjoyed cooking and housemaids enjoyed scrubbing. Those days are over; like master, like man, and still more so, like mistress, like maid. Mistress loathes scrubbing; in two generations, maid loathes scrubbing. But scrubbing must be done. At what price? – raise the price. The price is raised, the scrubbing goes a little better. But after a while, the loathing of scrubbing becomes again paramount in the kitchenmaid's breast, and then ensues a general state of tension, and a general outcry: Is it worth it? Is it really worth it?

What applies to scrubbing applies to all labour that cannot be mechanized or abstracted. A girl will slave over shorthand and typing for a pittance because it is not muscular work. A girl will not do housework well, not for a good wage. Why? Because, for some mysterious or obvious reason, the modern woman and the modern man hate physical work. Ask your husband to peel the potatoes, and earn his deep resentment. Ask your wife to wash your socks, and earn the same. There is still a certain thrill about 'mental' and purely mechanical work like attending a machine. But actual labour has become to us, with our education, abhorrent.

And it is here that science has not kept pace with human demand. It is here that progress is fatally threatened. There is an enormous, insistent demand on the part of the human being that mere labour, such as scrubbing, hewing and loading coal, navvying, the crude work that is the basis of all labour, shall be done away with. Even washing dishes. Science hasn't even learned how to wash dishes for us yet. The mistress who feels so intensely bitter about her maid who will not wash the dishes properly does so because she herself so loathes washing them. Science has rather left us in the lurch in these humble but basic matters. Before babies are conveniently bred in bottles, let the scientist find a *hey presto!* trick for turning dirty teacups into clean ones; since it is upon science we depend for our continued progress.

Progress, then, which proceeds so smoothly, and depends on science, does not proceed as rapidly as human feelings change. Beef-steaks are beef-steaks still, though all except the eating is horrible to us. A great deal must be done about a beef-steak besides the eating of it. And this great deal is done, we have to face the fact, unwillingly. When the mistress loathes trimming and grilling a beef-steak, or paring potatoes, or wringing the washing, the maid will likewise loathe these things, and do them at last unwillingly, and with a certain amount of resentment.

The one thing we don't sufficiently consider, in considering the march of human progress, is also the very dangerous march of human feeling that goes on at the same time and not always parallel. The change in human feeling! And one of the greatest changes that has ever taken place in man and woman is this revulsion from physical effort, physical labour and physical contact, which has taken place within the last thirty years. This change hits woman even harder than man, for she has always had to keep the immediate physical side going. And now it is repellent to her – just as nearly all physical activity is repellent to modern man. The film, the radio, the gramophone were all invented because physical effort and physical contact have become repulsive to man and woman alike. The aim is to abstract as far as possible. And science is our only help. And science still can't wash the dinner-things or darn socks, or even mend the fire. Electric heaters or central heating, of course! But that's not all.

What, then, is the result? In the abstract we sail ahead to bigger business and better jobs and babies bred in bottles and food in tabloid form. But meanwhile science hasn't rescued us from beef-steaks and dish-washing, heavy labour and howling babies. There is a great hitch. And owing to the great hitch, a great menace to progress. Because every day mankind hates the business of beef-steaks and dish-washing, heavy labour and howling babies more bitterly.

The housewife is full of resentment – she can't help it. The young husband is full of resentment – he can't help it, when he has to plant potatoes to eke out the family income. The housemaid is full of resentment, the navvy is full of resentment, the collier is full of resentment, and the collier's wife is full of resentment, because her man can't earn a proper wage. Resentment grows as the strange fastidiousness of modern men and women increases. Resentment, resentment, resentment – because the basis of life is still brutally physical, and that has become repulsive to us. Mr Ford, being in his own way a genius, has realized that what the modern workman wants, just like the modern gentleman, is abstraction. The modern workman doesn't *want* to be 'interested' in his job. He wants to be as little interested, as nearly perfectly mechanical as possible. This is the great will of the people, and there is no gainsaying it. It is precisely the same in woman as in man. Woman demands an electric cooker because it makes no call on her attention or her 'interest' at all. It is almost a pure abstraction, a few switches, and no physical contact, no *dirt*, which is the inevitable result of physical contact, at all. If only we could make housework a real abstraction, a matter of turning switches and guiding a machine, the housewife would again be more or less content. But it can't quite be done, even in America.

And the resentment is enormous. The resentment against *eating*, in the breast of modern woman who has to prepare food, is profound. Why all this work and bother about *mere eating*? Why, indeed? Because neither science nor evolution has kept up with the change in human feeling, and beef-steaks are beef-steaks still, no matter how detestable they may have become to the people who have to prepare them. The loathsome fuss of food continues, and will continue, in spite of all talk about tabloids. The loathsome digging of coal out of the earth, by half-naked men, continues, deep underneath Mr Ford's super-factories. There it is, and there it will be, and you can't get away from it. While men quite enjoyed hewing coal, which they did, and while women really enjoyed cooking, even with a coal range, which they did – then all was well. But suppose society *en bloc* comes to hate the thought of sweating cooking over a hot range, or sweating hacking at a coal-seam, then what are you to do? You have to ask, or to demand that a large section of society shall do something they

414

have come to hate doing, and which you would hate to do yourself. What then? Resentment and ill-feeling!

Social life means all classes of people living more or less harmoniously together. And private life means men and women, man and woman living together more or less congenially. If there is serious discord between the social classes, then society is threatened with confusion. If there is serious discord between man and woman, then the individual, and that means practically everybody, is threatened with internal confusion and unhappiness.

Now it is quite easy to keep the working classes in harmonious working order, so long as you don't ask them to do work they simply do not want to do. The Board Schools, however, did the fatal deed. They said to the boys: Work is noble, but what you want is to *get on*, you don't want to stick down a coal-mine all your life. Rise up, and do *clean* work! become a school-teacher or a clerk, not a common collier.

This is sound Board School education, and is in keeping with all the noblest social ideals of the last century. Unfortunately it entirely overlooks the unpleasant effect of such teaching on those who *cannot* get on, and who must perforce stick down a coal-mine all their lives. And these, in the Board Schools of a mining district, are at least ninety per cent of the boys; it must be so. So that ninety per cent of these Board School scholars are deliberately taught, at school, to be malcontents, taught to despise themselves for not having 'got on', for not having 'got out of the pit', for sticking down all their lives doing 'dirty work' and being 'common colliers'. Naturally, every collier, doomed himself, wants to get his boys out of the pit, to be gentlemen. And since this again is *impossible* in ninety per cent of the cases, the number of 'gentlemen', or clerks and school-teachers, being strictly proportionate to the number of colliers, there comes again the sour disillusion. So that by the third generation you have exactly what you've got today, the young malcontent collier. He has been deliberately produced by modern education coupled with modern conditions, and is logically, inevitably and naturally what he is: a malcontent collier. According to all the accepted teaching, he ought to have risen and bettered himself: equal opportunity, you know.

415

And he hasn't risen and bettered himself. Therefore he is more or less a failure in his own eyes even. He is doomed to do dirty work. He is a malcontent. Now even Mr Ford can't make coal-mines clean and shiny and abstract. Coal won't be abstracted. Even a Soviet can't do it. A coal-mine remains a hole in the black earth, where blackened men hew and shovel and sweat. You can't abstract it, or make it an affair of pulling levers, and, what is even worse, you can't abandon it, you can't do away with it. There it is, and it has got to be. Mr Ford forgets that his clean and pure and harmonious super-factory, where men only pull shining levers or turn bright handles, has all had to be grossly mined and smelted before it could come into existence. Mr Ford's is one of the various heavens of industry. But these heavens rest on various hells of labour, always did and always will. Science rather leaves us in the lurch in these matters. Science is supposed to remove these hells for us. And – it doesn't. Not at all!

If you had never taught the blackened men down in the various hells that they *were* in hell, and made them despise themselves for being there – a *common* collier, a *low* labourer – the mischief could never have developed so rapidly. But now we have it, all society resting on a labour basis of smouldering resentment. And the collier's question: How would *you* like to be a collier? – is unanswerable. We know perfectly well we should dislike it intensely. – At the same time, my father, who never went to a Board School, quite liked it. But he has been improved on. Progress! Human feeling has changed, changed rapidly and radically. And science has not changed conditions to fit.

What is to be done? We all loathe brute physical labour. We all think it is horrible to have to do it. We consider those that actually do it low and vile, and we have told them so, for fifty years, urging them to get away from it and 'better themselves', which would be very nice, if everybody *could* get on, and brute labour could be abandoned, as, scientifically, it ought to be. But actually, not at all. We are forced to go on forcing a very large proportion of society to remain 'unbettered', 'low and common', 'common colliers, common labourers', since a very large portion of humanity must still spend its life labouring, now and in the
416

future, science having let us down in this respect. You can't teach mankind to 'better himself' unless you'll better the gross earth to fit him. And the gross earth remains what it was, and man its slave. For neither science nor evolution shows any signs of saving us from our gross necessities. The labouring masses are and will be, even if all else is swept away: because they must be. They represent the gross necessity of man, which science has failed to save us from.

So then, what? The only thing that remains to be done is to make labour as likeable as possible, and try to teach the labouring masses to like it: which, given the trend of modern feeling, not only sounds, but is, fatuous. Mankind *en bloc* gets more fastidious and more 'nice' every day. Every day it loathes dirty work more deeply. And every day the whole pressure of social consciousness works towards making everybody more fastidious, more 'nice', more refined, and more unfit for dirty work. Before you make all humanity unfit for dirty work, you should first remove the necessity for dirty work.

But such being the condition of men and women with regard to work – a condition of repulsion in the breasts of men and women for the work that has got to be done – what about private life, the relation between man and woman? How does the new fastidiousness and nicety of mankind affect this?

Profoundly! The revulsion from physical labour, physical effort, physical contact has struck a death-blow at marriage and home-life. In the great trend of the times, a woman cannot save herself from the universal dislike of housework, housekeeping, rearing children and keeping a home going. Women make the most unselfish efforts in this direction, because it is generally expected of them. But this cannot remove the *instinctive* dislike of preparing meals and scouring saucepans, cleaning baby's bottles or darning the man's underwear, which a large majority of women feel today. It is something which there is no denying, a real physical dislike of doing these things. Many women school themselves and are excellent housewives, physically disliking it all the time. And this, though admirable, is wearing. It is an exhaustive process, with many ill results.

Can it be possible that women actually ever did like scouring saucepans and cleaning the range? – I believe some few women still do. I believe that twenty years ago, even, the majority of women enjoyed it. But what, then, has happened? Can human instincts really change?

They can, and in the most amazing fashion. And this is the great problem for the sociologist: the violent change in human instinct, especially in women. Woman's instinct used to be all for home, shelter, the protection of the man, and the happiness of running her own house. Now it is all against. Woman *thinks* she wants a lovely little home of her own, but her instinct is all against it, when it means matrimony. She *thinks* she wants a man of her own, but her instinct is dead against having him around all the time. She would like him on a long string, that she can let out or pull in, as she feels inclined. But she just doesn't want him inevitably and insidiously there all the time – not even every evening – not even for week-ends, if it's got to be a fixture. She wants him to be merely intermittent in her landscape, even if he is always present in her soul, and she writes him the most intimate letters every day. All well and good! But her instinct is against him, against his permanent and perpetual physical presence. She doesn't want to feel his presence as something material, unavoidable and permanent. It goes dead against her grain, it upsets her instinct. She loves him, she loves, even, being faithful to him. But she doesn't want him substantially around. She doesn't want his actual physical presence – except in snatches. What she *really* loves is the thought of him, the idea of him, the *distant* communion with him – varied with snatches of actually being together, like little festivals, which we are more or less glad when they are over.

Now a great many modern girls feel like this, even when they force themselves to behave in the conventional side-by-side fashion. And a great many men feel the same – though perhaps not so acutely as the women. Young couples may force themselves to be conventional husbands and wives, but the strain is often cruel, and the result often disastrous.

Now then we see the trend of our civilization, in terms of

human feeling and human relation. It is, and there is no denying it, towards a greater and greater abstraction from the physical, towards a further and further physical separateness between men and women, and between individual and individual. Young men and women today are together all the time, it will be argued. Yes, but they are together as good sports, good chaps, in strange independence of one another, intimate one moment, strangers the next, hands-off! all the time and as little connected as the bits in a kaleidoscope.

The young have the fastidiousness, the nicety, the revulsion from the physical, intensified. To the girl today, a man whose physical presence she is aware of, especially a bit *heavily* aware of, is or becomes really abhorrent. She wants to fly away from him to the uttermost ends of the earth. And as soon as women or girls get a bit female physical, young men's nerves go all to pieces. The sexes can't stand one another. They adore one another as spiritual or personal creatures, all talk and wit and back-chat, or jazz and motor-cars and machines, or tennis and swimming – even sitting in bathing-suits all day on a beach. But this is all peculiarly non-physical, a flaunting of the body in its non-physical, merely optical aspect. So much nudity, fifty years ago, would have made man and woman quiver through and through. Now, not at all! People flaunt their bodies to show how unphysical they are. The more the girls are not desired, the more they uncover themselves.

And this means, when we analyse it out, repulsion. The young are, in a subtle way, physically repulsive to one another, the girl to the man and the man to the girl. And they rather enjoy the feeling of repulsion, it is a sort of contest. It is as if the young girl said to the young man today: I rather like you, you know. You are so thrillingly repulsive to me. – And as if the young man replied: Same here! – There may be, of course, an intense bodiless sort of affection between young men and women. But as soon as either becomes a positive physical presence to the other, immediately there is repulsion.

And marriages based on the thrill of physical repulsion, as so many are today, even when coupled with mental 'adoring' or real

419

wistful, bodiless affection, are in the long run – not so very long, either – catastrophic. There you have it, the great 'spirituality', the great 'betterment' or refinement; the great fastidiousness; the great 'niceness' of feeling; when a girl must be a flat, thin, bodiless stick, and a boy a correct mannequin, each of them abstracted towards real caricature. What does it all amount to? What is its motive force?

What it amounts to, really, is physical repulsion. The great spirituality of our age means that we are all physically repulsive to one another. The great advance in refinement of feeling and squeamish fastidiousness means that we hate the *physical* existence of anybody and everybody, even ourselves. The amazing move into abstraction on the part of the whole of humanity – the film, the radio, the gramophone – means that we loathe the physical element in our amusements, we don't *want* the physical contact, we want to get away from it. We don't *want* to look at flesh and blood people – we want to watch their shadows on a screen. We don't *want* to hear their actual voices: only transmitted through a machine. We must get away from the physical.

The vast mass of the lower classes – and this is most extraordinary – are even more grossly abstracted, if we may use the term, than the educated classes. The uglier sort of working man today truly has no body and no real feelings at all. He eats the most wretched food, because taste has left him, he only *sees* his meal, he never *really* eats it. He drinks his beer by idea, he no longer tastes it at all. This must be so, or the food and beer could not be as bad as they are. And as for his relation to his women – his poor women – they are pegs to hang clothes on, and there's an end of them. It is a horrible state of feelingless depravity, atrophy of the senses.

But under it all, as ever, as everywhere, vibrates the one great impulse of our civilization, physical recoil from every other being and from every form of physical existence. Recoil, recoil, recoil. Revulsion, revulsion, revulsion. Repulsion, repulsion, repulsion. This is the rhythm that underlies our social activity, everywhere, with regard to physical existence.

Now we are all basically and permanently physical. So is the earth, so even is the air. What then is going to be the result of all this recoil and repulsion, which our civilization has deliberately fostered?

The result is really only one and the same: some form of collective social madness. Russia, being a very physical country, was in a frantic state of physical recoil and 'spirituality' twenty years ago. We can look on the revolution, really, as nothing but a great outburst of anti-physical insanity; we can look on Soviet Russia as nothing but a logical state of society established in anti-physical insanity. – Physical and material are, of course, not the same; in fact, they are subtly opposite. The machine is absolutely material, and absolutely anti-physical – as even our fingers know. And the Soviet is established on the image of the machine, 'pure' materialism. The Soviet hates the real physical body far more deeply than it hates Capital. It mixes it up with the bourgeois. But it sees very little danger in it, since all western civilization is now mechanized, materialized and ready for an outburst of insanity which shall throw us all into some purely machine-driven unity of lunatics.

What about it, then? What about it, men and women? The only thing to do is to get your bodies back, men and women. A great part of society is irreparably lost: abstracted into non-physical, mechanical entities whose motive power is still recoil, revulsion, repulsion, hate, and, ultimately, blind destruction. The driving force *underneath* our society remains the same: recoil, revulsion, hate. And let this force once run out of hand, and we know what to expect. It is not only in the working class. The well-to-do classes are just as full of the driving force of recoil, revulsion, which ultimately becomes hate. The force is universal in our spiritual civilization. Let it once run out of hand, and then –

It only remains for some men and women, individuals, to try to get back their bodies and preserve the other flow of warmth, affection and physical unison. There is nothing else to do.

# Matriarchy

*Evening News*, 5 October 1928; *Assorted Articles*, 1930

Whether they are aware of it or not, the men of today are a little afraid of the women of today; and especially the younger men. They not only see themselves in the minority, overwhelmed by numbers, but they feel themselves swamped by the strange un-loosed energy of the silk-legged hordes. Women, women everywhere, and all of them on the warpath! The poor young male keeps up a jaunty front, but his masculine soul quakes. Women, women, everywhere, silk-legged hosts that are up and doing, and no gainsaying them. They settle like silky locusts on all the jobs, they occupy the offices and the playing-fields like immensely active ants, they buzz round the coloured lights of pleasure in amazing bare-armed swarms, and the rather dazed young male is, naturally, a bit scared. Tommy may not be scared of his own in-dividual Elsie, but when he sees her with her scores of female 'pals', let him bluff as he may, he is frightened.

Being frightened, he begins to announce: Man must be master again! – The *must* is all very well. Tommy may be master of his own little Elsie in the stronghold of his own little home. But when she sets off in the morning to her job, and joins the hosts of her petticoatless, silk-legged 'pals', who is going to master her? Not Tommy!

It's not a question of petticoat rule. Petticoats no longer exist.

The unsheathed silky legs of the modern female are petticoatless, and the modern young woman is not going to spend her life managing some little husband. She is not interested. And as soon as a problem ceases to contain interest, it ceases to be a problem. So that petticoat rule, which was such a problem for our fathers and grandfathers, is for us nothing. Elsie is not interested.

No, the modern young man is not afraid of being petticoat-ruled. His fear lies deeper. He is afraid of being swamped, turned into a mere accessory of bare-limbed, swooping woman; swamped by her numbers, swamped by her devouring energy. He talks rather bitterly about rule of women, monstrous regiment of women, and about matriarchy, and, rather feebly, about man being master again. He knows perfectly well that he will never be master again. John Knox could live to see the head of his monstrous regiment of women, and the head of Mary of Scotland, just chopped off. But you can't chop off the head of the modern woman. As leave try to chop the head off a swarm of locusts. Woman has emerged, and you can't put her back again. And she's not going back of her own accord, not if she knows it.

So we are in for the monstrous rule of women, and a matriarchy. A matriarchy! This seems the last word of horror to the shuddering male. What it means, exactly, is not defined. But it rings with the hollow sound of man's subordination to woman. Woman cracks the whip, and the poor trained dog of a man jumps through the hoop. Nightmare!

Matriarchy, according to the dictionary, means mother-rule. The mother the head of the family. The children inherit the mother's name. The property is bequeathed from mother to daughter, with a small allowance for the sons. The wife, no doubt, swears to love and cherish her husband, and the husband swears to honour and obey his spouse.– It doesn't sound so very different from what already is: except that when Tommy Smith marries Elsie Jones, he becomes Mr Jones; quite right, too, nine cases out of ten.

And this is the matriarchy we are drifting into. No good trying to stem the tide. Woman is in flood.

But in this matter of matriarchy, let us not be abstract. Men and women will always be men and women. There is nothing new under the sun, not even matriarchy. Matriarchies have been and will be. And what about them, in living actuality? – It is said that in the ancient dawn of history there was nothing but matriarchy: children took the mother's name, belonged to the mother's clan, and the man was nameless. There is supposed to be a matriarchy today among the Berbers of the Sahara, and in Southern India, and one or two other rather dim places.

Yet, if you look at the photographs of Berbers, the men look most jaunty and cocky, with their spears, and the terrible matriarchal women look as if they did most of the work. It seems to have been so in the remote past. Under the matriarchal system that preceded the patriarchal system of Father Abraham, the men seem to have been lively sports, hunting and dancing and fighting, while the women did the drudgery and minded the brats.

Courage! Perhaps a matriarchy isn't so bad, after all. A woman deserves to possess her own children and have them called by her name. As for the household furniture and the bit of money in the bank, it seems naturally hers.

Far from being a thing to dread, matriarchy is a solution to our weary social problem. Take the Pueblo Indians of the Arizona desert. They still have a sort of matriarchy. The man marries into the woman's clan, and passes into *her* family house. His corn supply goes to *her* tribe. His children are the children of *her* tribe, and take *her* name, so to speak. Everything that comes into the house is hers, *her* property. The man has no claim on the house, which belongs to her clan, nor to anything within the house. The Indian woman's home is *her* castle.

So! And what about the man, in this dread matriarchy? Is he the slave of the woman? By no means. Marriage, with him, is a secondary consideration, a minor event. His first duty is not to his wife and children – they belong to the clan. His first duty is to the tribe. The man is first and foremost an active, religious member of the tribe. Secondarily, he is son or husband or father.

The real life of the man is not spent in his own little home, daddy in the bosom of the family, wheeling the perambulator on Sundays. His life is passed mainly in the khiva, the great underground religious meeting-house where only the males assemble, where the sacred practices of the tribe are carried on; then also he is away hunting, or performing the sacred rites on the mountains, or he works in the fields. But he spends only certain months of the year in his wife's house, sleeping there. The rest he spends chiefly in the great khiva, where he sleeps and lives, along with the men, under the tuition of the old men of the tribe.

The Indian is profoundly religious. To him, life itself is religion: whether planting corn or reaping it, scalping an enemy or begetting a child; even washing his long black hair is a religious act. And he believes that only by the whole united effort of the tribe, day in, day out, year in, year out, in sheer religious attention and practice, can the tribe be kept vitally alive. Of course, the religion is pagan, savage, and to our idea unmoral. But religion it is, and it is his charge.

Then the children. When the boys reach the age of twelve or thirteen, they are taken from the mother and given into the charge of the old men. They live now in the khiva, or they are taken to the sacred camps on the mountains, to be initated into manhood. Now their home is the khiva, the great sacred meeting-house underground. They may go and eat in their mother's house, but they live and sleep with the men.

And this is ancient matriarchy. And this is the instinctive form that society takes, even now. It seems to be a social instinct to send boys away to school at the age of thirteen, to be initiated into manhood. It is a social instinct in a man to leave his wife and children safe in the home, while he goes out and foregathers with other men, to fulfil his deeper social necessities. There is the club and the public-house, poor substitutes for the sacred khiva, no doubt, and yet absolutely necessary to most men. It is in the clubs and public-houses that men have really educated one another, by immediate contact, discussed politics and ideas, and made history. It is in the clubs and public-houses that men have tried to satisfy their deeper social instincts and intuitions. To satisfy his deeper social instincts and intuitions, a man must be able to get away from his family, and from women altogether, and foregather in the communion of men.

Of late years, however, the family has got hold of a man, and begun to destroy him. When a man is clutched by his family, his deeper social instincts and intuitions are all thwarted, he becomes a negative thing. Then the woman, perforce, becomes positive, and breaks loose into the world.

Let us drift back to matriarchy. Let the woman take the children and give them her name – it's a wise child that knows its own father. Let the woman take the property – what has a man to do with inheriting or bequeathing a grandfather's clock! Let the women form themselves into a great clan, for the preservation of themselves and their children. It is nothing but just.

And so, let men get free again, free from the tight littleness of family and family possessions. Give woman her full independence, and with it, the full responsibility of her independence. That is the only way to satisfy women once more: give them their full independence and full self-responsibility as mothers and heads of the family. When the children take the mother's name, the mother will look after the name all right.

And give the men a new foregathering ground, where they can meet and satisfy their deep social needs, profound social cravings which can only be satisfied apart from women. It is absolutely necessary to find some way of satisfying these ultimate social cravings in men, which are deep as religion in a man. It is necessary for the life of society, to keep us organically vital, to save us from the mess of industrial chaos and industrial revolt.

# 6. Consciousness, Being, Selfhood

## *From* Introduction to *Chariot of the Sun* by Harry Crosby

Written 1928, published as 'Chaos in Poetry' in
*Exchanges*, December 1929. The text used here was
first published in *Phoenix*, 1936

Poetry, they say, is a matter of words. And this is just as much true as that pictures are a matter of paint, and frescoes a matter of water and colour-wash. It is such a long way from being the whole truth that it is slightly silly if uttered sententiously.

Poetry is a matter of words. Poetry is a stringing together of words into a ripple and jingle and a run of colours. Poetry is an interplay of images. Poetry is the iridescent suggestion of an idea. Poetry is all these things, and still it is something else. Given all these ingredients, you have something very like poetry, something for which we might borrow the old romantic name of poesy. And poesy, like bric-à-brac, will for ever be in fashion. But poetry is still another thing.

The essential quality of poetry is that it makes a new effort of attention, and 'discovers' a new world within the known world. Man, and the animals, and the flowers, all live within a strange and for ever surging chaos. The chaos which we have got used to we call a cosmos. The unspeakable inner chaos of which we are composed we call consciousness, and mind, and even civilization. But it is, ultimately, chaos, lit up by visions, or not lit up by visions. Just as the rainbow may or may not light up the storm. And, like the rainbow, the vision perisheth.

But man cannot live in chaos. The animals can. To the animal

429

all is chaos, only there are a few recurring motions and aspects within the surge. And the animal is content. But man is not. Man must wrap himself in a vision, make a house of apparent form and stability, fixity. In his terror of chaos he begins by putting up an umbrella between himself and the everlasting whirl. Then he paints the under-side of his umbrella like a firmament. Then he parades around, lives and dies under his umbrella. Bequeathed to his descendants, the umbrella becomes a dome, a vault, and men at last begin to feel that something is wrong.

Man fixes some wonderful erection of his own between himself and the wild chaos, and gradually goes bleached and stifled under his parasol. Then comes a poet, enemy of convention, and makes a slit in the umbrella; and lo! the glimpse of chaos is a vision, a window to the sun. But after a while, getting used to the vision, and not liking the genuine draught from chaos, commonplace man daubs a simulacrum of the window that opens on to chaos, and patches the umbrella with the painted patch of the simulacrum. That is, he has got used to the vision; it is part of his house-decoration. So that the umbrella at last looks like a glowing open firmament, of many aspects. But alas! it is all simulacrum, in innumerable patches. Homer and Keats, annotated and with glossary.

This is the history of poetry in our era. Someone sees Titans in the wild air of chaos, and the Titan becomes a wall between succeeding generations and the chaos they should have inherited. The wild sky moved and sang. Even that became a great umbrella between mankind and the sky of fresh air; then it became a painted vault, a fresco on a vaulted roof, under which men bleach and go dissatisfied. Till another poet makes a slit on to the open and windy chaos.

But at last our roof deceives us no more. It is painted plaster, and all the skill of all the human ages won't take us in. Dante or Leonardo, Beethoven or Whitman: lo! it is painted on the plaster of our vault. Like St Francis preaching to the birds in Assisi. Wonderfully like air and birdy space and chaos of many things – partly because the fresco is faded. But even so, we are glad to get out of that church, and into the natural chaos.

From *Introduction to* Chariot of the Sun

This is the momentous crisis for mankind, when we have to get back to chaos. So long as the umbrella serves, and poets make slits in it, and the mass of people can be gradually educated up to the vision in the slit: which means they patch it over with a patch that looks just like the vision in the slit: so long as this process can continue, and mankind can be educated up, and thus built in, so long will a civilization continue more or less happily, completing its own painted prison. It is called completing the consciousness.

The joy men had when Wordsworth, for example, made a slit and saw a primrose! Till then, men had only seen a primrose dimly, in the shadow of the umbrella. They saw it through Wordsworth in the full gleam of chaos. Since then, gradually, we have come to see primavera nothing but primrose. Which means, we have patched over the slit.

And the greater joy when Shakespeare made a big rent and saw emotional, wistful man outside in the chaos, beyond the conventional idea and painted umbrella of moral images and iron-bound paladins, which had been put up in the Middle Ages. But now, alas, the roof of our vault is simply painted dense with Hamlets and Macbeths, the side walls too, and the order is fixed and complete. Man can't be any different from his image. Chaos is all shut out.

The umbrella has got so big, the patches and plaster are so tight and hard, it can be slit no more. If it were slit, the rent would no more be a vision, it would only be an outrage. We should dab it over at once, to match the rest.

So the umbrella is absolute. And so the yearning for chaos becomes a nostalgia. And this will go on till some terrific wind blows the umbrella to ribbons, and much of mankind to oblivion. The rest will shiver in the midst of chaos. For chaos is always there, and always will be, no matter how we put up umbrellas of visions.

What about the poets, then, at this juncture? They reveal the inward desire of mankind. What do they reveal? They show the desire for chaos, and the fear of chaos. The desire for chaos is the breath of their poetry. The fear of chaos is in their parade of

431

forms and technique. Poetry is made of words, they say. So they blow bubbles of sound and image, which soon burst with the breath of longing for chaos, which fills them. But the poetasters can make pretty shiny bubbles for the Christmas-tree, which never burst, because there is no breath of poetry in them, but they remain till we drop them.

# *From* The Crown

## IV

### *Within the Sepulchre*

The fourth of six essays written in 1915 for *The Signature*, 'a tiny monthly paper' launched by Lawrence and Middleton Murry by way of 'doing something' about the war. Only three issues, with three of Lawrence's essays, appeared; *The Crown* was printed in full in *Reflections on the Death of a Porcupine*, 1925

Within the womb of the established past, the light has entered the darkness, the future is conceived. It is conceived, the beginning of the end has taken place. Light is within the grip of darkness, darkness within the embrace of light, the Beginning and the End are closed upon one another.

They come nearer and nearer, till the oneness is full grown within the womb of the past, within the belly of Time, it must move out, must be brought forth, into timelessness.

But something withholds it. The pregnancy is accomplished, the hour of labour has come. Yet the labour does not begin. The loins of the past are withered, the young unborn is shut in.

All the time, within the womb, light has been travelling to the dark, the interfusion of the two into a oneness has continued. Now that it is fulfilled, it meets with some arrest. It is the dry walls of the womb which cannot relax.

There is a struggle. Then the darkness, having overcome the light, reaching the dead null wall of the womb, reacts into self-consciousness, and recoils upon itself. At the same time the light has surpassed its limit, become conscious, and starts in reflex to recoil upon itself. Thus the false I comes into being: the I which thinks itself supreme and infinite, and which is, in fact, a sick foetus shut up in the walls of an unrelaxed womb.

Here, at this moment when the birth pangs should begin, when the great opposition between the old and the young should take place, when the young should beat back the old body that surrounds it, and the old womb and loins should expel the young body, there is a deadlock. The two cannot fight apart. The walls of the old body are inflexible and insensible, the unborn does not know that there can be any travelling forth. It conceives itself as the whole universe, surrounded by dark nullity. It does not know that it is in prison. It believes itself to have filled up the whole of the universe, right to the extremes where is nothing but blank nullity.

It is tremendously conceited. It can only react upon itself. And the reaction can only take the form of self-consciousness. For the self is everything, universal, the surrounding womb is just the outer darkness in which that which *is*, exists. Therefore there remains either to die, to pass into the outer darkness, or to enter into self-knowledge.

So the unborn recoils upon itself, dark upon dark, light upon light. This is the horror of corruption begun already within the unborn, already dissolution and corruption set in before birth. And this is the triumph of the ego.

Mortality has usurped the Crown. The unborn, reacting upon the null walls of the womb, assumes that it has reached the limit of all space and all being. It concludes that its self is fulfilled, that all consummation is achieved. It takes for certain that itself has filled the whole of space and the whole of time.

And this is the glory of the ego.

There is no more fight to be fought, there is no more to be sought and embraced. All is fought and overcome, all is embraced and contained. It is all concluded, there is nothing remaining but the outer nothingness, the only activity is the reaction against the outer nothingness, into the achieved being of the self, all else is fulfilled and concluded. To die is merely to assume nothingness. The limit of all life is reached.

And this is the apotheosis of the ego.

So there is the great turning round upon the self, dark upon dark, light upon light, the flux of separation, corruption within the unborn. The tides which are set towards each other swirl back as from a promontory which intervenes. There has been no consummation. There can be no consummation. The only thing is to return, to go back – that which came from the Beginning to go back to the Beginning, that which came from the End to return to the End. In the return lies the fulfilment.

And this is the unconscious undoing of the ego.

That which we *are* is absolute. There is no adding to it, no superseding this accomplished self. It is final and universal. All that remains is thoroughly to explore it.

That is, to analyse it. Analysis presupposes a corpse.

It is at this crisis in the human history that tragic art appears again, that art becomes the only absolute, the only watchword among the people. This achieved self, which we are, is absolute and universal. There is nothing beyond. All that remains is to state this self, and the reactions upon this self, perfectly. And the perfect statement presumes to be art. It is aestheticism.

At this crisis there is a great cry of loneliness. Every man conceives himself as a complete unit surrounded by nullity. And he cannot bear it. Yet his pride is in this also. The greatest conceit of all is the cry of loneliness.

At this crisis, emotion turns into sentiment, and sentimentalism takes the place of feeling. The ego has no feeling, it has only sentiments. And the myriad egos sway in tides of sentimentalism.

But the *tacit* utterance of every man, when this state is reached, is '*Après moi le Déluge.*' And when the deluge begins to set in, there is profound secret satisfaction on every hand. For the ego in a man secretly hates every other ego. In a democracy where every little ego is crowned with the false crown of its own supremacy, every other ego is a false usurper, and nothing more. We can only tolerate those whose crowns are not yet manufactured, because they can't *afford* it.

And again, the supreme little ego in man hates an unconquered universe. We shall never rest till we have heaped tin cans on the North Pole and the South Pole, and put up barb-wire fences on the moon. Barb-wire fences are our sign of conquest. We have wreathed the world with them. The back of creation is broken.

We have killed the mysteries and devoured the secrets. It all lies now within our skin, within the ego of humanity.

So circumscribed within the outer nullity, we give ourselves up to the flux of death, to analysis, to introspection, to mechanical war and destruction, to humanitarian absorption in the body politic, the poor, the birth-rate, the mortality of infants, like a man absorbed in his own flesh and members, looking for ever at himself. It is the continued activity of disintegration – disintegration, separating, setting apart, investigation, research, the resolution back to the original void.

All this goes on within the glassy, insentient, insensible envelope of nullity. And within this envelope, like the glassy insects within their rind, we imagine we fill the whole cosmos, that we contain within ourselves the whole of time, which shall tick forth from us as from a clock, now everlastingly.

We are capable of nothing but reduction within the envelope. Our every activity is the activity of disintegration, of corruption, of dissolution, whether it be our scientific research, our social activity – (the social activity is largely concerned with reducing all the parts contained within the envelope to an equality, so that there shall be no unequal pressure, tending to rupture the envelope, which is divine) – our art, or our anti-social activity, sensuality, sensationalism, crime, war. Everything alike contributes to the flux of death, to corruption, and liberates the static data of the consciousness.

Whatever single act is performed by any man now, in this condition, it is an act of reduction, disintegration. The scientist in his laboratory, the artist in his study, the statesman, the artisan, the sensualist obtaining keen gratification, every one of these is reducing down that which is himself to its simpler elements, reducing the compound back to its parts. It is the pure process of corruption in all of us. The activity of death is the only activity. It is like the decay of our flesh, and every new step in decay liberates a sensation, keen, momentarily gratifying, or a conscious knowledge of the parts that made a whole; knowledge equally gratifying.

It is like Dmitri Karamazov, who seeks and experiences sensation after sensation, reduction after reduction, till finally he is stripped utterly naked before the police, and the quick of him perishes. There *is* no more any physical or integral Dmitri Karamazov. That which is in the hospital, afterwards, is a conglomeration of qualities, strictly an idiot, a nullity.

And Dostoyevsky has shown us perfectly the utter subjection of all human life to the flux of corruption. That is his theme, the theme of reduction through sensation after sensation, consciousness after consciousness, until nullity is reached, all complexity is broken down, an individual becomes an amorphous heap of elements, qualities.

There are the two types, the dark Dmitri Karamazov, or Rogozhin; and the Myshkin on the other hand. Dmitri Karamazov and Rogozhin will each of them plunge the flesh within the reducing agent, the woman, obtain the reduction within the flesh, add to the sensual experience, and progress towards utter dark disintegration, to nullity. Myshkin on the other hand will react upon the achieved consciousness or personality or ego of every one he meets, disintegrate this consciousness, this ego, and his own as well, obtaining the knowledge of the factors that made up the complexity of the consciousness, the ego, in the woman and in himself, reduce further and further back, till himself is a babbling idiot, a vessel full of disintegrated parts, and the woman is reduced to a nullity.

This is real death. The actual physical fact of death is part of the life-stream. It is an incidental point when the flux of light and dark has flowed sufficiently apart for the conjunction, which we call life, to disappear.

We live with the pure flux of death, it is part of us all the time. But our blossoming is transcendent, beyond death and life.

Only when we fall into egoism do we lose all chance of blossoming, and then the flux of corruption is the breath of our existence. From top to bottom, in the whole nation, we are engaged, fundamentally engaged in the process of reduction and dissolution. Our reward is sensational gratification in the flesh, or sensational gratification within the mind, the utter gratification we experience when we can pull apart the whole into its factors. This is the reward in scientific and introspective knowledge, this is the reward in the pleasure of cheap sensuality.

In each case, the experience remains as it were absolute. It is the statement of what is, or what was. And a statement of what *is*, is the absolute footstep in the progress backward towards the starting place, it is the *undoing* of a complete unit into the factors which previously went to making its oneness. It is the reduction of the iris back into its component waves.

There was the bliss when the iris came into being. There is now the bliss when the iris passes out of being, and the whole is torn apart. The secret of the whole is never captured. Certain data are captured. The secret escapes down the sensual, or the sensational, or intellectual, thrill of pleasure.

So there goes on reduction after reduction within the shell. And we, who find our utmost gratification in this process of reduction, this flux of corruption, this retrogression of death, we will preserve with might and main the glassy envelope, the insect rind, the tight-shut shell of the cabbage, the withered, null walls of the womb. For by virtue of this null envelope alone do we proceed uninterrupted in this process of gratifying reduction.

And this is utter evil, this secret, silent worship of the null envelope that preserves us intact for our gratification with the flux of corruption.

Intact within the null envelope, which we have come to worship as the preserver of this our life-activity of reduction, we react back upon what we are. We do not seek any more the consummation of union. We seek the consummation of reduction.

When a man seeks a woman in love, or in positive desire, he seeks a union, he seeks a consummation of himself with that which is not himself, light with dark, dark with light.

But within the glassy, null envelope of the enclosure, no union is sought, no union is possible; after a certain point, only reduction. Ego reacts upon ego only in friction. There are small egos, many small people, who have not reached the limit of the confines which we worship. They may still have small consummation in union. But all those who are strong and have travelled far have met and reacted from the nullity.

And then, when a man seeks a woman, he seeks not a consummation in union, but a frictional reduction. He seeks to plunge his compound flesh into the cold acid that will reduce him, in supreme sensual experience, down to his parts. This is Rogozhin seeking Nastasia Filippovna, Dmitri his Grushenka, or D'Annunzio in *Fuoco* seeking his Foscarina. This is more or less what happens when a soldier, maddened with lust of pure destructiveness, violently rapes the woman of his captivity. It is that he may destroy another being by the very act which is called the act of creation, or procreation. In the brute soldier it is cruelty-lust: as it was in the Red Indian. But when we come to civilized man, it is not so simple. His cruelty-lust is directed almost as much against himself as against his victim. He is destroying, reducing, breaking down that of himself which is within the envelope. He is immersing himself within a keen, fierce, terrible reducing agent. This is true of the hero in Edgar Allan Poe's tales, *Ligeia*, or *The Fall of the House of Usher*. The man seeks his own sensational reduction, but he disintegrates the woman even more, in the name of love. In the name of love, what horrors men perpetrate, and are applauded!

It is only in supreme crises that man reaches the supreme pitch of annihilation. The difference, however, is only a difference in degree, not in kind. The bank-clerk performs in a mild degree what Poe performed intensely and deathlily.

These are the men in whom the development is rather low, whose souls are coarsely compounded, so that the reduction is coarse, a sort of activity of coarse hate.

But the men of finer sensibility and finer development, sensuous or conscious, they must proceed more gradually and subtly and finely in the process of reduction. It is necessary for a finely compounded nature to reduce itself more finely, to know the subtle gratification of its own reduction.

A subtle nature like Myshkin's would find no pleasure of reduction in connexion with Grushenka, scarcely any with Nastasia. He must proceed more delicately. He must give up his soul to the reduction. It is his mind, his conscious self he wants to reduce. He wants to dissolve it back. He wants to become infantile, like a child, to reduce and resolve back all the complexity of his consciousness, to the rudimentary condition of childhood. That is his ideal.

So he seeks mental contacts, mental reactions. It is in his mental or conscious contacts that he seeks to obtain the gratification of self-reduction. He reaches his crisis in his monologue of self-analysis, self-dissolution, in the drawing-room scene where he falls in a fit.

And of course, all this reducing activity is draped in alluring sentimentalism. The most evil things in the world, today, are to be found under the chiffon folds of sentimentalism. Sentimentality is the garment of our vice. It covers viciousness as inevitably as greenness covers a bog.

With all our talk of advance, progress, we are all the time working backwards. Our heroines become younger and younger. In the movies, the heroine is becoming more and more childish, and touched with infantile idiocy. We cannot bear honest maturity. We want to reduce ourselves back, back to the *corruptive* state of childishness.

Now it is all very well for a child to be a child. But for a grown person to be slimily, pornographically reaching out for child-gratifications, is disgusting. The same with the prevalent love of boys. It is the desire to be reduced back, reduced back, in our accomplished ego: always within the unshattered rind of our completeness and complacency, to go backwards, in sentimentalized disintegration, to the states of childhood.

And no matter *what* happens to us, now, we sentimentalize it and use it as a means of sensational reduction. Even the great war does not alter our civilization one iota, in its total nature. The form, the whole form, remains intact. Only inside the complete envelope we writhe with sensational experiences of death, hurt, horror, reduction.

The goodness of anything depends on the direction in which it is moving. Childhood, like a bud, striving and growing and struggling towards blossoming full maturity, is surely beautiful. But childhood as a *goal*, for which grown people aim: childishness futile and sentimental, for which men and women lust, and

440

which always retreats when grasped, like the *ignis fatuus* of a poisonous marsh of corruption: this is disgusting.

While we live, we are balanced between the flux of life and the flux of death. All the while our bodies are being composed and decomposed. But while every man fully lives, all the time the two streams keep fusing into the third reality, of real creation. Every new gesture, every fresh smile of a child is a new emergence into creative being: a glimpse of the Holy Ghost.

But when grown people start grimacing with childishness, or lusting after child-gratifications, it is corruption pure and simple.

And the still clear look on an old face, and the stillness of old, withered hands, which have gathered the long repose of autumn, this is the purity of the two streams consummated, and the bloom, like autumn crocuses, of age.

But the painted, silly child-face that old women make nowadays: or the harpy's face that many have, lusting for the sensations of youth: the hard, voracious, selfish faces of old men, seeking their own ends, devouring the shoots of young life: this is vile.

While we live, we are balanced between the flux of life and the flux of death. But the real clue is the Holy Ghost, that moves us on into the state of blossoming. And each year the blossoming is different: from the delicate blue speedwells of childhood to the equally delicate, frail farewell flowers of old age: through all the poppies and sunflowers: year after year of difference.

While we live, we change, and our flowering is a constant change.

But once we fall into the state of egoism, we cannot change. The ego, the self-conscious ego remains fixed, a final envelope around us. And we are then safe inside the mundane egg of our own self-consciousness and self-esteem.

Safe we are! Safe as houses! Shut up like unborn chickens that cannot break the shell of the egg. That's how safe we are! And as we can't be born, we can only rot. That's how safe we are!

Safe within the everlasting walls of the egg-shell we have not the courage, nor the energy, to crack, we fall, like the shut-up chicken, into a pure flux of corruption, and the worms are our angels.

And mankind falls into the state of innumerable little worms bred within the unbroken shell: all clamouring for food, food, food, all feeding on the dead body of creation, all crying peace! peace! universal peace! brotherhood of man! Everything must be 'universal', to the conquering worm. It is only *life* which is different.

# Reflections on the Death of a Porcupine

Written 1924 or 1925, published in *Reflections on the Death of a Porcupine*, 1925

There are many bare places on the little pine trees, towards the top, where the porcupines have gnawed the bark away and left the white flesh showing. And some trees are dying from the top.

Everyone says porcupines should be killed; the Indians, Mexicans, Americans all say the same.

At full moon a month ago, when I went down the long clearing in the brilliant moonlight, through the poor dry herbage a big porcupine began to waddle away from me, towards the trees and the darkness. The animal had raised all its hairs and bristles, so that by the light of the moon it seemed to have a tall, swaying, moonlit aureole arching its back as it went. That seemed curiously fearsome, as if the animal were emitting itself demon-like on the air.

It waddled very slowly, with its white spiky spoon-tail steering flat, behind the round bear-like mound of its back. It had a lumbering, beetle's, squalid motion, unpleasant. I followed it into the darkness of the timber, and there, squat like a great tick, it began scrapily to creep up a pine-trunk. It was very like a great aureoled tick, a bug, struggling up.

I stood near and watched, disliking the presence of the creature. It is a duty to kill the things. But the dislike of killing him was greater than the dislike of him. So I watched him climb.

And he watched me. When he had got nearly the height of a man, all his long hairs swaying with a bristling gleam like an aureole, he hesitated, and slithered down. Evidently he had decided, either that I was harmless, or else that it was risky to go up any further, when I could knock him off so easily with a pole. So he slithered podgily down again, and waddled away with the same bestial, stupid motion of that white-spiky repulsive spoon-tail. He was as big as a middle-sized pig: or more like a bear.

I let him go. He was repugnant. He made a certain squalor in the moonlight of the Rocky Mountains. As all savagery has a touch of squalor, that makes one a little sick at the stomach. And anyhow, it seemed almost more squalid to pick up a pine-bough and push him over, hit him and kill him.

A few days later, on a hot, motionless morning when the pine-trees put out their bristles in stealthy, hard assertion; and I was not in a good temper, because Black-eyed Susan, the cow, had disappeared into the timber, and I had had to ride hunting her, so it was nearly nine o'clock before she was milked: Madame came in suddenly out of the sunlight, saying: 'I got such a shock! There are two strange dogs, and one of them has got the most awful beard, all round his nose.'

She was frightened, like a child, at something unnatural.

'Beard! Porcupine quills, probably! He's been after a porcupine.'

'Ah!' she cried in relief. 'Very likely! Very likely!' – then with a change of tone; 'Poor thing, will they hurt him?'

'They will. I wonder when he came.'

'I heard dogs bark in the night.'

'Did you? Why didn't you say so? I should have known Susan was hiding –'

The ranch is lonely, there is no sound in the night, save the innumerable noises of the night, that you can't put your finger on; cosmic noises in the far deeps of the sky, and of the earth.

I went out. And in the full blaze of sunlight in the field, stood two dogs, a black-and-white, and a big, bushy, rather handsome sandy-red dog, of the collie type. And sure enough, this latter did

444

look queer and a bit horrifying, his whole muzzle set round with white spines, like some ghastly growth; like an unnatural beard.

The black-and-white dog made off as I went through the fence. But the red dog whimpered and hesitated, and moved on hot bricks. He was fat and in good condition. I thought he might belong to some shepherds herding sheep in the forest ranges, among the mountains.

He waited while I went up to him, wagging his tail and whimpering and ducking his head, and dancing. He daren't rub his nose with his paws any more: it hurt too much. I patted his head and looked at his nose, and he whimpered loudly.

He must have had thirty quills, or more, sticking out of his nose, all the way round: the white, ugly ends of the quills protruding an inch, sometimes more, sometimes less, from his already swollen, blood-puffed muzzle.

The porcupines here have quills only two or three inches long. But they are devilish; and a dog will die if he does not get them pulled out. Because they work further and further in, and will sometimes emerge through the skin away in some unexpected place.

Then the fun began. I got him in the yard: and he drank up the whole half-gallon of the chickens' sour milk. Then I started pulling out the quills. He was a big, bushy, handsome dog, but his nerve was gone, and every time I got a quill out, he gave a yelp. Some long quills were fairly easy. But the shorter ones, near his lips, were deep in, and hard to get hold of, and hard to pull out when you did get hold of them. And with every one that came out, came a little spurt of blood and another yelp and writhe.

The dog wanted the quills out: but his nerve was gone. Every time he saw my hand coming to his nose, he jerked his head away. I quieted him, and stealthily managed to jerk out another quill, with the blood all over my fingers. But with every one that came out, he grew more tiresome. I tried and tried and tried to get hold of another quill, and he jerked and jerked, and writhed and whimpered, and ran under the porch floor.

It was a curiously unpleasant, nerve-trying job. The day was blazing hot. The dog came out and I struggled with him again for an hour or more. Then we blindfolded him. But either he smelled my hand approaching his nose, or some weird instinct told him. He jerked his head, this way, that way, up, down, sideways, roundwise, as one's fingers came slowly, slowly to seize a quill.

The quills on his lips and chin were deep in, only about a quarter of an inch of white stub protruding from the swollen, blood-oozed, festering black skin. It was very difficult to jerk them out.

We let him lie for an interval, hidden in the quiet cool place under the porch floor. After half an hour, he crept out again. We got a rope round his nose, behind the bristles, and one held while the other got the stubs with the pliers. But it was too trying. If a quill came out, the dog's yelp startled every nerve. And he was frightened of the pain, it was impossible to hold his head still any longer.

After struggling for two hours, and extracting some twenty quills, I gave up. It was impossible to quiet the creature, and I had had enough. His nose on the top was clear: a punctured, puffy, blood-darkened mess; and his lips were clear. But just on his round little chin, where the few white hairs are, was still a bunch of white quills, eight or nine, deep in.

We let him go, and he dived under the porch, and there he lay invisible: save for the end of his bushy, foxy tail, which moved when we came near. Towards noon he emerged, ate up the chicken-food, and stood with that doggish look of dejection, and fear, and friendliness, and greediness, wagging his tail.

But I had had enough.

'Go home!' I said. 'Go home! Go home to your master, and let him finish for you.'

He would not go. So I led him across the blazing hot clearing, in the way I thought he should go. He followed a hundred yards, then stood motionless in the blazing sun. He was not going to leave the place.

And I! I simply did not want him.

So I picked up a stone. He dropped his tail, and swerved towards the house. I knew what he was going to do. He was going to dive under the porch, and there stick, haunting the place.

I dropped my stone, and found a good stick under the cedar tree. Already in the heat was that sting-like biting of electricity, the thunder gathering in the sheer sunshine, without a cloud, and making one's whole body feel dislocated.

I could not bear to have that dog around any more. Going quietly to him, I suddenly gave him one hard hit with the stick, crying: 'Go home!' He turned quickly, and the end of the stick caught him on his sore nose. With a fierce yelp, he went off like a wolf, downhill, like a flash, gone. And I stood in the field full of pangs of regret, at having hit him, unintentionally, on his sore nose.

But he was gone.

And then the present moon came, and again the night was clear. But in the interval there had been heavy thunder-rains, the ditch was running with bright water across the field, and the night, so fair, had not the terrific, mirror-like brilliancy, touched with terror, so startling bright, of the moon in the last days of June.

We were alone on the ranch. Madame went out into the clear night, just before retiring. The stream ran in a cord of silver across the field, in the straight line where I had taken the irrigation ditch. The pine tree in front of the house threw a black shadow. The mountain slope came down to the fence, wild and alert.

'Come!' said she excitedly. 'There is a big porcupine drinking at the ditch. I thought at first it was a bear.'

When I got out he had gone. But among the grasses and the coming wild sunflowers, under the moon, I saw his greyish halo, like a pallid living bush, moving over the field, in the distance, in the moonlit *clair-obscur*.

We got through the fence, and following, soon caught him up. There he lumbered, with his white spoon-tail spiked with bristles, steering behind almost as if he were moving backwards, and this was his head. His long, long hairs above the quills quivering with a dim grey gleam, like a bush.

And again I disliked him.

'Should one kill him?'

She hesitated. Then with a sort of disgust:

447

'Yes!'

I went back to the house, and got the little twenty-two rifle. Now never in my life had I shot at any live thing: I never wanted to. I always felt guns very repugnant: sinister, mean. With difficulty I had fired once or twice at a target: but resented doing even so much. Other people could shoot if they wanted to. Myself, individually, it was repugnant to me even to try.

But something slowly hardens in a man's soul. And I knew now it had hardened in mine. I found the gun, and with rather trembling hands, got it loaded. Then I pulled back the trigger and followed the porcupine. It was still lumbering through the grass. Coming near, I aimed.

The trigger stuck. I pressed the little catch with a safety-pin I found in my pocket, and released the trigger. Then we followed the porcupine. He was still lumbering towards the trees. I went sideways on, stood quite near to him, and fired, in the clear-dark of the moonlight.

And as usual I aimed too high. He turned, went scuttling back whence he had come.

I got another shell in place, and followed. This time I fired full into the mound of his round back, below the glistening grey halo. He seemed to stumble on to his hidden nose, and struggled a few strides, ducking his head under like a hedgehog.

'He's not dead yet! Oh, fire again!' cried Madame.

I fired, but the gun was empty.

So I ran quickly, for a cedar pole. The porcupine was lying still, with subsiding halo. He stirred faintly. So I turned him and hit him hard over the nose; or where, in the dark, his nose should have been. And it was done. He was dead.

And in the moonlight, I looked down on the first creature I had ever shot.

'Does it seem mean?' I asked aloud, doubtful.

Again Madame hesitated. Then: 'No!' she said resentfully.

And I felt she was right. Things like the porcupine, one must be able to shoot them, if they get in one's way.

One must be able to shoot. I, myself, must be able to shoot, and to kill.

For me, this is a *volta face*. I have always preferred to walk round my porcupine, rather than kill it.

Now, I know it's no good walking around. One must kill.

I buried him in the adobe hole. But some animal dug down and ate him; for two days later there lay the spines and bones spread out, with the long skeletons of the porcupine-hands.

The only nice thing about him – or her, for I believe it was a female, by the dugs on her belly – were the feet. They were like longish, alert black hands, paw-hands. That is why a porcupine's tracks in the snow look almost as if a child had gone by, leaving naked little human footprints, like a little boy.

So, he is gone: or she is gone. But there is another one, bigger and blacker-looking, among the west timber. That too is to be shot. It is part of the business of ranching: even when it's only a little half-abandoned ranch like this one.

Wherever man establishes himself, upon the earth, he has to fight for his place, against the lower orders of life. Food, the basis of existence, has to be fought for even by the most idyllic of farmers. You plant, and you protect your growing crop with a gun. Food, food, how strangely it relates man with the animal and vegetable world! How important it is! And how fierce is the fight that goes on around it.

The same when one skins a rabbit, and takes out the inside, one realizes what an enormous part of the animal, comparatively, is intestinal, what a big part of him is just for food-apparatus; for *living on* other organisms.

And when one watches the horses in the big field, their noses to the ground, bite-bite-biting at the grass, and stepping absorbedly on, and bite-bite-biting without ever lifting their noses, cropping off the grass, the young shoots of alfalfa, the dandelions, with a blind, relentless, unwearied persistence, one's whole life pauses. One suddenly realizes again how all creatures devour, and *must* devour the lower forms of life.

So Susan, swinging across the field, snatches off the tops of the little wild sunflowers as if she were mowing. And down they go, down her black throat. And when she stands in her cowy oblivion chewing her cud, with her lower jaw swinging peacefully, and I

449

am milking her, suddenly the camomiley smell of her breath, as she glances round with glaring, smoke-blue eyes, makes me realize it is the sunflowers that are her ball of cud. Sunflowers! And they will go to making her glistening black hide, and the thick cream on her milk.

And the chickens, when they see a great black beetle, that the Mexicans call a *toro*, floating past, they are after it in a rush. And if it settles, instantly the brown hen stabs it with her beak. It is a great beetle two or three inches long: but in a second it is in the crop of the chicken. Gone!

And Timsy, the cat, as she spies on the chipmunks, crouches in another sort of oblivion, soft, and still. The chipmunks come to drink the milk from the chickens' bowl. Two of them met at the bowl. They were little squirrely things with stripes down their backs. They sat up in front of one another, lifting their inquisitive little noses and humping their backs. Then each put its two little hands on the other's shoulders, they reared up, gazing into each other's faces; and finally they put their two little noses together, in a sort of kiss.

But Miss Timsy can't stand this. In a soft, white-and-yellow leap she is after them. They skip, with the darting jerks of chipmunks, to the wood-heap, and with one soft, high-leaping sideways bound Timsy goes through the air. Her snow-flake of a paw comes down on one of the chipmunks. She looks at it for a second. It squirms. Swiftly and triumphantly she puts her two flowery little white paws on it, legs straight out in front of her, back arched, gazing concentratedly yet whimsically. Chipmunk does not stir. She takes it softly in her mouth, where it dangles softly, like a lady's tippet. And with a proud, prancing motion the Timsy sets off towards the house, her white little feet hardly touching the ground.

But she gets shooed away. We refuse to loan her the sitting-room any more, for her gladiatorial displays. If the chippy must be 'butchered to make a Timsy holiday', it shall be outside. Disappointed, but still high-stepping, the Timsy sets off towards the clay oven by the shed.

There she lays the chippy gently down, and soft as a little white cloud lays one small paw on its striped back. Chippy does not move. Soft as thistle-down she raises her paw a tiny, tiny bit, to release him.

And all of a sudden, with an elastic jerk, he darts from under the white release of her paw. And instantly, she is up in the air and down she comes on him, with the forward thrusting bolts of her white paws. Both creatures are motionless.

Then she takes him softly in her mouth again, and looks round, to see if she can slip into the house. She cannot. So she trots towards the wood-pile.

It is a game, and it is pretty. Chippy escapes into the wood-pile, and she softly, softly reconnoitres among the faggots.

Of all the animals, there is no denying it, the Timsy is the most pretty, the most fine. It is not her mere *corpus* that is beautiful; it is her bloom of aliveness. Her 'infinite variety'; the soft, snow-flakey lightness of her, and at the same time her lean, heavy ferocity. I had never realized the latter, till I was lying in bed one day moving my toe, unconsciously, under the bedclothes. Suddenly a terrific blow struck my foot. The Timsy had sprung out of no-where, with a hurling, steely force, thud upon the bedclothes where the toe was moving. It was as if someone had aimed a sudden blow, vindictive and unerring.

'Timsy!'

She looked at me with the vacant, feline glare of her hunting eyes. It is not even ferocity. It is the dilation of the strange, vacant arrogance of power. The power is in her.

And so it is. Life moves in circles of power and of vividness, and each circle of life only maintains its orbit upon the subjec-tion of some lower circle. If the lower cycles of life are not *mastered*, there can be no higher cycle.

In nature, one creature devours another, and this is an essen-tial part of all existence and of all being. It is not something to lament over, nor something to try to reform. The Buddhist who refuses to take life is really ridiculous, since if he eats only two grains of rice per day, it is two grains of life. We did not make creation, *we* are not the authors of the universe. And if we see that the whole of creation is established upon the fact that one life

451

devours another life, one cycle of existence can only come into existence through the subjugating of another cycle of existence, then what is the good of trying to pretend that it is not so? The only thing to do is to realize what is higher, and what is lower, in the cycles of existence.

It is nonsense to declare that there *is* no higher and lower. We know full well that the dandelion belongs to a higher cycle of existence than the hartstongue fern, that the ant's is a higher form of existence than the dandelion's, that the thrush is higher than the ant, that Timsy the cat is higher than the thrush, and that I, a man, am higher than Timsy.

What do we mean by higher? Strictly, we mean more alive. More vividly alive. The ant is more vividly alive than the pine-tree. We know it, there is no trying to refute it. It is all very well saying that they are both alive in two different ways, and therefore are incomparable, incommensurable. This is also true.

But one truth does not displace another. Even apparently contradictory truths do not displace one another. Logic is far too coarse to make the subtle distinctions life demands.

Truly, it is futile to compare an ant with a great pine-tree, in the absolute. Yet as far as *existence* is concerned, they are not only placed in comparison to one another, they are occasionally pitted against one another. And if it comes to a contest, the little ant will devour the life of the huge tree. If it comes to a contest.

And, in the cycles of *existence*, this is the test. From the lowest form of existence to the highest, the test question is: *Can thy neighbour finally overcome thee?*

If he can, then he belongs to a higher cycle of existence.

This is the truth behind the survival of the fittest. Every cycle of existence is established upon the overcoming of the lower cycles of existence. The real question is, wherein does *fitness* lie? Fitness for what? Fit merely to survive? That which is only fit to survive will survive only to supply food or contribute in some way to the existence of a higher form of life, which is able to do more than survive, which can really *vive*, live.

Life is more vivid in the dandelion than in the green fern, or than in a palm tree.

Life is more vivid in a snake than in a butterfly.

Life is more vivid in a wren than in an alligator.

Life is more vivid in a cat than in an ostrich.

Life is more vivid in the Mexican who drives the wagon, than in the two horses in the wagon.

Life is more vivid in me, than in the Mexican who drives the wagon for me.

We are speaking in terms of *existence*: that is, in terms of species, race, or type.

The dandelion can take hold of the land, the palm tree is driven into a corner, with the fern.

The snake can devour the fiercest insect.

The fierce bird can destroy the greatest reptile.

The great cat can destroy the greatest bird.

The man can destroy the horse, or any animal.

One race of man can subjugate and rule another race.

All this in terms of *existence*. As far as existence goes, that life-species is the highest which can devour, or destroy, or subjugate every other life-species against which it is pitted in contest.

This is a law. There is no escaping this law. Anyone, or any race, trying to escape it, will fall a victim: will fall into subjugation.

But let us insist and insist again, we are talking now of existence, of species, of types, of races, of nations, not of single individuals, nor of *beings*. The dandelion in full flower, a little sun bristling with sun-rays on the green earth, is a nonpareil, a nonsuch. Foolish, foolish, foolish to compare it to anything else on earth. It is itself incomparable and unique.

But that is the fourth dimension, of *being*. It is in the fourth dimension, nowhere else.

Because, in the time-space dimension, any man may tread on the yellow sun-mirror, and it is gone. Any cow may swallow it. Any bunch of ants may annihilate it.

This brings us to the inexorable law of life.

1. Any creature that attains to its own fulness of being, its own *living* self, becomes unique, a nonpareil. It has its place in

453

the fourth dimension, the heaven of existence, and there it is perfect, it is beyond comparison.

2. At the same time, every creature exists in time and space. And in time and space it exists relatively to all other existence, and can never be absolved. Its existence impinges on other existences, and is itself impinged upon. And in the struggle for existence, if an effort on the part of any one type or species or order of life can finally destroy the other species, then the destroyer is of a more vital cycle of existence than the one destroyed. (When speaking of existence we always speak in types, species, not individuals. Species exist. But even an individual dandelion has *being*.)

3. The force which we call *vitality*, and which is the determining factor in the struggle for existence, is, however, derived also from the fourth dimension. That is to say, the ultimate source of all vitality is in that other dimension, or region, where the dandelion blooms, and which men have called heaven, and which now they call the fourth dimension: which is only a way of saying that it is not to be reckoned in terms of space and time.

4. The primary way, in our existence, to get vitality, is to absorb it from living creatures lower than ourselves. It is thus transformed into a new and higher creation. (There are many ways of absorbing: devouring food is one way, love is often another. The best way is a pure relationship, which includes the *being* on each side, and which allows the transfer to take place in a living flow, enhancing the life in both beings.)

5. No creature is fully itself till it is, like the dandelion, opened in the bloom of pure relationship to the sun, the entire living cosmos.

So we still find ourselves in the tangle of existence and being, a tangle which man has never been able to get out of, except by sacrificing the one to the other.

Sacrifice is useless.

The clue to all existence is being. But you can't have being without existence, any more than you can have the dandelion flower without the leaves and the long tap root.

Being is *not* ideal, as Plato would have it: nor spiritual. It is a transcendent form of existence, and as much material as existence is. Only the matter suddenly enters the fourth dimension.

All existence is dual, and surging towards a consummation into being. In the seed of the dandelion, as it floats with its little umbrella of hairs, sits the Holy Ghost in tiny compass. The Holy Ghost is that which holds the light and the dark, the day and the night, the wet and the sunny, united in one little clue. There it sits, in the seed of the dandelion.

The seed falls to earth. The Holy Ghost rouses, saying *'Come!'* And out of the sky come the rays of the sun, and out of earth come dampness and dark and the death-stuff. They are called in, like those bidden to a feast. The sun sits down at the hearth, inside the seed; and the dark, damp death-returner sits on the opposite side, with the host between. And the host says to them: *'Come! Be merry together!'* So the sun looks with desirous curiosity on the dark face of the earth, and the dark damp one looks with wonder on the bright face of the other, who comes from the sun. And the host says: *'Here you are at home! Lift me up, between you, that I may cease to be a Ghost. For it longs me to look out, it longs me to dance with the dancers.'*

So the sun in the seed, and the earthy one in the seed take hands, and laugh, and begin to dance. And their dancing is like a fire kindled, a bonfire with leaping flame. And the treading of their feet is like the running of little streams, down to earth. So from the dance of the sun-in-the-seed with the earthy death-returner, green little flames of leaves shoot up, and hard little trickles of roots strike down. And the host laughs, and says: *'I am being lifted up! Dance harder! Oh wrestle, you two, like wonderful wrestlers, neither of which can win.'* So sun-in-the-seed and the death-returner, who is earthy, dance faster and faster and the leaves rising greener begin to dance in a ring above-ground, fiercely overwhelming any outsider, in a whirl of swords and lions' teeth. And the earthy one wrestles, wrestles with the sun-in-the-seed, so the long roots reach down like arms of a fighter gripping the power of earth, and strangles all intruders, strangling any intruder mercilessly. Till the two fall in one strange embrace, and from the centre the long flower-stem lifts like a phallus, budded with a bud. And out of the bud the voice of the Holy Ghost is heard crying: '*I am lifted up! Lo! I am lifted up! I am here!*' So the bud opens, and there is the flower poised in the very middle of the universe, with a ring of green swords below, to guard it, and the octopus, arms deep in earth, drinking and threatening. So the Holy Ghost, being a dandelion flower, looks round, and says: '*Lo! I am yellow! I believe the sun has lent me his body! Lo! I am sappy with golden, bitter blood! I believe death out of the damp black earth has lent me his blood! I am incarnate! I like my incarnation! But this is not all. I will keep this incarnation. It is good! But oh! if I can win to another incarnation, who knows how wonderful it will be! This one will have to give place. This one can help to create the next.*'

So the Holy Ghost leaves the clue of himself behind, in the seed, and wanders forth in the comparative chaos of our universe, seeking another incarnation.

And this will go on for ever. Man, as yet, is less than half grown. Even his flower-stem has not appeared yet. He is all leaves and roots, without any clue put forth. No sign of bud anywhere.

Either he will have to start budding, or he will be forsaken of the Holy Ghost: abandoned as a failure in creation, as the ichthyosaurus was abandoned. Being abandoned means losing his vitality. The sun and the earth-dark will cease rushing together in him. Already it is ceasing. To men, the sun is becoming stale, and the earth sterile. But the sun itself will never become stale, nor the earth barren. It is only that the *clue* is missing inside men. They are like flowerless, seedless fat cabbages, nothing inside.

Vitality depends upon the clue of the Holy Ghost inside a creature, a man, a nation, a race. When the clue goes, the vitality goes. And the Holy Ghost seeks for ever a new incarnation, and subordinates the old to the new. You will know that any creature or race is still alive with the Holy Ghost, when it can subordinate the lower creatures or races, and assimilate them into a new incarnation.

No man, or creature, or race can have vivid vitality unless it be moving towards a blossoming: and the most powerful is that which moves towards the as-yet-unknown blossom.

Blossoming means the establishing of a pure, *new* relationship with all the cosmos. This is the state of heaven. And it is the state of a flower, a cobra, a jenny-wren in spring, a man when he knows himself royal and crowned with the sun, with his feet gripping the core of the earth.

This too is the fourth dimension: this state, this mysterious other reality of things in a perfected relationship. It is into this perfected relationship that every straight line curves, as if to some core, passing out of the time-space dimension.

But any man, creature, or race moving towards blossoming will have to draw immense supplies of vitality from men, or creatures below, passionate strength. And he will have to accomplish a perfected relation with all things.

There will be conquest, always. But the aim of conquest is a perfect relation of conquerors with conquered, for a new blossoming. Freedom is illusory. Sacrifice is illusory. Almightiness is illusory. Freedom, sacrifice, almightiness, these are all human sidetracks, cul-de-sacs, bunk. All that is real is the overwhelmingness of a new inspirational command, a new relationship with all things.

Heaven is always there. No achieved consummation is lost. Procreation goes on for ever, to support the achieved revelation. But the torch of revelation itself is handed on. And this is all important.

Everything living wants to procreate more living things.

But more important than this is the fact that every revelation is a torch held out, to kindle new revelations. As the dandelion holds out the sun to me, saying: *'Can you take it!'*

Every gleam of heaven that is shown – like a dandelion flower, or a green beetle – quivers with strange passion to kindle a new gleam, never yet upheld. This is not self-sacrifice: it is self-contribution: in which the highest happiness lies.

The torch of existence is handed on, in the womb of procreation.

And the torch of revelation is handed on, by every living thing, from the protococcus to a brave man or a beautiful woman, handed to whomsoever can take it. He who can take it, has power beyond all the rest.

The cycle of procreation exists purely for the keeping alight

457

of the torch of perfection, in any species: the torch being the dandelion in blossom, the tree in full leaf, the peacock in all his plumage, the cobra in all his colour, the frog at full leap, woman in all the mystery of her fathomless desirableness, man in the fulness of his power: every creature become its pure self.

One cycle of perfection urges to kindle another cycle, as yet unknown.

And with the kindling from the torch of revelation comes the inrush of vitality, and the need to consume and *consummate* the lower cycles of existence, into a new thing. This consuming and this consummating means conquest, and fearless mastery. Freedom lies in the honourable yielding towards the new flame, and the honourable mastery of that which shall be new, over that which must yield. As I must master my horses, which are in a lower cycle of existence. And they, they are relieved and *happy* to serve. If I turn them loose into the mountain ranges, to run wild till they die, the thrill of real happiness is gone out of their lives.

Every lower order seeks in some measure to serve a higher order: and rebels against being conquered.

It is always conquest, and it always will be conquest. If the conquered be an old, declining race, they will have handed on their torch to the conqueror: who will burn his fingers badly, if he is too flippant. And if the conquered be a barbaric race, they will consume the fire of the conqueror, and leave him flameless, unless he watch it. But it is always conquest, conquered and conqueror, for ever. The Kingdom of heaven is the Kingdom of conquerors, who can serve the conquest for ever, after their own conquest is made.

In heaven, in the perfected relation, is peace: in the fourth dimension. But there is getting there. And that, for ever, is the process of conquest.

When the rose blossomed, then the great Conquest was made by the Vegetable Kingdom. But even this conqueror of conquerors, the rose, has to lend himself towards the caterpillar and the butterfly of a later conquest. A conqueror, but tributary to the later conquest.

There is no such thing as equality. In the Kingdom of heaven, in the fourth dimension, each soul that achieves a perfect relationship with the cosmos, from its own centre, is perfect, and incomparable. It has no superior, it is a conqueror, and incomparable.

But every man, in the struggle of conquest towards his own consummation, must master the inferior cycles of life, and never relinquish his mastery. Also, if there be men beyond him, moving on to a newer consummation than his own, he must yield to their greater demand, and serve their greater mystery, and so be faithful to the Kingdom of heaven which is within him, which is gained by conquest and by loyal service.

Any man who achieves his own being will, like the dandelion or the butterfly, pass into that other dimension which we call the fourth, and the old people called heaven. It is the state of perfected relationship. And here a man will have his peace for ever: whether he serve or command, in the process of living.

But even this entails his faithful allegiance to the Kingdom of heaven, which must be for ever and for ever extended, as creation conquers chaos. So that my perfection will but serve a perfection which still lies ahead, unrevealed and unconceived, and beyond my own.

We have tried to build walls round the Kingdom of heaven: but it's no good. It's only the cabbage rotting inside.

Our last wall is the golden wall of money. This is a fatal wall. It cuts us off from life, from vitality, from the alive sun and the alive earth, as *nothing* can. Nothing, not even the most fanatical dogmas of an iron-bound religion, can insulate us from the inrush of life and inspiration, as money can.

We are losing vitality: losing it rapidly. Unless we seize the torch of inspiration, and drop our moneybags, the moneyless will be kindled by the flame of flames, and they will consume us like old rags.

We are losing vitality, owing to money and money-standards. The torch in the hands of the moneyless will set our house on fire, and burn us to death, like sheep in a flaming corral.

# The Novel and the Feelings

Written after 1920, published in *Phoenix*, 1936

We think we are so civilized, so highly educated and civilized. It is farcical. Because, of course, all our civilization consists in harping on one string. Or at most on two or three strings. Harp, harp, harp, twingle, twingle-twang! That's our civilization, always on one note.

The note itself is all right. It's the exclusiveness of it that is awful. Always the same note, always the same note! 'Ah, how can you run after other women when your wife is so delightful, a lovely plump partridge?' Then the husband laid his hand on his waistcoat, and a frightened look came over his face. 'Nothing but partridge?' he exclaimed.

*Toujours perdrix!* It was up to that wife to be a goose and a cow, an oyster and an inedible vixen, at intervals.

Wherein are we educated? Come now, in what are we educated? In politics, in geography, in history, in machinery, in soft drinks and in hard, in social economy and social extravagance: ugh! a frightful universality of knowings.

But it's all France without Paris, *Hamlet* without the Prince, and bricks without straw. For we know nothing, or next to nothing, about ourselves. After hundreds of thousands of years we have learned how to wash our faces and bob our hair, and that is about all we *have* learned, *individually*. Collectively, of course, as

460

a species, we have combed the round earth with a tooth-comb, and pulled down the stars almost within grasp. And then what? Here sit I, a two-legged individual with a risky temper, knowing all about – take a pinch of salt – Tierra del Fuego and Relativity and the composition of celluloid, the appearance of the anthrax bacillus and solar eclipses, and the latest fashion in shoes; and it don't do me *no* good! as the charlady said of near beer. It doesn't leave me feeling no less lonesome inside! as the old Englishwoman said, long ago, of tea without rum.

Our knowledge, like the prohibition beer, is always near. But it never gets there. It leaves us feeling just as lonesome inside.

We are hopelessly uneducated in ourselves. We pretend that when we know a smattering of the Patagonian idiom we have in so far educated ourselves. What nonsense! The leather of my boots is just as effectual in turning me into a bull, or a young steer. Alas! we wear our education just as externally as we wear our boots, and to far less profit. It is all external education, anyhow.

What am I, when I am at home? I'm supposed to be a sensible human being. Yet I carry a whole waste-paper basket of ideas at the top of my head, and in some other part of my anatomy, the dark continent of myself. I have a whole stormy chaos of 'feelings'. And with these self-same feelings I simply don't get a chance. Some of them roar like lions, some twist like snakes, some bleat like snow-white lambs, some warble like linnets, some are absolutely dumb, but swift as slippery fishes, some are oysters that open on occasion: and lo! here am I, adding another scrap of paper to the ideal accumulation in the waste-paper basket, hoping to settle the matter that way.

The lion springs on me! I wave an idea at him. The serpent casts a terrifying glance at me, and I hand him a Moody and Sankey hymn-book. Matters go from bad to worse.

The wild creatures are coming forth from the darkest Africa inside us. In the night you can hear them bellowing. If you are a big game-hunter, like Billy Sunday, you may shoulder your elephant gun. But since the forest is inside all of us, and in every forest there's a whole assortment of big game and dangerous crea-

461

tures, it's one against a thousand. We've managed to keep clear of the darkest Africa inside us, for a long time. We've been so busy finding the North Pole and converting the Patagonians, loving our neighbour and devising new means of exterminating him, listening-in and shutting-out.

But now, my dear, dear reader, Nemesis is blowing his nose. And muffled roarings are heard out of darkest Africa, with stifled shrieks.

I say feelings, not emotions. Emotions are things we more or less recognize. We see love, like a woolly lamb, or like a decorative decadent panther in Paris clothes: according as it is sacred or profane. We see hate, like a dog chained to a kennel. We see fear, like a shivering monkey. We see anger, like a bull with a ring through his nose, and greed, like a pig. Our emotions are our domesticated animals, noble like the horse, timid like the rabbit, but all completely at our service. The rabbit goes into the pot, and the horse into the shafts. For we are creatures of circumstance, and must fill our bellies and our pockets.

Convenience! Convenience! There are convenient emotions and inconvenient ones. The inconvenient ones we chain up, or put a ring through their nose. The convenient ones are our pets. Love is our pet favourite.

And that's as far as our education goes, in the direction of feelings. We have no language for the feelings, because our feelings do not even exist for us.

Yet what is a man? Is he really just a little engine that you stoke with potatoes and beef-steak? Does all the strange flow of life in him come out of meat and potatoes, and turn into the so-called physical energy?

Educated! We are not even *born*, as far as our feelings are concerned.

You can eat till you're bloated, and 'get ahead' till you're a by-word, and still, inside you, will be the darkest Africa whence come roars and shrieks.

Man is not a little engine of cause and effect. We must put that out of our minds for ever. The *cause* in man is something we shall never fathom. But there it is, a strange dark continent that we do not explore, because we do not even allow that it exists. Yet all the time, it is within us: the *cause* of us, and of our days.

And our feelings are the first manifestations within the aboriginal jungle of us. Till now, in sheer terror of ourselves, we have turned our backs on the jungle, fenced it in with an enormous entanglement of barbed wire, and declared it did not exist.

But alas! we ourselves only exist because of the life that bounds and leaps into our limbs and our consciousness, from out of the original dark forest within us. We may wish to exclude this inbounding, inleaping life. We may wish to be as our domesticated animals are, tame. But let us remember that even our cats and dogs have, in each generation, to be tamed. They are not now a tame species. Take away the control, and they will cease to be tame. They will not tame *themselves*.

Man is the only creature who has deliberately tried to tame himself. He has succeeded. But alas! it is a process you cannot set a limit to. Tameness, like alcohol, destroys its own creator. Tameness is an effect of control. But the tamed thing loses the power of control, in itself. It must be controlled from without. Man has pretty well tamed himself, and he calls his tameness civilization. True civilization would be something very different. But man is now tame. Tameness means the loss of the peculiar power of command. The tame are always commanded by the untame. Man has tamed himself, and so has lost his power for command, the power to give himself direction. He has no choice in himself. He is tamed, like a tame horse waiting for the rein.

Supposing all horses were suddenly rendered masterless, what would they do? They would run wild. But supposing they were left still shut up in their fields, paddocks, corrals, stables, what would they do? They would go insane.

And that is precisely man's predicament. He is tamed. There are no untamed to give the commands and the direction. Yet he is shut up within all his barbed wire fences. He can only go insane, degenerate.

What is the alternative? It is nonsense to pretend we can untame ourselves in five minutes. That, too, is a slow and strange process, that has to be undertaken seriously. It is nonsense to pre-

463

tend we can break the fences and dash out into the wilds. There are no wilds left, comparatively, and man is a dog that returns to his vomit.

Yet unless we proceed to connect ourselves up with our own primeval sources, we shall degenerate. And degenerating, we shall break up into a strange orgy of feelings. They will be decomposition feelings, like the colours of autumn. And they will precede whole storms of death, like leaves in a wind.

There is no help for it. Man cannot tame himself and then stay tame. The moment he tries to stay tame he begins to degenerate, and gets the second sort of wildness, the wildness of destruction, which may be autumnal-beautiful for a while, like yellow leaves. Yet yellow leaves can only fall and rot.

Man tames himself in order to learn to un-tame himself again. To be civilized, we must not deny and blank out our feelings. Tameness is not civilization. It is only burning down the brush and ploughing the land. Our civilization has hardly realized yet the necessity for ploughing the soul. Later, we sow wild seed. But so far, we've been burning off and rooting out the old wild brush. Our civilization, as far as our own souls go, has been a destructive process, up to now. The landscape of our souls is a charred wilderness of burnt-off stumps, with a green bit of water here, and a tin shanty with a little iron stove.

Now we have to sow wild seed again. We have to cultivate our feelings. It is no good trying to be popular, to let a whole rank tangle of liberated, degenerate feelings spring up. It will give us no satisfaction.

And it is no use doing as the psychoanalysts have done. The psychoanalysts show the greatest fear of all, of the innermost primeval place in man, where God is, if he is anywhere. The old Jewish horror of the true Adam, the mysterious 'natural man', rises to a shriek in psychoanalysis. Like the idiot who foams and bites his wrists till they bleed. So great is the Freudian hatred of the oldest, old Adam, from whom God is not yet separated off, that the psychoanalyst sees this Adam as nothing but a monster of perversity, a bunch of engendering adders, horribly clotted.

This vision is the perverted vision of the degenerate tame:

tamed through thousands of shameful years. The old Adam is the for ever untamed: he who is of the tame hated, with a horror of fearful hate: but who is held in innermost respect by the fearless.

In the oldest of the old Adam, was God: behind the dark wall of his breast, under the seal of the navel. Then man had a revulsion against himself, and God was separated off, lodged in the outermost space.

Now we have to return. Now again the old Adam must lift up his face and his breast, and un-tame himself. Not in viciousness nor in wantonness, but having God within the walls of himself. In the very darkest continent of the body there is God. And from him issue the first dark rays of our feeling, wordless, and utterly previous to words: the innermost rays, the first messengers, the primeval, honourable beasts of our being, whose voice echoes wordless and for ever wordless down the darkest avenues of the soul, but full of potent speech. Our own inner meaning.

Now we have to educate ourselves, not by laying down laws and inscribing tables of stone, but by listening. Not listening-in to noises from Chicago or Timbuktu. But listening-in to the voices of the honourable beasts that call in the dark paths of the veins of our body, from the God in the heart. Listening inwards, inwards, not for words nor for inspiration, but to the lowing of the innermost beasts, the feelings, that roam in the forest of the blood, from the feet of God within the red, dark heart.

And how? How? How shall we even begin to educate ourselves in the feelings?

Not by laying down laws, or commandments, or axioms and postulates. Not even by making assertions that such and such is blessed. Not by words at all.

If we can't hear the cries far down in our own forests of dark veins, we can look in the real novels, and there listen-in. Not listen to the didactic statements of the author, but to the low, calling cries of the characters, as they wander in the dark woods of their destiny.

# Review of *The Social Basis of Consciousness* by Trigant Burrow

*Bookman* (New York), November 1927; *Phoenix*, 1936

Dr Trigant Burrow is well known as an independent psychologist through the essays and addresses he has published in pamphlet form from time to time. These have invariably shown the spark of original thought and discovery. The gist of all these essays now fuses into this important book, the latest addition to the International Library of Psychology, Philosophy and Scientific Method.

Dr Burrow is that rare thing among pyschiatrists, a humanly honest man. Not that practitioners are usually dishonest. They are intellectually honest, professionally honest: all that. But that other simple thing, human honesty, does not enter in, because it is primarily subjective; and subjective honesty, which means that a man is honest about his own inward experiences, is perhaps the rarest thing, especially among professionals. Chiefly, of course, because men, and especially men with a theory, don't know anything about their own inward experiences.

Here Dr Burrow is a rare and shining example. He set out, years ago, as an enthusiastic psychoanalyst and follower of Freud, working according to the Freudian method, in America. And gradually the sense that something was wrong, vitally wrong, in the theory and in the practice of psychoanalysis both, invaded him. Like any truly honest man, he turned and asked himself what it was that was wrong, with himself, with his methods, and with the theory according to which he was working.

This book is the answer, a book for every man interested in the human consciousness to read carefully. Because Dr Burrow's conclusions, sincere, almost naïve in their startled emotion, are far-reaching, and vital.

First, in the criticism of the Freudian method, Dr Burrow found, in his clinical experiences, that he was always applying a *theory*. Patients came to be analysed, and the analyst was there to examine with open mind. But the mind could not be open, because the patient's neurosis, all the patient's experience, *had* to be fitted to the Freudian theory of the inevitable incest-motive.

And gradually Dr Burrow realized that to fit life every time to a theory is in itself a mechanistic process, a process of unconscious repression, a process of image-substitution. All theory that has to be applied to life proves at last just another of these unconscious images which the repressed psyche uses as a substitute for life, and against which the psychoanalyst is fighting. The analyst wants to break all this image business, so that life can flow freely. But it is useless to try to do so by replacing in the unconscious another image – this time, the image, the fixed motive of the incest-complex.

Theory as theory is all right. But the moment you apply it to *life*, especially to the subjective life, the theory becomes mechanistic, a substitute for life, a factor in the vicious unconscious. So that while the Freudian theory of the unconscious and of the incest-motive is valuable as a *description* of our psychological condition, the moment you begin to *apply* it, and make it master of the living situation, you have begun to substitute one mechanistic or unconscious illusion for another.

In short, the analyst is just as much fixed in his vicious unconscious as is his neurotic patient, and the will to apply a mechanical incest-theory to every neurotic experience is just as sure an evidence of neurosis, in Freud or in the practitioner, as any psychologist could ask.

So much for the criticism of the psychoanalytic method.

If, then Dr Burrow asks himself, it is not sex-repression which

467

is at the root of the neurosis of modern life, what is it? For certainly, according to his finding, sex-repression is not the root of the evil.

The question is a big one, and can have no single answer. A single answer would only be another 'theory'. But Dr Burrow has struggled through years of mortified experience to come to some conclusion nearer the mark. And his finding is surely much deeper and more vital, and, also, much less spectacular than Freud's.

The real trouble lies in the inward sense of 'separateness' which dominates every man. At a certain point in his evolution, man became cognitively conscious: he bit the apple: he began to know. Up till that time his consciousness flowed unaware, as in the animals. Suddenly, his consciousness split.

It would appear that in his separativeness man has inadvertently fallen a victim to the developmental exigencies of his own consciousness. Captivated by the phylogenetically new and unwonted spectacle of his own image, it would seem he has been irresistibly arrested before the mirror of his own likeness and that in the present self-conscious phase of his mental evolution he is still standing spellbound before it. That such is the case with man is not remarkable. For the appearance of the phenomenon of consciousness marked a complete severance from all that was his past. Here was broken the chain of evolutionary events whose links extended back through the nebulous aeons of our remote ancestry, and in the first moment of his consciousness man stood, for the first time, *alone*. It was in this moment that he was 'created', as the legend runs, 'in the image and likeness of God'. For, breaking with the teleological traditions of his age-long biology, man now became suddenly *aware*.

Consciousness is self-consciousness. 'That is, consciousness in its inception entails the fallacy of *a self as over against other selves*.'

Suddenly aware of himself, and of other selves over against him, man is a prey to the division inside himself. Helplessly he must strive for more consciousness, which means, also, a more intensified aloneness, or individuality; and at the same time he has a horror of his own aloneness, and a blind, dim yearning for

468

the old togetherness of the far past, what Dr Burrow calls the preconscious state.

What man really wants, according to Dr Burrow, is a sense of togetherness with his fellow-men, which shall balance the secret but overmastering sense of separateness and aloneness which now dominates him. And therefore, instead of the Freudian method of personal analysis, in which the personality of the patient is pitted against the personality of the analyst in the old struggle for dominancy, Dr Burrow would substitute a method of group analysis, wherein the reactions were distributed over a group of people, and the intensely personal element eliminated as far as possible. For it is only in the intangible reaction of several people, or many people together, on one another that you can really get the loosening and breaking of the me-and-you tension and contest, the inevitable contest of two individualities brought into connexion. What must be broken is the egocentric absolute of the individual. We are all such hopeless little absolutes to ourselves. And if we are sensitive, it hurts us, and we complain, we are called neurotic. If we are complacent, we enjoy our own petty absolutism though we hide it and pretend to be quite meek and humble. But in secret, we are absolute and perfect to ourselves, and nobody could be better than we are. And this is called being normal.

Perhaps the most interesting part of Dr Burrow's book is his examination of normality. As soon as man became aware of himself, he made a picture of himself. Then he began to live according to the picture. Mankind at large made a picture of itself, and every man had to conform to the picture: the ideal.

This is the great image or idol which dominates our civilization, and which we worship with mad blindness. The idolatry of self. Consciousness should be a flow from within outwards. The organic necessity of the human being should flow into spontaneous action and spontaneous awareness, consciousness.

But the moment man became aware of himself he made a picture of himself, and began to live from the picture: that is, from without inwards. This is truly the reversal of life. And this is how we live. We spend all our time over the picture. All our education is but the elaborating of the picture. 'A good little girl' – ' a brave

469

boy' – ' a noble woman' – 'a strong man' – 'a productive society' – 'a progressive humanity' – it is all in the picture. It is all living from the outside to the inside. It is all the death of spontaneity. It is all, strictly, automatic. It is all the vicious unconscious which Freud postulated.

If we could once get into our heads – or if we once dare admit to one another – that we are *not* the picture, and the picture is not what we are, then we might lay a new hold on life. For the picture is really the death, and certainly the neurosis, of us all. We have to live from the outside in, idolatrously. And the picture of ourselves, the picture of humanity which has been elaborated through some thousands of years, and which we are still adding to, is just a huge idol. It is not real. It is a horrible compulsion set over us.

Individuals rebel: and these are the neurotics, who show some sign of health. The mass, the great mass, goes on worshipping the idol, and behaving according to the picture: and this is the normal. Freud tried to force his patients back to normal, and almost succeeded in shocking them into submission, with the incest-bogey. But the bogey is nothing compared to the actual idol.

As a matter of fact, the mass is more neurotic than the individual patient. This is Dr Burrow's finding. The mass, the normals, never live a life of their own. They cannot. They live entirely according to the picture. And according to the picture, each one is a little absolute unto himself: there is none better than he. Each lives for his own self-interest. The 'normal' activity is to push your own interest with every atom of energy you can command. It is 'normal' to get on, to go ahead, at whatever cost. The man who does disinterested work is abnormal. Every Johnny must look out for himself: that is normal. Luckily for the world, there still is a minority of individuals who do disinterested work, and are made use of by the 'normals'. But the number is rapidly decreasing.

And then the normals betray their utter abnormality in a crisis like the late war. There, there indeed the uneasy individual can look into the abysmal insanity of the normal masses. The same holds good of the Bolshevist hysteria of today: it is hysteria, incipient social insanity. And the last great insanity of all, which is going to tear our civilization to pieces, the insanity of class hatred, is almost entirely a 'normal' thing, and a 'social' thing. It is a state of fear, of ghastly collective fear. And it is absolutely a mark of the normal. To say that class hatred *need not exist* is to show abnormality. And yet it is true. Between man and man, class hatred hardly exists. It is an insanity of the mass, rather than of the individual.

But it is part of the picture. The picture says it is horrible to be poor, and splendid to be rich, and in spite of all individual experience to the contrary, we accept the terms of the picture, and thereby accept class war as inevitable.

Humanity, society has a picture of itself, and lives accordingly. The individual likewise has a private picture of himself, which fits into the big picture. In this picture he is a little absolute, and nobody could be better than he is. He must look after his own self-interest. And if he is a man, he must be very male. If she is a woman, she must be very female.

Even sex, today, is only part of the picture. Men and women alike, when they are being sexual, are only acting up. They are living according to the picture. If there is any dynamic, it is that of self-interest. The man 'seeketh his own' in sex, and the woman seeketh her own: in the bad, egoistic sense in which St Paul used the words. That is, the man seeks himself, the woman seeks herself, always, and inevitably. It is inevitable, when you live according to the picture, that you seek only yourself in sex. Because the picture is your own image of yourself: your *idea* of yourself. If you are quite normal, you don't have any true self, which 'seeketh not her own, is not puffed up'. The true self, in sex, would seek a *meeting*, would seek to meet the other. This would be the true flow: what Dr Burrow calls the 'societal consciousness', and what I would call the human consciousness, in contrast to the social, or image consciousness.

But today, all is image consciousness. Sex does not exist; there is only sexuality. And sexuality is merely a greedy, blind self-seeking. Self-seeking is the real motive of sexuality. And therefore, since the thing sought is the same, the self, the mode of

471

seeking is not very important. Heterosexual, homosexual, narcissistic, normal, or incest, it is all the same thing. It is just sexuality,
not sex. It is one of the universal forms of self-seeking. Every
man, every woman just seeks his own self, her own self, in the
sexual experience. It is the picture over again, whether in sexuality
or self-sacrifice, greed or charity, the same thing, the self, the
image, the idol, the image of me, and norm!

The true self is not aware that it is a self. A bird, as it sings,
sings itself. But not according to a picture. It has no idea of itself.

And this is what the analyst must try to do: to liberate his
patient from his own image, from his horror of his own isolation
and the horror of the 'stoppage' of his real vital flow. To do it, it is
no use rousing sex bogeys. A man is not neurasthenic or neurotic
because he loves his mother. If he desires his mother, it is because
he is neurotic, and the desire is merely a symptom. The cause of
the neurosis is further to seek.

And the cure? For myself, I believe Dr Burrow is right: the
cure would consist in bringing about a state of honesty and a
certain trust among a *group* of people, or many people – if possible, all the people in the world. For it is only when we can get
a man to fall back into his true relation to other men, and to
women, that we can give him an opportunity to be himself. So
long as men are inwardly dominated by their own isolation, their
own absoluteness, which after all is but a picture or an idea, nothing is possible but insanity more or less pronounced. Men must
get back into *touch*. And to do so they must forfeit the vanity and
the *noli me tangere* of their own absoluteness: also they must
utterly break the present great picture of a normal humanity:
shatter that mirror in which we all live grimacing: and fall again
into true relatedness.

I have tried more or less to give a *résumé* of Dr Burrow's book.
I feel there is a certain impertinence in giving these *résumés*. But
not more than in the affectation of 'criticizing' and being superior.
And it is a book one should read and assimilate, for it helps a
man in his own inward life.

# On Being a Man

*Vanity Fair*, June 1924; *Assorted Articles*, 1930

Man is a thought-adventurer.

Which isn't the same as saying that man has intellect. In intellect there is skill, and tricks. To the intellect the terms are given, as the chessmen and rules of the game are given in chess. Real thought is an experience. It begins as a change in the blood, a slow convulsion and revolution in the body itself. It ends as a new piece of awareness, a new reality in mental consciousness.

On this account, thought is an adventure, and not a practice. In order to think, man must risk himself. He must risk himself doubly. First, he must go forth and meet life in the body. Then he must face the result in his mind.

It is bad enough going out like a little David to meet the giant of life bodily. Take the war as an example of that. It is still harder, and bitterer, after a great encounter with life, to sit down and face out the result. Take war again. Many men went out and faced the fight. Who dared to face his own self afterwards?

The risk is double, because man is double. Each of us has two selves. First is this body which is vulnerable and never quite within our control. The body with its irrational sympathies and desires and passions, its peculiar direct communication, defying the mind. And second is the conscious ego, the self I KNOW I am.

The self that lives in my body I can never finally know. It has such strange attractions, and revulsions, and it lets me in for so much irrational suffering, real torment, and occasional frightening delight. The me that is in my body is a strange animal to me, and often a very trying one. My body is like a jungle in which dwells an unseen me, like a black panther in the night, whose two eyes glare green through my dreams, and, if a shadow falls, through my waking day.

Then there is this other me, that is fair-faced and reasonable and sensible and complex and full of good intentions. The known me, which can be seen and appreciated. I say of myself: 'Yes, I know I am impatient and rather intolerant in ideas. But in the ordinary way of life I am quite easy and really rather kindly. My kindliness makes me sometimes a bit false. But then I don't believe in mechanical honesty. There is an honesty of the feelings, of the sensibilities, as well as of the mind. If a man is lying to me, and I know it, it is a matter of choice whether I tell him so or not. If it would only damage his real feelings, and my own, then it would be *emotionally* dishonest to call him a liar to his face. I would rather be a bit mentally dishonest, and pretend to swallow the lie.'

This is the known me, having a talk with itself. It sees a reason for everything it does and feels. It has a certain unchanging belief in its own good intentions. It tries to steer a sensible and harmless course among all the other people and 'personalities' around itself.

To this known me, everything exists as a term of knowledge. A man is what I know he is. England is what I know it to be. I am what I know I am. And Bishop Berkeley is absolutely right: things only exist in our own consciousness. To the known me, nothing exists beyond what I know. True, I am always adding to the things I know. But this is because, in my opinion, knowledge begets knowledge. Not because anything has entered *from the outside*. There *is* no outside. There is only more knowledge to be added.

If I sit in the train and a man enters my compartment, he is already, in a great measure, known to me. He is, in the first place, A Man, and I know what that is. Then, he is old. And Old, I

474

know what that means. Then he is English and middle class, and so on, and so on. And I know it all.

There remains a tiny bit that is not known to me. He is a stranger. As a personality I don't yet know him. I glance at him quickly. It is a very small adventure, still an adventure in knowledge, a combination of certain qualities grouped in a certain way. At a glance I know as much about him as I want to know. It is finished, the adventure is over.

This is the adventure of knowing. People go to Spain, and 'know' Spain. People study entomology, and 'know' insects. People meet Lenin and 'know' Lenin. Lots of people 'know' me.

And this is how we live. We proceed from what we know already to what we know next. If we don't know the Shah of Persia, we think we have only to call at the palace in Teheran to accomplish the feat. If we don't know much about the moon, we have only to get the latest book on that orb, and we shall be *au courant*.

We know we know all about it, really. *Connu! Connu!* Remains only the fascinating little game of *understanding*, putting two and two together and being real little gods in the machine.

All this is the adventure of knowing and understanding. But it isn't the thought-adventure.

The thought-adventure starts in the blood, not in the mind. If an Arab or a Negro or even a Jew sits down next to me in the train, I cannot proceed so glibly with my knowing. It is not enough for me to glance at a black face and say: He is a Negro. As he sits next to me, there is a faint uneasy movement in my blood. A strange vibration comes from him, which causes a slight disturbance in my own vibration. There is a slight odour in my nostrils. And above all, even if I shut my eyes, there is a strange *presence* in contact with me.

I now can no longer proceed from what I am and what I know I am, to what I know him to be. I am not a nigger and so I can't quite know a nigger, and I can never fully 'understand' him.

What then? It's an *impasse*.

Then, I have three courses open. I can just plank down the word Nigger, and having labelled him, finish with him! Or I can try to track him down in terms of my own knowledge. That is, understand him as I understand any other individual.

Or I can do a third thing. I can admit that my blood is disturbed, that something comes from him and interferes with my normal vibration. Admitting so much, I can either put up a resistance and insulate myself. Or I can allow the disturbance to continue, because, after all, there is some peculiar alien sympathy between us.

In almost every case, of course, the nigger among white men will insulate himself, and not let his black aura reach the white neighbours. If I find myself in a train full of niggers, I shall no doubt do the same.

But apart from this, I shall admit a certain strange and incalculable reaction between me and him. This reaction causes a slight but unmistakable change in the vibration of my blood and nerves. This slight change in my blood develops in dreams and unconsciousness till, if I allow it, it struggles forward into light as a new bit of realization, a new term of consciousness.

Take the much commoner case of men and women. A man, proceeding from his known self, likes a woman because she is in sympathy with what he knows. He feels that he and she know one another. They marry. And then the fun begins. In so far as they know one another they can proceed from their known selves, they are as right as ninepence. Loving couple, etc. But the moment there is real blood contact, as likely as not a strange discord enters in. She is not what he thought her. He is not what she thought him. It is the other, primary or bodily self – appearing, very often like a black demon, out of the fair creature who was erst the beloved.

The man who before marriage seemed everything that is delightful, after marriage begins to come out in his true colours, a son of the old and rather hateful Adam. And she, who was an angel of loveliness and desirability, gradually emerges as an almost fiendlike daughter of the snake-frequenting Eve.

What has happened?

It is the invariable crucifixion. The Cross, as we know, stands for the body, for the dark self which lives in the body. And on the Cross of this bodily self is crucified the self which I know I am, my

476

so-called *real* self. The Cross, as an ancient symbol, has an inevitable phallic reference. But it is far deeper than sex. It is the self which darkly inhabits our blood and bone, and for which the ithyphallus is but a symbol. This self which lives darkly in my blood and bone is my *alter ego*, my other self, the homunculus, the second one of the Kabiri, the second of the Twins, the Gemini. And the sacred black stone at Mecca stands for this: the dark self that swells in the blood of a man and of a woman. Phallic if you like. But much more than phallic. And on this cross of division in the whole self is crucified the Christ. We are all crucified on it.

Marriage is the great puzzle of our day, It is our sphinx-riddle. Solve it, or to be torn to bits, is the decree.

We marry from the known self, taking the woman as an extension of our knowledge – an extension of our known self. And then, almost invariably, comes the jolt and crucifixion. The woman of the known self is fair and lovely. But the woman of the dark blood looks, to man, most malignant and horrific. In the same way, the fair daytime man of courtship days leaves nothing to be desired. But the husband, horrified by the serpent-advised Eve of the blood, obtuse and arrogant in his Adam obstinacy, is an enemy pure and simple.

Solve the puzzle. The quickest way is for the wife to smother the serpent-advised Eve which is in her, and for the man to talk himself out of his old arrogant Adam. Then they make a fair and above-board combination, called a successful marriage.

But Nemesis is on our track. The husband forfeits his arrogance, the wife has her children and her way to herself. But lo, the son of one woman is husband to the woman of the next generation! And oh, women, beware the mother's boy! Or else the wife forfeits the old serpent-advised Eve from her nature and becomes the instrument of the man. And then, oh, young husband of the next generation, prepare for the daughter's revenge.

What's to be done?

The thought-adventure! We've got to take ourselves as we are, not as we know ourselves to be. I am the son of the old red-earth Adam, with a black touchstone at the centre of me. And all the

477

fair words in the world won't alter it. Woman is the strange ser-pent-communing Eve, inalterable. We are a strange pair, who meet, but never mingle. I came, in the bath of birth, out of a mother. But I arose the old Adam, with the black old stone at the core of me. She had a father who begot her, but the column of her is pure enigmatic Eve.

In spite of all the things I know about her, in spite of my know-ing her so well, the serpent knows her better still. And in spite of my fair words, and my goodly pretences, she runs up against the black stone of Adam which is in the middle of me.

*Know thyself* means knowing at last that you *can't* know your-self. I can't know the Adam of red-earth which is me. It will always do things to me, beyond my knowledge. Neither can I know the serpent-listening Eve which is the woman, beneath all her modern glibness. I have to take her at that. And we have to meet as I meet a jaguar between the trees in the mountains, and advance, and touch, and risk it. When man and woman *actually* meet, there is always terrible risk to both of them. Risk for her, lest her womanhood be damaged by the hard dark stone which is unchangeable in his soul. Risk for him, lest the serpent drag him down, coiled round his neck, and kissing him with poison.

There is always risk, for him and for her. Take the risk, make the adventure. Suffer and enjoy the change in the blood. And, if you are a man, slowly, slowly make the great experience of realiz-ing. The final adventure and experience of realization, if you are a man. Fully conscious realization. If you are a woman, the strange, slumbrous serpentine realization, which knows without thinking.

But with man, it is a thought-adventure. He risks his body and blood. He withdraws and touches the black stone of his inner conscience. And in a new adventure he dares take thought. He dares take thought for what he has done and what has happened to him. And daring to take thought, he ventures on, and realizes at last.

To be a man! To risk your body and your blood first, and then to risk your mind. All the time, to risk your known self, and be-come once more a self you could never have known or expected.

To be a man, instead of being a mere personality. Today men don't risk their blood and bone. They go forth, panoplied in their own idea of themselves. Whatever they do, they perform it all in the full armour of their own idea of themselves. Their unknown bodily self is never for one moment unsheathed. All the time, the only protagonist is the known ego, the self-conscious ego. And the dark self in the mysterious labyrinth of the body is cased in a tight armour of cowardly repression.

Men marry and commit all their adulteries from the head. All that happens to them, all their reactions, all their experiences, happen only in the head. To the unknown man in them nothing happens. He remains shut up in armour, lest he might be hurt and give pain. And inside the armour he goes quite deranged.

All the suffering today is psychic: it happens in the mind. The red Adam only suffers the slow torture of compression and derangement. A man's wife is a mental thing, a known thing to him. The old Adam in him never sees her. She is just a thing of his own conscious ego. And not for one moment does he risk himself under the strange snake-infested bushes of her extraordinary Paradise. He is afraid.

He becomes extraordinarily clever and agile in his self-conscious panoply. With his mind he can dart about among the emotions as if he really felt something. It is all a lie, he feels nothing. He is just tricking you. He becomes extraordinarily acute at recognizing real feelings from false ones, knowing for certain the falsity of his own. He has always the touchstone of his own conscious falseness against which to test the reality or the falseness of others. And he is always exposing falseness in others. But not for the sake of liberating the real Adam and Eve. On the contrary. He is more terrified even than the ordinary frightened man in the street, of the real Adam and Eve. He is a greater coward still. But his greater cowardice makes him strive to appear a greater man. He denounces falsity in order to triumph in his own greater falsity. He praises the real thing in order to establish his own superiority even to the real thing. He must, must, must be superior. Because he knows himself absolutely and unspeakably and irremediably false. His spurious emotions are more like the real thing than

479

genuine emotions, and they have, for a time, greater effect. But all the time, somewhere, he knows they are false.

And this is his one point of power. Instead of having inside him, like the Adam of red earth, that heavy and immutable black stone which is the eternal touchstone of false and true, good and evil, he has this awful little tombstone of the knowledge of his own falsity. And in this ghastly little white tombstone which he erects to himself lies his peculiar infallibility among a false and mental people.

That's the widdishins way of being a man. To know so absolutely that you are *not* a man, that you dare almost anything on the strength of it. You dare anything, except being a man. So intense and final is the modern white man's conviction, his internal conviction, that he is *not* a man, that he dares anything on earth except be a man. There his courage drops to its grave. He daren't be a man: the old Adam of red earth, with the black touchstone at the middle of him.

He knows he's not a man. Hence his creed of harmlessness. He knows he is not a man of living red earth, to live onward through strange weather into new springtime. He knows there is extinction ahead: for nothing but extinction lies in wait for the conscious ego. Hence his creed of harmlessness, of relentless kindness. A little less than kin, and more than kind. There should be no danger in life *at all*, even no friction. This he asserts, while all the time he is slowly, malignantly undermining the tree of life.

# Enslaved by Civilization

*Vanity Fair*, September 1929; *Assorted Articles*, 1930

The one thing men have not learned to do is to stick up for their own instinctive feelings, against the things they are taught. The trouble is, we are all caught young. Little boys are trundled off to school at the age of five, and immediately the game begins, the game of enslaving the small chap. He is delivered over into the hands of schoolmistresses, young maids, middle-aged maids, and old maids, and they pounce on him, and with absolute confidence in their own powers, their own *rightness*, and their own superiority, they begin to 'form' the poor little devil. Nobody questions for a moment the powers of these women to mould the life of a young man. The Jesuits say: Give me a child till he is seven, and I will answer for him for the rest of his life. – Well, schoolmistresses are not as clever as Jesuits, and certainly not as clear as to what they are about, but they do the trick, nevertheless. They make the little boy into an incipient man, the man of today.

Now I ask you, do you really think that schoolmistresses are qualified to form the foundations of a *man*? They are almost all excellent women, and filled with the best of motives. And they have all passed some little exam or other. But what, in the name of heaven, qualifies them to be the makers of men? They are all maids: young maids, middling maids, or old maids. They none of them know anything about men: that is to say, they are not *supposed* to know anything about men. What knowledge they have must be surreptitious. They certainly know nothing about manhood. Manhood, in the eyes of the schoolmistress, and especially the elderly schoolmistress, is something uncalled-for and unpleasant. Men, in the pleasant opinions of schoolmistresses, are mostly grown-up babies. Haven't the babies all been through the mistress's hands, and aren't the men almost identically the same?

Well, it may be so! It may be that men nowadays are all grown-up babies. But if they are, it is because they were delivered over in their tenderest years, poor little devils, to absolute petticoat rule; mothers first, then schoolmistresses. But the mother very quickly yields to the schoolmistress. It is amazing what reverence ordinary women have for the excellent old-maid mistress of the infants' school. What the mistress says is gospel. Kings are no more kings by divine right, but queens are queens and mistresses, mistresses straight from God. It is amazing. It is fetish-worship. And the fetish is goodness.

'Oh, but Miss Teacher is so *good*, she's awfully *good*,' say the approving mothers, in luscious voices. 'Now, Johnny, you must mind what Miss Teacher says, she knows what is best for you. You must always listen to her!'

Poor Johnny, poor little devil! On the very first day it is: 'Now, Johnny dear, you must sit like a good little boy, like all the other good little boys.' And when he can't stand it, it is: 'Oh, Johnny dear, I wouldn't cry if I were you. Look at all the other good little boys, they don't cry, do they, dear? Be a good little boy, and teacher will give you a teddy-bear to play with. Would Johnny like a teddy-bear to play with? There, don't cry! Look at all the other good little boys. They are learning to write – to write! Wouldn't Johnny like to be a good little boy, and learn to write?'

As a matter of fact, Johnny wouldn't. At the bottom of his heart, he doesn't in the least want to be a good little boy and learn to write. But she comes it over him. Dear teacher, she starts him off in the way he must go, poor little slave. And once started, he goes on wheels, being a good little boy like all the other good little boys. School is a very elaborate railway system where good little boys are taught to run upon good lines till they are shunted off into life, at the age of fourteen, sixteen, or whatever it is. And by that age the running-on-lines habit is absolutely fixed. The good big boy merely turns off one set of rails on to another. And it is so easy, running on rails; he never realizes that he is a slave to the rails he runs on. Good boy!

Now the funny thing is that nobody, not even the most conscientious father, ever questions the absolute rightness of these school-marms. It is all for dear little Johnny's own good. And these school-marms know absolutely what Johnny's own good is. It is being a good little boy like all the other good little boys.

But to be a good little boy like all the other good little boys is to be at last a slave, or at least an automaton, running on wheels. It means that dear little Johnny is going to have all his own individual manhood nipped out of him, carefully plucked out, every time it shows a little peep. Nothing is more insidiously clever than an old maid's fingers at picking off the little shoots of manhood as they sprout out from a growing boy, and turning him into that neutral object, a good little boy. It is a subtle, loving form of mutilation, and mothers absolutely believe in it. 'Oh, but I *want* him to be a good boy!' She fails to remember how bored she gets with her good-boy husband. Good boys are very nice to mothers and schoolmistresses. But as men, they make a wishy-washy nation.

Of course, nobody wants Johnny to be a bad little boy. One would like him to be just a boy, with no adjective at all. But that is impossible. At the very best schools, where there is most 'freedom', the subtle, silent *compulsion* towards goodness is perhaps strongest. Children are all silently, steadily, relentlessly bullied into being good. They grow up good. And then they are no good.

For what does goodness mean? It means, in the end, being like everybody else, and not having a soul to call your own. Certainly you mustn't have a feeling to call your own. You must be good, and feel exactly what is expected of you, which is just what other people feel. Which means that in the end you feel nothing at all, all your feeling has been killed out of you. And all that is left is the artificial stock emotion which comes out with the morning papers.

I think I belong to the first generation of Englishmen that was really broken in. My father's generation, at least the miners where I was brought up, was still wild. But then my father had never been to anything more serious than a dame's school, and the dame, Miss Hight, had never succeeded in making him a good little boy. She had barely succeeded in making him able to write his name. As for his feelings, they had escaped her clutches entirely: as they escaped the clutches of his mother. The country was still open. He fled away from the women and rackapelted with his own gang. And to the end of his days his idea of life was to escape over the fringe of virtue and drink beer and perhaps poach an occasional rabbit.

But the boys of my generation were caught in time. We were sent at the ripe age of five to Board-schools, British schools, national schools, and though there was far less of the Johnny dear business, and no teddy-bear, we were forced to knuckle under. We were forced on to the rails. I went to the Board-school. Most of us, practically all, were miners' sons. The bulk were going to be miners themselves. And we all hated school.

I shall never forget the anguish with which I wept the first day. I was captured. I was roped in. The other boys felt the same. They hated school because they felt captives there. They hated the masters because they felt them as jailers. They hated even learning to read and write. The endless refrain was: 'When I go down pit you'll see what — sums I'll do.' That was what they waited for: to go down pit, to escape, to be men. To escape into the wild warrens of the pit, to get off the narrow lines of school.

The schoolmaster was an excellent, irascible old man with a white beard. My mother had the greatest respect for him. I remember he flew into a rage with me because I did not want to admit my first name, which is David. 'David! David!' he raved. 'David is the name of a great and good man. You don't like the name of David? You don't like the name of David!' He was purple with indignation. But I had an unreasonable dislike of the name David, and still have, and he couldn't force me into liking it. But he wanted to.

And there it was. David was the name of a great and good man, so I was to be *forced* to like it. If my first name had been Ananias or Ahab, I should have been excused. But David! no! My father, luckily, didn't know the difference between David and Davy of the safety-lamp.

But the old schoolmaster gradually got us under. There were occasional violent thrashings. But what really did the trick was not the thrashing, but the steady, persistent pressure of: Honest, decent lads behave in my way, and no other. – And he got the lads under. Because he was so absolutely sure he was right, and because mothers and fathers all agreed he was right, he managed pretty well to tame the uncouth colliery lads during the six or seven years he was responsible for them. They were the first generation to be really tamed.

With what result? They went down pit, but even pit was no more the happy subterranean warren it used to be. Down pit everything was made to run on lines, too, new lines, up-to-date lines; and the men became ever less men, more mere instruments. They married, and they made what the women of my mother's generation always prayed for, good husbands. But as soon as the men were good husbands, the women were a tiresome, difficult, unsatisfied lot of wives, so there you are! Without knowing it, they missed the old wildness, and were bored.

The last time I was back in the Midlands was during the great coal strike. The men of my age, the men just over forty, were there, standing derelict, pale, silent, with nothing to say, nothing to do, nothing to feel, and great hideous policemen from God-knows-where waiting in gangs to keep them on the lines. Alas, there was no need. The men of my generation were broken in; they'll stay on the lines and rust there. For wives, schoolmasters and employers of labour it is perhaps very nice to have men well broken in. But for a nation, for England, it is a disaster.

# Review of *Fallen Leaves* by V. V. Rozanov

*Everyman*, 23 January 1930; *Phoenix*, 1936

Rozanov is now acquiring something of a European reputation. There is a translation in French, and one promised in German, and the advanced young writers in Paris and Berlin talk of him as one of the true lights. Perhaps *Solitaria* is more popular than *Fallen Leaves*: but then, perhaps it is a little more sensational: *Fallen Leaves* is not sensational: it is on the whole quiet and sad, and truly Russian.

The book was written, apparently, round about 1912: and the author died a few years later. So that, from the western point of view, Rozanov seems like the last of the Russians. Post-revolution Russians are something different.

Rozanov is the last of the Russians, after Chekhov. It is the true Russian voice, become very plaintive now. Artzybashev, Gorky, Merejkovski are his contemporaries, but they are all three a little bit off the tradition. But Rozanov is right on it. His first wife had been Dostoyevsky's mistress: and somehow his literary spirit showed the same kind of connexion: a Dostoyevskian flicker that steadied and became a legal and orthodox light; yet always, of course, suspect. For Rozanov had been a real and perverse liar before he reformed and became a pious, yet suspected conservative. Perhaps he was a liar to the end: who knows? Yet *Solitaria* and *Fallen Leaves* are not lies, not so much lies as many more esteemed books.

The *Fallen Leaves* are just fragments of thought jotted down anywhere and anyhow. As to the importance of the where or how, perhaps it *is* important to keep throwing the reader out into the world, by means of the: At night: At work: In the tram: In the w.c. – which is sometimes printed after the reflections. Perhaps, to avoid any appearance of systematization, or even of philosophic abstraction, these little *addenda* are useful. Anyhow, it is Russian, and deliberate, done with the intention of keeping the reader – or Rozanov himself – in contact with the *moment*, the actual time and place. Rozanov says that with *Solitaria* he introduced a new *tone* into literature, the tone of manuscript, a manuscript being unique and personal, coming from the individual alone direct to the reader. And 'the secret (bordering on madness) that I am talking to myself: so constantly and attentively and *passionately*, that apart from this I practically hear nothing' – this is the secret of his newness, and of his book.

The description is just: and fortunately, on the whole, Rozanov talks sincerely to himself; he really does, on the whole, refrain from performing in front of himself. Of course he is self-conscious: he knows it and accepts it and tries to make it a stark-naked self-consciousness, between himself and himself as between himself and God. 'Lord, preserve in me that chastity of the writer: not to look in the glass.' From a professional liar it is a true and sincere prayer. 'I am coquetting like a girl before the whole world, hence my constant agitation.' 'A writer must suppress the writer in himself (authorship, literariness).'

He is constantly expressing his hatred of literature, as if it poisoned life for him, as if he felt he did not live, he was only *literary*.

The *most happy* moments of life I remember were those when I saw (heard) people in a state of happiness, Stakha and A.P.P. – va, 'My Friend's' story of her first love and marriage (the culminating point of my life). From this I conclude that I was born a contemplator, not an actor. I came into the world in order to *see*, and not to *accomplish*.

There is his trouble, that he felt he was always looking on at life, rather than partaking in it. And he felt this as a humiliation: and in his earlier days, it had made him act up, as the Americans say. He had acted up as if he were a real actor on life's stage. But it was too theatrical: his 'lying', his 'evil' were too much acted up. A liar and an evil bird he no doubt was, because the lies and the acting up to evil, whether they are 'pose' or spontaneous, have a vile effect. But he never got any real satisfaction even out of that. He never felt he had really been evil. He had only acted up, like all the Stavrogins, or Ivan Karamazovs of Dostoyevsky. Always acting up, trying to *act* feelings because you haven't really got any. That was the condition of the Russians at the end: even Chekhov. Being terribly emotional, terribly full of feeling, terribly good and pathetic or terribly evil and shocking, just to *make* yourself have feelings, when you have none. This was very Russian – and is very modern. A great deal of the world is like it today.

Rozanov left off 'acting up' and became quiet and decent, except, perhaps, for little bouts of hysteria, when he would be perfectly vicious towards a friend, or make a small splash of 'sin'. As far as a man who *has* no real fount of emotion can love he loved his second wife, 'My Friend'. He tried very, very hard to love her, and no doubt he succeeded. But there was always the taint of pity, and she, poor thing, must have been terribly emotionally overwrought, as a woman is with an emotional husband who has no real virile emotion or compassion, only 'pity'. 'European civilization will perish through compassion,' he says: but then goes on to say, profoundly, that it is not compassion but pseudo-compassion, with an element of perversity in it. This is very Dostoyevskian: and this pseudo-compassion tainted even Rozanov's love for his wife. There is somewhere an element of mockery. And oh, how Rozanov himself would have liked to escape it, and just to feel simple affection. But he couldn't. ' "Today" was completely absent in Dostoyevsky,' he writes. Which is a very succinct way of saying that Dostoyevsky never had any immediate feelings, only 'projected' ones, which are bound to destroy the immediate object, the actual 'today', the very body which is 'today'. So poor Rozanov saw his wife dying under his eyes with a paralysis due to a disease of the brain. She was his 'today', and he could not help, somewhere, jeering at her. But he suffered, and suffered deeply.

At the end, one feels his suffering *was* real: his grief over his wife *was* real. So he had gained that much reality: he really grieved for her, and that was love. It was a great achievement, after all, for the most difficult thing in the world is to achieve real feeling, especially real sympathy, when the sympathetic centres seem, from the very start, as in Rozanov, dead. But Rozanov knew his own nullity, and tried very hard to come through to real honest feeling. And in his measure, he succeeded. After all the Dostoyevskian hideous 'impurity' he did achieve a certain final purity, or genuineness, or true individuality, towards the end. Even at the beginning of *Fallen Leaves* he is often sentimental and false, repulsive.

And one cannot help feeling a compassion for the Russians of the old regime. They were such healthy barbarians in Peter the Great's time. Then the whole accumulation of western ideas, ideals, and inventions was poured in a mass into their hot and undeveloped consciousness, and worked like wild yeast. It produced a century of literature, from Pushkin to Rozanov, and then the wild working of this foreign leaven had ruined, for the time being, the very constitution of the Russian psyche. It was as if they had taken too violent a drug, or been injected with too strong a vaccine. The affective and effective centres collapsed, the control went all wrong, the energy died down in a rush, the nation fell, for the time being completely ruined. Too sudden civilization always kills. It kills the South Sea Islanders: it killed the Russians, more slowly, and perhaps even more effectually. Once the idea and the ideal become too strong for the spontaneous emotion in the individual, the civilizing influence ceases to be civilizing and becomes very harmful, like powerful drugs which ruin the balance and destroy the control of the organism.

Rozanov knew this well. What he says about revolution and democracy leaves nothing to be said. And what he says of 'officialdom' is equally final. I believe Tolstoy would be absolutely amazed if he could come back and see the Russia of today. I believe Rozanov would feel no surprise. He knew the inevitability of it. His attitude to the Jews is extraordinary, and shows uncanny penetration. And his sort of 'conservatism', which would be

489

Fascism today, was only a hopeless attempt to draw back from the way things were going.

But the disaster was inside himself already; there was no drawing back. Extraordinary is his note on his 'dreaminess'.

At times I am aware of something monstrous in myself. And that monstrous thing is my dreaminess. Then nothing can penetrate the circle traced by it.

I am all stone.

And a stone is a monster.

For one must love and be aflame.

From that dreaminess have come all my misfortunes in life (my former work in the Civil Service), the mistake of my whole proceedings (only when 'out of myself' was I attentive to My Friend [his wife] – and her pains), and also my sins.

In my dreaminess I could do nothing.

And on the other hand I could do anything ['sin'].

Afterwards I was sorry: but it was too late. Dreaminess has devoured me, and everything round me.

There is the clue to the whole man's life: this 'dreaminess' when he is like stone, insentient, and can do nothing, yet can do 'anything'. Over this dreaminess he has no control, nor over the stoniness. But what seemed to him dreaminess and stoniness seemed to others, from his actions, vicious malice and depravity. So that's that. It is one way of being damned.

And there we have the last word of the Russian, before the great *débâcle*. Anyone who understands in the least Rozanov's state of soul, in which, apparently, he was born, born with this awful insentient stoniness somewhere in him, must sympathize deeply with his real suffering and his real struggle to get back a positive self, a feeling self: to overcome the 'dreaminess', to dissolve the stone. How much, and how little, he succeeded we may judge from this book: and from his harping on the beauty of procreation and fecundity: and from his strange and self-revealing statements concerning Weininger. Rozanov is modern, terribly modern. And if he does not put the fear of God into us, he puts a real fear of destiny, or of doom: and of 'civilization' which does not come from within, but which is poured over the mind, by 'education'.

# Review of *A Second Contemporary Verse Anthology*

*New York Evening Post Literary Review*, 29 September 1923; *Phoenix*, 1936

'It is not merely an assembly of verse, but the spiritual record of an entire people.' – This from the wrapper of *A Second Contemporary Verse Anthology*. The spiritual record of an entire people sounds rather impressive. The book as a matter of fact is a collection of pleasant verse, neat and nice and easy as eating candy.

Naturally, any collection of contemporary verse in any country at any time is bound to be more or less a box of candy. Days of Horace, days of Milton, days of Whitman, it would be pretty much the same, more or less a box of candy. Would it be at the same time the spiritual record of an entire people? Why not? If we had a good representative anthology of the poetry of Whitman's day, and if it contained two poems by Whitman, then it would be a fairly true spiritual record of the American people of that day. As if the whole nation had whispered or chanted its inner experience into the horn of a gramophone.

And the bulk of the whisperings and murmurings would be candy: sweet nothings, tender trifles, and amusing things. For of such is the bulk of the spiritual experience of any entire people.

The Americans have always been good at 'occasional' verse. Sixty years ago they were very good indeed: making their little joke against themselves and their century. Today there are fewer jokes. There are also fewer footprints on the sands of time. Life is still earnest, but a little less real. And the soul has left off asserting that dust it isn't nor to dust returneth. The spirit of verse prefers now a 'composition salad' of fruits of sensation, in a cooked mayonnaise of sympathy. Odds and ends of feelings smoothed into unison by some prevailing sentiment:

> My face is wet with the rain
> But my heart is warm to the core...

Or you can call it a box of chocolate candies. Let me offer you a sweet! Candy! Isn't everything candy?

> There be none of beauty's daughters
> With a magic like thee –
> And like music on the waters
> Is thy sweet voice to me.

Is that candy? Then what about this?

> But you are a girl and run
> Fresh bathed and warm and sweet,
> After the flying ball
> On little, sandalled feet.

One of those two fragments is a classic. And one is a scrap from the contemporary spiritual record.

> The river boat had loitered down its way,
> The ropes were coiled, and business for the day
> Was done –

> Now fades the glimmering landscape on the sight,
> And all the air a solemn stillness holds;
> Save where –

Two more bits. Do you see any intrinsic difference between them? After all, the one *means* as much as the other. And what is there in the mere stringing together of words?

For some mysterious reason, there is everything.

> When lilacs last in the dooryard bloomed –

## Review of A Second Contemporary Verse Anthology

It is a string of words, but it makes me prick my innermost ear. So do I prick my ear to: 'Fly low, vermilion dragon.' But the next line: 'With the moon horns', makes me lower that same inward ear once more, in indifference.

There is an element of danger in all new utterance. We prick our ears like an animal in a wood at a strange sound.

Alas! though there is a modicum of 'strange sound' in this contemporary spiritual record, we are not the animal to prick our ears at it. Sounds sweetly familiar, linked in a new crochet pattern. 'Christ, what are patterns for?' But why invoke Deity? Ask the *Ladies' Home Journal*. You may know a new utterance by the element of danger in it. 'My heart aches,' says Keats, and you bet it's no joke.

> Why do I think of stairways
> With a rush of hurt surprise?

Heaven knows, my dear, unless you once fell down.

The element of danger. Man is always, all the time and for ever on the brink of the unknown. The minute you realize this, you prick your ears in alarm. And the minute any man steps alone, with his whole naked self, emotional and mental, into the everlasting hinterland of consciousness, you hate him and you wonder over him. Why can't he stay cozily playing word-games around the camp fire?

Now it is time to invoke the Deity, who made man an adventurer into the everlasting unknown of consciousness.

The spiritual record of any people is ninety-nine per cent a record of games around a camp fire: word-games and picture-games. But the one per cent is a step into the grisly dark, which is ever dangerous and wonderful. Nothing is wonderful unless it is dangerous. Dangerous to the *status quo* of the soul. And therefore to some degree detestable.

When the contemporary spiritual record warbles away about the wonder of the blue sky and the changing seas, etc., etc., etc., it is all candy. The sky is a blue hand-mirror to the modern poet and he goes on smirking before it. The blue sky of our particular heavens is painfully well known to us all. In fact, it is like the glass bowl to the goldfish, a *ne plus ultra* in which he sees himself as he goes round and round.

The actual heavens can suddenly roll up like the heavens of Ezekiel. That's what happened at the Renaissance. The old heavens shrivelled and men found a new empyrean above them. But they didn't get at it by playing word-games around the camp fire. Somebody has to jump like a desperate clown through the vast blue hoop of the upper air. Or hack a slow way through the dome of crystal.

Play! Play! Play! All the little playboys and playgirls of the western world, playing at goodness, playing at badness, playing at sadness, and playing deafeningly at gladness. Playboys and playgirls of the western world, harmlessly fulfilling their higher destinies and registering the spiritual record of an entire people. Even playing at death, and playing with death. Oh, poetry, you child in a bathing-dress, playing at ball!

You say nature is always nature, the sky is always the sky. But sit still and consider for one moment what sort of nature it was the Romans saw on the face of the earth, and what sort of heavens the medievals knew above them, and your sky will begin to crack like glass. The world is what it is, and the chimerical universe of the ancients was always child's play. The camera cannot lie. And the eye of man is nothing but a camera photographing the outer world in colour-process.

This sounds very well. But the eye of man photographs the chimera of nature, as well as the so-called scientific vision. The eye of man photographs gorgons and chimeras, as the eye of the spider photographs images unrecognizable to us and the eye of the horse photographs flat ghosts and looming motions. We are at the phase of scientific vision. This phase will pass and this vision will seem as chimerical to our descendants as the medieval vision seems to us.

The upshot of it all is that we are pot-bound in our consciousness. We are like a fish in a glass bowl, swimming round and round and gaping at our own image reflected on the walls of the infinite: the infinite being the glass bowl of our conception of life and the universe. We are prisoners inside our own conception of life and being. We have exhausted the possibilities of the universe, as we know it. All that remains is to telephone to Mars for a new word of advice.

Our consciousness is pot-bound. Our ideas, our emotions, our experiences are all pot-bound. For us there is nothing new under the sun. What there is to know, we know it already, and experience adds little. The girl who is going to fall in love knows all about it beforehand from books and the movies. She knows what she wants and she wants what she knows. Like candy. It is still nice to eat candy, though one has eaten it every day for years. It is still nice to eat candy. But the spiritual record of eating candy is a rather thin noise.

There is nothing new under the sun, once the consciousness becomes pot-bound. And this is what ails all art today. But particularly American art. The American consciousness is peculiarly pot-bound. It doesn't even have that little hole in the bottom of the pot through which desperate roots straggle. No, the American consciousness is not only potted in a solid and everlasting pot, it is placed moreover in an immovable ornamental vase. A double hide to bind it and a double bond to hide it.

European consciousness still has cracks in its vessel and a hole in the bottom of its absoluteness. It still has strange roots of memory groping down to the heart of the world.

But American consciousness is absolutely free of such danglers. It is free from all loop-holes and crevices of escape. It is absolutely safe inside a solid and ornamental concept of life. There it is Free! Life is good, and all men are meant to have a good time. Life is good! that is the flower-pot. The ornamental vase is : Having a good time.

So they proceed to have it, even with their woes. The young maiden knows exactly when she falls in love: she knows exactly how she feels when her lover or husband betrays her or when she betrays him: she knows precisely what it is to be a forsaken wife, an adoring mother, an erratic grandmother. All at the age of eighteen.

*Vive la vie!*

There is nothing new under the sun, but you can have a jolly

495

good old time all the same with old things. A nut sundae or a new beau, a baby or an automobile, a divorce or a troublesome appendix: my dear, that's Life! You've got to get a good time out of it, anyhow, so here goes!

In which attitude there is a certain piquant stoicism. The stoicism of having a good time. The heroism of enjoying yourself. But as I say, it makes rather thin hearing in a spiritual record. *Rechauffés* of *rechauffés*. Old soup of old bones of life, heated up again for a new consommé. Nearly always called *printanière*.

> I know a forest, stilly-deep ...

Mark the poetic novelty of stilly-deep, and then say there is nothing new under the sun.

> My soul-harp never thrills to peaceful tunes;

I should say so.

> For after all, the thing to do
> Is just to put your heart in song –

Or in pickle.

> I sometimes wish that God were back
>   In this dark world and wide;
> For though some virtues he might lack,
>   He had his pleasant side.

'Getting on the pleasant side of God, and how to stay there.' – Hints by a Student of Life.

> Oh, ho! Now I am masterful!
> Now I am filled with power.
> Now I am brutally myself again
>   And my own man.

> For I have been among my hills today,
> On the scarred dumb rocks standing;

And it made a man of him ...
Open confession is good for the soul.
The spiritual record of an entire ... what?

# Introduction to *Bottom Dogs*
## by Edward Dahlberg

Written and published 1929

When we think of America, and of her huge success, we never realize how many failures have gone, and still go, to build up that success. It is not till you live in America, and go a little under the surface, that you begin to see how terrible and brutal is the mass of failure that nourishes the roots of the gigantic tree of dollars. And this is especially so in the country, and in the newer parts of the land, particularly out west. There you see how many small ranches have gone broke in despair, before the big ranches scoop them up and profit by all the back-breaking, profitless, grim labour of the pioneer. In the west you can still see the pioneer work of tough, hard first-comers, individuals, and it is astounding to see how often these individuals, pioneer first-comers who fought like devils against their difficulties, have been defeated, broken, their efforts and their amazing hard work lost, as it were, on the face of the wilderness. But it is these hard-necked failures who really broke the resistance of the stubborn, obstinate country, and made it easier for the second wave of exploiters to come in with money and reap the harvest. The real pioneer in America fought like hell and suffered till the soul was ground out of him: and then, nine times out of ten, failed, was beaten. That is why pioneer literature, which, even from the glimpses one has of it, contains the amazing Odyssey of the brute fight with savage conditions of the western continent, hardly exists, and is absolutely unpopular. Americans will not stand for the pioneer stuff, except in small, sentimentalized doses. They know too well the grimness of it, the savage fight and the savage failure which broke the back of the country but also broke something in the human soul. The spirit and the will survived: but something in the soul perished: the softness, the floweriness, the natural tenderness. How could it survive the sheer brutality of the fight with that American wilderness, which is so big, vast and obdurate!

The savage America was conquered and subdued at the expense of the instinctive and intuitive sympathy of the human soul. The fight was too brutal. It is a great pity some publisher does not undertake a series of pioneer records and novels, the genuine, unsweetened stuff. The books exist. But they are shoved down into oblivion by the common will-to-forget. They show the strange brutality of the struggle, what would have been called in the old language the breaking of the heart. America was not colonized and 'civilized' until the heart was broken in the American pioneer. It was a price that was paid. The heart was broken. But the will, the determination to conquer the land and make it submit to productivity, this was not broken. The will-to-success and the will-to-produce became clean and indomitable once the sympathetic heart was broken.

By the sympathetic heart, we mean that instinctive belief which lies at the core of the human heart, that people and the universe itself are *ultimately* kind. This belief is fundamental and, in the old language, is embodied in the doctrine: God is good. Now given an opposition too ruthless, a fight too brutal, a betrayal too bitter, this belief breaks in the heart, and is no more. Then you have either despair, bitterness, and cynicism, or you have the much braver reaction which says: God is not good, but the human will is indomitable, it cannot be broken, it will succeed against all odds. It is not God's business to be good and kind, that is man's business. God's business is to be indomitable. And man's business is essentially the same.

This is, roughly, the American position today, as it was the position of the Red Indian, when the white man came, and of the

Aztec and of the Peruvian. So far as we can make out, neither Redskin nor Aztec nor Inca had any conception of a 'good' God. They conceived of implacable, indomitable Powers, which is very different. And that seems to me the essential American position today. Of course the white American believes that man should behave in a kind and benevolent manner. But this is a social belief and a social gesture, rather than an individual flow. The flow from the heart, the warmth of fellow-feeling which has animated Europe and been the best of her humanity, individual, spontaneous, flowing in thousands of little passionate currents often conflicting, this seems unable to persist on the American soil. Instead you get the social creed of benevolence and uniformity, a mass *will*, and an inward individual retraction, an isolation, an amorphous separateness like grains of sand, each grain isolated upon its own will, its own indomitableness, its own implacability, its own unyielding, yet heaped together with all the other grains. This makes the American mass the easiest mass in the world to rouse, to move. And probably, under a long stress, it would make it the most difficult mass in the world to hold together.

The deep psychic change which we call the breaking of the heart, the collapse of the flow of spontaneous warmth between a man and his fellows, happens of course now all over the world. It seems to have happened to Russia in one great blow. It brings a people into a much more complete social unison, for good or evil. But it throws them apart in their private, individual emotions. Before, they were like cells in a complex tissue, alive and functioning diversely in a vast organism composed of family, clan, village, nation. Now, they are like grains of sand, friable, heaped together in a vast inorganic democracy.

While the old sympathetic flow continues, there are violent hostilities between people, but they are not secretly repugnant to one another. Once the heart is broken, people become repulsive to one another, secretly, and they develop social benevolence. They smell in each other's nostrils. It has been said often enough of more primitive or old-world peoples, who live together in a state of blind mistrust but also of close physical connexion with one another, that they have no noses. They are so close, the flow from body to body is so powerful, that they hardly smell one another, and hardly are aware at all of offensive human odours that madden the new civilizations. As it says in this novel: The American senses other people by their sweat and their kitchens. By which he means, their repulsive effluvia. And this is basically true. Once the blood-sympathy breaks, and only the nerve-sympathy is left, human beings become secretly intensely repulsive to one another, physically, and sympathetic only mentally and spiritually. The secret physical repulsion between people is responsible for the perfection of American 'plumbing', American sanitation, and American kitchens, utterly white-enamelled and antiseptic. It is revealed in the awful advertisements such as those about 'halitosis', or bad breath. It is responsible for the American nausea at coughing, spitting, or any of those things. The American townships don't mind hideous litter of tin cans and paper and broken rubbish. But they go crazy at the sight of human excrement.

And it is this repulsion from the physical neighbour that is now coming up in the consciousness of the great democracies, in England, America, Germany. The old flow broken, men could enlarge themselves for a while in transcendentalism, Whitmanish 'adhesiveness' of the social creature, noble supermen, lifted above the baser functions. For the last hundred years man has been elevating himself above his 'baser functions' and posing around as a transcendentalist, a superman, a perfect social being, a spiritual entity. And now, since the war, the collapse has come.

Man has no ultimate control of his own consciousness. If his nose doesn't notice stinks, it just doesn't, and there's the end of it. If his nose is so sensitive that a stink overpowers him, then again he's helpless. He can't prevent his senses from transmitting and his mind from registering what it does register.

And now, man has begun to be overwhelmingly conscious of the repulsiveness of his neighbour, particularly of the physical repulsiveness. There it is, in James Joyce, in Aldous Huxley, in André Gide, in modern Italian novels like *Parigi* – in all the very modern novels, the dominant note is the repulsiveness, intimate physical repulsiveness of human flesh. It is the expression of absolutely genuine experience. What the young feel intensely, and no longer so secretly, is the extreme repulsiveness of other people.

It is, perhaps, the inevitable result of the transcendental bodiless brotherliness and social 'adhesiveness' of the last hundred years. People rose superior to their bodies, and soared along, till they had exhausted their energy in this performance. The energy once exhausted, they fell with a struggling plunge, not down into their bodies again, but into the cesspools of the body.

The modern novel, the very modern novel, has passed quite away from tragedy. An American novel like *Manhattan Transfer* has in it still the last notes of tragedy, the sheer spirit of suicide. An English novel like *Point Counter Point* has gone beyond tragedy into exacerbation, and continuous nervous repulsion. Man is so nervously repulsive to man, so screamingly, nerve-rackingly repulsive! This novel goes one further. Man just *smells*, offensively and unbearably, not to be borne. The human stink!

The inward revulsion of man away from man, which follows on the collapse of the physical sympathetic flow, has a slowly increasing momentum, a wider and wider swing. For a long time, the *social* belief and benevolence of man towards man keeps pace with the secret physical repulsion of man away from man. But ultimately, inevitably, the one outstrips the other. The benevolence exhausts itself, the repulsion only deepens. The benevolence is external and extra-individual. But the revulsion is inward and personal. The one gains over the other. Then you get a gruesome condition, such as is displayed in this book.

The only motive power left is the sense of revulsion away from people, the sense of the repulsiveness of the neighbour. It is a condition we are rapidly coming to – a condition displayed by the intellectuals much more than by the common people. Wyndham Lewis gives a display of the utterly repulsive effect people have on him, but he retreats into the intellect to make his display. It is a question of manner and manners. The effect is the same. It is the same exclamation: They stink! My God, they stink!

And in this process of recoil and revulsion, the affective con-

501

sciousness withers with amazing rapidity. Nothing I have ever read has astonished me more than the 'orphanage' chapters of this book. There I realized with amazement how rapidly the human psyche can strip itself of its awarenesses and its emotional contacts, and reduce itself to a sub-brutal condition of simple gross persistence. It is not animality – far from it. Those boys are much less than animals. They are cold wills functioning with a minimum of consciousness. The amount that they are *not* aware of is perhaps the most amazing aspect of their character. They are brutally and deliberately *unaware*. They have no hopes, no desires even. They have even no will-to-exist, for existence even is too high a term. They have a strange, stony will-to-persist, that is all. And they persist by reaction, because they still feel the repulsiveness of each other, of everything, even of themselves.

Of course the author exaggerates. The boy Lorry 'always had his nose in a book' – and he must have got things out of the books. If he had taken the intellectual line, like Mr Huxley or Mr Wyndham Lewis, he would have harped on the intellectual themes, the essential feeling being the same. But he takes the non-intellectual line, is in revulsion against the intellect too, so we have the stark reduction to a persistent minimum of the human consciousness. It is a minimum lower than the savage, lower than the African Bushman. Because it is a *willed* minimum, sustained from inside by resistance, brute resistance against any flow of consciousness except that of the barest, most brutal egoistic self-interest. It is a phenomenon, and pre-eminently an American phenomenon. But the flow or repulsion, inward physical revulsion of man away from man, is passing over all the world. It is only perhaps in America, and in a book such as this, that we see it most starkly revealed.

After the orphanage, the essential theme is repeated over a wider field. The state of revulsion continues. The young Lorry is indomitable. You can't destroy him. And at the same time, you can't catch him. He will recoil from everything, and nothing on earth will make him have a positive feeling, of affection or sympathy or connexion. His mother? – we see her in her decaying repulsiveness. He has a certain loyalty, because she is his sort: it is part of his will-to-persist. But he must turn his back on her with a certain disgust.

The tragedian, like Theodore Dreiser and Sherwood Anderson, still dramatizes his defeat and is in love with himself in his defeated role. But the Lorry Lewis is in too deep a state of revulsion to dramatize himself. He almost deliberately finds himself repulsive too. And he goes on, just to see if he can hit the world without destroying himself. Hit the world not to destroy it, but to experience in himself how repulsive it is.

Kansas City; Beatrice, Nebraska; Omaha; Salt Lake City; Portland, Oregon; Los Angeles, he finds them all alike, nothing if not repulsive. He covers the great tracts of prairie, mountain, forest, coast-range, without seeing anything but a certain desert scaliness. His consciousness is resistant, shuts things out, and reduces itself to a minimum.

In the Y.M.C.A. it is the same. He has his gang. But the last word about them is that they stink, their effluvia is offensive. He goes with women, but the thought of women is inseparable from the thought of sexual disease and infection. He thrills to the repulsiveness of it, in a terrified, perverted way. His associates – which means himself also – read Zarathustra and Spinoza, Darwin and Hegel. But it is with a strange external, superficial mind that has no connexion with the affective and effective self. One last desire he has – to write, to put down his condition in words. His will-to-persist is intellectual also. Beyond this, nothing.

It is a genuine book, as far as it goes, even if it is an objectionable one. It is, in psychic disintegration, a good many stages ahead of *Point Counter Point*. It reveals a condition that not many of us have reached, but towards which the trend of consciousness is taking us, all of us, especially the young. It is, let us hope, a *ne plus ultra*. The next step is legal insanity, or just crime. The book is perfectly sane: yet two more strides, and it is criminal insanity. The style seems to me excellent, fitting the matter. It is sheer bottom-dog style, the bottom-dog mind expressing itself direct, almost as if it barked. That directness, that unsentimental and non-dramatized thoroughness of setting down the under-dog mind surpasses anything I know. I don't want to read any more books like this. But I am glad to have read this one, just to know what is the last word in repulsive consciousness, consciousness in a state of repulsion. It helps one to understand the world, and saves one the necessity of having to follow out the phenomenon of physical repulsion any further, for the time being.

# Blessed Are the Powerful

*Reflections on the Death of a Porcupine*, 1925

The reign of love is passing, and the reign of power is coming again.

The day of popular democracy is nearly done. Already we are entering the twilight, towards the night that is at hand.

Before the darkness comes, it is as well to take our directions.

It is time to inquire into the nature of power, so that we do not crassly blunder into a new era: or fall down the gulf of anarchy, in the dark, as we cross the borders.

We have a confused idea, that *will* and power are somehow identical. We think we can have a will-to-power.

A will-to-power seems to work out as bullying. And bullying is something despicable and detestable.

Tyranny, too, which seems to us the apotheosis of power, is detestable.

It comes from our mistaken idea of power. It comes from the ancient mistake, old as Moses, of confusing power with *will*. The *pow*er of God, and the *will* of God, we have imagined identical. We need only think for a moment, and we can see the vastness of difference between the two.

The Jews, in Moses' time, and again particularly in the time of the Kings, came to look upon Jehovah as the apotheosis of arbitrary *will*. This is the root of a very great deal of evil; an old, old root.

Will is no more than an attribute of the ego. It is, as it were, the accelerator of the engine: or the instrument which increases the pressure. A man may have a strong will, an iron will, as we say, and yet be a stupid mechanical instrument, useful simply as an instrument, without any *power* at all.

An instrument, even an iron one, has no power. The power has to be put into it. This is true of men with iron wills, just the same.

The Jews made the mistake of deifying Will, the ethical Will of God. The Germans again made the mistake of deifying the egoistic Will of Man : the will-to-power.

There is a certain inherent stupidity in apotheosized Will, and a consequent inevitable inferiority in the devotees thereof. They all have an inferiority complex.

Because power is not in the least like Will. Power comes to us, we know not how, from beyond. Whereas our will is our own.

When a man prides himself on something that is just in himself, part of his own ego, he falls into conceit, and conceit carries an inferiority complex as its shadow.

If a man, or a race, or a nation is to be anything at all, he must have the generosity to admit that his strength comes to him from beyond. It is not his own, self-generated. It comes as electricity comes, out of nowhere into somewhere.

It is no good trying to intellectualize about it. All attempts to argue and intellectualize merely strangle the passages of the heart. We wish to keep our hearts open. Therefore we brush aside argument and intellectual haggling.

The intellect is one of the most curious instruments of the psyche. But, like the will, it is only an instrument. And it works only under pressure of the will.

By willing and by intellectualizing we have done all we can, for the time being. We only exhaust ourselves, and lose our lives – that is, our livingness, our power to live – by any further straining of the will and the intellect. It is time to take our hands off the throttle: knowing well enough what we are about, and choosing our course of action with a steady heart.

To take one's hand off the throttle is not the same as to let go the reins.

Man lives to live, and for no other reason. And life is not mere length of days. Many people hang on, and hang on, into a corrupt old age, just because they have *not* lived, and therefore cannot let go.

We must live. And to live, life must be in us. It must come to us, the power of life, and we must not try to get a strangle-hold upon it. From beyond comes to us the life, the power to live, and we must wisely keep our hearts open.

But the life will not come *unless* we live. That is the whole point. 'To him that hath shall be given.' To him that hath life shall be given life: on condition, of course, that he lives.

And again, life does not mean length of days. Poor old Queen Victoria had length of days. But Emily Brontë had life. She died of it.

And again 'living' doesn't mean just doing certain things: running after women, or digging a garden, or working an engine, or becoming a member of Parliament. Just because, for Lord Byron, to sleep with a 'crowned head' was life itself, it doesn't follow that it will be life for *me* to sleep with a crowned head, or even a head uncrowned. Sleeping with heads is no joke, anyhow. And living won't even consist in jazzing or motoring or going to Wembley, just because most folks do it. Living consists in doing what you really, vitally want to do: what the *life* in you wants to do, not what your ego imagines you want to do. And to find out *how* the life in you wants to be lived, and to live it, is terribly difficult. Somebody has to give us a clue.

And this is the real *exercise* of power.

That settles two points. First, power is life rushing in to us. Second, the exercise of power is the setting of life in motion.

And this is very far from *Will*.

If you want a dictator, whether it is Lenin, or Mussolini, or Primo de Rivera, ask, not whether he can set money in circulation, but if he can set life in motion, by dictating to his people.

Now, although we hate to admit it, Lenin did set life a good deal in motion, for the Russian proletariat. The Russian proletariat was like a child that had been kept under too much. So it was dying to be free. It was crazy to keep house for itself.

Now, like a child, it is keeping house for itself, without Papa or Mama to interfere. And naturally it enjoys it. For the time it's a game.

But for us, English or American or French or German people, it would not be a game. We have more or less kept house for ourselves for a long time, and it's not very thrilling after years of it.

So a Lenin wouldn't do us any good. He wouldn't set any life going in us at all.

The Gallic and Latin blood isn't thrilled about keeping house, anyhow. It wants Glory, or else ʎɹolפ. Glory on horse-back, or Glory upset. If there was any Glory to upset, either in France or Italy or Spain, then communism might flourish. But since there isn't even a spark of Glory to blow out – Alfonso! Victor Emmanuel! Poincaré! – what's the good of blowing?

So they set up a little harmless Glory in baggy trousers – Papa Mussolini – or a bit of fat, self-loving but amiable elder-brother Glory in General de Rivera: and they call it power. And the democratic world holds up its hands, and moans: *'Dictators! Tyranny!'* While the conservative world cheers loudly, and cries: *'The Man! The Man! El hombre! L'uomo! L'homme! Hooray!!!'*

Bunk!

We want life. And we want the power of life. We want to feel the power of life in ourselves.

We're sick of being soft, and amiable, and harmless. We're sick to death of even enjoying ourselves. We're a bit ashamed of our own existence. Or if we aren't we ought to be.

But what then? Shall we exclaim, in a fat voice: *'Aha! Power! Glory! Force! The Man!'* – and proceed to set up a harmless Mussolini, or a fat Rivera? Well, let us, if we want to. Only it won't make the slightest difference to our real living. Except it's probably a good thing to have the press – the newspaper press –

crushed under the up-to-date rubber heel of a tyrannous but harmless dictator.

We won't speak of poor old Hindenburg. Except, why didn't they set up his wooden statue with all the nails knocked into it, for a President? For surely they drove *something* in, with those nails!

We had a harmless dictator, in Mr Lloyd George. Better go ahead with the House of Representatives, than have another shot in that direction.

Power! How can there be power in politics, when politics is money?

Money is power, they say. Is it? Money is to power what margarine is to butter: a nasty substitute.

No, power is something you've got to respect, even revere, before you can have it. It isn't bossing, or bullying, hiring a man-servant or Salvationizing your social inferior, issuing loud orders and getting your own way, doing your opponent down. That isn't power.

Power is *pouvoir*: to be able to.

Might: the ability to make: to bring about that which may be.

And where are we to get Power, or Might, or Glory, or Honour, or Wisdom?

Out of Lloyd George, or Lenin, or Mussolini, or Rivera, or anything else political?

Bah! It has to be in the people, before it can come out in politics.

Do we *want* Power, Might, Glory, Honour, and Wisdom?

If we do, we'd better start to get them, each man for himself.

But if we don't, we'd better continue our lick-spittling course of being as happy, as happy as Kings.

> The world is so full of a number of things
> We ought all to be happy, as happy as Kings.

Which Kings, might we ask? Better be careful!

Myself I want Power. But I don't want to boss anybody.

I want Honour. But I don't see any existing nation or government that could give it me.

I want Glory. But heaven save me from mankind.

I want Might. But perhaps I've got it.

The first thing, of course, is to open one's heart to the source of Power, and Might, and Glory, and Honour. It just depends, which gates of one's heart one opens. You can open the humble gate, or the proud gate. Or you can open both, and see what comes.

Best open both, and take the responsibility. But set a guard at each gate, to keep out the liars, the snivellers, the mongrel and the greedy.

However smart we be, however rich and clever or loving or charitable or spiritual or impeccable, it doesn't help us at all. The real power comes in to us from beyond. Life enters us from behind, where we are sightless, and from below, where we do not understand.

And unless we yield to the beyond, and take our power and might and honour and glory from the unseen, from the unknown, we shall continue empty. We may have length of days. But an empty tin-can lasts longer than Alexander lived.

So, anomalous as it may sound, if we want power, we must put aside our own will, and our own conceit, and *accept* power, from the beyond.

And having admitted the power from the beyond into us, we must abide by it, and not traduce it. Courage, discipline, inward isolation, these are the conditions upon which power will abide in us.

And between brave people there will be the communion of power, prior to the communion of love. The communion of power does not exclude the communion of love. It includes it. The communion of love is only a part of the greater communion of power.

Power is the supreme quality of God and man: the power to cause, the power to create, the power to make, the power to do, the power to destroy. And then, between those things which are created or made, love is the supreme binding relationship. And between those who, with a single impulse, set out passionately to destroy what must be destroyed, joy flies like electric sparks, within the communion of power.

Love is simply and purely a relationship, and in a pure relationship there can be nothing but equality; or at least equipoise.

But Power is more than a relationship. It is like electricity, it has different degrees. Men are powerful or powerless, more or less: we know not how or why. But it is so. And the communion of power will always be a communion in inequality.

In the end, as in the beginning, it is always Power that rules the world! There *must* be rule. And only Power can rule. Love cannot, should not, does not seek to. The statement that love rules the camp, the court, the grove, is a lie; and the fact that such love has to rhyme with 'grove', proves it. Power rules and will always rule. Because it was Power that created us all. The act of love itself is an act of power, original as original sin. The power is given us.

As soon as there is an *act*, even in love, it is power. Love itself is purely a relationship.

But in an age that, like ours, has lost the mystery of power, and the reverence for power, a false power is substituted: the power of money. This is a power based on the force of human envy and greed, nothing more. So nations naturally become more envious and greedy every day. While individuals ooze away in a cowardice that they call love. They call it love, and peace, and charity, and benevolence, when it is mere cowardice. Collectively they are hideously greedy and envious.

True power, as distinct from the spurious power, which is merely the force of certain human vices directed and intensified by the human will: true power never belongs to us. It is given us, from the beyond.

Even the simplest form of power, physical strength, is not our own, to do as we like with. As Samson found.

But power is given differently, in varying degrees and varying kind to different people. It always was so, it always will be so. There will never be equality in power. There will always be unending inequality.

Nowadays, when the only power is the power of human greed and envy, the greatest men in the world are men like Mr Ford, who can satisfy the modern lust, we can call it nothing else, for owning a motor-car: or men like the great financiers, who can soar on wings of greed to uncanny heights, and even can spiritualize greed.

They talk about 'equal opportunity': but it is bunk, ridiculous bunk. It is the old fable of the fox asking the stork to dinner. All the food is to be served in a shallow dish, levelled to perfect equality, and you get what you can.

If you're a fox, like the born financier, you get a bellyful and more. If you're a stork, or a flamingo, or even a *man*, you have the food gobbled from under your nose, and you go comparatively empty.

Is the fox, then, or the financier, the highest animal in creation? Bah!

Humanity never bunked itself so thoroughly as with the bunk of equality, even qualified down to 'equal opportunity'.

In living life, we are all born with different powers, and different degrees of power: some higher, some lower. The only thing to do is honourably to accept it, and to live in the communion of power. Is it not better to serve a man in whom power lives, than to clamour for equality with Mr Motor-car Ford, or Mr Shady Stinnes? Pfui! to your equality with such men! It gives me gooseflesh.

How much better it must have been, to be a colonel under Napoleon than to be a Marshal Foch! Oh! how much better it must have been, to live in terror of Peter the Great – who was great – than to be a member of the proletariat under Comrade Lenin: or even to *be* Comrade Lenin: though even he was greatish, far greater than any extant millionaire.

Power is beyond us. Either it is given us from the unknown, or we have not got it. And better to touch it in another, than never to know it. Better be a Russian and shoot oneself out of sheer terror of Peter the Great's displeasure, than to live like a well-to-do American, and never know the mystery of Power at all. Live in blank sterility.

For Power is the first and greatest of all mysteries. It is the mystery that is behind all our being, even behind all our existence. Even the phallic erection is a first blind movement of power.

Love is said to call the power into motion: but it is probably the reverse: that the slumbering *power* calls love into being.

Power is manifold. There is physical strength, like Samson's. There is racial power, like David's or Mahomet's. There is mental power, like that of Socrates, and ethical power, like that of Moses, and spiritual power, like Jesus' or like Buddha's, and mechanical power, like that of Stephenson, or military power, like Napoleon's, or political power, like Pitt's. These are all true manifestations of power, coming out of the unknown.

Unlike the millionaire power, which comes out of the known forces of human greed and envy.

Power puts something new into the world. It may be Edison's gramophone, or Newton's Law or Caesar's Rome or Jesus' Christianity, or even Attila's charred ruins and emptied spaces. Something new displaces something old, and sometimes room has to be cleared beforehand.

Then power is obvious. Power is much more obvious in its destructive than in its constructive activity. A tree falls with a crash. It grew without a sound.

Yet true destructive power is power just the same as constructive. Even Attila, the Scourge of God, who helped to scourge the Roman world out of existence, was great with power. He was the scourge of *God*: not the scourge of the League of Nations, hired and paid in cash.

If it must be a scourge, let it be a scourge of God. But let it be power, the old divine power. The moment the divine power manifests itself, it is right: whether it be Attila or Napoleon or George Washington. But Lloyd George, and Woodrow Wilson, and Lenin, they never had the right smell. They never even roused real fear: no real passion. Whereas a manifestation of real power arouses passion, and always will.

Time it should again.

Blessed are the powerful, for theirs is the kingdom of earth.

# Democracy

Written towards 1920, published in *Phoenix*, 1936

## I

*The Average*

Whitman gives two laws or principles for the establishment of Democracy. We may epitomize them as:

(1) The Law of the Average; (2) The Principle of Individualism, or Personalism, or Identity.

The Law of the Average is well known to us. Upon this law rests all the vague dissertation concerning equality and social perfection. Rights of Man, Equality of Man, Social Perfectibility of Man: all these sweet abstractions, once so inspiring, rest upon the fatal little hypothesis of the Average.

What is the Average? As we are well aware, there is no such animal. It is a pure abstraction. It is the reduction of the human being to a mathematical unit. Every human being numbers one, one single unit. That is the grand proposition of the Average.

Let us further examine this mysterious One, this Unit, this Average; let us examine it corporeally. The average human being: put him on the table, the little monster, and let us see what his works are like. He is just a little monster. He has two legs, two eyes, one nose – all exact. He has a stomach and a penis. He is a little organism. He is one very complicated organ, a unit, an identity.

What is he for? If he's an organ, he must have a purpose. If he's an organism, he must have a purpose. The question is premature, yet it shall be answered. Since he has a mouth, he is made for eating. Since he has feet, he is made for walking. Since he has a penis, he is made for reproducing his species. And so on, and so on.

What a loathsome little beast he is, this Average, this Unit, this Homunculus. Yet he has his purposes. He is useful to measure by. That's the purpose of all averages. An average is not invented to be an Archetype. What a really comical mistake we have made about him. He is invented to serve as a standard in the business of comparison. He is invented to serve as a standard, just like any other standard, like the metre, or the gramme, or the English pound sterling. That's what he is for – nothing else. He was never intended to be worshipped. What comical, fetish-smitten savages we are.

We use a foot-rule to tell us how big our house is. We don't proceed to say that the foot-rule is the sceptre which sways the earth and all the stars. Yet we have said as much of this little standardized invention of ours, the Average Man, the man-in-the-street. We have made prime fools of ourselves.

Now let us pull the gilt off the image, and see exactly what it is, and what we want it for. It is a mathematical quantity, like the metre or the foot-rule: a purely arbitrary institution of the human mind. Let us be quite clear about that.

But the human mind has invented the institution for its own purposes. Granted. What are the purposes? Merely for the comparing of one *living* man with another *living* man, in case of necessity: just as money is merely a contrivance for comparing a leg of mutton with a volume of Keats's poems. The money in itself is nothing. It is simply the arbitrary static measure for human desires. We mistake the measure for the thing it measures, and proceed to base our desires on money. It is nonsensical materialism.

Now for the Average Man himself. He is five-feet-six-inches high: and therefore you, John, will take an over-size pair of trousers, reach-me-downs; and you, François, mon cher, will take an under-size. The Average Man also has a mouth and a stomach, which consume two pounds of bread and six ounces of meat per day: and therefore you, Fritz, exceed the normal consumption of food, while you, dear Emily, consume less than your share. The Average Man has also a penis; and therefore all of you, François, Fritz, John, and Giacomo, you may begin begetting children at the average age, let us say, of twenty-five.

The Average Man is somehow very unsatisfactory. He is not sufficiently worked out. It is astonishing that we have not perfected him before. But this is because we have mixed the issues. How could we scientifically establish the Average, whilst he had to stand draped upon a pedestal, as an Ideal? Haul him down at once. He is no Ideal. He is just a Standard, the creature on whom Standard suits and Standard boots are fitted, to whose stomach Standard bread is adjusted, and for whose eyes the Standard Lamps are lighted, the Standard Oil Company is busy refining its gallons. He comes under the Government Weights and Measures Act.

Perfect him quickly: the Average, the Normal, the Man-in-the-street. He is so many inches high, broad, deep; he weighs so many pounds. He must eat so much, and sleep so much, and work so much, and play so much, and love so much, and think so much, and argue so much, and read so many newspapers, and have so many children. Somebody, quick, – some Professor of Social Economy – draw us up a perfect Average, and let us have him before the middle of next week. He is urgently required at the moment.

This is all your Man-in-the-street amounts to: this tailor's dummy of an average. He is the image and effigy of all your equality. Men are not equal, and never were, and never will be, save by the arbitrary determination of some ridiculous human Ideal. But still, in the normal course of things, all men *do* have two eyes and one nose and a stomach and a penis. In the teeth of all opposition we assert it. In the normal course of things, all men *do* hunger and thirst and sleep and laugh and feel miserable and fall in love and ache for coition and ache to escape from the woman again. And the Average Man just represents what all men need and desire, physically, functionally, materially, and

516

socially. *Materially* need: that's the point. The Average Man is the standard of material need in the human being.

Please keep out all Spiritual and Mystical needs. They have nothing to do with the Average. You cannot Average such things. As far as the stomach goes, it is not really true that one man's meat is another man's poison. No. The law of the Average holds good for the stomach. All young mammals suck milk, without exception. But in the free, spontaneous self, one man's meat is truly another man's poison. And therefore you *can't* draw any average. You can't *have* an average: unless you are going to poison everybody.

Now we will settle for ever the Equality of Man, and the Rights of Man. Society means people living together. People *must* live together. And to live together, they must have some Standard, some *Material* Standard. This is where the Average comes in. And this is where Socialism and Modern Democracy come in. For Democracy and Socialism rest upon the Equality of Man, which is the Average. And this is sound enough, so long as the Average represents the real basic material needs of mankind: basic material needs: we insist and insist again. For Society, or Democracy, or any Political State or Community exists not for the sake of the individual, nor should ever exist for the sake of the individual, but simply to establish the Average, in order to make living together possible: that is, to make proper facilities for every man's clothing, feeding, housing himself, working, sleeping, mating, playing, according to his necessity as a common unit, an average. Everything beyond that common necessity depends on himself alone.

The proper adjustment of material means of existence: for this the State exists, but for nothing further. The State is a dead ideal. *Nation* is a dead ideal. Democracy and Socialism are dead ideals. They are one and all just *contrivances* for the supplying of the lowest material needs of a people. They are just vast hotels, or hostels, where every guest does some scrap of the business of the day's routine – if it's only lounging gracefully to give the appearance of ease – and for this contribution gets his suitable accommodation. England, France, Germany – these great nations, they have no vital meaning any more, except as great Food Committees and Housing Committees for a throng of people whose material tastes are somewhat in accord. No doubt they *had* other meanings. No doubt the French individuals of the seventeenth century still felt themselves gloriously expressed in stone, in Versailles. But man loses more and more his faculty for collective self-expression. Nay, the great development in collective expression in mankind has been a progress towards the possibility of purely individual expression. The highest Collectivity has for its true goal the purest individualism, pure individual spontaneity. But once more we have mistaken the means for the end: so that Presidents, those representatives of the collected masses, instead of being accounted the chief machine-section of society, which they are, are revered as ideal beings. The thing to do is not to raise the idea of Nation, or even of Internationalism, higher. The need is to take away every scrap of ideal drapery from nationalism and from internationalism, to show it all as a material contrivance for housing and feeding and conveying innumerable people. The housing and feeding, the method of conveyance and the rules of the road may be as different as you please – just as the methods of one great business house, and even of one hotel, are different from those of another. But that is all it is. Man no longer expresses himself in his form of government, and his President is strictly only his superlative butler. This is the true course of evolution: the great collective activities are at last merely auxiliary to the purely individual activities. Business houses may be magnificent, but there is nothing divine in it. This is why the Kaiser sounded so foolish. He was really only the head of a very great business concern. His God was the most intolerable part of his stock-in-trade. Genuine business houses may quarrel and compete, but they don't go to war. Why? Because they are not ideal concerns. They are just practical material concerns. It is only Ideal concerns which go to war, and slaughter indiscriminately with a feeling of exalted righteousness. But when a business concern masquerades as an ideal concern, and behaves in this fashion, it is really unbearable.

There are two things to do. Strip off at once all the ideal drapery

518

from nationality, from nations, peoples, states, empires, and even from Internationalism and Leagues of Nations. Leagues of Nations should be just flatly and simply committees where representatives of the various business houses, so-called Nations, meet and consult. Consultations, board-meetings of the State business men: no more. *Representatives of Peoples* – who can represent me? – I am myself. I don't intend anybody to represent me.

You, you Cabinet Minister – what are you? You are the arch-grocer, the super-hotel-manager, the foreman over the ships and railways. What else are you? You are the super-tradesman, same paunch, same ingratiating manner, same everything. Governments, what are they? Just board-meetings of big business men. Very useful, too – very thankful we are that somebody *will* look after this business. But Ideal! An Ideal Government? What nonsense. We might as well talk of an Ideal Cook's Tourist Agency, or an Ideal Achille Serre Cleaners and Dyers. Even the ideal Ford of America is only an ideal *average* motor-car. His employees are not spontaneous, nonchalant human beings, à la Whitman. They are just well-tested, well-oiled sections of the Ford automobile.

Politics – what are they? Just another, extra-large, commercial wrangle over buying and selling – nothing else. Very good to have the wrangle. Let us have the buying and selling well done. But *ideal!* Politics *ideal! Political Idealists!* What rank gewgaw and nonsense! We have just enough sense not to talk about Ideal Selfridges or Ideal Krupps or Ideal Heidsiecks. Then let us have enough sense to drop the ideal of England or Europe or anywhere else. Let us be men and women, and keep our house in order. But let us pose no longer as houses, or as England, or as housemaids, or democrats.

Pull the ideal drapery off Governments, States, Nations, and Inter-nations. Show them for what they are: big business concerns of manufacturing and retailing Standard goods. Put up a statue of the Average Man, something like those abominable statues of men in woollen underwear which surmount a shop at the corner of Oxford Street and Tottenham Court Road. Let your statue be grotesque: in fact, borrow those ignominious statues of men in pants and vests: the fat one for Germany, the thin one for England, the middling one for France, the gaunt one for America. Point to these statues, which guard the entrance to the House of Commons, to the Chamber, to the Senate, to the Reichstag – and let every Prime Minister and President know the quick of his own ignominy. Let every bursting politician see himself in his commercial pants. Let every senatorial idealist and saviour of mankind be reminded that his office depends on the quality of the underwear he supplies to the State. Let every fiery and rhetorical Deputy remember that he is only held together by his patent suspenders.

And then, when the people of the world have finally got over the state of giddy idealizing of governments, nations, inter-nations, politics, democracies, empires, and so forth; when they really understand that their collective activities are only cook-housemaid to their sheer individual activities; when they at last calmly accept a business concern for what it is; then, at last, we may actually see free men in the streets.

II

*Identity*

Let us repeat that Whitman establishes the true Democracy on two bases:

(1) The Average; (2) Individualism, Personalism, or Identity.

The Average is much easier to settle and define than is Individualism or Identity. The Average is the same as the Man-in-the-street, the unit of Humanity. This unit is in the first place just an abstraction, an invention of the human mind. In the first place, the Man-in-the-street is no more than an abstract idea. But in the second place, by application to Tom, Dick, and Harry, he becomes a substantial, material, functioning unit. This is how the ideal world is created. It is invented exactly as man invents machinery. First there is an idea; then the idea is substantiated, the inventor fabricates his machine; and then he proceeds to worship his fabrication, and himself as mouthpiece of the Logos.

This is how the world, the universe, was invented from the Logos: exactly as man has invented machinery and the whole ideal of humanity. The vital universe was never created from any Logos; but the ideal universe of man was certainly so invented. Man's overweening mind uttered the Word, and the Word was God. So that the world exists today as a flesh-and-blood-and-iron substantiation of this uttered word. This is all the trouble: that the invented *ideal* world of man is superimposed upon living men and women, and men and women are thus turned into abstracted, functioning, mechanical units. This is all the great ideal of Humanity amounts to: an aggregation of ideally functioning units; never a man or woman possible.

Ideals, all ideals and every ideal, are a trick of the devil. They are a superimposition of the abstracted, automatic, invented universe of man upon the spontaneous creative universe. So much for the Average, the Man-in-the-street, and the great ideal of Humanity: all a little trick men have played on us. But quite a useful little trick – so long as we merely use it as one uses the trick of making cakes or pies or bread, just for feeding purposes, and suchlike.

Let us leave the Average, and look at the second basis of democracy. With the Average we settle the cooking, eating, sleeping, housing, mating and clothing problem. But Whitman insisted on exalting his Democracy; he would not quite leave it on the cooking-eating-mating level. We cook to eat, we eat to sleep, we sleep to build houses, we build houses in order to beget and bear children in safety, we bear children in order to clothe them, we clothe them in order that they may start the old cycle over again, cook and eat and sleep and house and mate and clothe, and so on *ad infinitum*. That is the Average. It is the business of a government to superintend it.

But Whitman insisted on raising Democracy above government, or even above public service or humanity or love of one's neighbour. Heaven knows what his Democracy is – but something as yet unattained. It is something beyond governments and even beyond Ideals. It must be beyond Ideals, because it has never yet been stated. As an idea it doesn't yet exist. Even Whitman, with all his reiteration, got no further than *hinting*: and frightfully bad hints, many of them.

We've heard the Average hint – enough of that. Now for Individualism, Personalism, and Identity. We catch hold of the tail of the hint, and proceed with Identity.

What has Identity got to do with Democracy? It can't have anything to do with politics and governments. It can't much affect one's love for one's neighbour, or for humanity. Yet, stay – it can. Whitman says there is One Identity in all things. It is only the old dogma. All things emanate from the Supreme Being. All things, being all emanations from the Supreme Being, have One Identity.

Very nice. But we don't like the look of this Supreme Being. It is too much like the Man-in-the-street. This Supreme Being, this Anima Mundi, this Logos was surely just invented to suit the human needs. It is surely the magnified Average, abstracted from men, and then clapped on to them again, like identity-medals on wretched khaki soldiers. But instead of a magnified average-function-unit, we have a magnified unit of Consciousness, or Spirit.

Like the Average, this One Identity is useful enough, if we use it aright. It is not a matter of provisioning the body, this time, but of provisioning the spirit, the consciousness. We are all one, and therefore every bit partakes of all the rest. That is, the Whole is inherent in every fragment. That is, every human consciousness has the same intrinsic value as every other human consciousness, because each is an essential part of the Great Consciousness. This is the One Identity which identifies us all.

It is very nice theoretically. And it is a very great stimulus to universal comprehension; it leads us all to want to know everything; it even tempts us all to imagine we know everything beforehand, and need make no effort. It is the subtlest means of extending the consciousness. But when you have extended your consciousness, even to infinity, what then? Do you really become God? When in your understanding you embrace everything, then surely you are divine? But no! With a nasty bump you have to come down and realize that, in spite of your infinite comprehension, you are not really any other than you were before: not a

522

bit more divine or superhuman or enlarged. Your *consciousness* is not *you*: that is the sad lesson you learn in your superhuman flight of infinite understanding.

This big bump of falling out of the infinite back into your own old self leads you to suspect that the One Identity is not *the* identity. There is another, little sort of identity, which you can't get away from, except by breaking your neck. The One Identity is very like the Average. It is what you are when you aren't yourself. It is what you are when you imagine you're something hugely big – the Infinite, for example. And the consciousness is really capable of attaining infinity. But there you are! Your consciousness has to fly back to the old tree, to peck the old apples, and sleep under the leaves. It was all only an excursion. It was wearing a magic cap. You yourself invented the cap, and then puffed up your head to fit it. But a swelled head at last begins to ache, and you realize it's only your own old chump after all. All the extended consciousness that ranges the infinite heavens must sleep under the thatch of your hair at night: and you are only you; and your *spirit* is only a bird in your tree, that flies, and then settles, whistles, and then is silent.

Man is a queer beast. He spends dozens of centuries puffing himself up and drawing himself in, and at last he has to be content to be just his own size, neither infinitely big nor infinitely little. Man is tragi-comical. His insatiable desire to be *everything* has made him clean forget that he might be himself. To be everything – to be everything: the history of mankind is only a history of this insane craving in man. You can magnify yourself into a Jehovah and a huge Egyptian king-god: or you can reverse the spy-glass, and dwindle yourself away into a speck, lost in the Infinite of Love, as the later great races have done. But still you'll only be chasing the one mad reward, the reward of infinity: which, when you've got it, bursts like a bubble in your hand, and leaves you looking at your own fingers. Well, and what's wrong with your own fingers?

It is a bubble, the One Identity. But, chasing it, man gets his education. It is his education process, the chance of the All, the extension of the consciousness. He *learns* everything: except the last lesson of all, which he can't learn till the bubble has burst in his fingers.

The last lesson? – Ah, the lesson of his own fingers: himself: the little identity; little, but real. Better, far better, to be oneself than to be any bursting Infinite, or swollen One Identity.

It is a radical passion in man, however, the passion to include *everything* in himself, grasp it all. There are two ways of gratifying this passion. The first is Alexander's way, the way of power, power over the material universe. This is what the alchemists and magicians sought. This is what Satan offered Jesus, in the Temptations: power, mystic and actual, over the material world. And power, we know, is a bubble: a platitudinous bubble.

But Jesus chose the other way: not to *have* all, but to *be* all. Not to *grasp* everything into supreme possession: but to *be* everything, through supreme acceptance. It is the same thing, at the very last. The king-god and the crucified-God hold the same bubble in their hands: the bubble of the All, the Infinite. The king-god extends the dominion of his will and consciousness over all things: the crucified identifies his will and consciousness with all things. But the submission of love is at last a process of pure materialism, like the supreme extension of power. Up to a certain point, both in mastering, which is power, and in submitting, which is love, the soul *learns* and fulfils itself. Beyond a certain point, it merely collapses from its centrality, and lapses out into the material chain of cause and effect. The tyranny of Power is no worse than the tyranny of No-power. Government by the highest is no more fatal than government by the lowest. Let the Average govern, let him be called super-butler, let us have a faint but tolerant contempt for him. But let us keep our very self integral, greater than any having or knowing, centrally alive and quick.

The last lesson: the myriad, mysterious identities, no one of which can *comprehend* another. They can only exist side by side, as stars do. The lesson of lessons: not in any oneness with the rest of things do we have our pure being: but in clean, fine singleness. Oneness, and collectiveness, these are our lesser states, inferior: our impurity. They are mere states of consciousness and of having.

It is all very well to talk about a Supreme Being, an Anima Mundi, an Oversoul, an Infinite: but it is all just human invention. Come down to actuality. Where do you see Being? – In individual men and women. Where do you find an Animal? – In living individual creatures. Where would you look for a soul? – In a man, in an animal, in a tree or flower. And all the rest, about Supreme Beings and Anima Mundis and Oversouls, is just abstractions. Show me the very animal! – You can't. It is merely a trick of the human will, trying to get power over everything, and therefore making the wish father of the thought. The cart foals the horse, and there you are: a Logos, a Supreme Being, a What-not.

But there are two sorts of individual identity. Every factory-made pitcher has its own little identity, resulting from a certain mechanical combination of Matter with Forces. These are the material identities. They sum up to the material Infinite.

The true identity, however, is the identity of the living self. If we look for God, let us look in the bush where he sings. That is, in living creatures. Every living creature is single in itself, a *ne plus ultra* of creative reality, *fons et origo* of creative manifestation. Why go further? Why begin to abstract and generalize and include? There you have it. Every single living creature is a single creative unit, a unique, incommutable self. Primarily, in its own spontaneous reality, it knows no law. It is a law unto itself. Secondarily, in its material reality, it submits to all the laws of the material universe. But the primal, spontaneous self in any creature has ascendance, truly, over the material laws of the universe; it uses these laws and converts them in the mystery of creation.

This then is the true identity: the inscrutable, single self, the little unfathomable well-head that bubbles forth into being and doing. We cannot analyse it. We can only know it is there. It is not by any means a Logos. It precedes any knowing. It is the fountain-head of everything: the quick of the self.

Not people melted into a oneness: that is not the new Democracy. But people released into their single, starry identity, each one distinct and incommutable. This will never be an ideal; for of the living self you cannot make an idea, just as you have not been able to turn the individual 'soul' into an idea. Both are impossible to idealize. An idea is an abstraction from reality, a generalization. And you can't generalize the incommutable.

So the Whitman One Identity, the *En-Masse*, is a horrible nullification of true identity and being. At the best, our *en masse* activities can be but servile, serving the free soul. At the worst, they are sheer self-destruction. Let us put them in their place. Let us get over our rage of social activity, public being, universal self-estimation, republicanism, bolshevism, socialism, empire – all these mad manifestations of *En Masse* and One Identity. They are all self-betrayed. Let our Democracy be in the singleness of the clear, clean self, and let our *En Masse* be no more than an arrangement for the liberty of this self. Let us drop looking after our neighbour. It only robs him of his chance of looking after himself. Which is robbing him of his freedom, with a vengeance.

III

*Personality*

> One's-self I sing, a simple separate person,
> Yet utter the word Democratic, the word En-Masse.

Such are the opening words of *Leaves of Grass*. It is Whitman's whole *motif*, the key to all his Democracy. First and last he sings of 'the great pride of man in himself'. First and last he is Chanter of Personality. If it is not Personality, it is Identity; and if not Identity, it is the Individual: and along with these, Democracy and *En Masse*.

In Whitman, at all times, the true and the false are so near, so interchangeable, that we are almost inevitably left with divided feelings. The Average, one of his greatest idols, we flatly refuse to worship. Again, when we come to do real reverence to identity, we never know whether we shall be taking off our hats to that great mystery, the unique individual self, distinct and primal in every separate man, or whether we shall be saluting that old great idol of the past, the Supreme One which swallows up all true identity.

And now for Personality. What meaning does 'person' really carry? A *person* is given in the dictionary as an *individual human being*. But surely the words *person* and *individual* suggest very different things. It is not at all the same to have personality as to have individuality, though you may not be able to define the difference. And the distinction between a person and a human being is perhaps even greater. Some 'persons' hardly seem like human beings at all.

The derivation this time helps. *Persona*, in Latin, is a player's mask, or a character in a play: and perhaps the word is cognate with *sonare*, to sound. An *individual* is that which is not divided or not dividable. A *being* we shall not attempt to define, because it is indefinable.

So now, there must be a radical difference between something which was originally a player's mask, or a transmitted sound, and something which means 'the undivided'. The old meaning lingers in *person*, and is almost obvious in *personality*. A person is a human being *as he appears to others;* and personality is that which is transmitted from the person to his audience: the transmissible effect of a man.

A good actor can assume a personality; he can never assume an individuality. Either he has his own, or none. So that personality is something much more superficial, or at least more volatile than individuality. This volatile quality is the one we must examine.

Let us take a sentence from an American novel: 'My *ego* had played a trick on me, and made me think I wanted babies, when I only wanted the man.' This is a perfectly straight and lucid statement. But what is the difference between the authoress's *ego* and her *me*? The *ego* is obviously a sort of second self, which she carries about with her. It is her body of accepted consciousness, which she has inherited more or less ready-made from her father and grandfathers. This secondary self is very pernicious, dictating to her issues which are quite false to her true, deeper, spontaneous self, her creative identity.

Nothing in the world is more pernicious than the *ego* or spurious self, the conscious entity with which every individual is sad-

dled. He receives it almost *en bloc* from the preceding generation, and spends the rest of his life trying to drag his spontaneous
self from beneath the horrible incubus. And the most fatal part of
the incubus, by far, is the dead, leaden weight of handed-on
ideals. So that every individual is born with a mill-stone of ideals
round his neck, and, whether he knows it or not, either spends his
time trying to get his neck free, like a wild animal wrestling with a
collar to which a log is fastened; or else he spends his days de-
corating his mill-stone, his log, with fantastic colours.

And a finely or fantastically decorated mill-stone is called a
personality. Never trust for one moment any individual who has
unmistakable *personality*. He is sure to be a life-traitor. His personality is only a sort of actor's mask. It is his self-conscious *ego*,
his *ideal* self masquerading and prancing round, showing off. He
may not be aware of it. But that makes no matter. He is a painted
bug.

The *ideal* self: this is personality. The self that is begotten and
born from the *idea*, this is the *ideal* self: a spurious, detestable
product. This is man created from his own Logos. This is man
born out of his own head. This is the self-conscious ego, the entity of fixed ideas and ideals, prancing and displaying itself like
an actor. And this is personality. This is what makes the American authoress gush about babies. And this gush is her peculiar
form of personality, which renders her attractive to the American
men, who prefer so much to deal with personalities and *egos*,
rather than with real beings: because personalities and *egos*,
after all, are quite *reasonable*, which means, they are subject to the
laws of cause-and-effect; they are safe and calculable: materialists, units of the material world of Force and Matter.

Your idealist alone is a perfect materialist. This is no paradox.
What is the idea, or the ideal, after all? It is only a fixed, static
entity, an abstraction, an extraction from the living body of life.
Creative life is characterized by spontaneous mutability: it brings
forth unknown issues, impossible to preconceive. But an ideal is
just a machine which is in process of being built. A man gets the
idea for some engine, and proceeds to work it out in steel and
copper. In exactly the same way, man gets some ideal of man,

and proceeds to work it out in flesh-and-blood, as a fixed, static entity: just as a machine is a static entity, so is the ideal Humanity.

If we want to find the real enemy today, here it is: idealism. If we want to find this enemy incarnate, here he is: a personality. If we want to know the steam which drives this mechanical little incarnation, here it is: love of humanity, the public good.

There have been other ideals than ours, other forms of personality, other sorts of steam. We quite fail to see what sort of personality Rameses II had, or what sort of steam built the pyramids: chiefly, I suppose, because they are a very great load on the face of the earth.

Is love of humanity the same as real, warm, individual love? Nonsense. It is the moonshine of our warm day, a hateful reflection. Is personality the same as individual being? We know it is a mere mask. Is idealism the same as creation? Rubbish! Idealism is no more than a plan of a marvellous Human Machine, drawn up by the great Draughtsmen-Minds of the past. Give God a pair of compasses, and let the designs be measured and formed. What insufferable nonsense! As if creation proceeded from a pair of compasses. Better say that man is a forked radish, as Carlyle did: it's nearer the mark than this Pair of Compasses business.

You can have life two ways. Either everything is created from the mind, downwards; or else everything proceeds from the creative quick, outwards into exfoliation and blossom. Either a great Mind floats in space: God, the Anima Mundi, the Oversoul, drawing with a pair of compasses and making everything to scale, even emotions and self-conscious effusions; or else creation proceeds from the for ever inscrutable quicks of living beings, men, women, animals, plants. The actual living quick itself is alone the creative reality. Once you abstract from this, once you generalize and postulate Universals, you have departed from the creative reality, and entered the realm of static fixity, mechanism, materialism.

Now let us put salt on the tail of that sly old bird of 'attractive personality'. It isn't a bird at all. It is a self-conscious, self-important, befeathered snail: and salt is good for snails. It is the snail which has eaten off our flowers till none are left. Now let us no longer be taken in by the feathers. Anyhow, put salt on his tail.

No personalities in our Democracy. No ideals either. When still more Personalities come round hawking their pretty ideals, we must be ready to upset their apple-cart. I say, a man's self is a law unto itself: not unto *himself*, mind you, Itself. When a man talks about *himself*, he is talking about his idea of himself; his own ideal self, that fancy little homunculus he has fathered in his brain. When a man is conscious of himself he is trading his own personality.

You can't make an *idea* of the living self: hence it can never become an ideal. Thank heaven for that. There it is, an inscrutable, unfindable, vivid quick, giving us off as a life-issue. It is not *spirit*. Spirit is merely our mental consciousness, a finished essence extracted from our life-being, just as alcohol, spirits of wine, is the material, finished essence extracted from the living grape. The living self is not spirit. You cannot postulate it. How can you postulate that which is *there*? The moon might as well try to hold forth in heaven, postulating the sun. Or a child hanging on to his mother's skirt might as well commence in a long diatribe to postulate his mother's existence, in order to prove his own existence. Which is exactly what man has been busily doing for two thousand years. What amazing nonsense!

The quick of the self is *there*. You needn't try to get behind it. As leave try to get behind the sun. You needn't try to idealize it, for by so doing you will only slime about with feathers in your tail, a gorgeous befeathered snail of an *ego* and a personality. You needn't try to show it off to your neighbour: he'll put salt on your tail if you do. And you needn't go on trying to save the living soul of your neighbour. It's hands off. Do you think you are such a God-Almighty bird of paradise that you can grow your neighbour's goose-quills for him on your own loving house-sparrow wings? Every bird must grow his own feathers; you are not the almighty dodo; you've got nobody's wings to feather but your own.

IV

*Individualism*

It is obvious that Whitman's Democracy is not merely a political system, or a system of government – or even a social system. It is an attempt to conceive a new way of life, to establish new values. It is a struggle to liberate human beings from the fixed, arbitrary control of ideals, into free spontaneity.

No, the ideal of Oneness, the unification of all mankind into the homogeneous whole, is done away with. The great *desire* is that each single individual shall be incommutably himself, spontaneous and single, that he shall not in any way be reduced to a term, a unit of any Whole.

We must discriminate between an ideal and a desire. A desire proceeds from within, from the unknown, spontaneous soul or self. But an ideal is superimposed from above, from the mind; it is a fixed, arbitrary thing, like a machine control. The great lesson is to learn to break all the fixed ideals, to allow the soul's own deep desires to come direct, spontaneous into consciousness. But it is a lesson which will take many aeons to learn.

Our life, our being depends upon the incalculable issue from the central Mystery into indefinable *presence*. This sounds in itself an abstraction. But not so. It is rather the perfect absence of abstraction. The central Mystery is no generalized abstraction. It is each man's primal original soul or self, within him. And *presence* is nothing mystic or ghostly. On the contrary. It is the actual man present before us. The fact that an actual man present before us is an inscrutable and incarnate Mystery, untranslatable, this is the fact upon which any great scheme of social life must be based. It is the fact of *otherness*.

Each human self is single, incommutable, and unique. This is its *first* reality. Each self is unique, and therefore incomparable. It is a single well-head of creation, unquestionable: it cannot be compared with another self, another well-head, because, in its prime or creative reality, it can never be comprehended by any other self.

The living self has one purpose only: to come into its own fulness of being, as a tree comes into full blossom, or a bird into spring beauty, or a tiger into lustre.

But this coming into full, spontaneous being is the most difficult thing of all. Man's nature is balanced between spontaneous creativity and mechanical-material activity. Spontaneous being is subject to no law. But mechanical-material existence is subject to all the laws of the mechanical-physical world. Man has almost half his nature in the material world. His spontaneous nature *just* takes precedence.

The only thing man has to trust to in coming to himself is his desire and his impulse. But both desire and impulse tend to fall into mechanical automatism: to fall from spontaneous reality into dead or material reality. All our education should be a guarding against this fall.

The fall is possible in a two-fold manner. Desires tend to automatize into functional appetites, and impulses tend to automatize into fixed aspirations or ideals. These are the two great temptations of man. Falling into the first temptation, the whole human will pivots on some function, some material activity, which then works the whole being: like an *idée fixe* in the mental consciousness. This automatized, dominant appetite we call a lust: a lust for power, a lust for consuming, a lust for self-abnegation and merging. The second great temptation is the inclination to set up some fixed centre in the mind, and make the whole soul turn upon this centre. This we call idealism. Instead of the will fixing upon some sensational activity, it fixes upon some aspirational activity, and pivots this activity upon an idea or an ideal. The whole soul streams in the energy of aspiration and turns automatically, like a machine, upon the ideal.

These are the two great temptations of the fall of man, the fall from spontaneous, single, pure being, into what we call materialism or automatism or mechanism of the self. All education must tend against this fall; and all our efforts in all our life must be to preserve the soul free and spontaneous. The whole soul of man must *never* be subjected to one motion or emotion, the life-activity must never be degraded into a fixed activity, there must be *no fixed direction.*

There can be no ideal goal for human life. Any ideal goal means mechanization, materialism, and nullity. There is no pulling open the buds to see what the blossom will be. Leaves must unroll, buds swell and open, and *then* the blossom. And even after that, when the flower dies and the leaves fall, *still* we shall not know. There will be more leaves, more buds, more blossoms: and again, a blossom is an unfolding of the creative unknown. Impossible, utterly impossible to preconceive the unrevealed blossom. You cannot forestall it from the last blossom. We know the flower of today, but the flower of tomorrow is all beyond us. Only in the material-mechanical world can man foresee, foreknow, calculate, and establish laws.

So, we more or less grasp the first term of the new Democracy. We see something of what a man will be unto himself.

Next, what will a man be unto his neighbour? – Since every individual is, in his first reality, a single, incommutable soul, not to be calculated or defined in terms of any other soul, there can be no establishing of a mathematical ratio. We cannot say that all men are equal. We cannot say $A = B$. Nor can we say that men are unequal. We may not declare that $A = B + C$.

Where each thing is unique in itself, there can be no comparison made. One man is neither equal nor unequal to another man. When I stand in the presence of another man, and I am my own pure self, am I aware of the presence of an equal, or of an inferior, or of a superior? I am not. When I stand with another man, who is himself, and when I am truly myself, then I am only aware of a Presence, and of the strange reality of Otherness. There is me, and there is *another being*. That is the first part of the reality. There is no comparing or estimating. There is only this strange recognition of *present otherness*. I may be glad, angry, or sad, because of the presence of the other. But still no comparison enters in. Comparison enters only when one of us departs from his own integral being, and enters the material-mechanical world. Then equality and inequality starts at once.

So, we know the first great purpose of Democracy: that each

533

man shall be spontaneously himself – each man himself, each woman herself, without any question of equality or inequality entering in at all; and that no man shall try to determine the being of any other man, or of any other woman.

But, because of the temptation which awaits every individual – the temptation to fall out of being, into automatism and mechanization, every individual must be ready at all time to defend his own being against the mechanization and materialism forced upon him by those people who have fallen or departed from being. It is the long unending fight, the fight for the soul's own freedom of spontaneous being, against the mechanism and materialism of the fallen.

All the foregoing deals really with the integral, whole nature of man. If man would but *keep* whole, integral, everything could be left at that. There would be no need for laws and governments: agreement would be spontaneous. Even the great concerted social activities would be essentially spontaneous.

But in his present state of unspeakable barbarism, man is unable to distinguish his own spontaneous integrity from his mechanical lusts and aspirations. Hence there must still be laws and governments. But laws and governments henceforth, we see it clearly and we must never forget it, relate only to the material world: to property, the possession of property and the means of life, and to the material-mechanical nature of man.

In the past, no doubt, there were great ideals to fulfil: ideals of brotherhood, oneness, and equality. Great sections of humanity tended to cohere into particular brotherhoods, expressing their oneness and their equality and their united purpose in a manner peculiar to themselves. For no matter how single an ideal may be, even such a mathematical ideal as equality and oneness, it will find the most diverse and even opposite expressions. So that brotherhood and oneness in Germany never meant the same as brotherhood and oneness in France. Yet each was brotherhood, and each was oneness. Souls, as they work out the same ideal, work it out differently: always differently, until they reach the point where the spontaneous integrity of being finally breaks. And then, when pure mechanization or materialism sets in, the soul is

534

automatically pivoted, and the most diverse of creatures fall into a common mechanical unison. This we see in America. It is not a homogeneous, spontaneous coherence so much as a disintegrated amorphousness which lends itself to perfect mechanical unison.

Men have reached the point where, in further fulfilling their ideals, they break down the living integrity of their being and fall into sheer mechanical materialism. They become automatic units, determined entirely by mechanical law.

This is horribly true of modern democracy – socialism, conservatism, bolshevism, liberalism, republicanism, communism: all alike. The one principle that governs all the *isms* is the same: the principle of the idealized unit, the possessor of property. Man has his highest fulfilment as a possessor of property: so they all say, really. One half says that the uneducated, being the majority, should possess the property; the other half says that the educated, being the enlightened, should possess the property. There is no more to it. No need to write books about it.

This is the last of the ideals. This is the last phase of the ideal of equality, brotherhood, and oneness. All ideals work down to the sheer materialism which is their intrinsic reality, at last.

It doesn't matter, now, who has the property. They have all lost their being over it. Even property, that most substantial of realities, evaporates once man loses his integral nature. It is curious that it is so, but it is undeniable. So that property is now fast evaporating.

Wherein lies the hope? For with it evaporates the last ideal. Sometime, somewhere, man will wake up and realize that property is only there to be used, not to be possessed. He will realize that possession is a kind of illness of the spirit, and a hopeless burden upon the spontaneous self. The little pronouns 'my' and 'our' will lose all their mystic spell.

The question of property will never be settled till people cease to care for property. Then it will settle itself. A man only needs so much as will help him to his own fulfilment. Surely the individual who wants a motor-car merely for the sake of having it and riding in it is as hopeless an automaton as the motor-car itself.

When men are no longer obsessed with the desire to possess property, or with the parallel desire to prevent another man's possessing it, then, and only then shall we be glad to turn it over to the State. Our way of State-ownership is merely a farcical exchange of words, not of ways. We only intend our States to be Unlimited Liability Companies instead of Limited Liability Companies.

The Prime Minister of the future will be no more than a sort of steward, the Minister for Commerce will be the great housekeeper, the Minister for Transport the head-coachman: all just chief servants, no more: servants.

When men become their own decent selves again, then we can so easily arrange the material world. The arrangement will come, as it must come, spontaneously, not by previous ordering. Until such time, what is the good of talking about it? All discussion and idealizing of the possession of property, whether individual or group or State possession, amounts now to no more than a fatal betrayal of the spontaneous self. All settlement of the property question must arise spontaneously out of the new impulse in man, to free himself from the extraneous load of possession, and walk naked and light. Every attempt at preordaining a new material world only adds another last straw to the load that already has broken so many backs. If we are to keep our backs unbroken, we must deposit all property on the ground, and learn to walk without it. We must stand aside. And when many men stand aside, they stand in a new world; a new world of man has come to pass. This is the Democracy, the new order.

# 7. Myths

# Introduction to *The Dragon of the Apocalypse* by Frederick Carter

Written 1929, published in *London Mercury*, July 1930;
*Phoenix*, 1936
(Carter's book eventually appeared under a different
title and without Lawrence's Introduction)

It is some years now since Frederick Carter first sent me the
manuscript of his *Dragon of the Apocalypse*. I remember it
arrived when I was staying in Mexico, in Chapala. The village
post-master sent for me to the post-office: Will the honourable
Señor please come to the post-office. I went, on a blazing April
morning, there in the northern tropics. The post-master, a dark,
fat Mexican with moustaches, was most polite: but also rather
mysterious. There was a packet – did I know there was a packet?
No, I didn't. Well, after a great deal of suspicious courtesy, the
packet was produced; the rather battered typescript of the
*Dragon*, together with some of Carter's line-engravings, mainly
astrological, which went with it. The post-master handled them
cautiously. What was it? What was it? It was a book, I said, the
manuscript of a book, in English. Ah, but what sort of a book?
What was the book about? I tried to explain, in my hesitating
Spanish, what the *Dragon* was about, with its line-drawings. I
didn't get far. The post-master looked darker and darker, more
uneasy. At last he suggested, was it *magic*? I held my breath. It
seemed like the Inquisition again. Then I tried to accommodate
him. No, I said, it was not magic, but the *history* of magic. It was
the history of what magicians had thought, in the past, and these
were the designs they had used. Ah! The postman was relieved.

539

The history of magic! A scholastic work! And these were the designs they had used! He fingered them gingerly, but fascinated.

And I walked home at last, under the blazing sun, with the bulky package under my arm. And then, in the cool of the patio, I read the beginning of the first *Dragon*.

The book was not then what it is now. Then, it was nearly all astrology, and very little argument. It was confused: it was, in a sense, a chaos. And it hadn't very much to do with St John's Revelation. But that didn't matter to me. I was very often smothered in words. And then would come a page, or a chapter, that would release my imagination and give me a whole great sky to move in. For the first time I strode forth into the grand fields of the sky. And it was a real experience, for which I have been always grateful. And always the sensation comes back to me, of the dark shade on the veranda in Mexico, and the sudden release into the great sky of the old world, the sky of the zodiac.

I have read books of astronomy which made me dizzy with the sense of illimitable space. But the heart melts and dies – it is the disembodied mind alone which follows on through this horrible hollow void of space, where lonely stars hang in awful isolation. And this is not a release. It is a strange thing, but when science extends space *ad infinitum*, and we get the terrible sense of limitlessness, we have at the same time a secret sense of imprisonment. Three-dimensional space is homogeneous, and no matter *how* big it is, it is a kind of prison. No matter how vast the range of space, there is no release.

Why then, this sense of release, of marvellous release, in reading the *Dragon*? I don't know. But anyhow, the *whole* imagination is released, not a part only. In astronomical space, one can only *move*, one cannot be. In the astrological heavens, that is to say, the ancient zodiacal heavens, the whole man is set free, once the imagination crosses the border. The whole man, bodily and spiritual, walks in the magnificent fields of the stars, and the stars have names, and the feet tread splendidly upon – we know not what, but the heavens, instead of untreadable space.

It is an experience. To enter the astronomical sky of space is a great sensational experience. To enter the astrological sky of the zodiac and the living, roving planets is another experience, another *kind* of experience; it is truly imaginative, and to me, more valuable. It is not a mere extension of what we know: an extension that becomes awful, then appalling. It is the entry into another world, another kind of world, measured by another dimension. And we find some prisoned self in us coming forth to live in this world.

Now it is ridiculous for us to deny any experience. I well remember my first real experience of space, reading a book of modern astronomy. It was rather awful, and since then I rather hate the mere suggestion of illimitable space.

But I also remember very vividly my first experience of the astrological heavens, reading Frederick Carter's *Dragon*: the sense of being the Macrocosm, the great sky with its meaningful stars and its profoundly meaningful motions, its wonderful bodily vastness, not empty, but all alive and doing. And I value this experience more. For the sense of astronomical space merely paralyses me. But the sense of the living astrological heavens gives me an extension of my being, I become big and glittering and vast with a sumptuous vastness. I am the Macrocosm, and it is wonderful. And since I am not afraid to feel my own nothingness in front of the vast void of astronomical space, neither am I afraid to feel my own splendidness in the zodiacal heavens.

The *Dragon* as it exists now is no longer the *Dragon* which I read in Mexico. It has been made more – more argumentative, shall we say. Give me the old manuscript and let me write an introduction to that! I urge. But: No, says Carter. It isn't *sound*.

Sound what? He means his old astrological theory of the Apocalypse was not sound, as it was exposed in the old manuscript. But who cares? We do not care, vitally, about theories of the Apocalypse: what the Apocalypse means. What we care about is the release of the imagination. A real release of the imagination renews our strength and our vitality, makes us feel stronger and happier. Scholastic works don't release the imagination: at the best, they satisfy the intellect, and leave the body an unleavened lump. But when I get the release into the zodiacal cosmos my very feet feel lighter and stronger, my very knees are glad.

What does the Apocalypse matter, unless in so far as it gives us imaginative release into another vital world? After all, what meaning *has* the Apocalypse? For the ordinary reader, not much. For the ordinary student and biblical student, it means a prophetic vision of the martyrdom of the Christian Church, the Second Advent, the destruction of worldly power, particularly the power of the great Roman Empire, and then the institution of the Millennium, the rule of the risen Martyrs of Christendom for the space of one thousand years: after which, the end of everything, the Last Judgement, and souls in heaven; all earth, moon and sun being wiped out, all stars and all space. The New Jerusalem, and Finis!

This is all very fine, but we know it pretty well by now, so it offers no imaginative release to most people. It is the orthodox interpretation of the Apocalypse, and probably it is the true superficial meaning, or the final intentional meaning of the work. But what of it? It is a bore. Of all the stale buns, the New Jerusalem is one of the stalest. At the best, it was only invented for the Aunties of this world.

Yet when we read Revelation, we feel at once there are meanings behind meanings. The visions that we have known since childhood are not so easily exhausted by the orthodox commentators. And the phrases that have haunted us all our life, like: And I saw heaven opened, and behold! A white horse! – these are not explained quite away by orthodox explanations. When all is explained and expounded and commented upon, still there remains a curious fitful, half-spurious and half-splendid wonder in the work. Sometimes the great figures loom up marvellous. Sometimes there is a strange sense of incomprehensible drama. Sometimes the figures have a life of their own, inexplicable, which cannot be explained away or exhausted.

And gradually we realize that we are in the world of symbol as well as of allegory. Gradually we realize the book has no one meaning. It has meanings. Not meaning *within* meaning: but rather, meaning against meaning. No doubt the last writer left the Apocalypse as a sort of complete Christian allegory, a Pilgrim's Progress to the Judgement Day and the New Jerusalem: and the orthodox critics can explain the allegory fairly satisfactorily. But the Apocalypse is a compound work. It is no doubt the work of different men, of different generations and even different centuries.

So that we don't have to look for a *meaning*, as we can look for a meaning in an allegory like *Pilgrim's Progress*, or even like Dante. John of Patmos didn't *compose* the Apocalypse. The Apocalypse is the work of no one man. The Apocalypse began probably two centuries before Christ, as some small book, perhaps, of Pagan ritual, or some small pagan-Jewish Apocalypse written in symbols. It was written over by other Jewish apocalyptists, and finally came down to John of Patmos. He turned it more or less, rather less than more, into a Christian allegory. And later scribes trimmed up his work.

So the ultimate intentional, Christian meaning of the book is, in a sense, only plastered over. The great images incorporated are like the magnificent Greek pillars plastered into the Christian Church in Sicily: they are not merely allegorical figures: they are symbols, they belong to a bigger age than that of John of Patmos. And as symbols they defy John's superficial allegorical meaning. You can't give a great symbol a 'meaning', any more than you can give a cat a 'meaning', Symbols are organic units of consciousness with a life of their own, and you can never explain them away, because their value is dynamic, emotional, belonging to the sense – consciousness of the body and soul, and not simply mental. An allegorical image has a *meaning*. Mr Facing-both-ways has a meaning. But I defy you to lay your finger on the full meaning of Janus, who is a symbol.

It is necessary for us to realize very definitely the difference between allegory and symbol. Allegory is narrative description using, as a rule, images to express certain definite qualities. Each image means something, and is a term in the argument and nearly always for a moral or didactic purpose, for under the narrative of an allegory lies a didactic argument, usually moral. Myth likewise is descriptive narrative using images. But myth is never an argument, it never has a didactic nor a moral purpose, you can draw no conclusion from it. Myth is an attempt to narrate a whole human experience, of which the purpose is too deep, going

543

too deep in the blood and soul, for mental explanation or description. We *can* expound the myth of Chronos very easily. We can explain it, we can even draw the moral conclusion. But we only look a little silly. The myth of Chronos lives on beyond explanation, for it describes a profound experience of the human body and soul, an experience which is never exhausted and never will be exhausted, for it is being felt and suffered now, and it will be felt and suffered while man remains man. You may explain the myths away: but it only means you go on suffering blindly, stupidly, 'in the unconscious', instead of healthily and with the imaginative comprehension playing upon the suffering.

And the images of myth are symbols. They don't 'mean something'. They stand for units of human *feeling*, human experience. A complex of emotional experience is a symbol. And the power of the symbol is to arouse the deep emotional self, and the dynamic self, beyond comprehension. Many ages of accumulated experience still throb within a symbol. And we throb in response. It takes centuries to create a really significant symbol: even the symbol of the Cross, or of the horse-shoe, or the horns. No man can invent symbols. He can invent an emblem, made up of images: or metaphors: or images: but not symbols. Some images, in the course of many generations of men, become symbols, embedded in the soul and ready to start alive when touched, carried on in the human consciousness for centuries. And again, when men become unresponsive and half dead, symbols die.

Now the Apocalypse has many splendid old symbols, to make us throb. And symbols suggest schemes of symbols. So the Apocalypse, with its symbols, suggests schemes of symbols, deep underneath its Christian, allegorical surface meaning of the Church of Christ.

And one of the chief schemes of symbols which the Apocalypse will suggest to any man who has a feeling for symbols, as contrasted with the orthodox feeling for allegory, is the astrological scheme. Again and again the symbols of the Apocalypse are astrological, the movement is star-movement, and these suggest an astrological scheme. Whether it is worth while to work out the astrological scheme from the impure text of the Apocalypse depends on the man who finds it worth while. Whether the scheme *can* be worked out remains for us to judge. In all probability there was once an astrological scheme there.

But what is certain is that the astrological symbols and sugges-tions are still there, they give us the lead. And the lead leads us sometimes out into a great imaginative world where we feel free and delighted. At least, that is my experience. So what does it matter whether the astrological scheme can be restored intact or not? Who cares about explaining the Apocalypse, either allegori-cally or astrologically or historically or any other way. All one cares about is the lead, the lead that the symbolic figures give us, and their dramatic movement: the lead, and where it will lead us to. If it leads to a release of the imagination into some new sort of world, then let us be thankful, for that is what we want. It matters so little to us who care more about life than about scholarship, what is correct or what is not correct. What does 'correct' mean, anyhow? *Sanahorias* is the Spanish for carrots: I hope I am correct. But what are carrots correct for?

What the ass wants is carrots; not the idea of carrots, nor thought-forms of carrots, but carrots. The Spanish ass doesn't even know that he is eating *sanahorias*. He just eats and feels blissfully full of carrot. Now does *he* have more of the carrot, who eats it, or do I, who know that in Spanish it is called a *sana-horia* (I hope I am correct) and in botany it belongs to the *um-belliferae*?

We are full of the wind of thought-forms, and starved for a good carrot. I don't care *what* a man sets out to prove, so long as he will interest me and carry me away. I don't in the least care whether he proves his point or not, so long as he has given me a real imaginative experience by the way, and not another set of bloated thought-forms. We are starved to death, fed on the eternal sodom-apples of thought-forms. What we want is *com-plete* imaginative experience, which goes through the whole soul and body. Even at the expense of reason we want imaginative experience. For reason is certainly not the final judge of life.

Though, if we pause to think about it, we shall realize that it is not Reason herself whom we have to defy, it is her myrmidons, our accepted ideas and thought-forms. Reason can adjust herself to almost anything, if we will only free her from her crinoline and powdered wig, with which she was invested in the eighteenth and nineteenth centuries. Reason is a supple nymph, and slippery as a fish by nature. She had as leave give her kiss to an absurdity any day, as to syllogistic truth. The absurdity may turn out truer.

So we need not feel ashamed of flirting with the zodiac. The zodiac is well worth flirting with. But not in the rather silly modern way of horoscopy and telling your fortune by the stars. Telling your fortune by the stars, or trying to get a tip from the stables, before a horse-race. You want to know what horse to put your money on. Horoscopy is just the same. They want their 'fortune' told, never their misfortune.

Surely one of the greatest imaginative experiences the human race has ever had was the Chaldean experience of the stars, including the sun and moon. Sometimes it seems it must have been greater experience than any God-experience. For God is only a great imaginative experience. And sometimes it seems as if the experience of the living heavens, with a living yet not human sun, and brilliant living stars in *live* space must have been the most magnificent of all experiences, greater than any Jehovah or Baal, Buddha or Jesus. It may seem an absurdity to talk of *live* space. But is it? While we are warm and well and 'unconscious' of our bodies, are we not all the time ultimately conscious of our bodies in the same way, as live or living space? And is not this the reason why void space so terrifies us?

I would like to know the stars again as the Chaldeans knew them, two thousand years before Christ. I would like to be able to put my ego into the sun, and my personality into the moon, and my character into the planets, and live the life of the heavens, as the early Chaldeans did. The human consciousness is really homogeneous. There is no complete forgetting, even in death. So that somewhere within us the old experience of the Euphrates, Mesopotamia between the rivers, lives still. And in my Mesopotamian self I long for the sun again, and the moon and stars, for the Chaldean sun and the Chaldean stars. I long for them terribly.

Because *our* sun and *our* moon are only thought-forms to us, balls of gas, dead globes of extinct volcanoes, things we *know* but never feel by experience. By *experience*, we should feel the sun as the savages feel him, we should 'know' him as the Chaldeans knew him, in a terrific embrace. But our experience of the sun is dead, we are cut off. All we have now is the thought-form of the sun. He is a blazing ball of gas, he has spots occasionally, from some sort of indigestion, and he makes you brown and healthy if you let him. The first two 'facts' we should never have known if men with telescopes, called astronomers, hadn't told us. It is obvious, they are mere thought-forms. The third 'fact', about being brown and healthy, we believe because the doctors have told us it is so. As a matter of fact, many neurotic people become more and more neurotic, the browner and 'healthier' they become by sunbaking. The sun can rot as well as ripen. So the third fact is also a thought-form.

And that is all we have, poor things, of the sun. Two or three cheap and inadequate thought-forms. Where, for us, is the great and royal sun of the Chaldeans? Where even, for us, is the sun of the Old Testament, coming forth like a strong man to run a race? We have lost the sun. We have lost the sun, and we have found a few miserable thought-forms. A ball of blazing gas! With spots. He browns you!

To be sure, we are not the first to lose the sun. The Babylonians themselves began the losing of him. The great and living heavens of the Chaldeans deteriorated already in Belshazzar's day to the fortune-telling disc of the night skies. But that was man's fault, not the heavens'. Man always deteriorates. And when he deteriorates he always becomes inordinately concerned about his 'fortune' and his fate. While life itself is fascinating, fortune is completely uninteresting, and the idea of fate does not enter. When men become poor in life then they become anxious about their fortune and frightened about their fate. By the time of Jesus, men had become so anxious about their fortunes and so frightened about their fates, that they put up the grand declaration that life was one long misery and you couldn't expect your fortune till you got to heaven; that is, till after you were dead. This was acceped by all men, and has been the creed till our day, Buddha and Jesus alike. It has provided us with a vast amount of thought-forms, and landed us in a sort of living death.

So now we want the sun again. Not the spotted ball of gas that browns you like a joint of meat, but the living sun, and the living moon of the old Chaldean days. Think of the moon, think of Artemis and Cybele, think of the white wonder of the skies, so rounded, so velvety, moving so serene; and then think of the pock-marked horror of the scientific photographs of the moon!

But when we have seen the pock-marked face of the moon in scientific photographs, need that be the end of the moon for us? Even rationally? I think not. It is a great blow: but the imagination can recover from it. Even if we have to believe the pock-marked photograph, even if we believe in the cold and snow and utter deadness of the moon – which we *don't* quite believe – the moon is not therefore a dead nothing. The moon is a white strange world, great, white, soft-seeming globe in the night sky, and what she actually communicates to me across space I shall never fully know. But the moon that pulls the tides, and the moon that controls the menstrual periods of women, and the moon that touches the lunatics, she is not the mere dead lump of the astronomist. The moon is the great moon still, she gives forth her soft and feline influences, she sways us still, and asks for sympathy back again. In her so-called deadness there is enormous potency still, and power even over our lives. The Moon! Artemis! the great goddess of the splendid past of men! Are you going to tell me she is a dead lump?

She is not dead. But maybe we are dead, half-dead little modern worms stuffing our damp carcasses with thought-forms that have no sensual reality. When we describe the moon as dead, we are describing the deadness in ourselves. When we find space so hideously void, we are describing our own unbearable emptiness. Do we imagine that we, poor worms with spectacles and tele-scopes and thought-forms, are really more conscious, more vitally aware of the universe than the men in the past were, who called the moon Artemis, or Cybele, or Astarte? Do we imagine that we real-ly, livingly know the moon better than they knew her? That our knowledge of the moon is more real, more 'sound'? Let us disabuse ourselves. We know the moon in terms of our own telescopes and our own deadness. We know everything in terms of our own deadness.

But the moon is Artemis still, and a dangerous goddess she is, as she always was. She throws her cold contempt on you as she passes over the sky, poor, mean little worm of a man who thinks she is nothing but a dead lump. She throws back the cold white vitriol of her angry contempt on to your mean, tense nerves, nervous man, and she is corroding you away. Don't think you can escape the moon, any more than you can escape breathing. She is on the air you breathe. She is active within the atom. Her sting is part of the activity of the electron.

Do you think you can put the universe apart, a dead lump here, a ball of gas there, a bit of fume somewhere else? How puerile it is, as if the universe were the back yard of some human chemical works! How gibbering man becomes, when he is really clever, and thinks he is giving the ultimate and final description of the universe! Can't he see that he is merely describing himself, and that the self he is describing is merely one of the more dead and dreary states that man can exist in? When man changes his state of being, he needs an entirely different description of the universe, and so the universe changes its nature to him entirely. Just as the nature of our universe is entirely different from the nature of the Chaldean Cosmos. The Chaldeans described the Cosmos as they found it: Magnificent. We describe the universe as we find it: mostly void, littered with a certain number of dead moons and unborn stars, like the back yard of a chemical works.

Is our description true? Not for a single moment, once you change your state of mind: or your state of soul. It is true for our present deadened state of mind. Our state of mind is becoming unbearable. We shall have to change it. And when we have changed it, we shall change our description of the universe entirely. We shall not call the moon Artemis, but the new name will be nearer to Artemis than to a dead lump or an extinct globe. We shall not get back the Chaldean vision of the living heavens. But the heavens will come to life again for us, and the vision will express also the new men that we are.

And so the value of these studies in the Apocalypse. They wake the imagination and give us at moments a new universe to live in. We may think it is the old cosmos of the Babylonians, but it isn't. We can never recover an old vision, once it has been supplanted. But what we can do is to discover a new vision in harmony with the memories of old, far-off, far, far-off experience that lie within us. So long as we are not deadened or drossy, memories of Chaldean experience still live within us, at great depths, and can vivify our impulses in a new direction, once we awaken them.

Therefore we ought to be grateful for a book like this of the *Dragon*. What does it matter if it is confused? What does it matter if it repeats itself? What does it matter if in parts it is not very interesting, when in other parts it is intensely so, when it suddenly opens doors and lets out the spirit into a new world, even if it is a very old world! I admit that I cannot see eye to eye with Mr Carter about the Apocalypse itself. I cannot, myself, feel that old John of Patmos spent his time on his island lying on his back and gazing at the resplendent heavens; then afterwards writing a book in which all the magnificent cosmic and starry drama is deliberately wrapped up in Jewish-Christian moral threats and vengeances, sometimes rather vulgar.

But that, no doubt, is due to our different approach to the book. I was brought up on the Bible, and seem to have it in my bones. From early childhood I have been familiar with Apocalyptic language and Apocalyptic image: not because I spent my time reading Revelation, but because I was sent to Sunday School and to Chapel, to Band of Hope and to Christian Endeavour, and was always having the Bible read at me or to me. I did not even listen attentively. But language has a power of echoing and re-echoing in my unconscious mind. I can wake up in the night and 'hear' things being said – or hear a piece of music – to which I had paid no attention during the day. The very sound itself registers. And so the sound of Revelation had registered in me very early, and I was as used to: 'I was in the Spirit on the Lord's day, and heard behind me a great voice, as of a trumpet, saying: I am the Alpha and the Omega' – as I was to a nursery rhyme like 'Little Bo-Peep'! I didn't know the meaning, but then children so often prefer sound to sense. 'Alleluia: for the Lord God omnipotent reigneth.' The Apocalypse is full of sounding phrases, beloved by the uneducated in the chapels for their true liturgical powers. 'And he treadeth the winepress of the fierceness and wrath of Almighty God.'

No, for me the Apocalypse is altogether too full of fierce feeling, fierce and moral, to be a grand disguised star-myth. And yet it has intimate connexion with star-myths and the movement of the astrological heavens: a sort of submerged star-meaning. And nothing delights me more than to escape from the all-too-moral chapel meaning of the book, to another wider, older, more magnificent meaning. In fact, one of the real joys of middle age is in coming back to the Bible, reading a new translation, such as Moffatt's, reading the modern research and modern criticism of some Old Testament books, and of the Gospels, and getting a whole new conception of the Scriptures altogether. Modern research has been able to put the Bible back into its living connexions, and it is splendid: no longer the Jewish-moral book and a stick to beat an immoral dog, but a fascinating account of the adventure of the Jewish – or Hebrew or Israelite nation, among the great old civilized nations of the past, Egypt, Assyria, Babylon, and Persia: then on into the Hellenic world, the Seleucids, and the Romans, Pompey and Anthony. Reading the Bible in a new translation, with modern notes and comments, is more fascinating than reading Homer, for the adventure goes even deeper into time and into the soul, and continues through the centuries, and moves from Egypt to Ur and to Nineveh, from Sheba to Tarshish and Athens and Rome. It is the very quick of ancient history.

And the Apocalypse, the last and presumably the latest of the books of the Bible, also comes to life with a great new life, once we look at its symbols and take the lead that they offer us. The text leads most easily into the great chaotic Hellenic world of the first century: Hellenic, not Roman. But the symbols lead much further back.

They lead Frederick Carter back to Chaldea and to Persia,

chiefly, for his skies are the late Chaldean, and his mystery is chiefly Mithraic. Hints, we have only hints from the outside. But the rest is within us, and if we can take a hint, it is extraordinary how far and into what fascinating worlds the hints can lead us. The orthodox critics will say: Fantasy! Nothing but fantasy! But then, thank God for fantasy, if it enhances our life.

And even so, the 'reproach' is not quite just. The Apocalypse has an old, submerged astrological meaning, and probably even an old astrological scheme. The hints are too obvious and too splendid: like the ruins of an old temple incorporated in a Christian chapel. Is it any more fantastic to try to reconstruct the embedded temple, than to insist that the embedded images and columns are mere rubble in the Christian building, and have no meaning? It is as fantastic to deny meaning when meaning is there, as it is to invent meaning when there is none. And it is much duller. For the invented meaning may still have a life of its own.

# The Risen Lord

*Everyman*, 3 October 1929; *Assorted Articles*, 1930

> The risen lord, the risen lord
> has risen in the flesh,
> and treads the earth to feel the soil
> though his feet are still nesh.

The Churches loudly assert: We preach Christ crucified! – But in so doing, they preach only half of the Passion, and do only half their duty. The Creed says: 'Was crucified, dead, and buried ... the third day He rose again from the dead.' And again, 'I believe in the resurrection of the body ...' So that to preach Christ Crucified is to preach half the truth. It is the business of the Church to preach Christ born among men – which is Christmas; Christ Crucified, which is Good Friday; and Christ Risen, which is Easter. And after Easter, till November and All Saints, and till Annunciation, the year belongs to the Risen Lord: that is, all the full-flowering spring, all summer, and the autumn of wheat and fruit, all belong to Christ Risen.

But the Churches insist on Christ Crucified, and rob us of the blossom and fruit of the year. The Catholic Church, which has given us our images, has given us the Christ-child, in the lap of woman, and again, Christ Crucified: then the Mass, the mystery of atonement through sacrifice. Yet all this is really preparatory, these are the preparatory stages of the real living religion. The

Christ-child, enthroned in the lap of the Mother, is obviously only a preparatory image, to prepare us for Christ the Man. Yet a vast mass of Christians stick there.

What we have to remember is that the great religious images are only images of our own experiences, or of our own state of mind and soul. In the Catholic countries, where the Madonna-and-Child image overwhelms everything else, the man visions himself all the time as a child, a Christ-child, standing on the lap of a virgin mother. Before the war, if an Italian hurt himself, or suddenly fell into distress, his immediate cry was: *O mamma mia! mamma mia! – Oh, mother, mother!* – The same was true of many Englishmen. And what does this mean? It means that the man sees himself as a child, the innocent saviour-child enthroned on the lap of the all-pitying virgin mother. He lives according to this image of himself – the image of the guileless 'good' child sheltered in the arms of an all-sheltering mother – until the image breaks in his heart.

And during the war, this image broke in the hearts of most men, though not in the hearts of their women. During the war, the man who suffered most bitterly suffered beyond the help of wife or mother, and no wife nor mother nor sister nor any beloved could save him from the guns. This fact went home in his heart, and broke the image of mother and Christ-child, and left in its place the image of Christ Crucified.

It was not so, of course, for the woman. The image did not break for her. She visioned herself still as the all-pitying, all-sheltering Madonna, on whose lap the man was enthroned, as in the old pictures, like a Christ-child. And naturally the woman did not want to abandon this vision of herself. It gave her her greatest significance; and the greatest power. Break the image, and her significance and her power were gone. But the men came back from the war and denied the image – for them it was broken. So she fought to maintain it, the great vision of man, the Christ-child, enthroned in the lap of the all-pitying virginal woman. And she fought in vain, though not without disastrous result.

For the vision of the all-pitying and all-helpful Madonna was shattered in the hearts of men, during the war. The all-pitying and

554

all-helpful Woman actually did not, whether she could or not, prevent the guns from blowing to pieces the men who called upon her. So her image collapsed, and with it the image of the Christ-child. For the man who went through the war the resultant image inevitably was Christ Crucified, Christ tortured on the Cross. And Christ Crucified is essentially womanless.

True, many of the elderly men who never went through the war still insist on the Christ-child business, and most of the elderly women insist on their benevolent Madonna supremacy. But it is in vain. The guns broke the image in the hearts of middle-aged men, and the young were born, or are come to real consciousness, after the image was already smashed.

So there we are! We have three great image-divisions among men and women today. We have the old and the elderly, who never were exposed to the guns, still fatuously maintaining that man is the Christ-child and woman the infallible safeguard from all evil and all danger. It is fatuous, because it absolutely didn't work. Then we have the men of middle-age, who were all tortured and virtually put to death by the war. They accept Christ Crucified as their image, are essentially womanless, and take the great cry: *Consummatum est! It is finished!* – as their last word. – Thirdly, we have the young, who never went through the war. They have no illusions about it, however, and the death-cry of their elder generation: *It is finished!* rings cold through their blood. They cannot answer. They cannot even scoff. It is no joke, and never will be a joke.

And yet, neither of the great images is *their* image. They cannot accept the child-and-mother position which the old buffers still pose in. They cannot accept the Christ Crucified finality of the generations immediately ahead. For they, the young, came into the field of life after the death-cry *Consummatum est!* had rung through the world, and while the body, so to speak, was being put into the tomb. By the time the young came on to the stage, Calvary was empty, the tombs were closed, the women had lost for ever the Christ-child and the virgin savour, and it was altogether the day after, cold, bleak, empty, blank, meaningless, almost silly.

The young came into life, and found everything finished. Everywhere the empty crosses, everywhere the closed tombs, everywhere the manless, bitter or over-assertive woman, everywhere the closed grey disillusion of Christ Crucified, dead, and buried, those grey empty days between Good Friday and Easter.

And the Churches, instead of preaching the Risen Lord, go on preaching the Christ-child and Christ Crucified. Now man cannot live without some vision of himself. But still less can he live with a vision that is not true to his inner experience and inner feeling. And the vision of Christ-child and Christ Crucified are both untrue to the inner experience and feeling of the young. They don't feel that way. They show the greatest forbearance and tolerance of their elders, for whom the two images *are* livingly true. But for the post-war young, neither the Christ-child nor Christ Crucified means much.

I doubt whether the Protestant Churches, which supported the war, will ever have the faith and the power of life to take the great step onwards, and preach Christ Risen. The Catholic Church might. In the countries of the Mediterranean, Easter has always been the greatest of the holy days, the gladdest and holiest, not Christmas, the birth of the Child. Easter, Christ Risen, the Risen Lord, this, to the old faith, is still the first day in the year. The Easter festivities are the most joyful, the Easter processions the finest, the Easter ceremonies the most splendid. In Sicily the women take into church the saucers of growing corn, the green blades rising tender and slim like green light, in little pools, filling round the altar. It is Adonis. It is the re-born year. It is Christ Risen. It is the Risen Lord. And in the warm south still a great joy floods the hearts of the people on Easter Sunday. They feel it, they feel it everywhere. The Lord is risen. The Lord of the rising wheat and the plum blossoms is warm and kind upon earth again, after having been done to death by the evil and the jealous ones.

The Roman Catholic Church may still unfold this part of the Passion fully, and make men happy again. For Resurrection is indeed the consummation of all the passion. Not even Atonement, the being at one with Christ through partaking in his sacrifice, consummates the Passion finally. For even after Atonement men must still live, and must go forward with the vision. After we share in the body of Christ, we rise with him in the body. And that is the final vision that has been blurred to all the Churches.

Christ risen in the flesh! We must accept the image complete, if we accept it at all. We must take the mystery in its fulness and in fact. It is only the image of our own experience. Christ rises, when he rises from the dead, in the flesh, not merely as spirit. He rises with hands and feet, as Thomas knew for certain: and if with hands and feet, then with lips and stomach and genitals of a man. Christ risen, and risen in the whole of his flesh, not with some left out.

Christ risen in the full flesh! What for? It is here the gospels are all vague and faltering, and the Churches leave us in the lurch. Christ risen in the flesh in order to lurk obscurely for six weeks on earth, then be taken vaguely up into heaven in a cloud? Flesh, solid flesh, feet and bowels and teeth and eyes of a man, taken up into heaven in a cloud, and never put down again?

It is the only part of the great mystery which is all wrong. The virgin birth, the baptism, the temptation, the teaching, Gethsemane, the betrayal, the crucifixion, the burial and the resurrection, these are all true according to our inward experience. They are what men and women go through, in their different ways. But floated up into heaven as flesh-and-blood, and never set down again – this nothing in all our experience will ever confirm. If aeroplanes take us up, they bring us down, or let us down. Flesh and blood belong to the earth, and only to the earth. We know it.

And Jesus was risen flesh-and-blood. He rose a man on earth to live on earth. The greatest test was still before him : his life as a man on earth. Hitherto he had been a sacred child, a teacher, a messiah, but never a full man. Now, risen from the dead, he rises to be a man on earth, and live his life of the flesh, the great life, among other men. This is the image of our inward state today.

This is the image of the young: the Risen Lord. The teaching is over, the crucifixion is over, the sacrifice is made, the salvation is accomplished. Now comes the true life, man living his full life on earth, as flowers live their full life, without rhyme or reason except the magnificence of coming forth into fulness.

If Jesus rose from the dead in triumph, a man on earth triumphant in renewed flesh, triumphant over the mechanical anti-life convention of Jewish priests, Roman despotism, and universal money-lust; triumphant above all over his own self-absorption, self-consciousness, self-importance; triumphant and free as a man in full flesh and full, final experience, even the accomplished acceptance of his own death; a man at last full and free in flesh and soul, a man at one with death: then he rose to become at one with life, to live the great life of the flesh and the soul together, as peonies or foxes do, in their lesser way. If Jesus rose as a full man, in full flesh and soul, then he rose to take a woman to himself, to live with her, and to know the tenderness and blossoming of the twoness with her; he who had been hitherto so limited to his oneness, or his universality, which is the same thing. If Jesus rose in the full flesh, he rose to know the tenderness of a woman, and the great pleasure of her, and to have children by her. He rose to know the responsibility and the peculiar delight of children, and also the exasperation and nuisance of them. If Jesus rose as a full man, in the flesh, he rose to have friends, to have a manfriend whom he would hold sometimes to his breast, in strong affection, and who would be dearer to him than a brother, just out of the sheer mystery of sympathy. And how much more wonderful, this, than having disciples! If Jesus rose a full man in the flesh, he rose to do his share in the world's work, something he really liked doing. And if he remembered his first life, it would neither be teaching nor preaching, but probably carpentering again, with joy, among the shavings. If Jesus rose a full man in the flesh, he rose to continue his fight with the hard-boiled conventionalists like Roman judges and Jewish priests and moneymakers of every sort. But this time, it would no longer be the fight of self-sacrifice that would end in crucifixion. This time it would be a freed man fighting to shelter the rose of life from being trampled on by the pigs. This time, if Satan attempted temptation in the wilderness, the Risen Lord would answer: Satan, your silly temptations no longer tempt me. Luckily, I have died to that sort of self-importance and self-conceit. But let me tell you something, old man! Your name's Satan, isn't it? And your name is Mammon? You are the selfish hog that's got hold of all the world, aren't you? Well, look here, my boy, I'm going to take it all from you, so don't worry. The world and the power and the riches thereof, I'm going to take them all from you, Satan or Mammon or whatever your name is. Because you don't know how to use them. The earth is the Lord's, and the fulness thereof, and it's going to be. Men have risen from the dead and learned not to be so greedy and self-important. We left most of that behind in the late tomb. Men have risen beyond you, Mammon, they are your risen lords. And so, you hook-nosed, glisten-eyed, ugly, money-smelling anachronism, you've got to get out. Men have not died and risen again for nothing. Whom do you think the earth belongs to, you stale old rat? The earth is the Lord's and is given to the men who have died and had the power to rise again. The earth is given to the men who have risen from the dead, risen, you old grabber, and when did you ever rise? Never! So go you down to oblivion, and give your place to the risen men, and the women of the risen men. For man has been dispossessed of the full earth and the earth's fulness long enough. And the poor women, they have been shoved about manless and meaningless long enough. The earth is the Lord's and the fulness thereof, and I, the Risen Lord, am here to take possession. For now I am fully a man, and free above all from my own self-importance. I want life, and the pure contact with life. What are riches, and glory, and honour, and might, and power, to me who have died and lost my self-importance? That's why I am going to take them all from you, Mammon, because I care nothing about them. I am going to destroy all your values, Mammon; all your money values and conceit values, I am going to destroy them all.

Because only life is lovely, and you, Mammon, prevent life. I love to see a squirrel peep round a tree; and left to you, Mammon, there will soon be no squirrels to peep. I love to hear a man singing a song to himself, and if it is an old, improper song, about the fun between lads and girls, I like it all the better. But you, beastly mealy-mouthed Mammon, you would arrest any lad that sings a gay song. I love the movement of life, and the beauty of life, O Mammon, since I am risen, I love the beauty of life intensely; columbine flowers, for example, the way they dangle, or the delicate way a young girl sits and wonders, or the rage with which a man turns and kicks a fool dog that suddenly attacks him – beautiful that, the swift fierce turn and lunge of a kick, then the quivering pause for the next attack; or even the slightly silly glow that comes over some men as they are getting tipsy – it still is a glow, beautiful; or the swift look a woman fetches me, when she would really like me to go off with her, but she is troubled; or the real compassion I saw a woman express for a man who slipped and wrenched his foot: life, the beauty, the beauty of life! But that which is anti-life, Mammon, like you, and money, and machines, and prostitution, and all that tangled mass of self-importance and greediness and self-conscious conceit which adds up to Mammon, I hate it. I hate it, Mammon, I hate you and am going to push you off the face of the earth, Mammon, you great mob-thing, fatal to men.

# *From* Study of Thomas Hardy

Written 1914, published in *Phoenix*, 1936

## CHAPTER VII

*Of Being and Not-Being*

In life, then, no new thing has ever arisen, or can arise, save out of the impulse of the male upon the female, the female upon the male. The interaction of the male and female spirit begot the wheel, the plough, and the first utterance that was made on the face of the earth.

As in my flower, the pistil, female, is the centre and swivel, the stamens, male, are close-clasping the hub, and the blossom is the great motion outwards into the unknown, so in a man's life, the female is the swivel and centre on which he turns closely, producing his movement. And the female to a man is the obvious form, a woman. And normally, the centre, the turning pivot, of a man's life is his sex-life, the centre and swivel of his being is the sexual act. Upon this turns the whole rest of his life, from this emanates every motion he betrays. And that this should be so, every man makes his effort. The supreme effort each man makes, for himself, is the effort to clasp as a hub the woman who shall be the axle, compelling him to true motion, without aberration. The supreme desire of every man is for mating with a woman, such that the sexual act be the closest, most concentrated motion in his life, closest upon the axle, the prime movement of himself, of which all the rest of his motion is a continuance in the same kind. And the vital desire of every woman is that she shall be clasped as axle to the hub of the man, that his motion shall portray her motion-less, convey her static being into movement, complete and radiat-ing out into infinity, starting from her stable eternality, and reach-ing eternity again, after having covered the whole of time.

This is complete movement: man upon woman, woman within man. This is the desire, the achieving of which, frictionless, is im-possible, yet for which every man will try, with greater or less in-tensity, achieving more or less success.

This is the desire of every man, that his movement, the manner of his walk, and the supremest effort of his mind, shall be the pulsation outwards from stimulus received in the sex, in the sexual act, that the woman of his body shall be the begetter of his whole life, that she, in her female spirit, shall beget in him his idea, his motion, himself. When a man shall look at the work of his hands, that has succeeded, and shall know that it was begotten in him by the woman of his body, then he shall know what funda-mental happiness is. Just as when a woman shall look at her child, that was begotten in her by the man of her spirit, she shall know what it is to be happy, fundamentally. But when a woman looks at her children that were begotten in her by a strange man, not the man of her spirit, she must know what it is to be happy with an-guish, and to love with pain. So with a man who looks at his work which was not begotten in him by the woman of his body. He rejoices, troubles, and suffers an agony like death which contains resurrection.

For while, ideally, the soul of the woman possesses the soul of the man, procreates it and makes it big with new idea, motion, in the sexual act, yet, most commonly, it is not so. Usually, sex is only functional, a matter of relief or sensation, equivalent to eat-ing or drinking or passing of excrement.

Then, if a man must produce work, he must produce it to some other than the woman of his body: as, in the same case, if a woman produce children, it must be to some other than the man of her desire.

In this case, a man must seek elsewhere than in woman for the female to possess his soul, to fertilize him and make him try with increase. And the female exists in much more than his woman. And the finding of it for himself gives a man his vision, his God.

And since no man and no woman can get a perfect mate, nor obtain complete satisfaction at all times, each man according to his need must have a God, an idea, that shall compel him to the movement of his own being. And then, when he lies with his woman, the man may concurrently be with God, and so get increase of his soul. Or he may have communion with his God apart and averse from the woman.

Every man seeks in woman for that which is stable, eternal. And if, under his motion, this break down in her, in the particular woman, so that she be no axle for his hub, but be driven away from herself, then he must seek elsewhere for his stability, for the centre to himself.

Then either he must seek another woman, or he must seek to make conscious his desire to find a symbol, to create and define in his consciousness the object of his desire, so that he may have it at will, for his own complete satisfaction.

In doing this latter, he seeks with his desire the female elsewhere than in the particular woman. Since everything that is, is either male or female or both, whether it be clouds or sunshine or hills or trees or a fallen feather from a bird, therefore in other things and in such things man seeks for his complement. And he must at last always call God the unutterable and the inexpressible, the unknowable, because it is his unrealized complement.

But all gods have some attributes in common. They are the unexpressed Absolute: eternal, infinite, unchanging. Eternal, Infinite, Unchanging: the High God of all Humanity is this.

Yet man, the male, is essentially a thing of movement and time and change. Until he is stirred into thought, he is complete in movement and change. But once he thinks, he must have the Absolute, the Eternal, Infinite, Unchanging.

And Man is stirred into thought by dissatisfaction, or unsatisfaction, as heat is born of friction. Consciousness is the same effort in male and female to obtain perfect frictionless interaction, perfect as Nirvana. It is the reflex both of male and female from defect in their dual motion. Being reflex from the dual motion, consciousness contains the two in one, and is therefore in itself Absolute.

And desire is the admitting of deficiency. And the embodiment of the object of desire reveals the original defect or the defaulture. So that the attributes of God will reveal that which man lacked and yearned for in his living. And these attributes are always, in their essence, Eternality, Infinity, Immutability.

And these are the qualities man feels in woman, as a principle. Let a man walk alone on the face of the earth, and he feels himself like a loose speck blown at random. Let him have a woman to whom he belongs, and he will feel as though he had a wall to back up against; even though the woman be mentally a fool. No man can endure the sense of space, of chaos, on four sides of himself. It drives him mad. He must be able to put his back to the wall. And this wall is his woman.

From her he has a sense of stability. She supplies him with the feeling of Immutability, Permanence, Eternality. He himself is a raging activity, change potent within change. He dare not even conceive of himself, save when he is sure of the woman permanent beneath him, beside him. He dare not leap into the unknown save from the sure stability of the unyielding female. Like a wheel, if he turn without an axle, his motion is wandering neutrality.

So always, the fear of a man is that he shall find no axle for his motion, that no woman can centralize his activity. And always, the fear of a woman is that she can find no hub for her stability, no man to convey into motion her full stability. Either the particular woman breaks down before the stress of the man, becomes erratic herself, no stay, no centre; or else the man is insufficiently active to carry out the static principle of his female, of his woman.

So life consists in the dual form of the Will-to-Motion and the Will-to-Inertia, and everything we see and know and are is the resultant of these two Wills. But the One Will, of which they are dual forms, that is as yet unthinkable.

And according as the Will-to-Motion predominates in race, or the Will-to-Inertia, so must that race's conception of the One Will enlarge the attributes which are lacking or deficient in the race.

From *Study of Thomas Hardy*

Since there is never to be found a perfect balance or accord of the two Wills, but always one triumphs over the other, in life, according to our knowledge, so must the human effort be always to recover balance, to symbolize and so to possess that which is missing. Which is the religious effort of Man.

There seems to be a fundamental, insuperable division, difference, between man's artistic effort and his religious effort. The two efforts are mixed with each other, as they are revealed, but all the while they remain two, not one, all the while they are separate, single, never compounded.

The religious effort is to conceive, to symbolize that which the human soul, or the soul of the race, lacks, that which it is not, and which it requires, yearns for. It is the portrayal of that complement to the race-life which is known only as a desire: it is the symbolizing of a great desire, the statement of the desire in terms which have no meaning apart from the desire.

Whereas the artistic effort is the effort of utterance, the supreme effort of expressing knowledge, that which has been for once, that which was enacted, where the two wills met and intersected and left their result, complete for the moment. The artistic effort is the portraying of a moment of union between the two wills, according to knowledge. The religious effort is the portrayal or symbolizing of the eternal union of the two wills, according to aspiration. But in this eternal union, the features of one or the other Will are always salient.

The dual Will we call the Will-to-Motion and the Will-to-Inertia. These cause the whole of life, from the ebb and flow of a wave, to the stable equilibrium of the whole universe, from birth and being and knowledge to death and decay and forgetfulness. And the Will-to-Motion we call the male will or spirit, the Will-to-Inertia the female. This will to inertia is not negative, and the other positive. Rather, according to some conception, is Motion negative and Inertia, the static, geometric idea, positive. That is according to the point of view.

According to the race-conception of God, we can see whether in that race the male or the female element triumphs, becomes predominant.

But it must first be seen that the division into male and female is arbitrary, for the purpose of thought. The rapid motion of the rim of a wheel is the same as the perfect rest at the centre of the wheel. How can one divide them? Motion and rest are the same, when seen completely. Motion is only true of things outside oneself. When I am in a moving train, strictly, the land moves under me, I and the train are still. If I were both land and train, if I were large enough, there would be no motion. And if I were very very small, every fibre of the train would be in motion for me, the point of rest would be infinitely reduced.

How can one say, there is motion and rest? If all things move together in one infinite motion, that is rest. Rest and motion are only two degrees of motion, or two degrees of rest. Infinite motion and infinite rest are the same thing. It is obvious. Since, if motion were infinite, there would be no standing-ground from which to regard it as motion. And the same with rest.

It is easier to conceive that there is no such thing as rest. For a thing to us at rest is only a thing travelling at our own rate of motion: from another point of view, it is a thing moving at the lowest rate of motion we can recognize. But this table on which I write, which I call rest, I know is really in motion.

So there is no such thing as rest. There is only infinite motion. But infinite motion must contain every degree of rest. So that motion and rest are the same thing. Rest is the lowest speed of motion which I recognize under normal conditions.

So how can one speak of a Will-to-Motion or a Will-to-Inertia, when there is no such thing as rest or motion? And yet, starting from any given degree of motion, and travelling forward in ever-increasing degree, one comes to a state of speed which covers the whole of space instantaneously, and is therefore rest, utter rest. And starting from the same speed and reducing the motion infinitely, one reaches the same condition of utter rest. And the direction of method of approach to this infinite rest is different to our conception. And only travelling upon the slower, does the swifter reach the infinite rest of inertia: which is the same as the infinite rest of speed, the two things having united to surpass our comprehension.

So we may speak of Male and Female, of the Will-to-Motion and of the Will-to-Inertia. And so, looking at a race, we can say whether the Will-to-Inertia or the Will-to-Motion has gained the ascendancy, and in which direction this race tends to disappear.

For it is as if life were a double cycle, of men and women, facing opposite ways, travelling opposite ways, revolving upon each other, man reaching forward with outstretched hand, woman reaching forward with outstretched hand, and neither able to move till their hands have grasped each other, when they draw towards each other from opposite directions, draw nearer and nearer, each travelling in his separate cycle, till the two are abreast, and side by side, until even they pass on again, away from each other, travelling their opposite ways to the same infinite goal.

Each travelling to the same goal of infinity, but entering it from the opposite ends of space. And man, remembering what lies behind him, how the hands met and grasped and tore apart, utters his tragic art. Then moreover, facing the other way into the unknown, conscious of the tug of the goal at his heart, he hails the woman coming from the place whither he is travelling, searches in her for signs, and makes his God from the suggestion he receives, as she advances.

Then she draws near, and he is full of delight. She is so close, that they touch, and then there is a joyful utterance of religious art. They are torn apart, and he gives the cry of tragedy, and goes on remembering, till the dance slows down and breaks, and there is only a crowd.

It is as if this cycle dance where the female makes the chain with the male becomes ever wider, ever more extended, and the further they get from the source, from the infinity, the more distinct and individual do the dancers become. At first they are only figures. In the Jewish cycle, David, with his hand stretched forth, cannot recognize the woman, the female. He can only recognize some likeness of himself. For both he and she have not danced very far from the source and origin where they were both one. Though she is in the gross utterly other than he, yet she is

567

not very distinct from him. And he hails her Father, Almighty, God, Beloved, Strength, hails her in his own image. And with hand outstretched, fearful and passionate, he reaches to her. But it is Solomon who touches her hand, with rapture and joy, and cries out his gladness in the Song of Songs. Who is the Shulamite but God come close, for a moment, into physical contact? The Song may be a drama: it is still religious art. It is the development of the Psalms. It is utterly different from the Book of Job, which is remembrance.

Always the threefold utterance: the declaring of the God seen approaching, the rapture of contact, the anguished joy of remembrance, when the meeting has passed into separation. Such is religion, religious art, and tragic art.

But the chain is not broken by the letting-go of hands. It is broken by the overbearing of one cycle by the other. David, when he lay with a woman, lay also with God; Solomon, when he lay with a woman, knew God and possessed Him and was possessed by Him. For in Solomon and in the Woman, the male clasped hands with the female.

But in the terrible moment when they should break free again, the male in the Jew was too weak, the female overbore him. He remained in the grip of the female. The force of inertia overpowered him, and he remained remembering. But very true had been David's vision, and very real Solomon's contact. So that the living thing was conserved, kept always alive and powerful, but restrained, restricted, partial.

For centuries, the Jew knew God as David had perceived him, as Solomon had known him. It was the God of the body, the rudimentary God of physical laws and physical functions. The Jew lived on in physical contact with God. Each of his physical functions he shared with God; he kept his body always like the body of a bride ready to serve the bridegroom. He had become the servant of his God, the female, passive. The female in him predominated, held him passive, set utter bounds to his movement, to his roving, kept his mind as a slave to guard intact the state of sensation wherein he found himself. Which persisted century after century, the secret, scrupulous voluptuousness of the Jew, become

568

almost self-voluptuousness, engaged in the consciousness of his own physique, or in the extracted existence of his own physique. His own physique included the woman, naturally, since the man's body included the woman's, the woman's the man's. His religion had become a physical morality, deep and fundamental, but entirely of one sort. Its living element was this scrupulous physical voluptuousness, wonderful and satisfying in a large measure.

The conscious element was a resistance to the male or active principle. Being female, occupied in self-feeling, in realization of the age, in submission to sensation, the Jewish temper was antagonistic to the active male principle, which would deny the age and refuse sensation, seeking ever to make transformation, desiring to be an instrument of change, to register relationships. So this race recognized only male sins: it conceived only sins of commission, sins of change, of transformation. In the whole of the Ten Commandments, it is the female who speaks. It is natural to the male to make the male God a God of benevolence and mercy, susceptible to pity. Such is the male conception of God. It was the female spirit which conceived the saying: 'For I, the Lord thy God, am a jealous God, visiting the iniquities of the fathers upon the children unto the third and fourth generation of them that hate me, and showing mercy unto thousands of them that love me.'

It was a female conception. For is not man the child of woman? Does she not see in him her body, even more vividly than in her own? Man is more her body to her even than her own body. For the whole of flesh is hers. Woman knows that she is the fountain of all flesh. And her pride is that the body of man is of her issue. She can see the man as the One Being, for she knows he is of her issue.

It were a male conception to see God with a manifold Being, even though he be One God. For man is ever keenly aware of the multiplicity of things, and their diversity. But woman, issuing from the other end of infinity, coming forth as the flesh, manifest in sensation, is obsessed by the oneness of things, the One Being, undifferentiated. Man, on the other hand, coming forth as the

569

desire to single out one thing from another, to reduce each thing to its intrinsic self by process of elimination, cannot but be possessed by the infinite diversity and contrariety in life, by a passionate sense of isolation, and a poignant yearning to be at one.

That is the fundamental of female conception: that there is but One Being: this Being necessarily female. Whereas man conceives a manifold Being, the supreme of which is male. And owing to the complete Monism of the female, which is essentially static, self-sufficient, the expression of God has been left always to the male, so that the supreme God is forever he.

Nevertheless, in the God of the Ancient Jew, the female has triumphed. That which was born of Woman, that is indeed the God of the Old Testament. So utterly is he born of Woman that he scarcely needs to consider Woman: she is there unuttered.

And the Jewish race, continued in this Monism, stable, circumscribed, utterly unadventurous, utterly self-preservative, yet very deeply living, until the present century.

But Christ rose from the suppressed male spirit of Judea, and uttered a new commandment: Thou shalt love thy neighbour as thyself. He repudiated Woman: 'Who is my mother?' He lived the male life utterly apart from woman.

'Thou shalt love thy neighbour as thyself' – that is the great utterance against Monism, and the compromise with Monism. It does not say, 'Thou shalt love thy neighbour because he is thyself,' as the ancient Jew would have said. It commands 'Thou shalt recognize thy neighbour's distinction from thyself, and allow his separate being, because he also is of God, even though he be almost a contradiction to thyself.'

Such is the cry of anguish of Christianity: that man is separate from his brother, separate, maybe, even, in his measure, inimical to him. This the Jew had to learn. The old Jewish creed of identity, that Eve was identical with Adam, and all men children of one single parent, and therefore, in the absolute, identical, this must be destroyed.

Cunning and according to female suggestion is the story of the Creation: that Eve was born from the single body of Adam, without intervention of sex, both issuing from one flesh, as a child at birth seems to issue from one flesh of its mother. And the birth of Jesus is the retaliation to this: a child is born, not to the flesh, but to the spirit: and you. Woman, shall conceive, not to the body, but to the Word. 'In the beginning was the Word,' says the New Testament.

The great assertion of the Male was the New Testament, and, in its beauty, the Union of Male and Female. Christ was born of Woman, begotten by the Holy Spirit. This was why Christ should be called the Son of Man. For he was born of Woman. He was born to the Spirit, the Word, the Man, the Male.

And the assertion entailed the sacrifice of the Son of Woman. The body of Christ must be destroyed, that of him which was Woman must be put to death, to testify that he was Spirit, that he was Male, that he was Man, without any womanly part.

So the other great camp was made. In the creation, Man was driven forth from Paradise to labour for his body and for the woman. All was lost for the knowledge of the flesh. Out of the innocence and Nirvana of Paradise came, with the Fall, the consciousness of the flesh, the body of man and woman came into very being.

This was the first great movement of Man: the movement into the conscious possession of a body. And this consciousness of the body came through woman. And this knowledge, this possession, this enjoyment, was jealously guarded. In spite of all criticism and attack, Job remained true to this knowledge, to the utter belief in his body, in the God of his body. Though the Woman herself turned tempter, he remained true to it.

The senses, sensation, sensuousness, these things which are incontrovertibly Me, these are my God, these belong to God, said Job. And he persisted, and he was right. They issue from God on the female side.

But Christ came with his contradiction: That which is Not-Me, that is God. All is God, except that which I know immediately as Myself. First I must lose Myself, then I find God. Ye must be born again.

Unto what must man be born again? Unto knowledge of his

571

own separate existence, as in Woman he is conscious of his own incorporate existence. Man must be born unto knowledge of his own distinct identity, as in woman he was born to knowledge of his identification with the Whole. Man must be born to the knowledge, that in the whole being he is nothing, as he was born to know that in the whole being he was all. He must be born to the knowledge that other things exist beside himself, and utterly apart from all, and before he can exist himself as a separate identity, he must allow and recognize their distinct existence. Whereas previously, on the more female Jewish side, it had been said: 'All that exists is as Me. We are all one family, out of one God, having one being.'

With Christ ended the Monism of the Jew. God, the One God, became a Trinity, three-fold. He was the Father, the All-containing; He was the Son, the Word, the Changer, the Separator; and He was the Spirit, the Comforter, the Reconciliator between the Two.

And according to its conditions, Christianity has, since Christ, worshipped the Father or the Son, the one more than the other. Out of an over-female race came the male utterance of Christ. Throughout Europe, the suppressed, inadequate male desire, both in men and women, stretched to the idea of Christ, as a woman should stretch out her hands to a man. But Greece, in whom the female was overridden and neglected, became silent. So through the Middle Ages went on in Europe this fight against the body, against the senses, against this continual triumph of the senses. The worship of Europe, predominantly female, all through the medieval period, was to the male, to the incorporeal Christ, as a bridegroom, whilst the art produced was the collective, stupendous, emotional gesture of the Cathedrals, where a blind, collective impulse rose into concrete form. It was the profound, sensuous desire and gratitude which produced an art of architecture, whose essence is in utter stability, of movement resolved and centralized, of absolute movement, that has no relationship with any other form, that admits the existence of no other form, but is conclusive, propounding in its sum the One Being of All.

There was, however, in the Cathedrals, already the denial of the Monism which the Whole uttered. All the little figures, the gargoyles, the imps, the human faces, whilst subordinated within the Great Conclusion of the Whole, still, from their obscurity, jeered their mockery of the Absolute, and declared for multiplicity, polygeny. But all medieval art has the static, architectural, absolute quality, in the main, even whilst in detail it is differentiated and distinct. Such is Dürer, for example. When his art succeeds, it conveys the sense of Absolute Movement, movement proper only to the given form, and not relative to other movements. It portrays the Object, with its Movement content, and not the movement which contains in one of its moments the Object.

It is only when the Greek stimulus is received, with its addition of male influence, its addition of relative movement, its revelation of movement driving the object, the highest revelation which had yet been made, that medieval art became complete Renaissance art, that there was the union and fusion of the male and female spirits, creating a perfect expression for the time being.

During the medieval times, the God had been Christ on the Cross, the Body Crucified, the flesh destroyed, the Virgin Chastity combating Desire. Such had been the God of the Aspiration. But the God of Knowledge, of that which they acknowledged as themselves, had been the Father, the God of the Ancient Jew.

But now, with the Renaissance, the God of Aspiration became in accord with the God of Knowledge, and there was a great outburst of joy, and the theme was not Christ Crucified, but Christ born of Woman, the Infant Saviour and the Virgin; or of the Annunciation, the Spirit embracing the flesh in pure embrace.

This was the perfect union of male and female, in this the hands met and clasped, and never was such a manifestation of Joy. This Joy reached its highest utterance perhaps in Botticelli, as in his *Nativity of the Saviour*, in our National Gallery. Still there is the architectural composition, but what an outburst of movement from the source of motion. The Infant Christ is a centre, a radiating spark of movement, the Virgin is bowed in Absolute Movement, the earthly father, Joseph, is folded up, like a clod or a boulder, obliterated, whilst the Angels fly round in ecstasy, embracing and linking hands.

The bodily father is almost obliterated. As balance to the Virgin Mother he is there, presented, but silenced, only the movement of his loin conveyed. He is not the male. The male is the radiant infant, over which the mother leans. They two are the ecstatic centre, the complete origin, the force which is both centrifugal and centripetal.

This is the joyous utterance of the Renaissance, to which we listen for ever. Perhaps there is a melancholy in Botticelli, a pain of Woman mated to the Spirit, a nakedness of the Aphrodite issued exposed to the clear elements, to the fleshlessness of the male. But still it is joy transparent over pain. It is the utterance of complete, perfect religious art, unwilling, perhaps, when the true male and the female meet. In the Song of Solomon, the female was preponderant, the male was impure, not single. But here the heart is satisfied for the moment, there is a moment of perfect being.

And it seems to be so in other religions: the most perfect moment centres round the mother and the male child, whilst the physical male is deified separately, as a bull, perhaps.

After Botticelli came Correggio. In him the development from gesture to articulate expression was continued, unconsciously, the movement from the symbolic to the representation went on in him, from the object to the animate creature. The Virgin and Child are no longer symbolic, in Correggio: they no longer belong to religious art, but are distinctly secular. The effort is to render the living person, the individual perceived, and not the great aspiration, or an idea. Art now passes from the naïve, intuitive stage to the state of knowledge. The female impulse, to feel and to live in feeling, is now embraced by the male impulse – to know, and almost carried off by knowledge. But not yet. Still Correggio is unconscious, in his art; he is in that state of elation which represents the marriage of male and female, with the pride of the male perhaps predominant. In the *Madonna with the Basket*, of the National Gallery, the Madonna is most thoroughly a wife, the child is most triumphantly a man's child.

The Father is the origin. He is seen labouring in the distance, the true support of this mother and child. There is no Virgin worship, none of the mystery of woman. The artist has reached to a sufficiency of knowledge. He knows his woman. What he is now concerned with is not her great female mystery, but her individual character. The picture has become almost lyrical – it is the woman as known by the man, it is the woman as he has experienced her. But still she is also unknown, also she is the mystery. But Correggio's chief business is to portray the woman of his own experience and knowledge, rather than the woman of his aspiration and fear. The artist is now concerned with his own experience rather than with his own desire. The female is now more or less within the power and reach of the male. But still she is there, to centralize and control his movement, still the two react and are not resolved. But for the man, the woman is henceforth part of a stream of movement, she is herself a stream of movement, carried along with himself. He sees everything as motion, retarded perhaps by the flesh, or by the stable being of this life in the body. But still man is held and pivoted by the object, even if he tend to wear down the pivot to a nothingness.

Thus Correggio leads on to the whole of modern art, where the male still wrestles with the female, in unconscious struggle, but where he gains ever gradually over her, reducing her to nothing. Ever there is more and more vibration, movement, and less and less stability, centralization. Ever man is more and more occupied with his own experience, with his own overpowering of resistance, ever less and less aware of any resistance in the object, less and less aware of any stability, less and less aware of anything unknown, more and more preoccupied with that which he knows, till his knowledge tends to become an abstraction, because it is limited by no unknown.

It is the contradiction of Dürer, as the Parthenon Frieze was the contradiction of Babylon and Egypt. To Dürer woman did not exist; even as to a child at the breast, woman does not exist separately. She is the overwhelming condition of life. She was to Dürer that which possessed him, and not that which he possessed. Her being overpowered him, he could only see in her

575

terms, in terms of stability and of stable, incontrovertible being. He is overpowered by the vast assurance at whose breasts he is suckled, and, as if astounded, he grasps at the unknown. He knows that he rests within some great stability, and, marvelling at his own power for movement, touches the objects of this stability, becomes familiar with them. It is a question of the starting-point. Dürer starts with a sense of that which he does not know and would discover; Correggio with the sense of that which he has known, and would re-create.

And in the Renaissance, after Botticelli, the motion begins to divide in these two directions. The hands no longer clasp in perfect union, but one clasp overbears the other. Botticelli develops to Correggio and to Andrea del Sarto, develops forward to Rembrandt, and Rembrandt to the Impressionists, to the male extreme of motion. But Botticelli, on the other hand, becomes Raphael, Raphael and Michelangelo.

In Raphael we see the stable, architectural developing out further, and becoming the geometric: the denial or refusal of all movement. In the *Madonna degli Ansidei* the child is drooping, the mother stereotyped, the picture geometric, static, abstract. When there is any union of male and female, there is no goal of abstraction: the abstract is used in place, as a means of a real union. The goal of the male impulse is the announcement of motion, endless motion, endless diversity, endless change. The goal of the female impulse is the announcement of infinite oneness, of infinite stability. When the two are working in combination, as they must in life, there is, as it were, a dual motion, centrifugal for the male, fleeing abroad, away from the centre, outward to infinite vibration, and centripetal for the female, fleeing in to the eternal centre of rest. A combination of the two movements produces a sum of motion and stability at once, satisfying. But in life there tends always to be more of one than the other. The Cathedrals, Fra Angelico, frighten us or [bore] us with their final annunciation of centrality and stability. We want to escape. The influence is too female for us.

In Botticelli, the architecture remains, but there is the wonderful movement outwards, the joyous, if still clumsy, escape from

576

the centre. His religious pictures tend to be stereotyped, resigned. The Primavera herself is static, melancholy, a stability become almost a negation. It is as if the female, instead of being the great, unknown Positive, towards which all must flow, became the great Negative, the centre which denied all motion. And the Aphrodite stands there not as a force, to draw all things unto her, but as the naked, almost unwilling pivot, as the keystone which endured all thrust and remained static. But still there is the joy, the great motion around her, sky and sea, all the elements and living, joyful forces.

Raphael, however, seeks and finds nothing there. He goes to the centre to ask: 'What is this mystery we are all pivoted upon?' To Fra Angelico it was the unknown Omnipotent. It was a goal, to which man travelled inevitably. It was the desired, the end of the long horizontal journey. But to Raphael it was the negation. Still he is a seeker, an aspirant, still his art is religious art. But the Virgin, the essential female, was to him a negation, a neutrality. Such must have been his vivid experience. But still he seeks her. Still he desires the stability, the positive keystone which grasps the arch together, not the negative keystone neutralizing the thrust, itself a neutrality. And reacting upon his own desire, the male reacting upon itself, he creates the Abstraction, the geometric conception of life. The fundament of all is the geometry of all. Which is the Plato conception. And the desire is to formulate the complete geometry.

So Raphael, knowing that his desire reaches out beyond the range of possible experience, sensible that he will not find satisfaction in any one woman, sensible that the female impulse does not, or cannot unite in him with the male impulse sufficiently to create a stability, an eternal moment of truth for him, of realization, closes his eyes and his mind upon experience, and abstracting himself, reacting upon himself, produces the geometric conception of the fundamental truth, departs from religion, from any God idea, and becomes philosophic.

Raphael is the real end of Renaissance in Italy; almost he is the real end of Italy, as Plato was the real end of Greece. When the God-idea passes into the philosophic or geometric idea, then

577

there is a sign that the male impulse has thrown the female impulse, and has recoiled upon itself, has become abstract, asexual.

Michelangelo, however, too physically passionate, containing too much of the female in his body ever to reach the geometric abstraction, unable to abstract himself, and at the same time, like Raphael, unable to find any woman who in her being should resist him and reserve still some unknown from him, strives to obtain his own physical satisfaction in his art. He is obsessed by the desire of the body. And he must react upon himself to produce his own bodily satisfaction, aware that he can never obtain it through woman. He must seek the moment, the consummation, the keystone, the pivot, in his own flesh. For his own body is both male and female.

Raphael and Michelangelo are men of different nature placed in the same position and resolving the same question in their several ways. Socrates and Plato are a parallel pair, and, in another degree, Tolstoy and Turgenev, and, perhaps, St Paul and St John the Evangelist, and, perhaps, Shakespeare and Shelley.

The body it is which attaches us directly to the female. Sex, as we call it, is only the point where the dual stream begins to divide, where it is nearly together, almost one. An infant is of no very determinate sex: that is, it is of both. Only at adolescence is there a real differentiation, the one is singled out to predominate. In what we call happy natures, in the lazy, contented people, there is a fairly equable balance of sex. There is sufficient of the female in the body of such a man as to leave him fairly free. He does not suffer the torture of desire of a more male being. It is obvious even from the physique of such a man that in him there is a proper proportion between male and female, so that he can be easy, balanced, and without excess. The Greek sculptors of the 'best' period, Phidias and then Sophocles, Alcibiades, then Horace, must have been fairly well-balanced men, not passionate to any excess, tending to voluptuousness rather than to passion. So also Victor Hugo and Schiller and Tennyson. The real voluptuary is a man who is female as well as male, and who lives according to the female side of his nature, like Lord Byron.

The pure male is himself almost an abstraction, almost bodi-

less, like Shelley or Edmund Spenser. But, as we know humanity, this condition comes of an omission of some vital part. In
the ordinary sense, Shelley never lived. He transcended life. But
we do not want to transcend life, since we are of life.

Why should Shelley say of the skylark:

'Hail to thee, blithe Spirit! – bird thou never wert! –'? Why
should he insist on the bodilessness of beauty, when we cannot
know of any save embodied beauty? Who would wish that the
skylark were not a bird, but a spirit? If the whistling skylark were
a spirit, then we should all wish to be spirits. Which were impious and flippant.

I can think of no being in the world so transcendently male
as Shelley. He is phenomenal. The rest of us have bodies which
contain the male and the female. If we were so singled out as
Shelley, we should not belong to life, as he did not belong to life.
But it were impious to wish to be like the angels. So long as mankind exists it must exist in the body, and so long must each body
pertain both to the male and the female.

In the degree of pure maleness below Shelley are Plato and
Raphael and Wordsworth, then Goethe and Milton and Dante,
then Michelangelo, then Shakespeare, then Tolstoy, then St Paul.

A man who is well balanced between male and female, in his
own nature, is, as a rule, happy, easy to mate, easy to satisfy, and
content to exist. It is only a disproportion, or a dissatisfaction,
which makes the man struggle into articulation. And the articulation is of two sorts, the cry of desire or the cry of realization,
the cry of satisfaction, the effort to prolong the sense of satisfaction, to prolong the moment of consummation.

A bird in spring sings with the dawn, ringing out from the
moment of consummation in wider and wider circles. Dürer,
Fra Angelico, Botticelli, all sing of the moment of consummation, some of them still marvelling and lost in the wonder at the
other being, Botticelli poignant with distinct memory. Raphael
too sings of the moment of consummation. But he was not lost in
the moment, only sufficiently lost to know what it was. In the
moment, he was not completely consummated. He must strive to
complete his satisfaction from himself. So, whilst making his

great acknowledgement to the Woman, he must add to her to make her whole, he must give her his completion. So he rings her round with pure geometry, till she becomes herself almost of the geometric figure, an abstraction. The picture becomes a great ellipse crossed by a dark column. This is the *Madonna degli Ansidei*. The Madonna herself is almost insignificant. She and the child are contained within the shaft thrust across the ellipse.

This column must always stand for the male aspiration, the arch or ellipse for the female completeness containing this aspiration. And the whole picture is a geometric symbol of the consummation of life.

What we call the Truth is, in actual experience, that momentary state when in living the union between the male and the female is consummated. This consummation may be also physical, between the male body and the female body. But it may be only spiritual, between the male and female spirit.

And the symbol by which Raphael expresses this moment of consummation is by a dark, strong shaft or column leaping up into, and almost transgressing a faint, radiant, inclusive ellipse.

To express the same moment Botticelli uses no symbol, but builds up a complicated system of circles, of movements wheeling in their horizontal plane about their fixed centres, the whole builded up dome-shape, and then the dome surpassed by another singing cycle in the open air above.

This is Botticelli always: different cycles of joy, different moments of embrace, different forms of dancing round, all contained in one picture, without solution. He has not solved it yet.

And Raphael, in reaching the pure symbolic solution, has surpassed art and become almost mathematics. Since the business of art is never to solve, but only to declare.

There is no such thing as solution. Nietzsche talks about the *Ewige Wiederkehr*. It is like Botticelli singing cycles. But each cycle is different. There is no real recurrence.

And to single out one cycle, one moment, and to exclude from this moment all context, and to make this moment timeless, this is what Raphael does, and what Plato does. So that their absolute Truth, their geometric Truth, is only true in timelessness.

Michelangelo, on the other hand, seeks for no absolute Truth. His desire is to realize in his body, in his feeling, the moment-consummation which is for Man the perfect truth-experience. But he knows of no embrace. For him, personally, woman does not exist. For Botticelli she existed as the Virgin-Mother, and as the Primavera, and as Aphrodite. She existed as the pure origin of life on the female side, as the bringer of light and delight, and as the passionately Desired of every man, as the Known and Unknown in one: to Raphael she existed either as a minor part of his experience, having nothing to do with his aspiration, or else his aspiration merely used her as a statement included within the Great Abstraction.

To Michelangelo the female scarcely existed outside his own physique. There he knew of her and knew the desire of her. But Raphael, in his passion to be self-complete, roused his desire for consummation to a white-hot pitch, so that he became incandescent, reacting on himself, consuming his own flesh and his own bodily life, to reach the pitch of perfect abstraction, the resisting body holding back the raging stream of outward force, till the two formed a stable incandescence, a luminous geometric conception of permanence and inviolability. Meanwhile his body burned away, overpowered, in this state of incandescence.

Michelangelo's will was different. The body in him, that which knew of the female and therefore was the female, was stronger and most insistent. His desire for consummation was desire for the satisfying moment when the male and female spirits touch in closest embrace, vivifying each other, not one destroying the other, but still are two. He knew that for Man consummation is a temporal state. The pure male spirit must ever conceive of timelessness, the pure female of the moment. And Michelangelo, more mixed than Raphael, must always rage within the limits of time and of temporal forms. So he reacted upon himself, sought the female in himself, aggrandized it, and so reached a wonderful momentary stability of flesh exaggerated till it became tenuous, but filled and balanced by the outward-pressing force. And he reached his consummation in that way, reached the perfect moment, when he realized and revealed his figures in all their marvellous equilibrium. The Jewish tradition, with its great physical God, source of male and female, attracted him. By turning towards the female goal, of utter stability and permanence in Time, he arrived at his consummation. But only by reacting on himself, by withdrawing his own mobility. Thus he made his great figures, the Moses, static and looming, announcing, like the Jewish God, the magnificence and eternality of the physical law; the David, young, but with too much body for a young figure, the physique exaggerated, the clear, outward-leaping, essential spirit of the young man smothered over, the real maleness cloaked, so that the statue is almost a falsity. Then the slaves, heaving in body, fastened in bondage that refuses them movement; the motionless Madonna, no Virgin but Woman in the flesh, not the pure female conception, but the spouse of man, the mother of bodily children. The men are not male, nor the women female, to any degree.

The Adam can scarcely stir into life. That large body of almost transparent, tenuous texture is not established enough for motion. It is not that it is too ponderous: it is too unsubstantial, unreal. It is not motion, life, he craves, but body. Give him but a firm, concentrated physique. That is the cry of all Michelangelo's pictures.

But, powerful male as he was, he satisfies his desire by insisting upon and exaggerating the body in him, he reaches the point of consummation in the most marvellous equilibrium which his figures show. To attain this equilibrium he must exaggerate and exaggerate and exaggerate the flesh, make it ever more tenuous, keeping it really in true ratio. And then comes the moment, the perfect stable poise, the perfect balance between object and movement, the perfect combination of male and female in one figure.

It is wonderful, and peaceful, this equilibrium, once reached. But it is reached through anguish and self-battle and self-repression, therefore it is sad. Always, Michelangelo's pictures are full of joy, of self-acceptance and self-proclamation. Michelangelo fought and arrested the mobile male in him; Raphael was proud in the male he was, and gave himself utter liberty, at the female expense.

And it seems as though Italy had ever since the Renaissance been possessed by the Raphaelesque conception of the ultimate geometric basis of life, the geometric essentiality of all things. There is in the Italian, at the very bottom of all, the fundamental, geometric conception of absolute static combination. There is the shaft enclosed in the ellipse, as a permanent symbol. There exists no shaft, no ellipse separately, but only the whole complete thing; there is neither male nor female, but an absolute interlocking of the two in one, an absolute combination, so that each is gone in the complete identity. There is only the geometric abstraction of the moment of consummation, a moment made timeless. And this conception of a long, clinched, timeless embrace, this overwhelming conception of timeless consummation, of which there is no beginning nor end, from which there is no escape, has arrested the Italian race for three centuries. It is the source of its indifference and its fatalism and its positive abandon, and of its utter incapacity to be sceptical, in the Russian sense.

This conception contains also, naturally, as part of the same idea, Aphrodite-worship and Phallic-worship. But these are subordinate, and belong to a sort of initiatory period. The real conception, for the individual, is marriage, inviolable marriage, which always was and always has been, no matter what apparent aberrations there may or may not be. And the manifestation of divinity is the child. In marriage, in utter, interlocked marriage, man and woman cease to be two beings and become one, one and one only, not two in one as with us, but absolute One, a geometric absolute, timeless, the Absolute, the Divine. And the child, as issue of this divine and timeless state, is hailed with love and joy.

But the Italian is now beginning to withdraw from his clinched and timeless embrace, from his geometric abstraction, into the northern conception of himself and the woman as two separate identities, which meet, combine, but always must withdraw again.

So that the Futurist Boccioni now makes his sculpture, *Development of a Bottle through Space*, try to express the withdrawal, and at the same time he must adhere to the conception of this same interlocked state of marriage between centripetal and centrifugal forces, the geometric abstraction of the bottle. But he can neither do one thing nor the other. He wants to re-state the real abstraction. And at the same time he has an unsatisfied desire to satisfy. He must insist on the centrifugal force, and so destroy at once his abstraction. He must insist on the male spirit of motion outwards, because, during three static centuries, there has necessarily come to pass a preponderance of the female in the race, so that the Italian is rather more female than male now, as is the whole Latin race rather voluptuous than passionate, too much aware of their utter lockedness male with female, and too hopeless, as males, to act, to be passionate. So that when I look at Boccioni's sculpture, and see him trying to state the timeless abstract being of a bottle, the pure geometric abstraction of the bottle, I am fascinated. But then, when I see him driven by his desire for the male complement into portraying motion, simple motion, trying to give expression to the bottle in terms of mechanics, I am confused. It is for science to explain the bottle in terms of force and motion. Geometry, pure mathematics, is very near to art, and the vivid attempt to render the bottle as a pure geometric abstraction might give rise to a work of art, because of the resistance of the medium, the stone. But a representation in stone of the lines of force which create that state of rest called a bottle, that is a model in mechanics.

And the two representations require two different states of mind in the appreciator, so that the result is almost nothingness, mere confusion. And the portraying of a state of mind is impossible. There can only be made scientific diagrams of states of mind. A state of mind is a resultant between an attack and a resistance. And how can one produce a resultant without first causing the collision of the originating forces?

The attitude of the Futurists is the scientific attitude, as the attitude of Italy is mainly scientific. It is the forgetting of the old, perfect Abstraction, it is the departure of the male from the female, it is the act of withdrawal: the denying of consummation and the starting afresh, the learning of the alphabet.

CHAPTER VIII

*The Light of the World*

The climax that was reached in Italy with Raphael has never been reached in like manner in England. There has never been, in England, the great embrace, the surprising consummation, which Botticelli recorded and which Raphael fixed in a perfect Abstraction.

Correggio, Andrea del Sarto, both men of less force than those other supreme three, continued the direct line of development, turning no curve. They still found women whom they could not exhaust: in them, the male still reacted upon the incontrovertible female. But ever there was a tendency to greater movement, to a closer characterization, a tendency to individualize the human being, and to represent him as being embedded in some common, divine matrix.

Till after the Renaissance, supreme God had always been God the Father. The Church moved and had its being in Almighty God, Christ was only the distant, incandescent gleam towards which humanity aspired, but which it did not know.

Raphael and Michelangelo were both servants of the Father, of the Eternal Law, of the Prime Being. Raphael, faced with the question of Not-Being, when it was forced upon him that he would never accomplish his own being in the flesh, that he would never know completeness, the momentary consummation, in the body, accomplished the Geometrical Abstraction, which is the abstraction from the Law, which is the Father.

There was, however, Christ's great assertion of Not-Being, of No-Consummation, of life after death, to reckon with. It was after the Renaissance, Christianity began to exist. It had not existed before.

In God the Father we are all one body, one flesh. But in Christ we abjure the flesh, there is no flesh. A man must lose his life to save it. All the natural desires of the body, these a man must be able to deny, before he can live. And then, when he lives, he shall

585

live in the knowledge that he is himself, so that he can always say: 'I am I.'

In the Father we are one flesh, in Christ we are crucified, and rise again, and are One with Him in Spirit. It is the difference between Law and Love. Each man shall live according to the Law, which changeth not, says the old religion. Each man shall live according to Love, which shall save us from death and from the Law, says the new religion.

But what is Love? What is the deepest desire Man has yet known? It is always for this consummation, this momentary contact or union of male with female, of spirit with spirit and flesh with flesh, when each is complete in itself and rejoices in its own being, when each is in himself or in herself complete and single and essential. And love is the great aspiration towards this complete consummation and this joy; it is the aspiration of each man that all men, that all life, shall know it and rejoice. Since, until all men shall know it, no man shall fully know it. Since, by the Law, we are all one flesh. So that Love is only a closer vision of the Law, a more comprehensive interpretation: 'Think not I come to destroy the Law, or the Prophets: I come not to destroy, but to fulfil. For verily I say unto you, till heaven and earth pass, one jot or one tittle shall in no wise pass from the Law, till all be fulfilled.'

In Christ I must save my soul through love, I must lose my life, and thereby find it. The Law bids me preserve my life to the Glory of God. But Love bids me lose my life to the Glory of God. In Christ, when I shall have overcome every desire I know in myself, so that I adhere to nothing, but am loosed and set free and single, then, being without fear, and having nothing that I can lose, I shall know what I am, I, transcendent, intrinsic, eternal.

The Christian commandment: 'Thou shalt love thy neighbour as thyself' is a more indirect and moving, a more emotional form of the Greek commandment 'Know thyself.' This is what Christianity says, indirectly: 'Know thyself, and each man shall there-by know himself.'

Now in the Law, no man shall know himself, save in the Law. And the Law is the immediate law of the body. And the necessity of each man to know himself, to achieve his own consummation, shall be satisfied and fulfilled in the body. God, Almighty God, is the father, and in fatherhood man draws nearest to him. In the act of love, in the act of begetting, Man is with God and of God. Such is the Law. And there shall be no other God devised. That is the great obstructive commandment.

This is the old religious leap down, absolutely, even if not in direct statement. It is the Law. But through Christ it was at last declared that in the physical act of love, in the begetting of children, man does not necessarily know himself, nor become God-like, nor satisfy his deep, innate desire to B E. The physical act of love may fail utterly, may prove a sterility, a nothingness. Is a hood may be the least significant attribute to a man. And physical love may fail uttterly, may prove a sterility, a nothingness. Is a man then duped, and is his deepest desire a joke played on him?

There is a law, beyond the known law, there is a new Commandment. There is love. A man shall find his consummation the crucifixion of the body and the resurrection of the spirit.

Christ, the Bridegroom, or the Bride, as may be, awaits the desiring soul that shall seek him, and in him shall all men find their consummation, after their new birth. It is the New Law; the old Law is revoked.

'This is my Body, take, and eat,' says Christ, in the Communion, the ritual representing the Consummation. 'Come unto me all ye that labour and are heavy-laden, and I will give you rest.'

For each man there is the bride, for each woman the bridegroom, for all, the Mystic Marriage. It is the New Law. In the mystic embrace of Christ each man shall find fulfilment and relief, each man shall become himself, a male individual, tried, proved, completed, and satisfied. In the mystic embrace of Christ each man shall say, 'I am myself, and Christ is Christ'; each woman shall be proud and satisfied, saying, 'It is enough.'

So, by the New Law, man shall satisfy this his deepest desire. 'In the body ye must die, even as I die, on the cross,' says Christ, 'that ye may have everlasting life.' But this is a real contradiction of the Old Law, which says, 'In the life of the body we are one with the Father.' The Old Law bids us live: it is the old, original commandment, that we shall live in the Law, and not die. So that the new Christian preaching of Christ Crucified is indeed against the Law. 'And when ye are dead in the body, ye shall be one with the spirit, ye shall know the Bride, and be consummate in her Embrace, in the Spirit,' continues the Christian Commandment.

It is a larger interpretation of the Law, but, also, it is a breach of the Law. For by the Law, Man shall in no wise injure or deny or desecrate his living body of flesh, which is of the Father. Therefore, though Christ gave the Holy Ghost, the Comforter; though He bowed before the Father; though he said that no man should be forgiven the denial of the Holy Spirit, the Reconciler between the Father and the Son; yet did the Son deny the Father, must he deny the Father?

'Ye are my Spirit, in the Spirit ye know me, and in marriage of the Spirit I am fulfilled of you,' said the Son.

And it is the Unforgivable Sin to declare that these two are contradictions one of the other, though contradictions they are. Between them is linked the Holy Spirit, as a reconciliation, and whoso shall speak hurtfully against the Holy Spirit shall find no forgiveness.

So Christ, up in arms against the Father, exculpated himself and bowed to the Father. Yet man must insist either on one or on the other : either he must adhere to the Son or to the Father. And since the Renaissance, disappointed in the flesh, the northern races have sought the consummation through Love; and they have denied the Father.

The greatest and deepest human desire, for consummation, for Self-Knowledge, has sought a different satisfaction. In Love, in the act of love, that which is mixed in me becomes pure, that which is female in me is given to the female, that which is male in her draws into me, I am complete, I am pure male, she is pure female; we rejoice in contact perfect and naked and clear, singled out unto ourselves, and given the surpassing freedom. No longer we see through a glass, darkly. For she is she, and I am I, and, clasped together with her, I know how perfectly she is not me, how perfectly I am not her, how utterly we are two, the light and the darkness, and how infinitely and eternally not-to-be-comprehended by either of us is the surpassing One we make. Yet of this One, this incomprehensible, we have an inkling that satisfies us.

And through Christ Jesus, I know that I shall find my Bride, when I have overcome the impurity of the flesh. When the flesh in me is put away, I shall embrace the Bride, and I shall know as I am known.

But why the Schism? Why shall the Father say 'Thou shalt have no other God before Me'? Why is the Lord our God a jealous God? Why, when the body fails me, must I still adhere to the Law, and give it praise as the perfect Abstraction, like Raphael, announce it as the Absolute? Why must I be imprisoned within the flesh, like Michelangelo, till I must stop the voice of my crying out, and be satisfied with a little where I wanted completeness?

And why, on the other hand, must I lose my life to save it? Why must I die, before I can be born again? Can I not be born again, save out of my own ashes, save in resurrection from the dead? Why must I deny the Father, to love the Son? Why are they not One God to me, as we always protest they are?

It is time that the schism ended, that man ceased to oppose the Father to the Son, the Son to the Father. It is time that the Protestant Church, the Church of the Son, should be one again with the Roman Catholic Church, the Church of the Father. It is time that man shall cease, first to live in the flesh, with joy, and then, unsatisfied, to renounce and to mortify the flesh, declaring that the Spirit alone exists, that Christ he is God.

If a man find incomplete satisfaction in the body, why therefore shall he renounce the body and say it is of the devil? And why, at the start, shall a man say, 'The body, that is all, and the consummation, that is complete in the flesh, for me.'

Must it always be that a man set out with a worship of passion and a blindness to love, and that he end with a stern commandment to love and a renunciation of passion?

Does not a youth now know that he desires the body as the *via media*, that consummation is consummation of body and spirit, both?

How can a man say, 'I am this body,' when he will desire beyond the body tomorrow? And how can a man say, 'I am this spirit,' when his own mouth gives lie to the words it forms?

Why is a race, like the Italian race, fundamentally melancholy, save that it has circumscribed its consummation within the body? And the Jewish race, for the same reason, has become now almost hollow, with a pit of emptiness and misery in their eyes.

And why is the English race neutral, indifferent, like a thing that eschews life, save that it has said so insistently: 'I am this spirit. This body, it is not me, it is unworthy'? The body at last begins to wilt and become corrupt. But before it submits, half the life of the English race must be a lie. The life of the body, denied by the professed adherence to the spirit, must be something disowned, corrupt, ugly.

Why should the worship of the Son entail the denial of the Father?

Since the Renaissance, northern humanity has sought for consummation in the spirit, it has sought for the female apart from woman. 'I am I, and the Spirit is the Spirit; in the Spirit I am myself', and this has been the utterance of our art since Raphael.

There has been the ever-developing dissolution of form, the dissolving of the solid body within the spirit. He began to break the clear outline of the object, to seek for further marriage, not only between body and body, not the perfect, stable union of body with body, not the utter completeness and accomplishment of architectural form, with its recurrent cycles, but the marriage between body and spirit, or between spirit and spirit.

It is no longer the Catholic exultation 'God is God', but the Christian annunciation, 'Light is come into the world.' No longer has a man only to obey, but he has to die and be born again; he has to close his eyes upon his own immediate desires, and in the darkness receive the perfect light. He has to know himself in the spirit, he has to follow Christ to the Cross, and rise again in the light of the life.

And, in this light of life, he will see his Bride, he will embrace his complement and his fulfilment, and achieve his consummation. 'It is the spirit that quickeneth; the flesh forgetteth nothing; the words I speak unto you, they are the spirit, and they are life.'

And though in the Gospel, according to John particularly, Jesus constantly asserts that the Father has sent Him, and that He is of the Father, yet there is always the spirit of antagonism to the Father.

And it came to pass, as he spake these things, a certain woman of the company lifted up her voice and said unto him: 'Blessed is the womb that bare thee, and the paps thou hast sucked.'

But he said, Yea, rather, blessed are they that hear the word of God, and keep it.

And the woman who heard this knew that she was denied of the honour of her womb, and that the blessing of her breasts was taken away.

Again He said: 'And there be those that were born eunuchs, and there be those that were made eunuchs by men, and there be eunuchs which have made themselves eunuchs for the kingdom of heaven's sake. He that is able to receive it, let him receive it.' But before the Father a eunuch is blemished, even a childless man is without honour.

So that the spirit of Jesus is antagonistic to the spirit of the Father. And St John enhances this antagonism. But in St John there is the constant insistence on the Oneness of Father and Son, and on the Holy Spirit.

Since the Renaissance there has been the striving for the Light, and the escape from the Flesh, from the Body, the Object. And sometimes there has been the antagonism to the Father, sometimes reconciliation with him. In painting, the Spirit, the Word, the Love, all that was represented by John, has appeared as light. Light is the constant symbol of Christ in the New Testament. It is light, actual sunlight or the luminous quality of day, which has infused more and more into the defined body, fusing away the outline, absolving the concrete reality, making a marriage, an embrace between the two things, light and object.

In Rembrandt there is the first great evidence of this, the new exposition of the commandment 'Know thyself.' It is more than the 'Hail, holy Light! ' of Milton. It is the declaration that light is our medium of existence, that where the light falls upon our darkness, there we *are*: that I am but the point where light and darkness meet and break upon one another.

There is now a new conception of life, an utterly new conception, of duality, of two-fold existence, light and darkness, object and spirit two-fold, and almost inimical.

The old desire, for movement about a centre of rest, for stability, is gone, and in its place rises the desire for pure ambience, pure spirit of change, free from all laws and conditions of being.

Henceforward there are two things, and not one. But there is journeying towards the one thing again. There is no longer the One God who contains us all, and in whom we live and move and have our being, and to whom belongs each one of our movements. I am no longer a child of the Father, brother of all men. I am no longer part of the great body of God, as all men are part of it. I am no longer consummate in the body of God, identified with it and divine in the act of marriage.

The conception has utterly changed. There is the Spirit, and there is myself. I exist in contact with the Spirit, but I am not the Spirit. I am other, I am myself. Now I am become a man, I am no more a child of the Father. I am a man. And there are many men. And the Father has lost his importance. We are multiple, manifold men, we own only one Hope, one Desire, one Bride, one Spirit.

At last man insists upon his own separate Self, insists that he has a distinct, inconquerable being which stands apart even from Spirit, which exists other than the Spirit, and which seeks marriage with the Spirit.

And he must study himself and marvel over himself in the light of the Spirit, he must become lyrical: but he must glorify the Spirit, above all. Since that is the Bride. So Rembrandt paints his own portrait again and again, sees it again and again within the light.

He has no hatred of the flesh. That he was not completed in the flesh, even in the marriage of the body, is inevitable. But he is married in the flesh, and his wife is with him in the body, he loves his body, which she gave him complete, and he loves her body, which is not himself, but which he has known. He has known and rejoiced in the earthly bride, he will adhere to her always. But there is the Spirit beyond her : there is his desire which transcends her, there is the Bride still he craves for and courts. And he knows, this is the Spirit, it is not the body. And he paints it as the light. And he paints himself within the light. For he has a deep desire to know himself in the embrace of the spirit. For he does not know himself, he is never consummated.

In the Old Law, fulfilled in him, he is not appeased, he must transcend the Law. The Woman is embraced, caught up, and carried forward, the male spirit, passing on half satisfied, must seek a new bride, a further consummation. For there is no bride on earth for him.

To Dürer, the whole earth was as a bride, unknown and unaccomplished, offering satisfaction to him. And he sought out the earth endlessly, as a man seeks to know a bride who surpasses him. It was all: the Bride.

But to Rembrandt the bride was not to be found, he must react upon himself, he must seek in himself for his own consummation. There was the Light, the Spirit, the Bridegroom. But when Rembrandt sought the complete Bride, sought for his own consummation, he knew it was not to be found, he knew she did not exist in the concrete. He knew, as Michelangelo knew, that there was not on the earth a woman to satisfy him, to be his mate. He must seek for the Bride beyond the physical woman; he must seek for the great female principle in an abstraction.

But the abstraction was not the geometric abstraction, created from knowledge, a state of Absolute Remembering, making Absolute of the Consummation which had been, as in Raphael. It was the desired Unknown, the goodly Unknown, the Spirit, the Light. And with this Light Rembrandt must seek even the marriage of the body. Everything he did approximates to the Consummation, but never can realize it. He paints always faith, belief, hope; never Raphael's terrible, dead certainty.

To Dürer, every moment of his existence was occupied. He

existed within the embrace of the Bride, which embrace he could never fathom nor exhaust.

Raphael knew and outraged the Bride, but he harked back, obsessed by the consummation which had been.

To Rembrandt, woman was only the first acquaintance with the Bride. Of woman he obtained and expected no complete satisfaction. He knew he must go on, beyond the woman. But though the flesh could not find its consummation, still he did not deny the flesh. He was an artist, and in his art no artist ever could blaspheme the Holy Spirit, the Reconciler. Only a dogmatist could do that. Rembrandt did not deny the flesh, as so many artists try to do. He went on from her to the fuller knowledge of the Bride, in true progression. Which makes the wonderful beauty of Rembrandt.

But, like Michelangelo, owning the flesh, and a northern Christian being bent on personal salvation, personal consummation in the flesh, such as a Christian feels with us when he receives the Sacrament and hears the words 'This is my Body, take, and eat', Rembrandt craved to marry the flesh and the Spirit, to achieve consummation in the flesh through marriage with the Spirit.

Which is the great northern confusion. For the flesh is of the flesh, and the Spirit of the Spirit, and they are two, even as the Father and the Son are two, and not One.

Raphael conceived the two as One, thereby revoking Time. Michelangelo would have created the bridal Flesh, to satisfy himself. Rembrandt would have married his own flesh to the Spirit, taken the consummate Kiss of the Light upon his fleshly face.

Which is a confusion. For the Father cannot know the Son, nor the Son the Father. So, in Rembrandt, the marriage is always imperfect, the embrace is never close nor consummate, as it is in Botticelli or in Raphael, or in Michelangelo. There is an eternal non-marriage betwixt flesh and spirit. They are two; they are never Two-in-One. So that in Rembrandt there is never complete marriage betwixt the Light and the Body. They are contiguous, never.

This has been the confusion and the error of the northern countries, but particularly of Germany, this desire to have the spirit mate with the flesh, the flesh with the spirit. Spirit can mate with spirit, and flesh with flesh, and the two matings can take place separately, flesh with flesh, or spirit with spirit. But to try to mate flesh with spirit makes confusion.

The bride I mate with my body may or may not be the Bride in whom I find my consummation. It may be that, at times, the great female principle does not abide abundantly in woman: that, at certain periods, woman, in the body, is not the supreme representative of the Bride. It may be the Bride is hidden from Man, as the Light, or as the Darkness, which he can never know in the flesh.

It may be, in the same way, that the great male principle is only weakly evidenced in man during certain periods, that the Bridegroom be hidden away from woman, for a century or centuries, and that she can only find him as the voice, or the Wind. So I think it was with her during the medieval period; that the greatest women of the period knew that the Bridegroom did not exist for them in the body, but as the Christ, the Spirit.

And, in times of the absence of the bridegroom from the body, then woman in the body must either die in the body, or, mating in the body, she must mate with the Bridegroom in the Spirit, in a separate marriage. She cannot mate her body with the Spirit, nor mate her spirit with the Body. That is confusion. Let her mate the man in body, and her spirit with the Spirit, in a separate marriage. But let her not try to mate her spirit with the body of the man, that does not mate her Spirit.

The effort to mate spirit with body, body with spirit, is the crying confusion and pain of our times.

Rembrandt made the first effort. But art has developed to a clarity since then. It reached its climax in our own Turner. He did not seek to mate body with spirit. He mated his body easily, he did not deny it. But what he sought was the mating of the Spirit. Ever, he sought the consummation in the Spirit, and he reached it at last. Ever, he sought the Light, to make the light transfuse the body, till the body was carried away, a mere bloodstain, became a ruddy stain of red sunlight within white sunlight. This was perfect consummation in Turner, when, the body gone, the ruddy light meets the crystal light in a perfect fusion, the utter dawn, the utter golden sunset, the extreme of all life, where all is One, One-Being, a perfect glowing Oneness.

Like Raphael, it becomes an abstraction. But this, in Turner, is the abstraction from the spiritual marriage and consummation, the final transcending of all the Law, the achieving of what is to us almost a nullity. If Turner had ever painted his last picture, it would have been a white, incandescent surface, the same whiteness when he finished as when he began, proceeding from nullity to nullity, through all the range of colour.

Turner is perfect. Such a picture as his *Norham Castle, Sunrise*, where only the faintest shadow of life stains the light, is the last word that can be uttered, before the blazing and timeless silence.

He sought, and he found, perfect marriage in the spirit. It was apart from woman. His Bride was the Light. Or he was the bride himself, and the Light – the Bridegroom. Be that as it may, he became one and consummate with the Light, and gave us the consummate revelation.

Corot, also, nearer to the Latin tradition of utter consummation in the body, made a wonderful marriage in the spirit between light and darkness, just tinctured with life. But he contained more of the two consummations together, the marriage in the body, represented in geometric form, and the marriage in the spirit, represented by shimmering transfusion and infusion of light through darkness.

But Turner is the crisis in this effort: he achieves pure light, pure and singing. In him the consummation is perfect, the perfect marriage in the spirit.

In the body his marriage was other. He never attempted to mingle the two. The marriage in the body, with the woman, was apart from, completed away from the marriage in the Spirit, with the Bride, the Light.

But I cannot look at a later Turner picture without abstracting myself, without denying that I have limbs, knees and thighs and breast. If I look at the *Norham Castle*, and remember my own knees and my own breast, then the picture is a nothing to me. I must not know. And if I look at Raphael's *Madonna degli Ansidei*, I am cut off from my future, from aspiration. The gate is shut upon me, I can go no further. The thought of Turner's *Sunrise* becomes magic and fascinating, it gives the lie to this completed symbol. I know I am the other thing as well.

So that, whenever art or any expression becomes perfect, it becomes a lie. For it is only perfect by reason of abstraction from that context by which and in which it exists as truth.

So Turner is a lie, and Raphael is a lie, and the marriage in the spirit is a lie, and the marriage in the body is a lie, each is a lie without the other. Since each excludes the other in these instances, they are both lies. If they were brought together, and reconciled, then there were a jubilee. But where is the Holy Spirit that shall reconcile Raphael and Turner?

There must be marriage of body in body, and of spirit in spirit, and Two-in-One. And the marriage in the body must not deny the marriage in the spirit, for that is blasphemy against the Holy Ghost; and the marriage in the spirit shall not deny the marriage in the body, for that is blasphemy against the Holy Ghost. But the two must be for ever reconciled, even if they must exist on occasions apart one from the other.

For in Botticelli the dual marriage is perfect, or almost perfect, body and spirit reconciled, or almost reconciled, in a perfect dual consummation. And in all art there is testimony to the wonderful dual marriage, the true consummation. But in Raphael, the marriage in the spirit is left out so much that it is almost denied, so that the picture is almost a lie, almost a blasphemy. And in Turner, the marriage in the body is almost denied in the same way, so that his picture is almost a blasphemy. But neither in Raphael nor in Turner is the denial positive: it is only an over-affirmation of the one at the expense of the other.

But in some men, in some small men, like bishops, the denial of marriage in the body is positive and blasphemous, a sin against the Holy Ghost. And in some men, like Prussian army officers, the denial of marriage in the spirit is an equal blasphemy. But which of the two is a greater sinner, working better for the destruction of his fellow-man, that is for the One God to judge.

[Chapter IX can be found on p. 213 of this volume.]

CHAPTER X

It seems as if the history of humanity were divided into two epochs: the Epoch of the Law and the Epoch of Love. It seems as though humanity, during the time of its activity on earth, has made two great efforts: the effort to appreciate the Law and the effort to overcome the Law in Love. And in both efforts it has succeeded. It has reached and proved the Two Complementary Absolutes, the Absolute of the Father, of the Law, of Nature, and the Absolute of the Son, of Love, of Knowledge. What remains is to reconcile the two.

In the beginning, Man said: 'What am I, and whence is this world around me, and why is it as it is?' Then he proceeded to explore and to personify and to deify the Natural Law, which he called Father. And having reached the point where he conceived of the Natural Law in its purity, he had finished his journey, and was arrested.

But he found that he could not remain at rest. He must still go on. Then there was to discover by what principle he must proceed further than the Law. And he received an inkling of Love. All over the world the same, the second great epoch started with the incipient conception of Love, and continued until the principle of Love was conceived in all its purity. Then man was again at an end, in a cul-de-sac.

The Law it is by which we exist. It was the Father, the Law-Maker, Who said: 'Let there be Light': it was he who breathed life into the handful of dust and made man. 'Thus have I made man, in mine own image. I have ordered his outgoing and his incoming, and have cast the line whereby he shall walk.' So said the Father. And man went out and came in according to the ordering of the Lord; he walked by the line of the Lord and did not deviate. Till the path was worn barren, and man knew all the way, and the end seemed to have drawn nigh.

Then he said: 'I will leave the path. I will go out as the Lord
hath not ordained, and come in when my hour is fulfilled. For it
is written, a man shall eat and drink with the Lord: but I will
neither eat nor drink, I will go hungry, yet I will not die. It is
written, a man shall take himself a wife and beget him seed unto
the glory of God. But I will not take me a wife, nor beget seed,
but I will know no woman. Yet will I not die. And it is written,
a man shall save his body from harm, and preserve his flesh from
hurt, for he is made in the image and likeness of the Father. But
I will deliver up my body to hurt, and give my flesh unto the dust,
yet will I not die, but live. For man does not live by bread alone,
nor by the common law of the Father. Beyond this common law,
I am I. When my body is destroyed and my bones have perished,
then I am I. Yes, not until my body is consumed and my bones
have mingled with the dust, not until then am I whole, not until
then do I live. But I die in Christ, and rise again. And when I am
risen again, I live in the spirit. Neither hunger nor cold can lay
hold on me, nor desire lay hands on me. When I am risen again
then I shall *know*. Then I shall live in the ineffable bliss of knowledge. When the sun goes forth in the morning, I shall know the
glory of God, who passes the sun from his left hand to his right,
in the peace of his Understanding. As the night comes in her
divers shadows, I know the peace that passeth all understanding.
For God knoweth. Neither does he Will nor Command nor desire nor act, but exists perfect in the peace of knowledge.'

If a man must live still and act in the body, then let his action
be to the recognizing of the life in other bodies. Each man is to
himself the Natural Law. He can only conceive of the Natural
Law as he knows it in himself. The hardest thing for any man to
do is for him to recognize and to know that the natural law of his
neighbour is other than, and maybe even hostile to, his own
natural law, and yet is true. This hard lesson Christ tried to instil
in the doctrine of the other cheek. Orestes could not conceive
that it was the natural law of Clytemnestra's nature that she
should murder Agamemnon for sacrificing her daughter, and
for leaving herself abandoned in the pride of her womanhood,
unmated because he wanted the pleasure of war, and for his

unfaithfulness to her with other women; Clytemnestra could not understand that Orestes should want to kill her for fulfilling the law of her own nature. The law of the mother's nature was other than the law of the son's nature. This they could neither of them see: hence the killing. This Christianity would teach them: to recognize and to admit the law of the other person, outside and different from the law of one's own being. It is the hardest lesson of love. And the lesson of love learnt, there must be learned the next lesson, of reconciliation between different, maybe hostile, things. That is the final lesson. Christianity ends in submission, in recognizing and submitting to the law of the other person. 'Thou shalt love thy enemy.'

Therefore, since by the law man must act or move, let his motion be the utterance of the God of Peace, of the perfect, unutterable Peace of Knowledge.

And man has striven this way, to utter the Universal Peace of God. And, striving on, he has passed beyond the limits of utterance, and has reached once more the silence of the beginning.

After Sue, after Dostoyevsky's *Idiot*, after Turner's latest pictures, after the symbolist poetry of Mallarmé and the others, after the music of Debussy, there is no further possible utterance of the peace that passeth all understanding, the peace of God which is Perfect Knowledge. There is only silence beyond this.

Just as after Plato, after Dante, after Raphael, there was no further utterance of the Absoluteness of the Law, of the Immutability of the Divine Conception.

So that, as the great pause came over Greece, and over Italy, after the Renaissance, when the Law had been uttered in its absoluteness, there comes over us now, over England and Russia and France, the pause of finality, now we have seen the purity of Knowledge, the great, white, uninterrupted Light, infinite and eternal.

But that is not the end. The two great conceptions, of Law and of Knowledge or Love, are not diverse and accidental, but complementary. They are, in a way, contradictions each of the other. But they are complementary. They are the Fixed Absolute, the

600

Geometric Absolute, and they are the radiant Absolute, the Unthinkable Absolute of pure, free motion. They are the perfect Stability, and they are the perfect Mobility. They are the fixed condition of our being, and they are the transcendent condition of knowledge in us. They are our Soul, and our Spirit, they are our Feelings, and our Mind. They are our Body and our Brain. They are Two-in-One.

And everything that has ever been produced has been produced by the combined activity of the two, in humanity, by the combined activity of soul and spirit. When the two are acting together, then Life is produced, then Life, or Utterance, Something, is *created*. And nothing is or can be created save by combined effort of the two principles, Law and Love.

All through the medieval times, Law and Love were striving together to give the perfect expression to the Law, to arrive at the perfect conception of the Law. All through the rise of the Greek nation, to its culmination, the Law and Love were working in that nation to attain the perfect expression of the Law. They were driven by the Unknown Desire, the Holy Spirit, the Unknown and Unexpressed. But the Holy Spirit is the Reconciler and the Originator. Him we do not know.

The greatest of all Utterance of the Law has given expression to the Law as it is in relation to Love, both ruled by the Holy Spirit. Such is the Book of Job, such Aeschylus in the Trilogy, such, more or less, is Dante, such is Botticelli. Those who gave expression to the Law after these suppressed the contact, and achieved an abstraction. Plato, Raphael.

The greatest utterance of Love has given expression to Love as it is in relation to the Law: so Rembrandt, Shakespeare, Shelley, Wordsworth, Goethe, Tolstoy. But beyond these there has been Turner, who suppressed the context of the Law; also there have been Dostoyevsky, Hardy, Flaubert. These have shown Love in conflict with the Law, and only Death the resultant, no Reconciliation. So that humanity does not continue for long to accept the conclusions of these writers, nor even of Euripides and Shakespeare always. These great tragic writers endure by reason of the truth of the conflict they describe, because of its completeness, Law, Love, and Reconciliation, all active. But with regard to their conclusions, they leave the soul finally unsatisfied, unbelieving.

Now the aim of man remains to recognize and seek out the Holy Spirit, the Reconciler, the Originator, He who drives the twin principles of Law and of Love across the ages.

Now it remains for us to know the Law and to know the Love, and further to seek out the Reconciliation. It is time for us to build our temples to the Holy Spirit, and to raise our altars to the Holy Ghost, the Supreme, who is beyond us but is with us.

We know of the Law, and we know of Love, and to that little we know of each of these we have given our full expression. But have not completed one perfect utterance, not one. Small as is the circle of our knowledge, we are not able to cast it complete. In Aeschylus's *Eumenides,* Apollo is foolish, Athena mechanical. In Shakespeare's *Hamlet* the conclusion is all foolish. If we had conceived each party in his proper force, if Apollo had been equally potent with the Furies and no Pallas had appeared to settle the question merely by dropping a pebble, how would Aeschylus have solved his riddle? He could not work out the solution he knew must come, so he forced it.

And so it has always been, always : either a wrong conclusion, or one forced by the artist, as if he put his thumb in the scale to equalize a balance which he could not make level. Now it remains for us to seek the true balance, to give each party, Apollo and the Furies, Love and the Law, his due, and so to seek the Reconciler.

Now the principle of the Law is found strongest in Woman, and the principle of Love in Man. In every creature, the mobility, the law of change, is found exemplified in the male; the stability, the conservatism is found in the female. In woman man finds his root and establishment. In man woman finds her exfoliation and florescence. The woman grows downwards, like a root, towards the centre and the darkness and the origin. The man grows upwards, like the stalk, towards discovery and light and utterance.

Man and Woman are, roughly, the embodiment of Love and the Law: they are the two complementary parts. In the body

602

From *Study of Thomas Hardy*

they are most alike, in genitals they are almost one. Starting from the connexion, almost unification, of the genitals, and travelling towards the feelings and the mind, there becomes ever a greater difference and a finer distinction between the two, male and female, till at last, at the other closing in the circle, in pure utterance, the two are really one again, so that any pure utterance is a perfect unity, the two as one, united by the Holy Spirit.

We start from one side or the other, from the female side or the male, but what we want is always the perfect union of the two. That is the Law of the Holy Spirit, the law of Consummate Marriage. That every living thing seeks, individually and collectively. Every man starts with his deepest desire, a desire for consummation of marriage between himself and the female, a desire for completeness, that completeness of being which will give completeness of satisfaction and completeness of utterance. No man can as yet find perfect consummation of marriage between himself and the Bride, be the bride either Woman or an Idea, but he can approximate to it, and every generation can get a little nearer.

But it needs that a man shall first know in reverence and submit to the Natural Law of his own individual being: that he shall also know that he is but contained within the great Natural Law, that he is but a Child of God, and not God himself: that he shall then poignantly and personally recognize that the law of another man's nature is different from the law of his own nature, that it may be even hostile to him, and yet is part of the great Law of God, to be admitted: this is the Christian action of 'loving thy neighbour', and of dying to be born again: lastly, that a man shall know that between his law and the law of his neighbour there is an affinity, that all is contained in one, through the Holy Spirit.

It needs that a man shall know the natural law of his own being, then that he shall seek out the law of the female, with which to join himself as complement. He must know that he is half, and the woman is the other half: that they are two, but that they are two-in-one.

He must with reverence submit to the law of himself: and he

603

must with suffering and joy know and submit to the law of the woman: and he must know that they two together are one within the Great Law, reconciled within the Great Peace. Out of this final knowledge shall come his supreme art. There shall be the art which recognizes and utters his own law; there shall be the art which recognizes his own and also the law of the woman, his neighbour, utters the glad embraces and the struggle between them, and the submission of one; there shall be the art which knows the struggle between the two conflicting laws, and knows the final reconciliation, where both are equal, two in one, complete. This is the supreme art, which yet remains to be done. Some men have attempted it, and left us the results of efforts. But it remains to be fully done.

But when the two clasp hands, a moment, male and female, clasp hands and are one, the poppy, the gay poppy flies into flower again; and when the two fling their arms about each other, the moonlight runs and clashes against the shadow; and when the two toss back their hair, all the larks break out singing; and when they kiss on the mouth, a lovely human utterance is heard again – and so it is.

# Whistling of Birds

*Athenaeum*, 11 April 1919; *Phoenix*, 1936

The frost held for many weeks, until the birds were dying rapidly. Everywhere in the fields and under the hedges lay the ragged remains of lapwings, starlings, thrushes, redwings, innumerable ragged bloody cloaks of birds, whence the flesh was eaten by invisible beasts of prey.

Then, quite suddenly, one morning, the change came. The wind went to the south, came off the sea warm and soothing. In the afternoon there were little gleams of sunshine, and the doves began, without interval, slowly and awkwardly to coo. The doves were cooing, though with a laboured sound, as if they were still winter-stunned. Nevertheless, all the afternoon they continued their noise, in the mild air, before the frost had thawed off the road. At evening the wind blew gently, still gathering a bruising quality of frost from the hard earth. Then, in the yellow-gleamy sunset, wild birds began to whistle faintly in the blackthorn thickets of the stream-bottom.

It was startling and almost frightening after the heavy silence of frost. How could they sing at once, when the ground was thickly strewn with the torn carcasses of birds? Yet out of the evening came the uncertain, silvery sounds that made one's soul start alert, almost with fear. How could the little silver bugles sound the rally so swiftly, in the soft air, when the earth was yet bound? Yet the birds continued their whistling, rather dimly and brokenly, but throwing the threads of silver, germinating noise into the air.

It was almost a pain to realize, so swiftly, the new world. *Le monde est mort. Vive le monde!* But the birds omitted even the first part of the announcement, their cry was only a faint, blind, fecund *vive!*

There is another world. The winter is gone. There is a new world of spring. The voice of the turtle is heard in the land. But the flesh shrinks from so sudden a transition. Surely the call is premature while the clods are still frozen, and the ground is littered with the remains of wings! Yet we have no choice. In the bottoms of impenetrable blackthorn, each evening and morning now, out flickers a whistling of birds.

Where does it come from, the song? After so long a cruelty, how can they make it up so quickly? But it bubbles through them, they are like little well-heads, little fountain-heads whence the spring trickles and bubbles forth. It is not of their own doing. In their throats the new life distils itself into sound. It is the rising of silvery sap of a new summer, gurgling itself forth.

All the time, whilst the earth lay choked and killed and winter-mortified, the deep undersprings were quiet. They only wait for the ponderous encumbrance of the old order to give way, yield in the thaw, and there they are, a silver realm at once. Under the surge of ruin, unmitigated winter, lies the silver potentiality of all blossom. One day the black tide must spend itself and fade back. Then all-suddenly appears the crocus, hovering triumphant in the rear, and we know the order has changed, there is a new regime, sound of a new *vive! vive!*

It is no use any more to look at the torn remnants of birds that lie exposed. It is no longer any use remembering the sullen thunder of frost and the intolerable pressure of cold upon us. For whether we will or not, they are gone. The choice is not ours. We may remain wintry and destructive for a little longer, if we wish it, but the winter is gone out of us, and willy-nilly our hearts sing a little at sunset.

Even whilst we stare at the ragged horror of the birds scattered broadcast, part-eaten, the soft, uneven cooing of the pigeon ripples from the outhouses, and there is a faint silver whistling in the bushes come twilight. No matter, we stand and stare at the torn and unsightly ruins of life, we watch the weary, mutilated columns of winter retreating under our eyes. Yet in our ears are the silver vivid bugles of a new creation advancing on us from behind, we hear the rolling of the soft and happy drums of the doves.

We may not choose the world. We have hardly any choice for ourselves. We follow with our eyes the bloody and horrid line of march of extreme winter, as it passes away. But we cannot hold back the spring. We cannot make the birds silent, prevent the bubbling of the wood-pigeons. We cannot stay the fine world of silver-fecund creation from gathering itself and taking place upon us. Whether we will or no, the daphne tree will soon be giving off perfume, the lambs dancing on two feet, the celandines will twinkle all over the ground, there will be a new heaven and new earth.

For it is in us, as well as without us. Those who can may follow the columns of winter in their retreat from the earth. Some of us, we have no choice, the spring is within us, the silver fountain begins to bubble under our breast, there is gladness in spite of ourselves. And on the instant we accept the gladness! The first day of change, out whistles an unusual, interrupted paean, a fragment that will augment itself imperceptibly. And this in spite of the extreme bitterness of the suffering, in spite of the myriads of torn dead.

Such a long, long winter, and the frost only broke yesterday. Yet it seems, already, we cannot remember it. It is strangely remote, like a far-off darkness. It is as unreal as a dream in the night. This is the morning of reality, when we are ourselves. This is natural and real, the glimmering of a new creation that stirs in us and about us. We know there was winter, long, fearful. We know the earth was strangled and mortified, we know the body of life was torn and scattered broadcast. But what is this retrospective knowledge? It is something extraneous to us, extraneous to this that we are now. And what we are, and what, it seems, we always have been, is this quickening lovely silver plasm of pure creativity. All the mortification and tearing, ah yes, it was upon us, encompassing us. It was like a storm or a mist or a falling from a height. It was estrangled upon us, like bats in our hair, driving us mad. But it was never really our innermost self. Within, we were always apart, we were this, this limpid fountain of silver, then quiescent, rising and breaking now into the flowering.

It is strange, the utter incompatibility of death with life. Whilst there is death, life is not to be found. It is all death, one overwhelming flood. And then a new tide rises, and it is all life, a fountain of silvery blissfulness. It is one or the other. We are for life, or we are for death, one or the other, but never in our essence both at once.

Death takes us, and all is torn redness, passing into darkness. Life rises, and we are faint fine jets of silver running out to blossom. All is incompatible with all. There is the silver-speckled, incandescent-lovely thrush, whistling pipingly his first song in the blackthorn thicket. How is he to be connected with the bloody, feathered unsightliness of the thrush-remnants just outside the bushes? There is no connexion. They are not to be referred the one to the other. Where one is, the other is not. In the kingdom of death the silvery song is not. But where there is life, there is no death. No death whatever, only silvery gladness, perfect, the other-world.

The blackbird cannot stop his song, neither can the pigeon. It takes place in him, even though all his race was yesterday destroyed. He cannot mourn, or be silent, or adhere to the dead. Of the dead he is not, since life has kept him. The dead must bury their dead. Life has now taken hold on him and tossed him into the new ether of a new firmament, where he bursts into song as if he were combustible. What is the past, those others, now he is tossed clean into the new, across the untranslatable difference?

In his song is heard the first brokenness and uncertainty of the transition. The transit from the grip of death into new being is a death from death, in its sheer metempsychosis a dizzy agony. But only for a second, the moment of trajectory, the passage from one state to the other, from the grip of death to the liberty of newness. In a moment he is a kingdom of wonder, singing at the centre of a new creation.

The bird did not hang back. He did not cling to his death and his dead. There is no death, and the dead have buried their dead. Tossed into the chasm between two worlds, he lifted his wings in dread, and found himself carried on the impulse.

We are lifted to be cast away into the new beginning. Under our hearts the fountain surges, to toss us forth. Who can thwart the impulse that comes upon us? It comes from the unknown upon us, and it behoves us to pass delicately and exquisitely upon the subtle new wind from heaven, conveyed like birds in un-reasoning migrations from death to life.

# Index

# Index

Attila, 118, 167, 513
Attis, 357
Augustine, St, 347
Austen, Jane, 285–6, 359
Australia, 126–7, 130
Authority, 268–70, 275, 509
Average, the, 514–19, 521–2, 524, 526
Aztecs, 122–3, 128, 499

Babylonians, 547, 550
Baden-Baden, 118
Balzac, 162, 163
Barrie, J. M., 17
Baudelaire, 402
*Beasts, Men and Gods*, 117
Beethoven, 430
Being, 453–4, 532, 561–85
Benedict, St, 437
Benevolence, 383, 385, 436, 499, 501,
    529
    and Clym Yeobright, 198–9
Bennett, Arnold, 28
Berkeley, Bishop, 474
Besant, Annie, 172
Bestwood, *see* Eastwood
Bible
    novels in, 164
    a novel, 185–6
    in D.H.L.'s bones, 550
    quick of ancient history, 551
    *See* Jewish Religion, Job, Revela-
    tion, Old Testament
Blake, William, 201, 378
Boccaccio, 310, 311, 314, 326
Boccioni, 583–4
Bohemianism, 320–22, 333
Botticelli, 221, 224, 573, 576–7, 579–81,
    585, 594, 597, 601
    *Nativity of the Saviour*, 573–4
*Bridge of San Luis Rey, The*, 378
Brontë, Charlotte, 310
    *Jane Eyre*, 311, 314
Brontë, Emily, 507
Buddha, 356, 513
Bunyan, John
    *The Pilgrim's Progress*, 542–3
Burns, Robert, 319
Burrow, Dr Trigant, 466–72
Burton, Sir Richard, 325
Byron, Lord, 507, 578

Caesar, 393
California, 126
Cambridge, 49
Capri, 39–41, 45

Carlyle, Thomas, 529
Carter, Frederick, 539, 541, 551
Cathedrals, 572–3, 576
Cellini, Benvenuto, 46
    Life, 325
Ceylon, 126, 128, 129, 146
Chaldeans, 546–52
Chambers, Jessie, 14–15
Chambers, Robert W., 189
Character, 169–70
Chekhov, 263, 486, 488
Christ, *see* Jesus
Christian-socialism, 161–2
Christianity
    dogma and miracle, 22
    instinctive dream, 22
    and sentimentalism, 23–4
    the Evangelists, 164
    Dostoyevsky and, 269–71
    source of marriage, 345–6
    and individual salvation, 346
    killed animistic cosmos, 353–7
    asceticism has ended in living death,
        547–8
    successive images of Christ, 553–60
    essential separateness, 570
    as Not-Being, 585–8
    began to exist after Renaissance,
        585
    ends in submission, 600
    English sects contrasted, 22–3
    English and Mediterranean con-
        trasted, 341, 353–4, 556
    *See also* Bible, God, Jesus, Re-
        ligion, Roman Catholic Church
Chronos, 544
Class, 17, 54, 80–82, 141–2, 144, 150,
    156, 294–5 358–60, 367, 416,
    471
Clothes and sex, 339–41, 419
Colliers, 13–14, 17, 103–4, 106–9,
    154–5
    coal strike of 1926, 148–9, 152–4
    education of, 415–16, 485
Conrad, Joseph, *Lord Jim*, 164
Consciousness
    passional *v.* mental, 18, 53–5, 107,
        206–7, 259–60, 265, 333–4, 369,
        461, 474–5
    authentic *v.* societal, 187, 286–9,
        471–2
    cosmic *v.* personal, 286–7, 357, 376
    experience *v.* thoughtform, 545–7
    animistic *v.* scientific, 356–7, 540–
        41, 549

612

# Index

# Index

Jesus – *cont.*
  image as child, 553–5
    as crucified, 555–6
    as risen, 556–60
  as pale Galilean, 242–3
  as Son, 571–7
  and maleness, 223, 570–73
  and Mammon, 559–60
  and marriage, 349
  and monism, 571
  and power, 513
  and the Renaissance, 585–98
  imitators of among novelists, 165
  only relatively good, 171
  effortlessness of parables, 217–18
  Dostoyevsky on, 267–71
  supplanted physical with moral emotion, 273
  idealism, pessimism and abstractness, 356, 547–8
Jewish religion, 505–6, 567–70
  and psychoanalysis, 464
  and Michaelangelo, 582
  and melancholy, 590
Job, 219, 229, 568, 571, 601
John of Patmos, St, 543
John the Evangelist, St, 164, 578, 591
Joyce, James, 190, 266, 500
  *Ulysses*, 164, 189
Joynson-Hicks, Sir William (Lord Brentford), 311, 325
Judas, 171

Kant, 193
Keats, 19, 430, 515
Kennerley, Mitchell, 27
Knox, John, 423

Labour, 411–21
La Bruyère (*Caractères*), 302
Lasca (Grazzini), 314
Law and Love antithesis
  in Aeschylus, 214
  in English poets, 216
  in Tolstoy, 217
  in Hardy, 218–21
  in religion, 585–9
  two epochs, 598–604
Lawrence, Arthur, 13–14
  and D.H.L.'s writing, 26
  and mining, 106–7
  escapes education, 484–5

Lawrence, D. H.
  family and early life, 13–14, 103–6, 146–50, 390–91, 484–5
  chapel, 20–24, 550
  school, 14, 24, 484
  university, 14
  early literary life, 14–16, 25–7
  dislikes name David, 484–5
  class feeling, 17, 150–52
  early sexual confusion, 368–9
  at Florence, 30–39, 361–2
  at Monte Cassino, 42–59
  at Taormina, 60–77
  at Syracuse, 77–81
  in Malta, 84–6
  in Ceylon, 126, 128
  in U.S.A., 121
  in Mexico, 122–3, 539–40
  in New Mexico, 25, 125–31, 443–52
  in Paris, 112–15
  in Germany, 116–20
  returns to England, 137
  on Great Western Railway, 139–42
  returns to Eastwood, 146–54
  in Switzerland, 381
  never starved in a garret, 13
  feels not much of a human success, 16
  wrote first novel five or six times, 15
  poems which mean most to him, 19
  never read own published works, 25
  writes to some mysterious presence in the air, 27
  no belief in vast public, 28
  determined never to come to last shilling, 41
  at Cassino feels a child of the present, 48
  New Mexico his greatest experience, 126
  always depressed by and alien in Midlands, 146
  assesses himself at forty, 150–51
  police raid paintings, 326
  phoenix symbol, 360
  hostile correspondent, 370
  and porcupines, 443–9
  steeped in Apocalyptic language, 550
  works referred to:
    *Lady Chatterley's Lover*, first edition, 360–61; Italian printer's attitude, 361; pirated and cheap editions, 327–9; Clifford Chatterley not symbolic, 359

616

# Index

Mallarmé, 600
Malta, 81–91, 97
Manchester, 110
Mann, Thomas, 277–83
Marriage
  essentially personal, 229
  essentially impersonal, 350
  exhaustive yet enriching, 241
  eternal, 341, 583
  greatest contribution of Christianity, 345–6
  and Roman Catholic Church, 341–8
  and sex, 349
  and matriarchy, 423–6
  in *Jude the Obscure*, 248–9
  among colliers, 107–8
  French bourgeois, 113, 460
  modern, our sphinx-riddle, 477
    revolt against, 343–4
    counterfeit, 350–51
    overthrows expectations, 396, 477–8
    and music, 400–2
    and self-deception, 418, 479
    and repulsion, 419–20
  *See* Love, Male–female antithesis, Men and women, Sex
Marx, Karl, 164
Mascagni, 266
Masochism, 439
Masturbation, 316–19, 321–2, 352
Maupassant, 263, 399
Mazzaiba, Gabriel, 84–94
Melenga, Pancrazio, 66, 71–6
Men and women
  mutual need, 180, 374, 476, 561–4
  mutual hostility, 375, 419
  contrast in attitudes to work, home and family, 107, 425
    in attitudes to flowers, 108
    in need for purpose, 388
    in logic and development, 396
  and women's emancipation, 372–3
  male self-doubt, 373
  male fear, 423
  relation of, always the great relationship, 180
    stereotypes of, 168–9, 303–5
    sex *v.* copulation, 229–32, 400
    matriarchy, 423–6
    in Hardy's novels, 219–53
    in Verga's novels, 256
    as Love and Law, 602–4
    as Motion and Rest, 566–7

unreal now, 336
  among the young, 375–8, 408
  modern marriage, 418
  destroyed by egoism, 439
  *See* also Love, Male–female antithesis, Marriage, Sex, Women
Meredith, George, 286
  *Diana of the Crossways*, 14
Merejkovski, D. S., 486
Merimée, Prosper, 263
Methuen, 27–8
Mexico, 121–3, 146, 539–41
Michelangelo, 311, 576, 585
  and Raphael, 578–82
  and Rembrandt, 593–4
Middle Ages, 48–9, 56, 59, 572–3
Milton, John, 106, 491, 579, 592
Miners, *see* Colliers
Miracle, essential human need, 268–70, 273
Moffatt's translation of the Bible, 551
Money
  decent minimum essential, 155
  dominates education, 157
  mistaken for life, 270–71
  cuts us off from life as nothing can, 459
  nasty substitute for power, 509
  mere measure, 515
  Mammon, 559–60
  attitudes of D.H.L. and Magnus, 35–6, 40–41
  colliers, 107–8
  Jesus, 164, 559–60
  Hardy's heroes, 195
  the true human individual, 286
  the social being, 287
Monte Cassino monastery, 39, 42–50, 56–7, 98
Moody and Sankey hymn-book, 461
Moon, animistic and scientific
  accounts of, 20, 356, 548
Morality, essence of, 156–7
  balance between self and universe, 176
  in the novel, 177
  in Hardy, 205–6
  of tragedy, 212–13
  essential in art, yet also criticized, 214
  two levels, 354
  instinctive revulsion of the majority, 400
Moses, 505, 513, 582

# Index